3-D Computer Graphics

A Mathematical Introduction with OpenGL

This book is an introduction to 3-D computer graphics with particular emphasis on fundamentals and the mathematics underlying computer graphics. It includes descriptions of how to use the cross-platform OpenGL programming environment. It also includes source code for a ray tracing software package. (Accompanying software is available freely from the book's Web site.)

Topics include a thorough treatment of transformations and viewing, lighting and shading models, interpolation and averaging, Bézier curves and B-splines, ray tracing and radiosity, and intersection testing with rays. Additional topics, covered in less depth, include texture mapping and color theory. The book also covers some aspects of animation, including quaternions, orientation, and inverse kinematics. Mathematical background on vectors and matrices is reviewed in an appendix.

This book is aimed at the advanced undergraduate level or introductory graduate level and can also be used for self-study. Prerequisites include basic knowledge of calculus and vectors. The OpenGL programming portions require knowledge of programming in C or C++. The more important features of OpenGL are covered in the book, but it is intended to be used in conjunction with another OpenGL programming book.

Samuel R. Buss is Professor of Mathematics and Computer Science at the University of California, San Diego. With both academic and industrial expertise, Buss has more than 60 publications in the fields of computer science and mathematical logic. He is the editor of several journals and the author of a book on bounded arithmetic. Buss has years of experience in programming and game development and has acted as consultant for SAIC and Angel Studios.

3-D Computer Graphics

A Mathematical Introduction with OpenGL

SAMUEL R. BUSS
University of California, San Diego

CAMBRIDGE
UNIVERSITY PRESS

PUBLISHED BY THE PRESS SYNDICATE OF THE UNIVERSITY OF CAMBRIDGE
The Pitt Building, Trumpington Street, Cambridge, United Kingdom

CAMBRIDGE UNIVERSITY PRESS
The Edinburgh Building, Cambridge CB2 2RU, UK
40 West 20th Street, New York, NY 10011-4211, USA
477 Williamstown Road, Port Melbourne, VIC 3207, Australia
Ruiz de Alarcón 13, 28014 Madrid, Spain
Dock House, The Waterfront, Cape Town 8001, South Africa

http://www.cambridge.org

First published 2003

Printed in the United States of America

Typefaces Times New Roman PS 10/12 pt.   *System* LATEX 2$_\varepsilon$ [TB]

A catalog record for this book is available from the British Library.

Library of Congress Cataloging in Publication Data
Buss, Samuel R.
   3D computer graphics : a mathematical introduction with OpenGL / Samuel R. Buss.
      p.   cm.
   Includes bibliographical references and index.
   ISBN 0-521-82103-7
   1. Computer graphics.   2. OpenGL.   3. Three-dimensional display systems.   I. Title.
   T385 .B8695   2003

   006.6′93 – dc21   2002034804

ISBN 0 521 82103 7 hardback

To my family

Teresa, Stephanie, and Ian

Contents

Color art appears following page 256.

Preface

Computer graphics has grown phenomenally in recent decades, progressing from simple 2-D graphics to complex, high-quality, three-dimensional environments. In entertainment, computer graphics is used extensively in movies and computer games. Animated movies are increasingly being made entirely with computers. Even nonanimated movies depend heavily on computer graphics to develop special effects: witness, for instance, the success of the *Star Wars* movies beginning in the mid-1970s. The capabilities of computer graphics in personal computers and home game consoles have now improved to the extent that low-cost systems are able to display millions of polygons per second.

There are also significant uses of computer graphics in nonentertainment applications. For example, virtual reality systems are often used in training. Computer graphics is an indispensable tool for scientific visualization and for computer-aided design (CAD). We need good methods for displaying large data sets comprehensibly and for showing the results of large-scale scientific simulations.

The art and science of computer graphics have been evolving since the advent of computers and started in earnest in the early 1960s. Since then, computer graphics has developed into a rich, deep, and coherent field. The aim of this book is to present the mathematical foundations of computer graphics along with a practical introduction to programming using OpenGL. I believe that understanding the mathematical basis is important for any advanced use of computer graphics. For this reason, this book attempts to cover the underlying mathematics thoroughly. The principle guiding the selection of topics for this book has been to choose topics that are of practical significance for computer graphics practitioners – in particular for software developers. My hope is that this book will serve as a comprehensive introduction to the standard tools used in this field and especially to the mathematical theory behind these tools.

About This Book

The plan for this book has been shaped by my personal experiences as an academic mathematician and by my participation in various applied computer projects, including projects in computer games and virtual reality. This book was started while I was teaching a mathematics class at the University of California, San Diego (UCSD), on computer graphics and geometry. That course was structured as an introduction to programming 3-D graphics in OpenGL and to the mathematical foundations of computer graphics. While teaching that course, I became convinced of the need for a book that would bring together the mathematical theory underlying computer graphics in an introductory and unified setting.

The other motivation for writing this book has been my involvement in several virtual reality and computer game projects. Many of the topics included in this book are presented mainly because I have found them useful in computer game applications. Modern-day computer games and virtual reality applications are technically demanding software projects: these applications require software capable of displaying convincing three-dimensional environments. Generally, the software must keep track of the motion of multiple objects; maintain information about the lighting, colors, and textures of many objects; and display these objects on the screen at 30 or 60 frames per second. In addition, considerable artistic and creative skills are needed to make a worthwhile three-dimensional environment. Not surprisingly, this requires sophisticated software development by large teams of programmers, artists, and designers.

Perhaps it is a little more surprising that 3-D computer graphics requires extensive mathematics. This is, however, the case. Furthermore, the mathematics tends to be elegant and interdisciplinary. The mathematics needed in computer graphics brings together constructions and methods from several areas, including geometry, calculus, linear algebra, numerical analysis, abstract algebra, data structures, and algorithms. In fact, computer graphics is arguably the best example of a practical area in which so much mathematics combines so elegantly.

This book presents a blend of applied and theoretical topics. On the more applied side, I recommend the use of OpenGL, a readily available, free, cross-platform programming environment for 3-D graphics. The C and C++ code for OpenGL programs that can freely be downloaded from the Internet has been included, and I discuss how OpenGL implements many of the mathematical concepts discussed in this book. A ray tracer software package is also described; this software can also be downloaded from the Internet. On the theoretical side, this book stresses the mathematical foundations of computer graphics, more so than any other text of which I am aware. I strongly believe that knowing the mathematical foundations of computer graphics is important for being able to use tools such as OpenGL or Direct3D, or, to a lesser extent, CAD programs properly.

The mathematical topics in this book are chosen because of their importance and relevance to graphics. However, I have not hesitated to introduce more abstract concepts when they are crucial to computer graphics – for instance, the projective geometry interpretation of homogeneous coordinates. A good knowledge of mathematics is invaluable if you want to use the techniques of computer graphics software properly and is even more important if you want to develop new or innovative uses of computer graphics.

How to Use This Book

This book is intended for use as a textbook, as a source for self-study, or as a reference. It is strongly recommended that you try running the programs supplied with the book and write some OpenGL programs of your own. Note that this book is intended to be read in conjunction with a book on learning to program in OpenGL. A good source for learning OpenGL is the comprehensive *OpenGL Programming Guide* (Woo et al., 1999), which is sometimes called the "red book." If you are learning OpenGL on your own for the first time, the *OpenGL Programming Guide* may be a bit daunting. If so, the *OpenGL SuperBible* (Wright Jr., 1999) may provide an easier introduction to OpenGL with much less mathematics. The book *OpenGL: A Primer* (Angel, 2002) also gives a good introductory overview of OpenGL.

The outline of this book is as follows. The chapters are arranged more or less in the order the material might be covered in a course. However, it is not necessary to read the material in order. In particular, the later chapters can be read largely independently, with the exception that Chapter VIII depends on Chapter VII.

Chapter I. Introduction. Introduces the basic concepts of computer graphics; drawing points, lines, and polygons; modeling with polygons; animation; and getting started with OpenGL programming.

Chapter II. Transformations and Viewing. Discusses the rendering pipeline, linear and affine transformations, matrices in two and three dimensions, translations and rotations, homogeneous coordinates, transformations in OpenGL, viewing with orthographic and perspective transformations, projective geometry, pixelization, Gouraud and scan line interpolation, and the Bresenham algorithm.

Chapter III. Lighting, Illumination, and Shading. Addresses the Phong lighting model; ambient, diffuse, and specular lighting; lights and material properties in OpenGL; and the Cook–Torrance model.

Chapter IV. Averaging and Interpolation. Presents linear interpolation, barycentric coordinates, bilinear interpolation, convexity, hyperbolic interpolation, and spherical linear interpolation. This is a more mathematical chapter with many tools that are used elsewhere in the book. You may wish to skip much of this chapter on the first reading and come back to it as needed.

Chapter V. Texture Mapping. Discusses textures and texture coordinates, mipmapping, supersampling and jittering, bump mapping, environment mapping, and texture maps in OpenGL.

Chapter VI. Color. Addresses color perception, additive and subtractive colors, and RGB and HSL representations of color.

Chapter VII. Bézier Curves. Presents Bézier curves of degree three and of general degree; De Casteljau methods; subdivision; piecewise Bézier curves; Hermite polynomials; Bézier surface patches; Bézier curves in OpenGL; rational curves and conic sections; surfaces of revolution; degree elevation; interpolation with Catmull–Rom, Bessel–Overhauser, and tension-continuity-bias splines; and interpolation with Bézier surfaces.

Chapter VIII. B-Splines. Describes uniform and nonuniform B-splines and their properties, B-splines in OpenGL, the de Boor algorithm, blossoms, smoothness properties, rational B-splines (NURBS) and conic sections, knot insertion, relationship with Bézier curves, and interpolation with spline curves. This chapter has a mixture of introductory topics and more specialized topics. We include all proofs but recommend that many of the proofs be skipped on the first reading.

Chapter IX. Ray Tracing. Presents recursive ray tracing, reflection and transmission, distributed ray tracing, backwards ray tracing, and cheats to avoid ray tracing.

Chapter X. Intersection Testing. Describes testing rays for intersections with spheres, planes, triangles, polytopes, and other surfaces and addresses bounding volumes and hierarchical pruning.

Chapter XI. Radiosity. Presents patches, form factors, and the radiosity equation; the hemicube method; and the Jacobi, Gauss–Seidel, and Southwell iterative methods.

Chapter XII. Animation and Kinematics. Discusses key framing, ease in and ease out, representations of orientation, quaternions, interpolating quaternions, and forward and inverse kinematics for articulated rigid multibodies.

Appendix A. Mathematics Background. Reviews topics from vectors, matrices, linear algebra, and calculus.

Appendix B. RayTrace Software Package. Describes a ray tracing software package. The software is freely downloadable.

Exercises are scattered throughout the book, especially in the more introductory chapters. These are often supplied with hints, and they should not be terribly difficult. It is highly recommended that you do the exercises to master the material. A few sections in the book, as well as some of the theorems, proofs, and exercises, are labeled with an asterisk ($\star$). This indicates that the material is optional, less important, or both and can be safely skipped without affecting your understanding of the rest of the book. Theorems, lemmas, figures, and exercises are numbered separately for each chapter.

Obtaining the Accompanying Software

All software examples discussed in this book are available for downloading from the Internet at

```
http://math.ucsd.edu/~sbuss/MathCG/.
```

The software is available as source files and as PC executables. In addition, complete Microsoft Visual C++ project files are available.

The software includes several small OpenGL programs and a relatively large ray tracing software package.

The software may be used without any restriction except that its use in commercial products or any kind of substantial project must be acknowledged.

Getting Started with OpenGL

OpenGL is a platform-independent API (application programming interface) for rendering 3-D graphics. A big advantage of using OpenGL is that it is a widely supported industry standard. Other 3-D environments, notably Direct3D, have similar capabilities; however, Direct3D is specific to the Microsoft Windows operating system.

The official OpenGL Web site is `http://www.opengl.org`. This site contains a huge amount of material, but if you are just starting to learn OpenGL the most useful material is probably the tutorials and code samples available at

```
http://www.opengl.org/developers/code/tutorials.html.
```

The OpenGL programs supplied with this text use the OpenGL Utility Toolkit routines, called GLUT for short, which is widely used and provides a simple-to-use interface for controlling OpenGL windows and handling simple user input. You generally need to install the GLUT files separately from the rest of the OpenGL files.

If you are programming with Microsoft Visual C++, then the OpenGL header files and libraries are included with Visual C++. However, you will need to download the GLUT files yourself. OpenGL can also be used with other development environments such as Borland's C++ compiler.

The official Web site for downloading the latest version of GLUT for the Windows operating system is available from Nate Robin at

```
http://www.xmission.com/~nate/glut.html.
```

To install the necessary GLUT files on a Windows machine, you should put the header file `glut.h` in the same directory as your other OpenGL header files such as `glu.h`. You should likewise put the `glut32.dll` files and `glut32.lib` file in the same directories as the corresponding files for OpenGL, `glu32.dll`, and `glu32.lib`.

OpenGL and GLUT work under a variety of other operating systems as well. I have not tried out all these systems but list some of the prominent ones as an aid to the reader trying to run OpenGL in other environments. (However, changes occur rapidly in the software development world, and so these links may become outdated quickly.)

For Macintosh computers, you can find information about OpenGL and the GLUT libraries at the Apple Computer site

```
http://developer.apple.com/opengl/.
```

OpenGL and GLUT also work under the Cygwin system, which implements a Unix-like development environment under Windows. Information on Cygwin is available at `http://cygwin.com/` or `http://sources.redhat.com/cygwin/`.

OpenGL for Sun Solaris systems can be obtained from

```
http://www.sun.com/software/graphics/OpenGL/.
```

There is an OpenGL-compatible system, `Mesa3D`, which is available from `http://mesa3d.sourceforge.net/`. This runs on several operating systems, including Linux, and supports a variety of graphics boards.

Other Resources for Computer Graphics

You may wish to supplement this book with other sources of information on computer graphics. One rather comprehensive textbook is the volume by Foley et al. (1990). Another excellent recent book is Möller and Haines (1999). The articles by Blinn (1996; 1998) and Glassner (1999) are also interesting.

Finally, an enormous amount of information about computer graphics theory and practice is available on the Internet. There you can find examples of OpenGL programs and information about graphics hardware as well as theoretical and mathematical developments. Much of this can be found through your favorite search engine, but you may also use the ACM *Transactions on Graphics* Web site `http://www.acm.org/tog/` as a starting point.

For the Instructor

This book is intended for use with advanced junior- or senior-level undergraduate courses or introductory graduate-level courses. It is based in large part on my teaching of computer graphics courses at the upper division level and at the graduate level. In a two-quarter undergraduate course, I cover most of the material in the book more or less in the order presented here. Some of the more advanced topics would be skipped, however – most notably Cook–Torrance lighting and hyperbolic interpolation – and some of the material on Bézier and B-spline curves and patches is best omitted from an undergraduate course. I also do not cover the more difficult proofs in undergraduate courses.

It is certainly recommended that students studying this book get programming assignments using OpenGL. Although this book covers much OpenGL material in outline form, students will need to have an additional source for learning the details of programming in OpenGL. Programming prerequisites include some experience in C, C++, or Java. (As we write this, there is no standardized OpenGL API for Java; however, Java is close enough to C or C++ that students can readily make the transition required for mastering the simple programs included with this text.) The first quarters of my own courses have included programming assignments first on two-dimensional graphing, second on three-dimensional transformations based on the solar system exercise on page 40, third on polygonal modeling (students are asked to draw tori of the type in Figure I.11(b)), fourth on adding materials and lighting to a scene, and finally an open-ended assignment in which students choose a project of their own. The second quarter of the course has included assignments on modeling objects with Bézier patches (Blinn's article (1987) on how to construct the Utah teapot is used to help with this), on writing a program that draws Catmull–Rom and Overhauser spline curves that interpolate points picked with the mouse, on using the computer-aided design program *3D Studio Max* (this book does not cover any material about how to use CAD programs), on using the ray tracing software supplied with this book, on implementing some aspect of distributed ray tracing, and then ending with another final project of their choosing. Past course materials can be found on the Web from my home page http://math.ucsd.edu/~sbuss/.

Acknowledgments

Very little of the material in this book is original. The aspects that are original mostly concern organization and presentation: in several places, I have tried to present new, simpler proofs than those known before. Frequently, material is presented without attribution or credit, but in most instances this material is due to others. I have included references for items I learned by consulting the original literature and for topics for which it was easy to ascertain the original source; however, I have not tried to be comprehensive in assigning credit.

I learned computer graphics from several sources. First, I worked on a computer graphics project with several people at SAIC, including Tom Yonkman and my wife, Teresa Buss. Subsequently, I have worked for many years on computer games applications at Angel Studios, where I benefited greatly, and learned an immense amount, from Steve Rotenberg, Brad Hunt, Dave Etherton, Santi Bacerra, Nathan Brown, Ted Carson, Daniel Blumenthal, and others. I am particularly indebted to Steve Rotenberg, who has been my guru for advanced topics and current research in computer graphics.

I have taught computer graphics courses several times at UCSD, using at various times the textbooks by Watt and Watt (1992), Watt (1993), and Hill (2001). This book was written from notes developed while teaching these classes.

I am greatly indebted to Frank Chang and Malachi Pust for a thorough proofreading of an early draft of this book. In addition, I thank Michael Bailey, Stephanie Buss (my daughter), Chris Calabro, Joseph Chow, Daniel Curtis, Tamsen Dunn, Rosalie Iemhoff, Cyrus Jam, Jin-Su Kim, Vivek Manpuria, Jason McAuliffe, Jong-Won Oh, Horng Bin Ou, Chris Pollett, John Rapp, Don Quach, Daryl Sterling, Aubin Whitley, and anonymous referees for corrections to preliminary drafts of this book. Further thanks are due to Cambridge University Press for copyediting and final typesetting. As much as I would like to avoid it, the responsibility for all remaining errors is my own.

The figures in this book were prepared with several software systems. The majority of the figures were created using van Zandt's pstricks macro package for LaTeX. Some of the figures were created with a modified version of Geuzaine's program GL2PS for converting OpenGL images into PostScript files. A few figures were created from screen dump bitmaps and converted to PostScript images with Adobe Photoshop.

Partial financial support was provided by National Science Foundation grants DMS-9803515 and DMS-0100589.

I

Introduction

This chapter discusses some of the basic concepts behind computer graphics with particular emphasis on how to get started with simple drawing in OpenGL. A major portion of the chapter explains the simplest methods of drawing in OpenGL and various rendering modes. If this is your first encounter with OpenGL, it is highly suggested that you look at the included sample code and experiment with some of the OpenGL commands while reading this chapter.

The first topic considered is the different models for graphics displays. Of particular importance for the topics covered later in the book is the idea that an arbitrary three-dimensional geometrical shape can be approximated by a set of polygons – more specifically as a set of triangles. Second, we discuss some of the basic methods for programming in OpenGL to display simple two- and three-dimensional models made from points, lines, triangles, and other polygons. We also describe how to set colors and polygonal orientations, how to enable hidden surface removal, and how to make animation work with double buffering. The included sample OpenGL code illustrates all these capabilities. Later chapters will discuss how to use transformations, how to set the viewpoint, how to add lighting and shading, how to add textures, and other topics.

I.1 Display Models

We start by describing three models for graphics display modes: (1) drawing points, (2) drawing lines, and (3) drawing triangles and other polygonal patches. These three modes correspond to different hardware architectures for graphics display. Drawing points corresponds roughly to the model of a graphics image as a rectangular array of pixels. Drawing lines corresponds to vector graphics displays. Drawing triangles and polygons corresponds to the methods used by modern graphics display hardware for displaying three-dimensional images.

I.1.1 Rectangular Arrays of Pixels

The most common low-level model is to treat a graphics image as a rectangular array of pixels in which, each pixel can be independently set to a different color and brightness. This is the display model used for cathode ray tubes (CRTs) and televisions, for instance. If the pixels are small enough, they cannot be seen individually by the human viewer, and the image, although composed of points, can appear as a single smooth image. This technique is used in art as well – notably in mosaics and, even more so, in pointillism, where pictures are composed of small

Figure I.1. A pixel is formed from subregions or subpixels, each of which displays one of three colors. See Color Plate 1.

patches of solid color but appear to form a continuous image when viewed from a sufficient distance.

Keep in mind, however, that the model of graphics images as a rectangular array of pixels is only a convenient abstraction and is not entirely accurate. For instance, on a CRT or television screen, each pixel actually consists of three separate points (or dots of phosphor): each dot corresponds to one of the three primary colors (red, blue, and green) and can be independently set to a brightness value. Thus, each pixel is actually formed from three colored dots. With a magnifying glass, you can see the colors in the pixel as separate colors (see Figure I.1). (It is best to try this with a low-resolution device such as a television; depending on the physical design of the screen, you may see the separate colors in individual dots or in stripes.)

A second aspect of rectangular array model inaccuracy is the occasional use of subpixel image addressing. For instance, laser printers and ink jet printers reduce aliasing problems, such as jagged edges on lines and symbols, by micropositioning toner or ink dots. More recently, some handheld computers (i.e., palmtops) are able to display text at a higher resolution than would otherwise be possible by treating each pixel as three independently addressable subpixels. In this way, the device is able to position text at the subpixel level and achieve a higher level of detail and better character formation.

In this book however, issues of subpixels will never be examined; instead, we will always model a pixel as a single rectangular point that can be set to a desired color and brightness. Sometimes the pixel basis of a computer graphics image will be important to us. In Section II.4, we discuss the problem of approximating a straight sloping line with pixels. Also, when using texture maps and ray tracing, one must take care to avoid the aliasing problems that can arise with sampling a continuous or high-resolution image into a set of pixels.

We will usually not consider pixels at all but instead will work at the higher level of polygonally based modeling. In principle, one could draw any picture by directly setting the brightness levels for each pixel in the image; however, in practice this would be difficult and time consuming. Instead, in most high-level graphics programming applications, we do not have to think very much about the fact that the graphics image may be rendered using a rectangular array of pixels. One draws lines, or especially polygons, and the graphics hardware handles most of the work of translating the results into pixel brightness levels. A variety of sophisticated techniques exist for drawing polygons (or triangles) on a computer screen as an array of pixels, including methods for shading and smoothing and for applying texture maps. These will be covered later in the book.

I.1.2 Vector Graphics

In traditional vector graphics, one models the image as a set of lines. As such, one is not able to model solid objects, and instead draws two-dimensional shapes, graphs of functions,

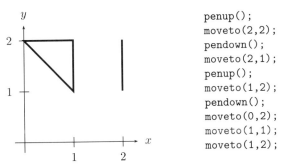

```
penup();
moveto(2,2);
pendown();
moveto(2,1);
penup();
moveto(1,2);
pendown();
moveto(0,2);
moveto(1,1);
moveto(1,2);
```

Figure I.2. Examples of vector graphics commands.

or wireframe images of three-dimensional objects. The canonical example of vector graphics systems are pen plotters; this includes the "turtle geometry" systems. Pen plotters have a drawing pen that moves over a flat sheet of paper. The commands available include (a) *pen up*, which lifts the pen up from the surface of the paper, (b) *pen down*, which lowers the point of the pen onto the paper, and (c) *move-to*(x, y), which moves the pen in a straight line from its current position to the point with coordinates $\langle x, y \rangle$. When the pen is up, it moves without drawing; when the pen is down, it draws as it moves (see Figure I.2). In addition, there may be commands for switching to a different color pen as well as convenience commands to make it easier to draw images.

Another example of vector graphics devices is vector graphics display terminals, which traditionally are monochrome monitors that can draw arbitrary lines. On these vector graphics display terminals, the screen is a large expanse of phosphor and does not have pixels. A traditional oscilloscope is also an example of a vector graphics display device.

Vector graphics displays and pixel-based displays use very different representations of images. In pixel-based systems, the screen image will be stored as a bitmap, namely, as a table containing all the pixel colors. A vector graphics system, on the other hand, will store the image as a list of commands – for instance as a list of pen up, pen down, and move commands. Such a list of commands is called a display list.

Nowadays, pixel-based graphics hardware is very prevalent, and thus even graphics systems that are logically vector based are typically displayed on hardware that is pixel based. The disadvantage is that pixel-based hardware cannot directly draw arbitrary lines and must approximate lines with pixels. On the other hand, the advantage is that more sophisticated figures, such as filled regions, can be drawn.

Modern vector graphics systems incorporate more than just lines and include the ability to draw curves, text, polygons, and other shapes such as circles and ellipses. These systems also have the ability to fill in or shade a region with a color or a pattern. They generally are restricted to drawing two-dimensional figures. Adobe's PostScript language is a prominent example of a modern vector graphics system.

I.1.3 Polygonal Modeling

One step up, in both abstraction and sophistication, is the polygonal model of graphics images. It is very common for three-dimensional geometric shapes to be modeled first as a set of polygons and then mapped to polygonal shapes on a two-dimensional display. The basic display hardware is generally pixel based, but most computers now have special-purpose graphics hardware for processing polygons or, at the very least, triangles. Graphics hardware for rendering triangles is also used in modern computer game systems; indeed, the usual measure of performance for graphics hardware is the number of triangles that can be rendered per second. At the time this book is being written, nominal peak performance rates of relatively cheap hardware is well above one million polygons per second!

Polygonal-based modeling is used in nearly every three-dimensional computer graphics systems. It is a central tool for the generation of interactive three-dimensional graphics and is used for photo-realistic rendering, including animation in movies.

The essential operation in a polygonal modeling system is drawing a single triangle. In addition, there are provisions for coloring and shading the triangle. Here, "shading" means varying the color across the triangle. Another important tool is the use of texture mapping, which can be used to paint images or other textures onto a polygon. It is very typical for color, shading, and texture maps to be supported by special-purpose hardware such as low-cost graphics boards on PCs.

The purpose of these techniques is to make polygonally modeled objects look more realistic. Refer to Figure III.1 on page 68. You will see six models of a teapot. Part (a) of the figure shows a wireframe teapot, as could be modeled on a vector graphics device. Part (b) shows the same shape but filled in with solid color; the result shows a silhouette with no three-dimensionality. Parts (c) through (f) show the teapot rendered with lighting effects: (c) and (e) show flat-shaded (i.e., unshaded) polygons for which the polygonal nature of the teapot is clearly evident; parts (d) and (f) incorporate shading in which the polygons are shaded with color that varies across the polygons. The shading does a fairly good job of masking the polygonal nature of the teapot and greatly increases the realism of the image.

I.2 Coordinates, Points, Lines, and Polygons

The next sections discuss some of the basic conventions of coordinate systems and of drawing points, lines, and polygons. Our emphasis will be on the conventions and commands used by OpenGL. For now, only drawing vertices at fixed positions in the xy-plane or in xyz-space is discussed. Chapter II will explain how to move vertices and geometric shapes around with rotations, translations, and other transformations.

I.2.1 Coordinate Systems

When graphing geometric shapes, one determines the position of the shape by specifying the positions of a set of vertices. For example, the position and geometry of a triangle are specified in terms of the positions of its three vertices. Graphics programming languages, including OpenGL, allow you to set up your own coordinate systems for specifying positions of points; in OpenGL this is done by specifying a function from your coordinate system into the screen coordinates. This allows points to be positioned at locations in either 2-space ($\mathbb{R}^2$) or 3-space ($\mathbb{R}^3$) and to have OpenGL automatically map the points into the proper location in the graphics image.

In the two-dimensional xy-plane, also called $\mathbb{R}^2$, a position is set by specifying its x- and y-coordinates. The usual convention (see Figure I.3) is that the x-axis is horizontal and pointing to the right and the y-axis is vertical and pointing upwards.

In three-dimensional space $\mathbb{R}^3$, positions are specified by triples $\langle a, b, c \rangle$ giving the x-, y-, and z-coordinates of the point. However, the convention for how the three coordinate axes are positioned is different for computer graphics than is usual in mathematics. In computer graphics, the x-axis points to the right, the y-axis points upwards, and the z-axis points toward the viewer. This is different from our customary expectations. For example, in calculus, the x-,

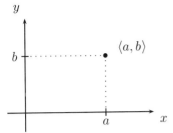

Figure I.3. The xy-plane, $\mathbb{R}^2$, and the point $\langle a, b \rangle$.

y-, and z-axes usually point forward, rightwards, and upwards (respectively). The computer graphics convention was adopted presumably because it keeps the x- and y-axes in the same position as for the xy-plane, but it has the disadvantage of taking some getting used to. Figure I.4 shows the orientation of the coordinate axes.

It is important to note that the coordinates axes used in computer graphics do form a right-handed coordinate system. This means that if you position your right hand with your thumb and index finger extended to make an L shape and place your hand so that your right thumb points along the positive x-axis and your index finger points along the positive y-axis, then your palm will be facing toward the positive z-axis. In particular, this means that the right-hand rule applies to cross products of vectors in $\mathbb{R}^3$.

I.2.2 Geometric Shapes in OpenGL

We next discuss methods for drawing points, lines, and polygons in OpenGL. We only give some of the common versions of the commands available in OpenGL. You should consult the OpenGL programming manual (Woo et al., 1999) for more complete information.

Drawing Points in OpenGL
OpenGL has several commands that define the position of a point. Two of the common ways to use these commands are[1]

```
glVertex3f(float x, float y, float z);
```

or

```
float v[3] = { x, y, z };
glVertex3fv( &v[0] );
```

The first form of the command, `glVertex3f`, specifies the point directly in terms of its x-, y-, and z-coordinates. The second form, `glVertex3fv`, takes a pointer to an array containing the coordinates. The "v" on the end of the function name stands for "vector." There are many other forms of the `glVertex*` command that can be used instead.[2] For instance, the "f,"

---

[1] We describe OpenGL commands with simplified prototypes (and often do not give the officially correct prototype). In this case, the specifiers "`float`" describe the types of the arguments to `glVertex3f()` but should be omitted in your C or C++ code.

[2] There is no function named `glVertex*`: we use this notation to represent collectively the many variations of the `glVertex` commands.

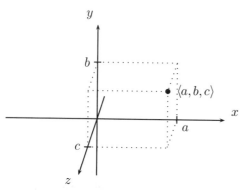

Figure I.4. The coordinate axes in $\mathbb{R}^3$ and the point $\langle a, b, c \rangle$. The z-axis is pointing toward the viewer.

which stands for "float," can be replaced by "s" for "short integer," by "i" for "integer," or by "d" for "double."[3]

For two-dimensional applications, OpenGL also allows you to specify points in terms of just x- and y-coordinates by using the commands

```
glVertex2f(float x, float y);
```

or

```
float v[2] = { x, y };
glVertex2fv( &v[0] );
```

glVertex2f is equivalent to glVertex3f but with $z = 0$.

All calls to glVertex* must be bracketed by calls to the OpenGL commands glBegin and glEnd. For example, to draw the three points shown in Figure I.5, you would use the commands

```
glBegin(GL_POINTS);
glVertex2f( 1.0, 1.0 );
glVertex2f( 2.0, 1.0 );
glVertex2f( 2.0, 2.0 );
glEnd();
```

The calls to the functions glBegin and glEnd are used to signal the start and end of drawing.

A sample OpenGL program, SimpleDraw, supplied with this text, contains the preceding code for drawing three points. If OpenGL is new to you, it is recommended that you examine the source code and try compiling and running the program. You will probably find that the points are drawn as very small, single-pixel points – perhaps so small as to be almost invisible. On most OpenGL systems, you can make points display as large, round dots by calling the following functions:

```
glPointSize(n);              // Points are n pixels in diameter
glEnable(GL_POINT_SMOOTH);
glHint(GL_POINT_SMOOTH_HINT, GL_NICEST);
glEnable(GL_BLEND);
glBlendFunc(GL_SRC_ALPHA, GL_ONE_MINUS_SRC_ALPHA);
```

---

[3] To be completely accurate, we should remark that, to help portability and future compatibility, OpenGL uses the types GLfloat, GLshort, GLint, and GLdouble, which are generally defined to be the same as float, short, int, and double. It would certainly be better programming practice to use OpenGL's data types; however, the extra effort is not really worthwhile for casual programming.

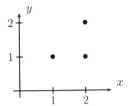

Figure I.5. Three points drawn in two dimensions.

(In the first line, a number such as 6 for *n* may give good results.) The `SimpleDraw` program already includes the preceding function calls, but they have been commented out. If you are lucky, executing these lines in the program before the drawing code will cause the program to draw nice round dots for points. However, the effect of these commands varies with different implementations of OpenGL, and thus you may see square dots instead of round dots or even no change at all.

The `SimpleDraw` program is set up so that the displayed graphics image is shown from the viewpoint of a viewer looking down the *z*-axis. In this situation, `glVertex2f` is a convenient method for two-dimensional graphing.

Drawing Lines in OpenGL
To draw a line in OpenGL, specify its endpoints. The `glBegin` and `glEnd` paradigm is still used. To draw individual lines, pass the parameter `GL_LINES` to `glBegin`. For example, to draw two lines, you could use the commands

```
glBegin( GL_LINES );
glVertex3f( x₁, y₁, z₁ );
glVertex3f( x₂, y₂, z₂ );
glVertex3f( x₃, y₃, z₃ );
glVertex3f( x₄, y₄, z₄ );
glEnd();
```

Letting $\mathbf{v}_i$ be the vertex $\langle x_i, y_i, z_i \rangle$, the commands above draw a line from $\mathbf{v}_1$ to $\mathbf{v}_2$ and another from $\mathbf{v}_3$ to $\mathbf{v}_4$. More generally, you may specify an even number, $2n$, of points, and the `GL_LINES` option will draw n lines connecting $\mathbf{v}_{2i-1}$ to $\mathbf{v}_{2i}$ for $i = 1, \ldots, n$.

You may also use `GL_LINE_STRIP` instead of `GL_LINES`: if you specify n vertices, a continuous chain of lines is drawn, namely, the lines connecting $\mathbf{v}_i$ and $\mathbf{v}_{i+1}$ for $i = 1, \ldots, n - 1$. The parameter `GL_LINE_LOOP` can also be used; it draws the line strip plus the line connecting $\mathbf{v}_n$ to $\mathbf{v}_1$. Figure I.6 shows the effects of these three line-drawing modes.

The `SimpleDraw` program includes code to draw the images in Figure I.6. When the program is run, you may find that the lines look much too thin and appear jagged because they

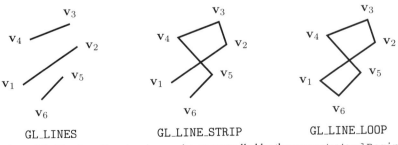

Figure I.6. The three line-drawing modes as controlled by the parameter to `glBegin`.

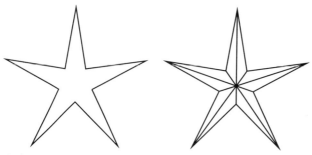

Figure I.7. Figures for Exercises I.2, I.3, and I.4.

were drawn only one pixel wide. By default, OpenGL draws thin lines, one pixel wide, and does not do any "antialiasing" to smooth out the lines. You can try making wider and smoother lines by using the following commands:

```
glLineWidth( n );        // Lines are n pixels wide
glEnable(GL_LINE_SMOOTH);
glHint(GL_LINE_SMOOTH_HINT, GL_NICEST);    // Antialias lines
glEnable(GL_BLEND);
glBlendFunc(GL_SRC_ALPHA, GL_ONE_MINUS_SRC_ALPHA);
```

(In the first line, a value such as 3 for n may give good results.) How well, and whether, the line-width specification and the antialiasing work will depend on your implementation of OpenGL.

Exercise I.1 *The OpenGL program* SimpleDraw *includes code to draw the images shown in Figures I.5 and I.6, and a colorized version of Figure I.12. Run this program, and examine its source code. Learn how to compile the program and then try enabling the code for making bigger points and wider, smoother lines. (This code is already present but is commented out.) Does it work for you?*

Exercise I.2 *Write an OpenGL program to generate the two images of Figure I.7 as line drawings. You will probably want to modify the source code of* SimpleDraw *for this.*

Drawing Polygons in OpenGL

OpenGL includes commands for drawing triangles, quadrilaterals, and convex polygons. Ordinarily, these are drawn as solid, filled-in shapes. That is, OpenGL does not just draw the edges of triangles, quadrilaterals, and polygons but instead draws their interiors.

To draw a single triangle with vertices $\mathbf{v}_i = \langle x_i, y_i, z_i \rangle$, you can use the commands

```
glBegin( GL_TRIANGLES );
glVertex3f( x_1, y_1, z_1 );
glVertex3f( x_2, y_2, z_2 );
glVertex3f( x_3, y_3, z_3 );
glEnd();
```

You may specify multiple triangles by a single invocation of the glBegin(GL_TRIANGLES) function by making $3n$ calls to glVertex* to draw n triangles.

Frequently, one wants to combine multiple triangles to form a continuous surface. For this, it is convenient to specify multiple triangles at once, without having to specify the same vertices repeatedly for different triangles. A "triangle strip" is drawn by invoking glBegin

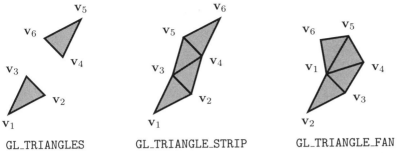

Figure I.8. The three triangle-drawing modes. These are shown with the default front face upwards. In regard to this, note the difference in the placement of the vertices in each figure, especially of v_5 and v_6 in the first two figures.

with GL_TRIANGLE_STRIP and specifying n vertices. This has the effect of joining up the triangles as shown in Figure I.8.

Another way to join up multiple triangles is to let them share the common vertex v_1. This is also shown in Figure I.8 and is invoked by calling glBegin with GL_TRIANGLE_FAN and giving vertices $v_1, \ldots, v_n$.

OpenGL allows you to draw convex quadrilaterals, that is, convex four-sided polygons. OpenGL does not check whether the quadrilaterals are convex or even planar but instead simply breaks the quadrilateral into two triangles to draw the quadrilateral as a filled-in polygon.

Like triangles, quadrilaterals are drawn by giving glBegin and glEnd commands and between them specifying the vertices of the quadrilateral. The following commands can be used to draw one or more quadrilaterals:

```
glBegin( GL_QUADS );
glVertex3f( x₁, y₁, z₁ );
    ...
glVertex3f( xₙ, yₙ, zₙ );
glEnd();
```

Here n must be a multiple of 4, and OpenGL draws the $n/4$ quadrilaterals with vertices v_{4i-3}, v_{4i-2}, v_{4i-1}, and v_{4i}, for $1 \leq i \leq n/4$. You may also use the glBegin parameter GL_QUAD_STRIP to connect the polygons in a strip. In this case, n must be even, and OpenGL draws the $n/2 - 1$ quadrilaterals with vertices v_{2i-3}, v_{2i-2}, v_{2i-1}, and v_{2i}, for $2 \leq i \leq n/2$. These are illustrated in Figure I.9.

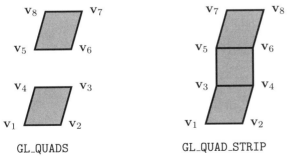

Figure I.9. The two quadrilateral-drawing modes. It is important to note that the order of the vertices is different in the two modes!

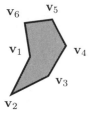

Figure I.10. A polygon with five vertices. This looks similar to the triangle fan of Figure I.8 but can give different results because the OpenGL standards do not specify how the polygon will be triangulated.

The vertices for GL_QUADS and for GL_QUAD_STRIP are specified in different orders. For GL_QUADS, vertices are given in counterclockwise order. For GL_QUAD_STRIP, they are given in pairs in left-to-right order suggesting the action of mounting a ladder.

OpenGL also allows you to draw polygons with an arbitrary number of sides. You should note that OpenGL assumes the polygon is planar, convex, and simple. (A polygon is *simple* if its edges do not cross each other.) Although OpenGL makes these assumptions, it does not check them in any way. In particular, it is quite acceptable to use nonplanar polygons (just as it is quite acceptable to use nonplanar quadrilaterals) as long as the polygon does not deviate too far from being simple, convex, and planar. What OpenGL does is to triangulate the polygon and render the resulting triangles.

To draw a polygon, you call glBegin with the parameter GL_POLYGON and then give the *n* vertices of the polygon. An example is shown in Figure I.10.

Polygons can be combined to generate complex surfaces. For example, Figure I.11 shows two different ways of drawing a torus as a set of polygons. The first torus is generated by using quad strips that wrap around the torus; 16 such strips are combined to make the entire torus. The second torus is generated by using a single long quadrilateral strip that wraps around the torus like a ribbon.

> **Exercise I.3** *Draw the five-pointed star of Figure I.7 as a solid, filled-in region. Use a single triangle fan with the initial point of the triangle fan at the center of the star. (Save your program to modify for Exercise I.4.)*

Colors

OpenGL allows you to set the color of vertices, and thereby the color of lines and polygons, with the glColor* commands. The most common syntax for this command is

```
glColor3f( float r, float g, float b );
```

The numbers r, g, b specify respectively the brightness of the red, green, and blue components of the color. If these three values all equal 0, then the color is black. If they all equal 1, then the color is white. Other colors can be generated by mixing red, green, and blue. For instance, here are some ways to specify some common colors:

```
glColor3f( 1, 0, 0 );          // Red
glColor3f( 0, 1, 0 );          // Green
glColor3f( 0, 0, 1 );          // Blue
glColor3f( 1, 1, 0 );          // Yellow
glColor3f( 1, 0, 1 );          // Magenta
glColor3f( 0, 1, 1 );          // Cyan
```

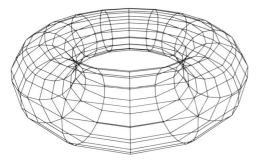

(a) Torus as multiple quad strips.

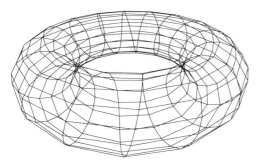

(b) Torus as a single quad strip.

Figure I.11. Two different methods of generating wireframe tori. The second torus is created with the supplied OpenGL program `WrapTorus`. In the second torus, the quadrilaterals are not quite planar.

The brightness levels may also be set to fractional values between 0 and 1 (and in some cases values outside the range [0, 1] can be used to advantage, although they do not correspond to actual displayable colors). These red, green, and blue color settings are used also by many painting and drawing programs and even many word processors on PCs. Many of these programs have color palettes that let you choose colors in terms of red, green, and blue values. OpenGL uses the same RGB system for representing color.

The `glColor*` command may be given inside the scope of `glBegin` and `glEnd` commands. Once a color is set by `glColor*`, that color will be assigned to all subsequent vertices until another color is specified. If all the vertices of a line or polygon have the same color, then the entire line or polygon is drawn with this color. On the other hand, it is possible for different vertices of line or polygon to have different colors. In this case, the interior of the line or polygon is drawn by blending colors; points in the interior of the line or polygon will be assigned a color by averaging colors of the vertices in such a way that the colors of nearby vertices will have more weight than the colors of distant vertices. This process is called *shading* and blends colors smoothly across a polygon or along a line.

You can turn off shading of lines and polygons by using the command

```
glShadeModel( GL_FLAT );
```

and turn it back on with

```
glShadeModel( GL_SMOOTH );
```

In the flat shading mode, an entire region gets the color of one of its vertices. The color of a line, triangle, or quadrilateral is determined by the color of the *last* specified vertex. The color of a general polygon, however, is set by the color of its first vertex.

The background color of the graphics window defaults to black but can be changed with the `glClearColor` command. One usually starts drawing an image by first calling the `glClear` command with the `GL_COLOR_BUFFER_BIT` set in its parameter; this initializes the color to black or whatever color has been set by the `glClearColor` command.

Later in the book we will see that shading is an important tool for creating realistic images, particularly when combined with lighting models that compute colors from material properties and light properties, rather than using colors that are explicitly set by the programmer.

> **Exercise I.4** *Modify the program you wrote for Exercise I.3, which drew a five-pointed star as a single triangle fan. Draw the star in the same way, but now make the triangles alternate between two colors.*

Hidden Surfaces

When we draw points in three dimensions, objects that are closer to the viewpoint may occlude, or hide, objects that are farther from the viewer. OpenGL uses a depth buffer that holds a distance or depth value for each pixel. The depth buffer lets OpenGL do hidden surface computations by the simple expedient of drawing into a pixel only if the new distance will be less than the old distance. The typical use of the depth buffer is as follows: When an object, such as a triangle, is rendered, OpenGL determines which pixels need to be drawn and computes a measure of the distance from the viewer to each pixel image. That distance is compared with the distance associated with the former contents of the pixel. The lesser of these two distances determines which pixel value is saved, because the closer object is presumed to occlude the farther object.

To better appreciate the elegance and simplicity of the depth buffer approach to hidden surfaces, we consider some alternative hidden surface methods. One such method, called the *painter's algorithm*, sorts the polygons from most distant to closest and renders them in back-to-front order, letting subsequent polygons overwrite earlier ones. The painter's algorithm is easy but not completely reliable; in fact, it is not always possible to sort polygons consistently according to their distance from the viewer (cf. Figure I.12). In addition, the painter's algorithm cannot handle interpenetrating polygons. Another hidden surface method is to work out all the information geometrically about how the polygons occlude each other and to render only the visible portions of each polygon. This, however, is quite difficult to design and implement robustly. The depth buffer method, in contrast, is very simple and requires only an extra depth, or distance, value to be stored per pixel. Furthermore, this method allows polygons to be rendered independently and in any order.

The depth buffer is not activated by default. To enable the use of the depth buffer, you must have a rendering context with a depth buffer. If you are using the OpenGL Utility Toolkit (as in the code supplied with this book), this is done by initializing your graphics window with a command such as

```
glutInitDisplayMode(GLUT_DEPTH | GLUT_RGB );
```

which initializes the graphics display to use a window with RGB buffers for color and with a depth buffer. You must also turn on depth testing with the command

```
glEnable( GL_DEPTH_TEST );
```

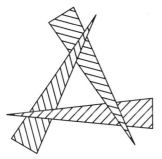

Figure I.12. Three triangles. The triangles are turned obliquely to the viewer so that the top portion of each triangle is in front of the base portion of another.

It is also important to clear the depth buffer each time you render an image. This is typically done with a command such as

```
glClear( GL_COLOR_BUFFER_BIT | GL_DEPTH_BUFFER_BIT );
```

which both clears the color (i.e., initializes the entire image to the default color) and clears the depth values.

The SimpleDraw program illustrates the use of depth buffering for hidden surfaces. It shows three triangles, each of which partially hides another, as in Figure I.12. This example shows why ordering polygons from back to front is not a reliable means of performing hidden surface computation.

Polygon Face Orientations

OpenGL keeps track of whether polygons are facing toward or away from the viewer, that is, OpenGL assigns each polygon a front face and a back face. In some situations, it is desirable for only the front faces of polygons to be viewable, whereas at other times you may want both the front and back faces to be visible. If we set the back faces to be invisible, then any polygon whose back face would ordinarily be seen is not drawn at all and, in effect, becomes transparent. (By default, both faces are visible.)

OpenGL determines which face of a polygon is the front face by the default convention that vertices on a polygon are specified in counterclockwise order (with some exceptions for triangle strips and quadrilateral strips). The polygons in Figures I.8, I.9, and I.10 are all shown with their front faces visible.

You can change the convention for which face is the front face by using the glFrontFace command. This command has the format

$$glFrontFace(\left\{ \begin{array}{l} GL\_CW \\ GL\_CCW \end{array} \right\});$$

where "CW" and "CCW" stand for clockwise and counterclockwise; GL_CCW is the default. Using GL_CW causes the conventions for front and back faces to be reversed on subsequent polygons.

To make front or back faces invisible, or to do both, you must use the commands

$$glCullFace(\left\{ \begin{array}{c} GL\_FRONT \\ GL\_BACK \\ GL\_FRONT\_AND\_BACK \end{array} \right\});$$

```
glEnable( GL_CULL_FACE );
```

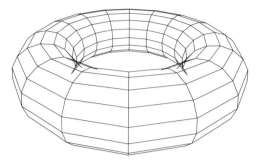

(a) Torus as multiple quad strips.

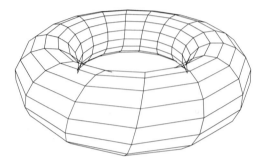

(b) Torus as a single quad strip.

Figure I.13. Two wireframe tori with back faces culled. Compare with Figure I.11.

You must explicitly turn on the face culling with the call to `glEnable`. Face culling can be turned off with the corresponding `glDisable` command. If both front and back faces are culled, then other objects such as points and lines are still drawn.

The two wireframe tori of Figure I.11 are shown again in Figure I.13 with back faces culled. Note that hidden surfaces are not being removed in either figure; only back faces have been culled.

Toggling Wireframe Mode

By default, OpenGL draws polygons as solid and filled in. It is possible to change this by using the `glPolygonMode` function, which determines whether to draw solid polygons, wireframe polygons, or just the vertices of polygons. (Here, "polygon" means also triangles and quadrilaterals.) This makes it easy for a program to switch between the wireframe and nonwireframe mode. The syntax for the `glPolygonMode` command is

$$\texttt{glPolygonMode(} \left\{ \begin{array}{c} \texttt{GL\_FRONT} \\ \texttt{GL\_BACK} \\ \texttt{GL\_FRONT\_AND\_BACK} \end{array} \right\} , \left\{ \begin{array}{c} \texttt{GL\_FILL} \\ \texttt{GL\_LINE} \\ \texttt{GL\_POINT} \end{array} \right\} \texttt{);}$$

The first parameter to `glPolygonMode` specifies whether the mode applies to front or back faces or to both. The second parameter sets whether polygons are drawn filled in, as lines, or as just vertices.

Exercise I.5 *Write an OpenGL program that renders a cube with six faces of different colors. Form the cube from six quadrilaterals, making sure that the front faces are facing* *outwards. If you already know how to perform rotations, let your program include the ability to spin the cube around. (Refer to Chapter II and see the* `WrapTorus` *program for code that does this.)*

If you rendered the cube using triangles instead, how many triangles would be needed?

Exercise I.6 *Repeat Exercise I.5 but render the cube using two quad strips, each containing three quadrilaterals.*

Exercise I.7 *Repeat Exercise I.5 but render the cube using two triangle fans.*

I.3 Double Buffering for Animation

The term "animation" refers to drawing moving objects or scenes. The movement is only a visual illusion, however; in practice, animation is achieved by drawing a succession of still scenes, called frames, each showing a static snapshot at an instant in time. The illusion of motion is obtained by rapidly displaying successive frames. This technique is used for movies, television, and computer displays. Movies typically have a frame rate of 24 frames per second. The frame rates in computer graphics can vary with the power of the computer and the complexity of the graphics rendering, but typically one attempts to get close to 30 frames per second and more ideally 60 frames per second. These frame rates are quite adequate to give smooth motion on a screen. For head-mounted displays, where the view changes with the position of the viewer's head, much higher frame rates are needed to obtain good effects.

Double buffering can be used to generate successive frames cleanly. While one image is displayed on the screen, the next frame is being created in another part of the memory. When the next frame is ready to be displayed, the new frame replaces the old frame on the screen instantaneously (or rather, the next time the screen is redrawn, the new image is used). A region of memory where an image is being created or stored is called a buffer. The image being displayed is stored in the *front buffer*, and the *back buffer* holds the next frame as it is being created. When the buffers are swapped, the new image replaces the old one on the screen. Note that swapping buffers does not generally require copying from one buffer to the other; instead, one can just update pointers to switch the identities of the front and back buffers.

A simple example of animation using double buffering in OpenGL is shown in the program `SimpleAnim` that accompanies this book. To use double buffering, you should include the following items in your OpenGL program: First, you need to have a graphics context that supports double buffering. This is obtained by initializing your graphics window by a function call such as

```
glutInitDisplayMode(GLUT_DOUBLE | GLUT_RGB | GLUT_DEPTH );
```

In `SimpleAnim`, the function `updateScene` is used to draw a single frame. It works by drawing into the back buffer and at the very end gives the following commands to complete the drawing and swap the front and back buffers:

```
glFlush();
glutSwapBuffers();
```

It is also necessary to make sure that `updateScene` is called repeatedly to draw the next frame. There are two ways to do this. The first way is to have the `updateScene` routine call `glutPostRedisplay()`. This will tell the operating system that the current window needs rerendering, and this will in turn cause the operating system to call the routine specified by `glutDisplayFunc`. The second method, which is used in `SimpleAnim`, is to use `glutIdleFunc` to request the operating system to call `updateScene` whenever the CPU is idle. If the computer system is not heavily loaded, this will cause the operating system to call `updateScene` repeatedly.

You should see the GLUT documentation for more information about how to set up callbacks, not only for redisplay functions and idle functions but also for capturing keystrokes, mouse button events, mouse movements, and so on. The OpenGL programs supplied with this book provide examples of capturing keystrokes; in addition, `ConnectDots` shows how to capture mouse clicks.

II

Transformations and Viewing

This chapter discusses the mathematics of linear, affine, and perspective transformations and their uses in OpenGL. The basic purpose of these transformations is to provide methods of changing the shape and position of objects, but the use of these transformations is pervasive throughout computer graphics. In fact, affine transformations are arguably the most fundamental mathematical tool for computer graphics.

An obvious use of transformations is to help simplify the task of geometric modeling. For example, suppose an artist is designing a computerized geometric model of a Ferris wheel. A Ferris wheel has considerable symmetry and includes many repeated elements such as multiple cars and struts. The artist could design a single model of the car and then place multiple instances of the car around the Ferris wheel attached at the proper points. Similarly, the artist could build the main structure of the Ferris wheel by designing one radial "slice" of the wheel and using multiple rotated copies of this slice to form the entire structure. Affine transformations are used to describe how the parts are placed and oriented.

A second important use of transformations is to describe animation. Continuing with the Ferris wheel example, if the Ferris wheel is animated, then the positions and orientations of its individual geometric components are constantly changing. Thus, for animation, it is necessary to compute time-varying affine transformations to simulate the motion of the Ferris wheel.

A third, more hidden, use of transformations in computer graphics is for rendering. After a 3-D geometric model has been created, it is necessary to render it on a two-dimensional surface called the *viewport*. Some common examples of viewports are a window on a video screen, a frame of a movie, and a hard-copy image. There are special transformations, called perspective transformations, that are used to map points from a 3-D model to points on a 2-D viewport.

To properly appreciate the uses of transformations, it is important to understand the *rendering pipeline*, that is, the steps by which a 3-D scene is modeled and rendered. A high-level description of the rendering pipeline used by OpenGL is shown in Figure II.1. The stages of the pipeline illustrate the conceptual steps involved in going from a polygonal model to an on-screen image. The stages of the pipeline are as follows:

Modeling. In this stage, a 3-D model of the scene to be displayed is created. This stage is generally the main portion of an OpenGL program. The program draws images by specifying their positions in 3-space. At its most fundamental level, the modeling in 3-space consists of describing vertices, lines, and polygons (usually triangles and quadrilaterals) by giving the x-, y-, z-coordinates of the vertices. OpenGL provides a flexible set of tools for positioning vertices, including methods for rotating, scaling, and reshaping objects.

17

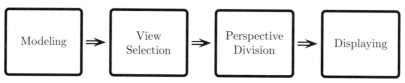

Figure II.1. The four stages of the rendering pipeline in OpenGL.

These tools are called "affine transformations" and are discussed in detail in the next sections. OpenGL uses a 4×4 matrix called the "model view matrix" to describe affine transformations.

View Selection. This stage is typically used to control the view of the 3-D model. In this stage, a camera or viewpoint position and direction are set. In addition, the range and the field of view are determined. The mathematical tools used here include "orthographic projections" and "perspective transformations." OpenGL uses another 4×4 matrix called the "projection matrix" to specify these transformations.

Perspective Division. The previous two stages use a method of representing points in 3-space by means of homogeneous coordinates. Homogeneous coordinates use vectors with four components to represent points in 3-space.

The perspective division stage merely converts from homogeneous coordinates back into the usual three x-, y-, z-coordinates. The x- and y-coordinates determine the position of a vertex in the final graphics image. The z-coordinates measure the distance to the object, although they can represent a "pseudo-distance," or "fake" distance, rather than a true distance.

Homogeneous coordinates are described later in this chapter. As we will see, perspective division consists merely of dividing through by a w value.

Displaying. In this stage, the scene is rendered onto the computer screen or other display medium such as a printed page or a film. A window on a computer screen consists of a rectangular array of pixels. Each pixel can be independently set to an individual color and brightness. For most 3-D graphics applications, it is desirable to not render parts of the scene that are not visible owing to obstructions of view. OpenGL and most other graphics display systems perform this hidden surface removal with the aid of depth (or distance) information stored with each pixel. During this fourth stage, pixels are given color and depth information, and interpolation methods are used to fill in the interior of polygons. This fourth stage is the only stage dependent on the physical characteristics of the output device. The first three stages usually work in a device-independent fashion.

The discussion in this chapter emphasizes the mathematical aspects of the transformations used by computer graphics but also sketches their use in OpenGL. The geometric tools used in computer graphics are mathematically very elegant. Even more important, the techniques discussed in this chapter have the advantage of being fairly easy for an artist or programmer to use and lend themselves to efficient software and hardware implementation. In fact, modern-day PCs typically include specialized graphics chips that carry out many of the transformations and interpolations discussed in this chapter.

II.1 Transformations in 2-Space

We start by discussing linear and affine transformations on a fairly abstract level and then see examples of how to use transformations in OpenGL. We begin by considering affine transformations in 2-space since they are much simpler than transformations in 3-space. Most of the important properties of affine transformations already apply in 2-space.

The xy-plane, denoted $\mathbb{R}^2 = \mathbb{R} \times \mathbb{R}$, is the usual Cartesian plane consisting of points $\langle x, y \rangle$. To avoid writing too many coordinates, we often use the vector notation $\mathbf{x}$ for a point in $\mathbb{R}^2$, with the usual convention being that $\mathbf{x} = \langle x_1, x_2 \rangle$, where $x_1, x_2 \in \mathbb{R}$. This notation is convenient but potentially confusing because we will use the same notation for vectors as for points.[1]

We write $\mathbf{0}$ for the origin, or zero vector, and thus $\mathbf{0} = \langle 0, 0 \rangle$. We write $\mathbf{x} + \mathbf{y}$ and $\mathbf{x} - \mathbf{y}$ for the componentwise sum and difference of $\mathbf{x}$ and $\mathbf{y}$. A real number $\alpha \in \mathbb{R}$ is called a *scalar*, and the product of a scalar and a vector is defined by $\alpha \mathbf{x} = \langle \alpha x_1, \alpha x_2 \rangle$.[2]

II.1.1 Basic Definitions

A *transformation* on $\mathbb{R}^2$ is any mapping $A : \mathbb{R}^2 \mapsto \mathbb{R}^2$. That is, each point $\mathbf{x} \in \mathbb{R}^2$ is mapped to a unique point, $A(\mathbf{x})$, also in $\mathbb{R}^2$.

Definition Let A be a transformation. A is a *linear transformation* provided the following two conditions hold:

1. For all $\alpha \in \mathbb{R}$ and all $\mathbf{x} \in \mathbb{R}^2$, $A(\alpha \mathbf{x}) = \alpha A(\mathbf{x})$.
2. For all $\mathbf{x}, \mathbf{y} \in \mathbb{R}^2$, $A(\mathbf{x} + \mathbf{y}) = A(\mathbf{x}) + A(\mathbf{y})$.

Note that $A(\mathbf{0}) = \mathbf{0}$ for any linear transformation A. This follows from condition 1 with $\alpha = 0$.

Examples: Here are five examples of linear transformations:

1. $A_1 : \langle x, y \rangle \mapsto \langle -y, x \rangle$.
2. $A_2 : \langle x, y \rangle \mapsto \langle x, 2y \rangle$.
3. $A_3 : \langle x, y \rangle \mapsto \langle x + y, y \rangle$.
4. $A_4 : \langle x, y \rangle \mapsto \langle x, -y \rangle$.
5. $A_5 : \langle x, y \rangle \mapsto \langle -x, -y \rangle$.

> **Exercise II.1** *Verify that the preceding five transformations are linear. Draw pictures of how they transform the* F *shown in Figure II.2.*

We defined transformations as acting on a single point at a time, but of course, a transformation also acts on arbitrary geometric objects since the geometric object can be viewed as a collection of points and, when the transformation is used to map all the points to new locations, this changes the form and position of the geometric object. For example, Exercise II.1 asked you to calculate how transformations acted on the F shape.

---

[1] Points and vectors in 2-space both consist of a pair of real numbers. The difference is that a point specifies a particular location, whereas a vector specifies a particular displacement, or change in location. That is, a vector is the difference of two points. Rather than adopting a confusing and nonstandard notation that clearly distinguishes between points and vectors, we will instead follow the more common, but ambiguous, convention of using the same notation for points as for vectors.

[2] In view of the distinction between points and vectors, it can be useful to form the sums and differences of two vectors, or of a point and a vector, or the difference of two points, but it is not generally useful to form the sum of two points. The sum or difference of two vectors is a vector. The sum or difference of a point and a vector is a point. The difference of two points is a vector. Likewise, a vector may be multiplied by a scalar, but it is less frequently appropriate to multiply a scalar and point. However, we gloss over these issues and define the sums and products on all combinations of points and vectors. In any event, we frequently blur the distinction between points and vectors.

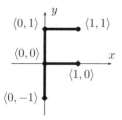

Figure II.2. An F shape.

One simple, but important, kind of transformation is a "translation," which changes the position of objects by a fixed amount but does not change the orientation or shape of geometric objects.

Definition A transformation A is a *translation* provided that there is a fixed $\mathbf{u} \in \mathbb{R}^2$ such that $A(\mathbf{x}) = \mathbf{x} + \mathbf{u}$ for all $\mathbf{x} \in \mathbb{R}^2$.

The notation $T_\mathbf{u}$ is used to denote this translation, thus $T_\mathbf{u}(\mathbf{x}) = \mathbf{x} + \mathbf{u}$.

The *composition* of two transformations A and B is the transformation computed by first applying B and then applying A. This transformation is denoted $A \circ B$, or just AB, and satisfies

$$(A \circ B)(\mathbf{x}) = A(B(\mathbf{x})).$$

The *identity* transformation maps every point to itself. The *inverse* of a transformation A is the transformation A^{-1} such that $A \circ A^{-1}$ and $A^{-1} \circ A$ are both the identity transformation. Not every transformation has an inverse, but when A is one-to-one and onto, the inverse transformation A^{-1} always exists.

Note that the inverse of $T_\mathbf{u}$ is $T_{-\mathbf{u}}$.

Definition A transformation A is *affine* provided it can be written as the composition of a translation and a linear transformation. That is, provided it can be written in the form $A = T_\mathbf{u} B$ for some $\mathbf{u} \in \mathbb{R}^2$ and some linear transformation B.

In other words, a transformation A is affine if it equals

$$A(\mathbf{x}) = B(\mathbf{x}) + \mathbf{u},   \tag{II.1}$$

with B a linear transformation and $\mathbf{u}$ a point.

Because it is permitted that $\mathbf{u} = \mathbf{0}$, every linear transformation is affine. However, not every affine transformation is linear. In particular, if $\mathbf{u} \neq \mathbf{0}$, then transformation II.1 is not linear since it does not map $\mathbf{0}$ to $\mathbf{0}$.

Proposition II.1 *Let A be an affine transformation. The translation vector $\mathbf{u}$ and the linear transformation B are uniquely determined by A.*

Proof First, we see how to determine $\mathbf{u}$ from A. We claim that in fact $\mathbf{u} = A(\mathbf{0})$. This is proved by the following equalities:

$$A(\mathbf{0}) \;=\; T_\mathbf{u}(B(\mathbf{0})) \;=\; T_\mathbf{u}(\mathbf{0}) \;=\; \mathbf{0} + \mathbf{u} \;=\; \mathbf{u}.$$

Then $B = T_\mathbf{u}^{-1} A = T_{-\mathbf{u}} A$, and so B is also uniquely determined.   □

II.1.2 Matrix Representation of Linear Transformations

The preceding mathematical definition of linear transformations is stated rather abstractly. However, there is a very concrete way to represent a linear transformation A – namely, as a 2×2 matrix.

Define $\mathbf{i} = \langle 1, 0 \rangle$ and $\mathbf{j} = \langle 0, 1 \rangle$. The two vectors $\mathbf{i}$ and $\mathbf{j}$ are the unit vectors aligned with the x-axis and y-axis, respectively. Any vector $\mathbf{x} = \langle x_1, x_2 \rangle$ can be uniquely expressed as a linear combination of $\mathbf{i}$ and $\mathbf{j}$, namely, as $\mathbf{x} = x_1\mathbf{i} + x_2\mathbf{j}$.

Let A be a linear transformation. Let $\mathbf{u} = \langle u_1, u_2 \rangle = A(\mathbf{i})$ and $\mathbf{v} = \langle v_1, v_2 \rangle = A(\mathbf{j})$. Then, by linearity, for any $\mathbf{x} \in \mathbb{R}^2$,

$$A(\mathbf{x}) = A(x_1\mathbf{i} + x_2\mathbf{j}) = x_1 A(\mathbf{i}) + x_2 A(\mathbf{j}) = x_1\mathbf{u} + x_2\mathbf{v}$$
$$= \langle u_1 x_1 + v_1 x_2, u_2 x_1 + v_2 x_2 \rangle.$$

Let M be the matrix $\left(\begin{smallmatrix} u_1 & v_1 \\ u_2 & v_2 \end{smallmatrix} \right)$. Then,

$$M \begin{pmatrix} x_1 \\ x_2 \end{pmatrix} = \begin{pmatrix} u_1 & v_1 \\ u_2 & v_2 \end{pmatrix} \begin{pmatrix} x_1 \\ x_2 \end{pmatrix} = \begin{pmatrix} u_1 x_1 + v_1 x_2 \\ u_2 x_1 + v_2 x_2 \end{pmatrix},$$

and so the matrix M computes the same thing as the transformation A. We call M the *matrix representation of A*.

We have just shown that every linear transformation A is represented by some matrix. Conversely, it is easy to check that every matrix represents a linear transformation. Thus, it is reasonable to think henceforth of linear transformations on $\mathbb{R}^2$ as being the same as 2×2 matrices.

One notational complication is that a linear transformation A operates on points $\mathbf{x} = \langle x_1, x_2 \rangle$, whereas a matrix M acts on column vectors. It would be convenient, however, to use both of the notations $A(\mathbf{x})$ and $M\mathbf{x}$. To make both notations be correct, we adopt the following rather special conventions about the meaning of angle brackets and the representation of points as column vectors:

Notation The point or vector $\langle x_1, x_2 \rangle$ is identical to the column vector $\left(\begin{smallmatrix} x_1 \\ x_2 \end{smallmatrix} \right)$. So "point," "vector," and "column vector" all mean the same thing. A column vector is the same as a single column matrix. A *row vector* is a vector of the form (x_1, x_2), that is, a matrix with a single row.

A superscript T denotes the matrix transpose operator. In particular, the transpose of a row vector is a column vector and vice versa. Thus, $\mathbf{x}^{\mathrm{T}}$ equals the row vector (x_1, x_2).

It is a simple, but important, fact that the columns of a matrix M are the images of $\mathbf{i}$ and $\mathbf{j}$ under M. That is to say, the first column of M is equal to $M\mathbf{i}$ and the second column of M is equal to $M\mathbf{j}$. This gives an intuitive method of constructing a matrix for a linear transformation, as shown in the next example.

Example: Let $M = \left(\begin{smallmatrix} 1 & 0 \\ 1 & 2 \end{smallmatrix} \right)$. Consider the action of M on the F shown in Figure II.3. To find the matrix representation of its inverse M^{-1}, it is enough to determine $M^{-1}\mathbf{i}$ and $M^{-1}\mathbf{j}$. It is not hard to see that

$$M^{-1} \begin{pmatrix} 1 \\ 0 \end{pmatrix} = \begin{pmatrix} 1 \\ -1/2 \end{pmatrix} \qquad \text{and} \qquad M^{-1} \begin{pmatrix} 0 \\ 1 \end{pmatrix} = \begin{pmatrix} 0 \\ 1/2 \end{pmatrix}.$$

Hint: Both facts follow from $M \left(\begin{smallmatrix} 0 \\ 1/2 \end{smallmatrix} \right) = \left(\begin{smallmatrix} 0 \\ 1 \end{smallmatrix} \right)$ and $M \left(\begin{smallmatrix} 1 \\ 0 \end{smallmatrix} \right) = \left(\begin{smallmatrix} 1 \\ 1 \end{smallmatrix} \right)$.

Therefore, M^{-1} is equal to $\left(\begin{smallmatrix} 1 & 0 \\ -1/2 & 1/2 \end{smallmatrix} \right)$.

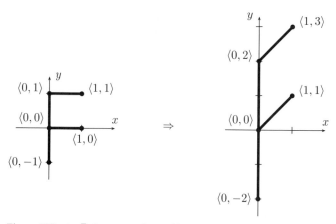

Figure II.3. An **F** shape transformed by a linear transformation.

The example shows a rather intuitive way to find the inverse of a matrix, but it depends on being able to find preimages of **i** and **j**. One can also compute the inverse of a 2×2 matrix by the well-known formula

$$\begin{pmatrix} a & b \\ c & d \end{pmatrix}^{-1} = \frac{1}{\det(M)} \begin{pmatrix} d & -b \\ -c & a \end{pmatrix},$$

where $\det(M) = ad - bc$ is the determinant of M.

> **Exercise II.2** *Figure II.4 shows an affine transformation acting on an* **F**. *(a) Is this a linear transformation? Why or why not? (b) Express this affine transformation in the form* $\mathbf{x} \mapsto M\mathbf{x} + \mathbf{u}$ *by explicitly giving M and $\mathbf{u}$.*

A *rotation* is a transformation that rotates the points in $\mathbb{R}^2$ by a fixed angle around the origin. Figure II.5 shows the effect of a rotation of θ degrees in the counterclockwise (CCW) direction. As shown in Figure II.5, the images of **i** and **j** under a rotation of θ degrees are $\langle \cos\theta, \sin\theta \rangle$ and $\langle -\sin\theta, \cos\theta \rangle$. Therefore, a counterclockwise rotation through an angle θ is represented by the matrix

$$R_\theta = \begin{pmatrix} \cos\theta & -\sin\theta \\ \sin\theta & \cos\theta \end{pmatrix}. \qquad\qquad \text{II.2}$$

> **Exercise II.3** *Prove the angle sum formulas for* sin *and* cos:
>
> $$\sin(\theta + \varphi) = \sin\theta \cos\varphi + \cos\theta \sin\varphi$$
>
> $$\cos(\theta + \varphi) = \cos\theta \cos\varphi - \sin\theta \sin\varphi,$$
>
> *by considering what the rotation R_θ does to the point* $\mathbf{x} = \langle \cos\varphi, \sin\varphi \rangle$.

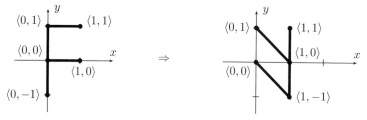

Figure II.4. An affine transformation acting on an **F**.

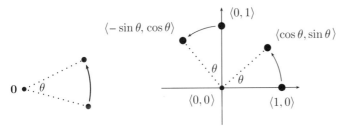

Figure II.5. Effect of a rotation through angle θ. The origin **0** is held fixed by the rotation.

Conventions on Row and Column Vectors and Transposes. The conventions adopted in this book are that points in space are represented by *column* vectors, and linear transformations with matrix representation M are computed as $M\mathbf{x}$. Thus, our matrices multiply on the left. Unfortunately, this convention is not universally followed, and it is also common in computer graphics applications to use *row* vectors for points and vectors and to use matrix representations that act on the right. That is, many workers in computer graphics use a *row* vector to represent a point: instead of using $\mathbf{x}$, they use the row vector $\mathbf{x}^{\mathsf{T}}$. Then, instead of multiplying on the left with M, they multiply on the right with its transpose M^{T}. Because $\mathbf{x}^{\mathsf{T}} M^{\mathsf{T}}$ equals $(M\mathbf{x})^{\mathsf{T}}$, this has the same meaning. Similarly, when multiplying matrices to compose transformations, one has to reverse the order of the multiplications when working with transposed matrices because $(MN)^{\mathsf{T}} = N^{\mathsf{T}} M^{\mathsf{T}}$.

OpenGL follows the same conventions as we do: points and vectors are column vectors, and transformation matrices multiply on the left. However, OpenGL does have some vestiges of the transposed conventions; namely, when specifying matrices with `glLoad-Matrix` and `glMultMatrix` the entries in the matrix are given in column order.

II.1.3 Rigid Transformations and Rotations

A rigid transformation is a transformation that only repositions objects, leaving their shape and size unchanged. If the rigid transformation also preserves the notions of "clockwise" versus "counterclockwise," then it is orientation-preserving.

Definition A transformation is called *rigid* if and only if it preserves both

1. Distances between points, and
2. Angles between lines.

The transformation is said to be *orientation-preserving* if it preserves the direction of angles, that is, if a counterclockwise direction of movement stays counterclockwise after being transformed by A.

Rigid, orientation-preserving transformations are widely used. One application of these transformations is in animation: the position and orientation of a moving rigid body can be described by a time-varying transformation $A(t)$. This transformation $A(t)$ will be rigid and orientation-preserving provided the body does not deform or change size or shape.

The two most common examples of rigid, orientation-preserving transformations are rotations and translations. Another example of a rigid, orientation-preserving transformation is a "generalized rotation" that performs a rotation around an arbitrary center point. We prove below that every rigid, orientation-preserving transformation over $\mathbb{R}^2$ is either a translation or a generalized rotation.

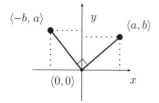

Figure II.6. A rigid, orientation-preserving, linear transformation acting on the unit vectors **i** and **j**.

For *linear* transformations, an equivalent definition of rigid transformation is that a linear transformation A is rigid if and only if it preserves dot products. That is to say, if and only if, for all $\mathbf{x}, \mathbf{y} \in \mathbb{R}^2$, $\mathbf{x} \cdot \mathbf{y} = A(\mathbf{x}) \cdot A(\mathbf{y})$. To see that this preserves distances, recall that $||\mathbf{x}||^2 = \mathbf{x} \cdot \mathbf{x}$ is the square of the magnitude of $\mathbf{x}$ or the square of $\mathbf{x}$'s distance from the origin.[3] Thus, $||\mathbf{x}||^2 = \mathbf{x} \cdot \mathbf{x} = A(\mathbf{x}) \cdot A(\mathbf{x}) = ||A(\mathbf{x})||^2$. From the definition of the dot product as $\mathbf{x} \cdot \mathbf{y} = ||\mathbf{x}|| \cdot ||\mathbf{y}|| \cos\theta$, where θ is the angle between $\mathbf{x}$ and $\mathbf{y}$, the transformation A must also preserve angles between lines.

Exercise II.4 *Which of the five linear transformations in Exercise II.1 on page 19 are rigid? Which ones are both rigid and orientation-preserving?*

Exercise II.5 *Let $M = (\mathbf{u}, \mathbf{v})$, that is, $M = \begin{pmatrix} u_1 & v_1 \\ u_2 & v_2 \end{pmatrix}$. Show that the linear transformation represented by the matrix M is rigid if and only if $||\mathbf{u}|| = ||\mathbf{v}|| = 1$, and $\mathbf{u} \cdot \mathbf{v} = 0$. Prove that if M represents a rigid transformation, then $\det(M) = \pm 1$.*

A matrix M of the type in the previous exercise is called an *orthonormal* matrix.

Exercise II.6 *Prove that the linear transformation represented by the matrix M is rigid if and only if $M^{\mathsf{T}} = M^{-1}$.*

Exercise II.7 *Show that the linear transformation represented by the matrix M is orientation-preserving if and only if $\det(M) > 0$. [Hint: Let $M = (\mathbf{u}, \mathbf{v})$. Let $\mathbf{u}'$ be $\mathbf{u}$ rotated counterclockwise $90°$. Then M is orientation-preserving if and only if $\mathbf{u}' \cdot \mathbf{v} > 0$.]*

Theorem II.2 *Every rigid, orientation-preserving, linear transformation is a rotation.*

The converse to Theorem II.2 holds too: every rotation is obviously a rigid, orientation-preserving, linear transformation.

Proof Let A be a rigid, orientation-preserving, linear transformation. Let $\langle a, b \rangle = A(\mathbf{i})$. By rigidity, $A(\mathbf{i}) \cdot A(\mathbf{i}) = a^2 + b^2 = 1$. Also, $A(\mathbf{j})$ must be the vector obtained by rotating $A(\mathbf{i})$ counterclockwise $90°$; thus, $A(\mathbf{j}) = \langle -b, a \rangle$, as shown in Figure II.6.

Therefore, the matrix M representing A is equal to $\begin{pmatrix} a & -b \\ b & a \end{pmatrix}$. Because $a^2 + b^2 = 1$, there must be an angle θ such that $\cos\theta = a$ and $\sin\theta = b$, namely, either $\theta = \cos^{-1} a$ or $\theta = -\cos^{-1} a$. From equation II.2, we see that A is a rotation through the angle θ. $\qquad\square$

Some programming languages, including C and C++, have a two-parameter version of the arctangent function that lets you compute the rotation angle as

$$\theta = \texttt{atan2}(b, a).$$

Theorem II.2 and the definition of affine transformations give the following characterization.

---

[3]   Appendix A contains a review of elementary facts from linear algebra, including a discussion of dot products and cross products.

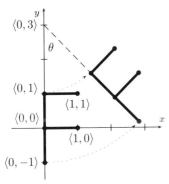

Figure II.7. A generalized rotation $R_\theta^{\mathbf{u}}$. The center of rotation is $\mathbf{u} = \langle 0, 3 \rangle$. The angle is $\theta = 45°$.

Corollary II.3 *Every rigid, orientation-preserving, affine transformation can be (uniquely) expressed as the composition of a translation and a rotation.*

Definition A *generalized rotation* is a transformation that holds a *center point* $\mathbf{u}$ fixed and rotates all other points around $\mathbf{u}$ through a fixed angle θ. This transformation is denoted $R_\theta^{\mathbf{u}}$.

An example of a generalized rotation is given in Figure II.7. Clearly, a generalized rotation is rigid and orientation-preserving.

One way to perform a generalized rotation is first to apply a translation to move the point $\mathbf{u}$ to the origin, then rotate around the origin, and then translate the origin back to $\mathbf{u}$. Thus, the generalized rotation $R_\theta^{\mathbf{u}}$ can be expressed as

$$R_\theta^{\mathbf{u}} = T_{\mathbf{u}} R_\theta T_{-\mathbf{u}}. \qquad\qquad\text{II.3}$$

You should convince yourself that formula II.3 is correct.

Theorem II.4 *Every rigid, orientation-preserving, affine transformation is either a translation or a generalized rotation.*

Obviously, the converse of this theorem holds too.

Proof Let A be a rigid, orientation-preserving, affine transformation. Let $\mathbf{u} = A(\mathbf{0})$. If $\mathbf{u} = \mathbf{0}$, A is actually a linear transformation, and Theorem II.2 implies that A is a rotation. So suppose $\mathbf{u} \neq \mathbf{0}$. It will suffice to prove that either A is a translation or there is some point $\mathbf{v} \in \mathbb{R}^2$ that is a fixed point of A, that is, such that $A(\mathbf{v}) = \mathbf{v}$. This is sufficient since, if there is a fixed point $\mathbf{v}$, then the reasoning of the proof of Theorem II.2 shows that A is a generalized rotation around $\mathbf{v}$.

Let L be the line that contains the two points $\mathbf{0}$ and $\mathbf{u}$. We consider two cases. First, suppose that A maps L to itself. By rigidity, and by choice of $\mathbf{u}$, $A(\mathbf{u})$ is distance $\|\mathbf{u}\|$ from $\mathbf{u}$, and so we must have either $A(\mathbf{u}) = \mathbf{u} + \mathbf{u}$ or $A(\mathbf{u}) = \mathbf{0}$. If $A(\mathbf{u}) = \mathbf{u} + \mathbf{u}$, then A must be the translation $T_{\mathbf{u}}$. This follows because, again by the rigidity of A, every point $\mathbf{x} \in L$ must map to $\mathbf{x} + \mathbf{u}$ and, by the rigidity and orientation-preserving properties, the same holds for every point not on L. On the other hand, if $A(\mathbf{u}) = \mathbf{0}$, then rigidity implies that $\mathbf{v} = \frac{1}{2}\mathbf{u}$ is a fixed point of A, and thus A is a generalized rotation around $\mathbf{v}$.

Second, suppose that the line L is mapped to a different line L'. Let L' make an angle of θ with L, as shown in Figure II.8. Since $L' \neq L$, θ is nonzero and is not a multiple of $180°$. Let L_2 be the line perpendicular to L at the point $\mathbf{0}$, and let L'_2 be the line perpendicular to L at the point $\mathbf{u}$. Note that L_2 and L'_2 are parallel. Now let L_3 be the line obtained by rotating L_2 around

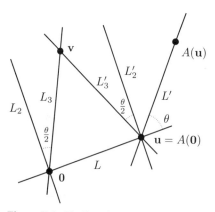

Figure II.8. Finding the center of rotation. The point **v** is fixed by the rotation.

the origin through a clockwise angle of $\theta/2$, and let L_3' be the line obtained by rotating L_2' around the point **u** through a counterclockwise angle of $\theta/2$. Because A is rigid and orientation-preserving and the angle between L and L_3 equals the angle between L' and L_3', the line L_3 is mapped to L_3' by A. The two lines L_3 and L_3' are not parallel and intersect in a point **v**. By the symmetry of the constructions, **v** is equidistant from **0** and **u**. Therefore, again by rigidity, $A(\mathbf{v}) = \mathbf{v}$. It follows that A is the generalized rotation $R_\theta^\mathbf{v}$, which performs a rotation through an angle θ around the center **v**. $\square$

II.1.4 Homogeneous Coordinates

Homogeneous coordinates provide a method of using a triple of numbers $\langle x, y, w \rangle$ to represent a point in $\mathbb{R}^2$.

Definition If $x, y, w \in \mathbb{R}$ and $w \neq 0$, then $\langle x, y, w \rangle$ is a *homogeneous coordinate representation* of the point $\langle x/w, y/w \rangle \in \mathbb{R}^2$.

Note that any given point in $\mathbb{R}^2$ has many representations in homogeneous coordinates. For example, the point $\langle 2, 1 \rangle$ can be represented by any of the following sets of homogeneous coordinates: $\langle 2, 1, 1 \rangle$, $\langle 4, 2, 2 \rangle$, $\langle 6, 3, 3 \rangle$, $\langle -2, -1, -1 \rangle$, and so on. More generally, the triples $\langle x, y, w \rangle$ and $\langle x', y', w' \rangle$ represent the same point in homogeneous coordinates if and only if there is a nonzero scalar α such that $x' = \alpha x$, $y' = \alpha y$, and $w' = \alpha w$.

So far, we have only specified the meaning of the homogeneous coordinates $\langle x, y, w \rangle$ when $w \neq 0$ because the definition of the meaning of $\langle x, y, w \rangle$ required dividing by w. However, we will see in Section II.1.8 that, when $w = 0$, $\langle x, y, w \rangle$ is the homogeneous coordinate representation of a "point at infinity." (Alternatively, graphics software such as OpenGL will sometimes use homogeneous coordinates with $w = 0$ as a representation of a direction.) However, it is always required that at least one of the components x, y, w be nonzero.

The use of homogeneous coordinates may at first seem somewhat strange or poorly motivated; however, it is an important mathematical tool for the representation of points in $\mathbb{R}^2$ in computer graphics. There are several reasons for this. First, as discussed next, using homogeneous coordinates allows an affine transformation to be represented by a single matrix. The second reason will become apparent in Section II.3, where perspective transformations and interpolation are discussed. A third important reason will arise in Chapters VII and VIII, where homogeneous coordinates will allow Bézier curves and B-spline curves to represent circles and other conic sections.

II.1.5 Matrix Representation of Affine Transformations

Recall that any affine transformation A can be expressed as a linear transformation B followed by a translation $T_{\mathbf{u}}$, that is, $A = T_{\mathbf{u}} \circ B$. Let M be a 2×2 matrix representing B, and suppose

$$M = \begin{pmatrix} a & b \\ c & d \end{pmatrix} \quad \text{and} \quad \mathbf{u} = \begin{pmatrix} e \\ f \end{pmatrix}.$$

Then the mapping A can be defined by

$$\begin{pmatrix} x_1 \\ x_2 \end{pmatrix} \mapsto M \begin{pmatrix} x_1 \\ x_2 \end{pmatrix} + \begin{pmatrix} e \\ f \end{pmatrix} = \begin{pmatrix} a & b \\ c & d \end{pmatrix} \begin{pmatrix} x_1 \\ x_2 \end{pmatrix} + \begin{pmatrix} e \\ f \end{pmatrix} = \begin{pmatrix} ax_1 + bx_2 + e \\ cx_1 + dx_2 + f \end{pmatrix}.$$

Now define N to be the 3×3 matrix

$$N = \begin{pmatrix} a & b & e \\ c & d & f \\ 0 & 0 & 1 \end{pmatrix}.$$

Using the homogeneous representation $\langle x_1, x_2, 1 \rangle$ of $\langle x_1, x_2 \rangle$, we see that

$$N \begin{pmatrix} x_1 \\ x_2 \\ 1 \end{pmatrix} = \begin{pmatrix} a & b & e \\ c & d & f \\ 0 & 0 & 1 \end{pmatrix} \begin{pmatrix} x_1 \\ x_2 \\ 1 \end{pmatrix} = \begin{pmatrix} ax_1 + bx_2 + e \\ cx_1 + dx_2 + f \\ 1 \end{pmatrix}.$$

The effect of N's acting on $\langle x, y, 1 \rangle$ is identical to the effect of the affine transformation A acting on $\langle x, y \rangle$. The only difference is that the third coordinate of "1" is being carried around. More generally, for any other homogeneous representation of the same point, $\langle \alpha x_1, \alpha x_2, \alpha \rangle$ with $\alpha \neq 0$, the effect of multiplying by N is

$$N \begin{pmatrix} \alpha x_1 \\ \alpha x_2 \\ \alpha \end{pmatrix} = \begin{pmatrix} \alpha(ax_1 + bx_2 + e) \\ \alpha(cx_1 + dx_2 + f) \\ \alpha \end{pmatrix},$$

which is another representation of the point $A(\mathbf{x})$ in homogeneous coordinates.

Thus, the 3×3 matrix N provides a representation of the affine map A because, when one works with homogeneous coordinates, multiplying by the matrix N provides exactly the same results as applying the transformation A. Further, N acts consistently on different homogeneous representations of the same point.

The method used to obtain N from A is completely general, and therefore any affine transformation can be represented as a 3×3 matrix that acts on homogeneous coordinates. So far, we have used only matrices that have the bottom row $(0\ 0\ 1)$; these matrices are sufficient for representing any affine transformation. In fact, an affine transformation may henceforth be viewed as being identical to a 3×3 matrix that has bottom row $(0\ 0\ 1)$.

When we discuss perspective transformations, which are more general than affine transformations, it will be necessary to have other values in the bottom row of the matrix.

> **Exercise II.8** *Figure II.9 shows an affine transformation acting on an* F. *(a) Is this a linear transformation? Why or why not? (b) Give a 3×3 matrix that represents the affine transformation.*
>
> *[Hint: In this case, the easiest way to find the matrix is to split the transformation into a linear part and a translation. Then consider what the linear part does to the vectors* $\mathbf{i}$ *and* $\mathbf{j}$.*]*

For the next exercise, it is not necessary to invert a 3×3 matrix. Instead, note that if a transformation is defined by $\mathbf{y} = A\mathbf{x} + \mathbf{u}$, then its inverse is $\mathbf{x} = A^{-1}\mathbf{y} - A^{-1}\mathbf{u}$.

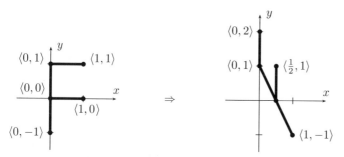

Figure II.9. An affine transformation acting on an F.

Exercise II.9 *Give the 3 × 3 matrix that represents the inverse of the transformation in Exercise II.8.*

Exercise II.10 *Give an example of how two different 3 × 3 homogeneous matrices can represent the same affine transformation.*

II.1.6 Two-Dimensional Transformations in OpenGL

We take a short break in this subsection from the mathematical theory of affine transformations and discuss how OpenGL specifies transformations. OpenGL maintains several matrices that control where objects are drawn, where the camera or viewpoint is positioned, and where the graphics image is displayed on the screen. For the moment we consider only a matrix called the `ModelView` matrix, which is used principally to position objects in 3-space. In this subsection, we are trying to convey only the idea, not the details, of how OpenGL handles transformations, and thus we will work in 2-space. OpenGL really uses 3-space, however, and so not everything we discuss is exactly correct for OpenGL.

We denote the `ModelView` matrix by M for the rest of this subsection. The purpose of M is to hold a homogeneous matrix representing an affine transformation. We therefore think of M as being a 3 × 3 matrix acting on homogeneous representations of points in 2-space. (However, in actuality, M is a 4 × 4 matrix operating on points in 3-space.) The OpenGL programmer specifies points in 2-space by calling a routine `glVertex2f(x,y)`. As described in Chapter I, this point, or "vertex," may be drawn as an isolated point or may be the endpoint of a line or a vertex of a polygon. For example, the following routine would specify three points to be drawn:

```
drawThreePoints() {
  glBegin(GL_POINTS);
  glVertex2f(0.0, 1.0);
  glVertex2f(1.0, -1.0);
  glVertex2f(-1.0, -1.0);
  glEnd();
}
```

The calls to `glBegin` and `glEnd` are used to bracket calls to `glVertex2f`. The parameter `GL_POINTS` specifies that individual points are to be drawn, not lines or polygons. Figure II.10(a) shows the indicated points.

However, OpenGL applies the transformation M before the points are drawn. Thus, the points will be drawn at the positions shown in Figure II.10(a) if M is the identity matrix. On

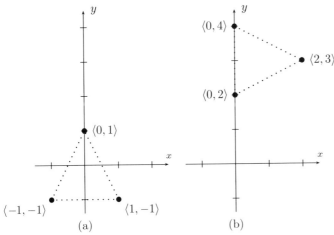

Figure II.10. Drawing points (a) without transformation by the model view matrix and (b) with transformation by the model view matrix. The matrix is as given in the text and represents a rotation of $-90°$ degrees followed by a translation of $\langle 1, 3 \rangle$.

the other hand, for example, if M is the matrix

$$\begin{pmatrix} 0 & 1 & 1 \\ -1 & 0 & 3 \\ 0 & 0 & 1 \end{pmatrix},$$ II.4

then the points will be drawn as shown in Figure II.10(b). Fortunately for OpenGL programmers, we do not often have to work directly with the component values of matrices; instead, OpenGL lets the programmer specify the model view matrix with a set of calls that implement rotations and translations. Thus, to use the matrix II.4, one can code as follows (function calls that start with "pgl" are not valid OpenGL[4]):

```
glMatrixMode(GL_MODELVIEW);        // Select model view matrix
glLoadIdentity();                  // M = Identity
pglTranslatef(1.0,3.0);            // M = M · T(1,3).⁵
pglRotatef(-90.0);                 // M = M · R₋₉₀°.⁵
drawThreePoints();                 // Draw the three points
```

When `drawThreePoints` is called, the model view matrix M is equal to $T_{(1,3)} \circ R_{-90°}$. This transformation is applied to the vertices specified in `drawThreePoints`, and thus the vertices are placed as shown in Figure II.10(b). It is important to note the order in which the two transformations are applied, since this is potentially confusing. The calls to the routines `pglTranslatef` and `pglRotatef` perform multiplications on the right; thus, when the vertices are transformed by M, the effect is that they are transformed first by the rotation and

---

[4] The prefix `pgl` stands for "pseudo-GL." The two `pgl` functions would have to be coded as `glTranslatef(1.0,3.0,0.0)` and `glRotatef(-90.0,0.0,0.0,1.0)` to be valid OpenGL function calls. These perform a translation and a rotation in 3-space (see Section II.2.2).

[5] We are continuing to identify affine transformations with homogeneous matrices, and so $T_{(1,3)}$ and $R_{-90°}$ can be viewed as 3×3 matrices.

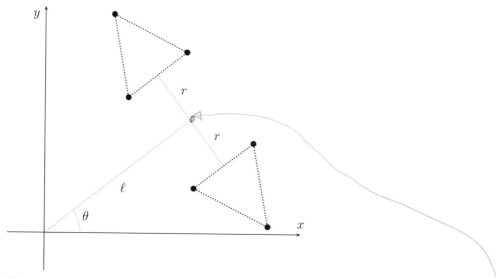

Figure II.11. The results of drawing the triangle with two different model view matrices. The dotted lines are not drawn by the OpenGL program and are present only to indicate the placement.

then by the translation. That is to say, the transformations are applied to the drawn vertices in the reverse order of the OpenGL function calls. The reason for this convention is that it makes it easier to transform vertices hierarchically.

Next, consider a slightly more complicated example of an OpenGL-style program that draws two copies of the triangle, as illustrated in Figure II.11. In the figure, there are three parameters, an angle θ, and lengths ℓ and r, which control the positions of the two triangles. The code to place the two triangles is as follows:

```
glMatrixMode(GL_MODELVIEW);        //  Select model view matrix
glLoadIdentity();                  //  M = Identity
pglRotatef(θ);                     //  M = M · R_θ
pglTranslatef(ℓ,0);                //  M = M · T_(ℓ,0)
glPushMatrix();                    //  Save M on a stack
pglTranslatef(0, r+1);             //  M = M · T_(0,r+1)
drawThreePoints();                 //  Draw the three points
glPopMatrix();                     //  Restore M from the stack
pglRotatef(180.0);                 //  M = M · R_180°
pglTranslatef(0, r+1);             //  M = M · T_(0,r+1)
drawThreePoints();                 //  Draw the three points
```

The new function calls `glPushMatrix` and `glPopMatrix` to save and restore the current matrix M with a stack. Calls to these routines can be nested to save multiple copies of the `ModelView` matrix in a stack. This example shows how the OpenGL matrix manipulation routines can be used to handle hierarchical models.

If you have never worked with OpenGL transformations before, then the order in which rotations and translations are applied in the preceding program fragment can be confusing. Note that the first time `drawThreePoints` is called, the model view matrix is equal to

$$M = R_\theta \circ T_{\langle \ell,0 \rangle} \circ T_{\langle 0,r+1 \rangle}.$$

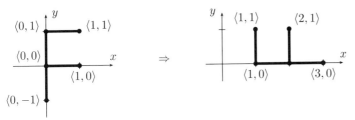

Figure II.12. The affine transformation for Exercise II.11.

The second time `drawThreePoints` is called

$$M = R_\theta \circ T_{\langle \ell, 0 \rangle} \circ R_{180°} \circ T_{\langle 0, r+1 \rangle}.$$

You should convince yourself that this is correct and that this way of ordering transformations makes sense.

> **Exercise II.11** *Consider the transformation shown in Figure II.12. Suppose that a function* `drawF()` *has been written to draw the* F *at the origin as shown in the left-hand side of Figure II.12.*
>
> a. *Give a sequence of pseudo-OpenGL commands that will draw the* F *as shown on the right-hand side of Figure II.12.*
> b. *Give the 3 × 3 homogeneous matrix that represents the affine transformation shown in the figure.*

II.1.7 Another Outlook on Composing Transformations

So far we have discussed the actions of transformations (rotations and translations) as acting on the objects being drawn and viewed them as being applied in reverse order from the order given in the OpenGL code. However, it is also possible to view transformations as acting not on objects but instead on coordinate systems. In this alternative viewpoint, one thinks of the transformations acting on local coordinate systems (and within the local coordinate system), and now the transformations are applied in the same order as given in the OpenGL code.

To explain this alternate view of transformations better, consider the triangle drawn in Figure II.10(b). That triangle is drawn by `drawThreePoints` when the model view matrix is $M = T_{\langle 1,3 \rangle} \cdot R_{-90°}$. The model view matrix was set by the two commands

```
pglTranslatef(1.0,3.0);        //  M = M · T(1,3)
pglRotatef(-90.0);             //  M = M · R−90° ,
```

and our intuition was that these transformations act on the triangle by first rotating it clockwise 90° around the origin and then translating it by the vector $\langle 1, 3 \rangle$.

The alternate way of thinking about these transformations is to view them as acting on a local coordinate system. First, the xy-coordinate system is translated by the vector $\langle 1, 3 \rangle$ to create a new coordinate system with axes x' and y'. Then the rotation acts on the coordinate system again to define another new local coordinate system with axes x'' and y'' by rotating the axes $-90°$ with the center of rotation at the origin of the $x'y'$-coordinate system. These new local coordinate systems are shown in Figure II.13. Finally, when `drawThreePoints` is invoked, it draws the triangle in the local coordinate axes x'' and y''.

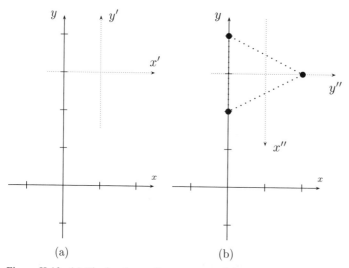

(a)   (b)

Figure II.13. (a) The local coordinate system $x'y'$ obtained by translating the xy-axes by $\langle 1, 3 \rangle$. (b) The coordinates further transformed by a clockwise rotation of 90°, yielding the local coordinate system with axes x'' and y''. In (b), the triangle's vertices are drawn according to the local coordinate axes x'' and y''.

When transformations are viewed as acting on local coordinate systems, the meanings of the transformations are to be interpreted within the framework of the local coordinate system. For instance, the rotation $R_{-90°}$ has its center of rotation at the origin of the current local coordinate system, not at the origin of the initial xy-axes. Similarly, a translation must be carried out relative to the current local coordinate system.

> **Exercise II.12** *Review the transformations used to draw the two triangles shown in Figure II.11. Understand how this works from the viewpoint that transformations act on local coordinate systems. Draw a figure showing all the intermediate local coordinate systems that are implicitly defined by the pseudocode that draws the two triangles.*

II.1.8 Two-Dimensional Projective Geometry★

Projective geometry provides an elegant mathematical interpretation of the homogeneous coordinates for points in the xy-plane. In this interpretation, the triples $\langle x, y, w \rangle$ do not represent points just in the usual flat Euclidean plane but in a larger geometric space known as the *projective plane*. The projective plane is an example of a projective geometry. A projective geometry is a system of points and lines that satisfies the following two axioms:[6]

P1. Any two distinct points lie on exactly one line.
P2. Any two distinct lines contain exactly one common point (i.e., the lines intersect in exactly one point).

Of course, the usual Euclidean plane, $\mathbb{R}^2$, does not satisfy the second axiom since parallel lines do not intersect in $\mathbb{R}^2$. However, by adding appropriate "points at infinity" and a "line at infinity," the Euclidean plane $\mathbb{R}^2$ can be enlarged so as to become a projective geometry. In addition, homogeneous coordinates are a suitable way of representing the points in the projective plane.

---

[6] This is not a complete list of the axioms for projective geometry. For instance, it is required that every line have at least three points, and so on.

The intuitive idea of projective plane construction is as follows: for each family of parallel lines in $\mathbb{R}^2$, we create a new point, called a *point at infinity*. This new point is added to each of these parallel lines. In addition, we add one new line: the *line at infinity*, which contains exactly all the new points at infinity. It is not hard to verify that the axioms P1 and P2 hold.

Consider a line L in Euclidean space $\mathbb{R}^2$: it can be specified by a point $\mathbf{u}$ on L and by a nonzero vector $\mathbf{v}$ in the direction of L. In this case, L consists of the set of points

$$\{\mathbf{u} + \alpha\mathbf{v} : \alpha \in \mathbb{R}\} = \{\langle u_1 + \alpha v_1, u_2 + \alpha v_2\rangle : \alpha \in \mathbb{R}\}.$$

For each value of α, the corresponding point on the line L has homogeneous coordinates $\langle u_1/\alpha + v_1, u_2/\alpha + v_2, 1/\alpha\rangle$. As $\alpha \to \infty$, this triple approaches the limit $\langle v_1, v_2, 0\rangle$. This limit is a point at infinity and is added to the line L when we extend the Euclidean plane to the projective plane. If one takes the limit as $\alpha \to -\infty$, then the triple $\langle -v_1, -v_2, 0\rangle$ is approached in the limit. This is viewed as being the same point as $\langle v_1, v_2, 0\rangle$ since multiplication by the nonzero scalar -1 does not change the meaning of homogeneous coordinates. Thus, the same point at infinity on the line is found at both ends of the line.

Note that the point at infinity, $\langle v_1, v_2, 0\rangle$, on the line L does not depend on $\mathbf{u}$. If the point $\mathbf{u}$ is replaced by some point not on L, then a different line is obtained; this line will be parallel to L in the Euclidean plane, and any line parallel to L can be obtained by appropriately choosing $\mathbf{u}$. Thus, any line parallel to L has the same point infinity as the line L.

More formally, the *projective plane* is defined as follows. Two triples, $\langle x, y, w\rangle$ and $\langle x', y', w'\rangle$, are *equivalent* if there is a nonzero $\alpha \in \mathbb{R}$ such that $x = \alpha x'$, $y = \alpha y'$, and $w = \alpha w'$. We write $\langle x, y, w\rangle^P$ to denote the equivalence class containing the triples that are equivalent to $\langle x, y, w\rangle$. The *projective points* are the equivalence classes $\langle x, y, w\rangle^P$ such that at least one of x, y, w is nonzero. A projective point is called a *point at infinity* if $w = 0$.

A *projective line* is either a usual line in $\mathbb{R}^2$ plus a point at infinity, or the line at infinity. Formally, for any triple a, b, c of real numbers, with at least one of a, b, c nonzero, there is a projective line L defined by

$$L = \{\langle x, y, w\rangle^P : ax + by + cw = 0, x, y, w \text{ not all zero}\}. \qquad \text{II.5}$$

If at least one of a, b is nonzero, then by considering only the $w = 1$ case, the line L is the line containing the Euclidean points $\langle x, y\rangle$ such that $ax + by + c = 0$. In addition, the line L contains the point at infinity $\langle -b, a, 0\rangle^P$. Note that $\langle -b, a\rangle$ is a Euclidean vector parallel to the line L.

The projective line defined with $a = b = 0$ and $c \neq 0$ is the *line at infinity*; it contains those points $\langle x, y, 0\rangle^P$ such that x and y are not both zero.

> **Exercise II.13**★ *Another geometric model for the two-dimensional projective plane is provided by the 2-sphere with antipodal points identified. The 2-sphere is the sphere in $\mathbb{R}^3$ that is centered at the origin and has radius 1. Points on the 2-sphere are represented by normalized triples $\langle x, y, w\rangle$, which have $x^2 + y^2 + w^2 = 1$. In addition, the antipodal points $\langle x, y, w\rangle$ and $\langle -x, -y, -w\rangle$ are treated as equivalent. Prove that lines in projective space correspond to great circles on the sphere, where a* great circle *is defined as the intersection of the sphere with a plane containing the origin. For example, the line at infinity corresponds to the intersection of the 2-sphere with the xy-plane. [Hint: Equation II.5 can be viewed as defining L in terms of a dot product with $\langle a, b, c\rangle$.]*

Yet another way of mathematically understanding the two-dimensional projective space is to view it as the space of linear subspaces of three-dimensional Euclidean space. To understand this, let $\mathbf{x} = \langle x_1, x_2, x_3\rangle$ be a homogeneous representation of a point in the projective plane. This point is equivalent to the points $\alpha\mathbf{x}$ for all nonzero $\alpha \in \mathbb{R}$; these points plus the origin form a line through the origin in $\mathbb{R}^3$. A line through the origin is of course a one-dimensional subspace, and we identify this one-dimensional subspace of $\mathbb{R}^3$ with the point $\mathbf{x}$.

Now consider a line L in the projective plane. If L is not the line at infinity, then it corresponds to a line in $\mathbb{R}^2$. One way to specify the line L is to choose $\mathbf{u} = \langle u_1, u_2 \rangle$ on L and a vector $\mathbf{v} = \langle v_1, v_2 \rangle$ in the direction of L. The line L then is the set of points $\{\mathbf{u} + \alpha \mathbf{v} : \alpha \in \mathbb{R}\}$. It is easy to verify that, after adding the point at infinity, the line L contains exactly the following set of homogeneous points:

$$\{\beta \langle u_1, u_2, 1 \rangle + \gamma \langle v_1, v_2, 0 \rangle : \beta, \gamma \in \mathbb{R} \text{ s.t. } \beta \neq 0 \text{ or } \gamma \neq 0\}.$$

This set of triples is, of course, a plane in $\mathbb{R}^3$ with a hole at the origin. Thus, we can identify this two-dimensional subspace of $\mathbb{R}^3$ (that is, the plane) with the line in the projective plane. If, on the other hand, L is the line at infinity, then it corresponds in the same way to the two-dimensional subspace $\{\langle x_1, x_2, 0 \rangle : x_1, x_2 \in \mathbb{R}\}$.

These considerations give rise to another way of understanding the two-dimensional projective plane. The "points" of the projective plane are one-dimensional subspaces of $\mathbb{R}^3$. The "lines" of the projective plane are two-dimensional subspaces of $\mathbb{R}^3$. A "point" lies on a "line" if and only if the corresponding one-dimensional subspace is a subset of the two-dimensional subspace.

The historical development of projective geometry arose from the development of the theory of perspective by Brunelleschi in the early fifteenth century. The basic tenet of the theory of perspective for drawings and paintings is that families of parallel lines point toward a common "vanishing point," which is essentially a point at infinity. The modern mathematical development of projective geometry based on homogeneous coordinates came much later of course through the work of Feuerbach and Möbius in 1827 and Klein in 1871. Homogeneous coordinates have long been recognized as useful for many computer graphics applications; see, for example, the early textbook (Newman and Sproull, 1979). An accessible mathematical introduction to abstract projective geometry is the textbook (Coxeter, 1974).

II.2 Transformations in 3-Space

We turn next to transformations in 3-space. This turns out to be very similar in many respects to transformations in 2-space. There are, however, some new features – most notably, rotations are more complicated in 3-space than in 2-space. First, we discuss how to extend the concepts of linear and affine transformations, matrix representations for transformations, and homogeneous coordinates to 3-space. We then explain the basic modeling commands in OpenGL for manipulating matrices. After that, we give a mathematical derivation of the rotation matrices needed in 3-space and give a proof of Euler's theorem.

II.2.1 Moving from 2-Space to 3-Space

In 3-space, points, or vectors, are triples $\langle x_1, x_2, x_3 \rangle$ of real numbers. We denote 3-space by $\mathbb{R}^3$ and use the notation $\mathbf{x}$ for a point with it being understood that $\mathbf{x} = \langle x_1, x_2, x_3 \rangle$. The origin, or zero vector, now is $\mathbf{0} = \langle 0, 0, 0 \rangle$. As before, we will identify $\langle x_1, x_2, x_3 \rangle$ with the column vector with the same entries. By convention, we always use a "right-handed" coordinate system, as shown in Figure I.4 on page 6. This means that if you position your right hand so that your thumb points along the x-axis and your index finger is extended straight and points along the y-axis, your palm will be facing in the positive z-axis direction. It also means that vector cross products are defined with the right-hand rule. As discussed in Section I.2.1, it is common in computer graphics applications to visualize the x-axis as pointing to the right, the y-axis as pointing upwards, and the z-axis as pointing toward you.

Homogeneous coordinates for points in $\mathbb{R}^3$ are vectors of four numbers. The homogeneous coordinates $\langle x, y, z, w \rangle$ represents the point $\langle x/w, y/w, z/w \rangle$ in $\mathbb{R}^3$. The two-dimensional projective geometry described in Section II.1.8 can be straightforwardly extended to a three-dimensional geometry by adding a "plane at infinity": each line has a single point at infinity, and each plane has a line of points at infinity (see Section II.2.5 for more on projective geometry).

A *transformation* on $\mathbb{R}^3$ is any mapping from $\mathbb{R}^3$ to $\mathbb{R}^3$. The definition of a *linear transformation* on $\mathbb{R}^3$ is identical to the definition used for $\mathbb{R}^2$ except that now the vectors **x** and **y** range over $\mathbb{R}^3$. Similarly, the definitions of *translation* and of *affine transformation* are word-for-word identical to the definitions given for $\mathbb{R}^2$ except that now the translation vector **u** is in $\mathbb{R}^3$. In particular, an affine transformation is still defined as the composition of a translation and a linear transformation.

Every linear transformation A in $\mathbb{R}^3$ can be represented by a 3×3 matrix M as follows. Let $\mathbf{i} = \langle 1, 0, 0 \rangle$, $\mathbf{j} = \langle 0, 1, 0 \rangle$, and $\mathbf{k} = \langle 0, 0, 1 \rangle$, and let $\mathbf{u} = A(\mathbf{i})$, $\mathbf{v} = A(\mathbf{j})$, and $\mathbf{w} = A(\mathbf{k})$. Set M equal to the matrix $(\mathbf{u}, \mathbf{v}, \mathbf{w})$, that is, the matrix whose columns are **u**, **v**, and **w**, and thus

$$M = \begin{pmatrix} u_1 & v_1 & w_1 \\ u_2 & v_2 & w_2 \\ u_3 & v_3 & w_3 \end{pmatrix}. \tag{II.6}$$

Then $M\mathbf{x} = A(\mathbf{x})$ for all $\mathbf{x} \in \mathbb{R}^3$, that is to say, M represents A. In this way, any linear transformation of $\mathbb{R}^3$ can be viewed as being a 3×3 matrix. (Compare this with the analogous construction for $\mathbb{R}^2$ explained at the beginning of Section II.1.2.)

A *rigid* transformation is one that preserves the size and shape of an object and changes only its position and orientation. Formally, a transformation A is defined to be rigid provided it preserves distances between points and angles between lines. Recall that the length of a vector **x** is equal to $||\mathbf{x}|| = \sqrt{\mathbf{x} \cdot \mathbf{x}} = \sqrt{x_1^2 + x_2^2 + x_3^2}$. An equivalent definition of rigidity is that a transformation A is rigid if it preserves dot products, that is to say, if $A(\mathbf{x}) \cdot A(\mathbf{y}) = \mathbf{x} \cdot \mathbf{y}$ for all $\mathbf{x}, \mathbf{y} \in \mathbb{R}^3$. It is not hard to prove that $M = (\mathbf{u}, \mathbf{v}, \mathbf{w})$ represents a rigid transformation if and only if $||\mathbf{u}|| = ||\mathbf{v}|| = ||\mathbf{w}|| = 1$ and $\mathbf{u} \cdot \mathbf{v} = \mathbf{v} \cdot \mathbf{w} = \mathbf{u} \cdot \mathbf{w} = 0$. From this, it is straightforward to show that M represents a rigid transformation if and only if $M^{-1} = M^{\mathrm{T}}$ (c.f. Exercises II.5 and II.6 on page 24).

We define an *orientation-preserving* transformation to be one that preserves "right-handedness." Formally, we say that A is orientation-preserving provided that $(A(\mathbf{u}) \times A(\mathbf{v})) \cdot A(\mathbf{u} \times \mathbf{v}) > 0$ for all noncollinear $\mathbf{u}, \mathbf{v} \in \mathbb{R}^3$. By recalling the right-hand rule used to determine the direction of a cross product, you should be able to convince yourself that this definition makes sense.

Exercise II.14 *Let $M = (\mathbf{u}, \mathbf{v}, \mathbf{w})$ be a 3×3 matrix. Prove that $\det(M)$ is equal to $(\mathbf{u} \times \mathbf{v}) \cdot \mathbf{w}$. Conclude that M represents an orientation-preserving transformation if and only if $\det(M) > 0$. Also, prove that if $\mathbf{u}$ and $\mathbf{v}$ are unit vectors that are orthogonal to each other, then setting $\mathbf{w} = \mathbf{u} \times \mathbf{v}$ makes $M = (\mathbf{u}, \mathbf{v}, \mathbf{w})$ a rigid, orientation-preserving transformation.*

Any affine transformation is the composition of a linear transformation and a translation. Since a linear transformation can be represented by a 3×3 matrix, any affine transformation can be represented by a 3×3 matrix and a vector in $\mathbb{R}^3$ representing a translation amount.

That is, any affine transformation can be written as

$$\begin{pmatrix} x \\ y \\ z \end{pmatrix} \mapsto \begin{pmatrix} a & b & c \\ d & e & f \\ g & h & i \end{pmatrix} \begin{pmatrix} x \\ y \\ z \end{pmatrix} + \begin{pmatrix} u \\ v \\ w \end{pmatrix}.$$

We can rewrite this using a single 4×4 homogeneous matrix that acts on homogeneous coordinates as follows:

$$\begin{pmatrix} x \\ y \\ z \\ 1 \end{pmatrix} \mapsto \begin{pmatrix} a & b & c & u \\ d & e & f & v \\ g & h & i & w \\ 0 & 0 & 0 & 1 \end{pmatrix} \begin{pmatrix} x \\ y \\ z \\ 1 \end{pmatrix}.$$

This 4×4 matrix contains the linear transformation in its upper left 3×3 submatrix and the translation in the upper three entries of the last column. Thus, affine transformations can be identified with 4×4 matrices with bottom row (0 0 0 1). When we study transformations for perspective, we will see some nontrivial uses of the bottom row of a 4×4 homogeneous matrix, but for now we are only interested in matrices whose fourth row is (0, 0, 0, 1).

As mentioned at the beginning of this section, rotations in 3-space are considerably more complicated than in 2-space. The reason for this is that a rotation can be performed about any axis whatsoever. This includes not just rotations around the x-, y- and z-axes but also rotations around an axis pointing in an arbitrary direction. A rotation that fixes the origin can be specified by giving a rotation axis $\mathbf{u}$ and a rotation angle θ, where the axis $\mathbf{u}$ can be any nonzero vector. We think of the base of the vector being placed at the origin, and the axis of rotation is the line through the origin parallel to the vector $\mathbf{u}$. The rotation angle θ specifies the magnitude of the rotation. The *direction* of the rotation is determined by the *right-hand rule*; namely, if one mentally grasps the vector $\mathbf{u}$ with one's right hand so that the thumb, when extended, is pointing in the direction of the vector $\mathbf{u}$, then one's fingers will curl around $\mathbf{u}$ pointing in the direction of the rotation. In other words, if one views the vector $\mathbf{u}$ headon, that is, down the axis of rotation in the opposite direction that $\mathbf{u}$ is pointing, then the rotation direction is counterclockwise (for positive values of θ). A rotation of this type is denoted $R_{\theta,\mathbf{u}}$. By convention, the axis of rotation always passes through the origin, and thus the rotation fixes the origin. Figure II.14 on page 37 illustrates the action of $R_{\theta,\mathbf{u}}$ on a point $\mathbf{v}$. Clearly, $R_{\theta,\mathbf{u}}$ is a linear transformation and is rigid and orientation-preserving.

Section II.2.4 below shows that every rigid, orientation-preserving, linear transformation in 3-space is a rotation. As a corollary, every rigid, orientation-preserving, affine transformation can be (uniquely) expressed as the composition of a translation and a rotation about a line through the origin.

It is of course possible to have rotations about axes that do not pass through the origin. These are discussed further in Section II.2.4.

II.2.2 Transformation Matrices in OpenGL

OpenGL has several function calls that enable you to conveniently manipulate the model view matrix, which transforms the positions of points specified with `glVertex*`. We have already seen much of the functionality of these routines in Section II.1.6, which explains the use of OpenGL matrix transformations in the two-dimensional setting. Actually, OpenGL really operates in three dimensions, although it supports a few two-dimensional functions, such as `glVertex2f`, which merely set the z-component to zero.

In three dimensions, the following commands are particularly useful for working with the model view matrix M.

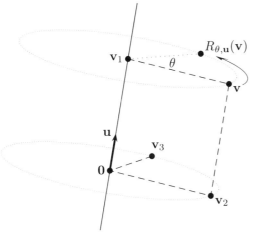

Figure II.14. The vector **v** being rotated around **u**. The vector $\mathbf{v}_1$ is **v**'s projection onto **u**. The vector $\mathbf{v}_2$ is the component of **v** orthogonal to **u**. The vector $\mathbf{v}_3$ is $\mathbf{v}_2$ rotated $90°$ around **u**. The dashed line segments in the figure all meet at right angles.

First, the command

```
glMatrixMode(GL_MODELVIEW);
```

selects the model view matrix as the currently active matrix. Other matrices that can be selected with this command include the projection matrix. The projection matrix and the model view matrix work together to position objects, and Section II.3.5 explains the interaction between these two matrices.

The following four commands provide simple ways to effect modeling transformations. All four commands affect the currently active matrix, which we assume is the matrix M for the sake of discussion.

`glLoadIdentity()`. Sets M equal to the 4×4 identity matrix.

`glTranslatef( float` u_1`, float` u_2`, float` u_3 `)`. This command sets M equal to $M \circ T_{\mathbf{u}}$, where $\mathbf{u} = \langle u_1, u_2, u_3 \rangle$ and $T_{\mathbf{u}}$ is the transformation that performs a translation by **u**. The 4×4 matrix representation for $T_{\mathbf{u}}$ in homogeneous coordinates is

$$\begin{pmatrix} 1 & 0 & 0 & u_1 \\ 0 & 1 & 0 & u_2 \\ 0 & 0 & 1 & u_3 \\ 0 & 0 & 0 & 1 \end{pmatrix}.$$

`glRotatef(float` θ`, float` u_1`, float` u_2`, float` u_3`)`. This sets M equal to $M \circ R_{\theta,\mathbf{u}}$, where $\mathbf{u} = \langle u_1, u_2, u_3 \rangle$ and, as discussed above, $R_{\theta,\mathbf{u}}$ is the transformation that performs a rotation around the axis through the origin in the direction of the vector **u**. The rotation angle is θ (measured in degrees), and the direction of the rotation is determined by the right-hand rule. The vector **u** must not equal **0**. For the record, if **u** is a unit vector, then the 4×4 matrix representation of $R_{\theta,\mathbf{u}}$ in homogeneous coordinates is

$$\begin{pmatrix} (1-c)u_1^2 + c & (1-c)u_1 u_2 - su_3 & (1-c)u_1 u_3 + su_2 & 0 \\ (1-c)u_1 u_2 + su_3 & (1-c)u_2^2 + c & (1-c)u_2 u_3 - su_1 & 0 \\ (1-c)u_1 u_3 - su_2 & (1-c)u_2 u_3 + su_1 & (1-c)u_3^2 + c & 0 \\ 0 & 0 & 0 & 1 \end{pmatrix}, \qquad \text{II.7}$$

where $c = \cos\theta$ and $s = \sin\theta$. OpenGL does not require that **u** be passed in as a unit vector: OpenGL will automatically compute the normalization of **u** in order to compute the rotation matrix. The formula II.7 for $R_{\theta,\mathbf{u}}$ will be derived below in Section II.2.3.

glScalef(float α_1, float α_2, float α_3). This command scales the x-, y-, z-coordinates of points independently. That is to say, it sets $M = M \circ S$, where S is the matrix

$$\begin{pmatrix} \alpha_1 & 0 & 0 & 0 \\ 0 & \alpha_2 & 0 & 0 \\ 0 & 0 & \alpha_3 & 0 \\ 0 & 0 & 0 & 1 \end{pmatrix}.$$

The matrix S will map $\langle x_1, x_2, x_3, 1 \rangle$ to $\langle \alpha_1 x_1, \alpha_2 x_2, \alpha_3 x_3, 1 \rangle$, so it allows scaling independently in each of the x-, y-, and z-directions.

OpenGL does not have any special function calls for reflections or shearing transformations. A reflection transformation is a transformation that transforms points to their "mirror image" across some plane, as illustrated in Figure II.16 on page 43. Reflections across the coordinate planes can easily be done with glScalef. For example,

glScalef(-1.0, 0.0, 0.0);

performs a reflection across the yz-plane by negating the x-coordinate of a point. A *shearing* transformation is a more complicated kind of transformation; some two-dimensional examples include the transformation A_3 of Exercise II.1 and the transformation shown in Figure II.3. In principle, one can use glScalef in combination with rotations and translations to perform arbitrary reflections and shearing transformations. In practice, this is usually more trouble than it is worth. Instead, you can just explicitly give the components of a 4×4 matrix that perform any desired affine transformation. For example, the formulas from Exercises II.18 and II.19 below can be used to get the entries of a 4×4 matrix that carries out a reflection.

OpenGL includes the following two commands that allow you to use any homogeneous 4×4 matrix you wish. Both of these commands take 16 floating point numbers as inputs and create a 4×4 homogeneous matrix with these components. The elements of the matrix are given in column order!

glLoadMatrixf(float* matEntries). This initializes M to be the matrix with entries the 16 numbers pointed to by matEntries.

glMultMatrixf(float* matEntries). This sets M equal to $M \cdot M'$, where M' is the matrix with entries equal to the 16 values pointed to by matEntries.

The variable matEntries can have its type defined by any one of the following lines:

```
float* matEntries;

float matEntries[16];

float matEntries[4][4];
```

In the third case, if one lets i and j range from 0 to 3, the entry in row i and column j is the value matEntries[j][i]. The indices i and j are reversed from what might normally be expected because the entries are specified in column order.

Solar System Examples in OpenGL. The Solar program contains some examples of using OpenGL's modeling transformations. This program creates a simple solar system with a central sun, a planet revolving around the sun every 365 days, and a moon revolving around the planet 12 times per year. In addition, the planet rotates on its axis once per day, that is, once per 24 hours. The program uses a combination of rotations and translations. In addition, it uses `glPushMatrix` and `glPopMatrix` to save and restore the model view matrix so as to isolate the transformations used to rotate the planet on its axis from the transformations used to position the moon as it revolves around the planet.

The central part of the `Solar` program code is as follows:

```
// Choose and clear Modelview matrix
glMatrixMode(GL_MODELVIEW);
glLoadIdentity();
// Move 8 units away to be able to view from the origin.
glTranslatef(0.0, 0.0, -8.0);
// Tilt system 15 degrees downward in order to view
//      from above the xy-plane.
glRotatef(15.0, 1.0,0.0,0.0);

// Draw the sun -- as a yellow, wireframe sphere
glColor3f( 1.0, 1.0, 0.0 );
glutWireSphere( 0.8, 15, 15 );          // Radius = 0.8 units.

// Draw the Earth
// First position it around the sun
// Use DayOfYear to determine its position
glRotatef( 360.0*DayOfYear/365.0, 0.0, 1.0, 0.0 );
glTranslatef( 4.0, 0.0, 0.0 );
// Second, rotate the earth on its axis.
// Use HourOfDay to determine its rotation.
glPushMatrix();                          // Save matrix state
glRotatef( 360.0*HourOfDay/24.0, 0.0, 1.0, 0.0 );
// Third, draw as a blue, wireframe sphere.
glColor3f( 0.2, 0.2, 1.0 );
glutWireSphere( 0.4, 10, 10);
glPopMatrix();                           // Restore matrix state

// Draw the moon.
// Use DayOfYear to control its rotation around the earth
glRotatef( 360.0*12.0*DayOfYear/365.0, 0.0, 1.0, 0.0 );
glTranslatef( 0.7, 0.0, 0.0 );
glColor3f( 0.3, 0.7, 0.3 );
glutWireSphere( 0.1, 5, 5 );
```

The complete code for `Solar.c` can be found with the software accompanying this book.

The code fragment draws wireframe spheres with commands

```
glutWireSphere( radius, slices, stacks );
```

The value of `radius` is the radius of the sphere. The integer values `slices` and `stacks` control the number of "wedges" and horizontal "stacks" used for the polygonal model of the sphere. The sphere is modeled with the "up" direction along the z-axis, and thus "horizontal" means parallel to the xy-plane.

The `glColor3f(red, green, blue)` commands are used to set the current drawing color.

The solar program code starts by specifying the `ModelView` matrix, M, as the current matrix and initializes it to the identity. The program then right multiplies M with a translation of -8 units in the z-direction and thereafter performs a rotation of $15°$ around the x-axis. This has the effect of centering the solar system at $\langle 0, 0, -8 \rangle$ with a small tilt, and so it is viewed from slightly above. The viewpoint, or camera position, is placed at the origin, looking down the negative z-axis.

The sun is drawn with `glutWireSphere`. This routine draws the wireframe sphere, issuing `glVertex*` commands for a sphere centered at the origin. Of course, the sphere is actually drawn centered at $\langle 0, 0, -8 \rangle$ because the position is transformed by the contents of the M matrix.

To draw the Earth and its moon, another `glRotatef` and `glTranslatef` are performed. These translate the Earth system away from the sun and revolve it around the sun. The angle of rotation depends on the day of the year and is specified in degrees. A further `glRotatef` rotates the Earth on its axis. This rotation is bracketed by commands pushing M onto the `ModelView` matrix stack and then restoring it with a pop. This prevents the rotation of the Earth on its axis from affecting the position of the moon. Finally, a `glRotatef` and `glTranslatef` control the position of the moon around the Earth.

To understand the effect of the rotations and translations on an intuitive level, you should think of their being applied in the reverse order of how they appear in the program. Thus, the moon can be thought of as being translated by $\langle 0.7, 0, 0 \rangle$, then rotated through an angle based on the day of the year (with exactly 12 months in a year), then translated by $\langle 4, 0, 0 \rangle$, then rotated by an angle that depends on the day of the year again (one revolution around the sun every 365 days), then rotated $15°$ around the x-axis, and finally translated by $\langle 0, 0, -8 \rangle$. That is, to see the order in which the transformations are logically applied, you have to read backward through the program, being sure to take into account the effect of matrix pushes and pops.

Exercise II.15 *Review the* `Solar` *program and understand how it works. Try making some of the following extensions to create a more complicated solar system.*

a. *Add one or more planets.*

b. *Add more moons. Make a geostationary moon, which always stays above the same point on the planet. Make a moon with a retrograde orbit. (A retrograde orbit means the moon revolves opposite to the usual direction, that is, in the clockwise direction instead of counterclockwise.)*

c. *Give the moon a satellite of its own.*

d. *Give the planet and its moon(s) a tilt. The tilt should be in a fixed direction. This is similar to the tilt of the Earth, which causes the seasons. The tilt of the Earth is always in the direction of the North Star, Polaris. Thus, during part of a year, the Northern Hemisphere tilts toward the sun, and during the rest of the year, the Northern Hemisphere tilts away from the sun.*

e. *Change the length of the year so that the planet revolves around the sun once every 365.25 days. Be sure not to introduce any discontinuities in the orientation of the planet at the end of a year.*

f. *Make the moon rotate around the planet every 29 days. Make sure there is no discontinuity in the moon's position at the end of a year.*

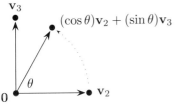

Figure II.15. The vector $\mathbf{v}_2$ being rotated around $\mathbf{u}$. This is the same situation as shown in Figure II.14 but viewed looking directly down the vector $\mathbf{u}$.

II.2.3 Derivation of the Rotation Matrix

This section contains the mathematical derivation of Formula II.7 for the matrix representing a rotation, $R_{\theta,\mathbf{u}}$, through an angle θ around axis $\mathbf{u}$. Recall that this formula was

$$
R_{\theta,\mathbf{u}} = \begin{pmatrix} (1-c)u_1^2 + c & (1-c)u_1u_2 - su_3 & (1-c)u_1u_3 + su_2 & 0 \\ (1-c)u_1u_2 + su_3 & (1-c)u_2^2 + c & (1-c)u_2u_3 - su_1 & 0 \\ (1-c)u_1u_3 - su_2 & (1-c)u_2u_3 + su_1 & (1-c)u_3^2 + c & 0 \\ 0 & 0 & 0 & 1 \end{pmatrix}, \qquad \text{II.7}
$$

where $c = \cos\theta$ and $s = \sin\theta$. The vector $\mathbf{u}$ must be a unit vector. There is no loss of generality in assuming that $\mathbf{u}$ is a unit vector since if not, it may be normalized by dividing by $||\mathbf{u}||$.

To derive the matrix for $R_{\theta,\mathbf{u}}$, let $\mathbf{v}$ be an arbitrary point and consider what $\mathbf{w} = R_{\theta,\mathbf{u}}\mathbf{v}$ is equal to. For this, we split $\mathbf{v}$ into two components, $\mathbf{v}_1$ and $\mathbf{v}_2$ so that $\mathbf{v} = \mathbf{v}_1 + \mathbf{v}_2$ with $\mathbf{v}_1$ parallel to $\mathbf{u}$ and $\mathbf{v}_2$ orthogonal to $\mathbf{u}$. The vector $\mathbf{v}_1$ is the projection of $\mathbf{v}$ onto the line of $\mathbf{u}$ and is equal to $\mathbf{v}_1 = (\mathbf{u} \cdot \mathbf{v})\mathbf{u}$ since the dot product $\mathbf{u} \cdot \mathbf{v}$ is equal to $||\mathbf{u}|| \cdot ||\mathbf{v}|| \cos(\varphi)$ where φ is the angle between $\mathbf{u}$ and $\mathbf{v}$, and since $||\mathbf{u}|| = 1$. (Refer to Figure II.14 on page 37.) We rewrite this as

$$
\mathbf{v}_1 = (\mathbf{u} \cdot \mathbf{v})\mathbf{u} = \mathbf{u}(\mathbf{u} \cdot \mathbf{v})
$$
$$
= \mathbf{u}(\mathbf{u}^{\mathsf{T}}\mathbf{v}) = (\mathbf{u}\mathbf{u}^{\mathsf{T}})\mathbf{v}.
$$

The equation above uses the fact that a dot product $\mathbf{u} \cdot \mathbf{v}$ can be rewritten as a matrix product $\mathbf{u}^{\mathsf{T}}\mathbf{v}$ (recall that our vectors are all column vectors) and that matrix multiplication is associative. The product $\mathbf{u}\mathbf{u}^{\mathsf{T}}$ is the symmetric 3×3 matrix

$$
\text{Proj}_{\mathbf{u}} = \mathbf{u}\mathbf{u}^{\mathsf{T}} = \begin{pmatrix} u_1 \\ u_2 \\ u_3 \end{pmatrix} (u_1\ u_2\ u_3) = \begin{pmatrix} u_1^2 & u_1u_2 & u_1u_3 \\ u_1u_2 & u_2^2 & u_2u_3 \\ u_1u_3 & u_2u_3 & u_3^2 \end{pmatrix}.
$$

Since $\mathbf{v} = \mathbf{v}_1 + \mathbf{v}_2$, we therefore have

$$
\mathbf{v}_1 = \text{Proj}_{\mathbf{u}}\mathbf{v} \qquad \text{and} \qquad \mathbf{v}_2 = (I - \text{Proj}_{\mathbf{u}})\mathbf{v},
$$

where I is the 3×3 identity matrix.

We know that $R_{\theta,\mathbf{u}}\mathbf{v}_1 = \mathbf{v}_1$ because $\mathbf{v}_1$ is a scalar multiple of $\mathbf{u}$ and is not affected by a rotation around $\mathbf{u}$. To compute $R_{\theta,\mathbf{u}}\mathbf{v}_2$, we further define $\mathbf{v}_3$ to be the vector

$$
\mathbf{v}_3 = \mathbf{u} \times \mathbf{v}_2 = \mathbf{u} \times \mathbf{v}. \qquad \left(= \mathbf{u} \times (\mathbf{v}_1 + \mathbf{v}_2) = \mathbf{u} \times \mathbf{v}_2 \right)
$$

The second equality holds since $\mathbf{v}$ and $\mathbf{v}_2$ differ by a multiple of $\mathbf{u}$. The vector $\mathbf{v}_3$ is orthogonal to both $\mathbf{u}$ and $\mathbf{v}_2$. Furthermore, because $\mathbf{u}$ is a unit vector orthogonal to $\mathbf{v}_2$, $\mathbf{v}_3$ has the same magnitude as $\mathbf{v}_2$. That is to say, $\mathbf{v}_3$ is equal to the rotation of $\mathbf{v}_2$ around the axis $\mathbf{u}$ through an angle of 90°. Figure II.15 shows a view of $\mathbf{v}_2$ and $\mathbf{v}_3$ oriented straight down the $\mathbf{u}$ axis of rotation. From the figure, it is obvious that rotating $\mathbf{v}_2$ through an angle of θ around $\mathbf{u}$ results in the vector

$$(\cos \theta)\mathbf{v}_2 + (\sin \theta)\mathbf{v}_3. \qquad \text{II.8}$$

Therefore, $R_{\theta,\mathbf{u}}\mathbf{v}$ is equal to

$$R_{\theta,\mathbf{u}}\mathbf{v} = R_{\theta,\mathbf{u}}\mathbf{v}_1 + R_{\theta,\mathbf{u}}\mathbf{v}_2$$

$$= \mathbf{v}_1 + (\cos \theta)\mathbf{v}_2 + (\sin \theta)\mathbf{v}_3$$

$$= \text{Proj}_{\mathbf{u}}\mathbf{v} + (\cos \theta)(I - \text{Proj}_{\mathbf{u}})\mathbf{v} + (\sin \theta)(\mathbf{u} \times \mathbf{v}).$$

To finish deriving the matrix for $R_{\theta,\mathbf{u}}$, we define the matrix

$$M_{\mathbf{u}\times} = \begin{pmatrix} 0 & -u_3 & u_2 \\ u_3 & 0 & -u_1 \\ -u_2 & u_1 & 0 \end{pmatrix}$$

and see, by a simple calculation, that $(M_{\mathbf{u}\times})\mathbf{v} = \mathbf{u} \times \mathbf{v}$ holds for all $\mathbf{v}$. From this, it is immediate that

$$R_{\theta,\mathbf{u}}\mathbf{v} = [\text{Proj}_{\mathbf{u}} + (\cos \theta)(I - \text{Proj}_{\mathbf{u}}) + (\sin \theta)M_{\mathbf{u}\times}]\mathbf{v}$$

$$= [(1 - \cos \theta)\text{Proj}_{\mathbf{u}} + (\cos \theta)I + (\sin \theta)M_{\mathbf{u}\times}]\mathbf{v}.$$

The quantity inside the square brackets is a 3×3 matrix, and so this completes the derivation of the matrix representation of $R_{\theta,\mathbf{u}}$. An easy calculation shows that this corresponds to the representation given earlier (in homogeneous form) by Equation II.7.

Exercise II.16 *Carry out the calculation to show that the formula for $R_{\theta,\mathbf{u}}$ above is equivalent to the formula in Equation II.7.*

Exercise II.17★ *Let $\mathbf{u}$, $\mathbf{v}$ and $\mathbf{w}$ be orthogonal unit vectors with $\mathbf{w} = \mathbf{u} \times \mathbf{v}$. Prove that $R_{\theta,\mathbf{u}}$ is represented by the following 3×3 matrix:*

$$\mathbf{u}\mathbf{u}^{\mathrm{T}} + (\cos \theta)(\mathbf{v}\mathbf{v}^{\mathrm{T}} + \mathbf{w}\mathbf{w}^{\mathrm{T}}) + (\sin \theta)(\mathbf{w}\mathbf{v}^{\mathrm{T}} - \mathbf{v}\mathbf{w}^{\mathrm{T}}).$$

It is also possible to convert a rotation matrix back into a unit rotation vector $\mathbf{u}$ and a rotation angle θ. For this, refer back to Equation II.7. Suppose we are given such a 4×4 rotation matrix $M = (m_{i,j})_{i,j}$ so that the entry in row i and column j is $m_{i,j}$. The sum of the first three entries on the diagonal of M (that is, the trace of the 3×3 submatrix representing the rotation) is equal to

$$m_{1,1} + m_{2,2} + m_{3,3} = (1 - c) + 3c = 1 + 2c$$

since $u_1^2 + u_2^2 + u_3^2 = 1$. Thus, $\cos \theta = (m_{1,1} + m_{2,2} + m_{3,3} - 1)/2$, or

$$\theta = \arccos(\alpha/2),$$

where $\alpha = m_{1,1} + m_{2,2} + m_{3,3} - 1$. Letting $s = \sin \theta$, we can determine $\mathbf{u}$'s components from

$$u_1 = \frac{m_{3,2} - m_{2,3}}{2s}$$

$$u_2 = \frac{m_{1,3} - m_{3,1}}{2s} \qquad \text{II.9}$$

$$u_3 = \frac{m_{2,1} - m_{1,2}}{2s}.$$

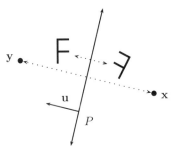

Figure II.16. Reflection across the plane P. The vector **u** is the unit vector perpendicular to the plane. A reflection maps a point to its mirror image across the plane. The point **x** is mapped to the point **y** directly across the plane and vice versa. Each F is mapped to the mirror image F.

The preceding method of computing θ and **u** from M will have problems with stability if θ is very close to 0 since, in that case, $\sin\theta \approx 0$, and thus the determination of the values of u_i requires dividing by values near zero. The problem is that dividing by a near-zero value tends to introduce unstable or inaccurate results, because small roundoff errors can have a large effect on the results of the division.

Of course, if θ, and thus $\sin\theta$, are exactly equal to zero, the rotation angle is zero and any vector **u** will work. Absent roundoff errors, this situation occurs only if M is the identity matrix.

To mitigate the problems associated with dividing by a near-zero value, one should instead compute

$$\beta = \sqrt{(m_{3,2} - m_{2,3})^2 + (m_{1,3} - m_{3,1})^2 + (m_{2,1} - m_{1,2})^2}.$$

Note that β will equal $2s = 2\sin\theta$ because dividing by $2s$ in Equations II.9 was what was needed to normalize the vector **u**. If β is zero, then the rotation angle θ is zero and, in this case, **u** may be an arbitrary unit vector. If β is nonzero, then

$$u_1 = (m_{3,2} - m_{2,3})/\beta$$
$$u_2 = (m_{1,3} - m_{3,1})/\beta$$
$$u_3 = (m_{2,1} - m_{1,2})/\beta.$$

This way of computing **u** makes it more likely that a (nearly) unit vector will be obtained for **u** when the rotation angle θ is near zero. From α and β, the angle θ can be computed as

$$\theta = \texttt{atan2}\,(\beta, \alpha).$$

This is a more robust way to compute θ than using the arccos function.

For an alternate, and often better, method of representing rotations in terms of 4-vectors, see the parts of Section XII.3 on quaternions (pages 298–307).

Exercise II.18★ *A plane P containing the origin can be specified by giving a unit vector **u** that is orthogonal to the plane. That is, let $P = \{\mathbf{x} \in \mathbb{R}^3 : \mathbf{u} \cdot \mathbf{x} = 0\}$. A reflection across P is the linear transformation that maps each point **x** to its "mirror image" directly across P, as illustrated in Figure II.16. Prove that, for a plane containing the origin, this reflection is represented by the 3×3 matrix $I - 2\mathbf{u}\mathbf{u}^{\mathsf{T}}$. Write out this matrix in component form too. [Hint: If $\mathbf{v} = \mathbf{v}_1 + \mathbf{v}_2$, as in the derivation of the rotation matrix, the reflection maps **v** to $\mathbf{v}_2 - \mathbf{v}_1$.]*

Exercise II.19★   *Now let P be the plane* $\{\mathbf{x} \in \mathbb{R}^3 : \mathbf{u} \cdot \mathbf{x} = a\}$ *for some unit vector* $\mathbf{u}$ *and scalar a, where P does not necessarily contain the origin. Derive the* 4×4 *matrix that represents the transformation reflecting points across P. [Hint: This is an affine transformation. It is the composition of the linear map from Exercise II.18 and a translation.]*

II.2.4 Euler's Theorem

A fundamental fact about rigid orientation-preserving linear transformations is that they are always equivalent to a rotation around an axis passing through the origin.

Theorem II.5 *If A is a rigid, orientation-preserving linear transformation of* $\mathbb{R}^3$*, then A is the same as some rotation* $R_{\theta,\mathbf{v}}$*.*

Proof The idea of the proof is similar to the proof of Theorem II.4, which showed that every rigid, orientation-preserving affine transformation is either a generalized rotation or a translation. However, now we consider the action of A on points on the unit sphere instead of on points in the plane.

Since A is rigid, unit vectors are mapped to unit vectors. So, A maps the unit sphere onto itself. In fact, it will suffice to show that A maps some point $\mathbf{v}$ on the unit sphere to itself, for if $\mathbf{v}$ is a fixed point, then A fixes the line through the origin containing $\mathbf{v}$. The rigidity and orientation-preserving properties then imply that A is a rotation around this line because the action of A on $\mathbf{v}$ and on a vector perpendicular to $\mathbf{v}$ determines all the values of A.

Assume that A is not the identity map. First, note that A cannot map every point $\mathbf{u}$ on the unit sphere to its *antipodal* point $-\mathbf{u}$; otherwise, A would not be orientation-preserving. Therefore, there is some unit vector $\mathbf{u}_0$ on the sphere such that $A(\mathbf{u}_0) \neq -\mathbf{u}_0$. Fix such a point, and let $\mathbf{u} = A(\mathbf{u}_0)$. If $\mathbf{u} = \mathbf{u}_0$, we are done; so suppose $\mathbf{u} \neq \mathbf{u}_0$. Let C be the great circle containing both $\mathbf{u}_0$ and $\mathbf{u}$ and let L be the shorter portion of C connecting $\mathbf{u}_0$ to $\mathbf{u}$, that is, L is spanning less than 180° around the unit sphere. Let L' be the image of L under A and let C' be the great circle containing L'. Suppose that $L = L'$, that is, that A maps this line to itself. In this case, rigidity implies that A maps $\mathbf{u}$ to $\mathbf{u}_0$. Then, rigidity further implies that the point $\mathbf{v}$ midway between $\mathbf{u}_0$ and $\mathbf{u}$ is a fixed point of A, and so A is a rotation around $\mathbf{v}$.

Otherwise, suppose $L \neq L'$. Let L' make an angle of θ with the great circle C, as shown in Figure II.17. Since $L \neq L'$, we have $-180° < \theta < 180°$. Let C_2, respectively C_2', be the great circle perpendicular to L at $\mathbf{u}_0$, respectively at $\mathbf{u}$. Let C_3 be C_2 rotated an angle of $-\theta/2$ around the vector $\mathbf{u}_0$, and let C_3' be C_2' rotated an angle of $\theta/2$ around $\mathbf{u}$. Then C_3 and C_3' intersect at a point $\mathbf{v}$ equidistant from $\mathbf{u}_0$ and $\mathbf{u}$. Furthermore, by rigidity considerations and the definition of θ, A maps C_3 to C_3' and $\mathbf{v}$ is a fixed point of A. Thus, A is a rotation around the vector $\mathbf{v}$. $\square$

One can define a *generalized rotation* in 3-space to be a transformation $R_{\theta,\mathbf{u}}^{\mathbf{v}}$ that performs a rotation through angle θ around the line L, where L is the line that contains the point $\mathbf{v}$ and is parallel to $\mathbf{u}$. However, unlike the situation for 2-space (see Theorem II.4), it is not the case that every rigid, orientation-preserving affine transformation in 3-space is equivalent to either a translation or a generalized rotation of this type. Instead, we need a more general notion of "glide rotation" that incorporates a screwlike motion. For example, consider a transformation that both rotates around the y-axis and translates along the y-axis.

A *glide rotation* is a mapping that can be expressed as a translation along an axis $\mathbf{u}$ composed with a rotation $R_{\theta,\mathbf{u}}^{\mathbf{v}}$ around the line that contains $\mathbf{v}$ and is parallel to $\mathbf{u}$.

Exercise II.20★ *Prove that every rigid, orientation-preserving affine transformation is a glide rotation. [Hint: First consider A's action on planes and define a linear transformation B as follows: let* $\mathbf{r}$ *be a unit vector perpendicular to a plane P and define* $B(\mathbf{r})$

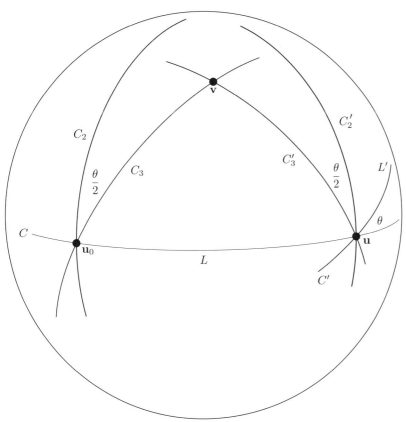

Figure II.17. Finding the axis of rotation. We have $\mathbf{u} = A(\mathbf{u}_0)$ and $\mathbf{v} = A(\mathbf{v})$. Compare this with Figure II.8.

> *to be the unit vector perpendicular to the plane $A(P)$. The transformation B is a rigid, orientation-preserving map on the unit sphere. Furthermore, $B(\mathbf{r}) = A(\mathbf{r}) - A(\mathbf{0})$, and so B is a linear transformation. By Euler's theorem, B is a rotation. Let $\mathbf{w}$ be a unit vector fixed by B and Q be the plane through the origin perpendicular to $\mathbf{w}$, and thus $A(Q)$ is parallel to Q. Let C be a transformation on Q defined by letting $C(\mathbf{x})$ be the value of $A(\mathbf{x})$ projected onto Q. Then C is a two-dimensional, generalized rotation around a point $\mathbf{v}$ in the plane Q. (Why?) From this, deduce that A has the desired form.]*

II.2.5 Three-Dimensional Projective Geometry*

Three-dimensional projective geometry can be developed analogously to the two-dimensional geometry discussed in Section II.1.8, and three-dimensional projective space can be viewed either as the usual three-dimensional Euclidean space augmented with points at infinity or as the space of linear subspaces of the four-dimensional $\mathbb{R}^4$.

We first consider how to represent three-dimensional projective space as $\mathbb{R}^3$ plus points at infinity. The new points at infinity are obtained as follows: let $\mathcal{F}$ be a family of parallel lines (i.e., let $\mathcal{F}$ be the set of lines parallel to a given line L, where L is a line in $\mathbb{R}^3$). We have a new point at infinity, $\mathbf{u}_\mathcal{F}$, and this point is added to every line in $\mathcal{F}$. The three-dimensional projective space consists of $\mathbb{R}^3$ plus these new points at infinity. Each plane P in $\mathbb{R}^3$ gets a new line of points at infinity in the projective space, namely, the points at infinity that belong to the lines in the plane P. The set of lines of the projective space are (a) the lines of $\mathbb{R}^3$ (including their new point at infinity), and (b) the lines at infinity that lie in a single plane. Finally, the set of all points at infinity forms the plane at infinity.

You should check that, in three-dimensional projective space, any two distinct planes intersect in a unique line.

Three-dimensional projective space can also be represented by linear subspaces of the four-dimensional space $\mathbb{R}^4$. This corresponds to the representation of points in $\mathbb{R}^3$ by homogeneous coordinates. A point in the projective space is equal to a one-dimensional subspace of $\mathbb{R}^4$, namely, a set of points of the form $\{\alpha\mathbf{u} : \alpha \in \mathbb{R}\}$ for $\mathbf{u}$ a *fixed* nonzero point of $\mathbb{R}^4$. The 4-tuple $\mathbf{u}$ is just a homogeneous representation of a point; if its fourth component (w-component) is zero, then the point is a point at infinity. The lines in projective space are just the two-dimensional subspaces of $\mathbb{R}^4$. A line is a line at infinity if and only if all its 4-tuples have zero as fourth component. The planes in projective space are precisely the three-dimensional subspaces of $\mathbb{R}^4$.

Exercise II.21 *Work out the correspondence between the two ways of representing three-dimensional projective space.*

OpenGL and other similar systems use 4-tuples as homogeneous coordinates for points in 3-space extensively. In OpenGL, the function call `glVertex4f(a,b,c,d)` is used to specify a point $\langle a, b, c, d \rangle$ in homogeneous coordinates. Of course, it is more common for a programmer to specify a point with only three (nonhomogeneous) coordinates, but then, whenever a point in 3-space is specified by a call to `glVertex3f(a,b,c)`, OpenGL translates this to the point $\langle a, b, c, 1 \rangle$.

However, OpenGL does not usually deal explicitly with points at infinity (although there are some exceptions, namely, defining Bézier and B-spline curves). Instead, points at infinity are typically used for indicating directions. As we will see later, when a light source is given a position, OpenGL interprets a point at infinity as specifying a direction. Strictly speaking, this is not a mathematically correct use of homogeneous coordinates, since taking the negative of the coordinates does not yield the same result but instead indicates the opposite direction for the light.

II.3 Viewing Transformations and Perspective

So far, we have used affine transformations as a method for placing geometric models of objects in 3-space. This is represented by the first stage of the rendering pipeline shown in Figure II.1 on page 18. In this first stage, points are placed in 3-space controlled by the model view matrix.

We now turn our attention to the second stage of the pipeline. This stage deals with how the geometric model in 3-space is viewed; namely, it places the camera or eye with a given position, view direction, and field of view. The placement of the camera or eye position determines what parts of the 3-D model will be visible in the final graphics image. Of course, there is no actual camera; it is only virtual. Instead, transformations are used to map the geometric model in 3-space into the xy-plane of the final image. Transformations used for this purpose are called *viewing transformations*. Viewing transformations include not only the affine transformations discussed earlier but also a new class of "perspective transformations."

To understand the purposes and uses of viewing transformations properly, it is necessary to consider the end result of the rendering pipeline (Figure II.1). The final output of the rendering pipeline is usually a rectangular array of pixels. Each pixel has an xy-position in the graphics image. In addition, each pixel has a color or grayscale value. Finally, it is common for each pixel to store a "depth value" or "distance value" that measures the distance to the object visible in that pixel.

Storing the depth is important because it is used by the hidden surface algorithm. When a scene is rendered, there may be multiple objects that lie behind a given pixel. As the objects are drawn onto the screen, the depth value, or distance, to the relevant part of the object is stored into each pixel location. By comparing depths, one can determine whether an object is in front of another object and thereby that the more distant object, being hidden behind the closer object, is not visible.

The use of the depth values is discussed more in Section II.4, but for now it is enough for us to keep in mind that it is important to keep track of the distance of objects from the camera position.

Stages 2 and 3 of the rendering pipeline are best considered together. These two stages are largely independent of the resolution of the screen or other output device. During the second stage, vertices are mapped by a 4×4 affine matrix into new homogeneous coordinates $\langle x, y, z, w \rangle$. The third stage, *perspective division*, further transforms these points by converting them back to points in $\mathbb{R}^3$ by the usual map

$$\langle x, y, z, w \rangle \;\mapsto\; \langle x/w, y/w, z/w \rangle.$$

The end result of the second and third stages is that they map the viewable objects into the $2 \times 2 \times 2$ cube centered at the origin, which contains the points with $-1 \le x \le 1, -1 \le y \le 1$, and $-1 \le z \le 1$. This cube will be mapped by simple rectangular scaling into the final graphics image during stage 4 of the rendering pipeline. The points with $x = 1$ (respectively, $x = -1$) are to be at the right (respectively, left) side of the screen or final image, and points with $y = 1$ (respectively, $y = -1$) are at the top (respectively, bottom) of the screen. Points with $z = 1$ are closest to the viewer, and points with $z = -1$ are farthest from the viewer.[7]

There are two basic kinds of viewing transformations: orthographic projections and perspective transformations. An orthographic projection is analogous to placing the viewer at an infinite distance (with a suitable telescope). Thus, orthographic projections map the geometric model by projecting at right angles onto a plane perpendicular to the view direction. Perspective transformations put the viewer at a finite position, and perspective makes closer objects appear larger than distant objects of the same size. The difference between orthographic and perspective transformations is illustrated in Figure II.18.

To simplify the definitions of orthographic and perspective transformations, it is convenient to define them only for a viewer who is placed at the origin and is looking in the direction of the negative z-axis. If the viewpoint is to be placed elsewhere or directed elsewhere, ordinary affine transformations can be used to adjust the view accordingly.

II.3.1 Orthographic Viewing Transformations

Orthographic viewing transformations carry out a parallel projection of a 3-D model onto a plane. Unlike the perspective transformations described later, orthographic viewing projections do not cause closer objects to appear larger and distant objects to appear smaller. For this reason, orthographic viewing projections are generally preferred for applications such as architecture or engineering applications, including computer-aided design and manufacturing (CAD/CAM) since the parallel projection is better at preserving relative sizes and angles.

---

[7] OpenGL uses the reverse convention on z with $z = -1$ for the closest objects and $z = 1$ for the farthest objects. Of course, this is merely a simple change of sign of the z component, but OpenGL's convention seems less intuitive because the transformation into the $2 \times 2 \times 2$ cube is no longer orientation-preserving. Since the OpenGL conventions are hidden from the programmer in most situations anyway, we will instead adopt the more intuitive convention.

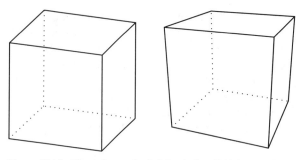

Figure II.18. The cube on the left is rendered with an orthographic projection, and the one on the right with a perspective transformation. With the orthographic projection, the rendered size of a face of the cube is independent of its distance from the viewer; compare, for example, the front and back faces. Under a perspective transformation, the closer a face is, the larger it is rendered.

For convenience, orthographic projections are defined in terms of an observer who is at the origin and is looking down the z-axis. The view direction is perpendicular to the xy-plane, and if two points differ in only their z-coordinate, then the one with higher z-coordinate is closer to the viewer.

An orthographic projection is generally specified by giving six axis-aligned "clipping planes," which form a rectangular prism. The geometry that lies inside the rectangular prism is scaled to have dimensions $2 \times 2 \times 2$ and translated to be centered at the origin. The rectangular prism is specified by six values $\ell, r, b, t, n,$ and f. These variable names are mnemonics for "left," "right," "bottom," "top," "near," and "far," respectively. The rectangular prism then consists of the points $\langle x, y, z \rangle$ such that

$$\ell \le x \le r,$$
$$b \le y \le t,$$
$$\text{and} \quad n \le -z \le f.$$

The $-z$ has a negative sign because of the convention that the viewer is looking down the z-axis facing in the negative z-direction. This means that the distance of a point $\langle x, y, z \rangle$ from the viewer is equal to $-z$. The usual convention is for n and f to be positive values; however, this is not actually required. The plane $z = -n$ is called the *near clipping plane*, and the plane $z = -f$ is called the *far clipping plane*. Objects closer than the near clipping plane or farther than the far clipping plane will be culled and not be rendered.

The orthographic projection must map points from the rectangular prism into the $2 \times 2 \times 2$ cube centered at the origin. This consists of (1) scaling along the coordinate axes and (2) translating so that the cube is centered at the origin. It is not hard to verify that this is accomplished by the following 4×4 homogeneous matrix:

$$\begin{pmatrix} \dfrac{2}{r-\ell} & 0 & 0 & -\dfrac{r+\ell}{r-\ell} \\ 0 & \dfrac{2}{t-b} & 0 & -\dfrac{t+b}{t-b} \\ 0 & 0 & \dfrac{2}{f-n} & \dfrac{f+n}{f-n} \\ 0 & 0 & 0 & 1 \end{pmatrix}. \qquad \text{II.10}$$

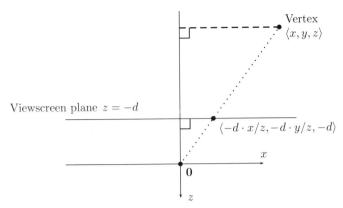

Figure II.19. Perspective projection onto a viewscreen at distance d. The viewer is at the origin looking in the direction of the negative z-axis. The point $\langle x, y, z \rangle$ is perspectively projected onto the plane $z = -d$, which is at distance d in front of the viewer at the origin.

II.3.2 Perspective Transformations

Perspective transformations are used to create the view when the camera or eye position is placed at a finite distance from the scene. The use of perspective means that an object will appear larger as it moves closer to the viewer. Perspective is useful for giving the viewer the sense of being "in" a scene because a perspective view shows the scene from a particular viewpoint. Perspective is heavily used in entertainment applications, where it is desired to give an immersive experience; it is particularly useful in dynamic situations in which the combination of motion and correct perspective gives a strong sense of the three-dimensionality of the scene. Perspective is also used in applications as diverse as architectural modeling and crime recreation to show the view from a particular viewpoint.

As was mentioned in Section II.1.8, perspective was originally discovered for applications in drawing and painting. An important principle in the classic theory of perspective is the notion of a "vanishing point" shared by a family of parallel lines. An artist who is incorporating perspective in a drawing will choose appropriate vanishing points to aid the composition of the drawing. In computer graphics applications, we are able to avoid all considerations of vanishing points and similar factors. Instead, we place objects in 3-space, choose a viewpoint (camera position), and mathematically calculate the correct perspective transformation to create the scene as viewed from the viewpoint.

For simplicity, we consider only a viewer placed at the origin looking down the negative z-axis. We mentally choose as a "viewscreen" the plane $z = -d$, which is parallel to the xy-plane at distance d from the viewpoint at the origin. Intuitively, the viewscreen serves as a display screen onto which viewable objects are projected. Let a vertex in the scene have position $\langle x, y, z \rangle$. We form the line from the vertex position to the origin and calculate the point $\langle x', y', z' \rangle$ where the line intersects the viewscreen (see Figure II.19). Of course, we have $z' = -d$. Referring to Figure II.19 and arguing on the basis of similar triangles, we have

$$ x' = \frac{d \cdot x}{-z} \quad \text{and} \quad y' = \frac{d \cdot y}{-z}. \qquad \text{II.11} $$

The values x', y' give the position of the vertex as seen on the viewscreen from the viewpoint at the origin.

So far, projective transformations have been very straightforward, but now it is necessary to incorporate also the "depth" of the vertex, that is, its distance from the viewer. The obvious first

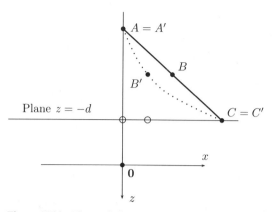

Figure II.20. The undesirable transformation of a line to a curve. The mapping used is $\langle x, y, z \rangle \mapsto \langle -d \cdot x/z, -d \cdot y/z, z \rangle$. The points A and C are fixed by the transformation, and B is mapped to B'. The dotted curve is the image of the line segment AC. (The small unlabeled circles show the images of A and B under the mapping of Figure II.19.)

attempt would be to use the value $-z$ for the depth. Another, albeit less appealing, possibility would be to record the true distance $\sqrt{x^2 + y^2 + z^2}$ as the depth. Both of these ideas, however, fail to work well. The reason is that, if perspective mappings are defined with a depth specified in either of these ways, then lines in the three-dimensional scene can be mapped to curves in the viewscreen space. That is, a line of points with coordinates x, y, z, will map to a curve that is not a line in the viewscreen space.

An example of how a line can map to a curve is shown in Figure II.20. For this figure, we use the transformation

$$x \mapsto \frac{d \cdot x}{-z} \qquad y \mapsto \frac{d \cdot y}{-z} \qquad z \mapsto z \qquad\qquad\qquad \text{II.12}$$

so that the z-coordinate directly serves a measure of depth. (Since the viewpoint is looking down the negative z-axis, greater values of z correspond to closer points.) In Figure II.20, we see points A, B, and C that are mapped by Transformation II.12 to points A', B', and C'. Obviously, A and C are fixed points of the transformation, and thus $A = A'$ and $C = C'$. However, the point B is mapped to the point B', which is not on the line segment from A' to C'. Thus, the image of the line segment is not straight.

One might question at this point why it is undesirable for lines to map to curves. The answer to this question lies in the way the fourth stage of the graphics-rendering pipeline works. In the fourth stage, the endpoints of a line segment are used to place a line in the screen space. This line in screen space typically has not only a position on the screen but also depth (distance) values stored in a *depth buffer*.[8] When the fourth stage processes a line segment, say as shown in Figure II.20, it is given only the endpoints A' and C' as points $\langle x_A, y_A, z_A \rangle$ and $\langle x_C, y_C, z_C \rangle$. It then uses linear interpolation to determine the rest of the points on the line segment. This then gives an incorrect depth to intermediate points such as B'. With incorrect depth values, the hidden surface algorithm can fail in dramatically unacceptable ways since the depth buffer values are used to determine which points are in front of other points.

Thus, we need another way to handle depth information. In fact, it is enough to find a definition of a "fake" distance or a "pseudo-distance" function that has the following two

---

[8]   Other information, such as color values, is also stored along with depth, but this does not concern the present discussion.

properties:

1. The pseudo-distance preserves relative distances, and
2. It causes lines to map to lines.

As it turns out, a good choice for this pseudo-distance is any function of the form

$$\text{pseudo-dist}(z) = A + B/z,$$

where A and B are constants such that $B < 0$. Since $B < 0$, property 1 certainly holds because pseudo-dist(z_1) < pseudo-dist(z_2) holds whenever $z_1 < z_2$.

It is a common convention to choose the values for A and B so that points on the near and far clipping planes have pseudo-distances equal to $+1$ and -1, respectively. The near and far clipping planes have $z = -n$ and $z = -f$, and so we need the following:

$$\text{pseudo-dist}(-n) = A - B/n = 1$$
$$\text{pseudo-dist}(-f) = A - B/f = -1.$$

Solving these two equations for A and B yields

$$A = \frac{-(f+n)}{f-n} \quad \text{and} \quad B = \frac{-2fn}{f-n}. \tag{II.13}$$

Before discussing property 2, it is helpful to see how this definition of the pseudo-distance function fits into the framework of homogeneous representation of points. With the use of the pseudo-dist function, the perspective transformation becomes the mapping

$$\langle x, y, z \rangle \mapsto \langle -d \cdot x/z, -d \cdot y/z, A + B/z \rangle.$$

We can rewrite this in homogeneous coordinates as

$$\langle x, y, z, 1 \rangle \mapsto \langle d \cdot x, d \cdot y, -A \cdot z - B, -z \rangle \tag{II.14}$$

since multiplying through by $(-z)$ does not change the point represented by the homogeneous coordinates. More generally, because the homogeneous representation $\langle x, y, z, w \rangle$ is equivalent to $\langle x/w, y/w, z/w, 1 \rangle$, the mapping II.14 acting on this point is

$$\langle x/w, y/w, z/w, 1 \rangle \mapsto \langle d \cdot x/w, \; d \cdot y/w, \; -A \cdot (z/w) - B, \; -z/w \rangle,$$

and, after multiplying both sides by w, this becomes

$$\langle x, y, z, w \rangle \mapsto \langle d \cdot x, \; d \cdot y, \; -(A \cdot z + B \cdot w), \; -z \rangle.$$

Thus, we have established that the perspective transformation incorporating the pseudo-dist function is represented by the following 4×4 homogeneous matrix:

$$\begin{pmatrix} d & 0 & 0 & 0 \\ 0 & d & 0 & 0 \\ 0 & 0 & -A & -B \\ 0 & 0 & -1 & 0 \end{pmatrix}. \tag{II.15}$$

That the perspective transformation based on pseudo-distance can be expressed as a 4×4 matrix has two unexpected benefits. First, homogeneous matrices provide a uniform framework for representing both affine and perspective transformations. Second, in Section II.3.3, we prove the following theorem:

Theorem II.6 *The perspective transformation represented by the 4×4 matrix II.15 maps lines to lines.*

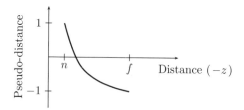

Figure II.21. Pseudo-distance varies nonlinearly with distance. Larger pseudo-distance values correspond to closer points.

In choosing a perspective transformation, it is important to select values for n and f, the near and far clipping plane distances, so that all the desired objects are included in the field of view. At the same time, it is also important not to choose the near clipping plane to be too near, or the far clipping plane to be too distant. The reason is that the depth buffer values need to have enough resolution so as to allow different (pseudo)distance values to be distinguished. To understand how the use of pseudo-distance affects how much resolution is needed to distinguish between different distances, consider the graph of pseudo-distance versus distance in Figure II.21. Qualitatively, it is clear from the graph that pseudo-distance varies faster for small distance values than for large distance values (since the graph of the pseudo-distance function is sloping more steeply at smaller distances than at larger distances). Therefore, the pseudo-distance function is better at distinguishing differences in distance at small distances than at large distances. In most applications this is good, for, as a general rule, small objects tend to be close to the viewpoint, whereas more distant objects tend to either be larger or, if not larger, then errors in depth comparisons for distant objects make less noticeable errors in the graphics image.

It is common for stage 4 of the rendering pipeline to convert the pseudo-distance into a value in the range 0 to 1, with 0 used for points at the near clipping plane and with 1 representing points at the far clipping plane. This number, in the range 0 to 1, is then represented in fixed point, binary notation, that is, as an integer with 0 representing the value at the near clipping plane and the maximum integer value representing the value at the far clipping plane. In modern graphics hardware systems, it is common to use a 32-bit integer to store the depth information, and this gives sufficient depth resolution to allow the hidden surface calculations to work well in most situations. That is, it will work well provided the near and far clipping distances are chosen wisely. Older systems used 16-bit depth buffers, and this tended occasionally to cause resolution problems. By comparison, the usual single-precision floating point numbers have 24 bits of resolution.

II.3.3 Mapping Lines to Lines⋆

As was discussed in the previous section, the fact that perspective transformations map lines in 3-space to lines in screen space is important for interpolation of depth values in the screen space. Indeed, more than this is true: any transformation represented by a 4×4 homogeneous matrix maps lines in 3-space to lines in 3-space. Since the perspective maps are represented by 4×4 matrices, as shown by Equation II.15, the same is true a fortiori of perspective transformations.

Theorem II.7 *Let M be a 4×4 homogeneous matrix acting on homogeneous coordinates for points in $\mathbb{R}^3$. If L is a line in $\mathbb{R}^3$, then the image of L under the transformation represented by M, if defined, is either a line or a point in $\mathbb{R}^3$.*

This immediately gives the following corollary.

Corollary II.8 *Perspective transformations map lines to lines.*

For proving Theorem II.7, the most convenient way to represent the three-dimensional projective space is as the set of linear subspaces of the Euclidean space $\mathbb{R}^4$, as was described in Section II.2.5. The "points" of the three-dimensional projective space are the one-dimensional subspaces of $\mathbb{R}^4$. The "lines" of the three-dimensional projective space are the two-dimensional subspaces of $\mathbb{R}^4$. The "planes" of the three-dimensional projective geometry are the three-dimensional subspaces of $\mathbb{R}^4$.

The proof of Theorem II.7 is now immediate. Since M is represented by a 4×4 matrix, it acts linearly on $\mathbb{R}^4$. Therefore, M must map a two-dimensional subspace representing a line onto a subspace of dimension at most two: that is, onto either a two-dimensional subspace representing a line, or a one-dimensional subspace representing a point, or a zero-dimensional subspace. In the last case, the value of M on points on the line is undefined because the point $\langle 0, 0, 0, 0 \rangle$ is not a valid set of homogeneous coordinates for a point in $\mathbb{R}^3$.

II.3.4 Another Use for Projection: Shadows

In the next chapter, we study local lighting and illumination models, which, because they track only local features, cannot handle phenomena such as shadows or indirect illumination. There are global methods for calculating lighting that do handle shadows and indirect illumination (see chapters IX and XI), but these methods are often computationally very difficult and cannot be used with ordinary OpenGL commands in any event. There are also some multipass rendering techniques for rendering shadows that can be used in OpenGL (see Section IX.3).

An alternative way to cast shadows that works well for casting shadows onto flat, planar surfaces is to render the shadow of an object explicitly. This can be done in OpenGL by setting the current color to black (or whatever shadow color is desired) and then drawing the shadow as a flat object on the plane. Determining the shape of a shadow of a complex object can be complicated since it depends on the orientation of the object and the position of the light source and object relative to the plane. Instead of attempting to calculate the shape of the shadow explicitly, you can first set the model view matrix to hold a projection transformation and then render the object in 3-space, letting the model view matrix map the rendered object down onto the plane.

This method has several advantages, chief among them being that it requires very little coding effort. One can merely render the object twice: once in its proper location in 3-space, and once with the model view matrix set to project it down flat onto the plane. This technique handles arbitrarily complex shapes properly, including objects that contain holes.

To determine what the model view matrix should be for shadow projections, suppose that the light is positioned at $\langle 0, y_0, 0 \rangle$, that is, at height y_0 up the y-axis, and that the plane of projection is the xz-plane, where $y = 0$. It is not difficult to see by using similar triangles that the projection transformation needed to cast shadows should be (see Figure II.22)

$$\langle x, y, z \rangle \mapsto \left\langle \frac{x}{1 - y/y_0}, 0, \frac{z}{1 - y/y_0} \right\rangle.$$

This transformation is represented by the following homogeneous matrix:

$$\begin{pmatrix} 1 & 0 & 0 & 0 \\ 0 & 0 & 0 & 0 \\ 0 & 0 & 1 & 0 \\ 0 & -\frac{1}{y_0} & 0 & 1 \end{pmatrix}.$$

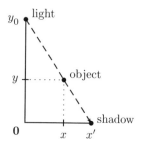

Figure II.22. A light is positioned at $\langle 0, y_0, 0 \rangle$. An object is positioned at $\langle x, y, z \rangle$. The shadow of the point is projected to the point $\langle x', 0, z' \rangle$, where $x' = x/(1 - y/y_0)$ and $z' = z/(1 - y/y_0)$.

Exercise II.22 *Prove the correctness of the formula above for the shadow transformation and the homogeneous matrix representation.*

One potential pitfall with drawing shadows on a flat plane is that, if the shadow is drawn exactly coincident with the plane, *z-fighting* may cause the plane and shadow to show through each other. The phenomenon of *z*-fighting occurs when two objects are drawn at the same depth from the viewer: owing to roundoff errors, it can happen that some pixel positions have the first object closer than the other and other pixels have the second closer than the first. The effect is a pattern of pixels in which one object shows through the other. One way to combat *z*-fighting is to lift the shadow up from the plane slightly, but this can cause problems from some viewpoints where the gap between the plane and the shadow can become apparent. To solve this problem, you can use the OpenGL polygon offset feature. The polygon offset mode perturbs the depth values (pseudo-distance values) of points before performing depth testing against the pixel buffer. This allows the depth values to be perturbed for depth comparison purposes without affecting the position of the object on the screen.

To use polygon offset to draw a shadow on a plane, you would first enable the polygon offset mode with a positive offset value, draw the plane, and disable the polygon offset mode. Finally, you would render the shadow without any polygon offset.

The OpenGL commands for enabling the polygon offset mode are

```
glPolygonOffset( 1.0, 1.0 );
```

$$
\text{glEnable(} \left\{ \begin{array}{l} \texttt{GL\_POLYGON\_OFFSET\_FILL} \\ \texttt{GL\_POLYGON\_OFFSET\_LINE} \\ \texttt{GL\_POLYGON\_OFFSET\_POINT} \end{array} \right\} \text{);}
$$

Similar options for `glDisable` will disable polygon offset. The amount of offset is controlled by the `glPolygonOffset()` command; setting both parameters to `1.0` is a good choice in most cases. You can also select negative values such as `-1.0` to use offset to pull objects closer to the view. For details on what these parameters mean, see the OpenGL programming manual (Woo et al., 1999).

II.3.5 The OpenGL Perspective Transformations

OpenGL provides special functions for setting up viewing transformations as either orthographic projections or perspective transformations. The direction and location of the camera can be controlled with the same affine transformations used for modeling transformations, and, in addition, there is a function, `gluLookAt`, that provides a convenient method to set the camera location and view direction.

The basic OpenGL command for creating an orthographic projection is

```
glOrtho ( float ℓ, float r, float b, float t, float n, float f );
```

As discussed in Section II.3.1, the intent of the `glOrtho` command is to set up the camera or eye position so that it is oriented to look down the negative z-axis at the rectangular prism of points with $\ell \leq x \leq r$ and $b \leq y \leq t$ and $n \leq -z \leq f$. Any part of the scene that lies outside this prism is clipped and not displayed. In particular, objects that are closer than the *near clipping plane*, defined by $(-z) = n$, are not visible and do not even obstruct the view of more distant objects. In addition, objects farther than the *far clipping plane*, defined by $(-z) = f$, are likewise not visible. Of course, objects, or parts of objects, outside the left, right, bottom, and top planes are not visible.

Internally, the effect of the `glOrtho` command is to multiply the current matrix, which is usually the projection matrix P, by the matrix

$$S = \begin{pmatrix} \dfrac{2}{r-\ell} & 0 & 0 & -\dfrac{r+\ell}{r-\ell} \\ 0 & \dfrac{2}{t-b} & 0 & -\dfrac{t+b}{t-b} \\ 0 & 0 & \dfrac{-2}{f-n} & -\dfrac{f+n}{f-n} \\ 0 & 0 & 0 & 1 \end{pmatrix}.$$

This is the same as the matrix shown in Equation II.10 on page 48, except the signs of the third row are reversed. This is because OpenGL's convention for the meaning of points in the $2 \times 2 \times 2$ cube is that $z = -1$ for the closest objects and $z = 1$ for the farthest objects, and thus the z values need to be negated. As usual, the multiplication is on the right; that is, it has the effect of performing the assignment $P = P \cdot S$, where P is the current matrix (presumably the projection matrix).

A special case of orthographic projections in OpenGL is provided by the following function:

```
gluOrtho2D( float ℓ, float r, float b, float t );
```

The function `gluOrtho2D` is exactly like `glOrtho`, but with $n = -1$ and $f = 1$. That is, `gluOrtho2D` views points that have z-value between -1 and 1. Usually, `gluOrtho2D` is used when drawing two-dimensional figures that lie in the xy-plane, with $z = 0$. It is a convenience function, along with `glVertex2*`, intended for drawing two-dimensional objects.

OpenGL has two commands that implement perspective transformations, `glFrustum` and `gluPerspective`. Both these commands make the usual assumption that the viewpoint is at the origin and the view direction is toward the negative z-axis. The most basic command is the `glFrustum` command, which has the following syntax:

```
glFrustum ( float ℓ, float r, float b, float t, float n, float f );
```

A *frustum* is a six-sided geometric shape formed from a rectangular pyramid by removing a top portion. In this case, the frustum consists of the points $\langle x, y, z \rangle$ satisfying the conditions II.16 and II.17. (Refer to Figure II.23).

a. The points lie between the near and far clipping planes:

$$n \leq -z \leq f. \hspace{8cm} \text{II.16}$$

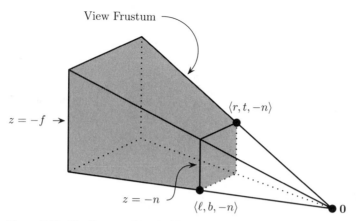

Figure II.23. The frustum viewed with `glFrustum(` ℓ `, ` r `, ` b `, ` t `, ` n `, ` f `)`. The near clipping plane is $z = -n$. The far clipping plane is $z = -f$. The frustum is the set of points satisfying Relations II.16 and II.17.

b. The perspective mapping, which performs a perspective projection onto the near clipping plane, maps $\langle x, y, z \rangle$ to a point $\langle x', y', z' \rangle$ with $\ell \leq x' \leq r$ and $b \leq y' \leq t$. On the basis of Equation II.11, this is the same as

$$\ell \leq \frac{n \cdot x}{-z} \leq r \qquad \text{and} \qquad b \leq \frac{n \cdot y}{-z} \leq t. \tag{II.17}$$

The effect of the `glFrustum` command is to form the matrix

$$S = \begin{pmatrix} \dfrac{2n}{r - \ell} & 0 & \dfrac{r + \ell}{r - \ell} & 0 \\ 0 & \dfrac{2n}{t - b} & \dfrac{t + b}{t - b} & 0 \\ 0 & 0 & \dfrac{-(f + n)}{f - n} & \dfrac{-2fn}{f - n} \\ 0 & 0 & -1 & 0 \end{pmatrix} \tag{II.18}$$

and then multiply the current matrix (usually the projection matrix) on the right by S. This matrix S is chosen so that the frustum is mapped onto the $2 \times 2 \times 2$ cube centered at the origin. The formula for the matrix S is obtained in nearly the same way as the derivation of Equation II.15 for the perspective transformation in Section II.3.2. There are three differences between Equations II.18 and II.15. First, the OpenGL matrix causes the final x and y values to lie in the range -1 to 1 by performing appropriate scaling and translation: the scaling is caused by the first two diagonal entries, and the translation is effected by the top two values in the third column. The second difference is that the values in the third row are negated because OpenGL negates the z values from our own convention. The third difference is that Equation II.15 was derived under the assumption that the view frustum was centered on the z-axis. For `glFrustum`, this happens if $\ell = -r$ and $b = -t$. But, `glFrustum` also allows more general-view frustums that are not centered on the z-axis.

Exercise II.23★ *Derive Formula II.18 for the* `glFrustum` *matrix.*

OpenGL provides a function `gluPerspective` that can be used as an alternative to `glFrustum`. The function `gluPerspective` limits you to perspective transformations for which the z-axis is in the center of the field of view, but this is usually what is wanted anyway. The function `gluPerspective` works by making a single call to `glFrustum`. The usage of `gluPerspective` is

    gluPerspective(float θ, float *aspectRatio*, float n, float ƒ);

where θ is an angle (measured in degrees) specifying the vertical field of view. That is to say, θ is the solid angle between the top bounding plane and the bottom bounding plane of the frustum in Figure II.23. The *aspect ratio* of an image is the ratio of its width to its height, and so the parameter *aspectRatio* specifies the ratio of the width of the frustum to the height of the frustum. It follows that a call to `gluPerspective` is equivalent to calling `glFrustum` with

$$t = n \cdot \tan(\theta/2)$$

$$b = -n \cdot \tan(\theta/2)$$

$$r = (aspectRatio) \cdot t$$

$$\ell = (aspectRatio) \cdot b$$

As an example of the use of `gluPerspective`, consider the following code fragment from the `Solar.c` program:

```
// Called when the window is resized
// Sets up the projection view matrix (somewhat poorly, however)
void ResizeWindow(int w, int h)
{
    glViewport( 0, 0, w, h );          // Viewport uses whole window

    float aspectRatio;
    h = (h == 0) ? 1 : h;              // Avoid divide by zero
    aspectRatio = (float)w/(float)h;

    // Set up the projection view matrix
    glMatrixMode( GL_PROJECTION );
    glLoadIdentity();
    gluPerspective( 60.0, aspectRatio, 1.0, 30.0 );
}
```

The routine `ResizeWindow` is called whenever the program window is resized[9] and is given the new width and height of the window in pixels. This routine first specifies that the *viewport* is to be the entire window, giving its lower left-hand corner as the pixel with coordinates $0, 0$ and its upper right-hand corner as the pixel with coordinates $w - 1, h - 1$.[10] The viewport is the area of the window in which the OpenGL graphics are displayed. The routine then makes the projection matrix the active matrix, restores it to the identity, and calls `gluPerspective`. This call picks a vertical field-of-view angle of $60°$ and makes the aspect ratio of the viewed scene equal to the aspect ratio of the viewport.

It is illuminating to consider potential problems with the way `gluPerspective` is used in the sample code. First, a vertical field of view of $60°$ is probably higher than optimal. By

---

[9]   This is set up by the earlier call to `glutReshapeFunc` in the main program of `Solar.c`.
[10] Pixel positions are numbered by values from 0 to $h - 1$ from the bottom row of pixels to the top row and are numbered from 0 to $w - 1$ from the left column of pixels to the right column.

making the field of view too large, the effects of perspective are exaggerated, causing the image to appear as if it were viewed through a wide-angle or "fish-eye" lens. On the other hand, if the field of view is too small, then the image does not have enough perspective and looks too close to an orthographic projection. Ideally, the field of view should be chosen to be equal to the angle that the final screen image takes up in the field of view of the person looking at the image. Of course, to set the field of view precisely in this way, one would need to know the dimensions of the viewport (in inches, say) *and* the distance of the person from the screen. In practice, one can usually only guess at these values.

The second problem with the preceding sample code is that the field of view angle is controlled by only the up–down, y-axis, direction. To see why this is a problem, try running the `Solar` program and resizing the window first to be wide and short and then to be narrow and tall. In the second case, only a small part of the solar system will be visible.

Exercise II.24 *Rewrite the* `ResizeWindow` *function in* `Solar.c` *so that the entire solar system is visible no matter what the aspect ratio of the window is.*

OpenGL provides another function `gluLookAt` to make it easy to position a viewpoint at an arbitrary location in 3-space looking in an arbitrary direction with an arbitrary orientation. This function is called with nine parameters:

```
gluLookAt(eye_x, eye_y, eye_z, center_x, center_y, center_z,
          up_x, up_y, up_z);
```

The three "eye" values specify a location in 3-space for the viewpoint. The three "center" values must specify a different location so that the view direction is toward the center location. The three "up" values specify an upward direction for the y-axis of the viewer. It is not necessary for the "up" vector to be orthogonal to the vector from the eye to the center, but it must not be parallel to it. The `gluLookAt` command should be used when the current matrix is the model view matrix, not the projection matrix. This is because the viewer should always be placed at the origin in order for OpenGL's lighting to work properly.

Exercise II.25 *Rewrite the* `Solar` *function on page 39 to use* `gluLookAt` *instead of the first translation and rotation.*

II.4 Mapping to Pixels

The fourth stage of the rendering pipeline (see Figure II.1 on page 18) takes polygons with vertices in 3-space and draws them into a rectangular array of pixels. This array of pixels is called the *viewport*. By convention, these polygons are specified in terms of their vertices; the three earlier stages of the pipeline have positioned these vertices in the $2 \times 2 \times 2$ cube centered at the origin. The x- and y-coordinates of a vertex determine its position in the viewport. The z-coordinate specifies a relative depth or distance value – possibly a pseudo-distance value. In addition, each vertex will usually have other values associated with it – most notably color values. The color values are commonly scalars r, g, b, α for the intensities of red, green, and blue light and the alpha channel value, respectively. Alternatively, the color may be a single scalar for gray-scale intensity in a black and white image. Other values may also be associated with pixels, for instance, u, v-values indexing into a texture map.

If the viewport has width w and height h, we index a pixel by a pair $\langle i, j \rangle$ with i, j integer values, $0 \leq i < w$ and $0 \leq j < h$. Suppose a vertex **v** has position $\langle x, y, z \rangle$ in the $2 \times 2 \times 2$ cube. It is convenient to remap the x, y values into the rectangle $[0, w) \times [0, h)$ so that the values of x, y correspond directly to pixel indices. Thus, we let

$$x' = \frac{x+1}{2} w \qquad \text{and} \qquad y' = \frac{y+1}{2} h.$$

Then the vertex $\mathbf{v}$ is mapped to the pixel $\langle i, j \rangle$, where[11]

$$i = \lfloor x' \rfloor \qquad \text{and} \qquad j = \lfloor y' \rfloor,$$

with the exceptions that $x' = w$ yields $i = w - 1$ and $y' = h$ yields $j = h - 1$. Thus, the pixel $\langle i, j \rangle$ corresponds to vertices with $\langle x', y' \rangle$ in the unit square centered at $\langle i + \frac{1}{2}, j + \frac{1}{2} \rangle$.

At the same time as the x' and y' values are quantized to pixel indices, the other values associated with the pixel are likewise quantized to integer values. The z-value is typically saved as a 16- or 32-bit integer with 0 indicating the closest visible objects and larger values more distant objects. Color values such as r, g, b are typically stored as either 8-bit integers (for "millions of colors" mode with 16,777,216 colors) or as 5-bit integers (for "thousands of colors" mode, with 32,768 colors). Texture coordinates are usually mapped to integer coordinates indexing a pixel in the texture.

Now suppose that a line segment has as endpoints the two vertices $\mathbf{v}_1$ and $\mathbf{v}_2$ and that these endpoints have been mapped to the pixels $\langle i_1, j_1 \rangle$ and $\langle i_2, j_2 \rangle$. Once the endpoints have been determined, it is still necessary to draw the pixels that connect the two endpoints in a straight line. The problem is that the pixels are arranged rectangularly thus, for lines that are not exactly horizontal or vertical, there is some ambiguity about which pixels belong to the line segment. There are several possibilities here for how to decide which pixels are drawn as part of the line segment. The usual solution is the following.

First, when drawing the pixels that represent a line segment, we work only with the values $\langle i_1, j_1 \rangle$ and $\langle i_2, j_2 \rangle$: the floating point numbers from which they were derived have been forgotten.[12] Then let

$$\Delta i = i_2 - i_1 \qquad \text{and} \qquad \Delta j = j_2 - j_1.$$

Of course, we may assume that $i_1 \le i_2$; otherwise, the vertices could be interchanged. We can also assume, without loss of any generality, that $j_1 \le j_2$, since the case $j_1 > j_2$ is symmetric. We then distinguish the cases of whether the slope of the line segment is ≤ 1 or ≥ 1, that is, whether $\Delta j / \Delta i \le 1$ or $\Delta i / \Delta j \le 1$. As illustrated in Figure II.24, in the first case, the line segment can be drawn so that there is exactly one pixel $\langle i, j \rangle$ drawn for each i between i_1 and i_2. In the second case, there is exactly one pixel $\langle i, j \rangle$ drawn for each j between j_1 and j_2.

Henceforth, it is assumed that the slope of the line is ≤ 1, that is, $\Delta j \le \Delta i$ and that, in particular, $i_1 \ne i_2$. This does not cause any loss of generality since the case of slope > 1 can be handled by interchanging the roles of the variables i and j. Our goal is to find values $j(i)$ so that the line segment can be drawn using the pixels $\langle i, j(i) \rangle$, for $i = i_1, i_1 + 1, \ldots, i_2$. This is done by using linear interpolation to define an "ideal" value $y(i)$ for $j(i)$ and then rounding to the nearest integer. Namely, suppose $i_1 \le i \le i_2$. Let $\alpha = \frac{i - i_1}{i_2 - i_1}$. Calculating the y-coordinate

[11] The notation $\lfloor a \rfloor$ denotes the least integer less than or equal to a.

[12] There is some loss of information in rounding to the nearest pixel and forgetting the floating point numbers. Some implementations of line drawing algorithms use subpixel levels of precision; that is, rather than rounding to the nearest pixel, they use a fixed number of bits of extra precision to address subpixel locations. This extra precision does not change the essential nature of the Bresenham algorithm for line drawing, which is described in the next section. In particular, the Bresenham algorithms can still work with integers.

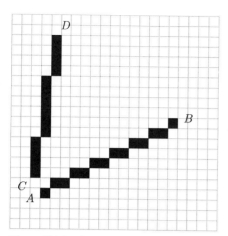

Figure II.24. The line segment AB has slope $\Delta j/\Delta i \leq 1$. The line segment CD has slope ≥ 1. The former segment is drawn with one pixel per column; the latter segment is drawn with one pixel per row.

of the line to be drawn on the viewport, we have that

$$y(i) - y(i_1) = \alpha \cdot (y(i_2) - y(i_1)),$$

that is,

$$y(i) = j_1 + \frac{1}{2} + \alpha(j_2 - j_1) = j_1 + \frac{1}{2} + \alpha\Delta j$$

because our best estimates for $y(i_1)$ and $y(i_2)$ are $y(i_1) = j_1 + \frac{1}{2}$ and $y(i_2) = j_2 + \frac{1}{2}$. We then obtain $j(i)$ by rounding down, namely,

$$j(i) = \left\lfloor j_1 + \frac{1}{2} + \alpha\Delta j \right\rfloor = \left\lfloor j_1 + \frac{1}{2} + \frac{i - i_1}{i_2 - i_1}\Delta j \right\rfloor. \qquad \text{II.19}$$

Another, and more suggestive, way to write the formula for $j(i)$ is to use the notation $[x]$ to denote x rounded to the nearest integer. Then $[x] = \lfloor x + \frac{1}{2} \rfloor$, and so Equation II.19 is equivalent to

$$j(i) = [(1 - \alpha)j_1 + \alpha j_2]. \qquad \text{II.20}$$

As we will see in Chapter IV, this is the usual formula for linear interpolation. (The additive $\frac{1}{2}$ in the earlier formulas is thus seen to be just an artifact of the rounding process.)

The other scalar values, such as the depth value z; the color values r, g, b; and the texture coordinates can be linearly interpolated in the same way. For the color values, this is what is called Gouraud interpolation.[13] For example, the interpolated values for the depth (pseudo-distance) z would be computed so that

$$z(i) = [(1 - \alpha)z_1 + \alpha z_2],$$

where z_1 and z_2 are the integer values at the first and last vertex obtained by appropriately scaling the z values and rounding down to the nearest integer. The value $z(i)$ is the calculated interpolating integer value at the pixel $\langle i, y(i) \rangle$.

---

[13] Gouraud interpolation is named after H. Gouraud, who proposed linear interpolation in 1971 as a method of blending colors across polygons in (Gouraud, 1971). His motivation was to apply smoothly varying colors to renderings of surface patches similar to the patches discussed in Section VII.10.

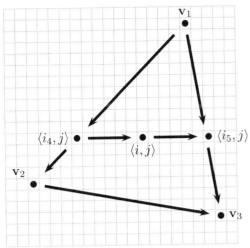

Figure II.25. The scan line interpolation method first interpolates along the edges of the triangle and then interpolates along the horizontal rows of pixels in the interior of the triangle. The interpolation directions are shown with arrows. If you look closely, you will note that the rightmost pixel $\langle i_5, j \rangle$ on the horizontal scan line is not exactly on the line segment forming the right edge of the triangle – this is necessary because its position must be rounded to the nearest pixel.

The next section will present the Bresenham algorithm, which gives an efficient, purely integer-based method for computing the interpolating values $y(i)$, $z(i)$, and so forth.

Before studying the Bresenham algorithm, we consider how interpolation is used to interpolate values across a triangle of pixels in the viewport. Let a triangle have vertices $\mathbf{v}_1$, $\mathbf{v}_2$, and $\mathbf{v}_3$. After projecting and rounding to integer values, the vertices map to points $\langle i_m, j_m \rangle$, for $m = 1, 2, 3$. By the linear interpolation formulas above, the three sides of the triangle can be drawn as pixels, and the other values such as depth and color are also interpolated to the pixels along the sides of the triangle. The remaining pixels in the interior of the triangle are filled in by interpolation along the horizontal rows of pixels. Thus, for instance, in Figure II.25, the scalar values at pixel $\langle i, j \rangle$ are interpolated from the values at the pixels $\langle i_4, j \rangle$ and $\langle i_5, j \rangle$. This method is called *scan line interpolation*.

The process of interpolating along a scan line is mathematically identical to the linear interpolation discussed above. Thus, it can also be carried out with the efficient Bresenham algorithm. In fact, the most natural implementation would involve nested loops that implement nested Bresenham algorithms.

Finally, there is a generalization of scan line interpolation that applies to general polygons rather than just to triangles. The general scan line interpolation interpolates values along all the edges of the polygon. Then, each horizontal scan line of pixels in the interior of the polygon begins and ends on an edge or vertex of course. The values on the horizontal scan line are filled in by interpolating from the values at the ends. With careful coding, general scan line interpolation can be implemented efficiently to carry out the interpolation along edges and across scan lines simultaneously. However, scan line interpolation suffers from the serious drawback that the results of the interpolation can change greatly as the polygon is rotated, and so it is generally not recommended for scenes that contain rotating polygons. Figure II.26 shows an example of how scan line interpolation can inconsistently render polygons as they rotate. There, a polygon is drawn twice – first upright and then rotated $90°$. Two of the vertices of the polygon are labeled W and are assigned the color white. The other two vertices are labeled B

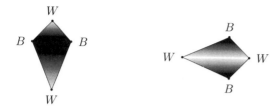

Figure II.26. Opposite vertices have the same black or white color. Scan line interpolation causes the appearance of the polygon to change radically when it is rotated. The two polygons are identical except for their orientation.

and are colored black. The scan line interpolation imposes a top-to-bottom interpolation that drastically changes the appearance of the rotated polygon.

Another problem with scan line interpolation is shown in Figure II.27. Here a nonconvex polygon has two black vertices and three white vertices. The nonconvexity causes a discontinuous shading of the polygon.

Scan line interpolation on triangles does not suffer from the problems just discussed. Indeed, for triangles, scan line interpolation is equivalent to linear interpolation – at least up to roundoff errors introduced by quantization.

II.4.1 Bresenham Algorithm

The Bresenham algorithm provides a fast iterative method for interpolating on integer values. It is traditionally presented as an algorithm for drawing pixels in a rectangular array to form a line. However, it applies equally well to performing linear interpolation of values in the depth buffer, linear interpolation for Gouraud shading, and so forth.

Before presenting the actual Bresenham algorithm, we present pseudocode for an algorithm based on real numbers. Then we see how to rewrite the algorithm to use integers instead. The algorithm will calculate the integer values $j(i)$ for $i = i_1, i_1 + 1, \ldots, i_2$ so that $j(i_1) = j_1$ and $j(i_2) = j_2$. We are assuming without loss of generality that $i_1 < i_2$ and $j_1 \le j_2$ and that $\Delta j = j_2 - j_1$ and $\Delta i = i_2 - i_1$ with $\Delta j / \Delta i \le 1$. The first algorithm to compute the $j(i)$ values is (in pseudo-C++):

```
float dJ = j2-j1;
float dI = i2-i1;
float m = dJ/dI;         // Slope
writePixel(i1, j1);
float y = j1;
int i, j;
for ( i=i1+1; i<=i2; i++ ) {
    y = y+m;
    j = round(y);        // Round to nearest integer
    writePixel( i, j );
}
```

In the preceding code, the function `writePixel(i,j)` is called to indicate that $j(i) = j$. The function `round(y)` is not a real C++ function but is intended to return y rounded to the nearest integer. The variables `i1` and `i2` are equal to i_1 and i_2.

The algorithm given above is very simple, but its implementation suffers from its using floating point and converting a floating point number to an integer number in each iteration

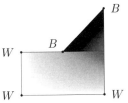

Figure II.27. Vertices are colored black or white as labeled. Scan line interpolation causes the nonconvex polygon to be shaded discontinuously.

of the loop. A more efficient algorithm, known as Bresenham's algorithm, can be designed to operate with only integers. The basic insight for Bresenham's algorithm is that the value of y in the algorithm is always a multiple of $1/(i_2 - i_1) = 1/\Delta i$. We rewrite the algorithm, using variables j and ry that have the property that $j + (ry/\Delta i)$ is equal to the value y of the previous pseudocode. Furthermore, j is equal to $[y] = \text{round}(y)$, and thus $-\Delta x/2 < ry \le \Delta x/2$, where $\Delta x = \Delta i$. With these correspondences, it is straightforward to verify that the next algorithm is equivalent to the previous algorithm.

```
int deltaX = i2-i1;
int thresh = deltaX/2;            // Integer division rounds down
int ry = 0;
int deltaY = j2 - j1;
writePixel( i1, j1 );
int i;
int j = j1;
for ( i=i1+1; i<=i2; i++ ) {
    ry = ry + deltaY;
    if ( ry > thresh ) {
        j = j + 1;
        ry = ry - deltaX;
    }
    writePixel( i, j );
}
```

The preceding algorithm, the Bresenham algorithm, uses only integer operations and straightforward operations such as addition, subtraction, and comparison. In addition, the algorithm is simple enough that it can readily be implemented efficiently in special-purpose hardware.

We also need a version of the Bresenham algorithm that works for interpolating other values such as depth buffer values, color values, and so on. When interpolating depth buffer values, for instance, it may well be the case that $\Delta z = z_2 - z_1$ is greater than Δx; however, there is, without loss of generality, only one z value per i value. (Since we are assuming that the line's slope is at most 1, there is only one pixel per i value.) To adapt the Bresenham algorithm to the case in which $\Delta z > \Delta x$, we let $q = \lfloor \Delta z/\Delta x \rfloor$ and $r = \Delta z - q\Delta x$. Then, the values $z(i)$ increase by approximately $q + r/\Delta x$ each time i is incremented. The resulting algorithm is as follows:

```
int deltaX = i2-i1;
int thresh = deltaX/2;
int rz = 0;
int q = (z2-z1)/deltaX;           // Integer division rounds down
```

```
int r= (z2-z1)-q*deltaX;
writePixelZ( i1, z1 );
int i;
int z = z1;
for ( i=i1+1; i<=i2; i++ ) {
    z = z + q;
    rz = rz + r;
    if ( rz > thresh ) {
        z = z + 1;
        rz = rz - deltaX;
    }
    writePixelZ( i, z );
}
```

The function `writePixelZ(i,z)` indicates that z is the interpolated value at the pixel $\langle i, j(i) \rangle$. This algorithm applies to the case in which $\Delta z < 0$ too, provided that the computation of q as `(z2-z1)/deltaX` always rounds *down* to the nearest integer. (However, the usual C/C++ rounding does not work this way!)

II.4.2 The Perils of Floating Point Roundoff

The preceding algorithm for line drawing has the property of attempting to draw lines that are "infinitely thin." Because of this, several unavoidable pitfalls can arise. The first and most common problem is that of aliasing. The term *aliasing* refers to a large variety of problems or effects that can occur when analog data is converted into digital data or vice versa. When drawing a line, we are converting floating point numbers representing positions into integers that signify pixel positions. The floating point numbers usually have much more precision than the integer values, and the conversion to integer values can cause problems.

For drawing lines on a screen, a major part of the problem is that the pixels on the screen are arranged rectangularly, whereas a line can be diagonal at an arbitrary angle. Therefore, a line at a diagonal is drawn as a "step function" consisting of straight segments that are horizontal (or vertical) with a 1-pixel jump between the segments. This can give the line drawn on the screen a jagged or sawtooth look, that is to say, the line has "jaggies." In addition, if the line is animated, the positions of the jaggies on the line move with the line. This can cause undesirable effects when the jaggies become annoyingly visible or where a moving line figure becomes "shimmery" from the changes in the digitization of the lines.

Several antialiasing methods can reduce the undesirable jaggies on lines, but we do not discuss these here (see Sections IX.2.1 and IX.3). Instead, we discuss another problem that can arise in rendering lines if the programmer is not careful to avoid inconsistent roundoff errors. An example is shown in Figure II.28. In the figure, the program has attempted to draw two polygons, $ABCD$ and $BAEF$, that share the common edge $\overline{AB}$. However, owing to roundoff errors, the second polygon was drawn as $B'A'EF$, where A' and B' are placed 1 pixel above and to the left of A and B, respectively. Because of this, the whole line segment $\overline{A'B'}$ is placed 1 pixel up and 1 pixel to the left of the segment $\overline{AB}$. The result is that the edges of the polygons do not exactly coincide, and there are pixels between the two polygons that are left undrawn. Each time the line segments "jog" up 1 pixel, an undrawn pixel is left behind. These undrawn pixels can create unsightly pixel-sized holes in the surface being formed from the two polygons.

In actuality, the problems of matching up edges between two abutting polygons is even more sensitive to roundoff error than is indicated in the previous paragraph. When two polygons share

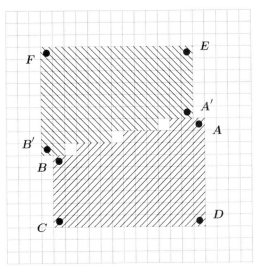

Figure II.28. The polygons $ABCD$ and $B'A'EF$ are supposed to share an edge, but arbitrarily small roundoff errors can cause a small displacement of the edge. This can lead to pixel-sized holes appearing between the two polygons. In the figure, the pixelized polygons are shown with different crosshatching: the three white pixels between the polygons are errors introduced by roundoff errors and will cause unwanted visual artifacts. This same effect can occur even in cases in which only one of the vertices is affected by roundoff errors.

an edge, the graphics display system should render them so that each pixel on the boundary edge belongs to exactly one of the two polygons. That is to say, the image needs to be drawn without leaving any gaps between the polgons *and* without having the polygons overlap in any pixel. There are several reasons it is important not to have the polygons overlap and share a pixel. First, it is desirable for the image to be drawn the same regardless of the order in which the two polygons are processed. Second, for some applications, such as blending or shadow volumes, polygons will leave visible seams where they overlap. Graphics hardware will automatically draw abutting polygons with no gaps and no overlaps; the edges are traced out by the Bresenham algorithm, but only the pixels whose centers are inside the polygon are drawn. (Some special handling is needed to handle the situation in which a pixel center lies exactly on a polygon edge.) This does mean, unfortunately, that almost any roundoff error that moves a vertex to a different pixel position can cause rendering errors.

This kind of misplacement from roundoff errors can happen no matter how small the roundoff error is. The only way to avoid this kind of roundoff error is to compute the positions A' and B' in *exactly* the same way that A and B were computed. By "exactly the same way," we do not mean by a mathematically equivalent way; rather, we mean by the same sequence of calculations.[14]

Figure II.29 shows another situation in which discretization errors can cause pixel-sized holes, even if there are no roundoff errors. In the figure, three triangles are being drawn: $\triangle\mathbf{uyx}$, $\triangle\mathbf{uzy}$, and $\triangle\mathbf{vxz}$. The point $\mathbf{y}$ lies on the boundary of the third triangle. Of course, if the color assigned to the vertex $\mathbf{y}$ is not the appropriate weighted average of the colors assigned to $\mathbf{x}$ and $\mathbf{z}$, then there will be a discontinuity in color across the line $\overline{\mathbf{xz}}$. But there can be problems even

---

[14] In rare cases, even using exactly the same sequence of calculations may not be good enough if the CPU or floating point coprocessor has flexibility in when it performs rounding of intermediate results, which is the default setting on many PCs.

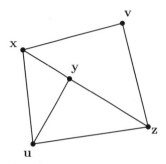

Figure II.29. Three triangles as placed by `glVertex*`. Even if no roundoff errors occur, the pixel-level discretization inherent in the Bresenham algorithm can leave pixel-sized gaps along the line $\overline{\mathbf{xz}}$.

if all vertices are assigned the same color. When the Bresenham algorithm draws the lines $\overline{\mathbf{xy}}$, $\overline{\mathbf{yz}}$, and $\overline{\mathbf{xz}}$, it starts by mapping the endpoints to the nearest pixel centers. This can sufficiently perturb the positions of the three points so that there are pixel-sized gaps left undrawn between the line $\overline{\mathbf{xz}}$ and the two lines $\overline{\mathbf{xy}}$ and $\overline{\mathbf{yz}}$.

This kind of discretization error can easily arise when approximating a curved surface with flat polygons (see the discussion on "cracking" in Section VII.10.2). It can also occur when two flat polygons that abut each other are subdivided into subpolygons, for example, in radiosity algorithms. If you look closely, you may be able to see examples of this problem in Figures XI.1–XI.3 on pages 273–274. (This depends on how precisely the figures were rendered in the printing process!)

To avoid this problem, you should subdivide the triangle $\triangle\mathbf{vxz}$ and draw the two triangles $\triangle\mathbf{vxy}$ and $\triangle\mathbf{vyz}$ instead.

III

Lighting, Illumination, and Shading

Lighting and shading are important tools for making graphics images appear more realistic and more understandable. Lighting and shading can provide crucial visual cues about the curvature and orientation of surfaces and are important in making three-dimensionality apparent in a graphics image. Indeed, good lighting and shading are probably more important than correct perspective in making a scene understandable.

Lighting and illumination models in computer graphics are based on a modular approach wherein the artist or programmer specifies the positions and properties of light sources, and, independently, specifies the surface properties of materials. The properties of the lights and the materials interact to create the illumination, color, and shading seen from a given viewpoint.

For an example of the importance of lighting and shading for rendering three-dimensional images, refer to Figure III.1. Figure III.1(b) shows a teapot rendered with a solid color with no shading. This flat, featureless teapot is just a silhouette with no three-dimensionality. Figure III.1(c) shows the same teapot but now rendered with the Phong lighting model. This teapot now looks three-dimensional, but the individual polygons are clearly visible. Figure III.1(d) further improves the teapot by using Gouraud interpolation to create a smooth, rounded appearance. Finally, Figures III.1(e) and (f) show the teapot with specular lighting added; the brightly reflecting spot shown in (e) and (f) is called a *specular highlight*.

"Shading" refers to the practice of letting colors and brightness vary smoothly across a surface. The two most popular kinds of shading are Gouraud interpolation (Gouraud, 1971) and Phong interpolation (Phong, 1975). Either of these shading methods can be used to give a smooth appearance to surfaces; even surfaces modeled as flat facets can appear smooth, as shown in Figure III.1(d) and (f).

This chapter discusses two *local* models of illumination and shading. The first model is the popular Phong lighting model. This model gives good shading and illumination; in addition, it lends itself to efficient implementation in either software or hardware. The Phong lighting model is almost universally used in real-time graphics systems – particularly for PCs and workstations. The Phong lighting model was introduced by Phong in the same paper (Phong, 1975) that also introduced Phong shading.

The second local lighting model is the Cook–Torrance lighting model. This is computationally more difficult to implement but gives better flexibility and the ability to model a wider variety of surfaces.

These lighting and shading models are at least partly based on the physics of how light reflects off surfaces. However, the actual physics of reflection is quite complicated, and it is

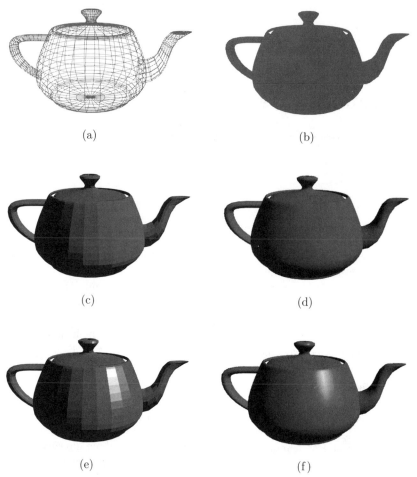

Figure III.1. Six teapots with various shading and lighting options. (a) Wireframe teapot. (b) Teapot drawn with solid color but no lighting or shading (c) Teapot with flat shading with only ambient and diffuse lighting. (d) Teapot drawn with Gouraud interpolation with only ambient and diffuse reflection. (e) Teapot drawn with flat shading with ambient, diffuse, and specular lighting. (f) Teapot with Gouraud shading with ambient, diffuse, and specular lighting. See Color Plate 4.

more accurate to say that the Phong and Cook–Torrance models are physically *inspired* rather than physically *correct*.

The Phong and Cook–Torrance models are both "local" models of lighting: they consider only the effects of a light source shining directly onto a surface and then being reflected directly to the viewpoint. Local lighting models do not consider secondary reflections, where light may reflect from several surfaces before reaching the viewpoint. Nor do the local lighting models, at least in their simplest forms, properly handle shadows cast by lights. We will discuss nonlocal, or "global," lighting models later: Chapter IX discusses ray tracing, and Chapter XI discusses radiosity.

III.1 The Phong Lighting Model

The Phong lighting model is the simplest, and by far the most popular, lighting and shading model for three-dimensional computer graphics. Its popularity is due, firstly, to its being flexible enough to achieve a wide range of visual effects, and, secondly, to the ease with which it can

Light source

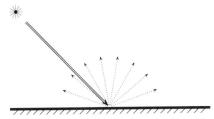

Figure III.2. Diffusely reflected light is reflected equally brightly in all directions. The double line is a beam of incoming light. The dotted arrows indicate outgoing light.

be efficiently implemented in software and especially hardware. It is the lighting model of choice for essentially all graphics hardware for personal computers, game consoles, and other realtime applications.

The Phong lighting model is, at its heart, a model of how light reflects off of surfaces. In the Phong lighting model, all light sources are modeled as point light sources. Also, light is modeled as consisting of the three discrete color components (red, green, and blue). That is to say, it is assumed that all light consists of a pure red component, a pure green component, and a pure blue component. By the *superposition principle*, we can calculate light reflection intensities independently for each light source and for each of the three color components.

The Phong model allows for two kinds of reflection:

Diffuse Reflection. Diffusely reflected light is light which is reflected evenly in all directions away from the surface. This is the predominant mode of reflection for nonshiny surfaces. Figure III.2 shows the graphical idea of diffuse reflection.

Specular Reflection. Specularly reflected light is light which is reflected in a mirror-like fashion, as from a shiny surface. As shown in Figure III.3, specularly reflected light leaves a surface with its angle of reflection approximately equal to its angle of incidence. This is the main part of the reflected light from a polished or glossy surface. Specular reflections are the cause of "specular highlights," that is, bright spots on curved surfaces where intense specular reflection occurs.

In addition to dividing reflections into two categories, the Phong lighting model treats light or illumination as being of three distinct kinds:

Specular Light. Specular light is light from a point light source that will be reflected specularly.

Diffuse Light. Diffuse light is light from a point light source that will be reflected diffusely.

Light source

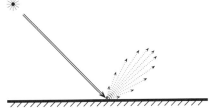

Figure III.3. Specularly reflected light is reflected primarily in the direction with the angle of incidence equal to the angle of reflection. The double line is a beam of incoming light. The dotted arrows indicate outgoing light; the longer the arrow, the more intense the reflection in that direction.

Light source

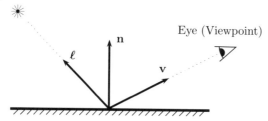

Eye (Viewpoint)

Figure III.4. The fundamental vectors of the Phong lighting model. The surface normal is the unit vector **n**. The point light source is in the direction of the unit vector ℓ. The viewpoint (eye) is in the direction of the unit vector **v**. The vectors ℓ, **n**, and **v** are not necessarily coplanar.

Ambient Light. Ambient light is light that arrives equally from all directions rather than from a point light source. Ambient light is intended to model light that has spread around the environment through multiple reflections.

As mentioned earlier, light is modeled as coming in a small number of distinct wavelengths, that is, in a small number of colors. In keeping with the fact that monitors have red, green, and blue pixels, light is usually modeled as consisting of a blend of red, green, and blue. Each of the color components is treated independently with its own specular, diffuse, and ambient properties.

Finally, the Phong lighting model gives material properties to each surface; the material properties control how lights illuminate the surface. Except for the specular exponent, these properties can be set independently for each of the three colors.

Specular Reflection Properties. A *specular reflectivity coefficient*, ρ_s, controls the amount of specular reflection. A *specular exponent*, f, controls the shininess of the surface by controlling the narrowness of the spread of specularly reflected light.

Diffuse Reflection Properties. A *diffuse reflectivity coefficient*, ρ_d, controls the relative intensity of diffusely reflected light.

Ambient Reflection Properties. An *ambient reflectivity coefficient*, ρ_a, controls the amount of ambient light reflected from the surface.

Emissive Properties. The *emissivity* of a surface controls how much light the surface emits in the absence of any incident light. Light emitted from a surface does not act as a light source that illuminates other surfaces; instead, it only affects the color seen by the observer.

The basic setup for reflection in the Phong reflection model is shown in Figure III.4. As shown in the figure, a particular point on a surface is being illuminated by a point light source and viewed from some viewpoint. The surface's orientation is specified by a unit vector **n** pointing perpendicularly up from the surface. The light's direction is specified by a unit vector ℓ that points from the point on the surface towards the light. The viewpoint direction is similarly specified by a unit vector **v** pointing from the surface towards the viewpoint. These three vectors, plus the properties of the light source and of the surface material, are used by the Phong model to determine the amount of light reaching the eye.

We assume that light from the point light source is shining with intensity I^{in}. The Phong lighting model provides methods to calculate the intensity of the light reflected from the surface that arrives at the eye. It is not particularly important to worry about how light intensity is measured except that it is useful to think of it as measuring the energy flux per unit area, where the area is measured perpendicularly to the direction of the light.

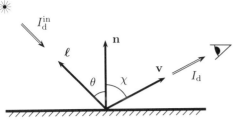

Figure III.5. The setup for diffuse reflection in the Phong model. The angle of incidence is θ, and I_d^{in} and I_d are the incoming and outgoing light intensities in the indicated directions.

The next two sections discuss how the Phong model calculates the reflection due to diffuse reflection and to specular reflection. For the time being, we will restrict attention to light at a single wavelength (i.e., of a single, pure color) and coming from a single light source. Section III.1.4 explains how the effects of multiple lights and of different colors are additively combined.

III.1.1 Diffuse Reflection

Diffuse reflection means that light is being reflected equally in all directions, as illustrated in Figure III.2. The fundamental Phong vectors are shown again in Figure III.5 but now with the angle between ℓ and $\mathbf{n}$ shown equal to θ: this is the angle of incidence of the light arriving from the point source. The amount of light that is diffusely reflected is modeled as

$$I_d = \rho_d I_d^{in} \cos\theta = \rho_d I_d^{in}(\ell \cdot \mathbf{n}), \qquad \text{III.1}$$

where the second equality holds because the vectors are unit vectors. Here, I_d^{in} is the intensity of the incoming diffuse light, and I_d is the intensity of the diffusely reflected light in the direction of the viewpoint. The value ρ_d is a constant, which is called the *diffuse reflectivity coefficient* of the surface. This value represents a physical property of the surface material.

A surface that diffusely reflects light according to Equation III.1 is called *Lambertian*, and most nonshiny surfaces are fairly close to Lambertian. The defining characteristic of a Lambertian surface is that, if a large flat region of the surface is uniformly lit, the surface should have the same apparent (or perceived) brightness and color from all viewing directions.

The presence of the $\cos\theta$ term in Equation III.1 requires some explanation. Recall that the incoming light intensity I_d^{in} is intended to measure energy flux per unit area with unit area measured *perpendicularly* to the direction of the light. Since the light is incident onto the surface at an angle of θ away from the normal vector $\mathbf{n}$, a "perpendicularly measured unit area's" worth of energy flux is spread over a larger area of the surface, namely, an area that is larger by a factor of $1/(\cos\theta)$. See Figure III.6 for an illustration of how the area increases by

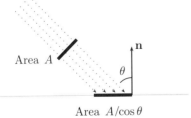

Figure III.6. The perpendicular cross-sectional area of a beam of light is A. The area of the surface tilted at an angle θ is larger by a factor of $1/\cos\theta$.

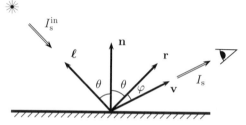

Figure III.7. The setup for specular reflection in the Phong model. The angle of incidence is θ. The vector **r** points in the direction of perfect mirror-like reflection, and I_s^{in} and I_s are the incoming and outgoing specular light intensities respectively, in the indicated directions.

a factor of $1/\cos\theta$. Because of this, the energy flux arriving per unit area of the surface is only $(\cos\theta)I_d^{in}$.

At this point, it would be reasonable to ask why there is not another cosine factor involving the angle of reflection. Of course, this is not what we generally perceive: that is, when one looks at a surface from a sharp angle we do not see the brightness of the surface drop off dramatically with the cosine of the angle of reflection. Otherwise, surfaces viewed from a sharply sidewise angle would appear almost black. Conversely, diffusely reflecting surfaces do not appear much brighter when viewed from straight on.[1]

However, more careful consideration of why there is no factor involving the angle of reflection reveals that Figure III.2 is a little misleading. It is not the case that the probability of a single photon's being reflected in a given direction is independent of the reflection direction. Instead, letting χ be the angle between the surface normal **n** and the outgoing light direction **v**, we find the probability that a photon reflects out in the direction **v** is proportional to $\cos\chi$. The viewer looking at the surface from this view angle of χ from the normal vector sees light coming from a surface area of $(1/\cos\chi)$ times the apparent field of view area. (This is similar to the justification of the $\cos\theta$ factor.) The two factors of $\cos\chi$ and $1/\cos\chi$ cancel out, and we are left with the Phong diffuse reflection formula III.1.

III.1.2 Specular Reflection

Specular reflection occurs when light reflects, primarily mirror-like, in the direction where the angle of incidence equals the angle of reflection. Specular reflection is used to model shiny surfaces. A perfect mirror would reflect all of its light in exactly that direction, but most shiny surfaces do not reflect nearly as well as a mirror, and so the specularly reflected light spreads out a little, as is shown in Figure III.3. (In any event, the Phong lighting model is not capable of modeling mirror-like reflections other than specular reflections from point light sources.)

Given the unit vector ℓ in the direction of the light source and the unit surface normal **n**, the direction of a perfect mirror-like reflection is given by the vector **r** shown in Figure III.7. The vector **r** is a unit vector coplanar with ℓ and **n**. The angle of perfect reflection is the angle between **r** and **n**, and this is equal to the angle of incidence θ, which is the angle between ℓ and **n**.

It is best to compute **r** using the following formula:

$$\mathbf{r} = 2(\ell \cdot \mathbf{n})\mathbf{n} - \ell.$$

To derive this formula, note that $(\ell \cdot \mathbf{n})\mathbf{n}$ is the projection of ℓ onto **n** and that $\ell - (\ell \cdot \mathbf{n})\mathbf{n}$ is equal to $(\ell \cdot \mathbf{n})\mathbf{n} - \mathbf{r}$.

---

[1] We are describing Lambertian surfaces. However, not all surfaces are Lambertian (e.g., the moon as illuminated by the sun and viewed from the Earth).

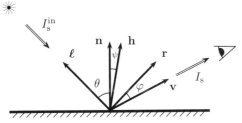

Figure III.8. The setup for calculating the specular reflection using the halfway vector **h**, the unit vector halfway between ℓ and **v**.

In Figure III.7, the angle between the view vector and the perfect reflection direction vector is φ. The guiding principle for determining specular reflection is that, the closer the angle φ is to zero, the more intense is the specular reflection in the direction of the viewpoint. The Phong lighting model uses the factor

$$(\cos\varphi)^f \qquad \qquad \text{III.2}$$

to model the dropoff in light intensity in a reflection direction that differs by an angle of φ from the direction **r** of perfect reflection. There is no particular physical justification for the use of the factor $(\cos\varphi)^f$; rather, it is used because the cosine can easily be computed by a dot product and the exponent f can be adjusted experimentally on an ad hoc basis to achieve the desired spread of specular light. The exponent f is ≥ 0, and values in the range 50 to 80 are typical for shiny surfaces; the larger the exponent, the narrower the beam of specularly reflected light. Higher exponent values make the specular highlights smaller and the surface appear shinier; however, exponents that are too high can lead to specular highlights being missed.

With the factor III.2, the Phong formula for the intensity I_s of specularly reflected light is

$$I_s = \rho_s I_s^{\text{in}}(\cos\varphi)^f = \rho_s I_s^{\text{in}}(\mathbf{v}\cdot\mathbf{r})^f, \qquad \qquad \text{III.3}$$

where ρ_s is a constant called the *specular reflectivity coefficient* and I_s^{in} is the intensity of the specular light from the light source. The value of ρ_s depends on the surface and on the wavelength of the light. For the time being, we are working under the assumption that all the light is a single pure color.

Often a computational shortcut, based on the "halfway" vector, is used to simplify the calculation of I_s. The *halfway vector* **h** is defined to be the unit vector halfway between light source direction and the view direction, namely,

$$\mathbf{h} = \frac{\ell+\mathbf{v}}{||\ell+\mathbf{v}||}.$$

Let ψ be the angle between **h** and the surface normal **n**. Referring to Figure III.8, one can easily see that if ℓ, **n**, and **v** are (approximately) coplanar, then ψ is (approximately) equal to $\varphi/2$. Therefore, it is generally acceptable to use ψ instead of φ in the calculation of I_s since the exponent f can be changed slightly to compensate for the factor of two change in the value of the angle. With the halfway vector, the Phong equation for the intensity of specular reflection becomes

$$I_s = \rho_s I_s^{\text{in}}(\cos\psi)^f = \rho_s I_s^{\text{in}}(\mathbf{h}\cdot\mathbf{n})^f. \qquad \qquad \text{III.4}$$

Although III.4 is not exactly equal to III.3, it gives qualitatively similar results.

For polygonally modeled objects, the calculation of the diffuse and specular components of Phong lighting is usually done at least once for each vertex in the geometric model. For points in the interior of polygons, Gouraud shading is used to determine the lighting and colors by averaging values from the vertices (see Section III.1.5 below). To apply the formula III.1 and the formulas III.3 or III.4 at each vertex, it is necessary to calculate the unit vectors ℓ and $\mathbf{v}$ at each vertex. To calculate these two vectors, one subtracts the surface position from the positions of the light and the viewpoint and then normalizes the resulting differences. This is computationally expensive, since, for each of ℓ and $\mathbf{v}$, this computation requires calculation of a square root and a division. One way to avoid this calculation is to make the simplifying approximation that the two vectors ℓ and $\mathbf{v}$ are constants and are the same for all vertices. In essence, this has the effect of placing the lights and the viewpoint at points at infinity so that the view direction $\mathbf{v}$ and the light direction ℓ are independent of the position of the surface being illuminated. When the light direction vector ℓ is held constant, we call the light a *directional light*. Nondirectional lights are called *positional* lights since the light's position determines the direction of illumination of any given point. If the view direction is computed using the position of the viewpoint, then we say there is a *local viewer*. Otherwise, the view direction $\mathbf{v}$ is held fixed, and we call it a *nonlocal viewer*. Note that a nonlocal viewer can be used in conjunction with a perspective. viewing transformation.

If we have a directional light and a nonlocal viewer, so that both ℓ and $\mathbf{v}$ are held constant, then the vector $\mathbf{h}$ also remains constant. This makes the use of the halfway vector and Formula III.4 even more advantageous: the only vector that needs to be calculated on a per-vertex basis is the surface normal $\mathbf{n}$.

III.1.3 Ambient Reflection and Emissivity

Ambient light is light that comes from all directions rather than from the direction of a light source. It is modeled as being reflected equally in all directions, and thus the ambient component of the surface lighting and shading is independent of the direction of view. We let I_a^{in} represent the total intensity of the incoming ambient light. In the Phong model, the surface has an associated *ambient reflectivity coefficient* ρ_a that specifies the fraction of the ambient light reflected. The formula for the intensity of the outgoing ambient light is

$$I_a = \rho_a I_a^{in}. \qquad\qquad\qquad\qquad \text{III.5}$$

Finally, a surface can also be given an *emissive intensity constant* I_e. This is equal to the intensity of the light emitted by the surface in addition to the reflected light.

III.1.4 Putting It Together: Multiple Lights and Colors

So far, the discussion of the Phong model has been restricted to a single wavelength (or pure color) of light with illumination from a single light source. According to the superposition principle, the various types of reflection and emission can be combined by simple addition. Furthermore, the effect of multiple lights is likewise determined by adding the illumination from the lights considered individually. Finally, different wavelengths may be considered independently with no interaction between the intensity of one wavelength and that of another.

First, for a single wavelength and a single light source, the total outgoing light intensity I is equal to

$$I = I_a + I_d + I_s + I_e$$
$$= \rho_a I_a^{in} + \rho_d I_d^{in}(\ell \cdot \mathbf{n}) + \rho_s I_s^{in}(\mathbf{r} \cdot \mathbf{v})^f + I_e. \qquad\qquad \text{III.6}$$

(The halfway vector formula for specular reflection may be used instead with $\mathbf{h} \cdot \mathbf{n}$ replacing $\mathbf{r} \cdot \mathbf{v}$ in the equation.)

Second, to adapt this formula to multiple wavelengths, we write I^λ, $I_a^{\lambda,\text{in}}$, $I_d^{\lambda,\text{in}}$, $I_s^{\lambda,\text{in}}$, I_e^λ for the intensities of the light at wavelength λ. In addition, the material properties are also dependent on the wavelength λ and can now be written as ρ_a^λ, and so forth. It is usual, however, to make the specular exponent independent of the wavelength. Equation III.6 can be specialized to a single wavelength, yielding

$$I^\lambda = \rho_a^\lambda I_a^{\lambda,\text{in}} + \rho_d^\lambda I_d^{\lambda,\text{in}}(\boldsymbol{\ell} \cdot \mathbf{n}) + \rho_s^\lambda I_s^{\lambda,\text{in}}(\mathbf{r} \cdot \mathbf{v})^f + I_e^\lambda. \qquad \text{III.7}$$

It is traditional to use the three wavelengths of red, green, and blue light since these are the three colors displayed by computer monitors; however, more wavelengths can be used for greater realism.

To write a single equation incorporating all three wavelengths at once, we use boldface variables to denote a 3-tuple: we let ρ_a denote the triple $\langle \rho_a^{\text{red}}, \rho_a^{\text{green}}, \rho_a^{\text{blue}} \rangle$; let $\mathbf{I}$ equal $\langle I^{\text{red}}, I^{\text{green}}, I^{\text{blue}} \rangle$, and so forth. We also momentarily use $*$ for component-wise multiplication on 3-tuples. Then Equation III.7 can be written as

$$\mathbf{I} = \rho_a * \mathbf{I}_a^{\text{in}} + \rho_d * \mathbf{I}_d^{\text{in}}(\boldsymbol{\ell} \cdot \mathbf{n}) + \rho_s * \mathbf{I}_s^{\text{in}}(\mathbf{r} \cdot \mathbf{v})^f + \mathbf{I}_e. \qquad \text{III.8}$$

Third, we consider the effect of multiple point light sources. We assume there are k light sources. When illuminating a given point on a surface, light number i has light direction vector $\boldsymbol{\ell}_i$. The ith light also has an intensity value $\mathbf{I}^{\text{in},i}$ that represents the intensity of the light reaching that point on the surface. This intensity may be moderated by the distance of the surface from the light and by various other effects such as spotlight effects. In addition, if $\mathbf{n} \cdot \boldsymbol{\ell}_i \leq 0$, then the light is not shining from above the surface, and in this case we take $\mathbf{I}^{\text{in},i}$ to be zero. We then merely add the terms of Equation III.8 over all light sources to get the overall illumination ($\mathbf{r}_i$ is the unit vector in the direction of perfect reflection for light i):

$$\mathbf{I} = \rho_a * \mathbf{I}_a^{\text{in}} + \rho_d * \sum_{i=1}^{k} \mathbf{I}_d^{\text{in},i}(\boldsymbol{\ell}_i \cdot \mathbf{n}) + \rho_s * \sum_{i=1}^{k} \mathbf{I}_s^{\text{in},i}(\mathbf{r}_i \cdot \mathbf{v})^f + \mathbf{I}_e. \qquad \text{III.9}$$

The 3-tuple $\mathbf{I}_a^{\text{in}}$ represents the incoming ambient light. It is common to specify a global value, $\mathbf{I}_a^{\text{in,global}}$, for global ambient light and to have each light source contribute some additional ambient light, $\mathbf{I}_a^{\text{in},i}$, to the scene. Then,

$$\mathbf{I}_a^{\text{in}} = \mathbf{I}_a^{\text{in,global}} + \sum_{i=1}^{k} \mathbf{I}_a^{\text{in},i}. \qquad \text{III.10}$$

This completes the theoretical description of the Phong lighting model. The next section takes up the two most common methods of interpolating, or shading, colors and brightness from the vertices of a triangle into the interior points of the triangle. Section III.1.8 explains in outline form how OpenGL commands are used to specify the material and light properties needed for the Phong lighting calculations.

Exercise III.1 *Why is it customary to use the same specular exponent for all wavelengths? What would a specular highlight look like if different wavelengths had different specular exponents?*

III.1.5 Gouraud and Phong Shading

The term "shading" refers to the use of interpolation to create a smoothly varying pattern of color and brightness on the surfaces of objects. Without shading, each polygon in a geometric model would be rendered as a solid, constant color; the resulting image would be noticeably

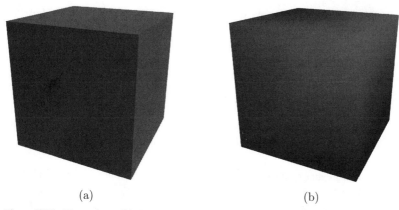

(a)   (b)

Figure III.9. Two cubes with (a) normals at vertices perpendicular to each face, and (b) normals outward from the center of the cube. Note that (a) is rendered with Gouraud shading, not flat shading. See Color Plate 5.

polygonal. One way to avoid this problem is to use extremely small polygons, say with each polygon so small that it spans only one pixel, but often this is prohibitively expensive in terms of computational time. Instead, good shading effects can be obtained even for moderately large polygons by computing the lighting and colors at only the vertices of the polygons and using interpolation, or averaging, to set the lighting and colors of pixels in the interior of the polygons.

There are several ways that interpolation is used to create shading effects. As usual, suppose a surface is modeled as a set of planar, polygonal patches and we render one patch at a time. Consider the problem of determining the color at a single vertex of one of the patches. Once the light source, viewpoint, and material properties are fixed, it remains only to specify the normal vector $\mathbf{n}$ at the vertex. If the surface is intended to be a smooth surface, then the normal vector at the vertex should, of course, be set to be the normal to the underlying surface. On the other hand, some surfaces are faceted and consist of flat polygonal patches – for example, the cube shown in part (a) of Figure III.9. For these surfaces, the normal vector for the vertex should be the same as the normal vector for the polygon being rendered. Since vertices typically belong to more than one polygon, this means that a vertex might be rendered with different normal vectors for different polygons.

Parts (d) and (f) of Figure III.1 show examples of Gouraud shading. Figure III.9 shows a more extreme example of how Gouraud shading can hide, or partially hide, the edges of polygons. Both parts of Figure III.9 show a reddish solid cube lit by only ambient and diffuse light, and both figures use Gouraud shading. The first cube was rendered by drawing each polygon independently with the normals at all four vertices of each polygon normal to the plane of the polygon. The second cube was drawn with the normal to each vertex pointing outward from the center point of the cube; that is, the normals at a vertex are an average of the normals of the three adjacent faces and thus are equal to $\langle \pm 1/\sqrt{3},\ \pm 1/\sqrt{3},\ \pm 1/\sqrt{3} \rangle$. The faces of the cube are clearly visible as flat surfaces in the first figure but are somewhat disguised in the second picture.

The question of how to determine the surface normal at a vertex of a polygonal model will be discussed further in Section III.1.6. For the moment, we instead consider the methods for interpolating the results of the Phong lighting model to shade interior points of a polygon. We assume the polygon is a triangle. This is a reasonable assumption, as rendering systems generally triangulate polygons. This assumption has the convenient effect that triangles are always planar, and so we do not need to worry about the pathological situation of nonplanar polygons.

Two kinds of shading are used with the Phong model, and both usually use the scan line interpolation described in Section II.4. Scan line interpolation is also equivalent to linear interpolation, which is discussed in Section IV.1.

The first kind of shading is *Gouraud shading*. In Gouraud shading, a color value is determined for each vertex, the color value being a triple $\langle r, g, b \rangle$ with red, green, and blue light intensities. After the three vertices of a triangle are rendered at pixel positions in the viewport, the interior pixels of the triangle in the viewport are shaded by simple linear interpolation. Recall that this means that if two vertices $\mathbf{x}_0$, $\mathbf{x}_1$ have color values $\langle r_i, g_i, b_i \rangle$ for $i = 0, 1$, and if another pixel is positioned on the line segment between the points at a fraction α of the way from $\mathbf{x}_0$ to $\mathbf{x}_1$, then the interpolated color is

$$(1 - \alpha)\langle r_0, g_0, b_0 \rangle + \alpha \langle r_1, g_1, b_1 \rangle.$$

Gouraud interpolation works reasonably well; however, for large polygons, it can miss specular highlights or at least miss the brightest part of the specular highlight if this falls in the middle of a polygon. Another example of how Gouraud shading can fail is that a spotlight shining on a wall can be completely overlooked by Gouraud interpolation: if the wall is modeled as a large polygon, then the four vertices of the polygon may not be illuminated by the spotlight at all. More subtly, Gouraud interpolation suffers from the fact that the brightness of a specular highlight depends strongly on how the highlight is centered on a vertex; this is particularly apparent when objects or lights are being animated. Nonetheless, Gouraud shading works well in many cases and can be implemented efficiently in hardware. For this reason, it is very popular and widely used.

The second kind of shading is *Phong shading*. In this technique, the surface normals are interpolated throughout the interior of the triangle, and the full Phong lighting is recalculated at each pixel in the triangle on the viewport. The interpolation is not as simple as the usual linear interpolation described in Section II.4 because the interpolated surface normals must be unit vectors to be used in the Phong lighting calculations.

The most common way to calculate interpolated surface normals is as follows: Suppose $\mathbf{x}_0$, $\mathbf{x}_1$ are pixels where the surface normals are $\mathbf{n}_0$ and $\mathbf{n}_1$, respectively. At a pixel a fraction α of the distance along the line from $\mathbf{x}_0$ to $\mathbf{x}_1$, the interpolated normal is

$$\mathbf{n}_\alpha = \frac{(1 - \alpha)\mathbf{n}_0 + \alpha \mathbf{n}_1}{||(1 - \alpha)\mathbf{n}_0 + \alpha \mathbf{n}_1||}. \tag{III.11}$$

This is computationally more work than Gouraud shading – especially because of the renormalization. However, the biggest disadvantage of Phong shading is that all the information about the colors and directions of lights needs to be kept until the final rendering stage so that lighting can be calculated at every pixel in the final image. On the other hand, the big advantage of Phong shading is that small specular highlights and spotlights are not missed when they occur in the interior of a triangle or polygon. In addition, the brightness of a specular highlight is not nearly so sensitive to whether the specular highlight is centered over a vertex or in the interior of a polygon.

A potential problem with both Gouraud and Phong shading is that they perform the interpolation in the coordinates of the screen or viewport. However, in perspective views, a large polygon that is angled from the viewpoint will have its more distant parts appear more compressed in the graphics image than its closer parts. Thus, the interpolation in screen coordinates does not properly reflect the size of the polygon. This can sometimes contribute to suboptimal shading with unwanted visual effects. The method of hyperbolic interpolation, which is discussed in Section IV.5, can be used to avoid these problems.

Yet another problem with Phong shading is that normals should not be interpolated linearly across the polygonal approximation to a surface because they tend to change less rapidly in areas where the normals are pointing towards the viewer and more rapidly in areas where the normals are pointing more sideways. One way to partly incorporate this observation in the Phong shading calculation is to use the following method to calculate normals. Let the normals be $\mathbf{n}_i = \langle n_{x,i}, n_{y,i}, n_{z,i} \rangle$, $i = 0, 1$. Then replace the calculation of Equation III.11 by

$$n_{x,\alpha} = (1 - \alpha)n_{x,0} + \alpha n_{x,1}$$

$$n_{y,\alpha} = (1 - \alpha)n_{y,0} + \alpha n_{y,1}$$

$$n_{z,\alpha} = \sqrt{1 - n_{x,\alpha}^2 - n_{y,\alpha}^2}\,.$$

The equations above calculate the x- and y-components of $\mathbf{n}_\alpha$ by linear interpolation and choose the z-component so as to make $\mathbf{n}_\alpha$ a unit vector.

Exercise III.2★ *Prove that these alternate equations for normal vector interpolation provide the correct unit normal vectors in the case of a spherical surface viewed orthographically.*

III.1.6 Computing Surface Normals

As we have seen, it is important to set the values of surface normals correctly to obtain good lighting and shading effects. In many cases, one can determine surface normals by understanding the surface clearly and using symmetry properties. For example, the surface normals for objects like spheres, cylinders, tori, and so forth, are easy to determine. However, for more complicated surfaces, it is necessary to use more general methods. We next consider three different methods for calculating surface normals on general surfaces.

First, suppose a surface has been modeled as a mesh of flat polygons with vertices that lie on the surface. Consider a particular vertex $\mathbf{v}$, and let $P_1, \ldots, P_k$ be the polygons that have that vertex as a corner. The unit surface normal $\mathbf{n}_i$ for each individual polygon P_i is easy to compute by taking two adjacent (and noncollinear) edges from the polygon, forming their cross product, and normalizing. Then we can estimate the unit normal $\mathbf{n}$ at the vertex as the average of the unit normals of the adjacent polygons, namely as

$$\mathbf{n} = \frac{\sum_i \mathbf{n}_i}{||\sum_i \mathbf{n}_i||}.$$

Note that it was necessary to renormalize since the Phong lighting model works with unit vectors.

Computing the normal vector by averaging the normals of adjacent polygons has the advantage that it can be done directly from the polygonal model of a surface without using any direct knowledge of the surface. It also works even when there is no mathematical surface underlying the polygonal data, say in situations in which the polygonal data has been generated by hand or by measurement of some object. Of course, this method does not generally give the exactly correct surface normal, but if the polygons are small enough compared with the rate of change of the surface curvature, this approach will give normals that are close to the correct surface normals.

The second method of computing surface normals can be used with surfaces that are defined parametrically. We say that a surface is defined *parametrically* if there is a function $\mathbf{f}(x, y)$ of two variables with a domain $A \subseteq \mathbb{R}^2$ such that the surface is the set of points $\{\mathbf{f}(x, y) : \langle x, y \rangle \in A\}$.

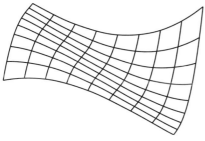

Figure III.10. A polygonal mesh defined by a parametric function. The horizontal and vertical curves are lines of constant y values and constant x values, respectively.

We write **f** in boldface because it is a function that takes values in $\mathbb{R}^3$, that is, it is a vector-valued function,

$$\mathbf{f}(x, y) = \langle f_1(x, y), f_2(x, y), f_3(x, y) \rangle.$$

The partial derivatives

$$\mathbf{f}_x := \frac{\partial \mathbf{f}}{\partial x} \qquad \text{and} \qquad \mathbf{f}_y := \frac{\partial \mathbf{f}}{\partial y}$$

are defined component-wise as usual and are likewise vectors in $\mathbb{R}^3$. The partial derivatives are the rates of change of **f** with respect to changes in one of the variables while the other is held fixed. In Figures III.10 and III.11, this is illustrated with the partial derivative tangent to the surface cross sections where the other variable is constant. Except in degenerate cases, the cross product of the two partial derivatives gives a vector perpendicular to the surface.

Theorem III.1 *Suppose* **f** *has partial derivatives at* $\langle x, y \rangle$. *If the cross-product vector* $\mathbf{f}_x(x, y) \times \mathbf{f}_y(x, y)$ *is nonzero, then it is perpendicular to the surface at* $\mathbf{f}(x, y)$.

To prove the theorem, note that $\mathbf{f}_x$ and $\mathbf{f}_y$ are noncollinear and are both tangent to the surface parametrically defined by **f**.

Usually, the vector $\mathbf{f}_x \times \mathbf{f}_y$ must be normalized, and care must be taken to choose the correct outward direction. Therefore, the unit vector normal to a parametrically defined surface is given

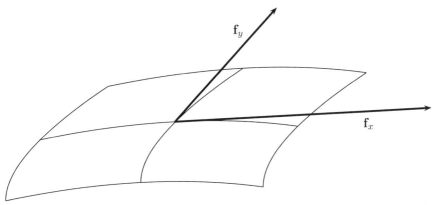

Figure III.11. A close-up view of a polygonal mesh. The partial derivatives are tangent to the horizontal and vertical cross-section curves.

by the formula

$$\pm \frac{\mathbf{f}_x(x, y) \times \mathbf{f}_y(x, y)}{||\mathbf{f}_x(x, y) \times \mathbf{f}_y(x, y)||} \qquad \text{III.12}$$

whenever the vector $\mathbf{f}_x(x, y) \times \mathbf{f}_y(x, y)$ is nonzero. The sign is chosen to make the vector point outward.

Exercise III.3 *Let T be a torus (doughnut shape) with major radius R and minor radius r. This torus is a tube going around the y-axis. The center of the tube stays distance R from the y-axis and lies in the xz-plane. The radius of the tube is r.*

(a) *Show that the torus T is parametrically defined by* $\mathbf{f}(\theta, \varphi)$, *for* $0 \le \theta \le 360°$ *and* $0 \le \varphi \le 360°$, *where*

$$\mathbf{f}(\theta, \varphi) = \langle (R + r \cos \varphi) \sin \theta, r \sin \varphi, (R + r \cos \varphi) \cos \theta \rangle. \qquad \text{III.13}$$

[Hint: θ controls the angle measured around the y-axis, starting with $\theta = 0$ at the positive z-axis. The angle φ specifies the amount of turn around the centerline of the torus.] Draw a picture of the torus and of a point on it for a representative value of θ and φ.

(b) *Use your picture and the symmetry of the torus to show that the unit normal vector to the torus at the point $\mathbf{f}(\theta, \varphi)$ is equal to*

$$\langle \sin \theta \cos \varphi, \sin \varphi, \cos \theta \cos \varphi \rangle. \qquad \text{III.14}$$

Exercise III.4 *Let T be the torus from the previous exercise. Use Theorem III.1 to compute a vector normal to the torus at the point $\mathbf{f}(\theta, \varphi)$. Compare your answer with equation III.14. Is it the same? If not, why not?*

The third method for computing surface normals applies to surfaces defined as level sets of functions. Such a surface can be defined as the set of points satisfying some equation and is sometimes called an *implicitly defined surface* (see Appendix A.4). Without loss of generality, there is a function $f(x, y, z)$, and the surface is the set of points $\{\langle x, y, z \rangle : f(x, y, z) = 0\}$. Recall that the gradient of f, ∇f, is defined by

$$\nabla f(x, y, z) = \left\langle \frac{\partial f}{\partial x}, \frac{\partial f}{\partial y}, \frac{\partial f}{\partial z} \right\rangle.$$

From multivariable calculus, it follows that the gradient of f is perpendicular to the level surface.

Theorem III.2 *Let S be the level set defined as above as the set of zeroes of f. Let $\langle x, y, z \rangle$ be a point on the surface S. If the vector $\nabla f(x, y, z)$ is nonzero, then it is perpendicular to the surface at $\langle x, y, z \rangle$.*

Exercise III.5 *Show that the torus T considered in the previous two exercises can be defined as the set of zeros of the function*

$$f(x, y, z) = (\sqrt{x^2 + z^2} - R)^2 + y^2 - r^2.$$

Use Theorem III.2 to derive a formula for a vector perpendicular to the surface at a point $\langle x, y, z \rangle$. Your answer should be independent of r. Does this make sense?

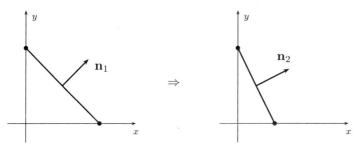

Figure III.12. An example of how a nonuniform scaling transformation affects a normal. The transformation maps $\langle x, y \rangle$ to $\langle \frac{1}{2}x, y \rangle$. The line with unit normal $\mathbf{n}_1 = \langle \frac{1}{\sqrt{2}}, \frac{1}{\sqrt{2}} \rangle$ is transformed to a line with unit normal $\mathbf{n}_2 = \langle \frac{2}{\sqrt{5}}, \frac{1}{\sqrt{5}} \rangle$.

III.1.7 Affine Transformations and Normal Vectors

When using affine transformations to transform the positions of geometrically modeled objects, it is important to also transform the normal vectors appropriately. After all, things could get very mixed up if the vertices and polygons are rotated but the normals are not!

For now, assume we have an affine transformation $A\mathbf{x} = B\mathbf{x} + \mathbf{u}_0$, where B is a linear transformation. Since translating a surface does not affect its normal vectors, we can ignore the translation $\mathbf{u}_0$ and just work with the linear mapping B.

If B is a rigid transformation (possibly not orientation-preserving), then it is clear that, after a surface is mapped by B, its normals are also mapped by B. That is to say, if a vertex $\mathbf{v}$ on the surface S has the normal $\mathbf{n}$, then on the transformed surface $B(S)$, the transformed vertex $B(\mathbf{v})$ has surface normal $B(\mathbf{n})$.

However, the situation is more complicated for nonrigid transformations. To understand this on an intuitive level, consider an example in the xy-plane. In Figure III.12(a), a line segment is shown with slope -1: the vector $\mathbf{n}_1 = \langle 1, 1 \rangle$ is perpendicular to this line. If B performs a scaling by a factor of $1/2$ in the x-axis dimension, then the line is transformed to a line with slope -2. But, the normal vector is mapped by B to $\langle \frac{1}{2}, 1 \rangle$, which is *not* perpendicular to the transformed line. Instead, the correct perpendicular direction is $\mathbf{n}_2 = \langle 2, 1 \rangle$; thus, it looks almost like the inverse of B needs to be applied to the normal vector. This is not quite correct though; as we will see next, it is the transpose of the inverse that needs to be applied to the normals.

We state the next theorem in terms of a vector normal to a plane, but the same results hold for a normal to a surface since we can just use the plane tangent to the surface at a given point. We may assume without much loss of applicability that the transformation B is invertible, for otherwise the image of B would be contained in a plane P and any normal to the plane P would be perpendicular to the surface.

Theorem III.3 *Let B be a linear transformation represented by the invertible matrix M. Let N equal $(M^T)^{-1} = (M^{-1})^T$. Let P be a plane and $\mathbf{n}$ be orthogonal to P. Then $N\mathbf{n}$ is orthogonal to the image $B(P)$ of the plane P under the map B.*

For the proof, it is helpful to recall that for any vectors $\mathbf{x}$ and $\mathbf{y}$, the dot product $\mathbf{x} \cdot \mathbf{y}$ is equal to $\mathbf{x}^T\mathbf{y}$ (see Appendix A).

Proof Suppose that $\mathbf{x}$ is a vector lying in the plane P, and so $\mathbf{n} \cdot \mathbf{x} = 0$. To prove the theorem, it will suffice to show that $(N\mathbf{n}) \cdot (M\mathbf{x}) = 0$. But this follows immediately from

$$(N\mathbf{n}) \cdot (M\mathbf{x}) = ((M^{-1})^T\mathbf{n}) \cdot (M\mathbf{x}) = ((M^{-1})^T\mathbf{n})^T(M\mathbf{x}) = (\mathbf{n}^T M^{-1})(M\mathbf{x})$$

$$= \mathbf{n}^T(M^{-1}M\mathbf{x}) = \mathbf{n}^T\mathbf{x} = \mathbf{n} \cdot \mathbf{x} = 0,$$

and the theorem is proved. $\square$

Recall that the adjoint of a matrix M is the transpose of the matrix formed from the cofactors of M (see Appendix A). In addition, the inverse of a matrix M is equal to the adjoint of M divided by the determinant of M. Therefore, it is immediate that Theorem III.3 also holds for the transpose of the adjoint of M in place of the transpose of the inverse of M.

To summarize, a normal vector transforms under an affine transformation $\mathbf{x} \mapsto M\mathbf{x} + \mathbf{u}_0$ according to the formula

$$\mathbf{n} \mapsto N\mathbf{n},$$

where N is the transpose of either the inverse or the adjoint of M. Note that $N\mathbf{n}$ may not be a unit vector.

Exercise III.6 *The linear transformation of $\mathbb{R}^2$ depicted in Figure III.12 is given by the matrix*

$$M = \begin{pmatrix} 1/2 & 0 \\ 0 & 1 \end{pmatrix}.$$

Compute the transposes of the adjoint of M and the inverse of M. Prove that, for any line L in $\mathbb{R}^2$, these matrices correctly map a vector normal to the line L to a vector normal to the image $M(L)$ of the line.

So far, we have only discussed how normal vectors are converted by *affine* transformations. However, the 4×4 homogeneous matrices allowed in OpenGL are more general than just affine transformations, and for these a different construction is needed. Given a 4×4 matrix M, let N be the transpose of either the inverse or the adjoint of M. Let $\mathbf{n}$ be orthogonal to a plane P. As discussed in Section II.2.5, the plane P in 3-space corresponds to a three-dimensional linear subspace P^H of $\mathbb{R}^4$ in homogeneous coordinates. Let $\mathbf{u}$ be a point on the plane P, and $\mathbf{x} = \langle x_1, x_2, x_3 \rangle$ and $\mathbf{y} = \langle y_1, y_2, y_3 \rangle$ be two noncollinear vectors parallel to P in 3-space. Form the vectors $\mathbf{x}^H = \langle x_1, x_2, x_3, 0 \rangle$ and $\mathbf{y}^H = \langle y_1, y_2, y_3, 0 \rangle$. These two vectors, plus $\mathbf{u}^H = \langle u_1, u_2, u_3, 1 \rangle$, span P^H.

Let $\mathbf{n} = \langle n_1, n_2, n_3 \rangle$ be orthogonal to P, and let $\mathbf{n}^H = \langle n_1, n_2, n_3, -\mathbf{u} \cdot \mathbf{n} \rangle$. Since $\mathbf{n}^H$ is orthogonal to $\mathbf{x}^H$, $\mathbf{y}^H$, and $\mathbf{u}^H$, it is perpendicular to the space P^H spanned by these three vectors. Therefore, by exactly the same proof as that of Theorem III.3, we have that $N\mathbf{n}^H$ is orthogonal to $M(P^H)$. Let $N\mathbf{n}^H = \langle n'_1, n'_2, n'_3, n'_4 \rangle$. Then clearly, $\langle n'_1, n'_2, n'_3 \rangle$ is a vector in 3-space orthogonal to the 3-space vectors parallel to $M(P)$. Therefore, $\langle n'_1, n'_2, n'_3 \rangle$ is perpendicular to the plane $M(P)$ in 3-space.

III.1.8 Light and Material Properties in OpenGL

OpenGL implements the full Phong lighting model with Gouraud interpolation. It supports all the material properties, including the ambient, diffuse, and specular reflectivity coefficients and emissivity. Light sources may be given independent ambient, diffuse, and specular intensities, and special effects for lights include spotlighting and distance attenuation.

This section is an outline of how lighting and surface material properties are specified and controlled in OpenGL. This is only an overview and you should refer to an OpenGL manual such as (Schreiner, 1999; Woo et al., 1999) for more information on the command syntax and operation. In particular, we do not include information on all the variations of the command syntax and only include the more common versions of the commands (usually the ones based on floating point inputs when appropriate).

Initializing the Lighting Model. By default, OpenGL does not compute Phong lighting effects. Instead, it just uses the color as given by a `glColor3f()` command to set the vertex color. To enable Phong lighting calculation, use the command

```
glEnable(GL_LIGHTING);
```

OpenGL includes eight point light sources; they must be explicitly enabled, or "turned on," by calling

```
glEnable(GL_LIGHTi); // 'i' should be 0,1,2,3,4,5,6, or 7
```

The light names are `GL_LIGHT0`, `GL_LIGHT1`, and so forth, and any OpenGL implementation should support at least eight lights. Lights can be disabled, or turned off, with the `glDisable(GL_LIGHTi)` command.

By default, OpenGL renders polygons with Gouraud shading. However, Gouraud shading can be turned off with the command

```
glShadeModel(GL_FLAT);
```

In this case, the usual convention is that the color of the *last* vertex of a polygon is used to color the entire polygon (but see page 12). The command

```
glShadeModel( GL_SMOOTH );
```

can be used to turn Gouraud shading back on. Usually, it is best to keep Gouraud shading turned on, but when rendering a faceted object it can be convenient to turn it off.

OpenGL gives you the option of rendering only one side or both sides of polygons. Recall that polygons are given a *front* face and a *back* face – usually according to the right-hand rule (see Section I.2.2 for more information). When applying lighting to the back face of a polygon, OpenGL reverses the normal vector direction at each vertex to get the surface normal vector for the back face. Frequently, however, the back faces are not visible or properly lit, and by default OpenGL does not shade the back faces according to the Phong lighting model. To tell OpenGL to use the Phong lighting model for the back faces too, use the command

```
glLightModeli(GL_LIGHT_MODEL_TWO_SIDE, GL_TRUE);
```

(This can be turned off by using `GL_FALSE` instead of `GL_TRUE`.) If the back faces are never visible, you may also want to cull them. For this, see `glCullFace` in Section I.2.2.

OpenGL can use the halfway vector computational shortcut mentioned at the end of Section III.1.2, which sets the light direction vectors ℓ and the view direction vector $\mathbf{v}$ to be constant vectors independent of vertex positions. To turn this off and allow the view vector $\mathbf{v}$ to be recalculated for each vertex position, use the command

```
glLightModeli(GL_LIGHT_MODEL_LOCAL_VIEWER, GL_TRUE);
```

To force OpenGL to use constant light direction vectors ℓ, make the lights directional rather than positional, using the commands discussed later in this section.

OpenGL's implementation of Phong lighting assumes that the view position, or camera, is positioned at the origin and, when the local viewer option is not used, that the view direction be oriented down the negative z-axis so that $\mathbf{v} = \langle 0, 0, 1 \rangle$. For this reason, the routines `gluPerspective`, `glFrustum`, and `glOrtho` should be invoked when the projection matrix is the current matrix, but `gluLookAt` should be invoked when the model view matrix is active.

Vertex Normals and Colors. Recall how `glBegin()` and `glEnd()` are used to bracket the specification of the geometric objects of points, lines, and polygons. OpenGL requires that all `glVertex*` commands be inside a `glBegin`, `glEnd` pair. In addition to the `glVertex*` commands giving the positions of vertices, you may also include commands that specify the surface normal and the surface material properties of a vertex. This can be done by commands of the following type:

```
glNormal3f( x,y,z );     // ⟨x,y,z⟩ is the normal
glMaterial*( ··· );      // Multiple glMaterial commands OK
glVertex*( ··· );        // Vertex position
```

The `glMaterial*()` commands are used to specify the reflectivity coefficients and the shininess exponent. The syntax of these commands is described later. The effect of a `glNormal3f()` or a `glMaterial*()` command is applied to all subsequent `glVertex*()` commands until it is overridden by another `glNormal3f()` or `glMaterial*()`.

The normal vector specified with `glNormal3f` should be a unit vector unless you have instructed OpenGL to normalize unit vectors automatically as described on page 87.

Light Properties. The global ambient light intensity, $\mathbf{I}_a^{in,global}$, is set by calling the OpenGL routines as follows:

```
float color[4] = { r, g, b, a };
glLightModelfv(GL_LIGHT_MODEL_AMBIENT, &color[0]);
```

Note how the color is passed in as a pointer to a float, that is, as the C/C++ type `float*`— in the OpenGL naming scheme, this is indicated by the suffix "fv" on the function name. The "v" stands for "vector."

The ambient color includes the levels of ambient light intensity for red, green, and blue and also a value for the "alpha" component of light. The alpha component is typically used for blending and transparency effects. We will not discuss it further here but remark only that it is handled just like the other color components until the final stage (stage 4) of the rendering pipeline. See Chapter V for more discussion on the uses of the alpha color channel. When specifying colors of lights and materials, OpenGL often requires you to set an alpha value; ordinarily, it is best just to set the alpha color equal to 1.

The positions, or alternatively the directions, of the point light sources are set with the OpenGL command

```
float pos[4] = { x, y, z, w };
glLightfv( GL_LIGHTi, GL_POSITION, &pos[0]);
```

The position has to be specified in homogeneous coordinates. If $w \neq 0$, then this indicates a *positional* light placed at the position $\langle x/w, y/w, z/w \rangle$. If $w = 0$, then the light is directional: the directional light is thought of as being placed at infinity in the $\langle x, y, z \rangle$ direction (not all of x, y, z, w should be zero). The light direction vector ℓ is thus equal to the constant vector $\langle x, y, z \rangle$ (recall that the vector ℓ points from the surface towards the light opposite to the direction the light is traveling). Note that, unlike the usual situation for homogeneous vectors, the vectors $\langle x, y, z, 0 \rangle$ and $\langle -x, -y, -z, 0 \rangle$ do not have the same meaning. Instead they indicate directional lights shining from opposite directions. The default value for lights is that they are directional, shining down the z-axis, that is, the default direction vector is $\langle 0, 0, 1, 0 \rangle$.

The positions and directions of lights are modified by the current contents of the model view matrix. Therefore, lights can be placed conveniently using the local coordinates of a model. It is important to keep in mind that the projection matrix does not affect the lights' positions and directions and that lights will work correctly only if the viewpoint is placed at the origin looking down the negative z-axis.

The colors, or, more properly speaking, the light intensity values, of lights are set by the following OpenGL command:

```
float color[4] = { r, g, b, a };

glLightfv(GL_LIGHTi, { GL_AMBIENT
                       GL_DIFFUSE }, &color[0] );
                       GL_SPECULAR
```

where the second parameter may be any of the three indicated possibilities. This command sets the values of the light's $\mathbf{I}_a^{in}$, $\mathbf{I}_d^{in}$, or $\mathbf{I}_s^{in}$ intensity vector.[2] The ambient light intensity defaults to $\langle 0, 0, 0, 1 \rangle$. The diffuse and specular light intensities default to $\langle 1, 1, 1, 1 \rangle$ for light 0 (GL_LIGHT0) and to $\langle 0, 0, 0, 0 \rangle$ for all other lights.

One might wonder why lights include an ambient color value when it would be computationally equivalent just to include the lights' ambient intensities in the global ambient light. The reasons are threefold. First, lights may be turned off and on, and this makes it convenient to adjust the ambient lighting automatically. Second, a light's ambient light intensity is adjusted by the distance attenuation and spotlight effects discussed later in this section. Finally, the purpose of ambient light is to model light after multiple bounces off of surfaces, and this logically goes with the light itself.

Material Properties. OpenGL's glMaterial*() commands are used to set the surface material properties. The ambient, diffuse, and specular reflectivity coefficients and the emissive intensity can be set by the following commands:

```
float color[4] = {r, g, b, a };

                   GL_FRONT                      GL_AMBIENT
glMaterialfv( {    GL_BACK           }, {         GL_DIFFUSE
              GL_FRONT_AND_BACK          GL_AMBIENT_AND_DIFFUSE },
                                                 GL_SPECULAR
                                                 GL_EMISSION

              &color[0] );
```

These set the indicated reflectivity coefficient or emissive intensity for either the front surface of polygons, the back surface of polygons, or both surfaces of polygons. The default values are $\langle 0.2, 0.2, 0.2, 1 \rangle$ for ambient reflectivity, $\langle 0.8, 0.8, 0.8, 1 \rangle$ for diffuse reflectivity, and $\langle 0, 0, 0, 1 \rangle$ for specular reflectivity and emissivity.

The specular exponent, or shininess coefficient, is set by a command

```
                GL_FRONT
glMaterialf( {  GL_BACK          }, GL_SHININESS, float f );
             GL_FRONT_AND_BACK
```

The default value for the specular exponent is 0, and the maximum value is 128.

You can still use glColor*() commands with Phong lighting, but they are less flexible than the glMaterial*() commands. First you have to call

```
glEnable(GL_COLOR_MATERIAL);
```

---

[2] However, before being used to calculate the illumination levels, as in Equation III.9, these light intensity values may be reduced by a distance attenuation factor or spotlight factor.

so that glColor* will affect material properties. Then you can code as follows:

```
glNormal3f( x, y, z );      // ⟨x,y,z⟩ is the normal
glColor3f( r, g, b );       // Change reflectivity parameter(s)
glVertex*( ··· );           // Vertex position
```

By default, the preceding glColor*() command changes the ambient and diffuse color of the material; however, this default can be changed with the glColorMaterial() command.

Special Effects: Attenuation and Spotlighting. OpenGL supports both distance attenuation and spotlighting as a means of achieving some special effects with lighting. Distance attenuation refers to making the light less intense, that is, less bright, as the distance increases from the light. The formula for the distance attenuation factor is

$$\frac{1}{k_c + k_\ell \mathrm{d} + k_q \mathrm{d}^2},$$

where d is the distance from the light, and the constant scalars k_c, k_ℓ and k_q are the *constant attenuation factor*, the *linear attenuation factor*, and the *quadratic attenuation factor*, respectively. All three of the light intensity values, $\mathbf{I}_a^{in}$, $\mathbf{I}_d^{in}$, and $\mathbf{I}_s^{in}$, are multiplied by the distance attenuation factor before being used in the Phong lighting calculations. The distance attenuation factors are set by the following OpenGL commands:

$$\text{glLightf(GL\_LIGHT}i, \begin{Bmatrix} \text{GL\_CONSTANT\_ATTENUATION} \\ \text{GL\_LINEAR\_ATTENUATION} \\ \text{GL\_QUADRATIC\_ATTENUATION} \end{Bmatrix}, \text{float}\,k\,);$$

A spotlight effect can be used to make a positional light act as a narrow beam of light. A spotlight effect is specified by giving (a) the direction of the spotlight; (b) the cutoff angle, which is the angle of the cone of light from the light source; and (c) a spotlight exponent, which controls how fast the light intensity decreases away from the center of the spotlight. The spotlight direction is set by the commands

```
float dir[3] = { x, y, z };
glLightfv( GL_LIGHTi, GL_SPOT_DIRECTION, &dir[0] );
```

The spotlight direction is modified by the model view matrix in exactly the same way that vertex normals are.

The spotlight cutoff angle controls the spread of the spotlight. A cutoff angle of θ specifies that the light intensity drops abruptly to zero for any direction more than θ degrees away from the spotlight direction. The spotlight cutoff angle is set by the command

```
glLightf(GL_LIGHTi, GL_SPOT_CUTOFF, float θ );
```

where, as usual for OpenGL, the angle is measured in degrees.

The spotlight exponent is used to reduce the intensity of the spotlight away from the center direction. The intensity of the light along a direction at an angle φ from the center of the spotlight (where φ is less than the spotlight cutoff angle) is reduced by a factor of $(\cos\varphi)^c$, where the constant c is the spotlight exponent. The command to set a spotlight exponent is

```
glLightf(GL_LIGHTi, GL_SPOT_EXPONENT, float c );
```

Normalizing Normal Vectors. By default, OpenGL treats normal vectors by assuming that they are already unit vectors and transforming them by the current model view matrix. As discussed in Section III.1.7, this is fine as long as the model view matrix holds a rigid transformation. However, this is not acceptable if the model view matrix holds a more general transformation, including a scaling transformation or a shear.

To make OpenGL transform normals by the procedure described in Section III.1.7, you must give the command

```
glEnable( GL_NORMALIZE );
```

This command should be given if you either use nonunit vectors with `glNormal3f()` or nonrigid transformations.

The latest version of OpenGL (version 1.2) has a new normalization option

```
glEnable( GL_RESCALE_NORMAL );
```

that rescales normal vectors under the assumption that the normal given with `glNormal3f()` is a unit vector and that the model view matrix consists of a rigid transformation composed with a uniform scaling, where the same scaling factor is used in all directions. This is considerably faster than the full `GL_NORMALIZE` option, which needs to compute the transpose of the inverse and then normalize the vector.

III.2 The Cook–Torrance Lighting Model★

The Cook–Torrance lighting model is an alternative to Phong lighting that can better capture reflectance properties of a wider range of surface materials. The Cook–Torrance lighting model was introduced by (Cook and Torrance, 1982) based partly on a lighting model developed by (Blinn, 1973). The Cook–Torrance lighting model incorporates the physical properties of reflection more fully than the Phong lighting model by using a microfacet model for rough surfaces and by incorporating the Fresnel equations in the calculation of reflection intensities. It thus can better handle rough surfaces and changes in reflection due to grazing view angles. In particular, the Cook–Torrance lighting model can be used to render metallic surfaces better than can be done with the Phong lighting model.

Several other local lighting models exist besides the Phong and the Cook–Torrance model. (He et al., 1991) have described a model that extends the Cook–Torrance model to include more physical aspects of light reflection. Another popular model by (Schlick, 1994) incorporates many features of the physically based models but is more efficient computationally.

III.2.1 Bidirectional Reflectivity

The central part of any local lighting model is to compute how light reflects off of a surface. To state this in a general form, we assume that a beam of light is shining on a point of the surface from the direction pointed to by a unit vector ℓ and that we wish to compute the intensity of the light that is reflected in the direction of a unit vector $\mathbf{v}$. Thus, the light reflectance calculation can be reduced to computing a single *bidirectional reflectivity function, BRIDF*. The initials "BRIDF" actually stand for "bidirectional reflected intensity distribution function." The parameters to the BRIDF function are (a) the incoming direction ℓ; (b) the outgoing direction $\mathbf{v}$, (c) the color or wavelength λ of the incoming light, and (d) the properties of the reflecting surface, including its normal and orientation. We write the BRIDF function

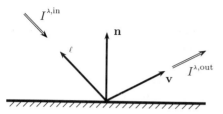

Figure III.13. The BRIDF function relates the outgoing light intensity and the incoming light intensity according to $\text{BRIDF}(\ell, \mathbf{v}, \lambda) = I^{\lambda,\text{out}}/I^{\lambda,\text{in}}$.

as just

$$\text{BRIDF}(\ell, \mathbf{v}, \lambda),$$

to signify a function of the light and view directions, and of the wavelength, suppressing in the notation the dependence on the surface properties. The value $\text{BRIDF}(\ell, \mathbf{v}, \lambda)$ is intended to be the ratio of the intensity of the outgoing light in the direction $\mathbf{v}$ to the intensity of the incoming light from the direction pointed to by ℓ.[3] As shown in Figure III.13, the bidirectional reflectivity function is defined by

$$\text{BRIDF}(\ell, \mathbf{v}, \lambda) = \frac{I^{\lambda,\text{out}}}{I^{\lambda,\text{in}}}.$$

An important characteristic of the BRIDF function is that the incoming and outgoing directions are completely arbitrary, and in particular, the outgoing direction $\mathbf{v}$ does not have to be in the direction of perfect reflection. By expressing the BRIDF function in this general form, one can define BRIDF functions for *anisotropic* surfaces, where the reflectance function is not circularly symmetric around the perpendicular. An example of an anisotropic surface would be a brushed metal surface that has parallel grooves: light will reflect from such a surface differently depending on the orientation of the incoming direction relative to the orientation of the grooves. Other examples of anisotropic surfaces include some types of cloth, where the weave pattern may create directional dependencies in reflection. Still other examples include hair, feathers, and fur. We will not consider anisotropic surfaces in this book, but the interested reader can consult (Kajiya, 1985) for an early treatment of anisotropic surfaces in computer graphics.

The bidirectional reflectivity function can be computed in several ways. First, if one is trying to simulate the appearance of a physical, real-world surface, the most direct way would be to perform experiments measuring the reflectivity function. This would require shining light from various directions and of various wavelengths onto a sample of the material and measuring the levels of reflected light in various directions. (Devices that perform these measurements are called goniometers.) Interpolation could then be used to fill in the values of the BRIDF function between the measured directions. In principle, this would give an accurate calculation of the

---

[3]   We are following (Trowbridge and Reitz, 1975) in using the BRIDF function, but many authors prefer to use a closely related function, $\text{BRDF}(\ell, \mathbf{v}, \lambda)$ instead. The BRDF function is called the "bidirectional reflectivity distribution function." These two functions are related by

$$\text{BRIDF}(\ell, \mathbf{v}, \lambda) = \text{BRDF}(\ell, \mathbf{v}, \lambda) \cdot (\mathbf{n} \cdot \ell).$$

Here, $\mathbf{n}$ is the unit surface normal, and so $\mathbf{n} \cdot \ell$ is the cosine of the angle between the surface normal and the incidence vector. Thus, the only difference between the two functions is that the BRIDF takes into account the reduction in intensity (per unit surface area) due to the angle of incidence, whereas the BRDF does not.

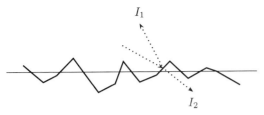

Figure III.14. A microfacet surface consists of small flat pieces. The horizontal line shows the average level of a flat surface, and the microfacets show the microscopic shape of the surface. Dotted lines show the direction of light rays. The incoming light can either be reflected in the direction of perfect mirror-like reflection (I_1) or can enter the surface (I_2). In the second case, the light is modeled as eventually exiting the material as diffusely reflected light.

bidirectional reflectivity function. In practice, the physical measurements are time consuming and inconvenient at best. And of course, physical measurements cannot be performed for materials that do not physically exist. There are published studies of reflectivity functions: these are typically performed at various wavelengths but usually only from perpendicular illumination and viewing directions.

A second way to calculate bidirectional reflectivity functions is to create a mathematical model of the reflectivity of the surface. We have already seen one example of this, namely, the Phong lighting model, which gives a simple and easy way to compute bidirectional reflectivity function. The Cook–Torrance model, which we discuss in detail in Section III.2.2, is another similar model but takes more aspects of the physics of reflection into account and thereby captures more features of reflectance.

The bidirectional reflectivity function is only an idealized model of reflection. To make physical sense of the way we have defined bidirectional reflectivity, one has to let the surface be an infinite flat surface and the distances to the light source and the viewer tend to infinity. Several more sophisticated local lighting models have been developed since the Cook–Torrance model. These models take into account more detailed aspects of the physics of reflectivity, such as subsurface scattering, polarization, and diffraction. To handle polarization, the BRIDF function needs to be redefined so as to incorporate polarization parameters (cf. (Wolff and Kurlander, 1990)).

III.2.2 Overview of Cook–Torrance★

The Cook–Torrance model and the earlier Blinn model are based on a microfacet model for surface reflection. According to this model, a surface consists of small flat pieces called *facets*. A one-dimensional cross section of a microfacet surface is shown in Figure III.14. The assumption is then made that light hitting a microfacet can either be immediately reflected or can enter into the surface. The light that is immediately reflected is presumed to reflect off the microfacet in the direction of perfect reflection, that is, in the direction of reflection from a mirror parallel to the microfacet. Light that is refracted and enters into the surface through the microfacet is assumed to penetrate deeper into the material and to reflect around inside the surface several times before exiting the surface. This portion of the light that is refracted and undergoes multiple reflections inside the material will exit the surface in an unpredictable direction. Thus, this part of the light is treated as being diffusely reflected.

Just like the Phong model, the Cook–Torrance model treats reflection as being composed of separate ambient, diffuse, and specular components. The ambient and diffuse components are essentially the same in the Cook–Torrance model as in the Phong lighting model. Thus, in the Cook–Torrance model, reflected light at a given wavelength can be expressed by

$$I = I_a + I_d + I_s$$
$$= \rho_a I_a^{\text{in}} + \rho_d I_d^{\text{in}}(\boldsymbol{\ell} \cdot \mathbf{n}) + I_s.$$

This is the same as in the Phong model (see Equation III.6) except that now the specularly reflected light will be calculated differently.

The calculation for specular light has the form

$$I_s = \frac{(\mathbf{n} \cdot \boldsymbol{\ell})}{(\mathbf{n} \cdot \mathbf{v})} s\, F\, G\, D \cdot I_s^{\text{in}},$$

where $\mathbf{n}$ is the unit vector normal to the surface, s is a scalar constant, and F, G, and D are scalar-valued functions that will be explained below. The constant s is used to scale the brightness of the specular reflection. Including the multiplicative factor $\mathbf{n} \cdot \boldsymbol{\ell}$ has the effect of converting the incoming light intensity into the incoming light energy flux per unit surface area; that is to say, the value $(\mathbf{n} \cdot \boldsymbol{\ell})I^{\text{in}}$ measures the amount of light energy hitting a unit area of the surface. Similarly, $(\mathbf{n} \cdot \mathbf{v})I_s$ measures the amount of light energy leaving a unit area of the surface, and for this reason we need to include the division by $\mathbf{n} \cdot \mathbf{v}$. Thus, the quantity $s \cdot F \cdot G \cdot D$ is the ratio of the energy hitting a unit area of the surface from the direction of $\boldsymbol{\ell}$ to the energy leaving the unit area in the direction of $\mathbf{v}$.

The function $D = D(\boldsymbol{\ell}, \mathbf{v})$ measures the distribution of the microfacets, namely, it equals the fraction of microfacets that are oriented correctly for specular reflection from the direction of $\boldsymbol{\ell}$ to the direction $\mathbf{v}$. Possible functions for D are discussed in Section III.2.3. The $G = G(\boldsymbol{\ell}, \mathbf{v})$ function measures the diminution of reflected light due to shadowing and masking, where the roughness of the surface creates shadowing that prevents reflection. This geometric term will be discussed in Section III.2.4. The function $F = F(\boldsymbol{\ell}, \mathbf{v}, \lambda)$ is the Fresnel coefficient, which shows what percentage of the incidence light is reflected. The Fresnel term is discussed in Section III.2.5.

The Fresnel coefficient is particularly important because it can be used to create the effect that light reflects more specularly at grazing angles than at angles near vertical. This kind of effect is easy to observe; for instance, a piece of white paper that usually reflects only diffusely will reflect specularly when viewed from a very oblique angle. An interesting additional effect is that the Fresnel term can cause the angle of greatest reflection to be different than the direction of perfect mirror-like reflection. The Fresnel term F, unlike the D and G functions, is dependent on the wavelength λ. This causes the color of specular reflections to vary with the angles of incidence and reflection.

In our description of the Cook–Torrance model, we have not followed exactly the conventions of (Blinn, 1973) and (Cook and Torrance, 1982). They did not distinguish between diffuse and specular incoming light but instead assumed that there is only one kind of incoming light. They then used a bidirectional reflectivity function of the form

$$\text{BRIDF} = d \cdot \rho_d(\mathbf{n} \cdot \boldsymbol{\ell}) + s \cdot \frac{(\mathbf{n} \cdot \boldsymbol{\ell})}{(\mathbf{n} \cdot \mathbf{v})} F\, G\, D,$$

where d and s are scalars, with $d + s = 1$, that control the fraction of diffuse versus specular reflection. We have changed this aspect of their model since it makes the model a little more general and also for the practical reason that it allows Cook–Torrance lighting to coexist with Phong lighting in the ray-tracing software described in Appendix B.

III.2.3 The Microfacet Distribution Term★

The microfacet model assumes that light incident from the direction of ℓ is specularly reflected independently by each individual microfacet. Hence, the amount of light reflected in the direction $\mathbf{v}$ is deemed to be proportional to the fraction of microfacets that are correctly oriented to cause mirror-like reflection in that direction. To determine the direction of these microfacets, recall that the halfway vector was defined by

$$\mathbf{h} = \frac{\mathbf{v} + \ell}{||\mathbf{v} + \ell||}$$

(see Figure III.8 on page 73). For a microfacet to be oriented properly for perfect reflection, the normal pointing outward from the microfacet must be equal to $\mathbf{h}$. We let ψ equal the angle between $\mathbf{h}$ and the overall surface normal $\mathbf{n}$, that is, $\psi = \cos^{-1}(\mathbf{h} \cdot \mathbf{n})$. Then, we use the function $D = D(\psi)$ to equal the fraction of microfacets that are correctly oriented for perfect reflection. There are several functions that have been suggested for D. One possibility is the Gaussian distribution function

$$D(\psi) = ce^{-\psi^2/m^2},$$

where c and m are positive constants. Another possibility is the Beckmann distribution

$$D(\psi) = \frac{1}{\pi \, m^2 \cos^4 \psi} e^{-(\tan^2 \psi)/m^2},$$

where again m is a constant. The Beckmann distribution is based on a mathematical model for a rough one-dimensional surface where the height of the surface is a normally distributed function and the autocorrelation of the surface makes the root mean value of the slope equal to $m/\sqrt{2}$. This sounds complicated, but what it means is that the constant m should be chosen to be approximately equal to the average slope of (microfacets of) the surface.[4] Bigger values of m correspond to rougher, more bumpy surfaces.

III.2.4 The Geometric Surface Occlusion Term★

The geometric term G in the Cook–Torrance model computes the fraction of the illuminated portion of the surface that is visible to the viewer, or, to be more precise, the geometric term computes the fraction of the light specularly reflected by the microfacets that is able to reach the viewer. Because the surface is rough and bumpy, it is probable that some of the illuminated area of the surface is not visible to the viewer, and this can reduce the amount of visible specularly reflected light.

To derive a formula for the geometric term, we make two simplifying assumptions. The first assumption is that the vectors ℓ, $\mathbf{n}$, and $\mathbf{v}$ are coplanar. We call this plane the *plane of reflection*. At the end of this section, we discuss how to remove this coplanarity assumption. The second, and more important, assumption is that the microfacets on the surface are arranged as symmetric 'V'-shaped grooves. These grooves are treated as being at right angles to the plane of reflection. In effect, this means we are adopting a one-dimensional model for the surface. We further assume that the tops of the grooves are all at the same height, that is, that the surface is obtained from a perfectly flat surface by etching the grooves into the surface. A view of the grooves is shown in Figure III.15.

---

[4] See (Beckmann and Spizzichino, 1963) for more details, including the details of the mathematical models.

Figure III.15. For the derivation of the geometric term G, the microfacets are modeled as symmetric, 'V'-shaped grooves with the tops of the grooves all at the same height. The horizontal line shows the overall plane of the surface.

The assumption about the microfacets being 'V'-shaped may seem rather drastic and unjustified, but the reason for the assumption is that it simplifies the calculation of the geometric factor G. In addition, it is hoped that the simplified model will qualitatively match the behavior of more complicated surfaces fairly well.

Some different kinds of specularly reflected light occlusion are illustrated in Figure III.16. Since the tops of the grooves are all at the same height, each groove may be considered independently. In Figure III.16, light is shown coming in from the direction pointed to by $\boldsymbol{\ell}$ and is reflected specularly in the direction of $\mathbf{v}$. This means that the side of the groove must have the normal vector equal to the halfway vector $\mathbf{h}$. In part (a) of the figure, the light falls fully onto the groove, and the entire groove is visible to the viewer. In part (b), the reflecting side of the groove is partly occluded by the other side, and thus some of the reflected light hits the opposite side of the groove and does not reach the viewer. In this case, we say that *masking* has occurred. In part (c), the reflecting side of the groove is partly shadowed by the other side of the groove so that the reflecting side of the groove is not fully illuminated: we call this *shadowing*. Finally, in part (d), both shadowing and masking are occurring.

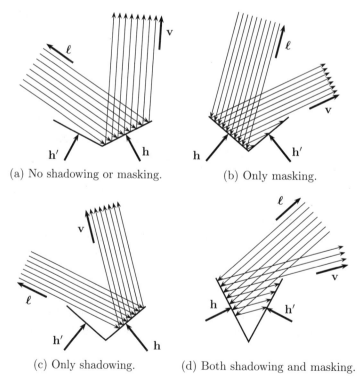

(a) No shadowing or masking.   (b) Only masking.

(c) Only shadowing.   (d) Both shadowing and masking.

Figure III.16. Shadowing and masking inside a single groove. The 'V' shape represents a groove; the unit vector $\mathbf{h}$ is normal to the facet where specular reflection occurs. Light from the direction of $\boldsymbol{\ell}$ is specularly reflected in the direction $\mathbf{v}$.

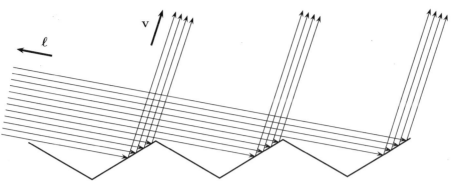

Figure III.17. Shadowing without masking does not reduce the intensity of the reflected light.

The usual formulation of the Cook–Torrance model calculates the percentage of light that is not shadowed and the percentage of the light that is not masked and uses the minimum of these for the G term. However, this usual formulation is incorrect because shadowing by itself should not cause any reduction in the intensity of reflected light. This is shown in Figure III.17, where the incoming light is partially shadowed, but, nonetheless, all of the incoming light is reflected to the viewer. Figure III.17 shows all the grooves having the same slope so as to make the situation clearer, but the same effect holds even if different grooves have different slopes (since the D term is used for the fraction of microfacets at a given slope, the G term does not need to take into account grooves that do not lead to perfect reflection).

Therefore, we present a version of the geometric term G that is different from the term used by (Blinn, 1973) and (Cook and Torrance, 1982) in that it uses a more correct treatment of shadowing. First, we need a geometric lemma due to (Blinn, 1973). This lemma will serve as the basis for calculating the fraction of the groove that is masked or shadowed. As stated with $\mathbf{v}$, the lemma computes the fraction that is not masked (if there is any masking), but replacing $\mathbf{v}$ with $\boldsymbol{\ell}$ gives the formula for the fraction of the groove that is not shadowed (if there is any shadowing).

Lemma III.4 *Consider the situation in Figure III.18. Let $\|AB\|$ be the distance from A to B, and so forth. Then,*

$$\frac{\|BC\|}{\|AC\|} = \frac{2(\mathbf{n} \cdot \mathbf{h})(\mathbf{n} \cdot \mathbf{v})}{(\mathbf{h} \cdot \mathbf{v})}. \qquad \text{III.15}$$

To prove the lemma, and for subsequent algorithms, it will be useful to define the vector $\mathbf{h}'$ to be the unit vector that is normal to the opposite side of the groove. By the symmetry of the

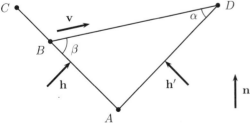

Figure III.18. The situation for Lemma III.4. The edges AC and AD form a symmetric groove, and AC and AD are of equal length. The vector $\mathbf{n}$ points upward, and the vector $\mathbf{v}$ is in the direction from B to D. The vectors $\mathbf{h}$ and $\mathbf{h}'$ are normal to the sides of the groove. All four vectors are unit vectors. The ratio of $\|BC\|$ to $\|AC\|$ measures the fraction of the groove that is not masked.

groove, the vector $\mathbf{h}'$ is easily seen to equal

$$\mathbf{h}' = 2(\mathbf{n} \cdot \mathbf{h})\mathbf{n} - \mathbf{h}. \hspace{4cm} \text{III.16}$$

We now prove the lemma.

Proof From the symmetry of the groove and the law of sines, we have

$$\frac{\|AB\|}{\|AC\|} = \frac{\|AB\|}{\|AD\|} = \frac{\sin\alpha}{\sin\beta}.$$

Clearly, we have $\sin\alpha = \cos(\frac{\pi}{2} - \alpha) = -\mathbf{v} \cdot \mathbf{h}'$. Similarly, we have $\sin\beta = \mathbf{v} \cdot \mathbf{h}$. From this, using Equation III.16, we get

$$\frac{\|BC\|}{\|AC\|} = 1 - \frac{\|AB\|}{\|AC\|} = 1 + \frac{\mathbf{v} \cdot (2(\mathbf{n} \cdot \mathbf{h})\mathbf{n} - \mathbf{h})}{\mathbf{v} \cdot \mathbf{h}},$$

and the lemma follows immediately.   □

With the aid of the lemma, we can now give a formula for the geometric term that describes the reduction in reflection due to masking. First, we note that masking occurs if, and only if, $\mathbf{v} \cdot \mathbf{h}' < 0$. To see this, note that $\mathbf{v} \cdot \mathbf{h}'$ is positive only if the vector $\mathbf{h}'$ is facing towards the viewer. When masking occurs, the fraction of the side of the groove that is not masked is given by Equation III.15 of the lemma.

For similar reasons, shadowing occurs if and only if we have $\boldsymbol{\ell} \cdot \mathbf{h}' < 0$. By Lemma III.4, with $\mathbf{v}$ replaced by $\boldsymbol{\ell}$, the fraction of the side of the groove that is not shadowed is equal to

$$\frac{2(\mathbf{n} \cdot \mathbf{h})(\mathbf{n} \cdot \boldsymbol{\ell})}{(\mathbf{h} \cdot \boldsymbol{\ell})}.$$

We can now describe how to compute the geometric factor G. In the case in which there is neither masking nor shadowing, we set G equal to 1. When there is masking, but no shadowing, we set G equal to the fraction of the reflected light that is not masked, that is,

$$G = \frac{2(\mathbf{n} \cdot \mathbf{h})(\mathbf{n} \cdot \mathbf{v})}{(\mathbf{h} \cdot \mathbf{v})}.$$

In the case in which both masking and shadowing occur, as illustrated in Figure III.16(d), we set G to equal the fraction of the reflected light that is not masked. This means that we set G equal to the ratio (note that $\mathbf{h} \cdot \mathbf{v} = \mathbf{h} \cdot \boldsymbol{\ell}$ by the definition of $\mathbf{h}$)

$$\left(\frac{2(\mathbf{n} \cdot \mathbf{h})(\mathbf{n} \cdot \mathbf{v})}{(\mathbf{h} \cdot \mathbf{v})}\right) \div \left(\frac{2(\mathbf{n} \cdot \mathbf{h})(\mathbf{n} \cdot \boldsymbol{\ell})}{(\mathbf{h} \cdot \boldsymbol{\ell})}\right) = \frac{\mathbf{n} \cdot \mathbf{v}}{\mathbf{n} \cdot \boldsymbol{\ell}}$$

if this value is less than 1. This is the case illustrated in part (d) of Figure III.16(d), and we are setting G equal to the ratio of the nonmasked amount to the nonshadowed amount. However, if the fraction is ≥ 1, then none of the nonshadowed part is masked, and so we just set $G = 1$.

To summarize, the geometric term G is defined by

$$G = \begin{cases} 1 & \text{if } \mathbf{v} \cdot \mathbf{h}' \geq 0 \text{ or } \mathbf{n} \cdot \mathbf{v} \geq \mathbf{n} \cdot \boldsymbol{\ell} \\[2mm] \dfrac{2(\mathbf{n} \cdot \mathbf{h})(\mathbf{n} \cdot \mathbf{v})}{(\mathbf{h} \cdot \mathbf{v})} & \text{if } \mathbf{v} \cdot \mathbf{h}' < 0 \text{ and } \boldsymbol{\ell} \cdot \mathbf{h}' \geq 0 \\[2mm] \dfrac{\mathbf{n} \cdot \mathbf{v}}{\mathbf{n} \cdot \boldsymbol{\ell}} & \text{if } \mathbf{v} \cdot \mathbf{h}' < 0, \boldsymbol{\ell} \cdot \mathbf{h}' < 0, \text{ and } \mathbf{n} \cdot \mathbf{v} < \mathbf{n} \cdot \boldsymbol{\ell}. \end{cases}$$

The formula for the geometric term was derived from a one-dimensional model of 'V'-shaped grooves. Although this assumption that the facets are arranged in grooves is unrealistic, it still works fairly well as long the vectors $\boldsymbol{\ell}$, $\mathbf{v}$, and $\mathbf{n}$ are coplanar. However, the formula breaks down when these vectors are not coplanar because the derivation of the formula for G made assumptions about how $\mathbf{h}$, $\mathbf{h}'$, and $\mathbf{n}$ interact that are no longer valid in the noncoplanar case. The coplanar case is actually quite common; for instance, these vectors are always coplanar in (nondistributed) ray tracing, as we will see in Chapter IX, since basic ray tracing follows rays in the direction of perfect mirror-like reflection.

In the noncoplanar case, we suggest that the vector $\mathbf{n}$ be replaced by projecting (actually, rotating) it down to the plane containing $\boldsymbol{\ell}$ and $\mathbf{v}$. That is to say, instead of $\mathbf{n}$, we use a unit vector $\mathbf{m}$ that is parallel to the projection of $\mathbf{n}$ onto the plane containing $\boldsymbol{\ell}$ and $\mathbf{v}$. The vector $\mathbf{h}$ is still computed as usual, but now $\mathbf{h}'$ is computed using $\mathbf{m}$ instead of $\mathbf{n}$. It is not hard to see that the projection of $\mathbf{n}$ onto the plane is equal to

$$\mathbf{n}_0 = \frac{(\mathbf{n} \cdot \boldsymbol{\ell})\boldsymbol{\ell} + (\mathbf{n} \cdot \mathbf{v})\mathbf{v} - (\mathbf{v} \cdot \boldsymbol{\ell})(\mathbf{v} \cdot \mathbf{n})\boldsymbol{\ell} - (\mathbf{v} \cdot \boldsymbol{\ell})(\boldsymbol{\ell} \cdot \mathbf{n})\mathbf{v}}{1 - (\mathbf{v} \cdot \boldsymbol{\ell})^2}. \qquad \text{III.17}$$

Then, $\mathbf{m} = \mathbf{n}_0/\|\mathbf{n}_0\|$. In the extreme case, where $\mathbf{v}$ and $\boldsymbol{\ell}$ are both perpendicular to $\mathbf{n}$, this gives a divide by zero, but this case can be handled by instead setting $\mathbf{n}_0 = \mathbf{v} + \boldsymbol{\ell}$.

Putting this together gives the following algorithm for the case in which $\mathbf{v}$, $\boldsymbol{\ell}$, and $\mathbf{n}$ are not coplanar:

```
ComputeG( n, ℓ, v ) {
    If ( ||ℓ + v|| == 0 ) { // if v · ℓ == −1
        Set G = 1;
        Return ( G );
    }
    Set h = (ℓ + v)/(||ℓ + v||);
    Set n₀ = (n · ℓ)ℓ + (n · v)v − (v · ℓ)(v · n)ℓ − (v · ℓ)(ℓ · n)v;
    If ( ||n₀|| ≠ 0 ) {
        Set m = n₀/||n₀||;
    }
    Else {
        Set m = h;
    }
    Set h' = 2(m · h)m − h;
```

$$\text{Set } G = \begin{cases} 1 & \text{if } \mathbf{v} \cdot \mathbf{h}' \geq 0 \text{ or } \mathbf{m} \cdot \mathbf{v} \geq \mathbf{m} \cdot \boldsymbol{\ell} \\[2mm] \dfrac{2(\mathbf{m} \cdot \mathbf{h})(\mathbf{m} \cdot \mathbf{v})}{(\mathbf{h} \cdot \mathbf{v})} & \text{if } \mathbf{v} \cdot \mathbf{h}' < 0 \text{ and } \boldsymbol{\ell} \cdot \mathbf{h}' \geq 0 \\[2mm] \dfrac{\mathbf{m} \cdot \mathbf{v}}{\mathbf{m} \cdot \boldsymbol{\ell}} & \text{otherwise.} \end{cases}$$

```
    Return ( G );
}
```

Although it is not part of the Cook–Torrance model, it is possible to use the geometric term to affect the diffuse part of the reflection too. (Oren and Nayar, 1994; 1995) use the same 'V'-shaped groove model of surface roughness to compute masking and shadowing effects for diffuse lighting; this allows them to render non-Lambertian surfaces.

Exercise III.7★ *Derive the formula III.17 for* $\mathbf{n}_0$.

III.2.5 The Fresnel Term★

The Fresnel equations describe what fraction of incident light is specularly reflected from a flat surface. For a particular wavelength λ, this can be defined in terms of a function $\mathcal{F}$

$$F(\ell, \mathbf{v}, \lambda) = \mathcal{F}(\varphi, \eta),$$

where $\varphi = \cos^{-1}(\ell \cdot \mathbf{h})$ is the angle of incidence, and η is the index of refraction of the surface. Here, φ is the angle of incidence of the incoming light with respect to the surface of the microfacets, not with respect to the overall plane of the whole surface. The index of refraction is the ratio of the speed of light above the surface to the speed of light inside the surface material and is discussed in more detail in Section IX.1.2 in connection with Snell's law. For materials that are not electrically conducting, Fresnel's law states that the fraction of light intensity that is specularly reflected is equal to

$$\mathcal{F} = \frac{1}{2}\left(\frac{\sin^2(\varphi - \theta)}{\sin^2(\varphi + \theta)} + \frac{\tan^2(\varphi - \theta)}{\tan^2(\varphi + \theta)} \right), \qquad \text{III.18}$$

where φ is the angle of incidence and θ is the angle of refraction. (We are not concerned with the portion of the light that is refracted, but the angle of refraction still appears in the Fresnel equation.) This form of the Fresnel equation applies to unpolarized light and is obtained by averaging the two forms of the Fresnel equations that apply to light polarized in two different orientations. The angles of incidence and refraction are related by Snell's law, which states that

$$\frac{\sin \varphi}{\sin \theta} = \eta.$$

Let

$$c = \cos \varphi \qquad \text{and} \qquad g = \sqrt{\eta^2 + c^2 - 1}. \qquad \text{III.19}$$

The most common situation is that $\eta > 1$, and in this case $\eta^2 + c^2 - 1 > 0$; thus, g is well defined.[5] A little work shows that $g = \eta \cos \theta$, and then using the trigonometric angle sum and difference formulas it is not hard to see that

$$\frac{\sin(\varphi - \theta)}{\sin(\varphi + \theta)} = \frac{(g - c)}{(g + c)} \qquad \text{III.20}$$

and

$$\frac{\cos(\varphi - \theta)}{\cos(\varphi + \theta)} = \frac{(c(g - c) + 1)}{(c(g + c) - 1)}. \qquad \text{III.21}$$

This lets us express the Fresnel equation III.18 in the following, easier to compute form:

$$\mathcal{F} = \frac{1}{2}\frac{(g - c)^2}{(g + c)^2}\left(1 + \frac{[c(g + c) - 1]^2}{[c(g - c) + 1]^2}\right). \qquad \text{III.22}$$

---

[5] However, the $\eta < 1$ case can arise in ray tracing when transmission rays are used, as described in Chapter IX. In that case, the condition $\eta^2 + c^2 - 1 \le 0$ corresponds to the case of total internal reflection. For total internal reflection, you should just set $\mathcal{F}$ equal to 1.

	Red	Green	Blue
Gold:	0.93	0.88	0.38
Iridium:	0.26	0.28	0.26
Iron:	0.44	0.435	0.43
Nickel:	0.50	0.47	0.36
Copper:	0.93	0.80	0.46
Platinum:	0.63	0.62	0.57
Silver:	0.97	0.97	0.96

Figure III.19. Experimentally measured reflectances for perpendicularly incident light. Values are based on (Touloukian and Witt, 1970).

The preceding form of the Fresnel equation makes several simplifying assumptions. First, the incoming light is presumed to be unpolarized. Second, conducting materials such as metals need to use an index of refraction that has an imaginary component called the *extinction coefficient*. For simplicity, the Cook–Torrance model just sets the extinction coefficient to zero.

If the index of refraction η is known, then Equations III.19 and III.22 provide a good way to compute the reflectance $\mathcal{F}$. On the other hand, the Fresnel equation is sometimes used in the context of ray tracing, and in that setting a slightly more efficient method can be used. For this, refer to Section IX.1.2. That section has a vector $\mathbf{v}$ giving the direction from which the light arrives and describes a method for computing the transmission direction $\mathbf{t}$. Then, we can calculate $c = \cos\varphi = \mathbf{v} \cdot \mathbf{n}$ and $g = \eta\cos\theta = -\eta\mathbf{t} \cdot \mathbf{n}$, instead of using Equation III.19.

Exercise III.8* *Prove that the reflectance $\mathcal{F}$ can also be computed by the formula*

$$\mathcal{F} = \frac{1}{2}\left[\left(\frac{\eta\cos\theta - \cos\varphi}{\eta\cos\theta + \cos\varphi}\right)^2 + \left(\frac{\eta\cos\varphi - \cos\theta}{\eta\cos\varphi + \cos\theta}\right)^2\right]. \qquad \text{III.23}$$

[Hint: Use Equation III.20 and use trignometry identities to show

$$\frac{\tan(\varphi - \theta)}{\tan(\varphi + \theta)} = \frac{\eta\cos\varphi - \cos\theta}{\eta\cos\varphi + \cos\theta}.] \qquad \text{III.24}$$

This still leaves the question of how to find the value of η, and Cook and Torrance suggest the following procedure for determining an index of refraction for metals. They first note that for perpendicularly incident light, $\varphi = \theta = 0$; thus, $c = 1$, $g = \eta$, and

$$\mathcal{F} = \left(\frac{\eta - 1}{\eta + 1}\right)^2.$$

Solving for η in terms of $\mathcal{F}$ gives

$$\eta = \frac{1 + \sqrt{\mathcal{F}}}{1 - \sqrt{\mathcal{F}}}. \qquad \text{III.25}$$

Reflectance values $\mathcal{F}$ for perpendicularly incident light have been measured for many materials (see (Touloukian and Witt, 1970; 1972; Touloukian, Witt, and Hernicz, 1972)). Given a reflectance value for perpendicularly incident light, Equation III.25 can be used to get an approximate value for the index of refraction. This value for η can then be used to calculate the Fresnel term for light incident at other angles. Figure III.19 shows reflectance values F for a few metals. These values are estimated from the graphs in (Touloukian and Witt, 1970)

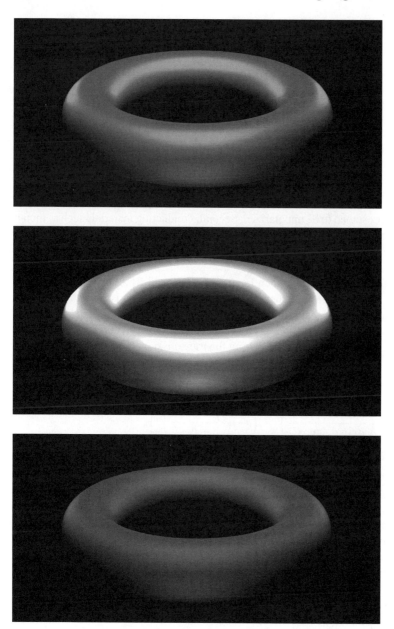

Figure III.20. Metallic tori with the specular component computed using the Cook–Torrance model. The materials are, from top to bottom, gold, silver, and platinum. The roughness is $m = 0.4$ for all three materials. The tori are each illuminated by five positional white lights. See Color Plate 16.

at red, green, and blue color values that correspond roughly to the red, green, and blue colors used by standard monitors.

Figures III.20 and V.8 show some examples of roughened metals rendered with the Cook–Torrance model. As can be seen from the figures, the Cook–Torrance model can do a fairly good job of rendering a metallic appearance, although the colors are not very accurate (and in any event, the colors in these figures have not been properly calibrated). The Cook–Torrance model works less well on shiny metals with low roughness.

IV

Averaging and Interpolation

This chapter takes up the subject of interpolation. For the purposes of the present chapter, the term "interpolation" means the process of finding intermediate values of a function by averaging its values at extreme points. Interpolation was already studied in Section II.4, where it was used for Gouraud and Phong interpolation to average colors or normals to create smooth lighting and shading effects. In Chapter V, interpolation is used to apply texture maps. More sophisticated kinds of interpolation will be important in the study of Bézier curves and B-splines in Chapters VII and VIII. Interpolation is also very important for animation, where both positions and orientations of objects may need to be interpolated.

The first three sections below address the simplest forms of interpolation; namely, linear interpolation on lines and triangles. This includes studying weighted averages, affine combinations, extrapolation, and barycentric coordinates. Then we turn to the topics of bilinear and trilinear interpolation with an emphasis on bilinear interpolation, including an algorithm for inverting bilinear interpolation. The next section has a short, abstract discussion on convex sets, convex hulls, and the definition of convex hulls in terms of weighted averages. After that, we take up the topic of weighted averages performed on points represented in homogeneous coordinates. It is shown that the effect of the homogeneous coordinate is similar to an extra weighting coefficient, and as a corollary, we derive the formulas for hyperbolic interpolation that are important for accurate interpolation in screen-space coordinates. The chapter concludes with a discussion of spherical linear interpolation ("slerping"), which will be used later for quaternion interpolation.

The reader may wish to skip many of the topics in this chapter on first reading and return to them as needed for topics taken up in later chapters.

IV.1 Linear Interpolation

IV.1.1 Interpolation between Two Points

Suppose that $\mathbf{x}_1$ and $\mathbf{x}_2$ are two distinct points, and consider the line segment joining them. We wish to parameterize the line segment between the two points by using a function $\mathbf{x}(\alpha)$ that maps the scalar α to a point on the line segment $\overline{\mathbf{x}_1 \mathbf{x}_2}$. We further want $\mathbf{x}(0) = \mathbf{x}_1$ and $\mathbf{x}(1) = \mathbf{x}_2$ and want $\mathbf{x}(\alpha)$ to interpolate linearly between $\mathbf{x}_1$ and $\mathbf{x}_2$ for values of α between 0 and 1.

Therefore, the function is defined by

$$\mathbf{x}(\alpha) = (1 - \alpha)\mathbf{x}_1 + \alpha\mathbf{x}_2. \hspace{2cm} \text{IV.1}$$

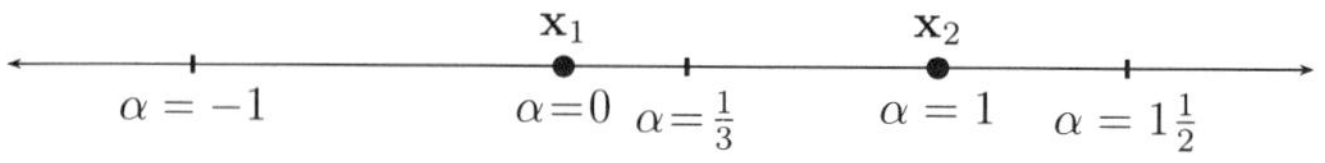

Figure IV.1. Interpolated and extrapolated points for various values of α. For $\alpha < 0$, $\mathbf{x}(\alpha)$ is to the left of $\mathbf{x}_1$. For $\alpha > 1$, $\mathbf{x}(\alpha)$ is to the right of $\mathbf{x}_2$. For $0 < \alpha < 1$, $\mathbf{x}(\alpha)$ is between $\mathbf{x}_1$ and $\mathbf{x}_2$.

Equivalently, we can also write

$$\mathbf{x}(\alpha) \; = \; \mathbf{x}_1 + \alpha(\mathbf{x}_2 - \mathbf{x}_1), \tag{IV.2}$$

where, of course, $\mathbf{x}_2 - \mathbf{x}_1$ is the vector from $\mathbf{x}_1$ to $\mathbf{x}_2$. Equation IV.1 is a more elegant way to express linear interpolation, but the equivalent formulation IV.2 makes it clearer how linear interpolation works.

We can also obtain points by *extrapolation*, by letting α be outside the interval $[0, 1]$. Equation IV.2 makes it clear how extrapolation works. When $\alpha > 1$, the point $\mathbf{x}(\alpha)$ lies past $\mathbf{x}_2$ on the line containing $\mathbf{x}_1$ and $\mathbf{x}_2$. And, when $\alpha < 0$, the point $\mathbf{x}(\alpha)$ lies before $\mathbf{x}_1$ on the line. All this is illustrated in Figure IV.1.

Now we consider how to invert the process of linear interpolation. Suppose that the points $\mathbf{x}_1$, $\mathbf{x}_2$, and $\mathbf{u}$ are given and we wish to find α such that $\mathbf{u} = \mathbf{x}(\alpha)$. Of course, this is possible only if $\mathbf{u}$ is on the line containing $\mathbf{x}_1$ and $\mathbf{x}_2$. Assuming that $\mathbf{u}$ is on this line, we solve for α as follows: From Equation IV.2, we have that

$$\mathbf{u} - \mathbf{x}_1 \; = \; \alpha(\mathbf{x}_2 - \mathbf{x}_1).$$

Taking the dot product of both sides of the equation with the vector $\mathbf{x}_2 - \mathbf{x}_1$ and solving for α, we obtain[1]

$$\alpha \; = \; \frac{(\mathbf{u} - \mathbf{x}_1) \cdot (\mathbf{x}_2 - \mathbf{x}_1)}{(\mathbf{x}_2 - \mathbf{x}_1)^2}. \tag{IV.3}$$

This formula for α is reasonably robust and will not have a divide-by-zero problem unless $\mathbf{x}_1 = \mathbf{x}_2$, in which case the problem was ill-posed. It is easy to see that if $\mathbf{u}$ is not on the line containing $\mathbf{x}_1$ and $\mathbf{x}_2$, then the effect of formula IV.3 is equivalent to first projecting $\mathbf{u}$ onto the line and then solving for α.

> **Exercise IV.1** *Let* $\mathbf{x}_1 = \langle -1, 0 \rangle$ *and* $\mathbf{x}_2 = \langle 2, 1 \rangle$. *Let* α *control the linear interpolation (and extrapolation) from* $\mathbf{x}_1$ *to* $\mathbf{x}_2$. *What points are obtained with* α *equal to* -2, -1, 0, $\frac{1}{10}$, $\frac{1}{3}$, $\frac{1}{2}$, 1, $1\frac{1}{2}$, *and* 2? *What value of* α *gives the point* $\langle 1, \frac{2}{3} \rangle$? *The point* $\langle 8, 3 \rangle$? *Graph your answers.*

Now we extend the notion of linear interpolation to linearly interpolating a function on the line segment $\overline{\mathbf{x}_1 \mathbf{x}_2}$. Let $f(\mathbf{u})$ be a function, and suppose that the values of $f(\mathbf{x}_1)$ and $f(\mathbf{x}_2)$ are known. To linearly interpolate the values of $f(\mathbf{u})$, we express $\mathbf{u}$ as $\mathbf{u} = (1 - \alpha)\mathbf{x}_1 + \alpha\mathbf{x}_2$. Then linear interpolation for f yields

$$f(\mathbf{u}) \; = \; (1 - \alpha)f(\mathbf{x}_1) + \alpha f(\mathbf{x}_2). \tag{IV.4}$$

This method works equally well when the function f is vector-valued instead of scalar-valued. For instance, in Gouraud interpolation, this method was used to interpolate color values. However, it does not work quite so well for Phong interpolation, where normals are interpolated, since the interpolated vectors have to be renormalized.

---

[1] We write $\mathbf{v}^2$ for $\mathbf{v} \cdot \mathbf{v} = ||\mathbf{v}||^2$. So $(\mathbf{x}_2 - \mathbf{x}_1)^2$ means the same as $||\mathbf{x}_2 - \mathbf{x}_1||^2$.

Equation IV.4 can also be used when α is less than zero or greater than one to extrapolate values of f.

The process of interpolating a function's values according to Formula IV.4 is often referred to as "lerping." "Lerp" is short for "*L*inear int*ERP*olation." Occasionally, when we want to stress the use of interpolation, we use the notation

$$\mathrm{lerp}(\mathbf{x}, \mathbf{y}, \alpha) = (1 - \alpha)\mathbf{x} + \alpha\mathbf{y}.$$

Thus, Formula IV.4 could be written as $f(\mathbf{u}) = \mathrm{lerp}(f(\mathbf{x}_1), f(\mathbf{x}_2), \alpha)$.

IV.1.2 Weighted Averages and Affine Combinations

The next two definitions generalize interpolation to interpolating between more than two points.

Definition Let $\mathbf{x}_1, \mathbf{x}_2, \ldots, \mathbf{x}_k$ be points. Let $a_1, a_2, \ldots, a_k$ be real numbers; then

$$a_1\mathbf{x}_1 + a_2\mathbf{x}_2 + \cdots + a_k\mathbf{x}_k \qquad \text{IV.5}$$

is called a *linear combination* of $\mathbf{x}_1, \ldots \mathbf{x}_k$.

If the coefficients sum to 1, that is, if $\sum_{i=1}^{k} a_i = 1$, the expression IV.5 is called an *affine combination* of $\mathbf{x}_1, \ldots, \mathbf{x}_k$.

If $\sum_{i=1}^{k} a_i = 1$ and, in addition, each $a_i \geq 0$, then expression IV.5 is called a *weighted average* of $\mathbf{x}_1, \ldots, \mathbf{x}_k$.

Theorem IV.1 *Affine combinations are preserved under affine transformations. That is, if*

$$\mathbf{f}(\mathbf{x}_1, \ldots, \mathbf{x}_k) = a_1\mathbf{x}_1 + a_2\mathbf{x}_2 + \cdots + a_k\mathbf{x}_k$$

is an affine combination, and if A is an affine transformation, then

$$\mathbf{f}(A(\mathbf{x}_1), A(\mathbf{x}_2), \ldots, A(\mathbf{x}_k)) = A(\mathbf{f}(\mathbf{x}_1, \mathbf{x}_2, \ldots, \mathbf{x}_k)).$$

Theorem IV.1 will turn out to be very important for Bézier curves and B-splines (as defined in Chapters VII and VIII). Bézier curves and B-spline curves will be defined as affine combinations of points called "control points," and Theorem IV.1 tells us that arbitrary rotations and translations of the control points just rotate and translate the spline curves in exactly the same way.

Proof Recall from Chapter II that the affine transformation A can be written as

$$A(\mathbf{x}) = B(\mathbf{x}) + A(\mathbf{0}),$$

where B is a linear transformation. Then,

$$A(a_1\mathbf{x}_1 + a_2\mathbf{x}_2 + \cdots + a_k\mathbf{x}_k)$$
$$= B(a_1\mathbf{x}_1 + a_2\mathbf{x}_2 + \cdots + a_k\mathbf{x}_k) + A(\mathbf{0})$$
$$= a_1 B(\mathbf{x}_1) + a_2 B(\mathbf{x}_2) + \cdots + a_k B(\mathbf{x}_k) + A(\mathbf{0})$$
$$= a_1 B(\mathbf{x}_1) + a_2 B(\mathbf{x}_2) + \cdots + a_k B(\mathbf{x}_k) + \sum_{i=1}^{k} a_i A(\mathbf{0})$$
$$= a_1 B(\mathbf{x}_1) + a_1 A(\mathbf{0}) + a_2 B(\mathbf{x}_2) + a_2 A(\mathbf{0}) + \cdots + a_k B(\mathbf{x}_k) + a_k A(\mathbf{0})$$
$$= a_1 A(\mathbf{x}_1) + a_2 A(\mathbf{x}_2) + \cdots + a_k A(\mathbf{x}_k).$$

The second equality above uses the linearity of B, and the third equality uses the fact that the combination is affine. $\square$

> **Exercise IV.2**[★] *By definition, a function $\mathbf{f}(\mathbf{x})$ is preserved under affine combinations if and only if, for all α and all $\mathbf{x}_1$ and $\mathbf{x}_2$,*
>
> $$\mathbf{f}((1-\alpha)\mathbf{x}_1 + \alpha\mathbf{x}_2) = (1-\alpha)\mathbf{f}(\mathbf{x}_1) + \alpha\mathbf{f}(\mathbf{x}_2).$$
>
> *Show that any function preserved under affine combinations is an affine transformation. [Hint: Show that $\mathbf{f}(\mathbf{x}) - \mathbf{f}(\mathbf{0})$ is a linear transformation.]*

> **Exercise IV.3**[★] *Show that any vector-valued function $\mathbf{f}(\mathbf{x}_1, \mathbf{x}_2)$ preserved under affine transformations is an affine combination. [Hint: Any such function is fully determined by the value of $\mathbf{f}(\mathbf{0}, \mathbf{i})$.] Remark: This result holds also for functions $\mathbf{f}$ with more than two inputs as long as the number of inputs is at most one more than the dimension of the underlying space.*

Theorem IV.1 states that affine transformations preserve affine combinations. On the other hand, *perspective* transformations do not in general preserve affine combinations. Indeed, if we try to apply affine combinations to points expressed in homogeneous coordinates, the problem arises that it makes a difference which homogeneous coordinates are chosen to represent the points. For example, consider the points $\mathbf{v}_0 = \langle 0, 0, 0, 1 \rangle$ and the point $\mathbf{v}_1 = \langle 1, 0, 0, 1 \rangle$. The first homogeneous vector represents the origin, and the second represents the vector $\mathbf{i}$. The second vector is also equivalent to $\mathbf{v}_1' = \langle 2, 0, 0, 2 \rangle$. If we form the linear combinations

$$\tfrac{1}{2}\mathbf{v}_0 + \tfrac{1}{2}\mathbf{v}_1 = \langle \tfrac{1}{2}, 0, 0, 1 \rangle \qquad\qquad\qquad\qquad \text{IV.6}$$

and

$$\tfrac{1}{2}\mathbf{v}_0 + \tfrac{1}{2}\mathbf{v}_1' = \langle 1, 0, 0, \tfrac{3}{2} \rangle, \qquad\qquad\qquad\qquad \text{IV.7}$$

the resulting two homogeneous vectors represent *different* points in 3-space even though they are weighted averages of representations of the same points! Thus, affine combinations of points in homogeneous coordinates have a different meaning than you might expect. We return to this subject in Section IV.4, where it will be seen that the w-component of a homogeneous vector serves as an additional weighting term. We will see later that affine transformations of homogeneous representations of points can be a powerful and flexible tool for rational Bézier curves and B-splines because it allows them to define circles and other conic sections.

IV.1.3 Interpolation on Three Points: Barycentric Coordinates

Section IV.1.1 discussed linear interpolation (and extrapolation) on a line segment between points. In this section, the notion of interpolation is generalized to allow linear interpolation on a triangle.

Let $\mathbf{x}$, $\mathbf{y}$, and $\mathbf{z}$ be three noncollinear points, and thus they are the vertices of a triangle T. Recall that a point $\mathbf{u}$ is a weighted average of these three points if it is equal to

$$\mathbf{u} = \alpha\mathbf{x} + \beta\mathbf{y} + \gamma\mathbf{z}, \qquad\qquad\qquad\qquad \text{IV.8}$$

where $\alpha + \beta + \gamma = 1$ and α, β, and γ are all nonnegative. As shown below (Theorems IV.2 and IV.3), a weighted average $\mathbf{u}$ of the three vertices $\mathbf{x}, \mathbf{y}, \mathbf{z}$ will always be in or on the triangle T. Furthermore, for each $\mathbf{u}$ in the triangle, there are unique values for α, β, and γ such that Equation IV.8 holds. The values α, β, and γ are called the *barycentric coordinates* of $\mathbf{u}$.

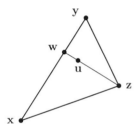

Figure IV.2. The point **u** in the interior of the triangle is on the line segment from **w** to **z**. The point **w** is a weighted average of **x** and **y**. The point **u** is a weighted average of **w** and **z**.

Theorem IV.2 *Let* **x**, **y**, **z** *be noncollinear points and let* T *be the triangle formed by these three points.*

(a) *Let* **u** *be a point on* T *or in the interior of* T. *Then* **u** *can be expressed as a weighted average of the three vertices* **x**, **y**, **z** *as in Equation IV.8 with* $\alpha, \beta, \gamma \geq 0$ *and* $\alpha + \beta + \gamma = 1$.
(b) *Let* **u** *be any point in the plane containing* T. *Then* **u** *can be expressed as an affine combination of the three vertices, as in Equation IV.8 but with only the condition* $\alpha + \beta + \gamma = 1$.

Proof (a) If **u** is on an edge of T, it is a weighted average of the two vertices on that edge. Suppose **u** is in the interior of T. Form the line containing **u** and **z**. This line intersects the opposite edge, $\overline{\mathbf{xy}}$, of T at a point **w**, as shown in Figure IV.2. Since **w** is on the line segment between **x** and **y**, it can be written as a weighted average

$$\mathbf{w} = a\mathbf{x} + b\mathbf{y},$$

where $a + b = 1$ and $a, b \geq 0$. Also, because **u** is on the line segment between **w** and **z**, it can be written as a weighted average

$$\mathbf{u} = c\mathbf{w} + d\mathbf{z},$$

where $c + d = 1$ and $c, d \geq 0$. Therefore, **u** is equal to

$$\mathbf{u} = (ac)\mathbf{x} + (bc)\mathbf{y} + d\mathbf{z},$$

and this is easily seen to be a weighted average because $ac + bc + d = 1$ and all three coefficients are nonnegative. This proves (a).

Part (b) could be proved by a method similar to the proof of (a), but instead we give a proof based on linear independence. First, note that the vectors $\mathbf{y} - \mathbf{x}$ and $\mathbf{z} - \mathbf{x}$ are linearly independent since they form two sides of a triangle and thus are noncollinear. Let P be the plane containing the triangle T: the plane P consists of the points **u** such that

$$\mathbf{u} = \mathbf{x} + \beta(\mathbf{y} - \mathbf{x}) + \gamma(\mathbf{z} - \mathbf{x}), \qquad\qquad\qquad \text{IV.9}$$

where $\beta, \gamma \in \mathbb{R}$. If we let $\alpha = (1 - \beta - \gamma)$, then **u** is equal to the affine combination $\alpha\mathbf{x} + \beta\mathbf{y} + \gamma\mathbf{z}$. $\square$

Exercise IV.4 *Let* $\mathbf{x} = \langle 0, 0 \rangle$, $\mathbf{y} = \langle 2, 3 \rangle$, *and* $\mathbf{z} = \langle 3, 1 \rangle$ *in* $\mathbb{R}^2$. *Determine the points represented by the following sets of barycentric coordinates.*

a. $\alpha = 0$, $\beta = 1$, $\gamma = 0$.
b. $\alpha = \frac{2}{3}$, $\beta = \frac{1}{3}$, $\gamma = 0$.

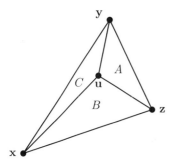

Figure IV.3. The barycentric coordinates α, β, and γ for the point **u** are proportional to the areas A, B and C.

    c. $\alpha = \frac{1}{3}$, $\beta = \frac{1}{3}$, $\gamma = \frac{1}{3}$.

    d. $\alpha = \frac{4}{5}$, $\beta = \frac{1}{10}$, $\gamma = \frac{1}{10}$.

    e. $\alpha = \frac{4}{3}$, $\beta = \frac{2}{3}$, $\gamma = -1$.

Graph your answers along with the triangle formed by **x**, **y**, *and* **z**.

The proof of part (b) of Theorem IV.2 constructed β and γ so that Equation IV.9 holds. In fact, because $\mathbf{y} - \mathbf{x}$ and $\mathbf{z} - \mathbf{x}$ are linearly independent, the values of β and γ are uniquely determined by **u**. This implies that the barycentric coordinates of **u** are unique, and so we have proved the following theorem.

Theorem IV.3 *Let* **x**, **y**, **z**, *and* T *be as in Theorem IV.2. Let* **u** *be a point in the plane containing* T. *Then there are unique values for* α, β, *and* γ *such that* $\alpha + \beta + \gamma = 1$ *and Equation IV.8 holds.*

One major application of barycentric coordinates and linear interpolation on three points is to extend the domain of a function f by linear interpolation. Suppose, as usual, that **x**, **y**, and **z** are the vertices of a triangle T and that f is a function for which we know the values of $f(\mathbf{x})$, $f(\mathbf{y})$, and $f(\mathbf{z})$. To extend f to be defined everywhere in the triangle by linear interpolation, we let

$$f(\mathbf{u}) = \alpha f(\mathbf{x}) + \beta f(\mathbf{y}) + \gamma f(\mathbf{z}),$$

where α, β, γ are the barycentric coordinates of **u**. Mathematically, this is the same computation as used in Gouraud shading based on scan line interpolation (at least, it gives the same results to within roundoff errors, which are due mostly to pixelization). The same formula can be used to linearly extrapolate f to be defined for all points **u** in the plane containing the triangle.

Area Interpretation of Barycentric Coordinates

There is a nice characterization of barycentric coordinates in terms of areas of triangles. Figure IV.3 shows a triangle with vertices **x**, **y**, and **z**. The point **u** divides the triangle into three subtriangles. The areas of these three smaller triangles are A, B, and C, and so the area of the entire triangle is equal to $A + B + C$. As the next theorem states, the barycentric coordinates of **u** are proportional to the three areas A, B, and C.

Theorem IV.4 *Suppose the situation shown in Figure IV.3 holds. Then the barycentric coordinates of* **u** *are equal to*

$$\alpha = \frac{A}{A + B + C} \qquad \beta = \frac{B}{A + B + C} \qquad \gamma = \frac{C}{A + B + C}.$$

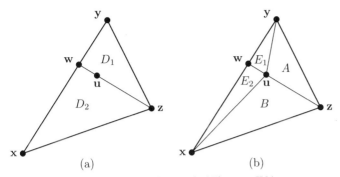

Figure IV.4. The areas used in the proof of Theorem IV.4.

Proof The proof is based on the construction used in the proof of part (a) of Theorem IV.2. In particular, recall the way the scalars a, b, c, and d were used to define the barycentric coordinates of $\mathbf{u}$. You should also refer to Figure IV.4, which shows additional areas D_1, D_2, E_1, and E_2.

As shown in part (a) of Figure IV.4, the line $\overline{\mathbf{zw}}$ divides the triangle into two subtriangles with areas D_1 and D_2. Let D be the total area of the triangle, and so $D = D_1 + D_2$. By using the usual "one-half base times height" formula for the area of a triangle with the base along the line $\overline{\mathbf{xy}}$, we have that

$$D_1 = aD \quad \text{and} \quad D_2 = bD. \qquad \qquad \text{IV.10}$$

(Recall a and b are defined so that $\mathbf{w} = a\mathbf{x} + b\mathbf{y}$.)

Part (b) of the figure shows the triangle with area D_1 further divided into two subtriangles with areas E_1 and A and the triangle with area D_2 divided into two subtriangles with areas E_2 and B. By exactly the same reasoning used for Equations IV.10, we have (recall that $\mathbf{u} = c\mathbf{w} + d\mathbf{z}$)

$$\begin{aligned} E_1 &= dD_1, \quad A = cD_1, \\ E_2 &= dD_2, \quad B = cD_2. \end{aligned} \qquad \qquad \text{IV.11}$$

Combining Equations IV.10 and IV.11 and using $C = E_1 + E_2$ and $a + b = 1$, we obtain

$$A = acD, \quad B = bcD, \quad \text{and} \quad C = dD.$$

This proves Theorem IV.4 since $D = A + B + C$ and $\alpha = ac$, $\beta = bc$, and $\gamma = d$. $\qquad \square$

Calculating Barycentric Coordinates

Now we take up the problem of how to find the barycentric coordinates of a given point $\mathbf{u}$. First consider the simpler case of 2-space, where all points lie in the xy-plane. (The harder 3-space case will be considered afterwards.) The points $\mathbf{x} = \langle x_1, x_2 \rangle$, $\mathbf{y} = \langle y_1, y_2 \rangle$, $\mathbf{z} = \langle z_1, z_2 \rangle$, and $\mathbf{u} = \langle u_1, u_2 \rangle$ are presumed to be known points. We are seeking coefficients α, β, and γ that express $\mathbf{u}$ as an affine combination of the other three points.

Recall (see Appendix A.2.1) that, in two dimensions, the (signed) area of a parallelogram with sides equal to the vectors $\mathbf{s}_1$ and $\mathbf{s}_2$ has area equal to the cross product $\mathbf{s}_1 \times \mathbf{s}_2$. Therefore, the area of the triangle shown in Figure IV.3 is equal to

$$D = \tfrac{1}{2}(\mathbf{z} - \mathbf{x}) \times (\mathbf{y} - \mathbf{x}).$$

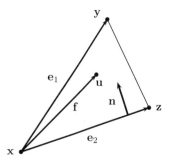

Figure IV.5. Calculating barycentric coordinates in $\mathbb{R}^3$.

Likewise, the area B is equal to

$$B = \tfrac{1}{2}(\mathbf{z} - \mathbf{x}) \times (\mathbf{u} - \mathbf{x}).$$

Thus, by Theorem IV.4,

$$\beta = \frac{(\mathbf{z} - \mathbf{x}) \times (\mathbf{u} - \mathbf{x})}{(\mathbf{z} - \mathbf{x}) \times (\mathbf{y} - \mathbf{x})}. \qquad\qquad \text{IV.12}$$

Similarly,

$$\gamma = \frac{(\mathbf{u} - \mathbf{x}) \times (\mathbf{y} - \mathbf{x})}{(\mathbf{z} - \mathbf{x}) \times (\mathbf{y} - \mathbf{x})}. \qquad\qquad \text{IV.13}$$

The barycentric coordinate α can be computed in the same way, but it is simpler just to let $\alpha = 1 - \beta - \gamma$.

Equations IV.12 and IV.13 can also be adapted for barycentric coordinates in 3-space except that you must use the *magnitudes* of the cross products instead of just the cross products. However, there is a simpler and faster method presented below by Equations IV.14 through IV.16.

To derive the better method, refer to Figure IV.5. The two sides of the triangle are given by the vectors

$$\mathbf{e}_1 = \mathbf{y} - \mathbf{x} \qquad \text{and} \qquad \mathbf{e}_2 = \mathbf{z} - \mathbf{x}.$$

In addition, the vector from $\mathbf{x}$ to $\mathbf{u}$ is $\mathbf{f} = \mathbf{u} - \mathbf{x}$. The vector $\mathbf{n}$ is the unit vector perpendicular to the side $\mathbf{e}_2$ pointing into the triangle. The vector $\mathbf{n}$ is computed by letting $\mathbf{m}$ be the component of $\mathbf{e}_1$ perpendicular to $\mathbf{e}_2$,

$$\mathbf{m} = \mathbf{e}_1 - (\mathbf{e}_1 \cdot \mathbf{e}_2)\mathbf{e}_2/e_2^2,$$

and setting $\mathbf{n} = \mathbf{m}/||\mathbf{m}||$. (The division by e_2^2 is needed since $\mathbf{e}_2$ may not be a unit vector.)

Letting $\mathbf{e}_2$ be the base of the triangle, we find that the height of the triangle is equal to $\mathbf{n} \cdot \mathbf{e}_1$. Thus, the area of the triangle is equal to

$$D = \tfrac{1}{2}(\mathbf{n} \cdot \mathbf{e}_1)||\mathbf{e}_2|| = \frac{(\mathbf{m} \cdot \mathbf{e}_1)||\mathbf{e}_2||}{2||\mathbf{m}||}.$$

Similarly, the area of the subtriangle B is equal to

$$B = \tfrac{1}{2}(\mathbf{n} \cdot \mathbf{f})||\mathbf{e}_2|| = \frac{(\mathbf{m} \cdot \mathbf{f})||\mathbf{e}_2||}{2||\mathbf{m}||}.$$

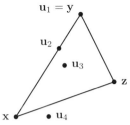

Figure IV.6. The points from Exercise IV.5.

Therefore, β is equal to

$$\beta = \frac{B}{D} = \frac{\mathbf{m} \cdot \mathbf{f}}{\mathbf{m} \cdot \mathbf{e}_1} = \frac{(\mathbf{e}_2^2 \mathbf{e}_1 - (\mathbf{e}_1 \cdot \mathbf{e}_2)\mathbf{e}_2) \cdot \mathbf{f}}{\mathbf{e}_1^2 \mathbf{e}_2^2 - (\mathbf{e}_1 \cdot \mathbf{e}_2)^2}.$$

IV.14

A similar formula holds for γ but with the roles of $\mathbf{e}_1$ and $\mathbf{e}_2$ reversed. We can further preprocess the triangle by letting

$$\mathbf{u}_\beta = \frac{\mathbf{e}_2^2 \mathbf{e}_1 - (\mathbf{e}_1 \cdot \mathbf{e}_2)\mathbf{e}_2}{\mathbf{e}_1^2 \mathbf{e}_2^2 - (\mathbf{e}_1 \cdot \mathbf{e}_2)^2} \quad \text{and} \quad \mathbf{u}_\gamma = \frac{\mathbf{e}_1^2 \mathbf{e}_2 - (\mathbf{e}_1 \cdot \mathbf{e}_2)\mathbf{e}_1}{\mathbf{e}_1^2 \mathbf{e}_2^2 - (\mathbf{e}_1 \cdot \mathbf{e}_2)^2}.$$

IV.15

Thus, the barycentric coordinates can be calculated by

$$\beta = \mathbf{u}_\beta \cdot \mathbf{f} \quad \text{and} \quad \gamma = \mathbf{u}_\gamma \cdot \mathbf{f},$$

IV.16

and of course $\alpha = 1 - \beta - \gamma$.

Note that the vectors $\mathbf{m}$ and $\mathbf{n}$ were used to derive the formulas for β and γ, but there is no need to actually compute them: instead, the vectors $\mathbf{u}_\beta$ and $\mathbf{u}_\gamma$ contain all the information necessary to compute the barycentric coordinates of the point $\mathbf{u}$ from $\mathbf{f} = \mathbf{u} - \mathbf{x}$. This allows barycentric coordinates to be computed very efficiently. A further advantage is that Equations IV.15 and IV.16 work in any dimension, not just in $\mathbb{R}^3$. When the point $\mathbf{u}$ does not lie in the plane containing the triangle, then the effect of using Equations IV.15 and IV.16 is the same as projecting $\mathbf{u}$ onto the plane containing the triangle before computing the barycentric coordinates.

Exercise IV.5 *Let* $\mathbf{x} = \langle 0, 0 \rangle$, $\mathbf{y} = \langle 2, 3 \rangle$, *and* $\mathbf{z} = \langle 3, 1 \rangle$. *Determine the barycentric coordinates of the following points (refer to Figure IV.6).*

a. $\mathbf{u}_1 = \langle 2, 3 \rangle$.
b. $\mathbf{u}_2 = \langle 1\frac{1}{3}, 2 \rangle$.
c. $\mathbf{u}_3 = \langle \frac{3}{2}, \frac{3}{2} \rangle$.
d. $\mathbf{u}_4 = \langle 1, 0 \rangle$.

Exercise IV.6★ *Generalize the notion of linear interpolation to allow interpolation between four noncoplanar points that lie in* $\mathbb{R}^3$.

IV.2 Bilinear and Trilinear Interpolation

IV.2.1 Bilinear Interpolation

The last section discussed linear interpolation between three points. However, often we would prefer to interpolate between four points that lie in a plane or on a two-dimensional surface rather than between only three points. For example, a surface may be tiled by a mesh of four-sided

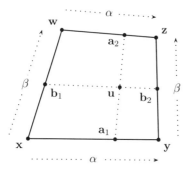

Figure IV.7. The point $\mathbf{u} = \mathbf{u}(\alpha, \beta)$ is formed by bilinear interpolation with the scalar coordinates α and β. The points $\mathbf{a}_1$ and $\mathbf{a}_2$ are obtained by interpolating with α, and $\mathbf{b}_1$ and $\mathbf{b}_2$ are obtained by interpolating with β.

polygons that are nonrectangular (or even nonplanar), but we may wish to parameterize the polygonal patches with values α and β both ranging between 0 and 1. This frequently arises when using texture maps. Another common use is in computer games such as in driving simulation games when the player follows a curved race track consisting of a series of approximately rectangular patches. The game programmer can use coordinates $\alpha, \beta \in [0, 1]$ to track the position within a given patch.

To interpolate four points, we use a method called *bilinear interpolation*. Suppose four points form a four-sided geometric patch, as pictured in Figure IV.7. Bilinear interpolation will be used to define a smooth surface; the four straight-line boundaries of the surface will be the four sides of the patch. We wish to index points on the surface with two scalar values, α and β, both ranging from 0 to 1; essentially, we are seeking a smooth mapping that has as its domain the unit square $[0, 1]^2 = [0, 1] \times [0, 1]$ and that maps the corners and the edges of the unit square to the vertices and the boundary edges of the patch. The value of α corresponds to the x-coordinate and that of β to the y-coordinate of a point $\mathbf{u}$ on the surface patch.

The definition of the bilinear interpolation function is as follows:

$$
\begin{aligned}
\mathbf{u} &= (1 - \beta) \cdot [(1 - \alpha)\mathbf{x} + \alpha\mathbf{y}] + \beta \cdot [(1 - \alpha)\mathbf{w} + \alpha\mathbf{z}] \\
&= (1 - \alpha) \cdot [(1 - \beta)\mathbf{x} + \beta\mathbf{w}] + \alpha \cdot [(1 - \beta)\mathbf{y} + \beta\mathbf{z}] \\
&= (1 - \alpha)(1 - \beta)\mathbf{x} + \alpha(1 - \beta)\mathbf{y} + \alpha\beta\mathbf{z} + (1 - \alpha)\beta\mathbf{w}.
\end{aligned}
\tag{IV.17}
$$

For $0 \leq \alpha \leq 1$ and $0 \leq \beta \leq 1$, this defines $\mathbf{u}$ as a weighted average of the vertices $\mathbf{x}$, $\mathbf{y}$, $\mathbf{z}$, and $\mathbf{w}$. We sometimes write $\mathbf{u}$ as $\mathbf{u}(\alpha, \beta)$ to indicate its dependence on α and β.

We defined bilinear interpolation with three equivalent equations in IV.17 to stress that bilinear interpolation can be viewed as linear interpolation with respect to α followed by linear interpolation with respect to β or, vice versa, as interpolation first with β and then with α. Thus, the first two lines of Equation IV.17 can be rewritten as

$$
\begin{aligned}
\mathbf{u} &= \text{lerp}(\,\text{lerp}(\mathbf{x}, \mathbf{y}, \alpha),\, \text{lerp}(\mathbf{w}, \mathbf{z}, \alpha),\, \beta) \\
&= \text{lerp}(\,\text{lerp}(\mathbf{x}, \mathbf{w}, \beta),\, \text{lerp}(\mathbf{y}, \mathbf{z}, \beta),\, \alpha).
\end{aligned}
\tag{IV.18}
$$

Bilinear interpolation may be used to interpolate the values of a function f. If the values of f are fixed at the four vertices, then bilinear interpolation is used to set the value of f at the point $\mathbf{u}$ obtained by Equation IV.17 to

$$
f(\mathbf{u}) = (1 - \alpha)(1 - \beta)f(\mathbf{x}) + \alpha(1 - \beta)f(\mathbf{y}) + \alpha\beta f(\mathbf{z}) + (1 - \alpha)\beta f(\mathbf{w}).
$$

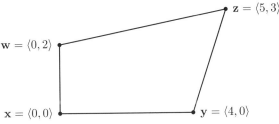

Figure IV.8. Figure for Exercise IV.7.

Exercise IV.7 *Let* $\mathbf{x} = \langle 0, 0 \rangle$, $\mathbf{y} = \langle 4, 0 \rangle$, $\mathbf{z} = \langle 5, 3 \rangle$, *and* $\mathbf{w} = \langle 0, 2 \rangle$, *as in Figure IV.8. For each of the following values of* α *and* β, *what point is obtained by bilinear interpolation? Graph your answers.*

a. $\alpha = 1$ *and* $\beta = 0$.

b. $\alpha = \frac{1}{3}$ *and* $\beta = 1$.

c. $\alpha = \frac{1}{2}$ *and* $\beta = \frac{1}{4}$.

d. $\alpha = \frac{2}{3}$ *and* $\beta = \frac{1}{3}$.

Equation IV.17 defining bilinear interpolation makes sense for an arbitrary set of vertices $\mathbf{x}$, $\mathbf{y}$, $\mathbf{z}$, $\mathbf{w}$. If the four vertices are coplanar and lie in a plane P, the bilinearly interpolated points $\mathbf{u}(\alpha, \beta)$ clearly lie in the same plane because they are weighted averages of the four vertices. If, on the other hand, the four vertices are not coplanar and are positioned arbitrarily in $\mathbb{R}^3$, then the points $\mathbf{u} = \mathbf{u}(\alpha, \beta)$ obtained by bilinear interpolation with $\alpha, \beta \in [0, 1]$ form a four-sided "patch," that is, a four-sided surface. The sides of the patch will be straight line segments, but the interior of the patch may be curved.

Exercise IV.8 *Suppose a surface patch in* $\mathbb{R}^3$ *is defined by bilinearly interpolating from four vertices. Derive the following formulas for the partial derivatives of* $\mathbf{u}$:

$$\frac{\partial \mathbf{u}}{\partial \alpha} = (1 - \beta)(\mathbf{y} - \mathbf{x}) + \beta(\mathbf{z} - \mathbf{w}) \qquad\qquad \text{IV.19}$$

$$\frac{\partial \mathbf{u}}{\partial \beta} = (1 - \alpha)(\mathbf{w} - \mathbf{x}) + \alpha(\mathbf{z} - \mathbf{y}).$$

In addition, give the formula for the normal vector to the patch at a point $\mathbf{u} = \mathbf{u}(\alpha, \beta)$.

Usually, bilinear interpolation uses vertices that are not coplanar but are not too far away from a planar, convex quadrilateral. A mathematical way to describe this is to say that a plane P exists such that, when the four vertices are orthogonally projected onto the plane, the result is a convex, planar quadrilateral. We call this condition the "projected convexity condition":

Projected Convexity Condition: *The projected convexity condition holds provided there exists a plane* P *such that the projection of the points* $\mathbf{x}$, $\mathbf{y}$, $\mathbf{z}$, $\mathbf{w}$ *onto the plane* P *are the vertices of a convex quadrilateral with the four vertices being in counterclockwise or clockwise order.*

To check that the projected convexity condition holds for a given plane, choose a unit vector $\mathbf{n}$ normal to the plane and assume, without loss of generality, that the plane contains the origin. Then project the four points onto the plane, yielding four points $\mathbf{x}_P$, $\mathbf{y}_P$, $\mathbf{z}_P$, and $\mathbf{w}_P$ by using the following formula (see Appendix A.2.2):

$$\mathbf{x}_P = \mathbf{x} - (\mathbf{n} \cdot \mathbf{x})\mathbf{n}.$$

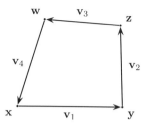

Figure IV.9. The vectors $\mathbf{v}_i$ are the directed edges around the quadrilateral.

Then check that the interior angles of the resulting quadrilateral are less than $180°$. (We discuss convexity more in Section IV.3, but for now we can take this test as being the definition of a convex quadrilateral.)

A mathematically equivalent method of checking whether the projected convexity condition holds for a plane with unit normal $\mathbf{n}$ is as follows. First define the four edge vectors by

$$\mathbf{v}_1 = \mathbf{y} - \mathbf{x}$$

$$\mathbf{v}_2 = \mathbf{z} - \mathbf{y}$$

$$\mathbf{v}_3 = \mathbf{w} - \mathbf{z}$$

$$\mathbf{v}_4 = \mathbf{x} - \mathbf{w}.$$

These give the edges in circular order around the quadrilateral, as shown Figure IV.9. The condition that the interior angles of the projected quadrilateral are less than $180°$ is equivalent to the condition that the four values

$$(\mathbf{v}_1 \times \mathbf{v}_2) \cdot \mathbf{n} \qquad (\mathbf{v}_3 \times \mathbf{v}_4) \cdot \mathbf{n}$$

$$(\mathbf{v}_2 \times \mathbf{v}_3) \cdot \mathbf{n} \qquad (\mathbf{v}_4 \times \mathbf{v}_1) \cdot \mathbf{n} \qquad\qquad \text{IV.20}$$

are either all positive or all negative. To verify this, suppose we view the plane down the normal vector $\mathbf{n}$. If the four values from IV.20 are all positive, then the projected vertices are in counterclockwise order. When the four values are all negative, the projected vertices are in clockwise order.

> **Exercise IV.9** *Prove that the values $(\mathbf{v}_i \times \mathbf{v}_j) \cdot \mathbf{n}$ are equal to $\ell_i \cdot \ell_j \sin\theta$ where ℓ_i is the magnitude of the projection of $\mathbf{v}_i$ onto the plane P and where θ is the angle between the projections of $\mathbf{v}_i$ and $\mathbf{v}_j$.*

The projected convexity condition turns out to be very useful, for instance, in the proof of Corollary IV.7 and for solving Exercise IV.10. Thus, it is a pleasant surprise that the projected convexity condition nearly always holds; indeed, it holds for *any* set of four noncoplanar vertices.

Theorem IV.5 *Suppose that $\mathbf{x}$, $\mathbf{y}$, $\mathbf{z}$, and $\mathbf{w}$ are not coplanar. Then the projected convexity condition is satisfied.*

Proof We call the two line segments $\overline{\mathbf{xz}}$ and $\overline{\mathbf{yw}}$ the *diagonals*. With reference to Figure IV.10, let $\mathbf{a}$ be the midpoint of the diagonal $\overline{\mathbf{xz}}$ so that $\mathbf{a} = \frac{1}{2}(\mathbf{x} + \mathbf{z})$. Likewise, let $\mathbf{b}$ be the midpoint of the other diagonal. The points $\mathbf{a}$ and $\mathbf{b}$ must be distinct, for otherwise the two diagonals would intersect and the four vertices would all lie in the plane containing the diagonals, contradicting the hypothesis of the theorem.

Form the unit vector $\mathbf{n}$ in the direction from $\mathbf{a}$ to $\mathbf{b}$, that is,

$$\mathbf{n} = \frac{\mathbf{b} - \mathbf{a}}{||\mathbf{b} - \mathbf{a}||}.$$

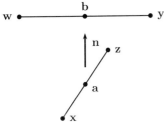

Figure IV.10. The line segments $\overline{\mathbf{xz}}$ and $\overline{\mathbf{yw}}$ have midpoints $\mathbf{a}$ and $\mathbf{b}$. The vector $\mathbf{n}$ is the unit vector in the direction from $\mathbf{a}$ to $\mathbf{b}$.

Let P be the plane containing the origin and perpendicular to $\mathbf{n}$, and consider the orthogonal projection of the four vertices onto P. The midpoints $\mathbf{a}$ and $\mathbf{b}$ project onto the same point of P because of the way $\mathbf{n}$ was chosen. Also, the projections of the two diagonals cannot be collinear, for otherwise all four vertices would lie in the plane that contains the projections of the diagonals and is perpendicular to P. That is, the projections of the diagonals are two line segments that cross each other (intersect in their interiors), as shown in Figure IV.11. In particular, neither diagonal projects onto a single point. The projections of the four vertices are the four endpoints of the projections of the diagonals. Clearly they form a convex quadrilateral with the vertices being in clockwise or counterclockwise order. □

For convex, planar quadrilaterals, we have the following theorem.

Theorem IV.6 *Let* $\mathbf{x}, \mathbf{y}, \mathbf{z}, \mathbf{w}$ *be the vertices of a planar, convex quadrilateral in counterclockwise (or clockwise) order. Then the bilinear interpolation mapping*

$$\langle \alpha, \beta \rangle \mapsto \mathbf{u}(\alpha, \beta)$$

is a one-to-one map from $[0, 1] \times [0, 1]$ *onto the quadrilateral.*

Proof We give a quick informal proof. If the value of β is fixed, then the second line in Equation IV.17 or IV.18 shows that the function $\mathbf{u}(\alpha, \beta)$ is just equal to the result of using α to interpolate linearly along the line segment L_β joining the two points

$$(1 - \beta)\mathbf{x} + \beta\mathbf{w} \quad \text{and} \quad (1 - \beta)\mathbf{y} + \beta\mathbf{z}.$$

These two points lie on opposite edges of the quadrilateral and thus are distinct. Furthermore, for $\beta \neq \beta'$, the two line segments L_β and $L_{\beta'}$ do not intersect, as may be seen by inspection of Figure IV.12. This uses the fact that the interior angles of the quadrilateral measure less than $180°$. Therefore, if $\beta \neq \beta'$, then $\mathbf{u}(\alpha, \beta) \neq \mathbf{u}(\alpha', \beta')$, since L_β and $L_{\beta'}$ are disjoint. On the other hand, if $\beta = \beta'$, but $\alpha \neq \alpha'$, then again $\mathbf{u}(\alpha, \beta) \neq \mathbf{u}(\alpha', \beta')$ because they are distinct points on the the line L_β.

To verify that the map is onto, note that the line segments L_β sweep across the quadrilateral as β varies from 0 to 1. Therefore, any $\mathbf{u}$ in the quadrilateral lies on some L_β. □

Figure IV.13 shows an example of how Theorem IV.6 fails for planar quadrilaterals that are not convex. The figure shows a sample line L_β that is not entirely inside the quadrilateral;

Figure IV.11. The projections of the two diagonals onto the plane P are noncollinear and intersect at their midpoints at the common projection of $\mathbf{a}$ and $\mathbf{b}$. The four projected vertices form a convex quadrilateral.

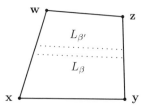

Figure IV.12. Since the polygon is convex, distinct values β and β' give nonintersecting "horizontal" line segments.

thus, the range of the bilinear interpolation map is not contained inside the quadrilateral. Furthermore, the bilinear interpolation map is not one-to-one; for instance, the point where the segments L_β and $\overline{\mathbf{zw}}$ intersect has two sets of bilinear coordinates.

However, the next corollary states that Theorem IV.6 does apply to any set of four noncoplanar points.

Corollary IV.7 *Suppose* $\mathbf{x}$, $\mathbf{y}$, $\mathbf{z}$, *and* $\mathbf{w}$ *are not coplanar. Then the function* $\mathbf{u}(\alpha, \beta)$ *is a one-to-one map on the domain* $[0, 1] \times [0, 1]$.

Proof By Theorem IV.5, the projected convexity condition holds for some plane P. Without loss of generality, the plane P is the xy-plane. The bilinear interpolation function $\mathbf{u}(\alpha, \beta)$ operates independently on the x-, y-, and z-components of the vertices. Therefore, by Theorem IV.6, the projection of the values of $\mathbf{u}(\alpha, \beta)$ onto the xy-plane is a one-to-one function from $[0, 1]^2$ into the xy-plane. It follows immediately that the function $\mathbf{u}(\alpha, \beta)$ is one-to-one. $\qquad\square$

Exercise IV.10★ *Let the vertices* $\mathbf{x}$, $\mathbf{y}$, $\mathbf{z}$, $\mathbf{w}$ *be four points in* $\mathbb{R}^3$ *and suppose that the projected convexity condition holds. Prove that*

$$\frac{\partial \mathbf{u}}{\partial \alpha} \times \frac{\partial \mathbf{u}}{\partial \beta}$$

is nonzero for all $\alpha, \beta \in [0, 1]$. *Conclude that this defines a nonzero vector normal to the surface. [Hint: Refer back to Exercise IV.8 on page 109. Prove that the cross product is equal to*

$$\alpha(1 - \beta)\mathbf{v}_1 \times \mathbf{v}_2 + \alpha\beta\mathbf{v}_2 \times \mathbf{v}_3 + (1 - \alpha)\beta\mathbf{v}_3 \times \mathbf{v}_4 + (1 - \alpha)(1 - \beta)\mathbf{v}_4 \times \mathbf{v}_1,$$

and use the fact that $(\mathbf{v}_i \times \mathbf{v}_j) \cdot \mathbf{n}$, *for* $j = (i \bmod 4) + 1$, *all have the same sign, for* $\mathbf{n}$ *normal to the plane from the projected convexity condition.]*

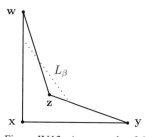

Figure IV.13. An example of the failure of Theorem IV.6 for nonconvex, planar quadrilaterals.

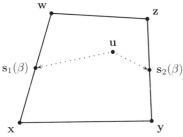

Figure IV.14. The three points $\mathbf{s}_1(\beta)$, $\mathbf{u}$, and $\mathbf{s}_2(\beta)$ will be collinear for the correct value of β. The value of β shown in the figure is smaller than the correct β coordinate of $\mathbf{u}$.

IV.2.2 Inverting Bilinear Interpolation

We now discuss how to invert bilinear interpolation. For this, we are given the four vertices $\mathbf{x}$, $\mathbf{y}$, $\mathbf{z}$, and $\mathbf{w}$, which are assumed to form a convex quadrilateral in a plane.[2] Without loss of generality, the points lie in $\mathbb{R}^2$, and so $\mathbf{x} = \langle x_1, x_2 \rangle$, and so on. In addition, we are given a point $\mathbf{u} = \langle u_1, u_2 \rangle$ in the interior of the quadrilateral formed by these four points. The problem is to find the values of $\alpha, \beta \in [0, 1]$ so that $\mathbf{u}$ satisfies the defining equation IV.17 for bilinear interpolation.

Our algorithm for inverting bilinear interpolation will be based on vectors. Let $\mathbf{s}_1 = \mathbf{w} - \mathbf{x}$ and $\mathbf{s}_2 = \mathbf{z} - \mathbf{y}$. Then let

$$\mathbf{s}_1(\beta) = \mathbf{x} + \beta \mathbf{s}_1 \qquad \text{and} \qquad \mathbf{s}_2(\beta) = \mathbf{y} + \beta \mathbf{s}_2,$$

as shown in Figure IV.14. To solve for the value of β, it is enough to find β such that $0 \le \beta \le 1$ and such that the three points $\mathbf{s}_1(\beta)$, $\mathbf{u}$, and $\mathbf{s}_2(\beta)$ are collinear.

Referring to Appendix A.2.1, we recall that two vectors in $\mathbb{R}^2$ are collinear if, and only if, their cross product is equal to zero.[3] Thus, for the three points to be collinear, we must have

$$
\begin{aligned}
0 &= (\mathbf{s}_1(\beta) - \mathbf{u}) \times (\mathbf{s}_2(\beta) - \mathbf{u}) \\
&= (\beta \mathbf{s}_1 - (\mathbf{u} - \mathbf{x})) \times (\beta \mathbf{s}_2 - (\mathbf{u} - \mathbf{y})) && \text{IV.21} \\
&= (\mathbf{s}_1 \times \mathbf{s}_2)\beta^2 + [\mathbf{s}_2 \times (\mathbf{u} - \mathbf{x}) - \mathbf{s}_1 \times (\mathbf{u} - \mathbf{y})]\beta + (\mathbf{u} - \mathbf{x}) \times (\mathbf{u} - \mathbf{y}).
\end{aligned}
$$

This quadratic equation can readily be solved for the desired value of β. In general, there will be two roots of the quadratic equation. To find these, let A, B, and C be the coefficients of β^2, β, and 1 in Equation IV.21, namely,

$$A = \mathbf{s}_1 \times \mathbf{s}_2 = (\mathbf{w} - \mathbf{x}) \times (\mathbf{z} - \mathbf{y})$$

$$B = (\mathbf{z} - \mathbf{y}) \times (\mathbf{u} - \mathbf{x}) - (\mathbf{w} - \mathbf{x}) \times (\mathbf{u} - \mathbf{y})$$

$$C = (\mathbf{u} - \mathbf{x}) \times (\mathbf{u} - \mathbf{y}).$$

The two roots of IV.21 are

$$\beta = \frac{-B \pm \sqrt{B^2 - 4AC}}{2A}. \qquad\qquad \text{IV.22}$$

---

[2] At the end of this section, we discuss how to modify the algorithm to work in three dimensions.

[3] Recall that the cross product for 2-vectors is defined to be the scalar value

$$\langle v_1, v_2 \rangle \times \langle w_1, w_2 \rangle = v_1 w_2 - v_2 w_1.$$

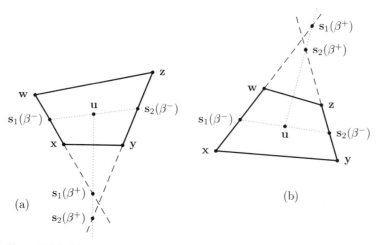

Figure IV.15. The two possibilities for the sign of $\mathbf{s}_1 \times \mathbf{s}_2$. In (a), $\mathbf{s}_1 \times \mathbf{s}_2 < 0$; in (b), $\mathbf{s}_1 \times \mathbf{s}_2 > 0$. In each case, there are two values for β where the points $\mathbf{s}_1(\beta)$, $\mathbf{s}_2(\beta)$, and $\mathbf{u}$ are collinear. The values β^+ and β^- are the solutions to Equation IV.22 obtained with the indicated choice of plus or minus sign. For (a) and (b), $\beta = \beta^-$ is between 0 and 1 and is the desired root.

There remains the question of which of the two roots is the right value for β. Of course, one way to decide this is to use the root between 0 and 1. But we can improve on this and avoid having to test the roots to see if they are between 0 and 1.[4] In fact, we will see that the right root is *always* the root

$$\beta = \frac{-B - \sqrt{B^2 - 4AC}}{2A}. \qquad\qquad \text{IV.23}$$

To prove this, consider the two cases $\mathbf{s}_1 \times \mathbf{s}_2 < 0$ and $\mathbf{s}_1 \times \mathbf{s}_2 > 0$ separately. (The case $\mathbf{s}_1 \times \mathbf{s}_2 = 0$ will be discussed later.) First, assume that $\mathbf{s}_1 \times \mathbf{s}_2 < 0$. This situation is shown in Figure IV.15(a), where the two vectors $\mathbf{s}_1$ and $\mathbf{s}_2$ are diverging, or pointing away, from each other since the angle from $\mathbf{s}_1$ to $\mathbf{s}_2$ must be negative if the cross product is negative. As shown in Figure IV.15(a), there are two values, β^- and β^+, where $\mathbf{s}_1(\beta)$, $\mathbf{u}$, and $\mathbf{s}_2(\beta)$ are collinear. The undesired root of Equation IV.21 occurs with a negative value of β, namely $\beta = \beta^+$, as shown in the figure. So in the case where $\mathbf{s}_1 \times \mathbf{s}_2 < 0$, the larger root of IV.22 is the correct one. And since the denominator $A = \mathbf{s}_1 \times \mathbf{s}_2$ of IV.22 is negative, the larger root is obtained by taking the negative sign in the numerator.

Now assume that $\mathbf{s}_1 \times \mathbf{s}_2 > 0$. This case is shown in Figure IV.15(b). In this case, the undesired root of Equation IV.21 is greater than 1; therefore, the desired root is the smaller of the two roots. Since the denominator is positive in this case, we again need to choose the negative sign in the numerator of IV.22.

This almost completes the mathematical description of how to compute the value of β. However, there is one further modification to be made to make the computation more stable. It is well known (c.f. (Higman, 1996)) that the usual formulation of the quadratic formula can be computationally unstable. This can happen to the formula IV.23 if value of B is negative and if B^2 is much larger than $4AC$, since the numerator will be computed as the difference of

[4] The problem with testing for being between 0 and 1 is that roundoff error may cause the desired root to be slightly less than 0 or slightly greater than 1. In addition, if one is concerned about minor differences in computation time, then comparison between real numbers can actually be slightly slower than other operations on real numbers.

two large numbers that mostly cancel out to yield a value close to 0. In this case, a more stable computation can be performed by using the formula

$$\beta = \frac{2C}{-B + \sqrt{B^2 - 4AC}}.$$ IV.24

This formula is equivalent to IV.23, as can be seen by multiplying both the numerator and denominator of IV.23 by $(-B + \sqrt{B^2 - 4AC})$, and it has the advantage of being computationally more stable when B is negative.

Once the value of β has been obtained, it is straightforward to find the value of α, since $\mathbf{u}$ is now the weighted average of $\mathbf{s}_1(\beta)$ and $\mathbf{s}_2(\beta)$. This can be done by just setting

$$\alpha = \frac{(\mathbf{u} - \mathbf{s}_1(\beta)) \cdot (\mathbf{s}_2(\beta) - \mathbf{s}_1(\beta))}{(\mathbf{s}_2(\beta) - \mathbf{s}_1(\beta))^2}$$

because this is the ratio of the distance from $\mathbf{s}_1(\beta)$ to $\mathbf{u}$ to the distance from $\mathbf{s}_1(\beta)$ to $\mathbf{s}_2(\beta)$. (See also Equation IV.3 on page 100.)

We now can present the algorithm for inverting bilinear interpolation. The input to the algorithm is five points in $\mathbb{R}^2$. For reliable results, the points $\mathbf{x}$, $\mathbf{y}$, $\mathbf{z}$, $\mathbf{w}$ should be the vertices of a convex quadrilateral, and $\mathbf{u}$ should be on or inside the quadrilateral.

```
// x, y, x, w, u lie in the plane R²
BilinearInvert( u, x, y, z, w ) {
    Set A = (w − x) × (z − y);
    Set B = (z − y) × (u − x) − (w − x) × (u − y);
    Set C = (u − x) × (u − y);
    If ( B > 0 ) {
        Set β = (−B − √(B² − 4AC)) / 2A ;
    }
    Else {
        Set β = 2C / (−B + √(B² − 4AC)) ;
    }
    Set s₁,β = (1 − β)x + βw;
    Set s₂,β = (1 − β)y + βz;
    Set α = ((u − s₁,β) · (s₂,β − s₁,β)) / (s₂,β − s₁,β)² ;
    Return α and β as the bilinear interpolation inverse.
}
```

We have omitted so far discussing the case where $A = \mathbf{s}_1 \times \mathbf{s}_2 = 0$: this happens whenever $\mathbf{s}_1$ and $\mathbf{s}_2$ are collinear so that the left and right sides of the quadrilateral are parallel. When A equals 0, the quadratic equation IV.21 becomes the linear equation $B\beta + C = 0$ with only one root, namely, $\beta = -C/B$. Thus, it would be fine to modify the preceding algorithm to test whether $A = 0$ and, if so, compute $\beta = -C/B$. However, the algorithm above will actually work correctly as written even when $A = 0$. To see this, note that, if $A = 0$, the left and right sides are parallel, so $(\mathbf{w} - \mathbf{x}) \times (\mathbf{u} - \mathbf{y}) \geq 0$ and $(\mathbf{z} - \mathbf{y}) \times (\mathbf{u} - \mathbf{x}) \leq 0$ since $\mathbf{u}$ is in the polygon. Furthermore, for a proper polygon these cross products are not both zero. Therefore, $B < 0$ and the algorithm above computes β according to the second case, which is mathematically equivalent to computing $-C/B$ and avoids the risk of a divide by zero.

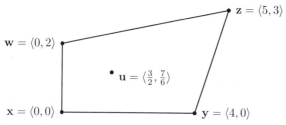

Figure IV.16. Figure for Exercise IV.11.

Exercise IV.11 *Let* $\mathbf{x} = \langle 0, 0 \rangle$, $\mathbf{y} = \langle 4, 0 \rangle$, $\mathbf{z} = \langle 5, 3 \rangle$, $\mathbf{w} = \langle 0, 2 \rangle$, *and* $\mathbf{u} = \langle \frac{3}{2}, \frac{7}{6} \rangle$, *as in Figure IV.16. What are the bilinear coordinates,* α *and* β, *of* $\mathbf{u}$?

Now we generalize the bilinear inversion algorithm to work in three dimensions instead of two. The key idea is that we just need to choose two orthogonal axes and project the problem onto those two axes, reducing the problem back to the two-dimensional case. For this, we start by choosing a unit vector $\mathbf{n}$ such that the projected convexity condition holds for a plane perpendicular to $\mathbf{n}$. To choose $\mathbf{n}$, you should *not* use the vector from the proof of Theorem IV.5, as this may give a poorly conditioned problem and lead to unstable computations. Indeed, this would give disastrous results if the points $\mathbf{x}, \mathbf{y}, \mathbf{z}$, and $\mathbf{w}$ were coplanar and would give unstable results if they were close to coplanar. Instead, in most applications, a better choice for $\mathbf{n}$ would be the vector

$$\frac{(\mathbf{z} - \mathbf{x}) \times (\mathbf{w} - \mathbf{y})}{\|(\mathbf{z} - \mathbf{x}) \times (\mathbf{w} - \mathbf{y})\|}.$$

Actually, it will turn out that there is no need to make $\mathbf{n}$ a unit vector, and so it is computationally easier just to set $\mathbf{n}$ to be the vector

$$\mathbf{n} = (\mathbf{z} - \mathbf{x}) \times (\mathbf{w} - \mathbf{y}). \qquad\qquad \text{IV.25}$$

This choice for $\mathbf{n}$ is likely to work well in most applications. In particular, if this choice for $\mathbf{n}$ does not give a plane satisfying the projected convexity condition, then the patches are probably poorly chosen and are certainly not very patchlike.

In some cases there are easier ways to choose $\mathbf{n}$. A common application of patches is to define a terrain or, more generally, a surface that does not vary too much from horizontal. In this case, the "up"-direction vector, say $\mathbf{j}$, can be used for the vector $\mathbf{n}$.

Once we have chosen the vector $\mathbf{n}$, we can convert the problem into a two-dimensional one by projecting onto a plane P orthogonal to $\mathbf{n}$. Fortunately, it is unnecessary to actually choose coordinate axes for P and project the five points $\mathbf{u}, \mathbf{x}, \mathbf{y}, \mathbf{z}$, and $\mathbf{w}$ onto P. Instead, we only need the three scalar values A, B, and C, and to compute these, it is mathematically equivalent to use the formulas in the `BilinearInvert` routine but then take the dot product with $\mathbf{n}$.

To summarize, the bilinear inversion algorithm for points in $\mathbb{R}^3$ is the same as the `BilinearInvert` program as given on page 115, except that now $\mathbf{u}, \mathbf{x}, \mathbf{y}, \mathbf{z}$, and $\mathbf{w}$ are vectors in $\mathbb{R}^3$, and the first three lines of the program are replaced by the following four lines:

Set $\mathbf{n} = (\mathbf{z} - \mathbf{x}) \times (\mathbf{w} - \mathbf{y})$;
Set $A = \mathbf{n} \cdot ((\mathbf{w} - \mathbf{x}) \times (\mathbf{z} - \mathbf{y}))$;
Set $B = \mathbf{n} \cdot ((\mathbf{z} - \mathbf{y}) \times (\mathbf{u} - \mathbf{x}) - (\mathbf{w} - \mathbf{x}) \times (\mathbf{u} - \mathbf{y}))$;
Set $C = \mathbf{n} \cdot ((\mathbf{u} - \mathbf{x}) \times (\mathbf{u} - \mathbf{y}))$;

The rest of `BilinearInvert` is unchanged. Other choices for $\mathbf{n}$ are possible too: the important point is that the projected convexity condition should hold robustly.

IV.2.3 Trilinear Interpolation

Trilinear interpolation is a generalization of bilinear interpolation to three dimensions. For trilinear interpolation, we are given eight points $x_{i,j,k}$, where $i, j, k \in \{0, 1\}$. Our goal is to define a smooth map $\mathbf{u}(\alpha, \beta, \gamma)$ from the unit cube $[0, 1]^3$ into 3-space so that $\mathbf{u}(i, j, k) = x_{i,j,k}$ for all $i, j, k \in \{0, 1\}$. The intent is that the eight points $x_{i,j,k}$ are roughly in the positions of the vertices of a rectangular prism and that the map $\mathbf{u}(\alpha, \beta, \gamma)$ should be a smooth interpolation function.

For trilinear interpolation, we define

$$\mathbf{u}(\alpha, \beta, \gamma) = \sum_{i,j,k} w_i(\alpha) w_j(\beta) w_k(\gamma) x_{i,j,k},$$

where the summation runs over all $i, j, k \in \{0, 1\}$, and where the values $w_n(\delta)$, for $n \in \{0, 1\}$, are defined by

$$w_n(\delta) = \begin{cases} 1 - \delta & \text{if } n = 0 \\ \delta & \text{if } n = 1. \end{cases}$$

Trilinear interpolation can also be used to interpolate the values of a function. Suppose a function f has its values specified at the vertices so that $f(x_{i,j,k})$ is fixed for all eight vertices. Then, we extend f to the unit cube $[0, 1]^3$ through trilinear interpolation by letting

$$f(\mathbf{u}(\alpha, \beta, \gamma)) = \sum_{i,j,k} w_i(\alpha) w_j(\beta) w_k(\gamma) f(x_{i,j,k}).$$

To the best of our knowledge, there is no good way to invert trilinear interpolation in closed form. However, it is possible to use an iterative method based on Newton's method to invert trilinear interpolation quickly.

IV.3 Convex Sets and Weighted Averages

The notion of a convex quadrilateral has already been discussed in the sections above. This section introduces the definition of convexity for general sets of points and proves that a set is convex if and only if it is closed under the operation of taking weighted averages.

The intuitive notion of a convex set is that it is a fully "filled in" region with no "holes" or missing interior points and that there are no places where the boundary bends inward and back outward. Figure IV.17 shows examples of convex and nonconvex sets in the plane. Nonconvex sets have the property that it is possible to find a line segment that has endpoints in the set but is not entirely contained in the set.

Definition Let A be a set of points (in R^d for some dimension d). The set A is *convex* if and only if the following condition holds: for any two points $\mathbf{x}$ and $\mathbf{y}$ in A, the line segment joining $\mathbf{x}$ and $\mathbf{y}$ is a subset of A.

Some simple examples of convex sets include: (a) any line segment, (b) any line or ray, (c) any plane or half-plane, (d) any half-space, (e) any linear subspace of $\mathbb{R}^d$, (f) the entire space $\mathbb{R}^d$, (g) any ball (i.e., a circle or sphere plus its interior), (h) the interior of a triangle or parallelogram, and so on. It is easy to check that the intersection of two convex sets must be convex. In fact, the intersection of an arbitrary collection of convex sets is convex. (You should supply a proof of this!) However, the union of two convex sets is not always convex.

Definition Let A be a set of points in $\mathbb{R}^d$. The *convex hull* of A is the smallest convex set containing A.

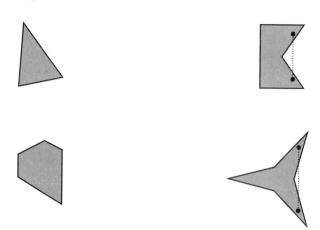

Figure IV.17. The shaded regions represent sets. The two sets on the left are convex, and the two sets on the right are not convex. The dotted lines show line segments with endpoints in the set that are not entirely contained in the set.

Every set A has a smallest enclosing convex set. In fact, if S is the set of convex sets containing A, then the intersection $\bigcap S$ of these sets is convex and contains A. It is therefore the smallest convex set containing A. (Note that the set S is nonempty because the whole space $\mathbb{R}^d$ is a convex set containing A.) Therefore, the notion of a convex hull is well-defined, and every set of points has a convex hull.

There is another, equivalent definition of *convex* that is sometimes used in place of the definition given above. Namely, a set is convex if and only if it is equal to the intersection of some set of half-spaces. In $\mathbb{R}^3$, a *half-space* is a set that lies on one side of a plane, or more precisely, a half-space is a set of the form $\{\mathbf{x} : \mathbf{n} \cdot \mathbf{x} > a\}$ for some nonzero vector $\mathbf{n}$ and scalar a. With this definition of convex set, the convex hull of A is the set of points that lie in every half-space that contains A. Equivalently, a point $\mathbf{y}$ is *not* in the convex hull of A if and only if there is a half-space such that A lies entirely in the half-space and y is not in the half-space.

It should be intuitively clear that the definition of convex hulls in terms of intersections of half-spaces is equivalent to our definition of convex hulls in terms of line segments. However, giving a formal proof that these two definitions of convexity are equivalent is fairly difficult: the proof is beyond the scope of this book, but the reader can find a proof in the texts (Grünbaum, 1967) or (Ziegler, 1995). (You might want to try your hand at proving this equivalence in dimensions 2 and 3 to get a feel for what is involved in the proof.) We have adopted the definition based on line segments since it makes it easy to prove that the convex hull of a set A is precisely the set of points that can be expressed as weighted averages of points from A.

Definition Let A be a set and $\mathbf{x}$ a point. We say that $\mathbf{x}$ is a weighted average of points in A if and only if there is a *finite* set of points $\mathbf{y}_1, \ldots, \mathbf{y}_k$ in A such that $\mathbf{x}$ is equal to a weighted average of $\mathbf{y}_1, \ldots, \mathbf{y}_k$.

Theorem IV.8 *Let A be a set of points. The convex hull of A is precisely the set of points that are weighted averages of points in A.*

Proof Let $WA(A)$ be the set of points that are weighted averages of points in A. We first prove that $WA(A)$ is convex, and since $A \subseteq WA(A)$, this implies that the convex hull of A is a subset of $WA(A)$. Let $\mathbf{y}$ and $\mathbf{z}$ be points in $WA(A)$. We wish to prove that the line segment between these points is also contained in $WA(A)$. Since this line segment is just the set of points that are weighted averages of $\mathbf{y}$ and $\mathbf{z}$, it is enough to show that if $0 \leq \alpha \leq 1$ and $\mathbf{w} = (1 - \alpha)\mathbf{y} + \alpha\mathbf{z}$, then $\mathbf{w}$ is in $WA(A)$. Since $\mathbf{y}$ and $\mathbf{z}$ are weighted averages of points in A, they are equal to

$$\mathbf{y} = \sum_{i=1}^{k} \beta_i \mathbf{x}_i \quad \text{and} \quad \mathbf{z} = \sum_{i=1}^{k} \gamma_i \mathbf{x}_i,$$

with each $\beta_i, \gamma_i \geq 0$ and $\sum_i \beta_i = 1$ and $\sum_i \gamma_i = 1$. We can assume the same k points $\mathbf{x}_1, \ldots, \mathbf{x}_k$ are used in both weighted averages because we can freely add extra terms with coefficients 0 to a weighted average. Now

$$\mathbf{w} = \sum_{i=1}^{k} ((1 - \alpha)\beta_i + \alpha\gamma_i)\mathbf{x}_i,$$

and the coefficients on the right-hand side are clearly nonnegative and sum to 1. Therefore, $\mathbf{w} \in WA(A)$. Thus, we have shown that $WA(A)$ is convex, and hence $WA(A)$ contains the convex hull of A.

For the second half of the proof, we need to show that every element of $WA(A)$ is in the convex hull of A. For this, we prove, by induction on k, that any weighted average of k points in A is in the convex hull. For $k = 1$, this is trivial because the convex hull of A contains A. For $k > 1$, let

$$\mathbf{w} = a_1\mathbf{x}_1 + a_2\mathbf{x}_2 + \cdots + a_k\mathbf{x}_k,$$

where $\alpha_k \neq 1$. This formula for $\mathbf{w}$ can be rewritten as

$$\mathbf{w} = (1 - a_k)\left[\frac{a_1}{1-a_k}\mathbf{x}_1 + \frac{a_2}{1-a_k}\mathbf{x}_2 + \cdots + \frac{a_{k-1}}{1-a_k}\mathbf{x}_{k-1}\right] + a_k\mathbf{x}_k.$$

Letting $\mathbf{w}'$ be the vector in square brackets in this last formula, we find that $\mathbf{w}'$ is a weighted average of $k - 1$ points in A and thus, by the induction hypothesis, $\mathbf{w}'$ is in the convex hull of A. Now, $\mathbf{w}$ is a weighted average of the two points $\mathbf{w}'$ and $\mathbf{x}_k$; in other words, $\mathbf{w}$ is on the line segment from $\mathbf{w}'$ to $\mathbf{x}_k$. Since $\mathbf{w}'$ and $\mathbf{x}_k$ are both in the convex hull of A, so is $\mathbf{w}$. $\square$

IV.4 Interpolation and Homogeneous Coordinates

This section takes up the question of what it means to form weighted averages of homogeneous vectors. The context is that we have a set of homogeneous vectors (4-tuples) representing points in $\mathbb{R}^3$. We then form a weighted average of the four tuples by calculating the weighted averages of the x-, y-, z, and w-components independently. The question is, What point in $\mathbb{R}^3$ is represented by the weighted average obtained in this way?

A key observation is that a given point in $\mathbb{R}^3$ has many different homogeneous representations, and the weighted average may give different results depending on which homogeneous representation is used. An example of this was already given above on page 102. In that example, we set $\mathbf{v}_0 = \langle 0, 0, 0, 1 \rangle$ and $\mathbf{v}_1 = \langle 1, 0, 0, 1 \rangle$ and $\mathbf{v}_1' = 2\mathbf{v}_1$; so $\mathbf{v}_0$ is a homogeneous representation of $\mathbf{0}$, and $\mathbf{v}_1$ and $\mathbf{v}'$ are both homogeneous representations of $\mathbf{i}$. In Equation IV.6, the average $\frac{1}{2}\mathbf{v}_0 + \frac{1}{2}\mathbf{v}_1$ was seen to be $\langle \frac{1}{2}, 0, 0, 1 \rangle$, which represents (not unexpectedly) the point midway between $\mathbf{0}$ and $\mathbf{i}$. On the other hand, the average $\frac{1}{2}\mathbf{v}_0 + \frac{1}{2}\mathbf{v}_1'$ is equal to $\langle 1, 0, 0, \frac{3}{2} \rangle$, which represents the point $\langle \frac{2}{3}, 0, 0 \rangle$: this is the point that is *two-thirds* of the way from $\mathbf{0}$ to $\mathbf{i}$. The intuitive reason for this is that the point $\mathbf{v}_1'$ has w-component equal to 2 and that the importance (or, weight) of the point $\mathbf{i}$ in the weighted average has therefore been doubled.

We next give a mathematical derivation of this intuition about the effect of forming weighted averages of homogeneous coordinates.

To help increase readability of formulas involving homogeneous coordinates, we introduce a new notation. Suppose $\mathbf{x} = \langle x_1, x_2, x_3 \rangle$ is a point in $\mathbb{R}^3$ and w is a nonzero scalar. Then the notation $\langle \mathbf{x}, w \rangle$ will denote the 4-tuple $\langle x_1, x_2, x_3, w \rangle$. In particular, if $\mathbf{x}$ is a point in $\mathbb{R}^3$, then the homogeneous representations of $\mathbf{x}$ all have the form $\langle w\mathbf{x}, w \rangle$.

Suppose $\mathbf{x}_1, \mathbf{x}_2, \ldots, \mathbf{x}_k$ are points in $\mathbb{R}^3$, and $w_1, w_2, \ldots, w_k$ are positive scalars so that the 4-tuples $\langle w_i \mathbf{x}_i, w_i \rangle$ are homogeneous representations of the points $\mathbf{x}_i$. Consider a weighted average of the homogeneous representations, that is

$$\alpha_1 \langle w_1 \mathbf{x}_1, w_1 \rangle + \alpha_2 \langle w_2 \mathbf{x}_2, w_2 \rangle + \cdots + \alpha_k \langle w_k \mathbf{x}_k, w_k \rangle.$$

The result is a 4-tuple; but the question is, What point $\mathbf{y}$ in $\mathbb{R}^3$ has this 4-tuple as its homogeneous representation? To answer this, calculate as follows:

$$\alpha_1 \langle w_1 \mathbf{x}_1, w_1 \rangle + \alpha_2 \langle w_2 \mathbf{x}_2, w_2 \rangle + \cdots + \alpha_k \langle w_k \mathbf{x}_k, w_k \rangle$$
$$= \langle \alpha_1 w_1 \mathbf{x}_1, \alpha_1 w_1 \rangle + \langle \alpha_2 w_2 \mathbf{x}_2, \alpha_2 w_2 \rangle + \cdots + \langle \alpha_k w_k \mathbf{x}_k, \alpha_k w_k \rangle$$
$$= \langle \alpha_1 w_1 \mathbf{x}_1 + \alpha_2 w_2 \mathbf{x}_2 + \cdots + \alpha_k w_k \mathbf{x}_k, \; \alpha_1 w_1 + \alpha_2 w_2 + \cdots + \alpha_k w_k \rangle$$
$$\equiv \left\langle \frac{\alpha_1 w_1 \mathbf{x}_1 + \alpha_2 w_2 \mathbf{x}_2 + \cdots + \alpha_k w_k \mathbf{x}_k}{\alpha_1 w_1 + \alpha_2 w_2 + \cdots + \alpha_k w_k}, \; 1 \right\rangle,$$

where the last equality ($\equiv$) means only that the homogeneous coordinates represent the same point in $\mathbb{R}^3$, namely the point

$$\mathbf{y} = \sum_{i=1}^{k} \frac{\alpha_i w_i}{\alpha_1 w_1 + \cdots + \alpha_k w_k} \cdot \mathbf{x}_i. \qquad\qquad \text{IV.26}$$

It is obvious that the coefficients on the $\mathbf{x}_i$'s sum to 1, and thus IV.26 is an affine combination of the $\mathbf{x}_i$'s. Furthermore, the α_i's are nonnegative, and at least one of them is positive. Therefore, each coefficient in IV.26 is in the interval [0,1], and thus IV.26 is a weighted average.

Equation IV.26 shows that a weighted average

$$\alpha_1 \langle w_1 \mathbf{x}_1, w_1 \rangle + \alpha_2 \langle w_2 \mathbf{x}_2, w_2 \rangle + \cdots + \alpha_k \langle w_k \mathbf{x}_k, w_k \rangle$$

gives a homogeneous representation of a point $\mathbf{y}$ in $\mathbb{R}^3$ such that $\mathbf{y}$ is a weighted average of $\mathbf{x}_1, \ldots, \mathbf{x}_k$:

$$\mathbf{y} = \beta_1 \mathbf{x}_1 + \beta_2 \mathbf{x}_2 + \cdots + \beta_k \mathbf{x}_k.$$

The coefficients $\beta_1, \ldots, \beta_k$ have the property that they sum to 1, and the ratios

$$\beta_1 : \beta_2 : \beta_3 : \cdots : \beta_{k-1} : \beta_k$$

are equal to the ratios

$$\alpha_1 w_1 : \alpha_2 w_2 : \alpha_3 w_3 : \cdots : \alpha_{k-1} w_{k-1} : \alpha_k w_k.$$

Thus, the w_i values serve as "weights" that adjust the relative importances of the $\mathbf{x}_i$'s in the weighted average.

The preceding discussion has established the following theorem:

Theorem IV.9 *Let A be a set of points in $\mathbb{R}^3$ and A^{H} a set of 4-tuples so that each member of A^{H} is a homogeneous representation of a point in A. Further suppose that the fourth component (the w-component) of each member of A^{H} is positive. Then any weighted average of 4-tuples from A^{H} is a homogeneous representation of a point in the convex hull of A.*

As we mentioned earlier, using weighted averages of homogeneous representations can greatly extend the power of Bézier and B-spline curves – these are the so-called rational Bézier curves and rational B-spline curves. In fact, it is only with the use of weighted averages in homogeneous coordinates that these spline curves can define conic sections such as circles, ellipses, parabolas, and hyperbolas.

A second big advantage of using weighted averages in homogeneous coordinates instead of in ordinary Euclidean coordinates is that weighted averages in homogeneous coordinates are preserved not only under affine transformations but also under perspective transformations. In fact, weighted averages (and more generally, linear combinations) of homogeneous representations are preserved under any transformation that is represented by a 4×4 homogeneous matrix. That is to say, for any 4×4 matrix M, any set of 4-tuples $\mathbf{u}_i$, and any set of scalars α_i,

$$M \left(\sum_i \alpha_i \mathbf{u}_i \right) = \sum_i \alpha_i M(\mathbf{u}_i).$$

Exercise IV.12 *Work out the following example of how weighted averages of Euclidean points in $\mathbb{R}^3$ are not preserved under perspective transformations. Let the perspective transformation act on points in $\mathbb{R}^3$ by mapping $\langle x, y, z \rangle$ to $\langle x/z, y/z, 0 \rangle$. Give a 4×4 homogeneous matrix that represents this transformation (cf. Section II.3.2). What are the values of the three points $\langle 0, 0, 3 \rangle$, $\langle 2, 0, 1 \rangle$ and $\langle 1, 0, 2 \rangle$ under this transformation? Explain how this shows that weighted averages are not preserved by the transformation.*

IV.5 Hyperbolic Interpolation

The previous section discussed the effect of interpolation in homogeneous coordinates and what interpolation of homogeneous coordinates corresponds to in terms of Euclidean coordinates. Now we discuss the opposite direction: how to convert interpolation in Euclidean coordinates into interpolation in homogeneous coordinates. This process is called "hyperbolic interpolation" or sometimes "rational linear interpolation" (see (Blinn, 1992) and (Heckbert and Moreton, 1991)).

The situation is the following: we have points in Euclidean space specified with homogeneous coordinates $\langle \mathbf{x}_i, w_i \rangle$, $i = 1, 2, \ldots, k$ (usually there are only two points, and so $k = 2$). These correspond to Euclidean points $\mathbf{y}_i = \mathbf{x}_i / w_i$. An affine combination of the points is given as

$$\mathbf{z} = \sum_i \alpha_i \mathbf{y}_i,$$

where $\sum_i \alpha_i = 1$. The problem is to find values of β_i so that $\sum \beta_i = 1$ and so the affine combination of homogeneous vectors

$$\sum_i \beta_i \langle \mathbf{x}_i, w_i \rangle$$

is a homogeneous representation of the same point $\mathbf{z}$. From our work in the previous section, we know that the values β_i and α_i must satisfy the condition that the values α_i are proportional to the products $\beta_i w_i$. Therefore, we may choose

$$\beta_i = \frac{\alpha_i / w_i}{\sum_j \alpha_j / w_j},$$

for $i = 1, 2, \ldots, n$.

Hyperbolic interpolation is useful for interpolating values in stage 4 of the rendering pipeline (see Chapter II). In stage 4, perspective division has already been performed, and thus we are working with points lying in the two-dimensional screen space. As described in Section II.4, linear interpolation is performed in screen space to fill in color, normal, and texture coordinate values for pixels inside a polygon. The linear interpolation along a line gives a weighted average

$$(1 - \alpha)\mathbf{y}_1 + \alpha\mathbf{y}_2$$

specifying a point in screen coordinates in terms of the endpoints of a line segment. However, linear interpolation in screen coordinates is not really correct; it is often better to interpolate in spatial coordinates because, after all, the object that is being modeled lies in 3-space. In addition, interpolating in screen coordinates means that the viewed object will change as the viewpoint changes.

Therefore, it is often desirable that values specified at the endpoints, such as color or texture coordinates, be interpolated using hyperbolic interpolation. For the hyperbolic interpolation, weights $(1 - \beta)$ and β are computed so that $(1 - \beta)\mathbf{x}_1 + \beta\mathbf{x}_2$ is a homogeneous representation of $(1 - \alpha)\mathbf{y}_1 + \alpha\mathbf{y}_2$. The weights $(1 - \beta)$ and β are used to obtain the other interpolated values. This does complicate the Bresenham algorithm somewhat, but it is still possible to use an extension of the Bresenham algorithm (cf. (Heckbert and Moreton, 1991)).

Hyperbolic interpolation is most useful when a polygon is being viewed obliquely with the near portion of the polygon much closer to the viewer than the far part. For an example of how hyperbolic interpolation can help with compensating for perspective distortion, see Figure V.2 on page 128.

IV.6 Spherical Linear Interpolation

This section discusses "spherical linear interpolation," also called "slerp"-ing, which is a method of interpolating between points on a sphere.[5] Fix a dimension $d > 1$ and consider the unit sphere in $\mathbb{R}^d$. This sphere consists of the unit vectors $\mathbf{x} \in \mathbb{R}^d$. In $\mathbb{R}^2$, the unit sphere is just the unit circle. In $\mathbb{R}^3$, the unit sphere is called S^2 or the "2-sphere" and is an ordinary sphere. In $\mathbb{R}^4$, it is called S^3 or the "3-sphere" and is a hypersphere.

Let $\mathbf{x}$ and $\mathbf{y}$ be points on the unit sphere and further assume that they are not antipodal (i.e., are not directly opposite each other on the sphere). Then, there is a unique shortest path from $\mathbf{x}$ to $\mathbf{y}$ on the sphere. This shortest path is called a geodesic and lies on a great circle. A *great circle* is defined to be the intersection of a plane containing the origin (i.e., a two-dimensional linear subspace of $\mathbb{R}^d$) and the unit sphere. Thus, a great circle is an ordinary circle of radius 1.

Now suppose also that α is between 0 and 1. We wish to find the point $\mathbf{z}$ on the sphere that is fraction α of the distance from the point $\mathbf{x}$ to $\mathbf{y}$ along the geodesic, as shown in Figure IV.18. This is sometimes called "slerp"-ing for "*S*pherical *L*inear int*ERP*olation," and is denoted by $\mathbf{z} = \text{slerp}(\mathbf{x}, \mathbf{y}, \alpha)$. The terminology comes from (Shoemake, 1985) who used slerping in $\mathbb{R}^4$ for interpolating quaternions on the 3-sphere (see Section XII.3.7).

An important aspect of spherical linear interpolation is that it is nonlinear: in particular, it is not good enough to form the interpolant by the formula

$$\frac{(1 - \alpha)\mathbf{x} + \alpha\mathbf{y}}{||(1 - \alpha)\mathbf{x} + \alpha\mathbf{y}||},$$

because this will traverse the geodesic at a nonconstant rate with respect to α. Instead, we want to let $\mathbf{z}$ be the result of rotating the vector $\mathbf{x}$ a fraction α of the way toward $\mathbf{y}$. That is, if the angle

---

[5] The material in this section is not needed until the discussion of interpolation of quaternions in Section XII.3.7.

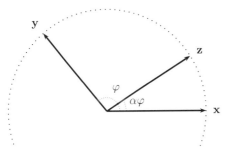

Figure IV.18. The angle between **x** and **y** is φ, and slerp(**x**, **y**, α) is the vector **z** obtained by rotating **x** a fraction α of the way toward **y**. All vectors are unit vectors because **x**, **y**, and **z** lie on the unit sphere.

between **x** and **y** is equal to φ, then **z** is the vector coplanar with **0**, **x**, and **y** that is obtained by rotating **x** through an angle of $\alpha\varphi$ toward **y**.

We now give a mathematical derivation of the formulas for spherical linear interpolation (slerping). Recall that φ is the angle between **x** and **y**; we have $0 \le \varphi < 180°$. If $\varphi = 180°$, then slerping is undefined, since there is no unique direction or shortest geodesic from **x** to **y**. Referring to Figure IV.19, we let **v** be the component of **y** that is perpendicular to **x** and let **w** be the unit vector in the same direction as **v**.

$$\mathbf{v} = \mathbf{y} - (\cos\varphi)\mathbf{x} = \mathbf{y} - (\mathbf{y} \cdot \mathbf{x})\mathbf{x},$$

$$\mathbf{w} = \frac{\mathbf{v}}{\sin\varphi} = \frac{\mathbf{v}}{\sqrt{\mathbf{v} \cdot \mathbf{v}}}.$$

Then we can define slerp(**x**, **y**, α) by

$$\text{slerp}(\mathbf{x}, \mathbf{y}, \alpha) = \cos(\alpha\varphi)\mathbf{x} + \sin(\alpha\varphi)\mathbf{w}, \qquad\qquad \text{IV.27}$$

since this calculation rotates **x** through an angle of $\alpha\varphi$.

An alternative formulation of the formula for slerping can be given by the following derivation:

$$\text{slerp}(\mathbf{x}, \mathbf{y}, \alpha) = \cos(\alpha\varphi)\mathbf{x} + \sin(\alpha\varphi)\mathbf{w}$$

$$= \cos(\alpha\varphi)\mathbf{x} + \sin(\alpha\varphi)\frac{\mathbf{y} - (\cos\varphi)\mathbf{x}}{\sin\varphi}$$

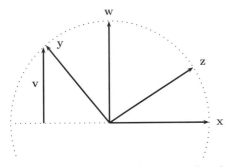

Figure IV.19. Vectors **v** and **w** are used to derive the formula for spherical linear interpolation. The vector **v** is the component of **y** perpendicular to **x**, and **w** is the unit vector in the same direction. The magnitude of **v** is $\sin\varphi$.

$$= \left(\cos(\alpha\varphi) - \sin(\alpha\varphi)\frac{\cos\varphi}{\sin\varphi} \right) \mathbf{x} + \frac{\sin(\alpha\varphi)}{\sin\varphi}\mathbf{y}$$

$$= \frac{\sin\varphi\cos(\alpha\varphi) - \sin(\alpha\varphi)\cos\varphi}{\sin\varphi}\mathbf{x} + \frac{\sin(\alpha\varphi)}{\sin\varphi}\mathbf{y}$$

$$= \frac{\sin(\varphi - \alpha\varphi)}{\sin\varphi}\mathbf{x} + \frac{\sin(\alpha\varphi)}{\sin\varphi}\mathbf{y}$$

$$= \frac{\sin((1-\alpha)\varphi)}{\sin\varphi}\mathbf{x} + \frac{\sin(\alpha\varphi)}{\sin\varphi}\mathbf{y}. \qquad\qquad \text{IV.28}$$

The next-to-last equality was derived using the sine difference formula $\sin(a - b) = \sin a \cos b - \sin b \cos a$.

The usual method for computing spherical linear interpolation is based on Equation IV.28. Since typical applications of slerping require multiple uses of interpolation between the same two points $\mathbf{x}$ and $\mathbf{y}$, it makes sense to precompute the values of φ and $s = \sin\varphi$. This is done by the following pseudocode:

```
Precompute_for_Slerp(x, y) {
    Set c = x·y;               // Cosine of φ
    Set φ = acos(c);           // Compute φ with arccos function
    Set s = sin(φ);            // Sine of φ
}
```

An alternative method for precomputing φ and s can provide a little more stability for very small angles φ without much extra computation:

```
Precompute_for_Slerp(x, y) {
    Set c = x·y;               // Cosine of φ
    Set v = y − cx;
    Set s = √v·v;              // Sine of φ
    Set φ = atan2(s,c);        // Compute φ = arctan(s/c)
}
```

Then, given any value for α, $0 \le \alpha \le 1$, compute $\text{slerp}(\mathbf{x}, \mathbf{y}, \alpha)$ by

```
Slerp(x, y, α) {
    // φ and s=sinφ have already been precomputed.
    Set z = sin((1−α)φ)/sinφ x + sin(αφ)/sinφ y;
    Return z;
}
```

As written above, there will a divide-by-zero error when $\varphi = 0$ because then $\sin\varphi = 0$. In addition, for φ close to zero, the division by a near-zero value can cause numerical instability. To avoid this, you should use the following approximations when $\varphi \approx 0$:

$$\frac{\sin((1-\alpha)\varphi)}{\sin\varphi} \approx (1-\alpha) \qquad \text{and} \qquad \frac{\sin(\alpha\varphi)}{\sin\varphi} \approx \alpha.$$

These approximations are obtained by using $\sin \psi \approx \psi$ when $\psi \approx 0$. The error in these approximations can be estimated from the Taylor series expansion of $\sin \psi$; namely, $\sin \psi \approx \psi - \frac{1}{6}\psi^3$. The test of $\varphi \approx 0$ can be replaced by the condition that roundoff error makes $1 - \frac{1}{6}\varphi^2$ evaluate to the value 1. For single-precision floating point, this condition can be replaced by the condition that $\varphi < 10^{-4}$. For double-precision floating point, the condition $\varphi < 10^{-9}$ can be used.

V

Texture Mapping

V.1 Texture Mapping an Image

Texture mapping, in its simplest form, consists of applying a graphics image, a picture, or a pattern to a surface. A texture map can, for example, apply an actual picture to a surface such as a label on a can or a picture on a billboard or can apply semirepetitive patterns such as wood grain or stone surfaces. More generally, a texture map can hold any kind of information that affects the appearance of a surface: the texture map serves as a precomputed table, and the texture mapping then consists simply of table lookup to retrieve the information affecting a particular point on the surface as it is rendered. If you do not use texture maps, your surfaces will either be rendered as very smooth, uniform surfaces or will need to be rendered with very small polygons so that you can explicitly specify surface properties on a fine scale.

Texture maps are often used to very good effect in real-time rendering settings such as computer games since they give good results with a minimum of computational load. In addition, texture maps are widely supported by graphics hardware such as graphics boards for PCs so that they can be used without needing much computation from a central processor.

Texture maps can be applied at essentially three different points in the graphics rendering process, which we list more or less in order of increasing generality and flexibility:

- A texture map can hold colors that are applied to a surface in "replace" or "decal" mode: the texture map colors just overwrite whatever surface colors are otherwise present. In this case, no lighting calculations should be performed, as the results of the lighting calculations would just be overwritten.
- A texture map can hold attributes such as color, brightness, or transparency that affect the surface appearance after the lighting model calculations are completed. In this case, the texture map attributes are blended with, or modulate, the colors of the surface as calculated by the lighting model. This mode and the first one are the most common modes for using texture maps.
- A texture map can hold attributes such as reflectivity coefficients, normal displacements, or other parameters for the Phong lighting model or the Cook–Torrance model. In this case, the texture map values modify the surface properties that are input to the lighting model. A prominent example of this is "bump mapping," which affects the surface normals by specifying virtual displacements to the surface.

Of course, there is no reason why you cannot combine various texture map techniques by applying more than one texture map to a single surface. For example, one might apply both an ordinary texture map that modulates the color of a surface together with a bump map that perturbs the normal vector. In particular, one could apply texture maps both before and after the calculation of lighting.

A texture map typically consists of a two-dimensional, rectangular array of data indexed with two coordinates s and t that both vary from 0 to 1. The data values are usually colors but could be any other useful value. The data in a texture map can be generated from an image such as a photograph, a drawing, or the output of a graphics program. The data can also be procedurally generated; for example, simple patterns like a checkerboard pattern can easily be computed. Procedurally generated data can either be precomputed and stored in a two-dimensional array or can be computed as needed. Finally, the texture map may be created during the rendering process itself; an example of this would be generating an environment map by prerendering the scene from one or more viewpoints and using the results to build a texture map used for the final rendering stage.

This chapter will discuss the following aspects of texture mapping. First, as a surface is rendered, it is necessary to assign texture coordinates s and t to vertices and then to pixels. These s and t values are used as coordinates to index into the texture and specify what position in the texture map is applied to the surface. Methods of assigning texture coordinates to positions on a surface are discussed in Section V.1.2. Once texture coordinates are assigned to vertices on a polygon, it is necessary to interpolate them to assign texture coordinates to rendered pixels: the mathematics behind this is discussed in Section V.1.1. Texture maps are very prone to bad visual effects from aliasing; this can be controlled by "mipmapping" and other techniques, as is discussed in Section V.1.3. Section V.2 discusses bump mapping, and Section V.3 discusses environment mapping. The remaining sections in this chapter cover some of the practical aspects of using texture mapping and pay particular attention to the most common methods of utilizing texture maps in OpenGL.

V.1.1 Interpolating a Texture to a Surface

The first step in applying a two-dimensional texture map to a polygonally modeled surface is to assign texture coordinates to the vertices of the polygons: that is to say, to assign s and t values to each vertex. Once this is done, texture coordinates for points in the interior of the polygon may be calculated by interpolation. If the polygon is a triangle (or is triangulated), you may use barycentric coordinates to linearly interpolate the values of the s and t coordinates across the triangle. If the polygon is a quadrilateral, you may use bilinear interpolation to interpolate the values of s and t across the interior of the quadrilateral. The former process is shown in Figure V.1, where a quadrilateral is textured with a region of a checkerboard texture map; the distortion is caused by the fact that the s and t coordinates do not select a region of the texture map that is the same shape as the quadrilateral. The distortion is different in the upper right and the lower left halves of the quadrilateral because the polygon was triangulated, and the linear interpolation of the texture coordinates was applied independently to the two triangles.

For either linear or bilinear interpolation of texture coordinates, it may be desirable to include the hyperbolic interpolation correction that compensates for the change in distance affecting the rate of change of texture coordinates. When a perspective projection is used, hyperbolic interpolation corrects for the difference between interpolating in screen coordinates and interpolating in the coordinates of the 3-D model. This is shown in Figure V.2, where hyperbolic interpolation makes more distant squares be correctly foreshortened. Refer to Section IV.5 for the mathematics of hyperbolic interpolation.

Hyperbolic interpolation can be enabled in OpenGL by using the command

```
glHint( GL_PERSPECTIVE_CORRECTION_HINT, GL_NICEST );
```

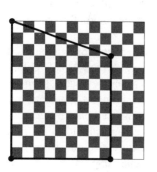

$\langle 0, 1 \rangle$ $\langle \frac{3}{4}, \frac{3}{4} \rangle$

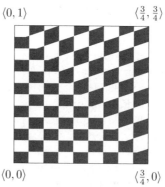

$\langle 0, 0 \rangle$ $\langle \frac{3}{4}, 0 \rangle$

Figure V.1. The square on the left is a texture map. The square on the right is filled with a quadrilateral region of this texture map. The coordinates labeling the corners of the square are s, t values indexing into the texture map. The subregion of the checkerboard texture map selected by the s and t coordinates is shown in the left square. This subregion of the texture map was converted to two triangles first, and each triangle was mapped by linear interpolation into the corresponding triangle in the square on the right: this caused the visible diagonal boundary between the triangles.

The disadvantage of hyperbolic interpolation is that it requires extra calculation and thus may be slower. Hyperbolic interpolation is necessary mostly when textures are applied to large, obliquely viewed polygons. For instance, if d_1 and d_2 are the minimum and maximum distances from the view position to points on the polygon, and if the difference in the distances, $d_2 - d_1$, is comparable to or bigger than the minimum distance d_1, then hyperbolic interpolation may be noticeably helpful.

V.1.2 Assigning Texture Coordinates

We next discuss some of the issues involved in assigning texture coordinates to vertices on a surface. In many cases, the choice of texture coordinates is a little ad hoc and depends greatly on the type of surface and the type of texture, as well as other factors. Because most surfaces are not flat, but we usually work with flat two-dimensional textures, there is often no single best method of assigning texture coordinates. We will deal with only some of the simplest examples of how texture map coordinates are assigned: namely, for cylinders, for spheres, and for tori. We also discuss some of the common pitfalls in assigning texture coordinates. For more sophisticated mathematical tools that can aid the process of assigning texture coordinates to more complex surfaces, consult the article (Bier and Sloan Jr., 1986) or the textbook (Watt and Watt, 1992).

First, consider the problem of mapping a texture map onto a shape whose faces are flat surfaces – for example, a cube. Since the faces are flat and a two-dimensional texture map is flat, the process of mapping the texture map to the surface does not involve any nonlinear stretching or distortion of the texture map. For a simple situation such as a cube, one can usually

Without hyperbolic interpolation   With hyperbolic interpolation

Figure V.2. The figure on the right uses hyperbolic interpolation to render the correct perspective fore-shortening. The figure on the left does not.

Figure V.3. A texture map and its application to a cylinder.

just set the texture coordinates explicitly by hand. Of course, a single vertex on a cube belongs to three different faces of the cube, and thus it generally is necessary to draw the faces of the cube independently so as to use the appropriate texture maps and different texture coordinates for each face.

To apply texture maps to surfaces other than individual flat faces, it is convenient if the surface can be parametrically defined by some function $\mathbf{p}(u, v)$, where $\langle u, v \rangle$ ranges over some region of $\mathbb{R}^2$. In most cases, one sets the texture coordinates s and t as functions of u and v, but more sophisticated applications might also let the texture coordinates depend on $\mathbf{p}(u, v)$, the surface normal, or both.

For the first example of a parametrically defined surface, consider how to map texture coordinates onto the surface of a cylinder. We will pay attention only to the problem of how to map a texture onto the side of the cylinder, not onto the top or bottom face. Suppose the cylinder has height h and radius r and that we are trying to cover the side of the cylinder by a texture map that wraps around the cylinder much as a label on a food can wraps around the can (see Figure V.3). The cylinder's side surface can be parametrically defined by the variables θ and y with the function

$$\mathbf{p}(\theta, y) = \langle r \sin\theta, y, r \cos\theta \rangle,$$

which places the cylinder in "standard" position with its center at the origin and with the y-axis as the central axis of the cylinder. We let y range from $-h/2$ to $h/2$ so the cylinder has height h.

One of the most natural choices for assigning texture coordinates to the cylinder would be to use

$$s = \frac{\theta}{360} \quad \text{and} \quad t = \frac{y + h/2}{h}. \tag{V.1}$$

This lets s vary linearly from 0 to 1 as θ varies from 0 to 360° (we are still using degrees to measure angles) and lets t vary from 0 to 1 as y varies from $-h/2$ to $h/2$. This has the effect of pasting the texture map onto the cylinder without any distortion beyond being scaled to cover the cylinder; the right and left boundaries meet at the front of the cylinder along the line where $x = 0$ and $z = r$.

Exercise V.1 *How should the assignment of cylinder texture coordinates be made to have the left and right boundaries of the texture map meet at the line at the rear of the cylinder where $x = 0$ and $z = -r$?*

Although mapping texture coordinates to the cylinder is very straightforward, there is one potential pitfall that can arise when drawing a patch on the cylinder that spans the line where

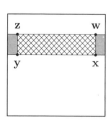
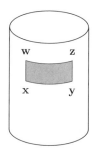

Figure V.4. The quadrilateral **x**, **y**, **z**, **w** selects a region of the texture map. The crosshatched region of the texture map is *not* the intended region of the texture map. The shaded area is the intended region.

the texture boundaries meet. This is best explained with an example. Suppose we are drawing the patch shown in Figure V.4, which has vertices **x**, **y**, **z**, and **w**. For **x** and **w**, the value of θ is, say, $-36°$, and, for **y** and **z**, the value of θ is $36°$. Now if you compute the texture coordinates with $0 \le s \le 1$, then we get $s = 0.9$ for the texture coordinate of **x** and **w** and $s = 0.1$ for the points **y** and **z**. This would have the unintended effect of mapping the long cross-hatched rectangular region of the texture map shown in Figure V.4 into the patch on the cylinder.

To fix this problem, one should use a texture map that repeats, or "wraps around." A repeating texture map is an infinite texture map that covers the entire st-plane by tiling the plane with infinitely many copies of the texture map. Then, you can let $s = 0.9$ for **x** and **w** and $s = 1.1$ for **y** and **z**. (Or you can use $s = -0.1$ and $s = 0.1$, respectively, or, more generally, you can add on any integer amount to the s values.) Of course this means that you need to use a certain amount of care in how you assign texture coordinates. Recall from Section II.4.2 that small roundoff errors in positioning a vertex can cause pixel-sized gaps in surfaces. Because of this, it is important that any point specified more than once by virtue of being part of more than one surface patch always has its position specified with exactly the same θ and y value. The calculation of the θ and y values must be done by exactly the same method each time to avoid roundoff error. However, the same point may be drawn multiple times with different texture values. An example of this is the point **y** of Figure V.4, which may need $s = 0.1$ sometimes and $s = 1.1$ sometimes. In particular, the texture coordinates s and t are not purely functions of θ and y; so you need to keep track of the "winding number," that is, the number of times that the cylinder has been wound around.

There is still a residual risk that roundoff error may cause $s = 0.1$ and $s = 1.1$ to correspond to different pixels in the texture map. This would be expected to cause serious visible defects in the image only rarely.

We now turn to the problem of assigning texture coordinates to a sphere. Unlike the case of a cylinder, a sphere is *intrinsically curved*, which means that there is no way to cover (even part of) a sphere with a flat piece paper without causing the paper to stretch, fold, tear, or otherwise distort. This is also a problem faced by map makers, since it means there is no completely accurate, distortion-free way to represent the surface of the Earth on a flat map. (The Mercator map is an often-used method to map a spherical surface to a flat map but suffers from the problem of distorting relative sizes as well as from the impossibility of using it to map all the way to the poles.)

The problem of assigning texture coordinates to points on a sphere is the problem faced by map makers, but in reverse: instead of mapping points on the sphere to a flat map, we are assigning points from a flat texture map onto a sphere. The sphere can be naturally parameterized by variables θ and φ using the parametric function

$$\mathbf{p}(\theta, \varphi) = \langle r \sin\theta \cos\varphi, r \sin\varphi, r \cos\theta \cos\varphi \rangle.$$

Figure V.5. Two applications of a texture map to a sphere. The sphere on the left has a checkerboard texture applied with texture coordinates given by the spherical map of Equation V.2. The sphere on the right uses texture coordinates given by the cylindrical projection of Equation V.3. The spheres are drawn with a tilt and a small rotation.

Here, θ represents the heading angle (i.e., the rotation around the y-axis), and φ represents the azimuth or "pitch" angle. As the value of θ varies from 0 to 360°, and the value of φ ranges from -90 to 90°, the points $\mathbf{p}(\theta, \phi)$ sweep out all of the sphere.

The first natural choice for assigning texture map coordinates would be

$$ s = \frac{\theta}{360} \quad \text{and} \quad t = \frac{\varphi}{180} + \frac{1}{2}. \qquad \text{V.2}$$

This assignment works relatively well.

A second choice for assigning texture coordinates would be to use the y value in place of the φ value for t. Namely,

$$ s = \frac{\theta}{360} \quad \text{and} \quad t = \frac{\sin \varphi}{2} + \frac{1}{2}. \qquad \text{V.3}$$

This assignment is mapping the sphere orthogonally outward to the surface of a cylinder and then unwrapping the cylinder to a flat rectangle. One advantage of this second map is that it is area preserving.

Figure V.5 shows a checkerboard pattern applied to a sphere with the two texture-coordinate assignment functions. Both methods of assigning texture coordinates suffer from the problem of bunching up at the poles of the sphere. Since the sphere is intrinsically curved, some kind of behavior of this type is unavoidable.

Finally, we consider the problem of how to apply texture coordinates to the surface of a torus. Like the sphere, the torus is intrinsically curved; thus, any method of assigning texture map coordinates on a torus must involve some distortion. Recall from Exercise III.3 on page 80 that the torus has the parametric equation

$$ \mathbf{p}(\theta, \varphi) = \langle (R + r \cos \varphi) \sin \theta, r \sin \varphi, (R + r \cos \varphi) \cos \theta \rangle, $$

where R is the major radius, r is the minor radius, and both θ and φ range from 0 to 360°. The most obvious way to assign texture coordinates to the torus would be

$$ s = \frac{\theta}{360} \quad \text{and} \quad t = \frac{\varphi}{360}. $$

Figure V.6 illustrates the application of a checkerboard texture map to a torus.

Exercise V.2 *Where would the center of the texture map appear on the torus under the preceding assignment of texture coordinates to the torus? How would you change the assignment so as to make the center of the texture map appear at the front of the torus (on the positive z-axis)?*

Figure V.6. A checkerboard texture map applied to a torus.

V.1.3 Mipmapping and Antialiasing

Texture maps often suffer from problems with aliasing. The term "aliasing" means, broadly speaking, any problem that results from conversion between digital and analog or from conversion between differently sampled digital formats. In the case of texture maps, aliasing problems can occur whenever there is not a one-to-one correspondence between screen pixels and texture pixels. For the sake of discussion, we assume that texture coordinates are interpolated from the vertices of a polygon to give a texture coordinate to each individual pixel in the interior of the polygon. We then assume that the texture coordinates for a screen pixel are rounded to the nearest pixel position in the texture and that the color of that texture map pixel is displayed on the screen in the given pixel location. In other words, each screen pixel holds the color from a single texture map pixel. We will shortly discuss better ways to assign color to screen pixels from the texture map colors, but we make this assumption for the moment to discuss how this straightforward method of copying from a texture map to the screen leads to problems.

First, consider the case in which the texture map resolution is less than the corresponding resolution of the screen. In this case, a single texture map pixel will correspond to a block of pixels on the screen. This will make each texture map pixel appear as a (probably more-or-less rectangularly shaped) region of the screen. The result is a blown up version of the texture map that shows each pixel as a too-large block.

Second, consider the (potentially much worse) case in which the screen pixel resolution is similar to, or is less than, the resolution of the texture map. At first thought, one might think that this is a good situation, for it means the texture map has plenty of resolution to be drawn on the screen. However, as it turns out, this case can lead to very bad visual effects such as interference and flashing. The problems arise from each screen pixel's being assigned a color from only one texture map pixel. When the texture map pixel resolution is higher than the screen resolution, this means that only a fraction of the texture map pixels are chosen to be displayed on the screen. As a result, several kinds of problems may appear, including unwanted interference patterns, speckled appearance, graininess, or other artifacts. When rendering a *moving* texture map, different pixels from the texture map may be displayed in different frames; this can cause further unwanted visual effects such as strobing, flashing, or scintillating. Similar effects can occur when the screen resolution is slightly higher than the texture map resolution owing to the fact that different texture map pixels may correspond to different numbers of screen pixels.

Several methods are available to fix, or at least partially fix, the aliasing problems with texture maps. We will discuss three of the more common ones: bilinear interpolation, mipmapping, and stochastic supersampling.

Interpolating Texture Map Pixels. One relatively easy way to smooth out the problems that occur when the screen resolution is about the same as the texture map resolution is to bilinearly interpolate the color values from several texture map pixels and use the resulting average color for the screen pixel. This is done by finding the exact s and t texture coordinates for the screen pixels, locating the four pixels in the texture map nearest to the $\langle s, t \rangle$ position of the texture map, and using bilinear interpolation to calculate a weighted average of the four texture map pixel colors.

For the case in which the texture map resolution is significantly greater (more than twice as great, say) than the screen resolution, one could use more than just four pixels from the texture map to form an average color to display on the screen. Indeed, from a theoretical point of view, this is more or less exactly what you would wish to do: namely, find the region of the texture map that corresponds to a screen pixel and then calculate the average color of the pixels in that region, taking care to properly average in fractions of pixels that lie on the boundary of the region. This can be a potentially expensive process, however, and thus instead it is common to use "mipmapping" to precompute some of the average colors.

Mipmapping. The term "mipmapping" was coined by (Williams, 1983), who introduced it as a technique of precomputing texture maps of reduced resolution – in other words, as a "level of detail" (LOD) technique. The term "mip" is an acronym for a Latin phrase, *multum in parvo*, or "many in one." Mipmapping tries to avoid the problems that arise when displaying a texture map that has greater resolution than the screen by precomputing a family of lower resolution texture maps and always displaying a texture map whose resolution best matches the the screen resolution.

The usual way to create mipmap textures is to start with a high resolution texture map of dimension $N \times M$. It is convenient to assume that N and M are powers of two. Then form a reduced resolution texture map of size $(N/2) \times (M/2)$ by letting the pixel in row i, column j in the reduced resolution texture map be given the average of the four pixels in rows $2i$ and $2i + 1$ and in columns $2j$ and $2j + 1$ of the original texture map. Then recursively apply this process as often as needed to get reduced resolution texture maps of arbitrarily low resolution.

When a screen pixel is to be drawn using a texture map, it can be drawn using a pixel from the mipmapped version of the texture map that has resolution no greater than that of the screen. Thus, when the texture-mapped object is viewed from a distance, a low-resolution mipmap will be used; whereas, when viewed up close, a high-resolution version will be used. This will get rid of many of the aliasing problems, including most problems with flashing and strobing. There can, however, be a problem when the distance from the viewer to the texture-mapped surface is changing, since switching from one mipmap version to another can cause a visible "pop" or "jump" in the appearance of the texture map. This can largely be avoided by rendering pixels using the *two* mipmap versions closest to the screen resolution and linearly interpolating between the results of the two texture maps.

A nice side benefit of the use of mipmaps is that it can greatly improve memory usage, provided the mipmap versions of texture maps are properly managed. Firstly, if each mipmap version is formed by halving the pixel dimensions of the previous mipmap, then the total space used by each successive mipmap is only one quarter the space of the previous mipmap. Since

$$1 + \frac{1}{4} + \frac{1}{16} + \frac{1}{64} + \cdots = 1\frac{1}{3},$$

this means that the use of mipmaps incurs only a 33 percent memory overhead. Even better, in any given scene, it is usual for only relatively few texture maps to be viewed from a close distance, whereas many texture maps may be viewed from a far distance. The more distant texture maps would be viewed at lower resolutions, and so only the lower resolution mipmap

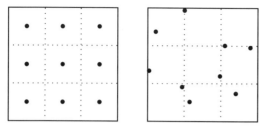

Figure V.7. In the first figure, the nine supersample points are placed at the centers of the nine subpixels. In the second figure, the supersample points are jittered but are constrained to stay inside their subpixel.

versions of these need to be stored in the more accessible memory locations (e.g., in the cache or on a graphics chip). This allows the possibility of more effectively using memory by keeping only the needed mipmap versions of texture maps available; of course, this may require sophisticated memory management.

One big drawback to mipmapping is that it does not fully address the problem that arises when surfaces are viewed obliquely. In this case, the ratio of the texture map resolution and the screen resolution may be quite different along different directions of the texture map, and thus no single mipmap version may be fully appropriate. Since the oblique view could come from any direction, there is no good way to generate enough mipmaps to accommodate all view directions.

V.1.4 Stochastic Supersampling

The term *supersampling* refers to rendering an image at a subpixel level of resolution and then averaging over multiple subpixels to obtain the color value for a single pixel. This technique can be adapted to reduce aliasing with texture maps by combining it with a stochastic, or randomized, sampling method.

The basic idea of nonstochastic supersampling is as follows. First, we divide each pixel into subpixels; for the sake of discussion, we assume each pixel is divided into nine subpixels, but other numbers of subpixels could be used instead. The nine subpixels are arranged in a 3×3 array of square subpixels. We render the image as usual into the subpixels, just as we would usually render the image for pixels, but use triple the resolution. Finally, we take the average of the results for the nine pixels and use this average for the overall pixel color.

Ninefold nonstochastic supersampling can be useful in reducing texture map aliasing problems or at least in delaying their onset until the resolution of the texture map is about three times as high as the resolution of the screen pixels. However, if the texture map contains regular patterns of features or colors, then even with supersampling there can be significant interference effects.

The supersampling method can be further improved by using *stochastic supersampling*. In its simplest form, stochastic supersampling chooses points at random positions inside a pixel, computes the image color at the points, and then averages the colors to set the color value for the pixel. This can cause unrepresentative values for the average if the randomly placed points are clumped poorly, and better results can be obtained by using a *jitter* method to select the supersampling points. The jitter method works as follows: Initially, the supersample points are distributed evenly across the pixel. Then each supersample point is "jittered" (i.e., has its position perturbed slightly). A common way to compute the jitter on nine supersample points is to divide the pixel into a 3×3 array of square subpixels and then place one supersample point randomly into each subpixel. This is illustrated in Figure V.7.

Figure V.8. A bump-mapped torus. Note the lack of bumps on the silhouette. Four white lights are shining on the scene plus a low level of ambient illumination. This picture was generated with the ray tracing software described in Appendix B. See Color Plate 6.

It is important that the positions of the supersampling points be jittered independently for each pixel; otherwise, interference patterns can still form.

Jittering is not commonly used for ordinary texture mapping but is often used for antialiasing in non-real-time environments such as ray-traced images. Figure IX.9 on page 245 shows an example of jittering in ray tracing. It shows three pool balls on a checkerboard texture; part (a) does not use supersampling, whereas part (b) does. Note the differences in the checkerboard pattern off towards the horizon on the sides of the image.

Jittering and other forms of stochastic supersampling decrease aliasing but at the cost of increased noise in the resulting image. This noise generally manifests itself as a graininess similar to that seen in a photograph taken at light levels that were too low. The noise can be reduced by using higher numbers of supersample points.

V.2 Bump Mapping

Bump mapping is used to give a smooth surface the appearance of having bumps or dents. It would usually be prohibitively expensive to model all the small dents and bumps on a surface with polygons because this would require a huge number of very small polygons. Instead, bump mapping works by using a "height texture" that modifies surface normals. When used in conjunction with Phong lighting or Cook–Torrance lighting, the changes in lighting caused by the perturbations in the surface normal will give the appearance of bumps or dents.

An example of bump mapping is shown in Figure V.8. Looking at the silhouette of the torus, you can see that the silhouette is smooth with no bumps. This shows that the geometric model for the surface is smooth: the bumps are instead an artifact of the lighting in conjunction with perturbed normals.

Bump mapping was first described by (Blinn, 1978), and this section presents his approach to efficient implementation of bump mapping. Suppose we have a surface that is specified parametrically by a function $\mathbf{p}(u, v)$. We also assume that the partial derivatives

$$\mathbf{p}_u = \frac{\partial \mathbf{p}}{\partial u} \quad \text{and} \quad \mathbf{p}_v = \frac{\partial \mathbf{p}}{\partial v},$$

are defined and nonzero everywhere and that we are able to compute them. (All the points and vectors in our discussion are functions of u and v even if we do not always indicate this explicitly.) As was discussed in Section III.1.6, a unit vector normal to the surface is given by

$$\mathbf{n}(u, v) = \frac{\mathbf{p}_u \times \mathbf{p}_v}{||\mathbf{p}_u \times \mathbf{p}_v||}.$$

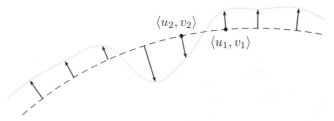

Figure V.9. The dashed curve represents a cross section of a two-dimensional surface. The surface is imagined to be displaced perpendicularly a distance $d(u, v)$ to form the dotted curve. The outward direction of the surface is upward, and thus the value $d(u_1, v_1)$ is positive and the value $d(u_2, v_2)$ is negative.

The bump map is a texture map of scalar values $d(u, v)$ that represent displacements in the direction of the normal vector. That is, a point on the surface $\mathbf{p}(u, v)$ is intended to undergo a "virtual" displacement of distance $d(u, v)$ in the direction of the normal vector. This process is shown in Figure V.9. However, remember that the surface is not actually displaced by the texture map, but rather we just imagine the surface as being displaced in order to adjust (only) the surface normals to match the normals of the displaced surface.

The formula for a point on the displaced surface is

$$\mathbf{p}^*(u, v) = \mathbf{p} + d\mathbf{n}.$$

The normals to the displaced surface can be calculated as follows. First, find the partial derivatives to the new surface by

$$\frac{\partial \mathbf{p}^*}{\partial u} = \frac{\partial \mathbf{p}}{\partial u} + \frac{\partial d}{\partial u}\mathbf{n} + d\frac{\partial \mathbf{n}}{\partial u},$$

$$\frac{\partial \mathbf{p}^*}{\partial v} = \frac{\partial \mathbf{p}}{\partial v} + \frac{\partial d}{\partial v}\mathbf{n} + d\frac{\partial \mathbf{n}}{\partial v}.$$

By taking the cross product of these two partial derivatives, we can obtain the normal to the perturbed surface; however, first we simplify the partial derivatives by dropping the last terms to obtain the approximations

$$\frac{\partial \mathbf{p}^*}{\partial u} \approx \frac{\partial \mathbf{p}}{\partial u} + \frac{\partial d}{\partial u}\mathbf{n},$$

$$\frac{\partial \mathbf{p}^*}{\partial v} \approx \frac{\partial \mathbf{p}}{\partial v} + \frac{\partial d}{\partial v}\mathbf{n}.$$

We can justify dropping the last term on the grounds that the displacement distances $d(u, v)$ are small because only small bumps and dents are being added to the surface and that the partial derivatives of $\mathbf{n}$ are not too large if the underlying surface is relatively smooth. Note, however, that the partial derivatives $\partial d/\partial u$ and $\partial d/\partial v$ cannot be assumed to be small since the bumps and dents would be expected to have substantial slopes. With this approximation, we can approximate the normal of the displaced surface by calculating

$$\mathbf{m} \approx \left(\frac{\partial \mathbf{p}}{\partial u} + \frac{\partial d}{\partial u}\mathbf{n}\right) \times \left(\frac{\partial \mathbf{p}}{\partial v} + \frac{\partial d}{\partial v}\mathbf{n}\right)$$

$$= \left(\frac{\partial \mathbf{p}}{\partial u} \times \frac{\partial \mathbf{p}}{\partial v}\right) + \left(\frac{\partial d}{\partial u}\mathbf{n} \times \frac{\partial \mathbf{p}}{\partial v}\right) - \left(\frac{\partial d}{\partial v}\mathbf{n} \times \frac{\partial \mathbf{p}}{\partial u}\right). \qquad \text{V.4}$$

The vector $\mathbf{m}$ is perpendicular to the displaced surface but is not normalized: the unit vector normal to the displaced surface is then just $\mathbf{n}^* = \mathbf{m}/\|\mathbf{m}\|$.

Note that Equation V.4 uses only the partial derivatives of the displacement function $d(u, v)$; the values $d(u, v)$ are not directly needed at all. One way to compute the partial derivatives is to approximate them using finite differences. However, a simpler and more straightforward method is not to store the displacement function values themselves but instead to save the partial derivatives as two scalar values in the texture map.

The algorithm for computing the perturbed normal $\mathbf{n}^*$ will fail when either of the partial derivatives $\partial\mathbf{p}/\partial u$ or $\partial\mathbf{p}/\partial v$ is equal to zero. This happens for exceptional points on many common surfaces; for instance, at the north and south poles of a sphere using either the spherical or the cylindrical parameterization. Thus, you need to be careful when applying a bump map in the neighborhood of a point where a partial derivative is zero.

It has been presupposed in the preceding discussion that the bump map displacement distance d is given as a function of the variables u and v. It is sometimes more convenient to have a bump map displacement distance function $D(s, t)$, which is a function of the texture coordinates s and t. The texture coordinates are of course functions of u and v, that is, we have $s = s(u, v)$ and $t = t(u, v)$, expressing s and t as either linear or bilinear functions of u and v. Then the bump map displacement function $d(u, v)$ is equal to $D(s(u, v), t(u, v))$. The chain rule then tells us that

$$\frac{\partial d}{\partial u} = \frac{\partial D}{\partial s}\frac{\partial s}{\partial u} + \frac{\partial D}{\partial t}\frac{\partial t}{\partial u}$$

$$\frac{\partial d}{\partial v} = \frac{\partial D}{\partial s}\frac{\partial s}{\partial v} + \frac{\partial D}{\partial t}\frac{\partial t}{\partial v}.$$

The partial derivatives of s and t are either constant in a given u, v-patch in the case of linear interpolation or can be found from Equation IV.19 on page 109 in the case of bilinear interpolation.

Bump-mapped surfaces can have aliasing problems when viewed from a distance – particularly when the distance is far enough that the bumps are rendered at about the size of an image pixel or smaller. As usual, stochastic supersampling can reduce aliasing. A more ad hoc solution is to reduce the height of the bumps gradually based on the level of detail at which the bump map is being rendered; however, this does not accurately render the specular highlights from the bumps.

Bump mapping is not supported in the standard version of OpenGL. This is because the design of the graphics-rendering pipeline in OpenGL only allows texture maps to be applied after the Phong lighting calculation has been performed. Bump mapping must precede Phong lighting model calculations because Phong lighting depends on the surface normal. For this reason, it would also make sense to combine bump mapping with Phong interpolation but not with Gouraud interpolation.

Bump mapping can be implemented in extensions of OpenGL that include support for programming modern graphics hardware boards with pixel shaders.

V.3 Environment Mapping

Environment mapping, also known as "reflection mapping," is a method of rendering a shiny surface showing a reflection of a surrounding scene. Environment mapping is relatively cheap compared with the global ray tracing discussed later in Chapter IX but can still give good effects – at least for relatively compact shiny objects.

The general idea of environment mapping is as follows: We assume we have a relatively small reflecting object. A small, flat mirror or spherical mirror (such as on a car's passenger side door), or a compact object with a mirror-like surface such as a shiny teapot, chrome faucet, toaster, or silver goblet are typical examples. We then obtain, either from a photograph or by

Figure V.10. An environment map mapped into a sphere projection. This is the kind of environment map supported by OpenGL. See Color Plate 7.

The scene is the same as is shown in Figure V.11. Note that the front wall has the most fidelity and the back wall the least. For this reason, spherical environment maps are best used when the view direction is close to the direction used to create the environment map.

computer rendering, a view of the world as seen from the center position of the mirror or object. From this view of the world, we create a texture map showing what is visible from the center position. Simple examples of such texture maps are shown in Figures V.10 and V.11.

When rendering a vertex on the reflecting object, one can use the viewpoint position, the vertex position, and surface normal to calculate a *view reflection direction*. The view reflection direction is the direction of perfect reflection from the viewpoint; that is, a ray of light emanating from the viewer's position to the vertex on the reflecting object would reflect in the view reflection direction. From the view reflection direction, one calculates the point in the texture map that corresponds to the view reflection direction. This gives the texture coordinates for the vertex.

The two most common ways of representing environment maps are shown in Figures V.10 and V.11. The first figure shows the environment map holding the "view of the world" in

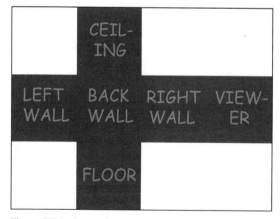

Figure V.11. An environment map mapped into a box projection consists of the six views from a point mapped to the faces of a cube and then unfolded to make a flat image. This scene shows the reflection map from the point at the center of a room. The room is solid blue except for yellow writing on the walls, ceiling, and floor. The rectangular white regions of the environment map are not used. See Color Plate 8.

a circular area. This is the same as you would see reflected from a perfectly mirror-like small sphere viewed orthogonally (from a point at infinity). The mathematics behind calculating the environment map texture coordinates is discussed a little more in Section V.4.6.

Figure V.11 shows the environment map comprising six square regions corresponding to the view seen through the six faces of a cube centered at the environment mapped object. This "box" environment map has a couple advantages over the former "sphere" environment map. Firstly, it can be generated for a computer-rendered scene using standard rendering methods by just rendering the scene six times from the viewpoint of the object in the directions of the six faces of a cube. Secondly, the "box" environment map can be used effectively from any view direction, whereas the "sphere" environment map can be used only from view directions close to the direction from which the environment was formed.

> **Exercise V.3★** *Derive formulas and an algorithm for converting the view reflection direction into texture coordinates for the "box" environment map. Make any assumptions necessary for your calculations.*

An interesting and fairly common use of environment mapping is to add specular highlights to a surface. For this, one first creates an environment texture map that holds an image of the specular light levels in each reflection direction. The specular light from the environment map can then be added to the rendered image based on the reflection direction at each point. A big advantage of this approach is that the specular reflection levels from multiple lights can be precomputed and stored in the environment map; the specular light can then be added late in the graphics pipeline without the need to perform specular lighting calculations again.

V.4 Texture Mapping in OpenGL

We now discuss the most basic uses of texture mapping in OpenGL. Three sample programs are supplied (`TextureBMP`, `FourTextures`, and `TextureTorus`) that illustrate simple uses of texture mapping. You should refer to these programs as you read the descriptions of the OpenGL commands below.

V.4.1 Loading a Texture Map

To use a texture map in OpenGL, you must first build an array holding the values of the texture map. This array will typically hold color values but can also hold values such as luminance, intensity, or alpha (transparency) values. OpenGL allows you to use several different formats for the values of the texture map, but the most common formats are floating point numbers (ranging from 0 to 1) or unsigned 8-bit integers (ranging from 0 to 255).

Once you have loaded the texture map information into an array (`pixelArray`), you must call an OpenGL routine to load the texture map into a "texture object." The most basic method for this is to call the routine `glTexImage2D`. A typical use of `glTexImage2D` might have the following form, with `pixelArray` an array of `float`'s:

```
glPixelStorei(GL_UNPACK_ALIGNMENT, 1);
glTexImage2D ( GL_TEXTURE_2D, 0, GL_RGBA, textureWidth, textureHeight,
                0, GL_RGBA, GL_FLOAT, pixelArray );
```

Another typical usage, with data stored in unsigned bytes, would have the form

```
glPixelStorei(GL_UNPACK_ALIGNMENT, 1);
glTexImage2D ( GL_TEXTURE_2D, 0, GL_RGB, textureWidth, textureHeight,
                0, GL_RGB, GL_UNSIGNED_BYTE, pixelArray );
```

but now with `pixelArray` an array of `unsigned char`'s. The call to `glPixelStorei` tells OpenGL not to expect any particular alignment of the texture data in the pixel array. (This is actually needed only for data stored in byte formats rather than floating point format.)

The parameters to `glTexImage2D` have the following meanings: The first parameter, `GL_TEXTURE_2D`, specifies that a texture is being loaded (as compared with using `GL_PROXY_TEXTURE_2D`, which checks if enough texture memory is available to hold the texture). The second parameter specifies the mipmapping level of the texture; the highest resolution image is level 0. The third parameter specifies what values are stored in the internal OpenGL texture map object: `GL_RGB` and `GL_RGBA` indicate that color (and alpha) values are stored. The next two parameters specify the width and height of the texture map in pixels; the minimum dimension of a texture map (for level 0) is 64×64. The sixth parameter is 0 or 1 and indicates whether a border strip of pixels has been added to the texture map; the value 0 indicates no border. The seventh and eighth parameters indicate the format of the texture values as stored in the programmer-created array of texture information. The last parameter is a pointer to the programmer-created array of texture values. The width and height of a texture map are required to equal a power of 2 or 2 plus a power of 2 if there is a border.

There are a huge number of options for the `glTexImage2D` command, and you should refer to the OpenGL programming manual (Woo et al., 1999) for more information.

Frequently, one also wants to generate mipmap information for textures. Fortunately, OpenGL has a utility routine `gluBuild2DMipmaps` that does all the work of generating texture maps at multiple levels of resolution for you: this makes the use of mipmapping completely automatic. The mipmap textures are generated by calling (for example):

```
gluBuild2DMipmaps( GL_TEXTURE_2D, GL_RGBA, textureWidth,
                   textureHeight, GL_RGBA, GL_FLOAT, pixelArray );
```

The parameters to `gluBuild2DMipmaps` have the same meanings as the parameters to `glTexImage2D` except that the level parameter is omitted since the `gluBuild2DMipmaps` is creating all the levels for you and that borders are not supported. The routine `gluBuild2DMipmaps` checks how much texture memory is available and decreases the resolution of the texture map if necessary; it also rescales the texture map dimensions to the nearest powers of two. It then generates all the mipmap levels down to a 1×1 texture map. It is a very useful routine and is highly recommended, at least for casual users.

OpenGL texture maps are always accessed with s and t coordinates that range from 0 to 1. If texture coordinates outside the range $[0, 1]$ are used, then OpenGL has several options of how they are treated: first, in `GL_CLAMP` mode, values of s and t outside the interval $[0, 1]$ will index into a 1-pixel-wide border of the texture map, or, if there is no border, then the pixels on the edge of the texture are used instead. Second, `GL_CLAMP_TO_EDGE` mode clamps s and t to lie in the range 0 to 1: this acts like `GL_CLAMP` except that, if a border is present, it is ignored (`CLAMP_TO_EDGE` is supported only in OpenGL 1.2 and later). Finally, `GL_REPEAT` makes the s and t wrap around, namely the fractional part of s or t is used; that is to say, $s - \lfloor s \rfloor$ and $t - \lfloor t \rfloor$ are used in "repeat" mode. The modes may be set independently for the s and t texture coordinates with the following command:

$$
\texttt{glTexParameteri(GL\_TEXTURE\_2D,} \left\{ \begin{array}{l} \texttt{GL\_TEXTURE\_WRAP\_S} \\ \texttt{GL\_TEXTURE\_WRAP\_T} \end{array} \right\}, \left\{ \begin{array}{c} \texttt{GL\_REPEAT} \\ \texttt{GL\_CLAMP} \\ \texttt{GL\_CLAMP\_TO\_EDGE} \end{array} \right\} \texttt{)};
$$

The default, and most useful, mode is the "repeat" mode for s and t values.

Section V.1.3 discussed the methods of averaging pixel values and of using mipmaps with multiple levels of detail to (partly) control aliasing problems and prevent interference effects and "popping." When only a single texture map level is used, with no mipmapping, the following OpenGL commands allow the averaging of neighboring pixels to be enabled or disabled:

$$\texttt{glTexParameteri(GL\_TEXTURE\_2D,} \begin{Bmatrix} \texttt{GL\_TEXTURE\_MAG\_FILTER} \\ \texttt{GL\_TEXTURE\_MIN\_FILTER} \end{Bmatrix}, \begin{Bmatrix} \texttt{GL\_NEAREST} \\ \texttt{GL\_LINEAR} \end{Bmatrix}\texttt{);}$$

The option `GL_NEAREST` instructs OpenGL to set a screen pixel color with just a single texture map pixel. The option `GL_LINEAR` instructs OpenGL to set the screen pixel by bilinearly interpolating from the immediately neighboring pixels in the texture map. The settings for "`GL_TEXTURE_MIN_FILTER`" apply when the screen pixel resolution is less than (that is, coarser than) the texture map resolution. The setting for "`GL_TEXTURE_MAG_FILTER`" applies when the screen resolution is higher than the texture map resolution.

When mipmapping is used, there is an additional option to set. OpenGL can be instructed either to use the "best" mipmap level (i.e., the one whose resolution is closest to the screen resolution) or to use linear interpolation between the two best mipmap levels. This is controlled with the following command:

```
glTexParameteri(GL_TEXTURE_2D,
```

$$\texttt{GL\_TEXTURE\_MIN\_FILTER,} \begin{Bmatrix} \texttt{GL\_NEAREST\_MIPMAP\_NEAREST} \\ \texttt{GL\_LINEAR\_MIPMAP\_NEAREST} \\ \texttt{GL\_NEAREST\_MIPMAP\_LINEAR} \\ \texttt{GL\_LINEAR\_MIPMAP\_LINEAR} \end{Bmatrix}\texttt{);}$$

This command is really setting two options at once. The first 'NEAREST' or 'LINEAR' controls whether only one pixel is used from a given mipmap level or whether neighboring pixels on a given mipmap level are averaged. The second part, 'MIPMAP_NEAREST' or 'MIPMAP_LINEAR', controls whether only the best mipmap level is used or whether the linear interpolation of two mipmap levels is used.

OpenGL has several additional advanced features that give you fine control over mipmapping; for documentation on these, you should again consult the OpenGL programming manual.

V.4.2 Specifying Texture Coordinates

It is simple to specify texture coordinates in OpenGL. Before a vertex is drawn with `glVertex*`, you give the *s* and *t* texture coordinates for that vertex with the command

```
glTexCoord2f( s, t );
```

This command is generally given along with a `glNormal3f` command if lighting is enabled. Like calls to `glNormal3f`, it must be given *before* the call to `glVertex*`.

V.4.3 Modulating Color

In OpenGL, the colors and Phong lighting calculations are performed before the application of textures. Thus, texture properties cannot be used to set parameters that drive Phong lighting calculations. This is unfortunate in that it greatly reduces the usability of textures; on the other hand, it allows the texture coordinates to be applied late in the graphics rendering pipeline, where it can be done efficiently by special purpose graphics hardware. As graphics hardware becomes more powerful, this situation is gradually changing; however, for the moment, OpenGL supports only a small amount of posttexture lighting calculations through the use of a separate specular color (as described in Section V.4.4).

The simplest form of applying a texture to a surface merely takes the texture map color and "paints" it on the surface being drawn with no change. In this situation, there is no need to set surface colors and normals or perform Phong lighting since the texture color will just overwrite any color already on the surface. To enable this simple "overwriting" of the surface color with the texture map color, you use the command

```
glTexEnvi( GL_TEXTURE_ENV, GL_TEXTURE_ENV_MODE, GL_DECAL );
```

There is a similar, less commonly used, option, GL_REPLACE, which acts just like GL_DECAL when the texture map does not have an alpha component.

The "decal" option, however, does not usually give very good results when used in a setting with lighting since the lighting does not affect the appearance of textured surfaces when the textures are applied in decal mode. The easiest and most common method of combining textures with lighting is to do the following: render the surface with Phong lighting enabled (turn this on with glEnable(GL_LIGHTING) as usual), give the surface material a white or gray ambient and diffuse color and a white or gray specular color, and then apply the texture map with the GL_MODULATE option. This option is activated by calling

```
glTexEnvi( GL_TEXTURE_ENV, GL_TEXTURE_ENV_MODE, GL_MODULATE );
```

What the "modulate" option does is take the colors r_s, g_s, and b_s that were calculated for the surface with the Phong lighting model and the colors r_t, g_t, and b_t from the texture map and form the products $r_s r_t$, $g_s g_t$, and $b_s b_t$. These products then become the new color of the screen pixel. This has the effect that the texture map color is modulated by the brightness of the lighting of the surface.

There are many other ways to control the interaction of texture map colors and surface colors. However, the two methods above are probably the most commonly used and the most useful. As usual, refer to the OpenGL programming manual (Woo et al., 1999) for more information on other ways to apply texture maps to surfaces.

V.4.4 Separate Specular Highlights

The previous section discussed the "GL_MODULATE" method for applying a texture map in conjunction with the use of Phong lighting. The main problem with this method is that the modulation of the Phong lighting color by the texture color tends to mute or diminish the visibility of specular highlights. Indeed, specular highlights tend to be the same color as the light; that is, they are usually white because lights are usually white. For instance, a shiny plastic object will tend to have white specular highlights, regardless of the color of the plastic itself. Unfortunately, when a white specular highlight is modulated (multiplied) by a texture color, it turns into the color of the texture and does not keep its white color.

Recent versions of OpenGL (since version 1.2) can circumvent this problem by keeping the specular component of the Phong lighting model separate from the diffuse, ambient, and emissive components of light. This feature is turned off by default and can be turned off and on with the commands

$$\texttt{glLightModeli(GL\_LIGHT\_MODEL\_COLOR\_CONTROL, } \begin{Bmatrix} \texttt{GL\_SINGLE\_COLOR} \\ \texttt{GL\_SEPARATE\_SPECULAR\_COLOR} \end{Bmatrix} \texttt{);}$$

When the separate specular color mode is enabled, the Phong lighting model stores both the sum of the ambient, diffuse, and emissive components from all light sources and the sum of specular light components from all light sources. When the texture map is applied, it is applied only to the nonspecular light component. After the texture has been applied, then the specular component of the light is added on unaltered by the texture.

Another way to add specular highlights after texturing is to use multiple texture maps, where the last texture map is an environment map that adds specular highlights (see the discussion of this in the last paragraph of Section V.3).

V.4.5 Managing Multiple Texture Maps

OpenGL provides a simple mechanism to manage multiple texture maps as "texture objects." This allows your program to load or create multiple texture maps and give them to OpenGL to be stored in OpenGL's texture memory. We sketch below the basic functionality of texture objects in OpenGL; you should look at the `FourTextures` program supplied with this book to see an example of how to use multiple texture maps in OpenGL.

The OpenGL commands for handling multiple texture maps are `glGenTextures()`, `glBindTexture()`, and `glDeleteTextures()`. The `glGenTextures` command is used to get the names (actually, integer indices) for one or more new texture objects. This has the effect of reserving texture map names for future use. The `glBindTextures()` function takes a texture map name as input and makes that texture the currently active texture map. Subsequent uses of commands such as `glTexImage*()`, `glTexParameter*()`, `gluBuild2DMipmaps()`, `glTexCoord*()`, and so on will apply to the currently active texture map.

To reserve new names for texture objects, use commands such as

```
GLuint textureNameArray[N];
glGenTextures( N, textureNameArray );
```

where N is the integer number of texture names requested. The call to `glGenTextures()` returns N texture names in the array. Each texture name is a `GLuint`, an unsigned integer. The texture name 0 is never returned by `glGenTextures`; instead, 0 is the texture name reserved for the default texture object.

To select a 2-D texture object, use the command

```
glBindTexture( GL_TEXTURE_2D, textureName );
```

The second parameter, `textureName`, is a `GLuint` unsigned integer that names a texture. When `glBindTexture` is called as above for the first time with a given `textureName` value, it sets the texture type to 2-D and sets the various parameters. On subsequent calls, it merely selects the texture object as the current texture object. It is also possible to use `GL_TEXTURE_1D` or `GL_TEXTURE_3D`: refer to the OpenGL programming manual (Woo et al., 1999) for information on one-dimensional and three-dimensional texture maps.

A texture object is freed with the command

```
glDeleteTextures( N, textureNameArray );
```

which frees the N texture names in the array pointed to by the second parameter.

Some implementations of OpenGL support "resident textures" as a means of managing a cache of textures: resident textures are intended mostly for use with special-purpose hardware (graphics boards) that incorporates special texture buffers.

V.4.6 Environment Mapping in OpenGL

OpenGL supports only the spherical projection version of environment maps (see Section V.3). The OpenGL programming manual (Woo et al., 1999) suggests the following procedure for generating a texture map for environment mapping: take a photograph of a perfectly reflecting sphere with a camera placed an infinite distance away; then scan in the resulting photograph. This, of course, is not entirely practical, but it is mathematically equivalent to what should be done to generate the texture map for OpenGL environment mapping.

To turn on environment mapping in OpenGL, you need to give the following commands (in addition to enabling texture mapping and loading a texture map):

```
glTexGeni(GL_S, GL_TEXTURE_GEN_MODE, GL_SPHERE_MAP);
glTexGeni(GL_T, GL_TEXTURE_GEN_MODE, GL_SPHERE_MAP);
glEnable(GL_TEXTURE_GEN_S);
glEnable(GL_TEXTURE_GEN_T);
```

When rendering an object with an environment map, the surface normal direction, the viewpoint, and the view direction are used to determine the texture coordinates.

If the viewer is not local, that is, if the view direction is fixed to be $\langle 0, 0, -1 \rangle$ with the viewer positioned at a point at infinity, then texture coordinates are generated in the following way: If the normal to the surface is equal to the unit vector $\langle n_x, n_y, n_z \rangle$, then the s and t texture coordinates are set equal to

$$ s = \frac{1}{2}n_x + \frac{1}{2} \quad \text{and} \quad t = \frac{1}{2}n_y + \frac{1}{2}. \qquad \text{V.5} $$

The effect is that the texture coordinates lie in the circle of radius $1/2$ centered at $\langle \frac{1}{2}, \frac{1}{2} \rangle$, and thus the values for s and t can range as low as 0 and as high as 1. For a sphere, this is the same as projecting the sphere orthogonally into a disk.

For a local viewer, the viewer is by convention placed at the origin, and the position and normal of the surface are used to compute the view reflection direction, that is, the direction in which a ray of light from the view position would be specularly reflected by the surface. Given the view reflection direction, one then computes the unit vector **n** that would cause a *nonlocal* viewer to have the same view reflection direction. The s, t texture coordinates are then set by Equation V.5.

The overall effect is that the view reflection direction is used to compute the s, t values generated for a nonlocal viewer with the same view reflection direction. That is to say, the texture coordinates s, t are determined by the view reflection direction.

> **Exercise V.4**★ *As in the Phong lighting model, let* **v** *be the unit vector in the direction of the viewer and* **n** *be the surface normal. Show that the view reflection direction is in the direction of the unit vector*
>
> $$ \mathbf{r}' = 2(\mathbf{n} \cdot \mathbf{v})\mathbf{n} - \mathbf{v}. $$
>
> *For a nonlocal viewer,* **v** *would be* $\langle 0, 0, 1 \rangle$; *for a local viewer, the vector* **v** *is the normalization of the position of the point on the surface (since the local viewer is presumed to be positioned at the origin).*
>
> *Let* $\mathbf{r}' = \langle r_1', r_2', r_3' \rangle$ *be a unit vector in the view reflection direction computed for a local viewer. Show that* $\mathbf{n}' = \langle r_1', r_2', r_3' + 1 \rangle$ *is perpendicular to the surface that gives the nonlocal viewer the same view reflection direction.*

The vector $\mathbf{n}'$ of the exercise can be normalized, and then its first two components give the s and t coordinates by the calculation in Equation V.5.

Other Texture Map Features of OpenGL. OpenGL supports many additional features for working with texture maps, too many for us to cover here. These other features include things such as

(a) The texture matrix – a homogeneous matrix for transforming texture coordinates. This is selected by setting the matrix mode to GL_TEXTURE.
(b) One-dimensional texture maps.
(c) Three-dimensional texture maps.
(d) Creation of texture maps by rendering into the frame buffer.
(e) Manipulation of a region or subimage of a texture map.
(f) More options for mipmapping and controlling level of detail.
(g) Numerous options for controlling the way a texture map modifies the color of a surface.
(h) Optional ability to perform "multitexturing," where multiple textures are successively applied to the same surface.
(i) Several ways of automatically generating texture coordinates (environment maps are only one example of this).
(j) Management of the available texture memory with texture proxies.
(k) Management of resident textures in graphics hardware systems.

For more information on these features, you should consult the OpenGL programming manual.

VI

Color

This chapter briefly discusses some of the issues in color perception and color representation that are important for computer graphics. Color perception and color representation are complicated topics, and more in-depth information can be found in references such as (Berns, Billmeyer, and Saltzman, 2000); (Jackson, MacDonald, and Freeman, 1994); (Foley et al., 1990); Volume I of (Glassner, 1995); or (Hall, 1989). Also recommended is the short, readable introduction to the physics of color and the physiological aspects of color perception in (Feynman, 1989). Some more detailed recommendations for further reading are given at the end of this chapter.

The first section of this chapter discusses the physiology of color perception and its implications for computer graphics. The second, more applied section discusses some of the common methods for representing color in computers.

VI.1 Color Perception

The basic theories of how humans perceive color were formulated already in the nineteenth century. There were two competing theories of color perception: the *trichromatic theory* and the *opponent color theory*. These two theories will appear contradictory at first glance, but in fact they are both correct in that they are grounded in different aspects of human color perception.

The Trichromatic Theory of Vision. The trichromatic theory was formulated by G. Palmer in 1777 and then again by T. Young in 1801; it was extended later by Helmholtz. This theory states that humans perceive color in three components: red, green, and blue. That is, that we see the colors red, green, and blue independently and that all other colors are formed from combinations of these three primary colors.

It was later discovered that the retina of the eye contains several kinds of light-sensitive receptors called cones and rods after their shapes. The human eye contains three kinds of cones: one kind is most sensitive to red light, one to green light, and one to blue light. Rods, the fourth kind of light-sensitive cell, are mostly used for vision in very low light levels and for peripheral vision and do not have the ability to distinguish different colors (thus, in very dark settings, you are unable to see colors but instead see only shades of gray and dark).

For direct viewing of objects in normal light levels, the cones are the primary color receptors, and, although the cones are each sensitive to a wide range of colors, the fact that the

146

three different kinds are selectively more sensitive to red, to green, and to blue provides a physiological basis for the trichromatic theory.

The Opponent Theory of Vision. The opponent theory was formulated by Ewald Hering in 1878. It states that humans perceive light in three opposing components: namely, light versus dark, red versus green, and blue versus yellow. This theory accounts for some aspects of our subjective perception of color such as that one cannot perceive mixtures of red and green or mixtures of blue and yellow (thus there are no colors that are reddish green or blueish yellow, for instance).

Although this theory would appear to be in conflict with the trichromatic theory, there is in fact a simple explanation of how both theories can be valid. The trichromatic theory applies to the different light sensitivities of cones in the retina, and the opponent color theory reflects the way the cells in the retina process color into signals sent to the brain. That is, the neurons in the retina encode color in "channels" so that the neural signals from the eyes to the brain have different channels for encoding the amount of light versus dark, the amount of red versus green, and the amount of blue versus yellow.

The trichromatic theory is the main theoretical foundation for computer graphics, whereas the opponent theory seems to have little impact on computer graphics.[1] Indeed, the principal system of color representation is the RGB system, which is obviously based directly on the trichromatic theory. For applications in computer graphics, the main implications of the trichromatic theory are twofold. First, the space of visible colors forms a three-dimensional vector space since colors are differentiated according to how much they stimulate the three kinds of cones.[2] Second, characterizing colors as being a combination of red, green, and blue light is a fairly good choice because these colors correspond to the light sensitivities of the different cones.

One consequence of the assumption that perceived colors form a three-dimensional space is that there are light sources that have different spectral qualities (i.e., have different intensities of visible light at given wavelengths) but that are indistinguishable to the human eye. This is a consequence of the fact that the set of possible visible light spectra forms an infinite dimensional space. It follows that there must be different light spectra that are equivalent in the sense that the human eye cannot perceive any difference in their colors. This phenomenon is called metamerism.

There have been extensive experiments to determine how to represent different light spectra as combinations of red, green, and blue light. These experiments use the *tristimulus method* and proceed roughly as follows: Fixed light sources of pure red, pure green, and pure blue are chosen as primary colors. Then, for a given color C, one tries to find a way to mix different intensities of the red, green, and blue lights so as to create a color that is equivalent to (i.e., visually indistinguishable from) the color C. The result is expressed by an equation

$$C = r_C R + g_C G + b_C B,$$

where r_C, g_C, b_C are scalars indicating the intensities of the red, green, and blue lights. This means that when the three reference lights are combined at the intensities given by the three scalars, the resulting light looks identical in color to C. It has been experimentally verified

---

[1] One exception to this is that the opponent theory was used in the design of color encoding for television. In order to compress the resolution of television signals suitably and retain backward compatibility with black and white television transmissions, the opponent theory was used to aid the decision of what information to remove from the color channels.

[2] The opponent theory of color also predicts that the perceivable colors form a three-dimensional space.

that all colors can be expressed as linear combinations of red, green, and blue in this way.[3] Furthermore, when colors are combined, they act as a vector space. Thus, the combination of two colors C_1 and C_2 is equivalent to the color

$$(r_{C_1} + r_{C_2})R + (g_{C_1} + g_{C_2})G + (b_{C_1} + b_{C_2})B.$$

There is one big, and unfortunate, problem: sometimes the coefficients r_C, g_C, b_C are negative! The physical interpretation of a negative coefficient, say if $b_C < 0$, is that the reference color (blue, say) must be added to the color C to yield a color that is equivalent to a combination of red and green colors. That is to say, the interpretation of negative coefficients on colors is that the formula should be rearranged by moving terms to the other side of the equality so as to make all coefficients positive.

The reason it is unfortunate that the tristimulus coefficients can be negative is that, since there is no way to make a screen or a drawing emit negative light intensities, it follows that there are some colors that cannot be rendered by a red–blue–green color scheme. That is to say, there are some colors that can be perceived by the human eye but that cannot be rendered on a computer screen, even in principle, at least as long as the screen is rendering colors using a system of three primary colors. The same considerations apply to any kind of color printing system based on three primary colors. Some high-quality printing systems use more than three primary colors to achieve a broader range of perceptual colors.[4]

So far our discussion has concerned the color properties of light. The color properties of materials are considerably more complicated. In Chapter III, the Phong and Cook–Torrance illumination models treated each material as having reflectance properties for the colors red, green, and blue, with each color treated independently. However, a more physically accurate approach would treat every spectrally pure color independently; that is, for each wavelength of light, the material has reflectance properties, and these properties vary with the wavelength. This more physically accurate model would allow for *illuminant metamerism*, where two materials may appear to be the same color under one illumination source and to be a different color under another illumination source. There seems to be no way to extend the Phong and Cook–Torrance light models easily to allow for reflectance properties that vary with wavelength except to use more than three primary colors. This is called *spectral sampling* and is sometimes used for high-quality, photorealistic renderings. For spectral sampling, each light source is treated as consisting of multiple pure components, and each surface has reflectance properties for each of the light components. The illumination equations are similar to those Chapter III described but are carried out for more wavelengths. At the end, it is necessary to reduce back to three

---

[3]   We are describing the standard, idealized model of color perception. The experiments only apply to colors at a constant level of intensity, and the experimental results are not as clear cut as we are making them sound. In addition, there is considerable variation in how different people distinguish colors.

[4]   It is curious, to this author at least, that we are so unconcerned about the quality of color reproduction. Most people are perfectly happy with the rather low range of colors available from a CRT or a television. In contrast, systems for sound reproduction are widespread, and home stereo systems routinely provide high-quality recording and reproduction of audio signals (music) accurately across the full audible spectrum. It is surprising that there has been no corresponding improvement in color reproduction systems for television nor even any demand for such improvement – at least from the general consumer.

It is certainly conceivable that improved color rendition could be developed for CRTs and televisions; for instance, one could envision a display system in which each pixel could emit a combination of two pure, narrow-spectrum, wavelengths of light, with the two wavelengths individually tunable. Such a system would be able to render nearly every perceptual color.

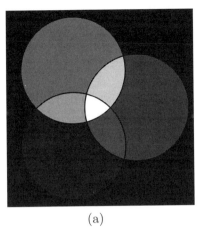 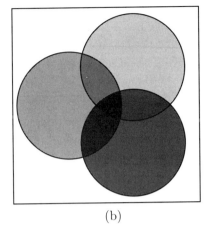

(a)   (b)

Figure VI.1. (a) The additive colors are red, green, and blue. (b) The subtractive colors are cyan, magenta, and yellow. See Color Plate 2.

primary colors for printing or display purposes. The book (Hall, 1989) discusses algorithms for spectral sampling devised by Hall and by Meyer.

VI.2 Representation of Color Values

This section discusses some of the principal ways in which colors are represented by computers. We discuss first the general theory of subtractive versus additive colors and then discuss how RGB values are typically encoded. Finally, we discuss alternate representations of color based on hue, saturation, and luminance.

VI.2.1 Additive and Subtractive Colors

The usual method of displaying red, green, and blue colors on a CRT monitor is called an *additive* system of colors. In an additive system of colors, the base or background color is black, and then varying amounts of three primary colors – usually red, green, and blue – are added. If all three colors are added at full intensity, the result is white. Additive colors are pictured in part (a) of Figure VI.1 in which the three circles should be viewed as areas that generate or emit light of the appropriate color. Where two circles overlap, they combine to form a color: red and green together make yellow, green and blue make cyan, and blue and red make magenta. Where all three circles overlap, the color becomes white. The additive representation of color is appropriate for display systems such as monitors, televisions, or projectors for which the background or default color is black and the primary colors are added in to form composite colors.

In the *subtractive* representation of light, the background or base color is white. Each primary color is subtractive in that it removes a particular color from the light by absorption or filtering. The subtractive primary colors are usually chosen as magenta, cyan, and yellow. Yellow represents the filtering or removal of blue light, magenta the removal of green light, and cyan the removal of red light. Subtractive primaries are relevant for settings such as painting, printing, or film, where the background or default color is white and primary colors remove a single color from the white light. In painting, for instance, a primary color consists of a paint that absorbs one color from the light and reflects the rest of the colors in the light. Subtractive colors are illustrated in part (b) of Figure VI.1. You should think of these colors as being in front of a white light source, and the three circles are filtering out components of the white light.

There can be confusion between the colors cyan and blue, or the colors magenta and red. Cyan is a light blue or greenish blue, whereas blue is a deep blue. Magenta is a purplish or bluish red; if red and magenta are viewed together, then the red frequently has an orangish appearance. Sometimes, cyan and magenta are referred to as blue and red, and this can lead to confusion over the additive and subtractive roles of the colors.

The letters RGB are frequently used to denote the additive red–green–blue primary colors, and CMY is frequently used for the subtractive cyan–magenta–yellow primary colors. Often, one uses these six letters to denote the intensity of the color on a scale 0 to 1. Then, the nominal way to convert from a RGB color representation to CMY is by the formulas

$$C = 1 - R$$
$$M = 1 - G$$
$$Y = 1 - B.$$

We call this the "nominal" way because it often gives poor results. The usual purpose of converting from RGB to CMY is to change an image displayed on a screen into a printed image. It is, however, very difficult to match colors properly as they appear on the screen with printed colors, and to do this well requires knowing the detailed spectral properties (or color equivalence properties) of both the screen and the printing process. A further complication is that many printers use CMYK colors, which use a K channel in addition to C,M,Y. The value of K represents the level of black in the color and is printed with a black ink rather than a combination of primary colors. There are several advantages to using a fourth black color: First, black ink tends to be cheaper than combining three colored inks. Second, less ink needs to be used, and thus the paper does not get so wet from ink, which saves drying time and prevents damage to the paper. Third, the black ink can give a truer black color than is obtained by combining three colored inks.

VI.2.2 Representation of RGB Colors

This section discusses the common formats for representing RGB color values in computers. An RGB color value typically consists of integer values for each of the R, G, B values, these values being rescaled from the interval [0, 1] and discretized to the resolution of the color values.

The highest commonly used resolution for RGB values is the so-called 32-bit or 24-bit color. On a Macintosh, this is called "millions of colors," and on a PC it is referred to variously as "32-bit color," "16,777,216 colors," or "true color." The typical storage for such RGB values is in a 32-bit word: 8 bits are reserved for specifying the red intensity, 8 bits for green, and 8 bits for blue. Since $2^{24} = 16, 777, 216$, there are that many possible colors. The remaining 8 bits in the 32-bit word are either ignored or are used for an alpha (α) value. Typical uses of the alpha channel are for transparency or blending effects (OpenGL supports a wide range of transparency and blending effects). Because each color has 8 bits, each color value may range from 0 to 255.

The second-highest resolution of the commonly used RGB color representations is the 16-bit color system. On a Macintosh, this is called "thousands of colors"; on a PC it will be called "high color," "32,768 colors," or "16-bit color." In 16-bit color, there are, for each of red, green, and blue, 5 bits that represent the intensity of that color. The remaining one bit is sometimes used to represent transparency. Thus, each color has its intensity represented by a number between 0 and 31, and altogether there are $2^{15} = 32,768$ possible color combinations.

The lowest resolution still extensively used by modern computers is 8-bit color. In 8-bit color, there are 256 possible colors. Usually, three of the bits are used to represent the red intensity, three bits represent the green intensity, and only two bits represent the blue intensity.

An alternative way to use eight bits per pixel for color representation is to use a *color lookup table*, often called a CLUT or a LUT, for short. This method is also called *indexed color*. A LUT is typically a table holding 256 distinct colors in 16-bit, 24-bit, or 32-bit format. Each pixel is then given an 8 bit color index. The color index specifies a position in the table, and the pixel is given the corresponding color. A big advantage of a LUT is that it can be changed in accordance with the contents of a window or image on the screen. Thus, the colors in the LUT can reflect the range of colors actually present in the image. For instance, if an image has many reds, the lookup table might be loaded with many shades of red and with relatively few nonred colors. For this reason, using 8-bit indexed color can give much better color rendition of a particular image than just using the standard 8-bit color representation with $3 + 3 + 2$ bits for red, green, and blue intensities.

Color lookup tables are useful in situations in which video memory is limited and only 8 bits of memory per pixel are available for storing color information. They are also useful for compressing files for transmission in bandwidth-limited or bandwidth-sensitive applications such as when files are viewed over the Internet. The widely used Compuserve GIF file format incorporates indexed color: a GIF file uses a k-bit index to specify the color of a pixel, where $1 \le k \le 8$. In addition, the GIF file contains a color lookup table of 2^k color values. Thus, with $k = 8$, there are 256 possible colors; however, smaller values for k can also be used to further reduce the file size at the cost of having fewer colors. This allows GIF files to be smaller than they would otherwise be and thereby faster to download without sacrificing too much in image quality. To be honest, we should mention that there is a second reason GIF files are so small: they use a sophisticated compression scheme, known as LZW (after its inventors Lempel, Ziv, and Welch) that further compresses the file by removing certain kinds of redundant information.

Internet software, such as *Netscape* or *Internet Explorer*, uses a standard color index scheme for "browser-safe" or "Web-safe" colors. This scheme is based on colors that are restricted to six levels of intensity for red, for green, and for blue, which makes a total of $6^3 = 216$ standard colors. In theory at least, browsers should render these 216 colors identically on all hardware.

VI.2.3 Hue, Saturation, and Luminance

Several methods exist for representing color other than in terms of its red, green, and blue components. These methods can be more intuitive and user-friendly for color specification and color blending.

We will discuss only one of the popular methods of this type, the "HSL" system, which specifies a color in terms of its hue, saturation, and luminance. The *hue* (or *chromaticity*) of a light is its dominant color. The *luminance* (also called *intensity*, or *value*, or *brightness*) specifies the overall brightness of the light. Finally, the *saturation* (also called *chroma* or *colorfulness*) of a color measures the extent to which the color consists of a pure color versus consists of white light. (These various terms with similar meanings are not precisely synonymous but instead have different technical definitions in different settings. For other methods of color specification similar in spirit to HSL, you may consult, for instance, (Foley et al., 1990).)

In the HSL system, hue is typically measured as an angle between 0 and 360°. A pure red color has hue equal to 0°, a pure green color has hue equal to 120°, and a pure blue color has hue equal to 240°. Intermediate angles for the hue indicate the blending of two of the primary colors. Thus, a hue of 60° indicates a color contains equal mixtures of red and green, that is, the color yellow. Figure VI.2 shows the hues as a function of angle.

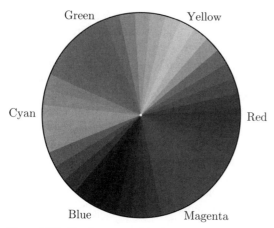

Figure VI.2. Hue is measured in degrees representing an angle around the color wheel. Pure red has hue equal to 0, pure green has hue equal to 120°, and pure blue has hue equal to 240°. See Color Plate 3.

The luminance refers to the overall brightness of the color. In the HSL system, luminance is calculated from RGB values by taking the average of the maximum and minimum intensities of the red, green, and blue colors.

The saturation is measured in a fairly complex fashion, but generally speaking, it measures the relative intensity of the brightest primary color versus the least bright primary color and scales the result into the range [0, 1].

The advantage of using HSL color specification is that it is a more intuitive method for defining colors. The disadvantage is that it does not correspond well to the physical processes of displaying colors on a monitor or printing colors with ink or dyes. For this, it is necessary to have some way of converting between HSL values and either RGB or CMY values.

The most common algorithm for converting RGB values into HSL values is the following:

```
// Input: R, G, B.     All in the range [0,1].
// Output: H, S, L.     H∈ [0,360], and S, L ∈ [0,1].
    Set Max = max{R, G, B};
    Set Min = min{R, G, B};
    Set Delta = Max - Min;
    Set L = (Max+Min)/2;                    // Luminance
    If (Max==Min) {
        Set S = 0;          // Achromatic, unsaturated.
        Set H = 0;          // Hue is undefined.
    }
    Else {
        If ( L<1/2 ) {
            Set S = Delta/(Max+Min);   // Saturation
        }
        Else {
            Set S = Delta/(2-Max-Min); // Saturation
        }
        If ( R == Max ) {
            Set H = 60*(G-B)/Delta;    // Hue
            If ( H<0 )
                Set H = 360+H;
        }
```

```
        Else if ( G == Max ) {
            Set H = 120 + 60*(B-R)/Delta;   // Hue
        }
        Else {
            Set H = 240 + 60*(R-G)/Delta;   // Hue
        }
    }
```

The H, S, and L values are often rescaled to be in the range 0 to 255.

To understand how the preceding algorithm works, consider the case in which R is the dominant color and B the least bright so that $R > G > B$. Then the hue will be calculated by

$$H = 60 \cdot \frac{G - B}{R - B} = 60 \cdot \frac{G - \text{Min}}{R - \text{Min}}.$$

Thus, the hue will range from 0 to 60° in proportion to $(G - \text{Min})/(R - \text{Min})$. If we think of the base intensity Min as the amount of white light, then $R - \text{Min}$ is the amount of red in the color and $G - \text{Min}$ is the amount of green in the color. So, in this case, the hue measures the ratio of the amount of green in the color to the amount of red in the color.

On the other hand, the conversion from RGB into HSL does not seem to be completely ideal in the way it computes brightness: for instance, the color yellow, which has R,G,B values of 1,1,0, has luminance $L = 1/2$. Likewise, the colors red and green, which have R,G,B values of 1,0,0 and of 0,1,0, respectively, also have luminance $L = 1/2$. However, the color yellow is usually a brighter color than either red or green. There seems to be no way of easily evading this problem.

The formulas for computing saturation from RGB values are perhaps a little mysterious. They are

$$S = \frac{\text{Max} - \text{Min}}{\text{Max} + \text{Min}} \qquad \text{and} \qquad S = \frac{\text{Max} - \text{Min}}{2 - (\text{Max} + \text{Min})},$$

where the formula on the left is used if $\text{Max} + \text{Min} \le 1$; otherwise, the formula on the right is used. Note that when $\text{Max} + \text{Min} = 1$, then the two formulas give identical results, and thus the saturation is a continuous function. Also note that if $\text{Max} = 1$, then $S = 1$. Finally, the formula on the right is obtained from the formula on the left by replacing Max by $1 - \text{Max}$ and Min by $1 - \text{Min}$.

It is not hard to see that the algorithm converting RGB into HSL can be inverted, and thus it is possible to calculate the RGB values from the HSL values. Or rather, the algorithm could be inverted if HSL values were stored as real numbers; however, the discretization to integer values means that the transformation from RGB to HSL is not one-to-one and cannot be exactly inverted.

Exercise VI.1 *Give an algorithm for converting HSL values to RGB values. You may treat all numbers as real numbers and consequently do not need to worry about discretization problems. [Hint: First compute* Min *and* Max *from L and S.]*

The translation from RGB into HSL is a nonlinear function; thus, a linear interpolation process such as Gouraud shading will give different results when applied to RGB values than to HSL values. Generally, Gouraud shading is applied to RGB values, but in some applications, it might give better results to interpolate in HSL space. There are potential problems with interpolating hue, however; for instance, how would one interpolate from a hue of 0° to a hue of 180°?

Further Reading: Two highly recommended introductions to color and its use in computer graphics are the book (Jackson, MacDonald, and Freeman, 1994) and the more advanced book (Berns, Billmeyer, and Saltzman, 2000); both are well written with plenty of color illustrations. They also include discussion of human factors and good design techniques for using color in a user-friendly way.

For a discussion of human abilities to perceive and distinguish colors, consult (Glassner, 1995), (Wyszecki and Stiles, 1982), or (Fairchild, 1998). Discussions of monitor and display design, as well as color printing, are given by (Glassner, 1995; Hall, 1989; Jackson, MacDonald, and Freeman, 1994).

A major tool for the scientific and engineering use of color is the color representation standards supported by the Commission International d'Eclairage (CIE) organization. For computer applications, the 1931 CIE $(\bar{x}, \bar{y}, \bar{z})$ representation is the most relevant, but there are several other standards, including the 1964 $10°$ observer standards and the CIELAB and CIELUV color representations, that better indicate human abilities to discriminate colors. The CIE standards are described to some extent in all of the aforementioned references. A particularly comprehensive mathematical explanation can be found in (Wyszecki and Stiles, 1982); for a shorter mathematical introduction, see Appendix B of (Berns, Billmeyer, and Saltzman, 2000). Also, (Fairman, Brill, and Hemmendinger, 1997) describe the mathematical definition of the 1931 CIE color standard and its historical motivations.

The early history of scientific theories of color is given by (Bouma, 1971, Chap. 12).

VII

Bézier Curves

A spline curve is a smooth curve specified succinctly in terms of a few points. These two aspects of splines, that they are smooth and that they are specified succinctly in terms of only a few points, are both important. First, the ability to specify a curve with only a few points reduces storage requirements. In addition, it facilitates the computer-aided design of curves and surfaces because the designer or artist can control an entire curve by varying only a few points. Second, the commonly used methods for generating splines give curves with good smoothness properties and without undesired oscillations. Furthermore, these splines also allow for isolated points where the curve is not smooth, such as points where the spline has a "corner." A third important property of splines is that there are simple algorithms for finding points on the spline curve or surface and simple criteria for deciding how finely a spline must be approximated by linear segments to obtain a sufficiently faithful representation of the spline. The main classes of splines discussed in this book are the Bézier curves and the B-spline curves. Bézier curves and patches are covered in this chapter, and B-splines in the next chapter.

Historically, splines were specified mechanically by systems such as flexible strips of wood or metal that were tied into position to record a desired curve. These mechanical systems were awkward and difficult to work with, and they could not be used to give a permanent, reproducible description of a curve. Nowadays, mathematical descriptions are used instead of mechanical devices because the mathematical descriptions are, of course, more useful and more permanent, not to mention more amenable to computerization. Nonetheless, some of the terminology of physical splines persists such as the use of "knots" in B-spline curves.

Bézier curves were first developed by automobile designers to describe the shape of exterior car panels. Bézier curves are named after Bézier for his work at Renault in the 1960s (Bézier, 1968; 1974). Slightly earlier, de Casteljau had already developed mathematically equivalent methods of defining spline curves at Citroën (de Casteljau, 1959; 1963).[1]

This chapter discusses Bézier curves, which are a simple kind of spline. For the sake of concreteness, the first five sections concentrate on the special case of degree three Bézier curves in detail. After that, we introduce Bézier curves of general degree. We then cover how to form Bézier surface patches and how to use Bézier curves and surfaces in OpenGL. In addition, we

---

[1] We do not attempt to give a proper discussion of the history of the development of Bézier curves and B-splines. The textbooks of (Farin, 1997), (Bartels, Beatty, and Barsky, 1987), and especially (Rogers, 2001) and (Schumaker, 1981) contain some historical material and many more references on the development of Bézier curves and B-splines.

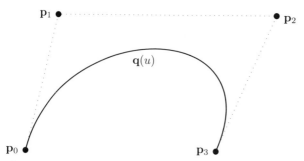

Figure VII.1. A degree three Bézier curve $\mathbf{q}(u)$. The curve is parametrically defined with $0 \leq u \leq 1$, and it interpolates the first and last control points with $\mathbf{q}(0) = \mathbf{p}_0$ and $\mathbf{q}(1) = \mathbf{p}_3$. The curve is "pulled towards" the middle control points $\mathbf{p}_1$ and $\mathbf{p}_2$. At $\mathbf{p}_0$, the curve is tangent to the line segment joining $\mathbf{p}_0$ and $\mathbf{p}_1$. At $\mathbf{p}_3$, it is tangent to the line segment joining $\mathbf{p}_2$ and $\mathbf{p}_3$.

describe rational Bézier curves and patches and how to use them to form conic sections and surfaces of revolution. The last sections of the chapter describe how to form piecewise Bézier curves and surfaces that interpolate a desired set of points.

For a basic understanding of degree three Bézier curves, you should start by reading Sections VII.1 through VII.4. After that, you can skip around a little. Sections VII.6–VII.9 and VII.12–VII.14 discuss general-degree Bézier curves and rational Bézier curves and are intended to be read in order. But it is possible to read Sections VII.10 and VII.11 about patches and about OpenGL immediately after Section VII.4. Likewise, Sections VII.15 and VII.16 on interpolating splines can be read immediately after Section VII.4. The mathematical proofs are not terribly difficult but may be skipped if desired.

VII.1 Bézier Curves of Degree Three

The most common Bézier curves are the *degree three* polynomial curves, which are specified by four points called *control points*. This is illustrated in Figure VII.1, where a parametric curve $\mathbf{q} = \mathbf{q}(u)$ is defined by four control points $\mathbf{p}_0$, $\mathbf{p}_1$, $\mathbf{p}_2$, $\mathbf{p}_3$. The curve starts from $\mathbf{p}_0$ initially in the direction of $\mathbf{p}_1$, then curves generally towards $\mathbf{p}_2$, and ends up at $\mathbf{p}_3$ coming from the direction of $\mathbf{p}_2$. Only the first and last points, $\mathbf{p}_0$ and $\mathbf{p}_3$, lie on $\mathbf{q}$. The other two control points, $\mathbf{p}_1$ and $\mathbf{p}_2$, influence the curve: the intuition is that these two middle control points "pull" on the curve. You can think of $\mathbf{q}$ as being a flexible, stretchable curve that is constrained to start at $\mathbf{p}_0$ and end at $\mathbf{p}_3$ and in the middle is pulled by the two middle control points. Figure VII.2 shows two more examples of degree three Bézier curves and their control points.

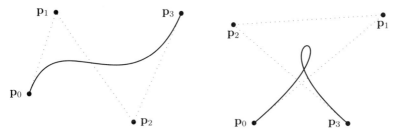

Figure VII.2. Two degree three Bézier curves, each defined by four control points. The curves interpolate only their first and last control points, $\mathbf{p}_0$ and $\mathbf{p}_3$. Note that, just as in Figure VII.1, the curves start off, and end up, tangent to line segments joining control points.

We say that a curve *interpolates* a control point if the control point lies on the curve. In general, Bézier curves do not interpolate their control points, except for the first and last points. For example, the degree three Bézier curves shown in Figures VII.1 and VII.2 interpolate the first and last control points $\mathbf{p}_0$ and $\mathbf{p}_3$ but not the middle control points.

Definition Degree three Bézier curves are defined parametrically by a function $\mathbf{q}(u)$: as u varies from 0 to 1, the values of $\mathbf{q}(u)$ sweep out the curve. The formula for a degree three Bézier curve is

$$\mathbf{q}(u) \;=\; B_0(u)\mathbf{p}_0 + B_1(u)\mathbf{p}_1 + B_2(u)\mathbf{p}_2 + B_3(u)\mathbf{p}_3, \qquad\qquad \text{VII.1}$$

where the four functions $B_i(u)$, called blending functions, are scalar-valued and are defined by

$$B_i(u) \;=\; \binom{3}{i} u^i (1-u)^{3-i}. \qquad\qquad \text{VII.2}$$

The notation $\binom{n}{m}$ represents the "choice function" counting the number of subsets of size m of a set of size n, namely,

$$\binom{n}{m} \;=\; \frac{n!}{m!(n-m)!}.$$

Much of the power and convenience of Bézier curves comes from their being defined in a uniform way independent of the dimension d of the space containing the curve. The control points $\mathbf{p}_i$ defining a Bézier curve lie in d-dimensional space $\mathbb{R}^d$ for some d. On the other hand, the blending functions $B_i(u)$ are scalar-valued functions. The Bézier curve itself is a parametrically defined curve $\mathbf{q}(u)$ lying in $\mathbb{R}^d$. Bézier curves can thus be curves in the plane $\mathbb{R}^2$ or in 3-space $\mathbb{R}^3$, and so forth. It is also permitted for d to equal 1, in which case a Bézier curve is a scalar-valued "curve." For instance, if u measures time and $d = 1$, then the "curve" represents a time-varying scalar value.

The functions $B_i(u)$ are special cases of the *Bernstein polynomials*. When we define Bézier curves of arbitrary degree in Section VII.6, the Bernstein polynomials of degree three will be denoted by B_i^3 instead of just B_i. But for now, we omit the superscript 3 to keep our notation from being overly cluttered.

The blending functions $B_i(u)$ are clearly degree three polynomials. Indeed, when their definitions are expanded they are equal to

$$B_0(u) = (1-u)^3 \qquad B_2(u) = 3u^2(1-u)$$
$$B_1(u) = 3u(1-u)^2 \qquad B_3(u) = u^3.$$

These four functions are graphed in Figure VII.3. Obviously, the functions take on values in the interval $[0, 1]$ for $0 \le u \le 1$. Less obviously, the sum of the four functions is always equal to 1: this can be checked by summing the polynomials, or, more elegantly, by the binomial theorem we have

$$\sum_{i=0}^{3} B_i(u) = \sum_{i=0}^{3} \binom{3}{i} u^i (1-u)^{3-i}$$

$$= (u + (1-u))^3 \;=\; 1.$$

In addition, $B_0(0) = 1$ and $B_3(1) = 1$. From this, we see immediately that $\mathbf{q}(u)$ is always computed as a weighted average of the four control points and that $\mathbf{q}(0) = \mathbf{p}_0$ and $\mathbf{q}(1) = \mathbf{p}_3$, confirming our observation that $\mathbf{q}(u)$ starts at $\mathbf{p}_0$ and ends at $\mathbf{p}_3$. The function $B_1(u)$ reaches its

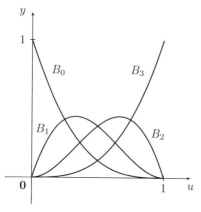

Figure VII.3. The four blending functions for degree three Bézier curves. We are only interested in their values in the interval $[0, 1]$. Each $B_i(u)$ is a degree three polynomial.

maximum value, namely $\frac{4}{9}$, at $u = \frac{1}{3}$; therefore, the control point $\mathbf{p}_1$ has the greatest influence over the curve at $u = \frac{1}{3}$. Symmetrically, $\mathbf{p}_2$ has the greatest influence over the curve at $u = \frac{2}{3}$. This coincides with the intuition that the control points $\mathbf{p}_1$ and $\mathbf{p}_2$ "pull" the hardest on the curve at $u = \frac{1}{3}$ and $u = \frac{2}{3}$.

If we calculate the derivatives of the four blending functions by hand, we of course find that their derivatives are degree two polynomials. If we then evaluate these derivatives at $u = 0$ and $u = 1$, we find that

$$B_0'(0) = -3 \qquad B_1'(0) = 3 \qquad B_2'(0) = 0 \qquad B_3'(0) = 0$$
$$B_0'(1) = 0 \qquad B_1'(1) = 0 \qquad B_2'(1) = -3 \qquad B_3'(1) = 3.$$

The derivative of the function $\mathbf{q}(u)$ can easily be expressed in terms of the derivatives of the blending functions, namely,

$$\mathbf{q}'(u) = B_0'(u)\mathbf{p}_0 + B_1'(u)\mathbf{p}_1 + B_2'(u)\mathbf{p}_2 + B_3'(u)\mathbf{p}_3.$$

This is of course a vector-valued derivative because $\mathbf{q}$ is a vector-valued function. At the beginning and end of the curve, the values of the derivatives are

$$\mathbf{q}'(0) = 3(\mathbf{p}_1 - \mathbf{p}_0) \hspace{10em} \text{VII.3}$$

$$\mathbf{q}'(1) = 3(\mathbf{p}_3 - \mathbf{p}_2).$$

Graphically, this means that the curve $\mathbf{q}(u)$ starts at $u = 0$ traveling in the direction of the vector from $\mathbf{p}_0$ to $\mathbf{p}_1$. Similarly, at the end, where $u = 1$, the curve $\mathbf{q}(u)$ is tangent to the vector from $\mathbf{p}_2$ to $\mathbf{p}_3$. Referring back to Figures VII.1 and VII.2, we note that this corresponds to the curve's starting at $\mathbf{p}_0$ initially tangent to the line segment joining the first control point to the second control point and ending at $\mathbf{p}_3$ tangent to the line segment joining the third and fourth control points.

Exercise VII.1 *A degree three Bézier curve in $\mathbb{R}^2$ satisfies $\mathbf{q}(0) = \langle 0, 1 \rangle$, $\mathbf{q}(1) = \langle 3, 0 \rangle$, $\mathbf{q}'(0) = \langle 3, 3 \rangle$ and $\mathbf{q}'(1) = \langle -3, 0 \rangle$. What are the control points for this curve? Give a rough freehand sketch of the curve, being sure to show the slopes at the beginning and end of the curve clearly.*

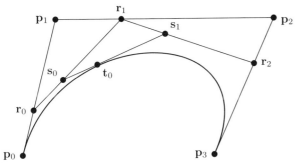

Figure VII.4. The de Casteljau method for computing $\mathbf{q}(u)$ for $\mathbf{q}$, a degree three Bézier curve. This illustrates the $u = 1/3$ case.

VII.2 De Casteljau's Method

The qualitative methods described above allow you to make a reasonable freehand sketch of a degree three Bezier curve based on the positions of its control points. In particular, the curve starts at $\mathbf{p}_0$, ends at $\mathbf{p}_3$, and has initial and final directions given by the differences $\mathbf{p}_1 - \mathbf{p}_0$ and $\mathbf{p}_3 - \mathbf{p}_2$. Finding the exact values of $\mathbf{q}(u)$ for a given value of u can be done by using Formulas VII.1 and VII.2 of course. However, an easier method, known as de Casteljau's method, can also be used to find values of $\mathbf{q}(u)$. De Casteljau's method is not only simpler for hand calculation but is also more stable numerically for computer calculations.[2] In addition, de Casteljau's method will be important later on as the basis for recursive subdivision.

Let $\mathbf{p}_0, \mathbf{p}_1, \mathbf{p}_2, \mathbf{p}_3$ define a degree three Bézier curve $\mathbf{q}$. Fix $u \in [0, 1]$ and suppose we want to compute $\mathbf{q}(u)$. The de Casteljau method for computing $\mathbf{q}(u)$ works as follows: First, form three points $\mathbf{r}_0, \mathbf{r}_1, \mathbf{r}_2$ by linear interpolation from the control points of $\mathbf{q}$ by

$$\mathbf{r}_i = (1 - u) \cdot \mathbf{p}_i + u \cdot \mathbf{p}_{i+1}. \qquad\qquad \text{VII.4}$$

Recall from Section IV.1.1 that this means that $\mathbf{r}_i$ lies between $\mathbf{p}_i$ and $\mathbf{p}_{i+1}$ with $\mathbf{r}_i$ at the point that is fraction u of the distance from $\mathbf{p}_i$ to $\mathbf{p}_{i+1}$. (This is illustrated in Figures VII.4 and VII.5.) Then define $\mathbf{s}_0$ and $\mathbf{s}_1$ by linear interpolation from the $\mathbf{r}_i$'s by

$$\mathbf{s}_i = (1 - u) \cdot \mathbf{r}_i + u \cdot \mathbf{r}_{i+1}. \qquad\qquad \text{VII.5}$$

Finally define $\mathbf{t}_0$ by linear interpolation from $\mathbf{s}_0$ and $\mathbf{s}_1$ by

$$\mathbf{t}_0 = (1 - u) \cdot \mathbf{s}_0 + u \cdot \mathbf{s}_1. \qquad\qquad \text{VII.6}$$

Then, it turns out that $\mathbf{t}_0$ is equal to $\mathbf{q}(u)$. We will prove a generalization of this fact as Theorem VII.6; however, for the special case of degree three Bézier curves, the reader can easily verify that $\mathbf{t}_0 = \mathbf{q}(u)$ by expressing $\mathbf{t}_0$ as an explicit function of u and the four control points.

In the special case of $u = 1/2$, the de Casteljau method becomes particularly simple. Then,

$$\mathbf{r}_i = \frac{\mathbf{p}_i + \mathbf{p}_{i+1}}{2}, \qquad\qquad \mathbf{s}_i = \frac{\mathbf{r}_i + \mathbf{r}_{i+1}}{2}, \qquad\qquad \mathbf{t}_0 = \frac{\mathbf{s}_0 + \mathbf{s}_1}{2}. \qquad \text{VII.7}$$

That is to say, $\mathbf{q}(\frac{1}{2}) = \mathbf{t}_0 = \frac{1}{8}\mathbf{p}_0 + \frac{3}{8}\mathbf{p}_1 + \frac{3}{8}\mathbf{p}_2 + \frac{1}{8}\mathbf{p}_3$.

Exercise VII.2 *Prove that $\mathbf{t}_0$, as computed by Equation VII.6, is equal to $\mathbf{q}(u)$.*

---

[2] See (Daniel and Daubisse, 1989; Farouki, 1991; Farouki and Rajan, 1987; 1988) for technical discussions on the stability of the de Casteljau methods. They conclude that the de Castaljau method is preferable to conventional methods for polynomial representation and evaluation, including Horner's method.

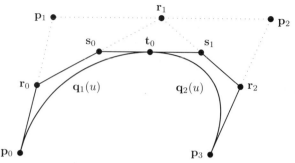

Figure VII.5. The de Casteljau method for computing $\mathbf{q}(u)$ for $\mathbf{q}$ a degree three Bézier curve is the basis for finding the new points needed for recursive subdivision. Shown here is the $u = 1/2$ case. The points $\mathbf{p}_0$, $\mathbf{r}_0$, $\mathbf{s}_0$, $\mathbf{t}_0$ are the control points for the Bézier curve $\mathbf{q}_1(u)$ that is equal to the first half of the curve $\mathbf{q}(u)$, that is, starting at $\mathbf{p}_0$ and ending at $\mathbf{t}_0$. The points $\mathbf{t}_0$, $\mathbf{s}_1$, $\mathbf{r}_2$, $\mathbf{p}_3$ are the control points for the curve $\mathbf{q}_2(u)$ equal to the second half of $\mathbf{q}(u)$, that is, starting at $\mathbf{t}_0$ and ending at $\mathbf{p}_3$.

Exercise VII.3 *Let $\mathbf{q}(u)$ be the curve from Exercise VII.1. Use the de Casteljau method to compute $\mathbf{q}(\frac{1}{2})$ and $\mathbf{q}(\frac{3}{4})$. (Save your work for Exercise VII.4.)*

VII.3 Recursive Subdivision

Recursive subdivision is the term used to refer to the process of splitting a single Bézier curve into two subcurves. Recursive subdivision is important for several reasons, but the most important, perhaps, is for the approximation of a Bézier curve by straight line segments. A curve that is divided into sufficiently many subcurves can be approximated by straight line segments without too much error. As we discuss in the latter part of this section, this can help with rendering and other applications such as intersection testing.

Suppose we are given a Bézier curve $\mathbf{q}(u)$ with control points $\mathbf{p}_0$, $\mathbf{p}_1$, $\mathbf{p}_2$, $\mathbf{p}_3$. This is a cubic curve of course, and if we let

$$\mathbf{q}_1(u) = \mathbf{q}(u/2) \qquad \text{and} \qquad \mathbf{q}_2(u) = \mathbf{q}((u+1)/2), \qquad\qquad \text{VII.8}$$

then both $\mathbf{q}_1$ and $\mathbf{q}_2$ are also cubic curves. We restrict $\mathbf{q}_1$ and $\mathbf{q}_2$ to the domain $[0, 1]$. Clearly, for $0 \leq u \leq 1$, $\mathbf{q}_1(u)$ is the curve that traces out the first half of the curve $\mathbf{q}(u)$, namely, the part of $\mathbf{q}(u)$ with $0 \leq u \leq 1/2$. Similarly, $\mathbf{q}_2(u)$ is the second half of $\mathbf{q}(u)$. The next theorem gives a simple way to express $\mathbf{q}_1$ and $\mathbf{q}_2$ as Bézier curves.

Theorem VII.1 *Let $\mathbf{q}(u)$, $\mathbf{q}_1(u)$, and $\mathbf{q}_2(u)$ be as above. Let $\mathbf{r}_i$, $\mathbf{s}_i$, and $\mathbf{t}_0$ be defined as in Section VII.2 for calculating $\mathbf{q}(u)$ with $u = 1/2$; that is to say, they are defined according to Equation VII.7. Then the curve $\mathbf{q}_1(u)$ is the same as the Bézier curve with control points $\mathbf{p}_0$, $\mathbf{r}_0$, $\mathbf{s}_0$, $\mathbf{t}_0$. And the curve $\mathbf{q}_2(u)$ is the same as the Bézier curve with control points $\mathbf{t}_0$, $\mathbf{s}_1$, $\mathbf{r}_2$, $\mathbf{p}_3$.*

Theorem VII.1 is illustrated in Figure VII.5.

One way to prove Theorem VII.1 is just to use a "brute force" evaluation of the definitions of $\mathbf{q}_1(u)$ and $\mathbf{q}_2(u)$. The two new Bézier curves are specified with control points $\mathbf{r}_i$, $\mathbf{s}_i$, and $\mathbf{t}_0$ that have been defined in terms of the $\mathbf{p}_i$'s. Likewise, from Equations VII.8, we get equations for $\mathbf{q}_1(u)$ and $\mathbf{q}_2(u)$ in terms of the $\mathbf{p}_i$'s. From this, the theorem can be verified by straightforward calculation. This brute force proof is fairly tedious and uninteresting, and so we omit it. The interested reader may work out the details or, better, wait until we give a proof of the more general Theorem VII.7.

Theorem VII.1 explained how to divide a Bézier curve into two halves with the subdivision breaking the curve at the middle position $u = 1/2$. Sometimes, one wishes to divide a Bézier curve into two parts of unequal size, at a point $u = u_0$. That is to say, one wants curves $\mathbf{q}_1(u)$ and $\mathbf{q}_2(u)$ defined on $[0, 1]$ such that

$$\mathbf{q}_1(u) = \mathbf{q}(u_0 u) \qquad \text{and} \qquad \mathbf{q}_2(u) = \mathbf{q}(u_0 + (1 - u_0)u).$$

The next theorem explains how to calculate control points for the subcurves $\mathbf{q}_1(u)$ and $\mathbf{q}_2(u)$ in this case.

Theorem VII.2 *Let $\mathbf{q}(u)$, $\mathbf{q}_1(u)$, and $\mathbf{q}_2(u)$ be as above. Let $0 < u_0 < 1$. Let $\mathbf{r}_i$, $\mathbf{s}_i$, and $\mathbf{t}_0$ be defined as in Section VII.2 for calculating $\mathbf{q}(u)$ with $u = u_0$. That is, they are defined by Equations VII.4–VII.6 so that $\mathbf{t}_0 = \mathbf{q}(u_0)$. Then the curve $\mathbf{q}_1(u)$ is the same as the Bézier curve with control points $\mathbf{p}_0, \mathbf{r}_0, \mathbf{s}_0, \mathbf{t}_0$. Also, the curve $\mathbf{q}_2(u)$ is the same as the Bézier curve with control points $\mathbf{t}_0, \mathbf{s}_1, \mathbf{r}_2, \mathbf{p}_3$.*

For an illustration of Theorem VII.2, refer to Figure VII.4, which shows the $u = 1/3$ case. The curve from $\mathbf{p}_0$ to $\mathbf{t}_0$ is the same as the Bézier curve with control points $\mathbf{p}_0, \mathbf{r}_0, \mathbf{s}_0$, and $\mathbf{t}_0$. The curve from $\mathbf{t}_0$ to $\mathbf{p}_3$ is the same as the Bézier curve with control points $\mathbf{t}_0, \mathbf{s}_1, \mathbf{r}_2$, and $\mathbf{p}_3$.

Like Theorem VII.1, Theorem VII.2 may be proved by direct calculation. Instead, we will prove a more general result later as Theorem VII.7.

> **Exercise VII.4** *Consider the curve $\mathbf{q}(u)$ of Exercise VII.1. Use recursive subdivision to split $\mathbf{q}(u)$ into two curves at $u_0 = \frac{1}{2}$. Repeat with $u_0 = \frac{3}{4}$.*

Applications of Recursive Subdivision

There are several important applications of recursive subdivision. The first, most prominent application is for rendering a Bézier curve as a series of straight line segments; this is often necessary because graphics hardware typically uses straight line segments as primitives. For this, we need a way to break a Bézier curve into smaller and smaller subcurves until each subcurve is sufficiently close to being a straight line so that rendering the subcurves as straight lines gives adequate results. To carry out this subdivision, we need to have a criterion for "sufficiently close to being a straight line." Generally, this criterion should depend not just on the curvature of the curve but also on the rendering context. For instance, when rendering to a rectangular array of pixels, there is probably no need to subdivide a curve that is so straight that the distance between the curve and a straight line approximation is less than a single pixel.

Here is one way of making this criterion of "sufficiently close to a straight line" more precise: first, based on the distance of the curve from the viewer and the pixel resolution of the graphics rendering context, calculate a value $\delta > 0$ so that any discrepancy in rendering of absolute value less than δ will be negligible. Presumably this δ would correspond to some fraction of a pixel dimension. Then recursively subdivide the curve into subcurves, stopping whenever the error in a straight line approximation to the curve is less than δ. A quick and dirty test to use as a stopping condition would be to check the position of the midpoint of the curve; namely, the stopping condition could be that

$$\|\mathbf{q}(\tfrac{1}{2}) - \tfrac{1}{2}(\mathbf{p}_0 + \mathbf{p}_3)\| < \delta.$$

In most cases, this condition can be checked very quickly: in the degree three Bézier case, $\mathbf{q}(\tfrac{1}{2})$ is equal to $\mathbf{t}_0 = \tfrac{1}{8}\mathbf{p}_0 + \tfrac{3}{8}\mathbf{p}_1 + \tfrac{3}{8}\mathbf{p}_2 + \tfrac{1}{8}\mathbf{p}_3$. A quick calculation shows that the stopping condition becomes merely

$$\|\mathbf{p}_0 - \mathbf{p}_1 - \mathbf{p}_2 + \mathbf{p}_3\|^2 < (8\delta/3)^2,$$

which can be efficiently computed.

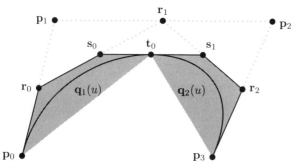

Figure VII.6. The convex hull of the control points of the Bézier curves shrinks rapidly during the process of recursive subdivision. The whole curve is inside its convex hull, that is, inside the quadrilateral $\mathbf{p}_0\mathbf{p}_1\mathbf{p}_2\mathbf{p}_3$. After one round of subdivision, the two subcurves are known to be constrained in the two convex shaded regions.

This "quick and dirty" test can occasionally fail since it is based on only the midpoint of the Bézier curve. A more reliable test would check whether the intermediate control points, $\mathbf{p}_1$ and $\mathbf{p}_2$, lie approximately on the line segment $\overline{\mathbf{p}_0\mathbf{p}_3}$.

A second important application of recursive subdivision involves combining it with convex hull tests to determine regions where the Bézier curve does *not* lie. For example, in Chapters IX and X, we are interested in determining when a ray (a half line) intersects a surface, and we will see that it is particularly important to have efficient methods of determining when a line does not intersect the surface. As another example, suppose we are rendering a large scene of which only a small part is visible at any given time. To render the scene quickly, it is necessary to be able to decide rapidly what objects are not visible by virtue, for example, of being outside the view frustum. A test for nonintersection or for nonvisibility would be based on the following fact: for a Bézier curve defined with control points $\mathbf{p}_i$, the points $\mathbf{q}(u)$, for $0 \le u \le 1$, all lie in the convex hull of the control points. This is a consequence of the fact that the points on the Bézier curve are computed as weighted averages of the control points.

To illustrate the principle of recursive subdivision combined with convex hull testing, we consider the two-dimensional analogue of the first example. The extension of these principles to three-dimensional problems is straightforward. Suppose we are given a Bézier curve $\mathbf{q}(u)$ and a line or ray L and want to decide whether the line intersects the Bézier curve and, if so, find where this intersection occurs. An algorithm based on recursive subdivision would work as follows: Begin by comparing the line L with the convex hull of the control points of $\mathbf{q}$.[3] Since the curve lies entirely in the convex hull of its control points, if L does not intersect the convex hull, then L does not intersect the Bézier curve: in this case the algorithm may return `false` to indicate no intersection occurs. If L does intersect the convex hull, then the algorithm performs recursive subdivision to divide the Bézier curve into two halves, $\mathbf{q}_1$ and $\mathbf{q}_2$. The algorithm then recursively calls itself to determine whether the line intersects either of the subcurves. However, before performing the recursive subdivision and recursive calls, the algorithm checks whether the Bézier curve is sufficiently close to a straight line and, if so, the algorithm merely performs a check for whether the line L intersects the straight line approximation to the Bézier curve. If so, this intersection, or nonintersection, is returned as the answer.

For algorithms using recursive subdivision for testing nonintersection or nonvisibility to perform well, it is necessary for the convex hulls to decrease rapidly in size with each successive subdivision. One step of this process is illustrated in Figure VII.6, which shows the convex

---

[3]   See Section X.1.4 for an efficient algorithm for finding the intersection of a line and polygon.

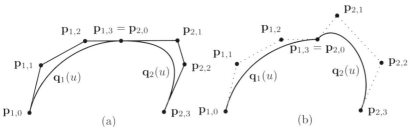

Figure VII.7. Two curves, each formed from two Bézier curves, with control points as shown. The curve in part (a) is G^1-continuous but not C^1-continuous. The curve in part (b) is neither C^1-continuous nor G^1-continuous. Compare these curves with the curves of Figures VII.5 and VII.6 which are both C^1-continuous and G^1-continuous.

hulls of the two subcurves $\mathbf{q}_1$ and $\mathbf{q}_2$ obtained by recursive subdivision. Actually, the shrinkage of the convex hulls of subcurves proceeds even more rapidly than is apparent in the figure: the "width" of the convex hull will decrease quadratically with the "length" of the convex hull. This fact can be proved by elementary calculus, just from the fact that Bézier curves have continuous second derivatives.

VII.4 Piecewise Bézier Curves

There is only a limited range of shapes that can described by a single degree-three Bézier curve. In fact, Figures VII.1 and VII.2 essentially exhaust the types of shapes that can be formed with a single Bézier curve. However, one frequently wants curves that are more complicated than can be formed with a single degree-three Bézier curve. For instance, in Section VII.15, we will define curves that interpolate an arbitrary set of points. One way to construct more complicated curves would be to use higher degree Bézier curves (look ahead to Figure VII.9(c), for an example). However, higher degree Bézier curves are not particularly easy to work with. So, instead, it is often better to combine multiple Bézier curves to form a longer, more complicated curve called a *piecewise Bézier curve*.

This section discusses how to join Bézier curves together – especially how to join them so as to preserve continuity and smoothness (i.e., continuity of the first derivative). For this, it is enough to show how to combine two Bézier curves to form a single smooth curve because generalizing the construction to combine multiple Bézier curves is straightforward. We already saw the converse process in the previous section, where recursive subdivision was used to split a Bézier curve into two curves.

Suppose we want to build a curve $\mathbf{q}(u)$ consisting of two constituent curves $\mathbf{q}_1(u)$ and $\mathbf{q}_2(u)$ that are both degree three Bézier curves. That is, we want to have $\mathbf{q}(u)$ defined in terms of $\mathbf{q}_1(u)$ and $\mathbf{q}_2(u)$ so that Equation VII.8 holds. Two examples of this are illustrated in Figure VII.7. Note that $\mathbf{q}(u)$ will generally not be a single Bézier curve; rather it is a union of two Bézier curves.

For $i = 1, 2$, let $\mathbf{p}_{i,0}$, $\mathbf{p}_{i,1}$, $\mathbf{p}_{i,2}$, and $\mathbf{p}_{i,3}$ be the control points for $\mathbf{q}_i(u)$. In order for $\mathbf{q}(u)$ to be a continuous curve, it is necessary for $\mathbf{q}_1(1)$ to equal $\mathbf{q}_2(0)$. Since Bézier curves begin and end at their first and last control points, this is equivalent to requiring that $\mathbf{p}_{1,3} = \mathbf{p}_{2,0}$. In order for $\mathbf{q}(u)$ to have a continuous first derivative at $u = \frac{1}{2}$, it is necessary to have $\mathbf{q}_1'(1) = \mathbf{q}_2'(0)$, that is, by Equation VII.3, to have

$$\mathbf{p}_{1,3} - \mathbf{p}_{1,2} = \mathbf{p}_{2,1} - \mathbf{p}_{2,0}.$$

If (and only if) these conditions are met, $\mathbf{q}(u)$ will be continuous and have continuous first derivatives. In this case, we say that $\mathbf{q}(u)$ is C^1-*continuous*.

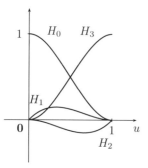

Figure VII.8. The degree three Hermite polynomials.

Definition Let $k \geq 0$. A function $\mathbf{f}(u)$ is C^k-*continuous* if $\mathbf{f}$ has kth derivative defined and continuous everywhere in the domain of $\mathbf{f}$. For $k = 0$, the convention is that the zeroth derivative of $\mathbf{f}$ is just $\mathbf{f}$ itself, and so C^0-continuity is the same as continuity.

The function $\mathbf{f}(u)$ is C^∞-*continuous* if it is C^k-continuous for all $k \geq 0$.

In some situations, having continuous first derivatives is important. For example, if the curve $\mathbf{q}(u)$ will be used to parameterize motion as a function of u, with u measuring time, then the C^1-continuity of $\mathbf{q}(u)$ will ensure that the motion proceeds smoothly with no instantaneous changes in velocity or direction. However, in other cases, the requirement that the first derivative be continuous can be relaxed somewhat. For example, if the curve $\mathbf{q}(u)$ is being used to define a shape, then we do not really need the full strength of C^1-continuity. Instead, it is often enough just to have the slope of $\mathbf{q}(u)$ be continuous. That is, it is often enough if the slope of $\mathbf{q}_1(u)$ at $u = 1$ is equal to the slope of $\mathbf{q}_2(u)$ at $u = 0$. This condition is known as G^1-continuity or *geometric continuity*. Intuitively, G^1-continuity means that when the curve is drawn as a static object, it "looks" smooth. A rather general definition of G^1-continuity can be given as follows.

Definition A function $\mathbf{f}(u)$ is G^1-*continuous* provided $\mathbf{f}$ is continuous and there is a function $t = t(u)$ that is continuous and strictly increasing such that the function $\mathbf{g}(u) = \mathbf{f}(t(u))$ has continuous, nonzero first derivative everywhere in its domain.

In practice, one rarely uses the full power of this definition. Rather, a sufficient condition for the G^1-continuity of the curve $\mathbf{q}(u)$ is that $\mathbf{p}_{1,3} - \mathbf{p}_{1,2}$ and $\mathbf{p}_{2,1} - \mathbf{p}_{2,0}$ both be nonzero and that one can be expressed as a positive scalar multiple of the other.

> **Exercise VII.5** *Give an example of a curve that is C^1-continuous but not G^1-continuous. [Hint: The derivative of the curve can be zero at some point.]*

VII.5 Hermite Polynomials

Hermite polynomials provide an alternative to Bézier curves for representing cubic curves. Hermite polynomials allow a curve to be defined in terms of its endpoints and its derivatives at its endpoints.

The degree three Hermite polynomials $H_0(u)$, $H_1(u)$, $H_2(u)$, and $H_3(u)$ are chosen so that

$$
\begin{array}{llll}
H_0(0)=1 & H_1(0)=0 & H_2(0)=0 & H_3(0)=0 \\
H_0'(0)=0 & H_1'(0)=1 & H_2'(0)=0 & H_3'(0)=0 \\
H_0'(1)=0 & H_1'(1)=0 & H_2'(1)=1 & H_3'(1)=0 \\
H_0(1)=0 & H_1(1)=0 & H_2(1)=0 & H_3(1)=1.
\end{array}
$$

The advantage of Hermite polynomials is that if we need a degree three polynomial $\mathbf{f}(u)$ that has value equal to $\mathbf{a}$ at $u = 0$ and equal to $\mathbf{d}$ at $u = 1$ and has first derivative equal to $\mathbf{b}$ at $u = 0$ and $\mathbf{c}$ at $u = 1$, then we can just define

$$\mathbf{f}(u) = \mathbf{a}H_0(u) + \mathbf{b}H_1(u) + \mathbf{c}H_2(u) + \mathbf{d}H_3(u).$$

Since a degree three polynomial is uniquely determined by its values and first derivatives at the two points $u = 0$ and $u = 1$, there is only one way to define the Hermite polynomials H_i to satisfy the preceding conditions. Some simple calculus and algebra shows that the degree three Hermite polynomials are[4]

$$H_0(u) = (1 + 2u)(1 - u)^2 = 2u^3 - 3u^2 + 1$$

$$H_1(u) = u(1 - u)^2 = u^3 - 2u^2 + u$$

$$H_2(u) = -u^2(1 - u) = u^3 - u^2$$

$$H_3(u) = u^2(3 - 2u) = -2u^3 + 3u^2.$$

The Hermite polynomials are scalar-valued functions but can be used to define curves in $\mathbb{R}^k$ by using vectors as coefficients. This allows any degree three Bézier curve to be expressed in a Hermite form. In fact, it is easy to convert a Bézier curve $\mathbf{q}(u)$ with control points $\mathbf{p}_0, \mathbf{p}_1, \mathbf{p}_2$, and $\mathbf{p}_3$ in $\mathbb{R}^k$ into a Hermite representation: because the initial derivative is $\mathbf{q}'(0) = 3(\mathbf{p}_1 - \mathbf{p}_0)$ and the ending derivative is $\mathbf{q}'(1) = 3(\mathbf{p}_3 - \mathbf{p}_2)$, the Hermite representation must be

$$\mathbf{q}(u) = \mathbf{p}_0 H_0(u) + 3(\mathbf{p}_1 - \mathbf{p}_0)H_1(u) + 3(\mathbf{p}_3 - \mathbf{p}_2)H_2(u) + \mathbf{p}_3 H_3(u).$$

Unlike Bézier curves, the Hermite representation of a curve is not a weighted average since the sum $H_1 + H_2 + H_3 + H_4$ does not generally equal 1. The coefficients of H_0 and H_3 are points (the starting and end points of the curve), but the coefficients of H_1 and H_2 are vectors. As a consequence, the Hermite polynomials lack many of the nice properties of Bézier curves; their advantage, however, is that sometimes it is more natural to define a curve in terms of its initial and ending positions and velocities than with control points.

For the opposite direction, converting a Hermite representation of a curve,

$$\mathbf{q}(u) = \mathbf{r}_0 H_0(u) + \mathbf{r}_1 H_1(u) + \mathbf{r}_2 H_2(u) + \mathbf{r}_3 H_3(u),$$

into a Bézier representation of the curve is also simple. Just let $\mathbf{p}_0 = \mathbf{r}_0$, let $\mathbf{p}_3 = \mathbf{r}_3$, let $\mathbf{p}_1 = \mathbf{p}_0 + \frac{1}{3}\mathbf{r}_1$, and let $\mathbf{p}_2 = \mathbf{p}_3 - \frac{1}{3}\mathbf{r}_2$.

> **Exercise VII.6** *Let $\mathbf{q}(u)$ be the curve of Exercise VII.1. Express $\mathbf{q}(u)$ with Hermite polynomials.*

VII.6 Bézier Curves of General Degree

We now take up the topic of Bézier curves of arbitrary degree. So far we have considered only degree three Bézier curves, but it is useful to consider curves of other degrees. For instance, in Section VII.13 we will use degree two, rational Bézier curves for rendering circles and other conic sections. As we will see, the higher (and lower) degree Bézier curves behave analogously to the already studied degree three Bézier curves.

---

[4] Another way to derive these formulas for the Hermite polynomials is to express them as Bézier curves that take values in $\mathbb{R}$. This is simple enough, as we know the functions' values and derivatives at the endpoints $u = 0$ and $u = 1$.

Definition Let $k \geq 0$. The *Bernstein polynomials of degree k* are defined by

$$B_i^k(u) = \binom{k}{i} u^i (1 - u)^{k-i}.$$

When $k = 3$, the Bernstein polynomials $B_i^3(u)$ are identical to the Bernstein polynomials $B_i(u)$ defined in Section VII.1. It is clear that the Bernstein polynomials $B_i^k(u)$ are degree k polynomials.

Definition Let $k \geq 1$. The *degree k Bézier curve* $\mathbf{q}(u)$ defined from $k + 1$ control points $\mathbf{p}_0, \mathbf{p}_1, \ldots, \mathbf{p}_k$ is the parametrically defined curve given by

$$\mathbf{q}(u) = \sum_{i=0}^{k} B_i^k(u)\mathbf{p}_i,$$

on the domain $u \in [0, 1]$.

The next theorem gives some simple properties of the Bernstein polynomials.

Theorem VII.3 *Let $k \geq 1$.*

a. $B_0^k(0) = 1 = B_k^k(1)$.

b. $\sum_{i=0}^{k} B_i^k(u) = 1$ *for all u.*

c. $B_i^k(u) \geq 0$ *for all $0 \leq u \leq 1$.*

Proof Parts a. and c. are easily checked. To prove part b., use the binomial theorem:

$$\sum_{i=0}^{k} B_i^k(u) = \sum_{i=0}^{k} \binom{k}{i} u^i (1 - u)^{k-i} = (u + (1 - u))^k = 1. \qquad \square$$

The properties of Bernstein functions in Theorem VII.3 immediately imply the corresponding properties of the curve $\mathbf{q}(u)$. By a., the curve starts at $\mathbf{q}(0) = \mathbf{p}_0$ and ends at $\mathbf{q}(1) = \mathbf{p}_k$. Properties b. and c. imply that each point $\mathbf{q}(u)$ is a weighted average of the control points. As a consequence, by Theorem IV.8, a Bézier curve lies entirely in the convex hull of its control points.

We have already seen several examples of degree three Bézier curves in Figures VII.1 and VII.2. Figure VII.9 shows some examples of Bézier curves of degrees 1, 2, and 8 along with their control points. The degree one Bézier curve is seen to have just two control points and to consist of linear interpolation between the two control points. The degree two Bézier curve has three control points, and the degree eight Bézier curve has nine.

In all the examples, the Bézier curve is seen to be tangent to the first and last line segments joining its control points at $u = 0$ and $u = 1$. This general fact can be proved from the following theorem, which gives a formula for the derivative of a Bézier curve.

Theorem VII.4 *Let $\mathbf{q}(u)$ be a degree k Bézier curve, with control points $\mathbf{p}_0, \ldots, \mathbf{p}_k$. Then its first derivative is given by*

$$\mathbf{q}'(u) = k \cdot \sum_{i=0}^{k-1} B_i^{k-1}(u)(\mathbf{p}_{i+1} - \mathbf{p}_i).$$

Therefore, the derivative $\mathbf{q}'(u)$ of a Bézier curve is itself a Bézier curve: the degree is decreased by one and the control points are $k(\mathbf{p}_{i+1} - \mathbf{p}_i)$. A special case of the theorem gives the following formulas for the derivatives of $\mathbf{q}(u)$ at its starting and end points:

Corollary VII.5 *Let $\mathbf{q}(u)$ be a degree k Bézier curve. Then*

$$\mathbf{q}'(0) = k(\mathbf{p}_1 - \mathbf{p}_0) \qquad and \qquad \mathbf{q}'(1) = k(\mathbf{p}_k - \mathbf{p}_{k-1}).$$

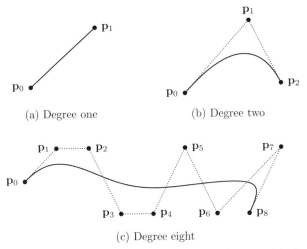

(a) Degree one   (b) Degree two

(c) Degree eight

Figure VII.9. (a) A degree one Bézier curve is just a straight line interpolating the two control points. (b) A degree two Bézier curve has three control points. (c) A degree eight Bézier curve has nine control points. The dotted straight line segments are called the *control polygon* of the Bézier curve.

This corollary proves the observation that the beginning and ending directions of the Bézier curve are in the directions of $\mathbf{p}_1 - \mathbf{p}_0$ and of $\mathbf{p}_k - \mathbf{p}_{k-1}$.

Proof The corollary is easily proved from Theorem VII.4 with the aid of Theorem VII.3. To prove Theorem VII.4, one may either obtain it as a special case of Theorem VIII.8 on page 221, which we will state and prove in the next chapter, or one can prove it directly by the following argument. Using the definition of the Bernstein polynomials, we have

$$\frac{d}{du} B_i^k(u) = \binom{k}{i} i u^{i-1}(1-u)^{k-i} - \binom{k}{i}(k-i)u^i(1-u)^{k-i-1}.$$

Note that the first term is zero if $i = 0$ and the second is zero if $i = k$. Thus, the derivative of $\mathbf{q}(u)$ is equal to

$$\sum_{i=0}^{k} \binom{k}{i} i u^{i-1}(1-u)^{k-i} \mathbf{p}_i - \sum_{i=0}^{k} \binom{k}{i}(k-i)u^i(1-u)^{k-1-i} \mathbf{p}_i$$

$$= \sum_{i=1}^{k} \binom{k}{i} i u^{i-1}(1-u)^{k-i} \mathbf{p}_i - \sum_{i=0}^{k-1} \binom{k}{i}(k-i)u^i(1-u)^{k-1-i} \mathbf{p}_i$$

$$= \sum_{i=0}^{k-1} \binom{k}{i+1}(i+1)u^i(1-u)^{k-1-i} \mathbf{p}_{i+1} - \sum_{i=0}^{k-1} \binom{k}{i}(k-i)u^i(1-u)^{k-1-i} \mathbf{p}_i$$

$$= \sum_{i=0}^{k-1} k\binom{k-1}{i} u^i(1-u)^{k-1-i} \mathbf{p}_{i+1} - \sum_{i=0}^{k-1} k\binom{k-1}{i} u^i(1-u)^{k-1-i} \mathbf{p}_i$$

$$= \sum_{i=0}^{k-1} k\binom{k-1}{i} u^i(1-u)^{k-1-i}(\mathbf{p}_{i+1} - \mathbf{p}_i)$$

$$= k \sum_{i=0}^{k-1} B_i^{k-1}(u)(\mathbf{p}_{i+1} - \mathbf{p}_i),$$

and Theorem VII.4 is proved.   □

Bézier curves of arbitrary degree k have many of the properties we discussed earlier in connection with degree three curves. These include the convex hull property mentioned previously. Another property is *invariance under affine transformations*; namely, if M is an affine transformation, then the result of applying M to a Bézier curve $\mathbf{q}(u)$ is identical to the result of applying M to the control points. In other words, the curve $M(\mathbf{q}(u))$ is equal to the Bézier curve formed from the control points $M(\mathbf{p}_i)$. The affine invariance property follows from the characterization of the point $\mathbf{q}(u)$ as a weighted average of the control points and from Theorem IV.1.

An additional property of Bézier curves is the *variation diminishing property*. Define the *control polygon* to be the series of straight line segments connecting the control points $\mathbf{p}_0, \mathbf{p}_1, \ldots, \mathbf{p}_k$ in sequential order (see Figure VII.9). Then the *variation diminishing property* states that, for any line L in $\mathbb{R}^2$ (or, any plane P in $\mathbb{R}^3$), the number of times the curve $\mathbf{q}(u)$ crosses the line (or the plane) is less than or equal to the number of times the control polygon crosses the line (or the plane). A proof of the variation diminishing property may be found in (Farin, 1997); this proof is also sketched in Exercise VII.9.

It is of course possible to create piecewise degree k Bézier curves using the same approach discussed in Section VII.4 for degree three curves. Let $\mathbf{p}_{1,i}$ be the control points for the first curve and $\mathbf{p}_{2,i}$ be the control points for the second curve (where $0 \le i \le k$). A necessary and sufficient condition for continuity is that $\mathbf{p}_{1,k} = \mathbf{p}_{2,0}$ so that the second curve will start at the end of the first curve. A necessary and sufficient condition for C^1-continuity is that $\mathbf{p}_{1,k} - \mathbf{p}_{1,k-1}$ equals $\mathbf{p}_{2,1} - \mathbf{p}_{2,0}$ so that the first derivatives will match up (see Corollary VII.5). A sufficient condition for G^1-continuity is that $\mathbf{p}_{1,k} - \mathbf{p}_{1,k-1}$ and $\mathbf{p}_{2,1} - \mathbf{p}_{2,0}$ are both nonzero and are positive scalar multiples of each other. These conditions are equivalent to those we encountered in the degree three case!

For the next exercise, we adopt the convention that two curves $\mathbf{q}_1(u)$ and $\mathbf{q}_2(u)$ are the same if and only if $\mathbf{q}_1(u) = \mathbf{q}_2(u)$ for all $u \in [0, 1]$. Otherwise, the two curves are said to be *different*.

> **Exercise VII.7** *Prove that, for a given degree k Bézier curve, there is a unique set of control points $\mathbf{p}_0, \ldots, \mathbf{p}_k$ that defines that Bézier curve. That is, two different sequences of $k + 1$ control points define two different Bézier curves. [Hint: This should be clear for $\mathbf{p}_0$ and $\mathbf{p}_k$; for the rest of the control points, use induction on the degree and the formula for the derivative of a Bézier curve.]*

A *degree k polynomial curve* is a curve of the form

$$\mathbf{q}(u) = \langle x(u), y(u), z(u) \rangle$$

with $x(u)$, $y(u)$, and $z(u)$ polynomials of degree $\le k$. A degree two (respectively, degree three) polynomial curve is also called a *quadratic curve* (respectively, *cubic curve*). Note that every degree k Bézier curve is a degree k polynomial curve.

> **Exercise VII.8** *Let $\mathbf{q}(u)$ be a degree k polynomial curve. Prove that there are control points $\mathbf{p}_0, \ldots, \mathbf{p}_k$ that represent $\mathbf{q}(u)$ as a degree k Bézier curve for $u \in [0, 1]$. [Hint: Prove that the dimension of the vector space of all degree k polynomial curves is equal to the dimension of the vector space of all degree k Bézier curves. You will need to use the previous exercise.]*

VII.7 De Casteljau's Method Revisited

Recall from Section VII.2 that de Casteljau gave a simple, and numerically stable, method for computing a point $\mathbf{q}(u)$ on a degree three Bézier curve for a particular value of u. As we show next, the de Casteljau method can be generalized to apply to Bézier curves of arbitrary degree in the more or less obvious way.

Let a degree k Bézier curve $\mathbf{q}(u)$ have control points $\mathbf{p}_i$, $i = 0, \ldots, k$. Fix $u \in [0, 1]$. We define points $\mathbf{p}_i^r(u)$ as follows. First, for $r = 0$, let $\mathbf{p}_i^0(u) = \mathbf{p}_i$. Second, for $r > 0$ and $0 \leq i \leq k - r$, let

$$\mathbf{p}_i^r(u) = (1 - u)\mathbf{p}_i^{r-1}(u) + u\mathbf{p}_{i+1}^{r-1}(u)$$

$$= \mathrm{lerp}(\mathbf{p}_i^{r-1}(u), \mathbf{p}_{i+1}^{r-1}(u), u).$$

In Section VII.2, for the degree $k = 3$ case, we used different names for the variables. Those variables can be translated into the new notation by $\mathbf{r}_i = \mathbf{p}_i^1$, $\mathbf{s}_i = \mathbf{p}_i^2$, and $\mathbf{t}_0 = \mathbf{p}_0^3$.

The next theorem generalizes the de Casteljau method to the general degree case.

Theorem VII.6 *Let $\mathbf{q}(u)$ and $\mathbf{p}_i^r$ be as above. Then, for all u, $\mathbf{q}(u) = \mathbf{p}_0^k(u)$.*

Proof To prove the theorem, we prove the following more general claim. The theorem is an immediate consequence of the $r = k$ case of the following claim.

Claim *Let $0 \leq r \leq k$ and $0 \leq i \leq k - r$. Then*

$$\mathbf{p}_i^r(u) = \sum_{j=0}^{r} B_j^r(u)\mathbf{p}_{i+j}. \qquad\qquad \text{VII.9}$$

We prove this claim by induction on r. The base case, $r = 0$, is obvious. Or, if you prefer to take $r = 1$ as the base case, the claim is also easily verified for $r = 1$. Now, suppose Equation VII.9 holds for r: we wish to prove it holds for $r + 1$. We have

$$\mathbf{p}_i^{r+1}(u) = (1 - u)\mathbf{p}_i^r(u) + u\mathbf{p}_{i+1}^r(u)$$

$$= \sum_{j=0}^{r}(1 - u)B_j^r(u)\mathbf{p}_{i+j} + \sum_{j=0}^{r} u B_j^r(u)\mathbf{p}_{i+j+1}$$

$$= \sum_{j=0}^{r+1} \left((1 - u)B_j^r(u) + u B_{j-1}^r(u)\right)\mathbf{p}_{i+j},$$

where the last sum should interpreted by letting the quantities $\binom{r}{r+1}$ and $\binom{r}{-1}$, and thus $B_{-1}^r(u)$ and $B_{r+1}^r(u)$, be defined to equal zero. Because $\binom{r}{j} + \binom{r}{j-1} = \binom{r+1}{j}$, it is easy to verify that

$$(1 - u)B_j^r(u) + u B_{j-1}^r(u) = B_j^{r+1}(u),$$

from whence the claim, and thus Theorem VII.6, are proved. $\qquad\qquad\square$

VII.8 Recursive Subdivision Revisited

The recursive subdivision technique of Section VII.3 can be generalized to Bézier curves of arbitrary degree. Let $\mathbf{q}(u)$ be a degree k Bézier curve, let $u_0 \in [0, 1]$, and let $\mathbf{q}_1(u)$ and $\mathbf{q}_2(u)$ be the curves satisfying

$$\mathbf{q}_1(u) = \mathbf{q}(u_0 u) \qquad \text{and} \qquad \mathbf{q}_2(u) = \mathbf{q}(u_0 + (1 - u_0)u).$$

Thus, $\mathbf{q}_1(u)$ is the first u_0-fraction of $\mathbf{q}(u)$ and $\mathbf{q}_2(u)$ is the rest of $\mathbf{q}(u)$: both curves $\mathbf{q}_1(u)$ and $\mathbf{q}_2(u)$ have domain $[0, 1]$. Also, let the points $\mathbf{p}_i^r = \mathbf{p}_i^r(u_0)$ be defined as in Section VII.7 with $u = u_0$.

Theorem VII.7 *Let* $\mathbf{q}$, $\mathbf{q}_1$, $\mathbf{q}_2$, *and* $\mathbf{p}_i^r$ *be as above.*

a. *The curve* $\mathbf{q}_1(u)$ *is equal to the degree k Bézier curve with control points* $\mathbf{p}_0^0$, $\mathbf{p}_0^1$, $\mathbf{p}_0^2$, ..., $\mathbf{p}_0^k$.
b. *The curve* $\mathbf{q}_2(u)$ *is equal to the degree k Bézier curve with control points* $\mathbf{p}_0^k$, $\mathbf{p}_1^{k-1}$, $\mathbf{p}_2^{k-2}$, ..., $\mathbf{p}_k^0$.

Proof We will prove part a.; part b. is completely symmetric. To prove a., we need to show that

$$\mathbf{q}(u_0 u) \;=\; \sum_{j=0}^{k} B_j^k(u)\mathbf{p}_0^j(u_0)$$

holds. Expanding the left-hand side with the definition of Bézier curves and the right-hand side with Equation VII.9 of the claim, we find this is equivalent to

$$\sum_{i=0}^{k} B_i^k(u_0 u)\mathbf{p}_i \;=\; \sum_{j=0}^{k} B_j^k(u)\sum_{i=0}^{j} B_i^j(u_0)\mathbf{p}_i.$$

With the summations reordered, the right-hand side of the equation is equal to

$$\sum_{i=0}^{k}\sum_{j=i}^{k} B_j^k(u)B_i^j(u_0)\mathbf{p}_i.$$

Therefore, equating coefficients of the $\mathbf{p}_i$'s, we need to show that

$$B_i^k(u_0 u) \;=\; \sum_{j=i}^{k} B_j^k(u)B_i^j(u_0),$$

that is,

$$\binom{k}{i}(u_0 u)^i(1 - u_0 u)^{k-i} \;=\; \sum_{j=i}^{k} \binom{k}{j}\binom{j}{i} u^j u_0^i (1 - u)^{k-j}(1 - u_0)^{j-i}.$$

If we divide both sides by $(u_0 u)^i$ and use the fact that $\binom{k}{j}\binom{j}{i} = \binom{k}{i}\binom{k-i}{j-i}$, this reduces to showing that

$$(1 - u_0 u)^{k-i} \;=\; \sum_{j=i}^{k} \binom{k-i}{j-i} u^{j-i}(1 - u)^{k-j}(1 - u_0)^{j-i}.$$

By a change of variables from "j" to "$j + i$" in the summation, the right-hand side is equal to

$$\sum_{j=0}^{k-i} \binom{k-i}{j} u^j (1 - u_0)^j (1 - u)^{k-i-j}$$

$$= \sum_{j=0}^{k-i} \binom{k-i}{j} (u - u_0 u)^j (1 - u)^{k-i-j}$$

$$= ((u - u_0 u) + (1 - u))^{k-i}$$

$$= (1 - u_0 u)^{k-i},$$

where the second equality follows from the binomial theorem. This is what we needed to show to complete the proof of Theorem VII.7.   □

Exercise VII.9★   *Fill in the details of the following sketch of a proof of the variation diminishing property of Bézier curves. First, fix a line (or, in $\mathbb{R}^3$, a plane) and a continuous curve (the curve may consist of straight line segments). Consider the following operation on the curve: choose two points on the curve and replace the part of the curve between the two points by the straight line segment joining the two points. Prove that this does not increase the number of times the curve crosses the line. Second, show that the process of going from the control polygon of a Bézier curve to the two control polygons of the two subcurves obtained by using recursive subdivision to split the curve at $u = 1/2$ involves only a finite number of uses of the operation from the first step. Therefore, the total number of times the two new control polygons cross the line is less than or equal to the number of times the original control polygon crossed the curve. Third, prove that, as the curve is repeatedly recursively subdivided, the control polygon approximates the curve. Fourth, argue that this suffices to prove the variation diminishing property (this last point is not entirely trivial).*

VII.9 Degree Elevation

The term "degree elevation" refers to the process of taking a Bézier curve of degree k and reexpressing the same curve as a higher degree Bézier curve. Degree elevation is useful for converting a low-degree Bézier curve into a higher degree representation. For example, Section VII.13 will describe several ways to represent a circle with degree two Bézier curves, and one may need to elevate their degree to three for use in a software program. The PostScript language, for example, supports only degree three Bézier curves, not degree two.

Of course, it should not be surprising that degree elevation is possible. Indeed, any degree k polynomial can be viewed also as a degree $k + 1$ polynomial by just treating it as having a leading term $0x^{k+1}$ with coefficient zero. It is not as simple to elevate the degree of Bézier curves, for we must define the curve in terms of its control points. To be completely explicit, the degree elevation problem is the following:

> We are given a degree k Bézier curve $\mathbf{q}(u)$ defined in terms of control points $\mathbf{p}_i$, $i = 0, \ldots, k$. We wish to find new control points $\widehat{\mathbf{p}}_i$, $i = 0, \ldots, k, k + 1$ so that the degree $k + 1$ Bézier curve $\widehat{\mathbf{q}}(u)$ defined by these control points is equal to $\mathbf{q}(u)$, that is, $\widehat{\mathbf{q}}(u) = \mathbf{q}(u)$ for all u.

It turns out that the solution to this problem is fairly simple. However, before we present the general solution, we first use the $k = 2$ case as an example. (See Exercise VII.17 on page 184 for an example of an application of this case.) In this case, we are given three control points, $\mathbf{p}_0, \mathbf{p}_1, \mathbf{p}_2$, of a degree two Bézier curve $\mathbf{q}(u)$. Since $\mathbf{q}(0) = \mathbf{p}_0$ and $\mathbf{q}(1) = \mathbf{p}_2$, we must have $\widehat{\mathbf{p}}_0 = \mathbf{p}_0$ and $\widehat{\mathbf{p}}_3 = \mathbf{p}_2$ so that the degree three curve $\widehat{\mathbf{q}}(u)$ will start at $\mathbf{p}_0$ and end at $\mathbf{p}_2$. Also, the derivatives at the beginning and end of the curve are equal to

$$\mathbf{q}'(0) = 2(\mathbf{p}_1 - \mathbf{p}_0)$$

$$\mathbf{q}'(1) = 2(\mathbf{p}_2 - \mathbf{p}_1).$$

Therefore, by Equation VII.3 for the derivative of a degree three Bézier curve, we must have

$$\widehat{\mathbf{p}}_1 = \widehat{\mathbf{p}}_0 + \frac{1}{3}\mathbf{q}'(0) = \tfrac{1}{3}\mathbf{p}_0 + \tfrac{2}{3}\mathbf{p}_1$$

$$\widehat{\mathbf{p}}_2 = \widehat{\mathbf{p}}_3 - \frac{1}{3}\mathbf{q}'(1) = \tfrac{2}{3}\mathbf{p}_1 + \tfrac{1}{3}\mathbf{p}_2,$$

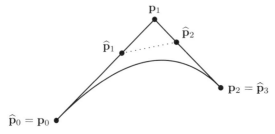

Figure VII.10. The curve $\mathbf{q}(u) = \widehat{\mathbf{q}}(u)$ is both a degree two Bézier curve with control points $\mathbf{p}_0$, $\mathbf{p}_1$, and $\mathbf{p}_2$ and a degree three Bézier curve with control points $\widehat{\mathbf{p}}_0$, $\widehat{\mathbf{p}}_1$, $\widehat{\mathbf{p}}_2$, and $\widehat{\mathbf{p}}_3$.

as shown in Figure VII.10. These choices for control points give $\widehat{\mathbf{q}}(u)$ the right starting and ending derivatives. Since $\mathbf{q}(u)$ and $\widehat{\mathbf{q}}(u)$ both are polynomials of degree ≤ 3, it follows that $\widehat{\mathbf{q}}(u)$ is equal to $\mathbf{q}(u)$.

Now, we turn to the general case of degree elevation. Suppose $\mathbf{q}(u)$ is a degree k curve with control points $\mathbf{p}_0, \ldots, \mathbf{p}_k$: we wish to find $k + 1$ control points $\widehat{\mathbf{p}}_0, \ldots, \widehat{\mathbf{p}}_{k+1}$ which define the degree $k + 1$ Bézier curve $\widehat{\mathbf{q}}(u)$ that is identical to $\mathbf{q}(u)$. For this, the following definitions work:

$$\widehat{\mathbf{p}}_0 = \mathbf{p}_0 \qquad \widehat{\mathbf{p}}_{k+1} = \mathbf{p}_k$$

$$\widehat{\mathbf{p}}_i = \frac{i}{k+1}\mathbf{p}_{i-1} + \frac{k-i+1}{k+1}\mathbf{p}_i.$$

Note that the first two equations, for $\widehat{\mathbf{p}}_0$ and $\widehat{\mathbf{p}}_{k+1}$, can be viewed as special cases of the third by defining $\mathbf{p}_{-1}$ and $\mathbf{p}_{k+1}$ to be arbitrary points.

Theorem VII.8 *Let $\mathbf{q}(u)$, $\widehat{\mathbf{q}}(u)$, $\mathbf{p}_i$, and $\widehat{\mathbf{p}}_i$ be as above. Then $\widehat{\mathbf{q}}(u) = \mathbf{q}(u)$ for all u.*

Proof We need to show that

$$\sum_{i=0}^{k+1} \binom{k+1}{i} u^i (1-u)^{k-i+1} \widehat{\mathbf{p}}_i = \sum_{i=0}^{k} \binom{k}{i} u^i (1-u)^{k-i} \mathbf{p}_i. \qquad \text{VII.10}$$

The left-hand side of this equation is also equal to

$$\sum_{i=0}^{k+1} \binom{k+1}{i} u^i (1-u)^{k-i+1} \left(\frac{i}{k+1}\mathbf{p}_{i-1} + \frac{k-i+1}{k+1}\mathbf{p}_i \right).$$

Regrouping the summation, we calculate the coefficient of $\mathbf{p}_i$ in this last equation to be equal to

$$\binom{k+1}{i+1}\frac{i+1}{k+1}u^{i+1}(1-u)^{k-i} + \binom{k+1}{i}\frac{k-i+1}{k+1}u^i(1-u)^{k-i+1}.$$

Using the identities $\binom{k+1}{i+1}\frac{i+1}{k+1} = \binom{k}{i} = \binom{k+1}{i}\frac{k-i+1}{k+1}$, we find this is further equal to

$$\binom{k}{i}(u + (1-u))u^i(1-u)^{k-i} = \binom{k}{i}u^i(1-u)^{k-i}.$$

Thus, we have shown that $\mathbf{p}_i$ has the same coefficient on both sides of Equation VII.10, which proves the desired equality. $\qquad \square$

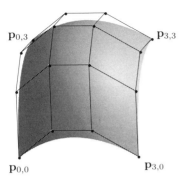

$\mathbf{p}_{0,3}$ $\mathbf{p}_{3,3}$

$\mathbf{p}_{0,0}$ $\mathbf{p}_{3,0}$

Figure VII.11. A degree three Bézier patch and its control points. The control points are shown joined by straight line segments.

VII.10 Bézier Surface Patches

This section extends the notion of Bézier curves to define Bézier patches. A Bézier curve is a one-dimensional curve; a Bézier patch is a two-dimensional parametric surface. Typically, a Bézier patch is parameterized by variables u and v, which both range over the interval $[0, 1]$. The patch is then the parametric surface $\mathbf{q}(u, v)$, where $\mathbf{q}$ is a vector-valued function defined on the unit square $[0, 1]^2$.

VII.10.1 Basic Properties of Bézier Patches

Bézier patches of degree three are defined using a 4×4 array of control points $\mathbf{p}_{i,j}$, where i, j take on values 0, 1, 2, 3. The Bézier patch with these control points is given by the formula

$$\mathbf{q}(u, v) = \sum_{i=0}^{3} \sum_{j=0}^{3} B_i(u) B_j(v) \mathbf{p}_{i,j}. \qquad \text{VII.11}$$

An example is shown in Figure VII.11. Intuitively, the control points act similarly to the control points used for Bézier curves. The four corner control points, $\mathbf{p}_{0,0}$, $\mathbf{p}_{3,0}$, $\mathbf{p}_{0,3}$, and $\mathbf{p}_{3,3}$ form the four corners of the Bézier patch, and the remaining twelve control points influence the patch by "pulling" the patch towards them.

Equation VII.11 can be equivalently written in either of the forms

$$\mathbf{q}(u, v) = \sum_{i=0}^{3} \left(B_i(u) \cdot \sum_{j=0}^{3} B_j(v) \mathbf{p}_{i,j} \right) \qquad \text{VII.12}$$

$$\mathbf{q}(u, v) = \sum_{j=0}^{3} \left(B_j(v) \cdot \sum_{i=0}^{3} B_i(u) \mathbf{p}_{i,j} \right). \qquad \text{VII.13}$$

Consider the cross sections of $\mathbf{q}(u, v)$ obtained by holding the value of v fixed and varying u. Some of these cross sections are shown going from left to right in Figure VII.12. Equation VII.12 shows that each such cross section is a degree three Bézier curve with control points $\mathbf{r}_i$ equal to the inner summation, that is,

$$\mathbf{r}_i = \sum_{j=0}^{3} B_j(v) \mathbf{p}_{i,j}.$$

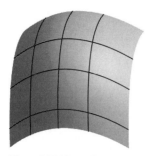

Figure VII.12. A degree three Bézier patch and some cross sections. The cross sections are Bézier curves.

Thus, the cross sections of the Bézier patch obtained by holding v fixed and letting u vary are ordinary Bézier curves. The control points $\mathbf{r}_i$ for the cross section are functions of v of course and are in fact given as Bézier curves of the control points $\mathbf{p}_{i,j}$.

Similarly, from Equation VII.13, if we hold u fixed and let v vary, then the cross sections are again Bézier curves and the control points $\mathbf{s}_j$ of the Bézier curve cross sections are computed as functions of u as Bézier curve functions:

$$\mathbf{s}_j = \sum_{i=0}^{3} B_i(u)\mathbf{p}_{i,j}.$$

Now consider what the boundaries of the Bézier patch look like. The "front" boundary is where $v = 0$ and $u \in [0, 1]$. For this front cross section, the control points $\mathbf{r}_i$ are equal to $\mathbf{p}_{i,0}$. Thus, the front boundary is the degree three Bézier curve with control points $\mathbf{p}_{0,0}$, $\mathbf{p}_{1,0}$, $\mathbf{p}_{2,0}$, and $\mathbf{p}_{3,0}$. Similarly, the "left" boundary where $u = 0$ is the Bézier curve with control points $\mathbf{p}_{0,0}$, $\mathbf{p}_{0,1}$, $\mathbf{p}_{0,2}$, and $\mathbf{p}_{0,3}$. Likewise, the other two boundaries are Bézier curves that have as control points the $\mathbf{p}_{i,j}$'s on the boundaries.

The first-order partial derivatives of the Bézier patch $\mathbf{q}(u, v)$ can be calculated with aid of Theorem VII.4 along with equations VII.12 and VII.13. This can be used to calculate the normal vector to the Bézier patch surface via Theorem III.1. Rather than carrying out the calculation of the general formula for partial derivatives here, we will instead consider only the partial derivatives at the boundary of the patches because these will be useful in the discussion about joining together Bézier patches with C^1- and G^1-continuity (see Section VII.10.2). By using Equation VII.3 for the derivatives of a Bézier curve at its endpoints and Equations VII.12 and VII.13, we can calculate the partial derivatives of $\mathbf{q}(u, v)$ at its boundary points as

$$\frac{\partial \mathbf{q}}{\partial v}(u, 0) = \sum_{i=0}^{3} 3B_i(u)(\mathbf{p}_{i,1} - \mathbf{p}_{i,0}) \qquad\qquad \text{VII.14}$$

$$\frac{\partial \mathbf{q}}{\partial v}(u, 1) = \sum_{i=0}^{3} 3B_i(u)(\mathbf{p}_{i,3} - \mathbf{p}_{i,2}) \qquad\qquad \text{VII.15}$$

$$\frac{\partial \mathbf{q}}{\partial u}(0, v) = \sum_{j=0}^{3} 3B_j(v)(\mathbf{p}_{1,j} - \mathbf{p}_{0,j}) \qquad\qquad \text{VII.16}$$

$$\frac{\partial \mathbf{q}}{\partial u}(1, v) = \sum_{j=0}^{3} 3B_j(v)(\mathbf{p}_{3,j} - \mathbf{p}_{2,j}). \qquad\qquad \text{VII.17}$$

These four partial derivatives are the partial derivatives in the directions pointing perpendicularly to the boundaries of the patch's domain. The other partial derivatives at the boundary, such as $(\partial \mathbf{q}/\partial u)(u, 0)$, can easily be calculated from the fact that the boundaries of the patch are Bézier curves.

Later, in Section VII.16, we will need to know the formulas for the second-order mixed partial derivatives at the corners of the patch. Using Equation VII.3 or Corollary VII.5 and Equation VII.14, we have

$$\frac{\partial^2 \mathbf{q}}{\partial u \partial v}(0, 0) = 9 \cdot (\mathbf{p}_{1,1} - \mathbf{p}_{0,1} - \mathbf{p}_{1,0} + \mathbf{p}_{0,0}). \qquad \text{VII.18}$$

Similarly, at the other three corners of the patch, we have

$$\frac{\partial^2 \mathbf{q}}{\partial u \partial v}(0, 1) = 9 \cdot (\mathbf{p}_{1,3} - \mathbf{p}_{0,3} - \mathbf{p}_{1,2} + \mathbf{p}_{0,2})$$

$$\frac{\partial^2 \mathbf{q}}{\partial u \partial v}(1, 0) = 9 \cdot (\mathbf{p}_{3,1} - \mathbf{p}_{2,1} - \mathbf{p}_{3,0} + \mathbf{p}_{2,0}) \qquad \text{VII.19}$$

$$\frac{\partial^2 \mathbf{q}}{\partial u \partial v}(1, 1) = 9 \cdot (\mathbf{p}_{3,3} - \mathbf{p}_{2,3} - \mathbf{p}_{3,2} + \mathbf{p}_{2,2}).$$

The second-order mixed partial derivatives at the corners are called *twist vectors*.

Exercise VII.10★ *Use Theorem VII.4 to work out the general formula for the first-order partial derivatives of a Bézier patch, $\partial \mathbf{q}(u, v)/\partial u$ and $\partial \mathbf{q}(u, v)/\partial v$.*

Exercise VII.11 *Derive an extension of the de Casteljau algorithm for degree three curves (see Section VII.2) that applies to Bézier patches of degree three.*

Exercise VII.12 *Derive a recursive subdivision method for degree three Bézier patches based on recursive subdivision for Bézier curves. Your method should either subdivide in the u direction or in the v direction and split a patch into two patches (i.e., it should not subdivide in both directions at once).*

VII.10.2 Joining Bézier Patches

A common use of Bézier patches is to combine multiple patches to make a smooth surface. With only 16 control points, a single Bézier patch can make only a limited range of surface shapes. However, by joining multiple patches, a wider range of surface shapes can be approximated. Let us start by considering how to join two patches together so as to make a continuous or C^1- or G^1-continuous surface. The situation is that we have two Bézier patches $\mathbf{q}_1(u, v)$ and $\mathbf{q}_2(u, v)$. The control points of $\mathbf{q}_1$ are $\mathbf{p}_{i,j}$, and those of $\mathbf{q}_2$ are the points $\mathbf{r}_{i,j}$. In addition, $\mathbf{q}_2$ has domain $[0, 1]^2$ as usual, but the surface $\mathbf{q}_1$ has been translated to have domain $[-1, 0] \times [0, 1]$ (by use of the change of variables $u \mapsto u + 1$). We wish to find conditions on the control points that will cause the two surfaces to join smoothly at their boundary where $u = 0$ and $0 \le v \le 1$, as shown in Figure VII.13.

Recall that the right boundary of $\mathbf{q}_1$ (where $u = 0$) is the Bézier curve with control points $\mathbf{p}_{3,j}$, $j = 0, 1, 2, 3$. Likewise, the left boundary of $\mathbf{q}_2$ is the Bézier curve with control points $\mathbf{r}_{0,j}$. Thus, in order for the two boundaries to match, it is necessary and sufficient that $\mathbf{p}_{3,j} = \mathbf{r}_{0,j}$ for $j = 0, 1, 2, 3$.

Now we assume that the patches are continuous at their boundary and consider continuity of the partial derivatives at the boundary between the patches. First, since the boundaries are equal, clearly the partials with respect to v are equal. For the partials with respect to u, it follows

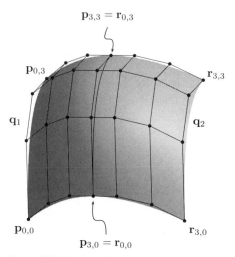

Figure VII.13. Two Bézier patches join to form a single smooth surface. The two patches $\mathbf{q}_1$ and $\mathbf{q}_2$ each have 16 control points. The four rightmost control points of $\mathbf{q}_1$ are the same as the four leftmost control points of $\mathbf{q}_2$. The patches are shown forming a C^1-continuous surface.

from Equations VII.16 and VII.17 that a necessary and sufficient condition for C^1-continuity, that is, for

$$\frac{\partial \mathbf{q}_2}{\partial u}(0, v) = \frac{\partial \mathbf{q}_1}{\partial u}(0, v)$$

to hold for all v, is that

$$\mathbf{p}_{3,j} - \mathbf{p}_{2,j} = \mathbf{r}_{1,j} - \mathbf{r}_{0,j} \qquad \text{for } j = 0, 1, 2, 3. \qquad\qquad \text{VII.20}$$

For G^1-continuity, it is sufficient that these four vectors are nonzero and that there is a scalar $\alpha > 0$ so that

$$\mathbf{p}_{3,j} - \mathbf{p}_{2,j} = \alpha(\mathbf{r}_{1,j} - \mathbf{r}_{0,j}) \qquad \text{for } j = 0, 1, 2, 3.$$

In Section VII.16, we will use the condition VII.20 for C^1-continuity to help make surfaces that interpolate points specified on a rectangular grid.

Subdividing Bézier Patches
In Exercise VII.12, you were asked to give an algorithm for recursively subdividing degree three Bézier patches. As in the case of Bézier curves, recursive subdivision is often used to divide a surface until it consists of small patches that are essentially flat. Each flat patch can be approximated as a flat quadrilateral (or, more precisely, can be divided into two triangles, each of which is necessarily planar). These flat patches can then be rendered as usual. In the case of recursive subdivision of patches, there is a new problem: since some patches may need to be subdivided further than others, it can happen that a surface is subdivided and its neighbor is not. This is pictured in Figure VII.14, where $\mathbf{q}_1$ and $\mathbf{q}_2$ are patches. After $\mathbf{q}_1$ is divided into two subpatches, there is a mismatch between the (formerly common) boundaries of $\mathbf{q}_1$ and $\mathbf{q}_2$. If this mismatch is allowed to persist, then we have a problem known as *cracking* in which small gaps or small overlaps can appear in the surface.

One way to fix cracking is to replace the boundary by a straight line. Namely, once the decision has been made that $\mathbf{q}_2$ needs no further subdivision (and will be rendered as a flat patch), replace the boundary between $\mathbf{q}_1$ and $\mathbf{q}_2$ with a straight line. This is done by redefining

$\mathbf{q}_1$ $\mathbf{q}_2$ $\mathbf{q}_1$ $\mathbf{q}_2$

Figure VII.14. Nonuniform subdivision can cause cracking. On the left, two Bézier patches share a common boundary. On the right, after subdivision of the left patch $\mathbf{q}_1$, the boundaries no longer match up.

the two middle control points along the common boundary. This forces the boundary of $\mathbf{q}_1$ also to be straight, and this straightness is preserved by subsequent subdivision.

Unfortunately, just replacing the boundary by a straight line is not enough to fix the cracking problem completely. First, as discussed at the end of Chapter II, there may be problems with pixel-size holes along the boundary (see the discussion accompanying Figure II.29 on page 66). Second, and more seriously, it is also important that the surface normals on the boundary between the two patches match up in order for lighting computations to be consistent. Still worse, being consistent about assigning surface normals to the vertices is not enough: this is because Gouraud interpolation is used to shade the results of the lighting calculation along the boundary between the patches. If the boundary is divided into two pieces in one patch and left as one piece in the other patch, Gouraud interpolation will give different results in the two patches. This could happen if three quadrilaterals were rendered as shown on the left in Figure VII.15 since the lighting calculated at the center vertex may not be consistent with the light values obtained by Gouraud interpolation when rendering patch $\mathbf{q}_2$. One possible solution to this problem is shown on the right in Figure VII.15, where the quadrilateral patch $\mathbf{q}_2$ has been split into a triangle and another quadrilateral. With this solution, the boundary is rendered only in separate pieces, never as a single edge, and Gouraud interpolation yields consistent results on both sides of the boundary.

We have discussed only degree three Bézier patches above, but of course, Bézier patches can also be defined with other degrees. In addition, a Bézier patch may have a different degree in u than in v. In general, if the Bézier patch has degree k_u in u and degree k_v in v, then there are $(k_u + 1)(k_v + 1)$ control points $\mathbf{p}_{i,j}$ with $0 \le i \le k_u$ and $0 \le j \le k_v$. The Bézier patch is given by

$$\mathbf{q}(u, v) \;=\; \sum_{i=0}^{k_u} \sum_{j=0}^{k_v} B_i^{k_u}(u) B_j^{k_v}(v) \mathbf{p}_{i,j}.$$

We will not develop the theory of Bézier patches of general degree any further; however, an example of a Bézier patch that is degree three in one direction and degree two in the other is shown in Section VII.14 on page 188.

$\mathbf{q}_1$ $\mathbf{q}_2$ $\mathbf{q}_1$ $\mathbf{q}_2$

Figure VII.15. Two solutions to the cracking problem. On the left, the subdivided $\mathbf{q}_1$ and the original $\mathbf{q}_2$ share a common straight boundary. However, the lighting and shading calculations may cause the surface to be rendered discontinuously at the boundary. On the right, the patch $\mathbf{q}_2$ has been subdivided in an ad hoc way to allow the common boundary to have the same points and normals with respect to both patches.

VII.11 Bézier Curves and Surfaces in OpenGL

VII.11.1 Bézier Curves

OpenGL has several routines for automatic generation of Bézier curves of any degree. However, OpenGL does not have generic Bézier curve support; instead, its Bézier curve functions are linked directly to drawing routines. Unfortunately, this means that the OpenGL Bézier curve routines can be used only for drawing; thus, if you wish to use Bézier curves for other applications, such as animation, you cannot use the built-in OpenGL routines.

Instead of having a single command for generating Bézier curves, OpenGL has separate commands for defining or initializing a Bézier curve from its control points and for displaying part or all of the Bézier curve.

Defining Bézier Curves. To define and enable (i.e., activate) a Bézier curve, the following two OpenGL commands are used:

```
glMap1f(GL_MAP1_VERTEX_3, float umin, float umax,
        int stride, int order, float* controlpointsptr );
glEnable(GL_MAP1_VERTEX_3);
```

The values of u_{min} and u_{max} give the range of u values over which the curve is defined. These are typically set to 0 and 1.

The last parameter points to an array of floats that contains the control points. A typical usage would define `controlpoints` as an array of x, y, z values,

```
float controlpoints[M][3];
```

and then the parameter `controlpointsptr` would be `&controlpoints[0][0]`. The `stride` value is the distance (in floats) from one control point to the next; that is, the control point $\mathbf{p}_i$ is pointed to by `controlpointsptr`+i*`stride`. For the preceding definition of `controlpoints`, `stride` equals 3.

The value of `order` is equal to one plus the degree of the Bézier curve; thus, it also equals the number of control points. Consequently, for the usual degree three Bézier curves, the order M equals 4.

As mentioned above, Bézier curves can be used only for drawing purposes. In fact, several Bézier curves can be active at one time to affect different aspects of the drawn curve such as its location and color. The first parameter to `glMap1f()` describes how the Bézier curve is used when the curve is drawn. The parameter `GL_MAP1_VERTEX_3` means that the Bézier curve is defining the x, y, z values of points in 3-space as a function of u. There are several other useful constants that can be used for the first parameter. These include `GL_MAP1_VERTEX_4`, which means that we are specifying x, y, z, w values of a curve, that is, a rational Bézier curve (see Sections VII.12 and VII.13 for information on rational curves). Also, one can use `GL_MAP1_COLOR_4` as the first parameter: this means that, as the Bézier curve is being drawn (by the commands described below), the color values will be specified as a Bézier function of u. You should consult the OpenGL documentation for other permitted values for this first parameter. Finally, a reminder: do not forget to give the `glEnable` command for any of these parameters you wish to activate!

Drawing Bézier Curves. Once the Bézier curve has been specified with `glMap1f()`, the curve can be drawn with the following commands. The most basic way to specify a point on the curve is with the command

```
glEvalCoord1f( float u );
```

which must be given between a glBegin() and glEnd(). The effect of this command is similar to specifying a point with glVertex* and, if the appropriate curves are enabled, with glNormal* and glTexCoord* commands. However, the currently active normal and texture coordinates are not changed by a call to glEvalCoord1f().

When you use glEvalCoord1f(), you are explicitly drawing the points on the curve. However, frequently you want to draw an entire curve or a portion of a curve at once instead of having to make multiple calls to glEvalCoord1f. For this, OpenGL has several commands that will automatically draw points at equally spaced intervals along the curve. To use these commands, after calling glMap1f and the corresponding glEnable, you must next tell OpenGL the "grid" or "mesh" of points on the curve to be drawn. This is done with the following command:

glMapGrid1f(int N, float u_{start}, float u_{end});

which tells OpenGL that you want the curve to be discretized as $N + 1$ equally spaced points starting with the value $u = u_{\text{start}}$ and ending with $u = u_{\text{end}}$. It is required that $u_{\text{min}} \leq u_{\text{start}} \leq u_{\text{end}} \leq u_{\text{max}}$.

A call to glMapGrid1f() only sets a grid of u values. To actually draw the curve, you should then call

glEvalMesh1(GL_LINE, int p_{start}, int p_{end});

This causes OpenGL to draw the curve at grid values, letting p range from p_{start} to p_{end} and drawing the points on the Bézier curve with coordinates

$$u = ((N - p)u_{\text{start}} + p \cdot u_{\text{end}})/N.$$

The first parameter, GL_LINE, tells OpenGL to draw the curve as a sequence of straight lines. This has the same functionality as drawing points after a call to glBegin(GL_LINE_STRIP). To draw only the points on the curve without the connecting lines, use GL_POINT instead (similar in functionality to using glBegin(GL_POINTS)). The values of p_{start} and p_{end} should satisfy $0 \leq p_{\text{start}} \leq p_{\text{end}} \leq N$.

You can also use glEvalPoint1(int p) to draw a single point from the grid. The functions glEvalPoint1 and glEvalMesh1 are *not* called from inside glBegin() and glEnd().

VII.11.2 Bézier Patches

Bézier patches, or Bézier surfaces, can be drawn using OpenGL commands analogous to the commands described in the previous section for Bézier curves. Since the commands are very similar, only very brief descriptions are given of the OpenGL routines for Bézier patches. The SimpleNurbs program in the software accompanying this book shows an example of how to render a Bézier patch in OpenGL.

To specify a Bézier patch, one uses the glMap2f() routine:

```
glMap2f(GL_MAP2_VERTEX_3,
        float umin, float umax, int ustride, int uorder,
        float vmin, float vmax, int vstride, int vorder,
        float* controlpoints );
glEnable(GL_MAP2_VERTEX_3);
```

The controlpoints array is now a (uorder)×(vorder) array and would usually be specified by

```
float controlpointsarray[Mu][Mv][3];
```

where M_u and M_v are the `uorder` and `vorder` values. In this case, the value `vstride` would equal 3, and `ustride` should equal $3M_v$. Note that the orders (which equal 1 plus the degrees) of the Bézier curves are allowed to be different for the u and v directions.

Other useful values for the first parameter to `glMap2f()` include `GL_MAP2_VERTEX_4` for rational Bézier patches, `GL_MAP2_COLOR_4` to specify colors, and `GL_MAP2_TEXTURE_COORD_2` to specify texture coordinates. Again, you must give the `glEnable` command to activate these settings for the parameter.

For many typical applications of texture coordinates to Bézier patches, one wants the texture coordinates s, t just to be equal to u and v. This is done by specifying a degree one (`order= 2`) Bézier curve; for instance,

```
float texpts[8]={0,0,  0,1,  1,0,  1,1};
glMap2f(GL_MAP2_TEXTURE_COORD_2,0,1,4,2,0,1,2,2,&texpts[0]);
glEnable(GL_MAP2_TEXTURE_COORD_2);
```

The normals to the patch may be specified by a Bézier formula using `GL_MAP2_NORMAL` as the first parameter to `glMap2f()`. However, this is rarely useful because typically one wants the true normals to the Bézier surface. OpenGL will calculate these true normals for you (according to Formula III.12 if applicable), if you give the command

```
glEnable(GL_AUTO_NORMAL);
```

To display the Bézier patch, or a portion of the Bézier surface, the following OpenGL commands are available:

```
glEvalCoord2f(float u,  float v);
glMapGrid2f(int Nu,  float ustart,  float uend,
                int Nv,  int vstart,  int vend);
glEvalMesh2(GL_FILL, int pstart,  pend,  qstart,  qend);
glEvalPoint2(int p,  int q);
```

The first parameter to `glEvalMesh2()` may be also `GL_LINE` or `GL_POINT`. These commands work analogously to the commands for one-dimensional Bézier curves. The most direct method of drawing a Bézier patch is to call `glMapGrid2f` and then `glEvalMesh2`.

> **Exercise VII.13** *Build a figure such as a teapot, coffee pot, vase, or other shape of similar complexity. The techniques described in Blinn's article (Blinn, 1987) on the famous Utah teapot can make this fairly straightforward. Make sure that normals are calculated so that lighting is applied correctly (OpenGL can compute the normal for you).*
>
> *Optionally, refer ahead to Sections VII.13 and VII.14 to learn how to make surfaces of revolution with rational Bézier patches. Apply this to make the cross sections of your object perfectly circular.*

One difficulty with completing the preceding exercise is that OpenGL does not always calculate normals on Bézier surfaces correctly. In particular, OpenGL has problems with normals when an edge of a Bézier patch consists of a single point. Remember that you should use `glEnable(GL_NORMALIZE)` when transforming illuminated objects. The sample program `SimpleNurbs` shows how to use OpenGL to render a Bézier patch with correct normals and illumination.

VII.12 Rational Bézier Curves

A Bézier curve is called *rational* if its control points are specified with homogeneous coordinates. Using homogeneous representations for control points may seem obscure or mystifying at first, but, in fact, there is nothing especially mysterious about the use of homogeneous

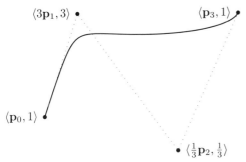

Figure VII.16. A degree three, rational Bézier curve. The control points are the same as in the left-hand side of Figure VII.2 on page 156, but now the control point $\mathbf{p}_1$ is weighted 3 and the control point $\mathbf{p}_2$ is weighted only $1/3$. The other two control points have weight 1. In comparison with the curve of Figure VII.2, this curve more closely approaches $\mathbf{p}_1$ but does not approach $\mathbf{p}_2$ nearly as closely.

coordinates for control points. In $\mathbb{R}^3$ (say), the control points are specified as 4-tuples $\mathbf{p}_i = \langle x, y, z, w \rangle$: the curve's values $\mathbf{q}(u)$ are expressed as weighted averages of the control points,

$$\mathbf{q}(u) = \sum_i B_i^k(u) \mathbf{p}_i,$$

and so the values of $\mathbf{q}(u)$ specify the points on the curve in homogeneous coordinates too.

There are several advantages to rational Bézier curves. These include the following:

a. The use of homogeneous coordinates allows the w-coordinate value to serve a weight factor that can be used to increase or decrease the relative weight of a control point. A higher weight for a control point causes the Bézier curve to be "pulled" harder by the control point.

b. The use of weights in this form allows rational Bézier curves to define circular arcs, ellipses, hyperbolas, and other conic curves.

c. Rational Bézier curves are preserved under perspective transformations, not just affine transformations. This is because the points on a Bézier curve are computed as weighted averages and affine combinations of homogeneous coordinates are preserved under perspective transformations (see Section IV.4).

d. Control points can be placed at infinity, giving extra flexibility in the definition of a Bézier curve.

To understand a., recall from Section IV.4 the notation $\langle w\mathbf{p}, w \rangle$, where $\mathbf{p} \in \mathbb{R}^3$ and $w \neq 0$, and where $\langle w\mathbf{p}, w \rangle$ is the 4-tuple that is the (unique) homogeneous representation of $\mathbf{p}$, which has w as its fourth component. Then a point $\mathbf{q}(u)$ on the curve is defined by a weighted average of homogeneous control points, namely

$$\mathbf{q}(u) = \sum_i B_i^k(u) \langle w_i \mathbf{p}_i, w_i \rangle.$$

The point $\mathbf{q}(u)$ is also a 4-tuple and thus is a homogeneous representation of a point in $\mathbb{R}^3$. By the earlier discussion in Section IV.4, it represents the following point in $\mathbb{R}^3$:

$$\sum_i \frac{w_i B_i^k(u)}{\sum_j w_j B_i^k(u)} \mathbf{p}_i.$$

Thus, the w-components of the control points act like extra weighting factors. Figure VII.16 shows an example of how weights can affect a Bézier curve.

$\mathbf{p}_0 = \langle 0, 1, 1 \rangle$

$\mathbf{q}(u)$

$\mathbf{p}_1 = \langle 1, 0, 0 \rangle$

$\mathbf{p}_2 = \langle 0, -1, 1 \rangle$

Figure VII.17. The situation of Theorem VII.9. The middle control point is actually a point at infinity, and the dotted lines joining it to the other control points are actually straight and are tangent to the circle at $\mathbf{p}_0$ and $\mathbf{p}_2$.

We used the representation $\langle w\mathbf{p}, w \rangle$ for the homogeneous representation of $\mathbf{p}$, with last component w. That is, if $\mathbf{p} = \langle p_1, p_2, p_3 \rangle \in \mathbb{R}^3$, then $\langle w\mathbf{p}, w \rangle$ is the 4-tuple $\langle wp_1, wp_2, wp_3, w \rangle$. This notation is a little confusing and user-unfriendly. Accordingly, drawing software or CAD programs usually use a different convention: these programs allow a user to set, independently, a control point $\mathbf{p}$ and a weight w, but they hide from the user the fact that the components of $\mathbf{p}$ are being multiplied by w. You can refer to Figure VII.19 for an example of this convention, where the control points in $\mathbb{R}^2$ are given in terms of their nonhomogeneous representation plus their weight.

VII.13 Conic Sections with Rational Bézier Curves

A major advantage to using rational Bézier curves is that they allow the definition of conic sections as quadratic Bézier curves. We start with an example that includes a point at infinity.[5]

Theorem VII.9 *Let* $\mathbf{p}_0 = \langle 0, 1, 1 \rangle$, $\mathbf{p}_1 = \langle 1, 0, 0 \rangle$, *and* $\mathbf{p}_2 = \langle 0, -1, 1 \rangle$ *be homogeneous representations of points in* $\mathbb{R}^2$. *Let* $\mathbf{q}(u)$ *be the degree two Bézier curve defined with these control points. Then, the curve* $\mathbf{q}(u)$ *traces out the right half of the unit circle* $x^2 + y^2 = 1$ *as u varies from 0 to 1.*

The situation of Theorem VII.9 is shown in Figure VII.17. Note that the middle control point is actually a point at infinity. However, we will see that the points $\mathbf{q}(u)$ on the curve are not points at infinity but are always finite points. To interpret the statement of the theorem properly, note that the points $\mathbf{q}(u)$ as computed from the three control points are actually homogeneous representations of points in $\mathbb{R}^2$. That is, $\mathbf{q}(u)$ is a triple $\langle q_1(u), q_2(u), q_3(u) \rangle$ and is the homogeneous representation of the point $\langle q_1(u)/q_3(u), q_2(u)/q_3(u) \rangle$ in $\mathbb{R}^2$. The import of the theorem is that the points $\mathbf{q}(u)$, when interpreted as homogeneous representations of points in $\mathbb{R}^2$, trace out the right half of the unit circle.

We now prove Theorem VII.9. From the definition of Bézier curves,

$$\mathbf{q}(u) = (1 - u)^2 \mathbf{p}_0 + 2u(1 - u)\mathbf{p}_1 + u^2 \mathbf{p}_2$$

$$= (1 - u)^2 \langle 0, 1, 1 \rangle + 2u(1 - u)\langle 1, 0, 0 \rangle + u^2 \langle 0, -1, 1 \rangle$$

$$= \langle 2u(1 - u), (1 - u)^2 - u^2, (1 - u)^2 + u^2 \rangle.$$

It is easy to check that the third component is nonzero for $0 \leq u \leq 1$. Thus, $\mathbf{q}(u)$ is the homogeneous representation of the point

$$\langle x(u), y(u) \rangle = \left\langle \frac{2u(1 - u)}{(1 - u)^2 + u^2}, \frac{(1 - u)^2 - u^2}{(1 - u)^2 + u^2} \right\rangle.$$

---

[5]   Most of our examples of constructions of circular arcs by Bézier curves in this section and by B-spline curves in Section VIII.11 can be found in the article (Piegl and Tiller, 1989).

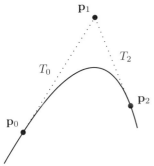

Figure VII.18. A portion of a branch of a conic section C is equal to a rational quadratic Bézier curve. Control points $\mathbf{p}_0$ and $\mathbf{p}_2$ have weight 1, and $\mathbf{p}_1$ gets weight $w_1 \geq 0$.

We need to show two things. The first is that each point $\mathbf{q}(u)$ lies on the unit circle. This is proved by showing that $x(u)^2 + y(u)^2 = 1$ for all u. For this, it is sufficient to prove that

$$[2u(1-u)]^2 + [(1-u)^2 - u^2]^2 = [(1-u)^2 + u^2]^2, \qquad \text{VII.21}$$

which is almost immediate. The second thing to show is that $\mathbf{q}(u)$ actually traces out the correct portion of the unit circle: for this we need to check that $x(u) \geq 0$ for all $u \in [0, 1]$ and that $y(u)$ is decreasing on the same interval $[0, 1]$. Both these facts can be checked readily, and we leave this to the reader.   □

Now that we have proved Theorem VII.9, the reader might reasonably ask how we knew to use the control point $\mathbf{p}_1 = \langle 1, 0, 0 \rangle$ for the middle control point. The answer is that we first tried the control point $\langle h, 0, 0 \rangle$ with h as a to-be-determined constant. We then carried out the construction of the theorem's proof but used the value h where needed. The resulting analogue of Equation VII.21 then had its first term multiplied by h^2; from this we noted that equality holds only with $h = \pm 1$, and $h = +1$ was needed to get the right half of the curve.

This construction generalizes to a procedure that can be used to represent any finite segment of any conic section as a quadratic Bézier curve. Let C be a portion of a conic section (a line, parabola, circle, ellipse, or hyperbola) in $\mathbb{R}^2$. Let $\mathbf{p}_0$ and $\mathbf{p}_2$ be two points on (one branch of) the conic section. Our goal is to find a third control point $\mathbf{p}_1$ with appropriate weight w_1 so that the quadratic curve with these three control points is equal to the portion of the conic section between $\mathbf{p}_0$ and $\mathbf{p}_1$ (refer to Figure VII.18).

Let T_0 and T_2 be the two lines tangent to the conic section at $\mathbf{p}_0$ and $\mathbf{p}_2$. Let $\mathbf{p}_1$ be the point in their intersection (or the appropriate point at infinity if the tangents are parallel, as in Theorem VII.9). We further assume that the segment of the conic section between $\mathbf{p}_0$ and $\mathbf{p}_2$ lies in the triangle formed by $\mathbf{p}_0$, $\mathbf{p}_1$, and $\mathbf{p}_2$ – this rules out the case in which the segment is more than $180°$ of a circle, for instance.

Theorem VII.10 *Let C, $\mathbf{p}_0$, $\mathbf{p}_2$, T_0, T_2, and $\mathbf{p}_1$ be as above. Let $\mathbf{p}_0$ and $\mathbf{p}_2$ be given weight 1. Then there is a value $w_1 \geq 0$ such that when $\mathbf{p}_1$ is given weight w_1, the rational degree two Bézier curve $\mathbf{q}(u)$ with control points $\mathbf{p}_0$, $\mathbf{p}_1$, and $\mathbf{p}_2$ traces out the portion of C between $\mathbf{p}_0$ and $\mathbf{p}_2$.*

Proof This was originally proved by (Lee, 1987); we give here only a quick and incomplete sketch of a proof. In the degenerate case in which C is a line, take $\mathbf{p}_1$ to be any point between $\mathbf{p}_0$ and $\mathbf{p}_2$; then any value for $w_1 \geq 0$ will work. Otherwise, for each $h \geq 0$, let $\mathbf{q}_h(u)$ be the Bézier curve obtained when $w_1 = h$. At $h = 0$, $\mathbf{q}_h(1/2)$ lies on the line segment from $\mathbf{p}_0$ to $\mathbf{p}_2$. As $h \to \infty$, $\mathbf{q}_h(1/2)$ tends to $\mathbf{p}_1$. Thus, there must be a value $h > 0$ such that $\mathbf{q}_h(1/2)$ lies on the conic section. By Theorem VII.11 below, the curve $\mathbf{q}_h(u)$ is a conic section. Furthermore,

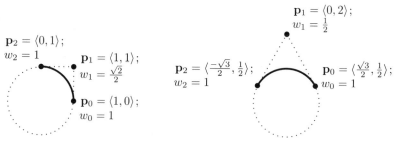

Figure VII.19. Two ways to define circular arcs with rational Bézier curves without control points at infinity.

there is a unique conic section that (a) contains the three points $\mathbf{p}_0$, $\mathbf{q}_h(1/2)$, and $\mathbf{p}_2$ and (b) is tangent to T_0 and T_2 at $\mathbf{p}_0$ and $\mathbf{p}_2$. Therefore, with $w_1 = h$, the resulting Bézier curve must trace out C. □

Theorem VII.10 gives the general framework for designing quadratic Bézier curves that form conic sections. Note that the fact that $\mathbf{p}_1$ lies at the intersection of the two tangent lines T_0 and T_2 is forced by the fact that the initial (respectively, the final) derivative of a Bézier curve points from the first (respectively, the second) control point towards the second point (respectively, the third point). It can be shown, using the equivalence of rational Bézier curves to Bézier curves with weighting, that this fact holds also for rational Bézier curves.

The next three exercises give some ways to form circles as quadratic Bézier curves that do not require the use of a point at infinity.

Exercise VII.14 *Let $\mathbf{q}(u)$ be the rational, degree two Bézier curve with homogeneous control points $\mathbf{p}_0 = \langle 1, 0, 1 \rangle$, $\mathbf{p}_1 = \langle \sqrt{2}/2, \sqrt{2}/2, \sqrt{2}/2 \rangle$ and $\mathbf{p}_2 = \langle 0, 1, 1 \rangle$. Prove that this Bézier curve traces out the $90°$ arc of the unit circle in $\mathbb{R}^2$ from the point $\langle 1, 0 \rangle$ to $\langle 0, 1 \rangle$. See Figure VII.19 where the control points are shown in $\mathbb{R}^2$ with their weights.*

Exercise VII.15 *Let $\mathbf{q}(u)$ be the rational, degree two Bézier curve defined with homogeneous control points $\mathbf{p}_0 = \langle \sqrt{3}/2, 1/2, 1 \rangle$, $\mathbf{p}_1 = \langle 0, 1, 1/2 \rangle$, and $\mathbf{p}_2 = \langle -\sqrt{3}/2, 1/2, 1 \rangle$. Prove that this Bézier curve traces out the $120°$ arc of the unit circle in $\mathbb{R}^2$ from $\langle \sqrt{3}/2, 1/2 \rangle$ to $\langle -\sqrt{3}/2, 1/2 \rangle$. See Figure VII.19.*

Exercise VII.16★ *Generalize the constructions of the previous two exercises. Suppose that $\mathbf{p}_0$ and $\mathbf{p}_2$ lie on the unit circle separated by an angle of θ, $0° < \theta < 180°$. Show that the arc from $\mathbf{p}_0$ to $\mathbf{p}_2$ can be represented by a degree two Bézier curve, where $\mathbf{p}_0$ and $\mathbf{p}_2$ are given weight 1, and $\mathbf{p}_1$ is given weight $w_1 = \cos(\theta/2)$. Also, give a formula expressing (or, if you prefer, an algorithm to compute) the position of $\mathbf{p}_1$ in terms of the positions of $\mathbf{p}_0$ and $\mathbf{p}_2$.*

Sometimes it is desirable to use degree three curves instead of degree two curves for conic sections. There are many ways to define conic sections with degree three curves: the next exercise suggests that one general method is first to form the curve as a degree two conic section and then to elevate the degree to degree three using the method of Section VII.9.

Exercise VII.17 *Apply degree elevation to the degree two Bézier curve of Theorem VII.9 (Figure VII.17) to prove that the following degree three Bézier curve traces out the right half of the unit circle: the degree three curve is defined with control points $\mathbf{p}_0 = \langle 0, 1 \rangle$, $\mathbf{p}_1 = \langle 2, 1 \rangle$, $\mathbf{p}_2 = \langle 2, -1 \rangle$ and $\mathbf{p}_3 = \langle 0, -1 \rangle$, with $\mathbf{p}_0$ and $\mathbf{p}_3$ having weight 1 and $\mathbf{p}_1$ and $\mathbf{p}_2$ having weight 1/3 (see Figure VII.20).*

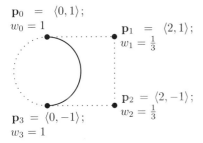

$$\mathbf{p}_0 = \langle 0, 1 \rangle;$$
$$w_0 = 1$$

$$\mathbf{p}_1 = \langle 2, 1 \rangle;$$
$$w_1 = \tfrac{1}{3}$$

$$\mathbf{p}_2 = \langle 2, -1 \rangle;$$
$$w_2 = \tfrac{1}{3}$$

$$\mathbf{p}_3 = \langle 0, -1 \rangle;$$
$$w_3 = 1$$

Figure VII.20. A semicircle as a degree three Bézier curve. See Exercise VII.17.

The next exercise shows that it is also possible to use negatively weighted control points for rational Bézier curves. This is more of an oddity than a genuinely useful construction; in particular, the convex hull property is lost when negatively weighted points are allowed (see Theorem IV.9).

> **Exercise VII.18** *Investigate what happens with negatively weighted control points. For instance, investigate what happens to the Bézier curve of Exercise VII.14 if the middle control point is redefined as $\mathbf{p}_1 = (-\sqrt{2}/2, -\sqrt{2}/2, -\sqrt{2}/2)$, that is, is a homogeneous representation of the same point but now in negated form. [Answer: You obtain the other three quarters of the unit circle.]*

Theorem VII.10 shows that finite portions of conic sections can be represented by quadratic Bézier curves. Its proof depended on the next theorem, which asserts that conic sections are the only curves that can be represented by quadratic Bézier curves.

Theorem VII.11 *Let $\mathbf{q}(u) = \langle x(u), y(u), w(u) \rangle$ be a rational quadratic curve in $\mathbb{R}^2$. Then there is a conic section such that every point of $\mathbf{q}(u)$ lies on the conic section.*

Proof Recall that a conic section is defined as the set of points $\langle x, y \rangle \in \mathbb{R}^2$ that satisfy

$$Ax^2 + Bxy + Cy^2 + Dx + Ey + F = 0$$

for some constants A, B, C, D, E, F not all zero. If we represent points with homogeneous coordinates $\langle x, y, w \rangle$, then this condition is equivalent to

$$Ax^2 + Bxy + Cy^2 + Dxw + Eyw + Fw^2 = 0. \qquad \text{VII.22}$$

Namely, a conic section is the set of points whose homogeneous representations satisfy equation VII.22.

Claim *Let $x = x(u)$, $y = y(u)$, and $w = w(u)$ be parametric functions of u. Let M be a transformation of $\mathbb{R}^2$ defined by an invertible 3×3 matrix that acts on homogeneous coordinates. Then, in $\mathbb{R}^2$, the curve $M(\mathbf{q}(u))$ lies on a conic section if and only if $\mathbf{q}(u)$ lies on a conic section.*

To prove the claim, let x_M, y_M, and w_M be the functions of u defined so that

$$\langle x_M, y_M, w_M \rangle = M \langle x, y, w \rangle.$$

Suppose that, for all u,

$$Ax_M^2 + Bx_M y_M + Cy_M^2 + Dx_M w_M + Ey_M w_M + Fw_M^2 = 0 \qquad \text{VII.23}$$

with not all the coefficients zero (i.e., $M(\mathbf{q})$ lies on a conic section). Since each of x_M, y_M, and w_M is a linear combination of x, y, and w, Equation VII.23 can be rewritten in the form of Equation VII.22 but with different values for the coefficients. Since M is invertible, this process can be reversed; therefore, the coefficients of Equation VII.22 for x, y, w are not all zero. Consequently, we have shown that if $M(\mathbf{q})$ lies on a conic section, then so does $\mathbf{q}$. Since M is invertible, the converse implication holds as well and the claim is proved.

We return to the proof of Theorem VII.11 and note that since $\mathbf{q}(u)$ is quadratic, it is equal to a Bézier curve (see Exercise VII.8 on page 168). Let $\mathbf{p}_0$, $\mathbf{p}_1$, and $\mathbf{p}_2$ be the homogeneous control points of this Bézier curve. If these three control points represent points in $\mathbb{R}^2$ that are collinear, then the curve $\mathbf{q}(u)$ lies in the line containing the control points and therefore on a (degenerate) conic section. Otherwise, since a line in $\mathbb{R}^2$ corresponds to a two-dimensional linear subspace of homogeneous xyw-space, the three points $\mathbf{p}_0$, $\mathbf{p}_1$, and $\mathbf{p}_2$ are linearly independent in homogeneous space (see Section II.2.5). Therefore, there is an invertible linear transformation M of homogeneous space, that is, a nonsingular 3×3 matrix M, that sends the three points $\mathbf{p}_0$, $\mathbf{p}_1$, and $\mathbf{p}_2$ to the three control points $\langle 0, 1, 1 \rangle$, $\langle 1, 0, 0 \rangle$, and $\langle 0, -1, 1 \rangle$ of Theorem VII.9. That is, the projective transformation M maps the curve $\mathbf{q}(u)$ to a circle. Therefore, $M(\mathbf{q})$ lies on a conic section, and thus, by the claim $\mathbf{q}(u)$ lies on a conic section. $\square$

The next two exercises show that we cannot avoid the use of homogeneous coordinates when representing conic sections.

Exercise VII.19 *Prove that there is no nonrational degree two Bézier curve that traces out a nontrivial part of a circle. [Hint: A quadratic curve consists of segments of the form $\langle x(u), y(u) \rangle$ with $x(u)$ and $y(u)$ degree two polynomials. To have only points on the unit circle, they must satisfy $(x(u))^2 + (y(u))^2 = 1$.]*

Exercise VII.20 *Prove that there is no nonrational Bézier curve of any degree that traces out a nontrivial part of a circle.*

Lest one get the overly optimistic impression that rational Bézier curves are universally good for everything, we end this section with one last exercise showing a limitation on what curves can be defined with (piecewise) Bézier curves.

Exercise VII.21* *(Requires advanced math.) Consider the helix spiraling around the z-axis, which is parametrically defined by $\mathbf{q}(u) = \langle \cos(u), \sin(u), u \rangle$. Prove that there is no rational Bézier curve that traces out a nontrivial portion of this spiral. [Hint: Suppose there is a rational curve $\mathbf{q}(u) = \langle x(u), y(u), z(u), w(u) \rangle$ that traces out a nontrivial portion of the helix. Then we must have*

$$\frac{x(u)}{w(u)} = \cos\left(\frac{z(u)}{w(u)}\right)$$

on some interval. But this is impossible because the lefthand side is a rational function and the righthand side is not.]

Another way to think about how to prove the exercise, at least for the quadratic case, is to note that if a nontrivial part of the helix is a Bézier curve, then its projection onto the xz-plane is a rational quadratic curve. But this projection is the graph of the function $x = \cos(z)$, which contradicts Theorem VII.11 because the graph of $\cos(z)$ is not composed of portions of conic sections.

(Farouki and Sakkalis, 1991) gave another approach to Exercise VII.21. They proved that there is no rational polynomial curve $\mathbf{q}(u)$, of any degree, that gives a parametric definition of any curve other than a straight line such that $\mathbf{q}(u)$ traverses the curve at a uniform speed with respect to the parameter u. In other words, it is not possible to parameterize any curve other than a straight line segment by rational functions of its arclength. For the special case of the circle, this means that there is no way to parameterize circular motion with a Bézier curve that traverses the circle at a uniform speed. For the circle, the impossibility of a Bézier curve's traversing a circle at uniform speed is equivalent to Exercise VII.21 because a Bézier curve tracing out the spiral could be reinterpreted with the z-value as time.

When we define B-splines in the next chapter, we will see that B-spline curves are equivalent to piecewise Bézier curves (in Section VIII.9). Therefore, the impossibility results of Exercises VII.19–VII.21 and of Farouki and Sakkalis also apply to B-spline curves.

VII.14 Surface of Revolution Example

This section presents an example of how to form a surface of revolution using rational Bézier patches with control points at infinity.

Our point of departure is Theorem VII.9, which showed how to form a semicircle with a single quadratic Bézier curve. We will extend this construction to form a surface of revolution using Bézier patches with quadratic cross sections. First, however, it useful to examine semicircles more closely; in particular, we want to understand how to translate, rotate, and scale circles.

Refer back to the semicircle shown in Figure VII.17 on page 182. That semicircle is centered at the origin. Suppose we want to translate the semicircle to be centered, for example, at $\langle 4, 2 \rangle$. We want to express the translated semicircle as a rational quadratic Bézier curve. Let $\mathbf{p}_0$, $\mathbf{p}_1$, and $\mathbf{p}_2$ be the control points shown in Figure VII.17. The question is, What are the control points $\mathbf{p}_i^*$ for the translated circle? Obviously, the first and last control points should now be $\mathbf{p}_0^* = \langle 4, 3, 1 \rangle$ and $\mathbf{p}_2 = \langle 4, 1, 1 \rangle$, as obtained by direct translation. But what is the point $\mathbf{p}_1^*$ at infinity? Here, it does not make sense to translate the point at infinity; instead, the correct control point is $\mathbf{p}_1^* = \mathbf{p}_1 = \langle 1, 0, 0 \rangle$. Intuitively, the reason for this is as follows: We chose the point $\mathbf{p}_1$ to be the point at infinity corresponding to the intersection of the two horizontal projective lines tangent to the circle at the top and bottom points (see Theorem VII.10). When the circle is translated, the tangent lines remain horizontal, and so they still contain the same point at infinity.

To be more systematic about translating the semicircle, we can work with the 3×3 homogeneous matrix that performs the translation, namely, the matrix

$$M = \begin{pmatrix} 1 & 0 & 4 \\ 0 & 1 & 2 \\ 0 & 0 & 1 \end{pmatrix}.$$

It is easy to check that

$$\mathbf{p}_0^* = M\mathbf{p}_0, \qquad \mathbf{p}_1^* = M\mathbf{p}_1, \qquad \text{and} \qquad \mathbf{p}_2^* = M\mathbf{p}_2.$$

This proves the correctness of the control points for the translated semicircle.

Exercise VII.22 *Consider the effect of rotating the semicircle from Figure VII.17 through a counterclockwise angle of $45°$ around the origin. Prove that the result is the same as the quadratic rational Bézier curve with control points*

$$\mathbf{p}_0^* = \langle -\tfrac{\sqrt{2}}{2}, \tfrac{\sqrt{2}}{2}, 1 \rangle, \quad \mathbf{p}_0^* = \langle \tfrac{\sqrt{2}}{2}, \tfrac{\sqrt{2}}{2}, 0 \rangle, \quad \text{and} \quad \mathbf{p}_2^* = \langle \tfrac{\sqrt{2}}{2}, -\tfrac{\sqrt{2}}{2}, 1 \rangle.$$

[Hint: The rotation is performed by the homogeneous matrix

$$\begin{pmatrix} \tfrac{\sqrt{2}}{2} & -\tfrac{\sqrt{2}}{2} & 0 \\ \tfrac{\sqrt{2}}{2} & \tfrac{\sqrt{2}}{2} & 0 \\ 0 & 0 & 1 \end{pmatrix}.$$

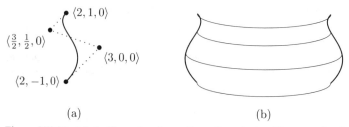

(a)   (b)

Figure VII.21. (a) A silhouette of a surface of revolution (the control points are in x, y, z-coordinates). (b) The front half of the surface of revolution. This example is implemented in the `SimpleNurbs` progam.

Exercise VII.23 *Consider the effect of scaling the semicircle from Figure VII.17 by a factor of r so that it has radius r. Prove that the result is the same as the quadratic rational Bézier curve with control points*

$$\mathbf{p}_0^* = \langle 0, r, 1\rangle, \quad \mathbf{p}_0^* = \langle r, 0, 0\rangle, \quad and \quad \mathbf{p}_2^* = \langle 0, -r, 1\rangle.$$

[Hint: The scaling is performed by the homogeneous matrix

$$\begin{pmatrix} r & 0 & 0 \\ 0 & r & 0 \\ 0 & 0 & 1 \end{pmatrix}.$$

We now give an example of how to form a surface of revolution. Figure VII.21 shows an example of a surface of revolution. The silhouette of the surface is defined by a cubic (nonrational) Bézier curve; the silhouette is defined as a curve in the xy-plane, and the surface is formed by revolving around the y-axis. We will show how to define a $180°$ arc of the surface with a single Bézier patch using control points at infinity. The entire surface can be formed with two such patches.

Section VII.10.1 discussed how the control points of a Bézier patch define the patch; most notably, each cross section is itself a Bézier curve and the control points of the cross sections are defined by Bézier curves. Considering the vertical cross sections (i.e., the cross sections that go up and down with the axis of revolution), we can see clearly that the control points of each vertical cross section must be obtained by revolving the control points shown in part (a) of Figure VII.21. Now these revolved control points can therefore be defined with Bézier curves that trace out semicircles.

These considerations let us define $180°$ of the surface of revolution shown in Figure VII.21(b) as a single rational Bézier patch that has order 4 in one direction and order 3 in the other direction. The control points for the patch are as follows:

$$\begin{array}{lll} \langle -2, -1, 0, 1\rangle & \langle 0, 0, 2, 0\rangle & \langle 2, -1, 0, 1\rangle \\ \langle -3, 0, 0, 1\rangle & \langle 0, 0, 3, 0\rangle & \langle 3, 0, 0, 1\rangle \\ \langle -\frac{3}{2}, \frac{1}{2}, 0, 1\rangle & \langle 0, 0, \frac{3}{2}, 0\rangle & \langle \frac{3}{2}, \frac{1}{2}, 0, 1\rangle \\ \langle -2, 1, 0, 1\rangle & \langle 0, 0, 2, 0\rangle & \langle 2, 1, 0, 1\rangle. \end{array}$$

Each of the four rows of the table holds three control points that define a semicircular curve in $\mathbb{R}^3$. Taking vertical cross sections of the four semicircles gives the four control points for the corresponding vertical cross section of the surface of revolution.

VII.15 Interpolating with Bézier Curves

Frequently, one wishes to define a smooth curve that interpolates (i.e., passes through, or contains) a given set of points. For example, suppose we are given a set of points that define the positions of some object at different times; if we then find a smooth curve that interpolates these points, we can use the curve to define (or estimate) the positions of the object at intermediate times.

The scenario is as follows. We are given a set of interpolation points $\mathbf{p}_0, \ldots, \mathbf{p}_m$ and a set of "knot values" $u_0, \ldots, u_m$. The problem is to define a piecewise (degree three) polynomial curve $\mathbf{q}(u)$, so that $\mathbf{q}(u_i) = \mathbf{p}_i$ for all i. There are several ways to define the interpolating curves as piecewise Bézier curves. The general idea is to define a series of Bézier curves connecting pairs of successive interpolation points. For each appropriate value of i, there will be a Bézier curve that starts at $\mathbf{p}_i$ and ends at $\mathbf{p}_{i+1}$. Putting these curves together forms the entire curve. This automatically makes a piecewise Bézier curve that interpolates the points $\mathbf{p}_i$ of course, but more work is needed to make the curve smooth at the points $\mathbf{p}_i$. For this, we need to use the methods of Section VII.4 to make the curve C^1-continuous.

We describe three ways to define interpolating piecewise Bézier curves. The first is the Catmull–Rom splines, and the second is a generalization of Catmull–Rom splines called Overhauser splines. Catmull–Rom splines are used primarily when the points $\mathbf{p}_i$ are more or less evenly spaced and with $u_i = i$. The Overhauser splines allow the use of more general values for u_i as well as chord-length parameterization to give better results when the distances between successive points $\mathbf{p}_i$ vary considerably. A more general variation on these splines is the tension–continuity–bias interpolation methods, which allow a user to vary parameters to obtain a desirable curve.

VII.15.1 Catmull–Rom Splines

Catmull–Rom splines are specified by a list of $m + 1$ interpolation points $\mathbf{p}_0, \ldots, \mathbf{p}_m$ and are piecewise degree three polynomial curves of the type described in Section VII.4 that interpolate all the points except the endpoints $\mathbf{p}_0$ and $\mathbf{p}_m$. For Catmull–Rom splines, $u_i = i$, and so we want $\mathbf{q}(i) = \mathbf{p}_i$ for $1 \leq i < m$. The Catmull–Rom spline will consist of $m - 2$ Bézier curves with the ith Bézier curve beginning at point $\mathbf{p}_i$ and ending at point $\mathbf{p}_{i+1}$. Catmull–Rom splines are defined by making an estimate for the first derivative of the curve passing through $\mathbf{p}_i$. These first derivatives are used to define additional control points for the Bézier curves.

Figure VII.22 illustrates the definition of a Catmull–Rom spline segment. Let

$$\mathbf{l}_i = \frac{1}{2}(\mathbf{p}_{i+1} - \mathbf{p}_{i-1})$$

and define

$$\mathbf{p}_i^+ = \mathbf{p}_i + \frac{1}{3}\mathbf{l}_i \qquad \text{and} \qquad \mathbf{p}_i^- = \mathbf{p}_i - \frac{1}{3}\mathbf{l}_i.$$

Then let $\mathbf{q}_i(u)$ be the Bézier curve – translated to have domain $i \leq u \leq i + 1$ – defined with control points $\mathbf{p}_i, \mathbf{p}_i^+, \mathbf{p}_{i+1}^-, \mathbf{p}_{i+1}$. Define the entire Catmull–Rom spline $\mathbf{q}(u)$ by piecing together these curves so that $\mathbf{q}(u) = \mathbf{q}_i(u)$ for $i \leq u \leq i + 1$.

Since Bézier curves interpolate their first and last control points, the curve $\mathbf{q}$ is continuous and $\mathbf{q}(i) = \mathbf{p}_i$ for all integers i such that $1 \leq i \leq m - 1$. In addition, $\mathbf{q}$ has continuous first derivatives with

$$\mathbf{q}'(i) = \mathbf{l}_i = (\mathbf{p}_{i+1} - \mathbf{p}_{i-1})/2.$$

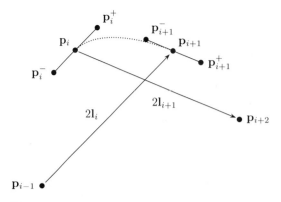

Figure VII.22. Defining the Catmull–Rom spline segment from the point $\mathbf{p}_i$ to the point $\mathbf{p}_{i+1}$. The points $\mathbf{p}_i^-$, $\mathbf{p}_i$, and $\mathbf{p}_i^+$ are collinear and parallel to $\mathbf{p}_{i+1} - \mathbf{p}_{i-1}$. The points $\mathbf{p}_i$, $\mathbf{p}_i^+$, $\mathbf{p}_{i+1}^-$, and $\mathbf{p}_{i+1}$ form the control points of a degree three Bézier curve, which is shown as a dotted curve.

It follows that $\mathbf{q}(u)$ is C^1-continuous. This formula for the first derivatives, $\mathbf{q}'(i)$, also explains the motivating idea behind the definition of Catmull–Rom splines. Namely, since $\mathbf{q}(i-1) = \mathbf{p}_{i-1}$ and $\mathbf{q}(i+1) = \mathbf{p}_{i+1}$, the *average* rate of change of $\mathbf{q}(u)$ between $u = i - 1$ and $u = i + 1$ must equal $(\mathbf{p}_{i+1} - \mathbf{p}_{i-1})/2$. Thus, the extra control points, $\mathbf{p}_i^+$ and $\mathbf{p}_i^-$, are chosen so as to make $\mathbf{q}'(i)$ equal to this average rate of change.

Figure VII.23 shows two examples of Catmull–Rom splines.

VII.15.2 Bessel–Overhauser Splines

Figure VII.23(b) shows that bad effects can result when the interpolated points are not more or less equally spaced; bad "overshoot" can occur when two close control points are next to widely separated control points. One way to solve this problem is to use *chord-length* parameterization. For chord-length parameterization, the knots u_i are chosen so that $u_{i+1} - u_i$ is equal to $||\mathbf{p}_{i+1} - \mathbf{p}_i||$. The idea is that the arclength of the curve between $\mathbf{p}_i$ and $\mathbf{p}_{i+1}$

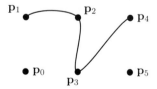

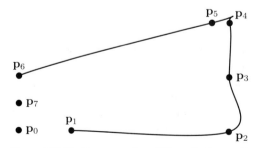

Figure VII.23. Two examples of Catmull–Rom splines with uniformly spaced knots.

will be approximately proportional to the distance from $\mathbf{p}_i$ to $\mathbf{p}_{i+1}$ and therefore approximately proportional to $u_{i+1} - u_i$. If one views the parameter u as time, then, as u varies, the curve $\mathbf{q}(u)$ will be traversed at roughly a constant rate of speed.[6]

Of course, to use chord-length parameterization, we need to modify the formalization of Catmull–Rom splines to allow for nonuniform knot positions: in particular, it is necessary to find an alternative definition of the extra control points $\mathbf{p}_i^-$ and $\mathbf{p}_i^+$. More generally, to handle arbitrary nonuniform knot positions, we use a method called the *Bessel tangent* method or the *Overhauser* method (Overhauser, 1968). Assume that we are given knot positions (not necessarily obtained from a chord-length parameterization) and that all knot positions are distinct with $u_i < u_{i+1}$. Define

$$\mathbf{v}_{i+\frac{1}{2}} = \frac{\mathbf{p}_{i+1} - \mathbf{p}_i}{u_{i+1} - u_i}.$$

The idea is that $\mathbf{v}_{i+\frac{1}{2}}$ is the average velocity at which the interpolating spline is traversed from $\mathbf{p}_i$ to $\mathbf{p}_{i+1}$. Of course, if we have defined the knot positions using a chord-length interpolation, then the velocities $\mathbf{v}_{i+\frac{1}{2}}$ will be unit vectors. Then we define a further velocity

$$\mathbf{v}_i = \frac{(u_{i+1} - u_i)\mathbf{v}_{i-\frac{1}{2}} + (u_i - u_{i-1})\mathbf{v}_{i+\frac{1}{2}}}{u_{i+1} - u_{i-1}},$$

which is a weighted average of the two velocities of the curve segments just before and just after the interpolated point $\mathbf{p}_i$. The weighted average is defined so that the velocities $\mathbf{v}_{i\pm\frac{1}{2}}$ are weighted more heavily when the elapsed time, $|u_{i\pm1} - u_i|$, between being at the control point $\mathbf{p}_{i\pm1}$ and being at the control point $\mathbf{p}_i$ is less. Finally, define

$$\mathbf{p}_i^- = \mathbf{p}_i - \tfrac{1}{3}(u_i - u_{i-1})\mathbf{v}_i$$

$$\mathbf{p}_i^+ = \mathbf{p}_i + \tfrac{1}{3}(u_{i+1} - u_i)\mathbf{v}_i.$$

These points are then used to define Bézier curves in exactly the manner used for the uniform Catmull–Rom curves. The ith segment, $\mathbf{q}_i(u)$, has control points $\mathbf{p}_i$, $\mathbf{p}_i^+$, $\mathbf{p}_{i+1}^-$, and $\mathbf{p}_{i+1}$ and is linearly transformed to be defined for u in the interval $[u_i, u_{i+1}]$. The entire piecewise Bézier curve $\mathbf{q}(u)$ is defined by patching these curves together, with $\mathbf{q}(u) = \mathbf{q}_i(u)$ for $u_i \leq u \leq u_{i+1}$.

Two examples of chord-length parameterization combined with the Overhauser method are shown in Figure VII.24. These interpolate the same points as the Catmull–Rom splines in Figure VII.23 but give a smoother and nicer curve – especially in the second example in the figures. Another example is given in Figure VII.25.

Exercise VII.24 *Let $\mathbf{p}_0 = \mathbf{p}_1 = \langle 0, 0 \rangle$, $\mathbf{p}_2 = \langle 10, 0 \rangle$ and $\mathbf{p}_3 = \mathbf{p}_4 = \langle 10, 1 \rangle$. Also, let $u_0 = 0$, $u_1 = 1$, $u_2 = 2$, $u_3 = 2.1$ and $u_4 = 3.1$. Find the control points for the corresponding Overhauser spline, $\mathbf{q}(u)$, with $\mathbf{q}(u_i) = \mathbf{p}_i$ for $i = 1, 2, 3$. Verify that your curve corresponds to the curve shown in Figure VII.25.*

Second, draw the Catmull–Rom curve defined by these same interpolation points. Qualitatively compare the Catmull–Rom curve with the Overhauser spline.

Exercise VII.25 *Investigate the chord-length parameterization Overhauser method curve from $\mathbf{p}_0$ to $\mathbf{p}_2$ when $\mathbf{p}_0$, $\mathbf{p}_1$, $\mathbf{p}_2$ are collinear. What is the velocity at $\mathbf{p}_1$? Consider separately the cases in which $\mathbf{p}_1$ is, and is not, between $\mathbf{p}_0$ and $\mathbf{p}_2$.*

---

[6] Another common choice for knot parameterization is the *centripetal parameterization* where $u_{i+1} - u_i$ is set equal to $\sqrt{\|\mathbf{p}_{i+1} - \mathbf{p}_i\|}$. This presumably has an effect intermediate between uniform knot spacing and chord-length parameterization.

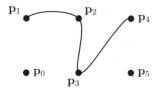

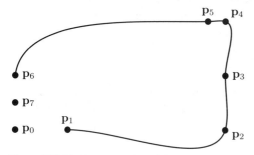

Figure VII.24. Two examples of Overhauser spline curves. The knot positions were set by chord-length parameterization. These are defined from exactly the same control points as the Catmull–Rom curves in Figure VII.23.

Exercise VII.26 *It should be clear that the Overhauser method gives G^1-continuous curves. Prove that, in fact, the Overhauser method gives C^1-continuous curves. [Hint: Prove that $\mathbf{q}'(u_i) = \mathbf{v}_i$. You will need to take into account the fact that $\mathbf{q}_i(u)$ has domain $[u_i, u_{i+1}]$.]*

There is another nice characterization of the Overhauser method in terms of blending two quadratic polynomials that provides a second justification for its appropriateness. Define $\mathbf{f}_i(u)$ to be the (unique) quadratic polynomial such that $\mathbf{f}_i(u_{i-1}) = \mathbf{p}_{i-1}$, $\mathbf{f}_i(u_i) = \mathbf{p}_i$, and $\mathbf{f}_i(u_{i+1}) = \mathbf{p}_{i+1}$. Similarly define $\mathbf{f}_{i+1}(u)$ to be the quadratic polynomial with the values $\mathbf{p}_i$, $\mathbf{p}_{i+1}$, $\mathbf{p}_{i+2}$ at $u = u_i, u_{i+1}, u_{i+2}$. Then define

$$\mathbf{q}_i(u) \;=\; \frac{(u_{i+1} - u)\mathbf{f}_i(u) + (u - u_i)\mathbf{f}_{i+1}(u)}{u_{i+1} - u_i}.$$ VII.24

Clearly $\mathbf{q}_i(u)$ is a cubic polynomial and, further, for $u_i \leq u \leq u_{i+1}$, $\mathbf{q}_i(u)$ is equal to the curve $\mathbf{q}_i(u)$ obtained with the Overhauser method.

Exercise VII.27★ *Prove the last assertion about the Overhauser method. [Suggestion: verify that $\mathbf{q}_i(u)$ has the correct values and derivatives at its endpoints u_i and u_{i+1}.]*

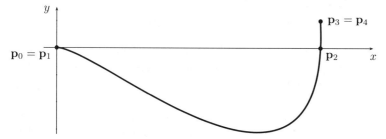

Figure VII.25. The Overhauser spline that is the solution to Exercise VII.24.

Exercise VII.28 *Write a program that takes a series of positions specified with mouse clicks and draws a Cutmull–Rom curve, Bessel–Overhauser spline, or both so that the curve interpolates them. Make the curves also interpolate the first and last point by doubling the first and last points (i.e., treat the first and last points as if they occur twice). The supplied program* ConnectDots *can be used as a starting point; it accepts mouse clicks and joins the points with straight line segments.*

VII.15.3 Tension–Continuity–Bias Splines

There are a variety of modified versions of Catmull–Rom interpolation schemes. Many of these are tools that let a curve designer specify a broader range of shapes for curves. For instance, someone may want to design a curve that is "tighter" at some points and "looser" at other points. One widely used method is the TCB (tension–continuity–bias) method of (Kochanek and Bartels, 1984), which uses the three parameters of tension, continuity, and bias that affect the values of the tangents and thereby the extra control points $\mathbf{p}_i^+$ and $\mathbf{p}_i^-$. The parameter of tension is used to control the tightness of curve, the continuity parameter controls the (dis)continuity of first derivatives, and the bias controls how the curve overshoots or undershoots an interpolation point.

The TCB method is a refinement of Catmull–Rom splines that adjusts the control points $\mathbf{p}_i^-$ and $\mathbf{p}_i^+$ according to the three new parameters. To describe how the TCB method works, we first reformulate the Catmull–Rom method slightly by introducing notations for the left and right first derivatives of the curve at an interpolation point $\mathbf{p}_i$ as follows:

$$D\mathbf{q}_i^- = \lim_{u \to u_i^-} \frac{\mathbf{q}(u_i) - \mathbf{q}(u)}{u_i - u} = 3(\mathbf{p}_i - \mathbf{p}_i^-),$$

$$D\mathbf{q}_i^+ = \lim_{u \to u_i^+} \frac{\mathbf{q}(u) - \mathbf{q}(u_i)}{u - u_i} = 3(\mathbf{p}_i^+ - \mathbf{p}_i).$$

If we set values for $D\mathbf{q}_i^+$ and $D\mathbf{q}_i^-$, then this determines $\mathbf{p}_i^+$ and $\mathbf{p}_i^-$ by

$$\mathbf{p}_i^+ = \mathbf{p}_i + \tfrac{1}{3} D\mathbf{q}_i^+ \qquad \text{and} \qquad \mathbf{p}_i^- = \mathbf{p}_i - \tfrac{1}{3} D\mathbf{q}_i^-.$$

The basic Catmull–Rom splines can be defined by setting

$$D\mathbf{q}_i^- = D\mathbf{q}_i^+ = \frac{1}{2}\mathbf{v}_{i-\frac{1}{2}} + \frac{1}{2}\mathbf{v}_{i+\frac{1}{2}}, \qquad\qquad \text{VII.25}$$

where $\mathbf{v}_{i-\frac{1}{2}} = \mathbf{p}_i - \mathbf{p}_{i-1}$. The TCB splines work by modifying Equation VII.25 but leaving the rest of the definition of the splines unchanged.

The tension parameter, denoted t, adjusts the tightness or looseness of the curve. The default value is $t = 0$; positive values should be less than 1 and make the curve tighter, and negative values make the curve looser. Mathematically, this has the effect of setting

$$D\mathbf{q}_i^- = D\mathbf{q}_i^+ = (1 - t)\left(\frac{1}{2}\mathbf{v}_{i-\frac{1}{2}} + \frac{1}{2}\mathbf{v}_{i+\frac{1}{2}}\right),$$

that is, of multiplying the derivative by $(1 - t)$. Positive values of t make the derivative smaller: this has the effect of making the curve's segments between points $\mathbf{p}_i$ straighter and making the velocity of the curve closer to zero at the points $\mathbf{p}_i$. Negative values of t make the curve looser and can cause it to take bigger swings around interpolation points. The effect of setting tension to $1/2$ and to $-1/2$ is shown in Figure VII.26.

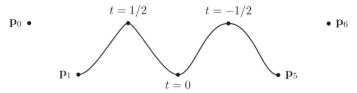

Figure VII.26. The effects of the tension parameter.

The continuity parameter is denoted c. If $c = 0$, then the curve is C^1-continuous; otherwise, the curve has a corner at the control point $\mathbf{p}_i$ and thus a discontinuous first derivative. The mathematical effect of the continuity parameter is to set

$$D\mathbf{q}_i^- = \frac{1-c}{2}\mathbf{v}_{i-\frac{1}{2}} + \frac{1+c}{2}\mathbf{v}_{i+\frac{1}{2}}$$

$$D\mathbf{q}_i^+ = \frac{1+c}{2}\mathbf{v}_{i-\frac{1}{2}} + \frac{1-c}{2}\mathbf{v}_{i+\frac{1}{2}}.$$

Typically, $-1 \leq c \leq 0$, and values $c < 0$ have the effect of turning the slope of the curve towards the straight line segments joining the interpolation points. Setting $c = -1$ would make the curve's left and right first derivatives at $\mathbf{p}_i$ match the slopes of the line segments joining $\mathbf{p}_i$ to $\mathbf{p}_{i-1}$ and $\mathbf{p}_{i+1}$.

The effect of $c = -1/2$ and $c = -1$ is shown in Figure VII.27. The effect of $c = -1/2$ in this figure looks very similar to the effect of tension $t = 1/2$ in Figure VII.26; however, the effects are not as similar as they look. With $t = 1/2$, the curve still has a continuous first derivative, and the velocity of a particle following the curve with u measuring time will be slower near the point where $t = 1/2$. On the other hand, with $c = -1/2$, the curve has a "corner" where the first derivative is discontinuous, but there is no slowdown of velocity in the vicinity of the corner.

The bias parameter b weights the two average velocities $\mathbf{v}_{i-\frac{1}{2}}$ and $\mathbf{v}_{i+\frac{1}{2}}$ differently to cause either undershoot or overshoot. The mathematical effect is

$$D\mathbf{q}_i^- = D\mathbf{q}_i^+ = \frac{1+b}{2}\mathbf{v}_{i-\frac{1}{2}} + \frac{1-b}{2}\mathbf{v}_{i+\frac{1}{2}}.$$

The curve will have more tendency to overshoot $\mathbf{p}_i$ if $b > 0$ and to undershoot it if $b < 0$. The effect of bias $b = 1/2$ and bias $b = -1/2$ is shown in Figure VII.28.

The tension, continuity, and bias parameters can be set independently to individual interpolation points or uniformly applied to an entire curve. This allows the curve designer to modify the curve either locally or globally. The effects of the three parameters can be applied together.

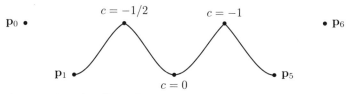

Figure VII.27. The effects of the continuity parameter.

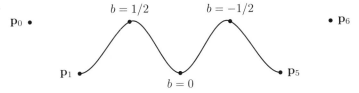

Figure VII.28. The effects of the bias parameter.

This results in the following composite formula, which replaces Equation VII.25:

$$D\mathbf{q}_i^- = \frac{(1-t)(1-c)(1+b)}{2}\mathbf{v}_{i-\frac{1}{2}} + \frac{(1-t)(1+c)(1-b)}{2}\mathbf{v}_{i+\frac{1}{2}}$$

$$D\mathbf{q}_i^+ = \frac{(1-t)(1+c)(1+b)}{2}\mathbf{v}_{i-\frac{1}{2}} + \frac{(1-t)(1-c)(1-b)}{2}\mathbf{v}_{i+\frac{1}{2}}.$$

Exercise VII.29★ *Extend the TCB parameters to apply to Overhauser splines instead of Catmull–Rom splines.*

VII.16 Interpolating with Bézier Surfaces★

The previous sections have discussed methods of interpolating points with a series of Bézier curves that connects the interpolated points together with a smooth curve. The analogous problem for surfaces is to interpolate a two-dimensional mesh of control points with a smooth surface formed from Bézier patches. For this, suppose we are given control points $\mathbf{p}_{i,j}$ for $i = 0, \ldots, m$ and $j = 0, \ldots, n$ and we want to find a smooth surface $\mathbf{q}(u, v)$ so that $\mathbf{q}(i, j) = \mathbf{p}_{i,j}$ for all appropriate i and j.

To formulate the problem a little more generally, let $\mathcal{I}$ and $\mathcal{J}$ be finite sets of real numbers,

$$\mathcal{I} = \{u_0, u_1, \ldots, u_m\} \qquad \text{and} \qquad \mathcal{J} = \{v_0, v_1, \ldots, v_n\},$$

where $u_i < u_{i+1}$ and $v_j < v_{j+1}$ for all i, j. For $0 \le i \le m$ and $0 \le j \le n$, let $\mathbf{p}_{i,j}$ be a point in $\mathbb{R}^3$. Then, we are seeking a smooth surface $\mathbf{q}(u, v)$ so that $\mathbf{q}(u_i, v_j) = \mathbf{p}_{i,j}$ for all $0 < i < m$ and $0 < j < n$.

We define the surface $\mathbf{q}(u, v)$ as a collection of Bézier patches analogous to the Catmull–Rom and Bessel–Overhauser splines defined with multiple Bézier curves that interpolate a sequence of points. The corners of the Bézier patches comprising $\mathbf{q}(u, v)$ will meet at the interpolation points $\mathbf{p}_{i,j}$, and the Bézier patches will form a mesh of rectangular patches. One big advantage of this method is that the Bézier patches are defined locally, that is, each Bézier patch depends only on nearby interpolation points.

We discuss primarily the case in which the interpolation positions u_i and v_j are equally spaced with $u_i = i$ and $v_j = j$, but we will also discuss how to generalize to the non-equally-spaced case.

We define degree three Bézier patches $Q_{i,j}(u, v)$ with domains the rectangles $[u_i, u_{i+1}] \times [v_j, v_{j+1}]$. The complete surface $\mathbf{q}(u, v)$ will be formed as the union of these patches $Q_{i,j}$. Of course, we will need to be sure that the patches have the right continuity and C^1-continuity properties. The control points for the Bézier patch $Q_{i,j}$ will be 16 points, $\mathbf{p}_{\alpha,\beta}$, where $\alpha \in \{i, i + \frac{1}{3}, i + \frac{2}{3}, i + 1\}$, and $\beta \in \{j, j + \frac{1}{3}, j + \frac{2}{3}, j + 1\}$. Of course, this means that the patch $Q_{i,j}$ will interpolate the points $\mathbf{p}_{i,j}, \mathbf{p}_{i+1,j}, \mathbf{p}_{i,j+1}$, and $\mathbf{p}_{i+1,j+1}$, which is exactly what we want. It remains to define the other 12 control points of the patch.

As the first step towards defining the other 12 control points for each patch, we define the control points that lie on the boundary, that is, the control points $\mathbf{p}_{\alpha,\beta}$, where either α or β is an integer. Fix, for the moment, the value of j and the value of v as $v = v_j$. Consider the cross section of the surface $\mathbf{q}(u, v)$ for this value of v, namely, the curve $\mathbf{q}_j(u) = \mathbf{q}(u, v_j)$. This cross section is piecewise degree three Bézier curves defined with control points $\mathbf{p}_{\alpha,j}$. It also interpolates the point $\mathbf{p}_{i,j}$ at $\alpha = u_i$. Thus, it seems natural to define the other control points $\mathbf{p}_{i\pm\frac{1}{3},j}$, for all values of i, using the Catmull–Rom or Bessel–Overhauser method. (Recall that the Catmull–Rom and Bessel–Overhauser methods are identical in the equally spaced case. The Bessel–Overhauser method should be used in the non-equally-spaced case.) The control points $\mathbf{p}_{i\pm\frac{1}{3},j}$ are chosen so that the curve $\mathbf{q}_j$ smoothly interpolates the points $\mathbf{p}_{i,j}$ for this fixed value of j.

Dually, if i is held fixed and $u = u_i$, the cross-sectional curves of $\mathbf{q}(u_i, v)$ are likewise piecewise degree three Bézier curves. Thus, the control points $\mathbf{p}_{i,\beta}$ can be defined using the Catmull–Rom or Bessel–Overhauser method to obtain a curve that interpolates the points $\mathbf{p}_{i,j}$ for a fixed value of i.

It now remains to pick the four interior control points for each patch $Q_{i,j}$, namely, the control points $\mathbf{p}_{i+\frac{1}{3},j+\frac{1}{3}}$, $\mathbf{p}_{i+\frac{2}{3},j+\frac{1}{3}}$, $\mathbf{p}_{i+\frac{1}{3},j+\frac{2}{3}}$, and $\mathbf{p}_{i+\frac{2}{3},j+\frac{2}{3}}$. As we will see, these four control points can be determined by choosing appropriate *twist vectors*. To simplify the details of how to set these control points, we now make the assumption that the interpolation positions u_i and v_j are equally spaced: in fact, we assume that $u_i = i$ and $v_j = j$ for all i and j.

The patches $Q_{i,j}$ and $Q_{i-1,j}$ share a common border. In order to have C^1-continuity between the two patches, it is necessary that the partial derivatives match up along the boundary. As was discussed in Section VII.10.2, to match up partial derivatives, it is necessary and sufficient to ensure that

$$\mathbf{p}_{i,\beta} - \mathbf{p}_{i-\frac{1}{3},\beta} = \mathbf{p}_{i+\frac{1}{3},\beta} - \mathbf{p}_{i,\beta} \qquad\qquad\qquad \text{VII.26}$$

for each $\beta \in \{j, j + \frac{1}{3}, j + \frac{2}{3}, j + 1\}$. Likewise, in joining up patches $Q_{i,j}$ and $Q_{i,j-1}$, we must have

$$\mathbf{p}_{\alpha,j} - \mathbf{p}_{\alpha,j-\frac{1}{3}} = \mathbf{p}_{\alpha,j+\frac{1}{3}} - \mathbf{p}_{\alpha,j}, \qquad\qquad\qquad \text{VII.27}$$

for $\alpha \in \{i, i + \frac{1}{3}, i + \frac{2}{3}, i + 1\}$. Equations VII.26 and VII.27 were derived for a particular patch $Q_{i,j}$, but since all the patches must join up smoothly these equations actually hold for all values of i and j. We define the *twist vector* $\boldsymbol{\tau}_{i,j}$ by

$$\boldsymbol{\tau}_{i,j} = 9(\mathbf{p}_{i+\frac{1}{3},j+\frac{1}{3}} - \mathbf{p}_{i,j+\frac{1}{3}} - \mathbf{p}_{i+\frac{1}{3},j} + \mathbf{p}_{i,j}).$$

Then, by Equation VII.26, with $\beta = j$ and $\beta = j + \frac{1}{3}$, we obtain

$$\boldsymbol{\tau}_{i,j} = 9(\mathbf{p}_{i,j+\frac{1}{3}} - \mathbf{p}_{i-\frac{1}{3},j+\frac{1}{3}} - \mathbf{p}_{i,j} + \mathbf{p}_{i-\frac{1}{3},j}).$$

By similar reasoning, with Equation VII.27 for α equal to $i + \frac{1}{3}$, i and $i - \frac{1}{3}$, we have also

$$\boldsymbol{\tau}_{i,j} = 9(\mathbf{p}_{i+\frac{1}{3},j} - \mathbf{p}_{i,j} - \mathbf{p}_{i+\frac{1}{3},j-\frac{1}{3}} + \mathbf{p}_{i,j-\frac{1}{3}})$$

$$\boldsymbol{\tau}_{i,j} = 9(\mathbf{p}_{i,j} - \mathbf{p}_{i-\frac{1}{3},j} - \mathbf{p}_{i,j-\frac{1}{3}} + \mathbf{p}_{i-\frac{1}{3},j-\frac{1}{3}}).$$

Rewriting these four equations, we get formulas for the inner control points:

$$\mathbf{p}_{i+\frac{1}{3},j+\frac{1}{3}} = \frac{1}{9}\boldsymbol{\tau}_{i,j} + \mathbf{p}_{i,j+\frac{1}{3}} + \mathbf{p}_{i+\frac{1}{3},j} - \mathbf{p}_{i,j} \qquad\qquad \text{VII.28}$$

$$\mathbf{p}_{i-\frac{1}{3},j+\frac{1}{3}} = -\frac{1}{9}\boldsymbol{\tau}_{i,j} + \mathbf{p}_{i,j+\frac{1}{3}} + \mathbf{p}_{i-\frac{1}{3},j} - \mathbf{p}_{i,j}$$

$$\mathbf{p}_{i+\frac{1}{3},j-\frac{1}{3}} = -\frac{1}{9}\tau_{i,j} + \mathbf{p}_{i,j-\frac{1}{3}} + \mathbf{p}_{i+\frac{1}{3},j} - \mathbf{p}_{i,j}$$

$$\mathbf{p}_{i-\frac{1}{3},j-\frac{1}{3}} = \frac{1}{9}\tau_{i,j} + \mathbf{p}_{i,j-\frac{1}{3}} + \mathbf{p}_{i-\frac{1}{3},j} - \mathbf{p}_{i,j}.$$

Thus, once the twist vectors $\tau_{i,j}$ have been fixed, the remaining control points for the Bézier patches are completely determined.

The twist vector has a simple geometric meaning as the second-order partial derivatives of the Bézier surfaces; namely, by equations VII.18 and VII.19 on page 175 and by the definition of the twist vector,

$$\frac{\partial^2 Q_{i,j}}{\partial u \partial v}(u_i, v_j) = \tau_{i,j}.$$

Thus, the twist vector $\tau_{i,j}$ is just the second-order mixed partial derivative at the corners of the patches that meet at $\langle u_i, v_j \rangle$.

To finish specifying all the control points, it only remains to set the value of the twist vector. The simplest method is just to set the twist vectors $\tau_{i,j}$ all equal to zero. This yields the so-called Ferguson patches since it is equivalent to a construction from (Ferguson, 1964). The disadvantage of just setting the twist vector to zero is that it tends to make the surface $\mathbf{q}(u, v)$ too flat around the interpolation points. For specular surfaces in particular, this can make artifacts on the surface, known as "flats," where the surface is noticeably flattened around interpolation points.

It is better to set the twist vector by estimating the second-order mixed partial derivative of $\mathbf{q}(u, v)$ at an interpolation point $\langle u_i, v_j \rangle$. Here we are still making the assumption that interpolation positions are equally spaced, that is, that $u_i = i$ and $v_j = j$. Then, a standard estimate for the partial derivative is

$$\frac{\partial^2 \mathbf{q}}{\partial u \partial v}(i, j) = \frac{1}{4}(\mathbf{q}(i+1, j+1) - \mathbf{q}(i-1, j+1) - \mathbf{q}(i+1, j-1) + \mathbf{q}(i-1, j-1))$$

$$= \frac{1}{4}(\mathbf{p}_{i+1,j+1} - \mathbf{p}_{i-1,j+1} - \mathbf{p}_{i+1,j-1} + \mathbf{p}_{i-1,j-1}). \qquad \text{VII.29}$$

Using this value as the value of τ can give a better quality interpolating surface.

The estimate of Equation VII.29 is not entirely ad hoc: indeed, it can be justified as a generalization of the Bessel–Overhauser curve method. For surface interpolation, we refer to it as just the *Bessel twist method*, and the idea is as follows. Let $f_{i,j}(u, v)$ be the degree two polynomial ("degree two" means degree two in each of u and v separately) that interpolates the nine control points $\mathbf{p}_{\alpha,\beta}$ for $\alpha \in \{u_{i-1}, u_i, u_{i+1}\}$ and $\beta \in \{v_{j-1}, v_j, v_{j+1}\}$; thus, $f_{i,j}(\alpha, \beta) = \mathbf{p}_{\alpha,\beta}$ for these nine values of α and β. Then define the patch $Q_{i,j}$ by blending four of these functions, namely,

$$Q_{i,j}(u, v)$$
$$= \frac{(u - u_i)(v - v_j)}{\Delta u_i \Delta v_j} f_{i+1,j+1}(u, v) + \frac{(u - u_i)(v_{j+1} - v)}{\Delta u_i \Delta v_j} f_{i+1,j}(u, v)$$
$$+ \frac{(u_{i+1} - u)(v - v_j)}{\Delta u_i \Delta v_j} f_{i,j+1}(u, v) + \frac{(u_{i+1} - u)(v_{j+1} - v)}{\Delta u_i \Delta v_j} f_{i,j}(u, v), \qquad \text{VII.30}$$

where $\Delta u_i = u_{i+1} - u_i$ and $\Delta v_j = v_{j+1} - v_j$. Note that this way of defining $Q_{i,j}$ is a direct generalization of the Bessel–Overhauser method of Equation VII.24. The patch $Q_{i,j}$ defined by Equation VII.30 is obviously a bicubic patch (i.e., is degree three in each of u and v separately).

As a bicubic patch it can be expressed as a degree three Bézier patch. In view of Exercise VII.27, the corners and boundary control points of $Q_{i,j}$ defined by Equation VII.30 are equal to the control points defined using the first method. We claim also that the four interior control points of the patch $Q_{i,j}$ as defined by Equation VII.30 are the same as the control points calculated by using Equation VII.29 with the twist vector estimate of Equation VII.29. To prove this for the case of equally spaced interpolation positions, we can evaluate the mixed partial derivatives of the right-hand side of Equation VII.30 and use the fact that the four functions $f_{i+1,j+1}$, $f_{i,j+1}$, $f_{i+1,j}$ and $f_{i,j}$ are equal at $\langle u_i, v_j \rangle$, that $(\partial f_{i,j}/\partial u)(u_i, v_j) = (\partial f_{i,j+1}/\partial u)(u_i, v_j)$, and that $(\partial f_{i,j}/\partial v)(u_i, v_j) = (\partial f_{i+1,j}/\partial v)(u_i, v_j)$. We find that

$$\frac{\partial^2 Q_{i,j}}{\partial u \partial v}(u_i, v_j) = \frac{\partial^2 f_{i,j}}{\partial u \partial v}(u_i, v_j).$$

This holds even in the case of non-equally-spaced interpolation positions. We leave the details of the calculations to the reader.

Finally, we claim that

$$\frac{\partial^2 f_{i,j}}{\partial u \partial v}(u_i, v_j) = \frac{1}{4}(\mathbf{p}_{i+1,j+1} - \mathbf{p}_{i-1,j+1} - \mathbf{p}_{i+1,j-1} + \mathbf{p}_{i-1,j-1}) \qquad \text{VII.31}$$

when the interpolation positions are equally spaced. This is straightforward to check, and we leave its verification to the reader, too. With this, the Bessel method is seen to be equivalent to using the last formula of Equation VII.29 to calculate the twist vector.

We now generalize to the case of non-equally-spaced interpolation positions. We have already described how to set the corner and boundary control points of each patch $Q_{i,j}$. We still let the twist vector $\tau_{i,j}$ be the mixed partial derivative at $\langle u_i, v_j \rangle$. Now the Equations VII.28 become

$$\mathbf{p}_{i+\frac{1}{3},j+\frac{1}{3}} = \Delta u_i \Delta v_j \frac{\tau_{i,j}}{9} + \mathbf{p}_{i,j+\frac{1}{3}} + \mathbf{p}_{i+\frac{1}{3},j} - \mathbf{p}_{i,j} \qquad \text{VII.32}$$

$$\mathbf{p}_{i-\frac{1}{3},j+\frac{1}{3}} = -\Delta u_{i-1} \Delta v_j \frac{\tau_{i,j}}{9} + \mathbf{p}_{i,j+\frac{1}{3}} + \mathbf{p}_{i-\frac{1}{3},j} - \mathbf{p}_{i,j}$$

$$\mathbf{p}_{i+\frac{1}{3},j-\frac{1}{3}} = -\Delta u_i \Delta v_{j-1} \frac{\tau_{i,j}}{9} + \mathbf{p}_{i,j-\frac{1}{3}} + \mathbf{p}_{i+\frac{1}{3},j} - \mathbf{p}_{i,j}$$

$$\mathbf{p}_{i-\frac{1}{3},j-\frac{1}{3}} = \Delta u_{i-1} \Delta v_{j-1} \frac{\tau_{i,j}}{9} + \mathbf{p}_{i,j-\frac{1}{3}} + \mathbf{p}_{i-\frac{1}{3},j} - \mathbf{p}_{i,j}.$$

In addition, Equation VII.31 is no longer correct: instead, we let

$$T_{i,j} = \mathbf{p}_{i+1,j+1} - \mathbf{p}_{i+1,j} - \mathbf{p}_{i,j+1} + \mathbf{p}_{i,j},$$

and then we have

$$\frac{\partial^2 f_{i,j}}{\partial u \partial v}(u_i, v_j)$$

$$= \frac{\Delta u_i \Delta v_j T_{i-1,j-1} + \Delta u_i \Delta v_{j-1} T_{i-1,j} + \Delta u_{i-1} \Delta v_j T_{i,j-1} + \Delta u_{i-1} \Delta v_{j-1} T_{i,j}}{(\Delta u_i + \Delta u_{i-1})(\Delta v_j + \Delta v_{j-1})}$$

$$= \frac{\Delta u_i \Delta v_j T_{i-1,j-1} + \Delta u_i \Delta v_{j-1} T_{i-1,j} + \Delta u_{i-1} \Delta v_j T_{i,j-1} + \Delta u_{i-1} \Delta v_{j-1} T_{i,j}}{(u_{i+1} - u_{i-1})(v_{j+1} - v_{j-1})}.$$

Thus, for non-equally-spaced interpolation points, we recommend setting the twist vector $\tau_{i,j}$ equal to this last equation and setting the control points with Equations VII.32.

There are several other ways of computing twist vectors: see (Farin, 1997) and the references cited therein.

Further Reading: The preceding discussion has been limited to surfaces formed by regular patterns of retangular patches. Not all surfaces can be conveniently approximated by rectangular patches, however; in fact, some cannot be approximated by a single array of rectangular patches at all. One alternative is to work with triangular patches; for example, the books (Farin, 1997) and (Hoschek and Lasser, 1993) discuss Bézier patches defined on triangles. More generally, it is desirable to be able to model surfaces containing an arbitrary topology of triangles, rectangles, and other polygons. Extensive work has been conducted on *subdivision surfaces* for the purpose of modeling surfaces with a wide range of topologies. Subdivision surfaces are beyond the scope of this book, but for an introduction you can consult the Siggraph course notes (Schröder, Zorin, et al., 1998) or the book (Warren and Weimer, 2002).

VIII

B-Splines

This chapter covers uniform and nonuniform B-splines, including rational B-splines (NURBS). B-splines are widely used in computer-aided design and manufacturing and are supported by OpenGL. B-splines are a powerful tool for generating curves with many control points and provide many advantages over Bézier curves – especially because a long, complicated curve can be specified as a single B-spline. Furthermore, a curve designer has much flexibility in adjusting the curvature of a B-spline curve, and B-splines can be designed with sharp bends and even "corners." In addition, it is possible to translate piecewise Bézier curves into B-splines and vice versa. B-splines do not usually interpolate their control points, but it is possible to define interpolating B-splines. Our presentation of B-splines is based on the Cox–de Boor definition of blending functions, but the blossoming approach to B-splines is also presented.

The reader is warned that this chapter is a mix of introductory topics and more advanced, specialized topics. You should read at least the first parts of Chapter VII before this chapter. Sections VIII.1–VIII.4 give a basic introduction to B-splines. The next four sections cover the de Boor algorithm, blossoming, smoothness properties, and knot insertion; these sections are fairly mathematical and should be read in order. If you wish, you may skip these mathematical sections at first, for the remainder of the chapter can be read largely independently. Section VIII.9 discusses how to convert a piecewise Bézier curves into a B-spline. The very short Section VIII.10 discusses degree elevation. Section VIII.11 covers rational B-splines. Section VIII.12 very briefly describes using B-splines in OpenGL. Section VIII.13 gives a method for interpolating points with B-splines. You should feel free to skip most of the proofs if you find them confusing; most of the proofs, especially the more difficult ones, are not needed for the practical use of splines.

Splines – especially interpolating splines – have a long history, and we do not try to describe it here. B-spline functions were defined by (Shoenberg, 1946; Curry and Shoenberg, 1947). The name "B-spline," with the "B" standing for "basis," was coined by (Shoenberg, 1967). The terminology "basis spline" refers to the practice of defining B-splines in terms of "basis functions." (We use the term "blending function" instead of "basis function.") B-splines became popular after de Boor (de Boor, 1972), Cox (Cox, 1972), and Mansfield discovered the fundamental Cox–de Boor formula for recursively defining the blending functions.

Figure VIII.1 shows one of the simplest possible examples of how B-spline curves can be used. There are nine control points, $\mathbf{p}_0, \ldots, \mathbf{p}_8$, that completely define the B-spline curves. The curve shown in part (a) is a uniform degree two B-spline curve; the curve in part (b) is

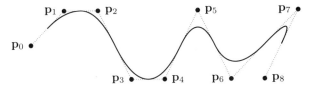

(a) Degree two B-spline curve.

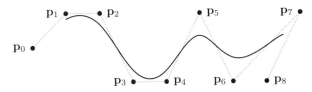

(b) Degree three B-spline curve.

Figure VIII.1. Degree two and degree three B-spline curves with uniformly spaced knots and nine control points. The degree three curve is smoother than the degree two curve, whereas, the degree two curve approaches the control points a little more closely. Compare with the degree eight Bézier curve of Figure VII.9(c) on page 167.

a uniform degree three curve. (The mathematical definitions of these curves are in Sections VIII.1 and VIII.2.) Qualitatively, the curves are "pulled towards" the control points in much the same way that a Bézier curve is pulled towards its interior control points. Unlike Bézier curves, B-spline curves do not necessarily interpolate their first and last control points; rather, the degree two curve starts and ends midway between two control points, and the degree three curve starts and ends near the control points adjacent to the starting and ending points. However, there are ways of defining B-spline curves that ensure that the first and last control points are interpolated.

A big advantage of B-spline curves over Bézier curves is that they act more flexibly and intuitively with a large number of control points. Indeed, if you compare the curves of Figure VIII.1 with the degree eight Bézier curve of Figure VII.9(c) on page 167, you will see that the B-spline curves are pulled more definitely by the control points. The Bézier curve seems to be barely affected by the placement of individual control points, whereas the B-spline curves are clearly affected directly by the control points. This makes B-spline curves much more useful for designing curves.

We will first treat the case of uniform B-splines and then the more general case of nonuniform B-splines.

VIII.1 Uniform B-Splines of Degree Three

Before presenting the general definition of B-splines in Section VIII.2, we first introduce one of the simplest and most useful cases of B-splines, namely, the *uniform B-splines of degree three*. Such a B-spline is defined with a sequence $\mathbf{p}_0, \mathbf{p}_1, \mathbf{p}_2, \ldots, \mathbf{p}_n$ of *control points*. Together with a set of blending (or basis) functions $N_0(u), N_1(u), \ldots, N_n(u)$, this parametrically defines a curve $\mathbf{q}(u)$ by

$$\mathbf{q}(u) = \sum_{i=0}^{n} N_i(u) \cdot \mathbf{p}_i \qquad 3 \leq u \leq n+1.$$

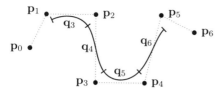

Figure VIII.2. A degree three uniform B-spline curve with seven control points.

We define these blending functions later in this section, but for the moment, just think of the blending functions N_i as having an effect analogous to the Bernstein polynomials B_i used in the definition of Bézier curves.

An important property of the uniform degree three blending functions N_i is that $N_i(u)$ will equal zero if either $u \le i$ or $i + 4 \le u$. That is, the support of $N_i(u)$ is the open interval $(i, i + 4)$. In particular, this means that we can rewrite the formula for $\mathbf{q}(u)$ as

$$\mathbf{q}(u) = \sum_{i=j-3}^{j} N_i(u) \cdot \mathbf{p}_i \qquad \text{provided } u \in [j, j+1], 3 \le j \le n \qquad \text{VIII.1}$$

since the terms omitted from the summation are all zero. This means that the B-spline has *local control*; namely, if a single control point $\mathbf{p}_i$ is moved, then only the portion of the curve $\mathbf{q}(u)$ with $i < u < i + 4$ is changed, and the rest of the B-spline remains fixed. Local control is an important feature enhancing the usefulness of B-spline curves: it allows a designer or artist to edit one portion of a curve without causing changes to distant parts of the curve. In contrast, Bézier curves of higher degree do not have local control, for each control point affects the entire curve.

Figure VIII.2 shows an example of a degree three B-spline curve $\mathbf{q}(u)$ defined with seven control points and defined for $3 \le u \le 7$. The curve $\mathbf{q}$ is split into four subcurves $\mathbf{q}_3, \ldots, \mathbf{q}_6$, where $\mathbf{q}_3$ is the portion of $\mathbf{q}(u)$ corresponding to $3 \le u \le 4$, $\mathbf{q}_4$ is the portion with $4 \le u \le 5$, and so on. More generally, $\mathbf{q}_i(u) = \mathbf{q}(u)$ for $i \le u \le i + 1$.

The intuition of how the curve $\mathbf{q}(u)$ behaves is as follows. The beginning point of $\mathbf{q}_3$, where $u = 3$, is being pulled strongly towards the point $\mathbf{p}_1$ and less strongly towards the points $\mathbf{p}_0$ and $\mathbf{p}_2$. The other points on $\mathbf{q}_3$ are calculated as weighted averages of $\mathbf{p}_0, \mathbf{p}_1, \mathbf{p}_2, \mathbf{p}_3$. The other segments are similar; namely, the beginning of $\mathbf{q}_i$ is being pulled strongly towards $\mathbf{p}_{i-2}$, the end of $\mathbf{q}_i$ is being pulled strongly towards $\mathbf{p}_{i-1}$, and the points interior to $\mathbf{q}_i$ are computed as weighted averages of the four control points $\mathbf{p}_{i-3}, \mathbf{p}_{i-2}, \mathbf{p}_{i-1}, \mathbf{p}_i$. Finally, the segments $\mathbf{q}_i(u)$ are degree three polynomial curves; thus, $\mathbf{q}(u)$ is piecewise a degree three polynomial curve. Furthermore, $\mathbf{q}(u)$ has continuous second derivatives everywhere it is defined.

These properties of the curve $\mathbf{q}(u)$ all depend on properties of the blending functions $N_i(u)$.[1] Figure VIII.3 shows the graphs of the functions $N_i(u)$. At $u = 3$, we have $N_1(3) > N_0(3) = N_2(3) > 0$, and $N_i(3) = 0$ for all other values of i. In fact, we will see that $N_1(3) = 2/3$ and $N_0(3) = N_2(3) = 1/6$. Therefore, $\mathbf{q}(3)$ is equal to the weighted average $(\mathbf{p}_0 + 4\mathbf{p}_1 + \mathbf{p}_2)/6$, which is consistent with what we earlier observed in Figure VIII.2 about the beginning point of the curve $\mathbf{q}_3$. The other assertions we made about the curves $\mathbf{q}_3, \ldots, \mathbf{q}_6$ can likewise be seen to follow from the properties of the blending functions $N_i(u)$. Note that Equation VIII.1 is borne out by the behavior of the blending functions in Figure VIII.3. Similarly, it is also clear that a control point $\mathbf{p}_i$ affects only the four segments $\mathbf{q}_i, \mathbf{q}_{i+1}, \mathbf{q}_{i+2}, \mathbf{q}_{i+3}$.

---

[1] When we develop the theory of B-splines of arbitrary degree, these blending functions $N_i(u)$ will be denoted $N_{i,4}(u)$. Another mathematical derivation of these blending functions is given in the first example of Section VIII.3.

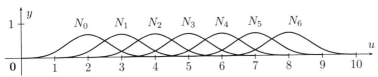

Figure VIII.3. The blending functions for a uniform, degree three B-spline. Each function N_i has support $(i, i + 4)$.

The blending functions should have the following properties:

(a) The blending functions are translates of each other, that is,

$$N_i(u) = N_0(u - i).$$

(b) The functions $N_i(u)$ are piecewise degree three polynomials. The breaks between the pieces occur only at integer values of i.
(c) The functions $N_i(u)$ have continuous second derivatives, that is, they are C^2-continuous.
(d) The blending functions are a *partition of unity*, that is,

$$\sum_i N_i(u) = 1$$

for $3 \leq u \leq 7$. (Or, for $3 \leq u \leq n + 1$ when there are $n + 1$ control points $\mathbf{p}_0, \ldots, \mathbf{p}_n$.) This property is necessary for points on the B-spline curve to be defined as weighted averages of the control points.
(e) $N_i(u) \geq 0$ for all u. Therefore, $N_i(u) \leq 1$ for all u.
(f) $N_i(u) = 0$ for $u \leq i$ and for $i + 4 \leq u$. This property of the blending functions gives the B-spline curves their local control properties.

Because of conditions (a) and (f), the blending functions will be fully specified once we define the function $N_0(u)$ on the domain $[0, 4]$. For this purpose, we will define four functions $R_0(u)$, $R_1(u)$, $R_2(u)$, $R_3(u)$ for $0 \leq u \leq 1$ by

$$R_0(u) = N_0(u) \qquad\qquad R_2(u) = N_0(u + 2)$$
$$R_1(u) = N_0(u + 1) \qquad R_3(u) = N_0(u + 3).$$

Thus, the functions $R_i(u)$ are the translates of the four segments of $N_0(u)$ to the interval $[0, 1]$ and, to finish the definition of $N_0(u)$ it suffices to define the four functions $R_i(u)$. These four functions are degree three polynomials by condition (b). In fact, we claim that the following choices for the R_i functions work (and this is the unique way to define these functions to satisfy the six conditions (a)–(f)):

$$R_0(u) = \tfrac{1}{6}u^3$$

$$R_1(u) = \tfrac{1}{6}(-3u^3 + 3u^2 + 3u + 1)$$

$$R_2(u) = \tfrac{1}{6}(3u^3 - 6u^2 + 4)$$

$$R_3(u) = \tfrac{1}{6}(1 - u)^3.$$

It takes a little work to verify that conditions (a)–(f) hold when $N_0(u)$ is defined from these choices for $R_0, \ldots, R_3$. Straightforward calculation shows that $\sum_i R_i(u) = 1$; thus, (d) holds. Also, it can be checked that $R_i(u) \geq 0$ for $i = 0, 1, 2, 3$ and all $u \in [0, 1]$; hence (e) holds. For (c) to hold, $N_0(u)$ needs to have continuous second derivative. Of course, this also means $N_0(u)$ is continuous and has continuous first derivative. These facts are proved by noticing that when the R_i functions are pieced together, their values and their first and second derivatives match up. That is,

$$
\begin{array}{lll}
R_0(0)=0 & R_0'(0)= 0 & R_0''(0)= 0 \\
R_0(1)=\frac{1}{6}=R_1(0) & R_0'(1)= \frac{1}{2} =R_1'(0) & R_0''(1)= 1 =R_1''(0) \\
R_1(1)=\frac{2}{3}=R_2(0) & R_1'(1)= 0 =R_2'(0) & R_1''(1)=-2=R_2''(0) \\
R_2(1)=\frac{1}{6}=R_3(0) & R_2'(1)= \frac{-1}{2}=R_3'(0) & R_2''(1)= 1 =R_3''(0) \\
R_3(1)=0 & R_3'(1)= 0 & R_3''(1)= 0
\end{array}
$$

Exercise VIII.1 *Graph the four functions R_i on the interval $[0, 1]$. [Hint: These are portions of the blending functions shown in Figure VIII.3.]*

Exercise VIII.2 *Give formulas for the first and second derivatives of the R_i functions. Verify the 15 conditions needed for the C^2-continuity of the blending function $N_0(u)$.*

Exercise VIII.3 *Verify that $\sum_i R_i(u) = 1$. Prove that $R_i(u) > 0$ for $i = 0, 1, 2, 3$ and for all $u \in (0, 1)$.*

Exercise VIII.4 *Verify that $R_0(u) = R_3(1 - u)$ and that $R_1(u) = R_2(1 - u)$. Show that this means that uniform B-splines have left–right symmetry in that, if the order of the control points is reversed, the curve $\mathbf{q}$ is unchanged except for being traversed in the opposite direction.*

Exercise VIII.5 *Describe the effect of repeating control points in degree three uniform B-splines. Qualitatively describe the curve obtained if one control point is repeated – for instance, if $\mathbf{p}_3 = \mathbf{p}_4$.*

Secondly, suppose $\mathbf{p}_2 \neq \mathbf{p}_3 = \mathbf{p}_4 = \mathbf{p}_5 \neq \mathbf{p}_6$. Show that the curve $\mathbf{q}$ interpolates the point $\mathbf{p}_3$ with $\mathbf{q}(6) = \mathbf{p}_3$. Further show that the segments $\mathbf{q}_5$ and $\mathbf{q}_6$ are straight lines.

VIII.2 Nonuniform B-Splines

The degree three uniform B-splines of the previous section were defined so that the curve $\mathbf{q}(u)$ was "pulled" by the control points in such way that $\mathbf{q}(i)$ is close to (or at least, strongly affected by) the control point $\mathbf{p}_{i-2}$. These splines are called "uniform" since the values u_i where the curve $\mathbf{q}(u)$ is most strongly affected by control points are evenly spaced at integer values $u_i = i$. These values u_i are called *knots*. A *nonuniform* spline is one for which the knots u_i are not necessarily uniformly spaced. The ability to space knots nonuniformly makes it possible to define a wider range of curves, including curves with sharp bends or discontinuous derivatives. The uniform B-splines are just the special case of nonuniform B-splines where $u_i = i$.

We define a *knot vector* to be a sequence

$$[u_0, u_1, \ldots, u_{\ell-1}, u_\ell]$$

of real numbers $u_0 \leq u_1 \leq u_2 \leq \cdots \leq u_{\ell-1} \leq u_\ell$ called *knots*. A knot vector is used with a sequence of $n + 1$ control points $\mathbf{p}_0, \mathbf{p}_1, \ldots, \mathbf{p}_n$ to define a nonuniform B-spline curve. (When defining an order m Bézier curve, that is, a curve of degree $k = m - 1$, we have $n = \ell - m$.) You should think of the spline curve as being a flexible and stretchable curve: its flexibility is limited and thus it resists being sharply bent. The curve is parameterized by the variable u, and we can think of u as measuring the time spent traversing the length of the curve. The control points "pull" on parts of the curve; you should think of there being a stretchable string, or

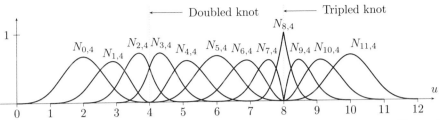

Figure VIII.4. Example of order four (degree three) blending functions with repeated knots. The knot vector is [0, 1, 2, 3, 4, 4, 5, 6, 7, 8, 8, 8, 9, 10, 11, 12] so that the knot 4 has multiplicity two and the knot 8 has multiplicity three.

rubber band, attached to a point on the curve and tied also to the control point $\mathbf{p}_i$. These pull on the spline, and the spline settles down into a smooth curve.

Now, you might expect that the "rubber bands" tie the control point $\mathbf{p}_i$ to the point on the curve where $u = u_i$. This, however, is not correct. Instead, when defining a B-spline curve of order m, you should think of the control point $\mathbf{p}_i$ as being tied to the curve at the position $u = u_{i+m/2}$. If m is odd, we need to interpret the position $u_{i+m/2}$ as lying somewhere between the two knots $u_{i+(m-1)/2}$ and $u_{i+(m+1)/2}$. This corresponds to what we observed in the case of uniformly spaced knots defining a degree three curve, where $m = 4$: the curve $\mathbf{q}(u)$ is most strongly influenced by the control point $\mathbf{p}_i$ at the position with $u = u_{i+2}$.

It is possible for knots to be repeated multiple times. If a knot position has multiplicity two, that is, if it occurs twice with $u_{i-1} < u_i = u_{i+1} < u_{i+2}$, then the curve will be affected more strongly by the corresponding control point. The curve will also lose some continuity properties for its derivatives. For instance, if $\mathbf{q}(u)$ is a degree three curve with a knot $u_i = u_{i+1}$ of multiplicity two, then $\mathbf{q}(u)$ will generally no longer have continuous second derivatives at u_i, although it will still have a continuous first derivative at u_i. Further, if $\mathbf{q}(u)$ has a a knot of multiplicity three, with $u_{i-1} < u_i = u_{i+1} = u_{i+2} < u_{i+3}$, then $\mathbf{q}(u)$ will interpolate the point $\mathbf{p}_{i+2}$ and will generally have a "corner" at $\mathbf{p}_{i+2}$ and thus not be C^1- or G^1-continuous. However, unlike the situation in Exercise VIII.5, the adjacent portions of the B-spline curve will not be straight line segments. These behaviors are exhibited in Figures VIII.4 and VIII.5.

If a knot position occurs four times (in a degree three curve), then the curve can actually become discontinuous! Knots that repeat four times are usually used only at the beginning or end of the knot vector and thus do not cause a discontinuity in the curve.

Next, we give the Cox–de Boor mathematical definition of nonuniform B-spline blending functions. So far, all of our examples have been degree three splines, but it is now convenient to generalize to splines of degree $k = m - 1$, which are also called *order m* splines. Assume the knot vector $u_0 \leq u_1 \leq \cdots \leq u_\ell$ has been fixed. The blending functions $N_{i,m}(u)$ for order m splines depend only on the knot positions, not on the control points, and are defined by induction

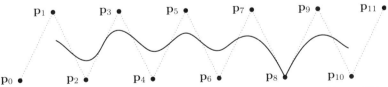

Figure VIII.5. Example of an order four B-spline created with repeated knots. This curve is created with the knot vector and blending functions shown in Figure VIII.4. It has domain [3, 9].

on $m \geq 1$ as follows. First, for $i = 0, \ldots, \ell - 1$, let

$$
N_{i,1}(u) = \begin{cases} 1 & \text{if } u_i \leq u < u_{i+1} \\ 0 & \text{otherwise.} \end{cases}
$$

There is one minor exception to the preceding definition, which is to include the very last point $u = u_\ell$ in the domain of the last nonzero function: namely, if $u_{i-1} < u_i = u_\ell$, then we let $N_{i-1,1}(u) = 1$ when $u_{i-1} \leq u \leq u_i$. In this way, the theorems stated below hold also for $u = u_\ell$. Second, for $m \geq 1$, letting $m = k + 1$, $N_{i,k+1}(u)$ is defined by the Cox–de Boor formula:

$$
N_{i,k+1}(u) = \frac{u - u_i}{u_{i+k} - u_i} N_{i,k}(u) + \frac{u_{i+k+1} - u}{u_{i+k+1} - u_{i+1}} N_{i+1,k}(u)
$$

The Cox–de Boor formula

When there are repeated knots, some of the denominators above may be zero: we adopt the convention that $0/0 = 0$ and $(a/0)0 = 0$. Since $N_{i,k}(u)$ will be identically zero when $u_{i+k} = u_i$ (see the next paragraph), this means that any term with denominator equal to zero may be ignored.

The form of the Cox–de Boor recursive formulas for the blending functions immediately implies that the functions $N_{i,m}(u)$ are piecewise degree $m - 1$ polynomials and that the breaks between pieces occur at the knots u_i. Secondly, it is easy to prove, by induction on $m \geq 1$, that the function $N_{i,m}(u)$ has support in $[u_i, u_{i+m}]$ (i.e., $N_{i,m}(u) = 0$ for $u < u_i$ and for $u_{i+m} < u$). From similar considerations, it is easy to see that the definition of the blending function $N_{i,m}(u)$ depends only on the knots $u_i, u_{i+1}, \ldots, u_{i+m}$.

VIII.3 Examples of Nonuniform B-Splines

To gain a qualitative understanding of how nonuniform B-splines work, it is helpful to do some simple examples.

Example: Uniformly Spaced Knots

We start with what is perhaps the simplest example, namely, the case in which the knots are uniformly spaced with the knot vector equal to just $[0, 1, 2, 3, \ldots, \ell]$. That is, the knots are $u_i = i$. Of course, we expect this case to give the same degree three results as the uniform B-splines discussed in Section VIII.1 with the functions $N_{i,4}(u)$ equal to the functions $N_i(u)$ of that section.

To define the blending functions, $N_{i,m}(u)$, we start with the order $m = 1$ case, that is, the degree $k = 0$ case. For this we have merely the step functions, for $i = 0, \ldots, \ell - 1$,

$$
N_{i,1}(u) = \begin{cases} 1 & \text{if } i \leq u < i + 1 \\ 0 & \text{otherwise.} \end{cases}
$$

These functions are piecewise degree zero (i.e., piecewise constant); of course, they are discontinuous at the knot positions $u_i = i$.

Next, we compute the order two (piecewise degree one) blending functions $N_{i,2}(u)$. Using the fact that $u_i = i$, we define these from the Cox–de Boor formula as

$$
N_{i,2}(u) = \frac{u - i}{1} N_{i,1}(u) + \frac{i + 2 - u}{1} N_{i+1,1}(u),
$$

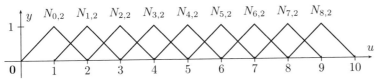

Figure VIII.6. The order two (piecewise degree one) blending functions with uniformly spaced knots, $u_i = i$. Here $\ell = 10$, and there are $\ell + 1$ knots and $\ell - 1$ blending functions. The associated B-spline curve of Equation VIII.2 is defined for $1 \le u \le \ell - 1$.

for $i = 0, \ldots, \ell - 2$. Specializing to the case $i = 0$, we have

$$N_{0,2}(u) = u N_{0,1}(u) + (2 - u) N_{1,1}(u),$$

and from the definitions of $N_{0,1}(u)$ and $N_{1,1}(u)$, this means that

$$N_{0,2}(u) = \begin{cases} u & \text{if } 0 \le u < 1 \\ 2 - u & \text{if } 1 \le u < 2 \\ 0 & \text{otherwise.} \end{cases}$$

Because the knots are uniformly spaced, similar calculations apply to the rest of the order two blending functions $N_{i,2}(u)$, and these are all just translates of $N_{0,2}(u)$ with $N_{i,2}(u) = N_{0,2}(u - i)$. The order two blending functions are graphed in Figure VIII.6.

Note that the order two blending functions are continuous (C^0-continuous) and piecewise linear. Since clearly $N_{i,2}(u) \ge 0$ and $\sum_i N_{i,2}(u) = 1$ for all $u \in [1, \ell - 1]$, we can define a "curve" $\mathbf{q}(u)$ as

$$\mathbf{q}(u) = \sum_{i=0}^{\ell-2} N_{i,2}(u) \mathbf{p}_i, \qquad 1 \le u \le \ell - 1, \tag{VIII.2}$$

with control points $\mathbf{p}_0, \ldots, \mathbf{p}_{\ell-2}$. By inspection, this "curve" consists of straight line segments connecting the control points $\mathbf{p}_0, \ldots, \mathbf{p}_{\ell-2}$ in a "connect-the-dots" fashion with $\mathbf{q}(u_{i+1}) = \mathbf{p}_i$ for $i = 0, \ldots, \ell - 2$.

Next, we compute the order three (piecewise degree two) blending functions, $N_{i,3}(u)$. From the Cox–de Boor formula with $m = 3$ or $k = 2$,

$$N_{i,3}(u) = \frac{u - i}{2} N_{i,2}(u) + \frac{i + 3 - u}{2} N_{i+1,2}(u).$$

These are defined for $i = 0, \ldots, \ell - 3$. As before, we specialize to the case $i = 0$ and have

$$N_{0,3}(u) = \tfrac{1}{2} u N_{0,2}(u) + \tfrac{1}{2}(3 - u) N_{1,2}(u).$$

Considering separately the cases $0 \le u < 1$ and $1 \le u < 2$ and $2 \le u < 3$, we have

$$N_{0,3}(u) = \begin{cases} \tfrac{1}{2} u^2 & \text{if } 0 \le u < 1 \\ \tfrac{1}{2} u(2 - u) + \tfrac{1}{2}(3 - u)(u - 1) = \tfrac{1}{2}(6u - 2u^2 - 3) & \text{if } 1 \le u < 2 \\ \tfrac{1}{2}(3 - u)^2 & \text{if } 2 \le u < 3 \\ 0 & \text{otherwise.} \end{cases}$$

It is straightforward to check that $N_{0,3}(u)$ has a continuous first derivative. In addition, direct calculation shows that $N_{0,3}(u) \ge 0$ for all u. Because the knots are uniformly spaced, the rest of the order three blending functions, $N_{i,3}(u)$, are just translates of $N_{0,3}(u)$, with $N_{i,3}(u) = N_{0,3}(u - i)$: these functions are shown in Figure VIII.7. It is also straightforward to check that $\sum_{i=0}^{\ell-3} N_{i,3}(u) = 1$ for $2 \le u \le \ell - 2$. Also note that the function $N_{i,3}(u)$ is maximized at $u = i + 3/2$, where it takes on the value $3/4$. A degree two B-spline curve can be defined with

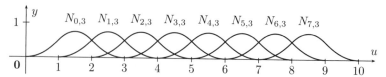

Figure VIII.7. The order three (piecewise degree two) blending functions with uniform knot positions $u_i = i$. We still have $\ell = 10$; there are $\ell + 1$ knots and $\ell - 2$ blending functions. The associated B-spline curve of Equation VIII.3 is defined for $2 \le u \le \ell - 2$.

these blending functions as

$$\mathbf{q}(u) = \sum_{i=0}^{\ell-3} N_{i,3}(u)\mathbf{p}_i, \qquad 2 \le u \le \ell - 2. \tag{VIII.3}$$

By using the Cox–de Boor formula again, we could define the order four (piecewise degree three) blending functions $N_{i,4}(u)$. We do not carry out this computation; however, the results obtained would be identical to the blending functions $N_i(u)$ used in Section VIII.1 and shown in Figure VIII.3. We leave it as an exercise for the reader to verify this fact.

Example: Bézier Curve as B-Spline

For our second example, we let the knot vector be $[0, 0, 0, 0, 1, 1, 1, 1]$ and compute the order 1, 2, 3, and 4 blending functions for this knot vector. Here we have $u_i = 0$ for $i = 0, 1, 2, 3$ and $u_i = 1$ for $i = 4, 5, 6, 7$. The order one blending functions are just

$$N_{3,1}(u) = \begin{cases} 1 & \text{if } 0 \le u \le 1 \\ 0 & \text{otherwise} \end{cases}$$

and $N_{i,1}(u) = 0$ for $i \ne 3$.

The order two blending functions $N_{i,2}(u)$ are zero except for $i = 2, 3$. Also, for every order $m \ge 1$, every blending function will be zero for $u < 0$ and $u > 1$. Both these facts use the conventions for the Cox–de Boor equations that $0/0 = 0$ and $(a/0) \cdot 0$. (The reader should verify all our assertions!) For $i = 2, 3$ and $0 \le u \le 1$, the Cox–de Boor equations with $k = 1$ give

$$\begin{aligned} N_{2,2}(u) &= \frac{u - u_2}{u_3 - u_2} \cdot N_{2,1}(u) + \frac{u_4 - u}{u_4 - u_3} \cdot N_{3,1}(u) \\ &= \frac{u - 0}{0 - 0} \cdot 0 + \frac{1 - u}{1 - 0} \cdot 1 = 1 - u \end{aligned}$$

$$\begin{aligned} N_{3,2}(u) &= \frac{u - u_3}{u_4 - u_3} \cdot N_{3,1}(u) + \frac{u_5 - u}{u_5 - u_4} \cdot N_{4,1}(u) \\ &= \frac{u - 0}{1 - 0} \cdot 1 + \frac{1 - u}{1 - 1} \cdot 0 = u. \end{aligned}$$

The order three blending functions are zero except for $i = 1, 2, 3$, and $N_{1,3}(u)$, $N_{2,3}(u)$, and $N_{3,3}(u)$ are zero outside the domain $[0, 1]$. Calculations from the Cox–de Boor equations, similar to the preceding, give, for $0 \le u \le 1$,

$$N_{1,3}(u) = (1 - u)^2$$

$$N_{2,3}(u) = 2u(1 - u) \tag{VIII.4}$$

$$N_{3,3}(u) = u^2.$$

The order four (piecewise degree three) blending functions $N_{i,4}(u)$ are nonzero for $i = 0, 1, 2, 3$ and have support contained in $[0, 1]$. Further calculations from the Cox–de Boor equations give

$$N_{0,4}(u) = (1 - u)^3$$

$$N_{1,4}(u) = 3u(1 - u)^2$$

$$N_{2,4}(u) = 3u^2(1 - u)$$

$$N_{3,4}(u) = u^3$$

for $0 \le u \le 1$. Surprisingly, these four blending functions are equal to the Bernstein polynomials of degree three, namely, $B_i^3(u) = N_{i,4}(u)$. Therefore, the B-spline curve defined with the four control points $\mathbf{p}_0, \mathbf{p}_1, \mathbf{p}_2, \mathbf{p}_3$ and knot vector $[0, 0, 0, 0, 1, 1, 1, 1]$ is exactly the same as the degree three Bézier curve with the same control points.

Some generalizations of this example are given later in the first half of Section VIII.9, where it is shown how to represent multiple Bézier curves as a single B-spline curve: see Theorem VIII.12 on page 226.

Example: Nonuniformly Spaced and Repeated Knots

Consider the nonuniform knot vector

$$[0, 0, 0, 0, 1, 2, 2\tfrac{4}{5}, 3\tfrac{1}{5}, 4, 5, 6, 7, 7, 8, 9, 10, 10, 10, 10].$$

This was obtained by starting with knots at integer values 0 through 10, quadrupling the first and last knots, doubling the knots at $u = 3$ and $u = 7$, and then separating the knots at 3 slightly to be at $2\tfrac{4}{5}$ and $3\tfrac{1}{5}$. As usual, for $i = 0, \ldots, 18$, u_i denotes the ith knot as shown:

i:	0	1	2	3	4	5	6	7	8	9	10	11	12	13	14	15	16	17	18
u_i:	0	0	0	0	1	2	$2\tfrac{4}{5}$	$3\tfrac{1}{5}$	4	5	6	7	7	8	9	10	10	10	10

The degree zero blending functions $N_{i,1}(u)$ are defined for $0 \le i \le 17$. These are the step functions defined to have value 1 on the half-open interval $[u_i, u_{i+1})$ and value zero elsewhere. For values i such that $u_i = u_{i+1}$, this means that $N_{i,1}(u)$ is equal to zero for all u. This happens for i equal to 0, 1, 2, 11, 15, 16, 17.

The degree one blending functions are $N_{i,2}(u)$, for $0 \le i \le 16$, and are shown in Figure VIII.8. When u_i, u_{i+1}, and u_{i+2} are distinct, then the graph of the function $N_{i,2}(u)$ rises linearly from zero at u_i to 1 at u_{i+1} and then decreases linearly back to zero at u_{i+2}. It is zero outside the interval (u_i, u_{i+2}). On the other hand, when $u_i = u_{i+1} \neq u_{i+2}$, then $N_{i,2}$ is discontinuous at u_i: it jumps from the value zero for $u < u_i$ to the value 1 at u_i. It then decreases linearly back to zero at u_{i+2}. The situation is dual when $u_i \neq u_{i+1} = u_{i+2}$. In Figure VIII.8, $N_{10,2}$ and $N_{11,2}$ are both discontinuous at $u = 7$. If $u_i = u_{i+2}$, as happens for $i = 0, 1, 15, 16$, then $N_{i,2}(u)$ is equal to the constant zero everywhere.

The degree two blending functions are $N_{i,3}(u)$, for $0 \le i \le 15$, and are shown in part (b) of Figure VIII.8. The functions $N_{i,3}(u)$ have support in the interval $[u_i, u_{i+3}]$. More than this is true: if $u_i \neq u_{i+1}$, then $N_{i,3}(u_i) = 0$, and similarly, if $u_{i+2} \neq u_{i+3}$, then $N_{i,3}(u_{i+3}) = 0$. Even further, if $u_i = u_{i+1} \neq u_{i+2}$, then $N_{i,3}(u_i) = 0$: this happens when $i = 2, 11$. However, in this case, $N_{i,3}(u)$ has discontinuous first derivative at u_i. The symmetric case of $u_{i+1} \neq u_{i+2} = u_{i+3}$ can be seen with $i = 9$ and $i = 13$.

When there is a knot of multiplicity ≥ 3 and $u_i = u_{i+2} \neq u_{i+3}$, then we have $N_{i,3}(u_i) = 1$: in our example, this happens for $i = 1$. Dually, when $u_i \neq u_{i+1} = u_{i+3}$, as happens with $u = 14$,

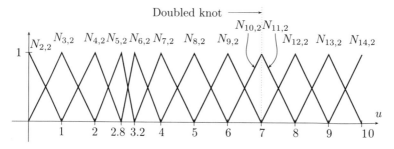

(a) Degree one blending functions.

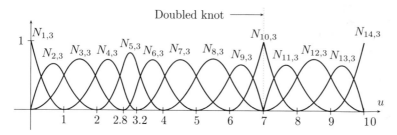

(b) Degree two blending functions.

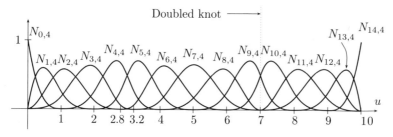

(c) Degree three blending functions.

Figure VIII.8. Degree one, two, and three blending functions for a nonuniform knot sequence. The knot 7 has multiplicity two, and the knots 0 and 10 have multiplicity 4.

then $N_{i,3}(u_{i+2}) = 1$. For $i = 0, 15$, $N_{i,3}(u)$ is just the constant zero everywhere. At the doubled knot $u_{11} = u_{12} = 7$, the blending function $N_{10,3}(u)$ is continuous and equal to 1 but has a discontinuous first derivative. A degree two B-spline curve formed with this knot vector will interpolate $\mathbf{p}_{10}$ at $u = 7$ but will, in general, have a corner there.

The degree three blending functions, $N_{i,4}(u)$, are shown in part (c) of Figure VIII.8. They are defined for $0 \leq i \leq 14$ and have support in the interval $[u_i, u_{i+4}]$. Where a knot has multiplicity ≥ 4, say if $u_i = u_{i+3} \neq u_{i+4}$, then the right limit $\lim_{u \to u_i^+} N_{i,4}(u)$ is equal to 1. Likewise, if $u_i \neq u_{i+1} = u_{i+4}$, then the left limit $\lim_{u \to u_{i+1}^-} N_{i,4}(u)$ equals 1. In this example, these situations happen only at the endpoints of the curve.

The degree three blending functions are C^2-continuous everywhere *except* at the doubled knot position $u = 7$, where $N_{8,4}(u)$, $N_{9,4}(u)$, $N_{10,4}(u)$, and $N_{11,4}(u)$ are only C^1-continuous.

The next two exercises ask you to work out some details of the standard knot vectors for degree two and degree three. For general degree k, the standard knot vectors have the form

$$[0, 0, \ldots, 0, 1, 2, 3, \ldots, s - 2, s - 1, s, s, \ldots, s],$$

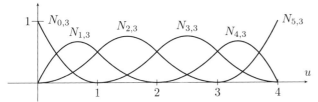

Figure VIII.9. The degree two blending functions, $N_{i,3}(u)$, for the knot vector of Exercise VIII.6.

where the knots 0 and s have multiplicity $k + 1$ and the rest of the knots have multiplicity 1. For these knot vectors, the B-spline curve will interpolate the first and last control points: the exercises ask you to verify this for some particular examples. In Section VIII.13, we will work again with the standard knot vector for degree three B-spline curves to interpolate a set of control points.

Exercise VIII.6 *Derive the formulas for the quadratic (order three, degree two) B-spline blending functions for the knot vector* $[0, 0, 0, 1, 2, 3, 4, 4, 4]$. *How many control points are needed for a quadratic B-spline curve with this knot vector? What is the domain of the B-spline curve? Show that the curve begins at the first control point and ends at the last control point. Check your formulas for the blending functions against Figure VIII.9.*

Exercise VIII.7 *Repeat the previous exercise, but with cubic B-spline curves with the knot vector* $[0, 0, 0, 0, 1, 2, 3, 4, 5, 6, 6, 6, 6]$. *The graph of the blending functions for this curve is shown in Figure VIII.10. (If you actually do this exercise, you might wish to use a computer algebra program to derive the formulas to avoid excessive hand calculation.)*

VIII.4 Properties of Nonuniform B-Splines

We now introduce some of the basic properties of the B-spline blending functions. Theorem VIII.1 describes the domain of definition for B-spline blending functions and shows they can be used to form weighted averages. Theorem VIII.2 explains the continuity properties of derivatives of B-splines.

Throughout this section, we use m to denote the order of the blending functions, that is, m is 1 plus the degree k of the blending functions.

Theorem VIII.1 *Let* $u_0 \leq u_1 \leq \cdots \leq u_\ell$ *be a knot vector. Then the blending functions* $N_{i,m}(u)$, *for* $0 \leq i \leq \ell - m$, *satisfy the following properties.*

(a) $N_{i,m}$ *has support in* $[u_i, u_{i+m}]$ *for all* $m \geq 1$.
(b) $N_{i,m}(u) \geq 0$ *for all* u.
(c) $\sum_{i=0}^{\ell-m} N_{i,m}(u) = 1$ *for all* u *such that* $u_{m-1} \leq u \leq u_{\ell-m+1}$.

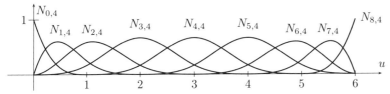

Figure VIII.10. The degree three blending functions, $N_{i,4}(u)$, for the knot vector $[0, 0, 0, 0, 1, 2, 3, 4, 5, 6, 6, 6, 6]$ of Exercise VIII.7.

It can become very confusing to keep track of all the precise values for subscripts and their ranges. Referring to Figures VIII.3, VIII.6, and VIII.7 can help with this.

Proof As discussed earlier, conditions (a) and (b) are readily proved by induction on m. Condition (c) is also proved by induction on m by the following argument. The base case, with $m = 1$, is obviously true. For the induction step, we assume condition (c) holds and then prove it with $m + 1$ in place of m. Assume $u_m \leq u \leq u_{\ell-m}$. By the Cox–de Boor formula,

$$\sum_{i=0}^{\ell-m-1} N_{i,m+1}(u)$$

$$= \sum_{i=0}^{\ell-m-1} \left(\frac{u - u_i}{u_{i+m} - u_i} N_{i,m}(u) + \frac{u_{i+m+1} - u}{u_{i+m+1} - u_{i+1}} N_{i+1,m}(u) \right)$$

$$= \frac{u - u_0}{u_m - u_0} N_{0,m}(u) + \sum_{i=1}^{\ell-m-1} \frac{(u - u_i) + (u_{i+m} - u)}{u_{i+m} - u_i} N_{i,m}(u)$$

$$\qquad\qquad + \frac{u_\ell - u}{u_\ell - u_{\ell-m}} N_{\ell-m,m}(u)$$

$$= N_{0,m}(u) + \sum_{i=1}^{\ell-m-1} 1 \cdot N_{i,m}(u) + N_{\ell-m,m}(u)$$

$$= \sum_{i=0}^{\ell-m} N_{i,m}(u) = 1.$$

The final equality follows from the induction hypothesis. The derivation of the next to last line needed the fact that $\frac{u-u_0}{u_m-u_0} N_{0,m}(u) = N_{0,m}(u)$. This holds since $u_m \leq u$; in particular, if $u_m < u$ then $N_{0,m}(u) = 0$ by (a), and if $u_m = u$ then $\frac{u-u_0}{u_m-u_0} = 1$. Similarly, the fact that $\frac{u_\ell - u}{u_\ell - u_{\ell-m}} N_{\ell-m,m}(u) = N_{\ell-m,m}(u)$ is justified by $u \leq u_{\ell-m}$. □

The importance of conditions (b) and (c) is that they allow the blending functions to be used as coefficients of control points to give a weighted average of control points. To define an order m (degree $m - 1$) B-spline curve, one needs $n + m + 1$ knot positions $u_0, \ldots, u_{n+m}$ and $n + 1$ control points $\mathbf{p}_0, \ldots, \mathbf{p}_n$. Then $\ell = n + m$ and the B-spline curve equals

$$\mathbf{q}(u) = \sum_{i=0}^{n} N_{i,m}(u)\mathbf{p}_i$$

for $u_{m-1} \leq u \leq u_{\ell-m+1} = u_{n+1}$.

The bounded interval of support given in condition (a) means that

$$\mathbf{q}(u) = \sum_{i=j-m+1}^{j} N_{i,m}(u)\mathbf{p}_i$$

provided $u_j \leq u < u_{j+1}$. Thus, the control points provide local control over the B-spline curve, since changing one control point only affects m segments of the B-spline curve.

The next theorem describes the smoothness properties of a B-spline curve. Because a B-spline consists of pieces that are degree $m - 1$ polynomials, it is certainly C^∞-continuous at all values of u that are not knot positions. If there are no repeated knots and if $m > 1$, then, as we will prove, the curve is in fact continuous everywhere in its domain and, even more, the curve is C^{m-2}-continuous everywhere in its domain. For instance, a degree three B-spline with no repeated knots has its second derivatives defined and continuous everywhere in its domain, including at the knot positions.

The case of repeated knots is more complicated. We say that a knot has *multiplicity* μ if it occurs μ times in the knot vector. Since the knots are linearly ordered, these μ occurrences must be consecutive values in the knot vector. That is, we have

$$u_{i-1} < u_i = u_{i+1} = \cdots = u_{i+\mu-1} < u_{i+\mu}.$$

In this case, the curve will have its $(m - \mu - 1)$th derivative defined and continuous at $u = u_i$. For instance, a degree three B-spline will have a continuous first derivative at a twice repeated knot position but in general will be only continuous at a knot position of multiplicity three. In the latter case, the curve will generally have a "corner" or "bend" at that knot position. A B-spline curve of degree three can be discontinuous at a knot position of multiplicity four.

The ability to repeat knots and make the curve have fewer continuous derivatives is important for the usefulness of B-splines because it allows a single curve to include both smooth portions and sharply bending portions.

We combine the assertions above about the smoothness of B-splines into the next theorem.

Theorem VIII.2 *Let* $\mathbf{q}(u)$ *be a B-spline curve of order* m, *and let the knot* u_i *have multiplicity* μ. *Then the curve* $\mathbf{q}(u)$ *has continuous* $(m - \mu - 1)$*th derivative at* $u = u_i$.

It is fairly difficult to give a direct proof of this theorem, and so the proof of Theorem VIII.2 is postponed until Section VIII.7, where we present a proof based on the use of the blossoms introduced in Section VIII.6.

The last property of B-splines discussed in this section concerns the behavior of blending functions near repeated knots. In general, if a degree k B-spline curve has a knot of multiplicity $\geq k$, then there is a blending function $N_{i,k+1}(u)$ that goes to 1 at the knot. Examples of this are the blending functions shown in Figures VIII.8–VIII.10, where the first and last knots are repeated many times and the first and last blending functions reach the value 1 at the first and last knots, respectively. It can also happen that interior knot positions have multiplicity k as well, and at such knots the appropriate blending function(s) will reach the value 1; see Figures VIII.4 and VIII.8(b) for examples of this.

The next theorem formalizes these facts. In addition to helping us understand the behavior of B-spline curves at their endpoints, the theorem will be useful in the next two sections for the development of the de Boor algorithm and for the proof of Theorem VIII.2.

Theorem VIII.3 *Let* $k \geq 1$.

(a) *Suppose that* $u_i = u_{i+k-1} < u_{i+k}$, *and so* u_i *has multiplicity at least* k. *Then*

$$\lim_{u \to u_i^+} N_{i-1,k+1}(u) = 1 \qquad\qquad \text{VIII.5}$$

and, for $j \neq i - 1$,

$$\lim_{u \to u_i^+} N_{j,k+1}(u) = 0.$$

(b) *Dually, suppose* $u_{i-1} < u_i = u_{i+k-1}$, *and so* u_i *has multiplicity at least* k. *Then*

$$\lim_{u \to u_i^-} N_{i-1,k+1}(u) = 1 \qquad\qquad \text{VIII.6}$$

and, for $j \neq i - 1$,

$$\lim_{u \to u_i^-} N_{j,k+1}(u) = 0.$$

Proof To prove (a) and (b), it will suffice to prove that equations VIII.5 and VIII.6 hold since the fact that the other limits equal zero will then follow from the partition of unity property of Theorem VIII.1(c).

We prove VIII.5 by induction on k. The base case is $k = 1$. (Refer to figures VIII.6 and VIII.8(a).) Using the definitions of the $N_{j,1}(u)$ blending functions as step functions, that $u_{i+1} - u_i \neq 0$, and the Cox–de Boor formula, we have

$$\lim_{u \to u_i^+} N_{i-1,2}(u) = \lim_{u \to u_i^+} \left(\frac{u - u_{i-1}}{u_i - u_{i-1}} N_{i-1,1}(u) + \frac{u_{i+1} - u}{u_{i+1} - u_i} N_{i,1}(u) \right)$$

$$= 0 + 1 \cdot 1 = 1.$$

The induction step applies to $k \geq 2$. In this case, we have

$$\lim_{u \to u_i^+} N_{i-1,k+1}(u)$$

$$= \lim_{u \to u_i^+} \left(\frac{u - u_{i-1}}{u_{i+k-1} - u_{i-1}} N_{i-1,k}(u) + \frac{u_{i+k} - u}{u_{i+k} - u_i} N_{i,k}(u) \right)$$

$$= 1 \cdot 1 + 1 \cdot 0 = 1.$$

Here we have used the induction hypothesis and the fact that $u_i = u_{i+k-1}$.

The proof of VIII.6 is completely dual, and we omit it. □

> **Exercise VIII.8** *Use Theorem VIII.3 to prove that B-splines defined with the standard knot vector interpolate their first and last control points. [Hint: Use $i = 0$ and $i = s + k - 1$.]*

VIII.5 The de Boor Algorithm

The de Boor algorithm is a method for evaluating a B-spline curve $\mathbf{q}(u)$ at a single value of u. The de Boor algorithm is similar in spirit to the de Casteljau method for Bézier curves in that it works by repeatedly linearly interpolating between pairs of points. This makes the de Boor algorithm stable, robust, and less prone to roundoff errors than methods that work by calculating values of the blending functions $N_{i,m}(u)$. The de Boor algorithm is also an important construction for understanding the mathematical properties of B-spline curves, and it will be used to establish the "blossoming" method for B-splines in the next section.

Suppose that $\mathbf{q}(u)$ is a B-spline curve of degree $k \geq 1$ and is defined by the control points $\mathbf{p}_0, \mathbf{p}_1, \ldots, \mathbf{p}_n$ and the knot vector $[u_0, \ldots, u_{n+m}]$, where $m = k + 1$ is the order of $\mathbf{q}(u)$. Therefore, the curve's domain of definition is $[u_k, u_{n+1}]$. As usual, $\mathbf{q}(u)$ is defined by

$$\mathbf{q}(u) = \sum_{i=0}^{n} N_{i,k+1}(u)\mathbf{p}_i. \qquad \text{VIII.7}$$

The next theorem provides the main tool needed to derive the de Boor algorithm.

Theorem VIII.4 *For all $u \in [u_k, u_{n+1}]$ (or, for all $u \in [u_k, u_{n+1})$ if $k = 1$),*

$$\mathbf{q}(u) = \sum_{i=1}^{n} N_{i,k}(u)\mathbf{p}_i^{(1)}(u), \qquad \text{VIII.8}$$

where

$$\mathbf{p}_i^{(1)}(u) = \frac{u_{i+k} - u}{u_{i+k} - u_i}\mathbf{p}_{i-1} + \frac{u - u_i}{u_{i+k} - u_i}\mathbf{p}_i. \qquad \text{VIII.9}$$

If any knot has multiplicity $> k$; we can have $u_i = u_{i+k}$; the value $\mathbf{p}_i^{(1)}(u)$ is undefined. With our conventions on division by zero, the theorem still makes sense in this case, for then the function $N_{i,k}(u)$ is the constant zero function.

Proof We expand equation VIII.7 using the Cox–de Boor formula.

$$\mathbf{q}(u) = \sum_{i=0}^{n} N_{i,k+1}(u)\mathbf{p}_i$$

$$= \sum_{i=0}^{n} \left(\frac{u - u_i}{u_{i+k} - u_i} N_{i,k}(u) + \frac{u_{i+k+1} - u}{u_{i+k+1} - u_{i+1}} N_{i+1,k}(u) \right) \mathbf{p}_i$$

$$= \sum_{i=0}^{n} \frac{u - u_i}{u_{i+k} - u_i} N_{i,k}(u)\mathbf{p}_i + \sum_{i=1}^{n+1} \frac{u_{i+k} - u}{u_{i+k} - u_i} N_{i,k}(u)\mathbf{p}_{i-1}$$

$$= \sum_{i=1}^{n} \frac{u - u_i}{u_{i+k} - u_i} N_{i,k}(u)\mathbf{p}_i + \sum_{i=1}^{n} \frac{u_{i+k} - u}{u_{i+k} - u_i} N_{i,k}(u)\mathbf{p}_{i-1}$$

$$= \sum_{i=1}^{n} \left(\frac{u_{i+k} - u}{u_{i+k} - u_i} \mathbf{p}_{i-1} + \frac{u - u_i}{u_{i+k} - u_i} \mathbf{p}_i \right) N_{i,k}(u).$$

It is necessary to justify the fourth equality above, which reduces the domains of the summations. First note that, since $N_{0,k}(u)$ has support contained in $[u_0, u_k]$ and is right continuous at u_k, $N_{0,k}(u) = 0$ for $u \geq u_k$. This justifies dropping the $i = 0$ term from the first summation. For the second summation, we need to show that $N_{n+1,k}(u) = 0$. Note that $N_{n+1,k}(u)$ has support in $[u_{n+1}, u_{n+m}]$, and so the desired equality $N_{n+1,k}(u) = 0$ certainly holds if $u < u_{n+1}$. It remains to consider the case where $k > 1$ and $u = u_{n+1}$. Now, if $u_{n+1} < u_{n+m}$, then $N_{n+1,k}(u_{n+1}) = 0$ by the Cox–de Boor formula. On the other hand, if $u_{n+1} = u_{n+m}$, then $N_{n+1,k}(u)$ is the constant zero function.

That suffices to prove the theorem. $\square$

It is possible restate Theorem VIII.4 without the special case for $k = 1$. For this, let the order k functions $N_{i,k}(u)$ be defined from the knot vector $[u_0, \ldots, u_{n+m-1}]$ instead of the knots $[u_0, \ldots, u_{n+m}]$. Then Equation VIII.8 holds for all $u \in [u_k, u_{n+1}]$ for all $k \geq 1$.

At first glance, Equation VIII.8 may appear to define $\mathbf{q}(u)$ as a degree $k - 1$ B-spline curve. This is not quite correct however, since the new "control points" $\mathbf{p}_i^{(1)}(u)$ depend on u. Nonetheless, it is convenient to think of the theorem as providing a method of "degree lowering," and we can iterate the construction of the theorem to lower the degree all the way down to degree one. For this, we define

$$\mathbf{p}_i^{(0)}(u) = \mathbf{p}_i,$$

and, for $1 \leq j \leq k$, we generalize Equation VIII.9 to

$$\mathbf{p}_i^{(j)}(u) = \frac{u_{i+k-j+1} - u}{u_{i+k-j+1} - u_i} \mathbf{p}_{i-1}^{(j-1)} + \frac{u - u_i}{u_{i+k-j+1} - u_i} \mathbf{p}_i^{(j-1)}. \qquad \text{VIII.10}$$

The following theorem shows that, for a particular value of j and a particular u, $\mathbf{q}(u)$ can be expressed in terms of a B-spline curve of degree $k - j$.

Theorem VIII.5 *Let $0 \leq j \leq k$. Let $u \in [u_k, u_{n+1}]$ (or $u \in [u_k, u_{n+1})$ if $j = k$). Then*

$$\mathbf{q}(u) = \sum_{i=j}^{n} N_{i,k+1-j}(u)\mathbf{p}_i^{(j)}(u). \qquad \text{VIII.11}$$

This theorem is proved by induction on j using Theorem VIII.4. $\square$

$$\begin{array}{l}
\mathbf{p}_{s-k}^{(0)} \;=\; \mathbf{p}_{s-k} \\[2pt]
\;\;\;\;\swarrow \\
\mathbf{p}_{s-k+1}^{(1)} \longleftarrow \\
\;\;\swarrow \\
\mathbf{p}_{s-k+2}^{(2)} \longleftarrow \qquad\qquad \vdots \qquad \vdots \\
\;\;\vdots \\
\;\;\vdots \qquad\qquad \mathbf{p}_{s-2}^{(1)} \longleftarrow \mathbf{p}_{s-2}^{(0)} \;=\; \mathbf{p}_{s-2} \\
\mathbf{p}_{s-1}^{(k-1)} \swarrow \qquad \mathbf{p}_{s-1}^{(2)} \longleftarrow \mathbf{p}_{s-1}^{(1)} \swarrow \mathbf{p}_{s-1}^{(0)} \;=\; \mathbf{p}_{s-1} \\
\mathbf{p}_{s}^{(k)} \longleftarrow \mathbf{p}_{s}^{(k-1)} \longleftarrow \cdots \quad \mathbf{p}_{s}^{(2)} \longleftarrow \mathbf{p}_{s}^{(1)} \longleftarrow \mathbf{p}_{s}^{(0)} \;=\; \mathbf{p}_{s}
\end{array}$$

Figure VIII.11. The control points obtained as $\mathbf{q}(u)$ is expressed as B-spline curves of lower degrees. For $j > 0$, the values $\mathbf{p}_i^{(j)}$ depend on u.

For the rest of this section, we suppose $\mathbf{q}(u)$ has degree k and that every knot position has multiplicity $\leq k$ except that possibly the first and last knot positions have multiplicity $k + 1$. It follows from Theorem VIII.2 that $\mathbf{q}(u)$ is a continuous curve. These assumptions can be made without loss of generality since the B-spline curve can be discontinuous at any knot with multiplicity $\geq k + 1$, and if such knots do occur the B-spline curve can be split into multiple B-spline curves.

We are now ready to describe the de Boor algorithm. Suppose we are given a value for u such that $u_s \leq u < u_{s+1}$, and we wish to compute $\mathbf{q}(u)$. By Theorem VIII.5, with $j = k$, we have $\mathbf{q}(u) = \mathbf{p}_s^{(k)}(u)$. This is because the degree zero blending function $N_{s,1}(u)$ is equal to 1 on the interval containing u. The de Boor algorithm thus consists of evaluating $\mathbf{p}_s^{(k)}(u)$ by using equation VIII.10 recursively. As shown in Figure VIII.11, $\mathbf{p}_s^{(k)}(u)$ does not in general depend on all of the original control points $\mathbf{p}_i$ but instead only on the control points $\mathbf{p}_i$ with $s - k \leq i \leq s$. The de Boor algorithm presented at the conclusion of this section works by computing the control points $\mathbf{p}_i^{(j)}(u)$, which are shown in Figure VIII.11. That is, it computes $\mathbf{p}_i^{(j)}(u)$ for $j = 1, \ldots, k$ and for $i = s - k + j, \ldots, s$. An example of the de Boor algorithm is also illustrated in Figure VIII.12.

There is one special case in which the de Boor algorithm can be made more efficient. When u is equal to the knot u_s, it is not necessary to iterate all the way to $j = k$. Instead, suppose

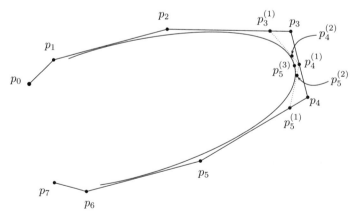

Figure VIII.12. The use of the de Boor algorithm to compute $\mathbf{q}(u)$. The degree three spline has the uniform knot vector $u_i = i$ for $0 \leq i \leq 10$ and control points $\mathbf{p}_i$. The points $\mathbf{p}_i^{(j)}$ are computed by the de Boor algorithm with $u = 5\frac{1}{2}$ and $\mathbf{p}_5^{(3)} = \mathbf{q}(5\frac{1}{2})$.

the knot $u = u_s$ has multiplicity μ. Since $u_s < u_{s+1}$, we have $u_{s-\mu+1} = u_s$, and applying Theorem VIII.3(b) with $i = s - \mu + 1$ gives

$$\mathbf{q}(u) = \mathbf{p}_{s-\mu}^{(k-\mu)}.$$

The pseudocode for the de Boor algorithm is presented below. The algorithm works by computing values $\mathbf{p}_i^{(j)}(u)$ for successive values of j up to $j = k - \mu$; these values are stored in an array r[]. For a given value of j, r[ℓ] is computed to equal $\mathbf{p}_{s-k+j+\ell}^{(j)}(u)$. To find the formula for computing successive values of r[ℓ], make the change of variables $\ell = i - (s - k + j)$ in Equation VIII.10 to obtain

$$\mathbf{p}_{s-k+j+\ell}^{(j)}(u) = \frac{u_{s+\ell+1} - u}{u_{s+\ell+1} - u_{s-k+j+\ell}}\mathbf{p}_{s-k+j+\ell-1}^{(j-1)} + \frac{u - u_{s-k+j+\ell}}{u_{s+\ell+1} - u_{s-k+j+\ell}}\mathbf{p}_{s-k+j+\ell}^{(j-1)}. \quad \text{VIII.12}$$

```
De Boor Algorithm
Input:  A degree k B-spline curve q (thus of order m = k + 1), given by:
              Control points p₀, p₁, ..., pₙ,
              Knot positions u₀, u₁, ..., uₙ₊ₘ.
        A value u such that uₖ ≤ u ≤ uₙ₊₁.
Result: Return value is q(u).
Algorithm:
        If ( u==uₙ₊ₘ ) { // If so, also u = uₙ₊₁ holds.
              Return pₙ;
        }
        Set s to be the value such that uₛ ≤ u < uₛ₊₁;
        If ( u==uₛ ) {
              Set μ = the multiplicity of uₛ;
        }
        Else {
              Set μ = 0;
        }
        // Initialize for j=0:
        For ℓ = 0, 1, ..., k − μ {
              Set r[ℓ] = pₛ₋ₖ₊ℓ;
        }
        // Main loop:
        For j = 1,2,..., k − μ {
              For ℓ = 0, 1, ..., k − μ − j {
                    Set α = (u − uₛ₋ₖ₊ⱼ₊ℓ)/(uₛ₊ℓ₊₁ − uₛ₋ₖ₊ⱼ₊ℓ);
                    Set r[ℓ] = lerp(r[ℓ],r[ℓ+1],α);
              }
        }
        Return r[0];
```

VIII.6 Blossoms

Blossoms are a method of representing polynomial curves with symmetric, multiaffine functions. As such they provide an elegant tool for working with B-splines. Apart from mathematical elegance, the most important aspect of blossoms for us is that they give a simple algorithm for computing the control points of a B-spline curve from the polynomial segments of the curve. Blossoms will be useful for obtaining formulas for the derivative of a B-spline. In addition, they give an easy method for deriving algorithms for knot insertion.

Suppose $\mathbf{q}(u)$ is a degree k B-spline curve and that $u_s < u_{s+1}$ are two knots. The curve $\mathbf{q}(u)$ consists of polynomial pieces; on the interval $[u_s, u_{s+1}]$, $\mathbf{q}(u)$ is defined by a (single) polynomial, which we call $\mathbf{f}(u)$. We will find a new function $\mathbf{b}(x_1, x_2, \ldots, x_k)$ that takes k real numbers as arguments but has the *diagonal* property that

$$\mathbf{b}(u, u, \ldots, u) = \mathbf{f}(u). \qquad \qquad \text{VIII.13}$$

This function $\mathbf{b}(x_1, \ldots, x_k)$ is called the "blossom" of $\mathbf{f}$. The blossom $\mathbf{b}$ will also satisfy the following two properties:

> **Symmetry Property:** Changing the order of the inputs to $\mathbf{b}$ does not change the value of $\mathbf{b}$; namely, for any permutation π of $\{1, \ldots, k\}$ and for all values of $x_1, \ldots x_k$,
>
> $$\mathbf{b}(x_{\pi(1)}, x_{\pi(2)}, \ldots, x_{\pi(k)}) = \mathbf{b}(x_1, x_2, \ldots, x_k).$$
>
> A function with this property is called a *symmetric function*.
>
> **Multiaffine Property:** For any scalars α and β with $\alpha + \beta = 1$, the blossom satisfies
>
> $$\mathbf{b}(\alpha x_1 + \beta x_1', x_2, x_3, \ldots, x_k) = \alpha \mathbf{b}(x_1, x_2, x_3, \ldots, x_k) + \beta \mathbf{b}(x_1', x_2, x_3, \ldots, x_k).$$
>
> By the symmetry property, the same property holds for any of the other inputs $x_2, \ldots, x_k$ in place of x_1.

Normally, the term "affine" is used for a function of a single variable that is defined by a polynomial of degree one. (This is equivalent to how "affine" was defined in Chapter II; however, now we are working with functions that take scalar inputs instead of inputs from $\mathbb{R}^2$ or $\mathbb{R}^3$.) In other words, a function $h(x)$ is *affine* if it is of the form $h(x) = ax + b$. Such functions h are precisely the functions that satisfy $h(\alpha x + \beta y) = \alpha h(x) + \beta h(y)$ for all values of x, y, α, and β with $\alpha + \beta = 1$. Since blossoms are affine in each input variable separately, they are called "multiaffine."

We next define the blossom of a polynomial curve $\mathbf{q}(u)$ in $\mathbb{R}^d$. First, some notation is necessary. For $k > 0$, we let $[k] = \{1, 2, \ldots, k\}$. For J a subset of $[k]$, we define the term x_J to be the product

$$x_J = \prod_{j \in J} x_j.$$

For example, if $J = \{1, 3, 6\}$, then $x_J = x_1 x_3 x_6$. For the empty set, we define $x_\emptyset = 1$.

Definition Let $\mathbf{q}$ have degree $\leq k$ so that

$$\mathbf{q}(u) = \mathbf{r}_k u^k + \mathbf{r}_{k-1} u^{k-1} + \cdots + \mathbf{r}_2 u^2 + \mathbf{r}_1 u^1 + \mathbf{r}_0,$$

where the coefficients $\mathbf{r}_i$ are points from $\mathbb{R}^d$ for some d. (These coefficients $\mathbf{r}_i$ should not be confused with the control points of a B-spline curve.) We define the *degree k blossom* of $\mathbf{q}(u)$ to be the k variable polynomial

$$\mathbf{b}(x_1, \ldots, x_k) = \sum_{i=0}^{k} \sum_{\substack{J \subseteq [k] \\ |J| = i}} \binom{k}{i}^{-1} \mathbf{r}_i x_J, \qquad \qquad \text{VIII.14}$$

where $|J|$ denotes the cardinality of J. We need to check that the definition of the blossom $\mathbf{b}$ satisfies the three properties described above. First, it is immediate, just from the form of the definition, that $\mathbf{b}$ is a symmetric function. Second, the terms in the polynomial defining $\mathbf{b}$

contain at most one occurrence of each variable; therefore, $\mathbf{b}$ is degree one in each variable separately and thus is affine in each variable. Finally, since there are $\binom{k}{i}$ many subsets J of k of size i, it is easy to see that $\mathbf{b}(u, u, \ldots, u) = \mathbf{q}(u)$.

As an example, let $\mathbf{q}(u)$ be the quadratic curve

$$\mathbf{q}(u) = \mathbf{a}u^2 + \mathbf{b}u + \mathbf{c}.$$

Then, the degree two blossom of $\mathbf{q}(u)$ is the polynomial

$$\mathbf{b}(x_1, x_2) = \mathbf{a}x_1 x_2 + \tfrac{1}{2}\mathbf{b}(x_1 + x_2) + \mathbf{c}.$$

There is also a degree three blossom for $\mathbf{q}(u)$. For this, we think of $\mathbf{q}(u)$ as being a degree three polynomial with leading coefficient zero. Then the degree three blossom of $\mathbf{q}(u)$ equals

$$\mathbf{b}(x_1, x_2, x_3) = \tfrac{1}{3}\mathbf{a}(x_1 x_2 + x_1 x_3 + x_2 x_3) + \tfrac{1}{3}\mathbf{b}(x_1 + x_2 + x_3) + \mathbf{c}.$$

Exercise VIII.9 *Let* $\mathbf{q}(u) = \mathbf{a}u^3 + \mathbf{b}u^2 + \mathbf{c}u + \mathbf{d}$. *What is the degree three blossom of* $\mathbf{q}(u)$?

The key reason that blossom functions are useful is that they can be used to compute the control points of a B-spline curve from the polynomial equation of the curve. This is expressed by the next theorem.

Theorem VIII.6 *Let* $\mathbf{q}(u)$ *be a degree* k, *order* $m = k + 1$ *B-spline curve with knot vector* $[u_0, \ldots, u_{n+m}]$ *and control points* $\mathbf{p}_0, \ldots, \mathbf{p}_n$. *Suppose* $u_s < u_{s+1}$, *where* $k \le s \le n$. *Let* $\mathbf{q}(u)$ *be equal to the polynomial* $\mathbf{q}_s(u)$ *for* $u \in [u_s, u_{s+1})$. *Let* $\mathbf{b}(x_1, \ldots, x_k)$ *be the blossom of* $\mathbf{q}_s(u)$.[2] *Then the control points* $\mathbf{p}_{s-k}, \ldots, \mathbf{p}_s$ *are equal to*

$$\mathbf{p}_i = \mathbf{b}(u_{i+1}, u_{i+2}, \ldots, u_{i+k}), \qquad\qquad \text{VIII.15}$$

for $i = s - k, \ldots, s$.

This theorem lets us obtain the control points that affect a single segment of a B-spline from the blossom of the segment. In particular, it means that $k + 1$ consecutive control points can be calculated from just the one segment that they all affect!

Proof To prove Theorem VIII.6, we relate the blossom's values to the intermediate values obtained in the de Boor algorithm. For this, it is convenient to make a change of variables by setting $i = s - k + \ell$ and rewriting equation VIII.15 as

$$\mathbf{p}_{s-k+\ell} = \mathbf{b}(u_{s-k+\ell+1}, u_{s-k+\ell+2}, \ldots, u_{s+\ell}). \qquad\qquad \text{VIII.16}$$

It will thus suffice to prove Equation VIII.16 holds for $\ell = 0, 1, \ldots, k$.

Consider the values of the blossom function, as shown in Figure VIII.13. To save space, we have used two notational conveniences. First, the notation $u^{(i)}$ is used to denote i occurrences of the parameter u; for example, the diagonal property VIII.13 can be reexpressed as $\mathbf{b}(u^{(k)}) = \mathbf{q}_s(u)$. Second, for $i < j$, the notation $u_{[i,j]}$ denotes the sequence of values $u_i, u_{i+1}, \ldots, u_j$.

Figure VIII.13 looks very much like Figure VIII.11, which describes the de Boor algorithm. Indeed, the next lemma shows that it corresponds exactly to Figure VIII.11.

Lemma VIII.7 *Suppose the equality VIII.16 holds for all* $\ell = 0, \ldots, k$. *Then, for* $j = 0, \ldots, k$ *and* $\ell = 0, \ldots, k - j$,

$$\mathbf{p}_{s-k+j+\ell}^{(j)}(u) = \mathbf{b}(u_{s-k+j+\ell+1}, \ldots, u_{s+\ell}, u^{(j)}).$$

---

[2] The B-spline curve $\mathbf{q}(u)$ is only piecewise polynomial, and so it does not have a blossom. But, of course the subcurve $\mathbf{q}_s(u)$ does have a blossom.

$$\mathbf{b}(u_{[s-k+3,s]}, u^{\langle 2\rangle}) \longleftarrow \quad\quad \mathbf{b}(u_{[s-k+2,s]}, u) \longleftarrow \quad\quad \mathbf{b}(u_{[s-k+1,s]})$$

$$\vdots \quad\quad\quad \vdots \quad\quad\quad \vdots$$

$$\cdots \quad\quad \vdots \quad\quad \mathbf{b}(u_{[s-1,s+k-3]}, u) \longleftarrow \mathbf{b}(u_{[s-1,s+k-2]})$$

$$\mathbf{b}(u_{[s,s+k-3]}, u^{\langle 2\rangle}) \longleftarrow \mathbf{b}(u_{[s,s+k-2]}, u) \longleftarrow \mathbf{b}(u_{[s,s+k-1]})$$

$$\mathbf{b}(u^{\langle k\rangle}) \longleftarrow \cdots \mathbf{b}(u_{[s+1,s+k-2]}, u^{\langle 2\rangle}) \longleftarrow \mathbf{b}(u_{[s+1,s+k-1]}, u) \longleftarrow \mathbf{b}(u_{[s+1,s+k]})$$

Figure VIII.13. A table of blossom values. The value $\mathbf{b}(u^{\langle k\rangle})$ on the left is equal to $\mathbf{q}_s(u)$. The blossom values in the right column are equal to the control points of the B-spline curve. The symmetry and multiaffine properties of the blossom function mean that each blossom value is a weighted average of the two blossom values that point to it as expressed in Equation VIII.17.

The lemma is proved by induction on j. The base case is $j = 0$, and for this case, the lemma holds by the hypothesis that VIII.16 holds. To prove the induction step for $j > 0$, note that the symmetry and multiaffine properties of $\mathbf{b}$ imply that $\mathbf{b}(u_{s-k+j+\ell+1}, \ldots, u_{s+\ell}, u^{\langle j\rangle})$ equals

$$\mathbf{b}(u_{s-k+j+\ell+1}, \ldots, u_{s+\ell}, u, u^{\langle j-1\rangle})$$

$$= \frac{u_{s+\ell+1} - u}{u_{s+\ell+1} - u_{s-k+j+\ell}} \mathbf{b}(u_{s-k+j+\ell}, \ldots, u_{s+\ell}, u^{\langle j-1\rangle}) \qquad\qquad \text{VIII.17}$$

$$+ \frac{u - u_{s-k+j+\ell}}{u_{s+\ell+1} - u_{s-k+j+\ell}} \mathbf{b}(u_{s-k+j+\ell+1}, \ldots, u_{s+\ell+1}, u^{\langle j-1\rangle}).$$

The induction hypothesis tells us that $\mathbf{b}(u_{s-k+j+\ell}, \ldots, u_{s+\ell}, u^{\langle j-1\rangle})$ and $\mathbf{b}(u_{s-k+j+\ell+1}, \ldots, u_{s+\ell+1}, u^{\langle j-1\rangle})$ are equal to $\mathbf{p}_{s-k+j+\ell-1}^{(j-1)}(u)$ and $\mathbf{p}_{s-k+j+\ell}^{(j-1)}(u)$, respectively. Therefore, by Equation VIII.12,

$$\mathbf{b}(u_{s-k+j+\ell+1}, \ldots, u_{s+\ell}, u^{\langle j\rangle}) = \mathbf{p}_{s-k+j+\ell}^{(j)}(u).$$

That completes the proof of the lemma.

The lemma immediately implies that, if the control points $\mathbf{p}_{s-k}, \ldots, \mathbf{p}_s$ satisfy Equation VIII.16, then the correct curve $\mathbf{q}_s(u)$ is obtained. That is, the values $\mathbf{b}(u_{s-k+\ell+1}, u_{s-k+\ell+2}, \ldots, u_{s+\ell})$ are a *possible* set of control points for $\mathbf{q}_s(u)$. On the other hand, vector space dimensionality considerations imply that there is at most a single set of possible control points for $\mathbf{q}_s(u)$. Namely, for a curve lying in $\mathbb{R}^d$, the vector space of all degree k polynomials has dimension $(k+1)d$, and the space of possible control points $\mathbf{p}_{s-k}, \ldots, \mathbf{p}_s$ has the same dimension. Thus, Theorem VIII.6 is proved. $\qquad\qquad\qquad\qquad\qquad\qquad\qquad\qquad\qquad\square$

Exercise VIII.10 *Verify the following special case of Theorem VIII.6. Let*

$$\mathbf{q}(u) = (1-u)^2\mathbf{p}_0 + 2u(1-u)\mathbf{p}_1 + u^2\mathbf{p}_2$$

be the degree two B-spline with the knot vector $[0, 0, 0, 1, 1, 1]$ *and control points* $\mathbf{p}_0, \mathbf{p}_1, \mathbf{p}_2$. *(See Equations VIII.4 on page 208.) Give the formula for the blossom* $\mathbf{b}(x_1, x_2)$ *of* $\mathbf{q}$. *What are the values of* $\mathbf{b}(0, 0)$, $\mathbf{b}(0, 1)$, *and* $\mathbf{b}(1, 1)$?

It is possible to develop the theory of Bézier curves and B-spline curves using the blossoms as the central concept. This alternate approach differs from our treatment in this book by using blossoms instead of blending functions $N_{i,k}$ as the main tool for defining B-splines. The textbook (Farin, 1997) describes this alternate approach. Two early papers describing the use of blossoms are (Seidel, 1988; 1989); his work is based on the original developments by de Casteljau and Ramshaw.

VIII.7 Derivatives and Smoothness of B-Spline Curves

This section derives formulas for the derivative of a B-spline curve and proves Theorem VIII.2 about the number of continuous derivatives of a B-spline. It is a pleasant discovery that the derivative of a degree k B-spline curve is itself a B-spline curve of degree $k - 1$.

Theorem VIII.8 *Let* $\mathbf{q}(u)$ *be a degree* $k = m - 1$ *B-spline curve with control points* $\mathbf{p}_0, \ldots, \mathbf{p}_n$. *Then its first derivative is*

$$\mathbf{q}'(u) = \sum_{i=1}^{n} k N_{i,k}(u) \frac{\mathbf{p}_i - \mathbf{p}_{i-1}}{u_{i+k} - u_i}. \qquad \text{VIII.18}$$

In particular, $\mathbf{q}'(u)$ *is the degree* $k - 1$ *B-spline curve with control points equal to*

$$\mathbf{p}_i^* = \frac{k}{u_{i+k} - u_i}(\mathbf{p}_i - \mathbf{p}_{i-1}). \qquad \text{VIII.19}$$

We prove Theorem VIII.8 in stages. First, we prove that Equation VIII.18 is valid for all values of u that are not knots. We then use continuity considerations to conclude that Equation VIII.18 holds also for u a knot.[3] After proving Theorem VIII.8, we use it to help prove Theorem VIII.2.

The next lemma will be used for the first stage of the proof of Theorem VIII.8. This lemma explains how to express the blossom of the first derivative of a function in terms of the blossom of the function.

Lemma VIII.9 *Let* $\mathbf{f}(u)$ *be a polynomial curve of degree* $\leq k$, *and let* $\mathbf{b}(x_1, \ldots, x_k)$ *be its degree* k *blossom.*

(a) *Let* $\mathbf{b}^*(x_1, \ldots, x_{k-1})$ *be the degree* $k - 1$ *blossom of the first derivative* $\mathbf{f}'(u)$ *of* $\mathbf{f}(u)$. *Then,*

$$\mathbf{b}^*(x_1, \ldots, x_{k-1}) = k \cdot (\mathbf{b}(x_1, \ldots, x_{k-1}, 1) - \mathbf{b}(x_1, \ldots, x_{k-1}, 0)). \qquad \text{VIII.20}$$

(b) *More generally, for all* $s \neq t$,

$$\mathbf{b}^*(x_1, \ldots, x_{k-1}) = \frac{k}{t - s}(\mathbf{b}(x_1, \ldots, x_{k-1}, t) - \mathbf{b}(x_1, \ldots, x_{k-1}, s)). \qquad \text{VIII.21}$$

Proof Let $\mathbf{f}(u) = \sum_{i=0}^{k} \mathbf{r}_i u^i$. The definition of the degree k blossom of $\mathbf{f}(u)$ given by equation VIII.14 can be rewritten as

$$\mathbf{b}(x_1, \ldots, x_k) = \sum_{J \subseteq [k]} \binom{k}{|J|}^{-1} \mathbf{r}_{|J|} x_J. \qquad \text{VIII.22}$$

---

[3] (For any practical use of splines, you can ignore this footnote.) To be completely rigorous, it is not quite true that $\mathbf{q}'(u)$ is always the degree $k - 1$ B-spline curve with control points $\mathbf{p}_i^*$. Namely, at points where the degree $k - 1$ curve is discontinuous, the first derivative of $\mathbf{q}$ is undefined. However, if the first derivative is extended to isolated points by taking right limits, we have equality. For similar reasons, Equation VIII.18 does not always hold either. A more correct way to say this is that Equation VIII.18 holds whenever the expression on the right-hand side is continuous at u as well as whenever $\mathbf{q}'(u)$ is defined.

The first derivative of $\mathbf{f}(u)$ is $\mathbf{f}'(u) = \sum_{i=0}^{k-1}(i+1)\mathbf{r}_{i+1}u^i$, and its degree $k-1$ blossom is

$$\mathbf{b}^*(x_1, \ldots, x_{k-1}) = \sum_{J \subseteq [k-1]} \binom{k-1}{|J|}^{-1} (|J|+1)\mathbf{r}_{|J|+1}x_J. \qquad \text{VIII.23}$$

Now consider the difference $\mathbf{b}(x_1, \ldots, x_{k-1}, 1) - \mathbf{b}(x_1, \ldots, x_{k-1}, 0)$. Examining the formula VIII.22 for $\mathbf{b}$, we see that terms for subsets J's that do not contain x_k cancel out in the difference, and terms for J's that do contain x_k survive but with the factor x_k removed. Thus,

$$\mathbf{b}(x_1, \ldots, x_{k-1}, 1) - \mathbf{b}(x_1, \ldots, x_{k-1}, 0) = \sum_{J \subseteq [k-1]} \binom{k}{|J|+1}^{-1} r_{|J|+1}x_J. \qquad \text{VIII.24}$$

Now, VIII.20 follows immediately from VIII.23 and VIII.24 and the identity $k \cdot \binom{k-1}{i} = (i+1) \cdot \binom{k}{i+1}$. So (a) is proved.

Part (b) is proved using (a). By the multiaffine property, since $s + (1 - s) = 1$ and $s \cdot 1 + (1 - s) \cdot 0 = s$,

$$\mathbf{b}(x_1, \ldots, x_{k-1}, s) = s \cdot \mathbf{b}(x_1, \ldots, x_{k-1}, 1) + (1 - s) \cdot \mathbf{b}(x_1, \ldots, x_{k-1}, 0).$$

Therefore,

$$\mathbf{b}(x_1, \ldots, x_{k-1}, s) - \mathbf{b}(x_1, \ldots, x_{k-1}, 0) = s \cdot (\mathbf{b}(x_1, \ldots, x_{k-1}, 1) - \mathbf{b}(x_1, \ldots, x_{k-1}, 0)).$$
$$\text{VIII.25}$$

Similarly, with t in place of s,

$$\mathbf{b}(x_1, \ldots, x_{k-1}, t) - \mathbf{b}(x_1, \ldots, x_{k-1}, 0) = t \cdot (\mathbf{b}(x_1, \ldots, x_{k-1}, 1) - \mathbf{b}(x_1, \ldots, x_{k-1}, 0)).$$
$$\text{VIII.26}$$

Equation VIII.21 follows from Equations VIII.20, VIII.25, and VIII.26. $\square$

Returning to the proof of Theorem VIII.8, we can now show that $\mathbf{q}'(u)$ is the B-spline curve with control points $\mathbf{p}_i^*$. For this, by Theorem VIII.6, it will suffice to prove the following: For two distinct adjacent knots, $u_s < u_{s+1}$, if $\mathbf{b}$ and $\mathbf{b}^*$ are the blossoms of $\mathbf{q}(u)$ and $\mathbf{q}'(u)$ on the interval (u_s, u_{s+1}), then $\mathbf{p}_i^* = \mathbf{b}^*(u_{i+1}, \ldots, u_{i+k-1})$ for all i such that $i \le s < i + k$. This is proved as follows using Lemma VIII.9(b) with $s = u_i$ and $t = u_{i+k}$:

$$\mathbf{b}^*(u_{i+1}, \ldots, u_{i+k-1})$$

$$= \frac{k}{u_{i+k} - u_i}(\mathbf{b}(u_{i+1}, \ldots, u_{i+k-1}, u_{i+k}) - \mathbf{b}(u_{i+1}, \ldots, u_{i+k-1}, u_i))$$

$$= \frac{k}{u_{i+k} - u_i}(\mathbf{b}(u_{i+1}, \ldots, u_{i+k-1}, u_{i+k}) - \mathbf{b}(u_i, u_{i+1}, \ldots, u_{i+k-1}))$$

$$= \frac{k}{u_{i+k} - u_i}(\mathbf{p}_i - \mathbf{p}_{i-1}) = \mathbf{p}_i^*.$$

It follows from what we have proved so far that Equation VIII.18 holds for all values of u that are not knots. It remains to establish the appropriate continuity conditions. This will complete the proof of Theorem VIII.8, since a function that is continuous and whose first derivative is equal to a continuous function except at isolated points has a continuous first derivative. This is formalized by the following fact from real analysis (which we leave to the reader to prove):

Lemma VIII.10 *Let f be a continuous function, whose first derivative is defined in a neighborhood of u_i such that the left and right limits of $f'(u)$ at $u = u_i$ satisfy $\lim_{u \to u_i^+} f'(u) = L = \lim_{u \to u_i^-} f'(u)$. Then $f'(u_i)$ exists and is equal to L.*

That concludes the proof of Theorem VIII.8.

We are now ready to prove Theorem VIII.2. It is certainly enough to prove the following statement: For all B-spline curves $\mathbf{q}(u)$ of degree k, if a knot u_i has multiplicity μ, then $\mathbf{q}(u)$ has continuous $(k - \mu)$th derivative at $u = u_i$. We prove this statement by holding the knot vector and thus the multiplicity μ of u_i fixed and using induction on k starting at $k = \mu$.

The base case, $k = \mu$, is a direct consequence of Theorem VIII.3. $N_{i-1,k+1}(u)$ has limit 1 on both sides of u_i and thus value 1 at $u = u_i$. For $j \neq i - 1$, $N_{j,k+1}(u)$ is continuous and equal to zero at u_i. So, in this case, $\mathbf{q}(u)$ is continuous at $u = u_i$ with $\mathbf{q}(u_i) = \mathbf{p}_{i-1}$.

The induction step uses the Cox–de Boor formula to establish continuity and Theorem VIII.8 and Lemma VIII.10 to establish the continuity of the derivatives. Assume $k > \mu$. The induction hypothesis implies that, for all j, $N_{j,k}(u)$ is continuous and is $C^{k-\mu-1}$-continuous at u_i (the induction hypothesis applies to $N_{j,k}(u)$ since it is a real-valued, degree $k - 1$ B-spline curve). The Cox–de Boor formula expresses each $N_{j,k+1}(u)$ in terms of $N_{j,k}(u)$ and $N_{j+1,k}(u)$, and so the induction hypothesis applied to these two functions implies that $N_{j,k+1}(u)$ has continuous $(k - \mu - 1)$th derivative at u_i. Thus, any degree k B-spline curve $\mathbf{q}(u)$ with this knot vector is $C^{k-\mu-1}$-continuous at u_i. Theorem VIII.8 further implies that the first derivative of $\mathbf{q}(u)$ is equal to a degree $k - 1$ B-spline curve, except possibly at knots. By the induction hypothesis, this degree $k - 1$ curve is $C^{k-\mu-1}$-continuous at u_i. It follows that $\mathbf{q}(u)$ has a continuous $(k - \mu)$th derivative, by using Lemma VIII.10 with $\mathbf{f}(u)$ equal to the $(k - \mu - 1)$th derivative of $\mathbf{q}(u)$. $\square$

VIII.8 Knot Insertion

An important tool for practical interactive use of B-spline curves is the technique of *knot insertion*, which allows one to add a new knot to a B-spline curve without changing the curve or its degree. For instance, when editing a B-spline curve with a CAD program, one may wish to insert additional knots in order to be able to make further adjustments to a curve: having additional knots in the area of the curve that needs adjustment allows more flexibility in editing the curve. Knot insertion also allows the multiplicity of a knot to be increased, which provides more control over the smoothness of the curve at that point. A second use of knot insertion is to convert a B-spline curve into a series of Bézier curves, as will be seen in Section VIII.9. A third use of knot insertion is that, by adding more knots and control points, the control polygon will more closely approximate the B-spline curve. This can be useful, for instance, in combination with the convex hull property, since the convex hull will be smaller and will more closely approximate the curve. This is similar to the way recursive subdivision can be used for Bézier curves. However, one complication is that, for B-spline curves with many knot positions, you should not work with the convex hull of the entire set of control points. Instead, you should use the local support property and define a sequence of convex hulls of $k + 1$ consecutive control points so that the union of these convex hulls contains the B-spline curve. A fourth use of knot insertion is for knot refinement, whereby two curves with different knot vectors can each have new knot positions inserted until the two curves have the same knot vectors.

There are two commonly used methods for knot insertion. The Böhm method (Böhm, 1980; Böhm and Prautsch, 1985) allows a single knot at a time to be inserted into a curve, and the Oslo method (Cohen, Lyche, and Riesenfeld, 1980; Prautsch, 1984) allows multiple knots to be inserted at once. We will discuss only the Böhm method; of course, multiple knots may be inserted by iterating this method. The proof of the Böhm method's correctness will be based

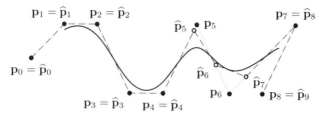

(a) Knot vector becomes $[0, 1, 2, 3, 4, 5, 6, 7, 7\frac{3}{4}, 8, 9, 10, 11]$.

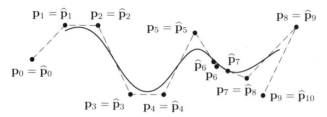

(b) Knot vector becomes $[0, 1, 2, 3, 4, 5, 6, 7, 7\frac{3}{4}, 7\frac{3}{4}, 8, 9, 10, 11]$.

Figure VIII.14. Showing the insertion of knots into a degree three curve. The original knot vector is the uniform knot vector $[0, 1, 2, 3, 4, 5, 6, 7, 8, 9, 10, 11]$. We insert the value $7\frac{3}{4}$ into the curve twice, each time adding a new control point and making the control polygon more closely approximate the curve near $7\frac{3}{4}$. The dotted straight lines show the control polygon before the insertion of the new knot position. The dashed straight lines are the control polygon after the insertion. (In (b), the dashed line from $\widehat{\mathbf{p}}_6$ to $\widehat{\mathbf{p}}_7$ is so close to the curve that it cannot be seen in the graph.) The filled circles are the original control point positions. The open circles are the changed control point positions. The control points $\widehat{\mathbf{p}}_i$ of (a) are renamed $\mathbf{p}_i$ in (b). In both figures, one new knot has been inserted and some of the control points have been moved, but the B-spline curve itself is unchanged. If we inserted $7\frac{3}{4}$ a third time, then the new control point $\widehat{\mathbf{p}}_7$ would be equal to the point on the curve at $u = 7\frac{3}{4}$.

on blossoming. For other methods of knot insertion, the reader can consult (Farin, 1997) and (Piegl and Tiller, 1997) and the references cited therein.

Suppose $\mathbf{q}(u)$ is an order m, degree $k = m - 1$, B-spline curve defined with knot vector $[u_0, \ldots, u_{n+m}]$ and control points $\mathbf{p}_0, \ldots, \mathbf{p}_n$. We wish to insert a new knot position $\widehat{u}$ where $u_s \leq \widehat{u} < u_{s+1}$ and then choose new control points so that the curve $\mathbf{q}(u)$ remains unchanged. The new knot vector is denoted $[\widehat{u}_0, \ldots, \widehat{u}_{n+m+1}]$, where, of course,

$$\widehat{u}_i = \begin{cases} u_i & \text{if } i \leq s \\ \widehat{u} & \text{if } i = s + 1 \\ u_{i-1} & \text{if } i > s + 1. \end{cases}$$

The method of choosing the new control points is less obvious, for we must be sure not to change the curve. The Böhm algorithm gives the following definition of the control points: (remember, $k = m - 1$):

$$\widehat{\mathbf{p}}_i = \begin{cases} \mathbf{p}_i & \text{if } i \leq s - k \\ \dfrac{u_{i+k} - \widehat{u}}{u_{i+k} - u_i}\mathbf{p}_{i-1} + \dfrac{\widehat{u} - u_i}{u_{i+k} - u_i}\mathbf{p}_i & \text{if } s - k < i \leq s \\ \mathbf{p}_{i-1} & \text{if } s < i. \end{cases} \qquad \text{VIII.27}$$

It is implicit in the definitions of the $\widehat{\mathbf{p}}_i$'s that $u_{s+1} > u_s$. This can always be arranged by inserting a new repeated knot at the end of a block of repeated knots rather than the beginning or the middle. Note that the new control points $\widehat{\mathbf{p}}_i$ are defined as weighted averages of pairs of old control points $\mathbf{p}_{i-1}$ and $\mathbf{p}_i$.

The correctness of the Böhm algorithm for knot insertion is stated by the next theorem.

Theorem VIII.11 *Suppose $k \geq 1$ and let $\widehat{\mathbf{q}}(u)$ be the degree k B-spline curve defined with the knot vector $[\widehat{u}_0, \ldots, \widehat{u}_{n+m+1}]$ and control points $\widehat{\mathbf{p}}_0, \ldots, \widehat{\mathbf{p}}_{n+1}$. Then, $\widehat{\mathbf{q}}(u) = \mathbf{q}(u)$ for all u.*

Proof Because of the way blossoms determine control points, it will suffice to show that

$$\mathbf{q}(u) = \widehat{\mathbf{q}}(u) \qquad \text{for } u \in [u_s, u_{s+1}).$$

For this, it is enough to show that the blossom $\mathbf{b}$ of $\mathbf{q}$ on the interval $[u_s, u_{s+1})$ is also the blossom for $\widehat{\mathbf{q}}$ on the intervals $[u_s, \widehat{u})$ and $[\widehat{u}, u_{s+1})$. To prove this, it is necessary and sufficient to show that the blossom $\mathbf{b}$ has the properties given by Theorem VIII.6 with respect to the knot positions and control points of $\widehat{\mathbf{q}}$, namely, that for all i such that $s - k \leq i \leq s + 1$,

$$\widehat{\mathbf{p}}_i = \mathbf{b}(\widehat{u}_{i+1}, \widehat{u}_{i+2}, \ldots, \widehat{u}_{i+k}).$$

For $i = s - k$, this is easily shown by

$$\widehat{\mathbf{p}}_{s-k} = \mathbf{p}_{s-k}$$
$$= \mathbf{b}(u_{s-k+1}, u_{s-k+2}, \ldots, u_s)$$
$$= \mathbf{b}(\widehat{u}_{s-k+1}, \widehat{u}_{s-k+2}, \ldots, \widehat{u}_s)$$

since $u_j = \widehat{u}_j$ for $j \leq s$. Likewise, for $i = s + 1$,

$$\widehat{\mathbf{p}}_{s+1} = \mathbf{p}_s$$
$$= \mathbf{b}(u_{s+1}, u_{s+2}, \ldots, u_{s+k})$$
$$= \mathbf{b}(\widehat{u}_{s+2}, \widehat{u}_{s+3}, \ldots, \widehat{u}_{s+k+1}).$$

It remains to consider the case in which $s - k < i \leq s$. Let

$$\alpha = \frac{u_{i+k} - \widehat{u}}{u_{i+k} - u_i} \qquad \text{and} \qquad \beta = \frac{\widehat{u} - u_i}{u_{i+k} - u_i}.$$

Then, by the definition of $\widehat{\mathbf{p}}_i$ and since $i \leq s < i + k$,

$$\widehat{\mathbf{p}}_i = \alpha \mathbf{p}_{i-1} + \beta \mathbf{p}_i$$
$$= \alpha \mathbf{b}(u_i, u_{i+1}, \ldots, u_{i+k-1}) + \beta \mathbf{b}(u_{i+1}, u_{i+2}, \ldots, u_{i+k})$$
$$= \mathbf{b}(u_{i+1}, u_{i+2}, \ldots, u_s, \widehat{u}, u_{s+1}, \ldots, u_{i+k-1})$$
$$= \mathbf{b}(\widehat{u}_{i+1}, \widehat{u}_{i+2}, \ldots, \widehat{u}_{i+k}).$$

The third equality above is justified by the symmetry and multiaffine properties of the blossom and because $\alpha + \beta = 1$ and $\alpha u_i + \beta u_{i+k} = \widehat{u}$. $\qquad \square$

Exercise VIII.11 *In Exercise VII.17 on page 184, a half-circle is expressed as a quadratic rational Bézier curve. Rewrite this as a degree two rational B-spline with knot vector $[0, 0, 0, 1, 1, 1]$. Insert $u = \frac{1}{2}$ as a new knot position. What are the new control points? Graph the curve and its new control polygon. Compare with Figure VIII.17 on page 229.*

Exercise VIII.12★ *Prove that B-spline curves satisfy the variation diminishing property. [Hint: Combine the ideas of Exercise VII.9 with the fact that repeatedly inserting knots in the correct sequence can make the control polygon approximate the B-spline curve arbitrarily well.]*

VIII.9 Bézier and B-Spline Curves

We now discuss methods for translating between Bézier curves and B-spline curves. These methods are degree preserving in that they will transform a degree k Bézier curve into a degree k B-spline and vice versa. Of course, there is a bit of a mismatch: a Bézier curve consists of a single degree k curve specified by $k + 1$ control points whereas a B-spline curve consists of a series of pieces, each piece a degree k polynomial. Accordingly, the translation between B-spline curves and Bézier curves will transform a series of degree k pieces that join together to make a single curve. Such a series of curve pieces can be viewed as either a single B-spline curve or as a collection of Bézier curves.

From Bézier Curves to B-Spline Curves

First, we consider the problem of converting a single Bézier curve into a B-spline curve. Suppose we have a degree three Bézier curve $\mathbf{q}(u)$ defined with control points $\mathbf{p}_0, \mathbf{p}_1, \mathbf{p}_2, \mathbf{p}_3$ that are defined over the range $0 \le u \le 1$. To construct a definition of this curve as a B-spline curve with the same control points, we let $[0, 0, 0, 0, 1, 1, 1, 1]$ be the knot vector and keep the control points as $\mathbf{p}_0, \mathbf{p}_1, \mathbf{p}_2, \mathbf{p}_3$. It can be verified by direct computation that the B-spline curve is in fact the same curve $\mathbf{q}(u)$ as the Bézier curve (see pages 208–209). In fact, we have the following general theorem.

Theorem VIII.12 *Let $k \ge 1$ and $\mathbf{q}(u)$ be a degree k Bézier curve defined by control points $\mathbf{p}_0, \ldots, \mathbf{p}_k$. Then $\mathbf{q}(u)$ is identical to the degree k B-spline curve defined with the same control points over the knot vector consisting of the knot 0 with multiplicity $k + 1$ followed by the knot 1 also with multiplicity $k + 1$.*

To prove this theorem, let $N_{i,k+1}(u)$ be the basis functions for the B-spline with the knot vector $[0, \ldots, 0, 1, \ldots, 1]$ containing $2k + 2$ many knots. Then we claim that

$$N_{i,k+1}(u) = \binom{k}{i} u^i (1 - u)^{k-i}. \qquad\qquad \text{VIII.28}$$

The right-hand side of this equation is just the same as the Bernstein polynomials used to define Bézier curves, and so the theorem follows immediately from Equation VIII.28. Equation VIII.28 is easy to prove by induction on k, and we leave the proof to the reader. $\square$

The most useful cases of the previous theorem are when $k = 2$ and $k = 3$. As we saw in Section VII.13, the $k = 2$ case is frequently used for defining conic sections, including circles, via Bézier curves. In the $k = 2$ case, a degree two Bézier curve with the three control points $\mathbf{p}_0, \mathbf{p}_1, \mathbf{p}_2$ is equivalent to the degree two B-spline curve with the same three control points and with knot vector $[0, 0, 0, 1, 1, 1]$.

Often one wants to combine two or more Bézier curves into a single B-spline curve. For instance, suppose one has degree two Bézier curves $\mathbf{q}_0(u)$ and $\mathbf{q}_1(u)$ defined with control points $\mathbf{p}_0, \mathbf{p}_1, \mathbf{p}_2$ and $\mathbf{p}_0', \mathbf{p}_1', \mathbf{p}_2'$. We wish to combine these curves into a single curve $\mathbf{q}(u)$ that consists of $\mathbf{q}_1(u)$ followed by $\mathbf{q}_2(u)$. That is, $\mathbf{q}(u) = \mathbf{q}_1(u)$ for $0 \le u \le 1$, and $\mathbf{q}(u) = \mathbf{q}_2(u - 1)$ for $1 \le u \le 2$. By Theorem VIII.12, $\mathbf{q}(u)$ is equivalent to the degree two B-spline curve with knot vector $[0, 0, 0, 1, 1, 1, 2, 2, 2]$ and with the six control points $\mathbf{p}_0, \ldots, \mathbf{p}_2'$. However, usually the two Bézier curves form a single continuous curve, that is, $\mathbf{p}_2 = \mathbf{p}_0'$. In this case, $\mathbf{q}(u)$ is the same as the B-spline curve with knot vector $[0, 0, 0, 1, 1, 2, 2, 2]$ and with five control points $\mathbf{p}_0, \mathbf{p}_1, \mathbf{p}_2, \mathbf{p}_1', \mathbf{p}_2'$. Note that one knot position and the duplicate control point have been omitted. This construction is demonstrated by the calculation in the next exercise.

Exercise VIII.13 *Calculate the degree two blending functions for the knot vector* [0, 0, 0, 1, 1, 2, 2, 2]. *Show that the results are the degree two Bernstein polynomials on the interval* [0, 1], *followed by the same degree two Bernstein polynomials translated to the interval* [1, 2]. *Conclude that a quadratic B-spline formed with this knot vector and control points* $\mathbf{p}_0$, $\mathbf{p}_1$, $\mathbf{p}_2$, $\mathbf{p}_3$, $\mathbf{p}_4$ *will be the concatenation of the two quadratic Bézier curves with control points* $\mathbf{p}_0$, $\mathbf{p}_1$, $\mathbf{p}_2$ *and with control points* $\mathbf{p}_2$, $\mathbf{p}_3$, $\mathbf{p}_4$.

The construction in this exercise can be generalized in several ways. First, if one has three degree two Bézier curves that form a single continuous curve, then they are equivalent to a degree two B-spline curve with knot vector [0, 0, 0, 1, 1, 2, 2, 3, 3, 3]. This generalizes to allow a continuous curve that consists of any number of quadratic Bézier curves to be expressed as a single B-spline curve. Second, the construction generalizes to other degrees: for instance, a continuous curve that consists of two degree three Bézier curves is the same as the degree three B-spline curve that has knot vector [0, 0, 0, 0, 1, 1, 1, 2, 2, 2, 2] and has the same seven points as its control points. We leave the proofs of these statements to the reader.

Exercise VIII.14 *Prove that the de Casteljau algorithm for a Bézier curve is the same as the de Boor algorithm for the equivalent B-spline curve.*

From B-Spline Curve to Piecewise Bézier Curve

We now discuss how to convert a general B-spline curve into constituent Bézier curves. A priori, it is always possible to convert a degree k B-spline curve into a series of degree k Bézier curves merely because the B-spline curve consists of piecewise polynomials of degree k and any finite segment of a degree k polynomial can be represented as a degree k Bézier curve (see Exercise VII.8).

Here is an algorithm to convert a B-spline curve into multiple Bézier pieces: use repeated knot insertion to insert multiple occurrences of the knots until the first and last knots have multiplicity $k + 1$ and each interior knot has multiplicity k. By the discussion about combining multiple Bézier curves into a B-spline curve, this means that the control points of the resulting B-spline curve (that is, the control points that result from the knot insertion) are also the control points for Bézier curves between the knot positions.

VIII.10 Degree Elevation

Section VII.9 discussed degree elevation for Bézier curves. Degree elevation can also be applied to B-spline curves. In analogy to the situation with Bézier curves, suppose are given a degree k B-spline curve $\mathbf{q}(u)$ and wish to find a way to describe the (same) curve as a degree $k + 1$ B-spline curve.

The first thing to notice is that if a knot u has multiplicity μ in the degree k curve, then $\mathbf{q}(u)$ has continuous $(k - \mu)$th derivative at u (by Theorem VIII.2) but may well not have a continuous $(k - \mu + 1)$th derivative at u. Thus, to represent $\mathbf{q}(u)$ as a degree $k + 1$ curve, it is necessary for the knot position u to have multiplicity $\mu + 1$. In other words, to elevate the degree of a curve, it will generally be necessary to increase the multiplicity of all the knots by one.

Because of the need to add so many (duplicate) knot positions, the algorithms for degree elevation are not particularly simple. We do not cover them but instead refer the reader to (Farin, 1997) or (Piegl and Tiller, 1997) for algorithms and references for other algorithms. Piegl and Tiller suggest the following algorithm: first, use knot insertion or knot refinement to make all knots have multiplicity $k - 1$ in order to convert the curve into degree k Bézier curve segments; second, use the degree elevation algorithm for Bézier

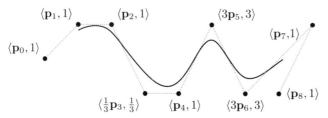

Figure VIII.15. A degree three, rational B-spline curve. The control points are the same as in Figure VIII.1 on page 201, but now the control point $\mathbf{p}_3$ is weighted only $1/3$, and the two control points $\mathbf{p}_5$ and $\mathbf{p}_6$ are weighted 3. All other control points have weight 1. In comparison with the curve of Figure VIII.1(b), this curve more closely approaches $\mathbf{p}_5$ and $\mathbf{p}_6$ but does not approach $\mathbf{p}_3$ as closely.

curves; and then, third, reduce the knot multiplicities by a process called "knot elimination." Other algorithms are available that do not need to add excess knots, for example, based on blossoms.

VIII.11 Rational B-Splines and NURBS

A B-spline curve is called a *rational curve* if its control points are specified with homogeneous coordinates. These curves are sometimes called "NURBS," which is an acronym for "nonuniform, rational B-splines."

Rational Bézier curves were already discussed earlier in Sections VII.12 and VII.13; much of what was said about rational Bézier curves also applies to rational B-splines. A rational B-spline has 4-tuples $\langle x, y, z, w \rangle$ as control points; the curve's values $\mathbf{q}(u)$ are expressed as weighted averages of the control points,

$$\mathbf{q}(u) \; = \; \sum_i N_{i,m}(u)\mathbf{p}_i,$$

and so $\mathbf{q}(u)$ represents the points on the curve in homogeneous coordinates.

As with rational Bézier curves, the w component of a control point acts as a weight factor: a control point $\langle w\mathbf{p}_i, w \rangle$ weights the point $\mathbf{p}_i$ by a factor of w. This is illustrated in Figure VIII.15. Also, like rational Bézier curves, rational B-splines are preserved under perspective transformations and may have control points at infinity.

Section VII.13 described the construction of Bézier curves that trace out a semicircle or, more generally, a portion of a conic section. B-splines can do better in that a single B-spline can define an entire circle or an entire conic section. This is done by patching together several quadratic Bézier curves to form a quadratic B-spline curve that traces out an entire circle or conic section. As was shown in Section VIII.9, two quadratic Bézier curves may be patched together into a single B-spline curve by using the knot vector $[0, 0, 0, 1, 1, 2, 2, 2]$. Similarly, three quadratic Bézier curves can be combined into a single B-spline curve using the knot vector $[0, 0, 0, 1, 1, 2, 2, 3, 3, 3]$, and a similar construction works for combining four Bézier curves into a single B-spline curve, and so forth. As an example, Theorem VII.9 on page 182 implies that if we use the knot vector $[0, 0, 0, 1, 1, 2, 2, 2]$ and the control points

$$\begin{aligned}
\mathbf{p}_0 &= \langle 0, 1, 1 \rangle & \mathbf{p}_3 &= \langle -1, 0, 0 \rangle \\
\mathbf{p}_1 &= \langle 1, 0, 0 \rangle & \mathbf{p}_4 &= \mathbf{p}_0, \\
\mathbf{p}_2 &= \langle 0, -1, 1 \rangle
\end{aligned}$$

then the resulting B-spline will trace out the unit circle.

Similar constructions also give the unit circle as a B-spline consisting of either three or four Bézier segments without using control points at infinity. These are based on the results

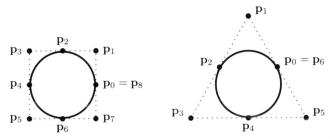

Figure VIII.16. Two ways to form a complete circle with a quadratic B-spline curve. The first curve has knot vector $[0, 0, 0, 1, 1, 2, 2, 3, 3, 4, 4, 4]$, and the control points $\mathbf{p}_i$ have weight 1 when i is even and weight $\frac{\sqrt{2}}{2}$ when i is odd. The second curve has knot vector $[0, 0, 0, 1, 1, 2, 2, 3, 3, 3]$, and the control points $\mathbf{p}_i$ have weight 1 when i is even and weight $\frac{1}{2}$ when i is odd.

from Exercises VII.14 and VII.15 and are pictured in Figure VIII.16. Compare this Figure with VII.19 on page 184.

Another well-known construction of the unit circle by a degree two B-spline curve is shown in Figure VIII.17; we leave the proof of its correctness to the reader (see Exercise VIII.11 on page 225).

VIII.12 B-Splines and NURBS Surfaces in OpenGL

OpenGL provides routines for drawing (nonuniform) B-spline surfaces in the `glu` library. By specifying the control points in homogeneous coordinates, this includes the ability to render NURBS surfaces. The B-spline routines include `gluNewNurbsRenderer` and `gluDeleteNurbsRenderer` to allocate and deallocate, respectively, a B-spline renderer; these routines are misnamed, for they can also be used to render nonrational B-splines. The routines `gluBeginSurface()` and `gluEndSurface()` are used to bracket one or more calls to `gluNurbsSurface`. The latter routine allows specification of an array of knots and control points. Since it renders a surface, it uses two knot arrays and a two-dimensional array of control points. The routine `gluNurbsProperty` allows you to control the level of detail at which the B-spline surface is rendered.

The interested reader should refer to the OpenGL documentation for more details.

VIII.13 Interpolating with B-Splines

Frequently, one wishes to define a smooth curve that interpolates (i.e., passes through, or contains) a given set of points. Chapter VII explained ways of forming interpolating curves using the Catmull–Rom and Overhauser splines, which consist of piecewise Bézier curves. The Catmull–Rom and Overhauser curves are C^1-continuous but generally do not have

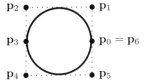

Figure VIII.17. Another way to form a complete circle with a quadratic B-spline curve. The curve has knot vector $[0, 0, 0, 1, 2, 2, 3, 4, 4, 4]$, the control points $\mathbf{p}_0$, $\mathbf{p}_3$, and $\mathbf{p}_6$ have weight 1, and the other control points $\mathbf{p}_1$, $\mathbf{p}_2$, $\mathbf{p}_4$, and $\mathbf{p}_5$ have weight $\frac{1}{2}$. Exercise VIII.11 on page 225 shows a way to prove the correctness of this B-spline curve.

continuous second derivatives. On the other hand, we know (see Section VIII.4) that degree three splines can have continuous second derivatives provided the knots have multiplicity one. Thus, we might hope to get better, smoother curves by using B-splines to interpolate a set of points.

Unfortunately, the B-spline curves that have been defined so far are not particularly convenient for this purpose; they have been defined from control points, which merely influence the curve and usually are not interpolated; thus, the control points usually do not lie on the curve. When control points are interpolated, it is generally because of repeated knot values, but then the curve loses its good smoothness properties and may even have discontinuous first derivatives.

Our strategy for constructing interpolating B-spline curves with good smoothness properties will be first to choose knot positions and then solve for control points that will make the B-spline curve interpolate the desired points. The algorithm for finding the control points will be based on solving a system of linear equations, which will be tridiagonal and thus easily solved.

Consider the following problem. We are given points $\mathbf{q}_0, \mathbf{q}_1, \mathbf{q}_2, \ldots, \mathbf{q}_n$ and positions $u_0, u_1, u_2, \ldots, u_n$ with $u_i < u_{i+1}$ for all i. The problem is to find a degree three B-spline curve $\mathbf{q}(u)$ so that $\mathbf{q}(u_i) = \mathbf{q}_i$ for all i. This still leaves too many possibilities, and so we further make the rather arbitrary assumption that the B-spline curve is to be formed with the standard knot vector

$$[u_0, u_0, u_0, u_0, u_1, u_2, u_3, \ldots, u_{n-2}, u_{n-1}, u_n, u_n, u_n, u_n],$$

where the first and last knots have multiplicity 4 and the rest of the knots have multiplicity 1. (Refer to Exercises VIII.6 and VIII.7 for a qualitative understanding of the blending functions defined from this knot vector.) Note that there are $n + 7$ knot positions, and thus there must be $n + 3$ control points. The conditions are still not strong enough to determine the B-spline, fully for there are only $n + 1$ conditions $\mathbf{q}(u_i) = \mathbf{q}_i$ but $n + 3$ control points to be determined. Therefore, we make one more arbitrary assumption, namely, that the first derivative of $\mathbf{q}(u)$ at u_0 and at u_n is equal to zero. This means that the first two control points must be equal so that $\mathbf{q}'(u_0) = 0$, and the last two control points must be equal so that $\mathbf{q}'(u_n) = 0$.

The control points can thus be denoted

$$\mathbf{p}_0, \mathbf{p}_0, \mathbf{p}_1, \mathbf{p}_2, \ldots, \mathbf{p}_{n-2}, \mathbf{p}_{n-1}, \mathbf{p}_n, \mathbf{p}_n.$$

The equation for the curve $\mathbf{q}(u)$ based on these knot positions and control points is

$$\mathbf{q}(u) = (N_{0,4}(u) + N_{1,4}(u))\mathbf{p}_0 + \sum_{i=1}^{n-1} N_{i+1,4}(u)\mathbf{p}_i + (N_{n+2,4}(u) + N_{n+3,4}(u))\mathbf{p}_n.$$

Since the first and last knots have multiplicity 4, we have

$$\mathbf{q}(u_0) = \mathbf{p}_0 \quad \text{and} \quad \mathbf{q}(u_n) = \mathbf{p}_n$$

and thus need $\mathbf{p}_0 = \mathbf{q}_0$ and $\mathbf{p}_n = \mathbf{q}_n$. Theorem VIII.1 and the continuity of the blending functions tell us where these blending functions are nonzero, and so we have, for $1 \le i \le n - 1$,

$$\mathbf{q}(u_i) = N_{i,4}(u_i)\mathbf{p}_{i-1} + N_{i+1,4}(u_i)\mathbf{p}_i + N_{i+2,4}(u_i)\mathbf{p}_{i+1}.$$

Of course, we want this value to equal $\mathbf{q}_i$. Letting $\alpha_i = N_{i,4}(u_i)$, $\beta_i = N_{i+1,4}(u_i)$, and $\gamma_i = N_{i+2,4}(u_i)$, we want

$$\mathbf{q}_i = \alpha_i \mathbf{p}_{i-1} + \beta_i \mathbf{p}_i + \gamma_i \mathbf{p}_{i+1}.$$

We can write the desired conditions as a single matrix equation:

$$
\begin{pmatrix}
1 & 0 & 0 & \cdots & & \cdots & 0 \\
\alpha_1 & \beta_1 & \gamma_1 & 0 & \cdots & & \vdots \\
0 & \alpha_2 & \beta_2 & \gamma_2 & 0 & \cdots & \\
0 & 0 & \alpha_3 & \beta_3 & \gamma_3 & 0 & \cdots \\
\vdots & & & \ddots & \ddots & \ddots & \\
& & \cdots & 0 & \alpha_{n-1} & \beta_{n-1} & \gamma_{n-1} \\
0 & & \cdots & & 0 & 0 & 1
\end{pmatrix}
\begin{pmatrix}
\mathbf{p}_0 \\ \mathbf{p}_1 \\ \mathbf{p}_2 \\ \mathbf{p}_3 \\ \vdots \\ \mathbf{p}_{n-1} \\ \mathbf{p}_n
\end{pmatrix}
=
\begin{pmatrix}
\mathbf{q}_0 \\ \mathbf{q}_1 \\ \mathbf{q}_2 \\ \mathbf{q}_3 \\ \vdots \\ \mathbf{q}_{n-1} \\ \mathbf{q}_n
\end{pmatrix}.
$$

We need to solve this matrix equation to find values for the control points $\mathbf{p}_i$. Because the matrix equation is tridiagonal, it is particularly easy to solve for the $\mathbf{p}_i$'s. The algorithm that calculates the $\mathbf{p}_i$'s uses two passes: first, we transform the matrix into an upper diagonal matrix by subtracting a multiple of the ith row from the $(i+1)$st row, for $i = 1, 2, \ldots, n-1$. This makes the matrix upper diagonal and in the form

$$
\begin{pmatrix}
1 & 0 & 0 & \cdots & & \cdots & 0 \\
0 & \beta_1' & \gamma_1 & 0 & \cdots & & \vdots \\
0 & 0 & \beta_2' & \gamma_2 & 0 & \cdots & \\
0 & 0 & 0 & \beta_3' & \gamma_3 & 0 & \cdots \\
\vdots & & & \ddots & \ddots & \ddots & \\
& & \cdots & 0 & 0 & \beta_{n-1}' & \gamma_{n-1} \\
0 & & \cdots & & 0 & 0 & 1
\end{pmatrix}
\begin{pmatrix}
\mathbf{p}_0 \\ \mathbf{p}_1 \\ \mathbf{p}_2 \\ \mathbf{p}_3 \\ \vdots \\ \mathbf{p}_{n-1} \\ \mathbf{p}_n
\end{pmatrix}
=
\begin{pmatrix}
\mathbf{q}_0' \\ \mathbf{q}_1' \\ \mathbf{q}_2' \\ \mathbf{q}_3' \\ \vdots \\ \mathbf{q}_{n-1}' \\ \mathbf{q}_n'
\end{pmatrix}.
$$

Second, we can easily solve the upper diagonal matrix by setting $\mathbf{p}_n = \mathbf{q}_n'$ and setting $\mathbf{p}_i = (\mathbf{q}_i' - \gamma_i \mathbf{p}_{i+1})/\beta_i'$, for $i = n-1, n-2, \ldots, 0$.

The complete algorithm for calculating the $\mathbf{p}_i$'s is as follows:

```
// Pass One
Set β'₀ = 1;
Set γ₀ = 0;
Set q'₀ = q₀;
For i = 1, 2, ..., n-1 {
    Set mᵢ = αᵢ/β'ᵢ₋₁;
    Set β'ᵢ = βᵢ - mᵢγᵢ₋₁;
    Set q'ᵢ = qᵢ - mᵢq'ᵢ₋₁;
}
Set q'ₙ = qₙ;

// Pass two
Set pₙ = q'ₙ;        // Same as qₙ.
For i = n-1, n-2, ..., 2, 1 {
    Set pᵢ = (q'ᵢ - γᵢpᵢ₊₁)/β'ᵢ;
}
Set p₀ = q'₀;        // Same as q₀.
```

Note that the algorithm is only linear time, that is, has runtime $O(n)$. This is possible because the matrix is tridiagonal. For general matrices, matrix inversion is much more difficult.

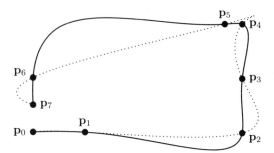

Figure VIII.18. Degree three interpolating spline. The dotted curve uses uniform knot spacing. The solid curve uses chord-length parameterization. It is clear that chord-length parameterization gives much better results. The interpolation points are the same as used for the interpolating Catmull–Rom and Overhauser splines shown in Figures VII.23 and VII.24 on pages 190 and 192.

The B-spline interpolating curve does not enjoy local control properties: moving a single interpolation point $\mathbf{q}_i$ can affect the curve along its entire length. However, in usual cases, moving a control point has only slight effects on distant parts of the B-spline.

Figure VIII.18 shows an interpolating B-spline and can be compared with the earlier examples of interpolating Catmull–Rom and Overhauser splines. The figure shows two curves. The dotted curve is based on uniformly spaced values for u_i, with $u_i = i$. The solid curve uses *chord-length parameterization* with the values u_i chosen so that $u_i - u_{i-1} = ||\mathbf{p}_i - \mathbf{p}_{i-1}||$. Evidently, just like the Overhauser splines, B-spline interpolation can benefit from the use of chord-length parameterization.

IX

Ray Tracing

Ray tracing is a technique that performs, by a single unified technique, global calculations of lighting and shading, hidden surface elimination, reflection and transmission of light, casting of shadows, and other effects. As such, it significantly extends the local lighting models such as the Phong and Cook–Torrance lighting models from Chapter III. Ray tracing also eliminates the use of a depth buffer for hidden surface determination. In addition, it allows for many special effects and can create images that are more realistic looking than those that can be easily obtained by the methods we have discussed so far.

With all these advantages, ray tracing sounds too wonderful to be true; however, it has the big disadvantage of being computationally very expensive. Indeed, a single ray-traced image may take minutes, hours, or occasionally even days to render. For example, modern computer-animated movies routinely use ray tracing to render scenes; it is not unusual for an *average* frame of a movie to require an hour of computation time to render, and individual frames might require 10 hours or more to render. A quick calculation shows that this means that a movie with 24 frames per second, lasting for 100 minutes, may require 6,000 CPU days to render, which is over 16 CPU years! It is fortunate that individual frames can be ray traced independently in parallel, and it is common for animated movies to be developed with the aid of hundreds of computers dedicated to rendering images. Despite the high computational costs of ray tracing, it has become a widely used technique for generating high quality and photorealistic images – especially because computers are becoming cheaper and faster and ray tracing techniques are becoming more sophisticated.

The basic idea behind ray tracing is to follow the paths of light rays around a 3-D scene. Typically, one follows the light rays' paths from the position of the viewer back to their source. When light rays hit objects in the 3-D scene, one computes the reflection direction for the light ray and continues to follow the light ray in the reflection direction. Continuing this process, perhaps through multiple reflections (and possibly transmissions through transparent media), one can trace the path of a light ray from its origination at a light source until it reaches the view position.

Ray tracing is generally combined with a local lighting model such as the Phong or the Cook–Torrance model but adds many global lighting effects that cannot be achieved with just these local lighting models. The global lighting phenomena that can be obtained with basic ray tracing include the following:

- Reflections – glossy or mirror-like reflections.
- Shadows – sharp shadows cast by lights.
- Transparency and refraction.

The basic form of ray tracing is covered in Section IX.1. That section discusses the way rays are traced backwards from the view position to the light sources. It also discusses the mathematical models for transmission of light through semitransparent materials. The basic ray tracing method can generate effects such as reflection, transparency, refraction, and shadows.

There are many more advanced models of ray tracing. Many of these go under the name of "distributed ray tracing" and involve tracing a multiplicity of rays. Applications of distributed ray tracing include antialiasing, depth of field, motion blur, and simulation of diffuse lighting. Distributed ray tracing is covered in Section IX.2.1. Section IX.2.2 covers the so-called backwards ray tracing, where light rays are traced starting from the positions of the lights.

OpenGL does not support ray tracing, and so it is necessary to use custom code (such as the ray tracing code provided with this book) to perform all the rendering calculations from scratch. However, a variety of tricks, or "cheats," exist that can be used in OpenGL to give effects similar to ray tracing with substantially less computation. Some of these are surveyed in Section IX.3.

Appendix B covers the features of a ray tracing software package developed for this book. The software package is freely available from the Internet and may be used without restriction.

Radiosity is another global lighting method that is complementary in many ways to ray tracing. Whereas ray tracing is good at handling specular lighting effects and less good at handling special diffuse lighting effects, radiosity is very good at diffuse lighting effects but does not handle specularity. Radiosity will be covered in Chapter XI.

IX.1 Basic Ray Tracing

The basic idea behind ray tracing is to follow the paths taken by rays of light, or photons, as they travel from the light sources until they eventually reach the viewer's eye position. Of course, most light rays never reach the eye position at all but instead either leave the scene or are absorbed into a material. Thus, from a computational point of view, it makes more sense to trace the paths traveled by rays of light from the eye by going backwards until eventually a light source is reached since, in this way, we do not waste time on tracing rays that do not ever reach the viewer.[1]

The simplest kind of ray tracing is illustrated in Figure IX.1. The figure shows, first, a 3-D scene containing two boxes and a sphere (which are represented by two rectangles and a circle); second, a single light source; and, third, a viewer. The viewer is looking at the scene through a virtual viewport rectangle, and our task is to render the scene as seen through the viewport. To determine the color of a pixel P in the viewport, a ray is sent from the eye through the center of the pixel, and then we determine the first point of intersection of the ray with the objects in the scene. In the figure, the ray would intersect both the lower rectangle and the circle. However, it intersects the rectangle first, and thus this is what is seen through the pixel. The point of intersection on the rectangle is shaded (colored) according to a local lighting model such as the Phong model, and the result is the contents of the pixel P.

In the simple form described so far, ray tracing would not achieve any new visual effects beyond those already obtainable by a local lighting model and the depth buffer hidden-surface algorithm. Indeed, so far all that has changed is that the depth buffer method of culling hidden

---

[1] In a confusing twist of terminology, the process of following rays from the eye position back to their point of origin from a light is sometimes called *forward ray tracing*, whereas, tracing paths from a light up to the viewpoint is called *backwards ray tracing*. To add to the confusion, many authors reverse the meaning of these terms. Section IX.2.2 covers backwards ray tracing.

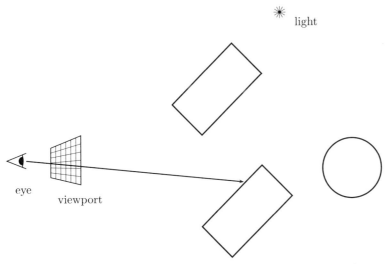

Figure IX.1. The simplest kind of ray tracing, nonrecursive ray tracing, involves casting rays of light from the view position through pixel positions. A local lighting model is used to calculate the illumination of the surface intersected by the ray.

surfaces has been replaced by a ray tracing method for determining visible surfaces. More interesting effects are obtained with ray tracing as we add reflection rays, transmission rays, and shadow feelers.

Shadow Feelers

A *shadow feeler* is a ray sent from a point **u** on the surface of an object towards a light source to determine whether the light is visible from the point **u** or whether it is occluded by intervening objects. As you will recall from Chapter III, the local lighting models (Phong or Cook–Torrance) do not form any shadows; instead, they assume that every light is visible at all times and that no objects are blocking the light and creating shadows. Examples of shadow feelers are shown in Figure IX.2: four rays are traced from the eye through the centers of four pixels in the viewport (not shown) until they hit points in the scene. From each of these four points, a ray, called a shadow feeler, is traced from the point to the light source. If the shadow feeler hits an object before reaching the light, then the light is presumed to be occluded by the object so that the point is in a shadow and is not directly lit by the light. In the figure, two of the shadow feelers find intersections; these rays are marked with an "**X**" to show they are blocked. In one case, a point on the box surface is being shadowed by the box itself.

Reflection Rays

What we have described so far accounts for light rays that originate from a point light, hit a surface, and then reflect from the surface to the eye. However, light can also travel more complicated paths, perhaps bouncing multiple times from surfaces before reaching the eye. This phenomenon can be partially simulated by adding reflection rays to the ray tracing algorithm. When a ray from the eye position hits a surface point, we generate a further *reflection ray* in the direction of perfect specular reflection. This reflection ray is handled in the same way as the ray from the eye; namely, we find the first point where it hits an object in the scene and calculate that point's illumination from all the light sources. This process can continue recursively with reflection rays themselves spawning their own reflection rays.

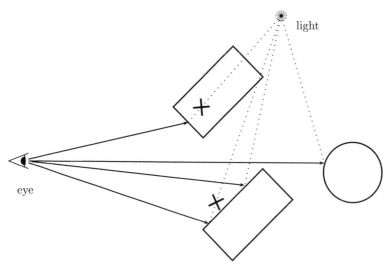

Figure IX.2. Shadow feelers: Rays from the eye are traced to their intersections with objects in the scene. Shadow feeler rays, shown as dotted lines, are sent from the points in the scene to each light to determine whether the point is directly illuminated by the point light source or whether it is in a shadow. The two shadow feelers marked with an "**X**" show that the light is not directly visible from the point.

This process is illustrated in Figure IX.3, where a single ray from the eye hits an object, and from this point another ray is sent in the direction of perfect specular reflection. This second ray hits another object, then generates another reflection ray, and so on.

Although it is not shown in Figure IX.3, each time a ray hits an object, we generate shadow feelers to all the light sources to determine which lights, if any, are illuminating the surface. In Figure IX.3, the first and third points hit by the ray are directly illuminated by the light; the second point is not directly illuminated.

The purpose of tracing reflections is to determine the illumination of the point that is visible to the viewer (i.e., of the point hit by the ray from the eye through the pixel position). This is

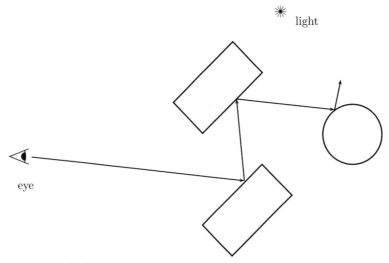

Figure IX.3. Reflection rays: The path of the ray from the eye is traced through multiple reflections. This calculates approximations to the lighting effects of multiple reflections.

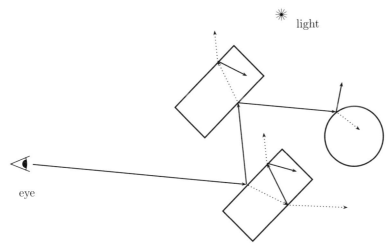

Figure IX.4. Transmission and reflection rays: The path of the ray from the eye is traced through multiple reflections and transmissions. Reflection rays are shown as solid lines, and transmission rays as dotted lines. The shadow feeler rays would still be used but are not shown.

computed by a formula of the form

$$I = I_{\text{local}} + \rho_{\text{rg}} I_{\text{reflect}}. \tag{IX.1}$$

Here, I_{local} is the lighting as computed by the local illumination model (Phong lighting, say), and I_{reflect} is the lighting of the point in the direction of the reflection ray. The scalar ρ_{rg} is a new material property: it is a factor specifying what fraction of the light from the reflection direction is reflected. Like the diffuse and specular material properties, the ρ_{rg} value is wavelength dependent, and thus there are separate reflection coefficients for red, green, and blue. The subscript "rg" stands for "reflection, global." The intensity of the incoming reflected light, I_{reflect}, is computed recursively by Equation IX.1.

Sections IX.1.1 and IX.1.3 give more details about how the local lighting is calculated and about the recursive calculations.

Transmission Rays

Ray tracing can also model transparency effects by using *transmission rays* in addition to reflection rays. Transmission rays can simulate *refraction*, the bending of light that occurs when light passes from one medium to another (e.g., from air into water).

A transmission ray is generated when a ray hits the surface of a transparent object: the transmission ray continues on through the surface. Refraction causes the direction of the transmitted ray to change. This change in direction is caused physically by the difference in the speed of light in the two media (air and water, for instance). The amount of refraction is calculated using the *index of refraction*, as discussed in Section IX.1.2.

Transmitted rays are recursively traced in the same manner as reflected rays. Of course, the transmission rays may be inside an object, and their first intersection with the scene could be the boundary of an object hit from the inside. When the transmitted ray hits a point, it will again spawn a reflection ray and a transmission ray. This process continues recursively. Figure IX.4 illustrates the generation of both reflection and transmission rays. In the figure, a single ray from the eye is traced through three bounces, spawning a total of 12 additional rays: the transmission rays are shown as dotted lines to distinguish them from reflection rays.

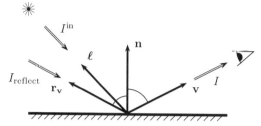

Figure IX.5. The usual setup for reflection rays in basic recursive ray tracing. The vector **v** points in the direction opposite to the incoming ray. The direction of perfect reflection is shown by the vector $\mathbf{r_v}$. The vector $\boldsymbol{\ell}$ points to a point light source, I is the outgoing light intensity as seen from the direction given by **v**, I_{reflect} is the incoming light from the reflection direction $\mathbf{r_v}$. and I^{in} is the intensity of the light from the light source. (Compare this with Figure III.7 on page 72.)

When transmission rays are used, the lighting formula has the form

$$I = I_{\text{local}} + \rho_{\text{rg}} I_{\text{reflect}} + \rho_{\text{tg}} I_{\text{xmit}}.$$

The new term $\rho_{\text{tg}} I_{\text{xmit}}$ includes the effect of recursively calculating the lighting in the transmission direction scaled by the material property ρ_{tg}. The scalar ρ_{tg} is wavelength dependent and specifies the fraction of light transmitted through the surface. The subscript "tg" stands for "transmission, global."

IX.1.1 Local Lighting and Reflection Rays

We now give more details about the calculation of reflection rays and the associated lighting calculations. The basic setup is shown in Figure IX.5, where we are tracing the path of a ray whose direction is determined by the vector **v**. In keeping with our usual conventions that the vectors are pointing away from the point of intersection with the surface, the vector **v** is actually pointing in the opposite direction of the ray being traced. (The figure shows the traced ray as emanating from an eye position, but the ray could more generally emanate from another intersection point instead.) We assume **v** is a unit vector. Also, **n** is the unit vector normal to the surface at the point of intersection.

The direction of perfect reflection is shown as the vector $\mathbf{r_v}$. This is calculated according to the formula

$$\mathbf{r_v} = 2(\mathbf{v} \cdot \mathbf{n})\mathbf{n} - \mathbf{v}, \qquad\qquad\qquad\qquad\qquad \text{IX.2}$$

which is derived in the same way as the formula for the reflection vector in Section III.1.2.[2]

The basic ray tracing algorithms depend on the use of a particular local lighting model: this is commonly either the Phong lighting model or the Cook–Torrance lighting model; the discussion that follows will presume the use of the Phong lighting model (it is straightforward to substitute the Cook–Torrance model in its place). The illumination of the point on the surface as seen from the ray trace direction **v** is given by the formula

$$I = I_{\text{local}} + \rho_{\text{rg}} I_{\text{reflect}}. \qquad\qquad\qquad\qquad\qquad \text{IX.3}$$

The I_{local} term is the lighting due to direct illumination by the lights that are visible from the intersection point.

For a given light i, let $\boldsymbol{\ell}_i$ be the unit vector in the direction of the light. Then let let δ_i equal 1 if the light is above the surface and is directly illuminating the point as determined by a shadow

---

[2]   The reflection vector is named $\mathbf{r_v}$ instead of **r** to avoid confusion with the reflection of the light vector $\boldsymbol{\ell}$ of Section III.1.2.

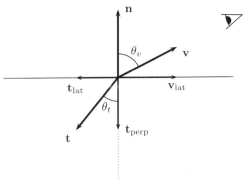

Figure IX.6. Computing the transmission ray direction **t**. The horizontal line represents the surface of a transmissive material; **n** is the unit vector normal to the surface. The vector **v** points in the direction opposite to the incoming ray. The direction of perfect transmission is shown by the vector **t**. The vectors $\mathbf{v}_{\text{lat}}$ and $\mathbf{t}_{\text{lat}}$ are the projections of these vectors onto the plane tangent to the surface, and, $\mathbf{t}_{\text{perp}}$ is the projection of **t** onto the normal vector.

feeler; otherwise, let δ_i equal 0. The value of δ_i is computed by determining whether the light is above the surface by checking whether $\boldsymbol{\ell}_i \cdot \mathbf{n} > 0$; if so, a shadow feeler is used to determine visibility of the light. The illumination due to the light i is defined as

$$I_{\text{local}}^{i} = \rho_a I_a^{\text{in},i} + \delta_i \cdot \left(\rho_d I_d^{\text{in},i} (\boldsymbol{\ell}_i \cdot \mathbf{n}) + \rho_s I_s^{\text{in},i} (\mathbf{r_v} \cdot \boldsymbol{\ell}_i)^f \right). \qquad \text{IX.4}$$

You should compare this to Equation III.6 on page 74. We are here using the notations $I_-^{\text{in},i}$ for the light coming from the ith light. The term $\mathbf{r} \cdot \mathbf{v}$ has been replaced by $\mathbf{r_v} \cdot \boldsymbol{\ell}_i$, which is clearly mathematically equivalent.

The net local lighting due to all the lights above the surface and incorporating all the wavelengths is obtained by summing the illumination from all the lights:

$$\mathbf{I}_{\text{local}} = \rho_a * \mathbf{I}_a^{\text{in}} + \rho_d * \sum_{i=1}^{k} \delta_i \mathbf{I}_d^{\text{in},i} (\boldsymbol{\ell}_i \cdot \mathbf{n}) + \rho_s * \sum_{i=1}^{k} \delta_i \mathbf{I}_s^{\text{in},i} (\mathbf{r_v} \cdot \boldsymbol{\ell}_i)^f + \mathbf{I}_e,$$

which is similar to Equation III.9 on page 75. As before, the values ρ_a, ρ_d, ρ_s are tuples of coefficients with one entry per color, and $*$ denotes a component-wise product. The value of $\mathbf{I}_a^{\text{in}}$ is still given according to Formula III.10.

The second term in Equation IX.3 contains the new material property ρ_{rg}: this coefficient is a scalar and can vary with wavelength (i.e., it is different for each color). The light intensity I_{reflect} is computed recursively by iterating the ray tracing algorithm.

IX.1.2 Transmission Rays

Now we turn to the details of how the ray tracing calculations work for transmission rays. First, we discuss how to compute the direction **t** of perfect transmission. The setup is shown in Figure IX.6.

The direction of the transmission vector **t** is found using the incoming direction **v** and the surface normal **n** with the aid of Snell's law. Snell's law relates the angle of incidence with the angle of refraction by the formula

$$\frac{\sin \theta_v}{\sin \theta_t} = \eta.$$

Here, θ_v, the angle of incidence, is the angle between $\mathbf{v}$ and the normal $\mathbf{n}$; and θ_t, the angle of refraction, is the angle between the transmission direction $\mathbf{t}$ and the negated normal. The *index of refraction*, η, is the ratio of the speed of light in the medium above the surface (the side where $\mathbf{v}$ is) to the speed of light in the medium below the surface (the side where $\mathbf{t}$ is). Typical values for η are approximately equal to 1.3 for rays going from air to water, and approximately equal to 1.5 for rays going from air to glass. For the reverse direction you need the reciprocal, and so when traveling from water or glass to air the index of refraction would be approximately $1/1.3$ or $1/1.5$. Snell's law can be derived from the wave model for light and can be found in many elementary physics books.

Snell's law can be rewritten as

$$\sin\theta_t = \eta^{-1}\sin\theta_v.$$

Now, if $\eta < 1$, it can happen that $\eta^{-1}\sin\theta_v$ is greater than 1. Of course in this case there is no possible angle θ_t that satisfies Snell's law. This corresponds to total internal reflection, where there is no transmission but only reflection. This happens only if $\eta < 1$, which is the case if light is traveling in a region of lower light speed (e.g., inside a medium such as glass or water) and is exiting to a medium, such as air, with a higher speed of light. In addition, this happens only when the angle of incidence is sufficiently large that the quantity $\eta^{-1}\sin\theta_v$ is larger than 1.

We can derive a method of computing $\mathbf{t}$ from $\mathbf{n}$ and $\mathbf{v}$ as follows. Let $\mathbf{v}_{\text{lat}}$ be the component of $\mathbf{v}$ that is orthogonal to the normal vector, namely,

$$\mathbf{v}_{\text{lat}} = \mathbf{v} - (\mathbf{v}\cdot\mathbf{n})\mathbf{n}.$$

(The subscript "lat" stands for "lateral.") Note that $||\mathbf{v}_{\text{lat}}|| = \sin\theta_v$. Therefore, the component, $\mathbf{t}_{\text{lat}}$, of $\mathbf{t}$ orthogonal to $\mathbf{n}$ has magnitude equal to

$$||\mathbf{t}_{\text{lat}}|| = \sin\theta_t = \eta^{-1}\sin\theta_v = \eta^{-1}||\mathbf{v}_{\text{lat}}||.$$

If $||\mathbf{t}_{\text{lat}}|| \geq 1$, then total internal reflection occurs. Otherwise, if $||\mathbf{t}_{\text{lat}}|| < 1$, we can continue the computation of the transmission direction. Since $\mathbf{t}_{\text{lat}}$ points in the direction opposite to $\mathbf{v}_{\text{lat}}$, this means that

$$\mathbf{t}_{\text{lat}} = -\eta^{-1}\mathbf{v}_{\text{lat}}.$$

The component of $\mathbf{t}$ in the direction of the negation of the normal vector has magnitude equal to

$$\cos\theta_t = \sqrt{1 - \sin^2\theta_t} = \sqrt{1 - ||\mathbf{t}_{\text{lat}}||^2},$$

and therefore is equal to

$$\mathbf{t}_{\text{perp}} = -\sqrt{1 - ||\mathbf{t}_{\text{lat}}||^2}\cdot\mathbf{n}.$$

Finally, we have

$$\mathbf{t} = \mathbf{t}_{\text{lat}} + \mathbf{t}_{\text{perp}},$$

which completes the calculation of the transmission direction.

Exercise IX.1 *An alternative calculation of the transmission vector uses*
$$\mathbf{t}_{\text{perp}} = -\sqrt{1 - \eta^{-2}(1 - (\mathbf{v}\cdot\mathbf{n})^2)}\cdot\mathbf{n}.$$
Prove that this formula is correct too.

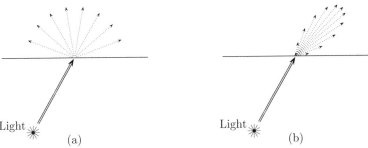

Figure IX.7. (a) Diffusely transmitted light. (b) Specularly transmitted light. The specularly transmitted light is centered around the transmission direction from Snell's law.

The exercise lets us give a closed form expression for **t**:

$$\mathbf{t} = \eta^{-1}((\mathbf{v} \cdot \mathbf{n})\mathbf{n} - \mathbf{v}) - \sqrt{1 - \eta^{-2}(1 - (\mathbf{v} \cdot \mathbf{n})^2)} \cdot \mathbf{n} \qquad \text{IX.5}$$

provided the formula in the square root is nonnegative. If the value in the square root is negative, then there is no transmission ray at all and we have total internal reflection.

To summarize, here is our preferred algorithm for computing the transmission ray:

```
CalcTransmissionDirection( v, n, η ) {
    Set t_lat = ((v · n)n − v)/η;
    Set sinSq = ||t_lat||²;              // sin²(θₜ)
    If ( sinSq>1 ) {
        Return(``No transmission --- total internal reflection!'');
    }
    Set t  =  t_lat − √(1 − sinSq) · n;
    Return t;
}
```

Next, we give details on how to extend the Phong lighting model to apply to transmission of light. (The Cook–Torrance or other local lighting models could be used instead, but we only discuss the Phong-style lighting model.) The new aspect of local lighting is that a transparent surface may now be illuminated by a light that lies on the far side of the surface. That is to say, the light may be on the opposite side of the surface from the viewer or incoming ray. As in the case of reflective illumination, transmitted illumination is modeled as having separate diffuse and specular components. These two kinds of illumination are shown in Figure IX.7; you should compare these with Figures III.2 and III.3 on page 69. The diffusely transmitted light is transmitted equally in all directions; the specularly transmitted light is transmitted primarily in the direction of perfect transmission.

The I_{local} term for the transmitted illumination from a light i that is on the opposite side of the surface is given by

$$I_{\text{local}}^i = \rho_a I_a^{\text{in},i} + \delta_i' \cdot \left(\rho_{\text{dt}} I_d^{\text{in},i} (\boldsymbol{\ell}_i \cdot (-\mathbf{n})) + \rho_{\text{st}} I_s^{\text{in},i} (\mathbf{t} \cdot \boldsymbol{\ell}_i)^f \right), \qquad \text{IX.6}$$

where ρ_{dt} and ρ_{st} are material properties for diffuse and specular transmitted light (these can reasonably be taken to just equal ρ_d and ρ_s in some cases). The value δ_i' is equal to 1 if the light is below the surface and the surface point is visible from the light, as determined by a shadow feeler. Otherwise δ_i' is equal to zero. Equation IX.6 needs to be used only when the light is behind the surface and $\delta_i' = 1$, and so $\boldsymbol{\ell}_i \cdot \mathbf{n} < 0$; otherwise, Equation IX.4 would be used instead. Figure IX.8 shows the vectors used in the application of Equation IX.6.

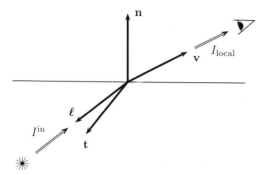

Figure IX.8. The vectors used in the computation of transmitted light are **v**, $\boldsymbol{\ell}$, **t**, and **n**. The vector **v** points in the direction opposite to the incoming ray. The direction of perfect transmission is shown by the vector **t**. The direction opposite to the incoming light is given by $\boldsymbol{\ell}$.

The full local lighting formula, incorporating both reflected and transmitted illumination as well as all wavelengths, can be given as

$$\mathbf{I}_{\text{local}} = \rho_a * \mathbf{I}_a^{\text{in}} + \rho_d * \sum_{i=1}^{k} \delta_i \mathbf{I}_d^{\text{in},i} (\boldsymbol{\ell}_i \cdot \mathbf{n}) + \rho_s * \sum_{i=1}^{k} \delta_i \mathbf{I}_s^{\text{in},i} (\mathbf{r_v} \cdot \boldsymbol{\ell}_i)^f$$

$$+ \rho_{dt} * \sum_{i=1}^{k} \delta_i' \mathbf{I}_d^{\text{in},i} (\boldsymbol{\ell}_i \cdot (-\mathbf{n})) + \rho_{st} * \sum_{i=1}^{k} \delta_i' \mathbf{I}_s^{\text{in},i} (\mathbf{t} \cdot \boldsymbol{\ell}_i)^f + \mathbf{I}_e. \qquad \text{IX.7}$$

For each particular light i, at most one of δ_i and δ_i' can be nonzero since the light source cannot be both above and below the surface.

IX.1.3 Putting It All Together

We have finished the discussion of all the features of the basic form of recursive ray tracing. These are combined into a recursive routine for ray tracing. The main loop of the recursive routine loops over every pixel in the image and forms the ray from the eye through that pixel. With that ray, a routine `RayTrace` is called, which does the following:

1. Finds the first place where the ray intersects the scene. If the ray does not hit any object in the scene, then a default "background color" is used for the illumination level.
2. Calculates the illumination of that point according to the local lighting model.
3. Spawns a reflection ray and a transmission ray as appropriate.
4. Calls itself recursively with the reflection ray and with the transmission ray.
5. Combines the resulting illumination levels and returns.

In addition, a stopping criterion is needed to terminate the recursive calls to `RayTrace`: an easy, albeit rather arbitrary, stopping criterion is just to trace recursively to only a fixed number of levels, or "bounces." This is the approach we take in the pseudocode that follows.

Here is the main program for basic recursive ray tracing:

```
RayTraceMain() {
    // Let x be the position of the viewer.
    // Let maxDepth be a positive integer.
    For each pixel p in the viewport, do {
        Set u = unit vector in the direction from x to p.
```

```
            Call RayTrace( x, u, maxDepth );
            Assign pixel p the color returned by RayTrace.
    }
}
```

The recursive ray tracing routine is given next.

```
RayTrace( s, u, depth ) {
    // s is the starting position of the ray.
    // u is unit vector in the direction of the ray.
    // depth  is the trace depth.
    // Return value is a 3-tuple of color values (R,G,B).

    // Part I - Nonrecursive computations
    Check the ray with starting position s and direction u
        against the surfaces of the objects in the scene.
        If it intersects any point, let z be the first intersection point
        and n be the surface normal at the intersection point.
    If no point was intersected {
        Return the background color.
    }
    For each light {
        Generate a shadow feeler from z to the light.
        Check if the shadow feeler intersects any object.
        Set δ_i and δ'_i appropriately.
    }
    Set color = I_local;                    // Use equation IX.7

    // Part II - Recursive computations
    If ( depth==0 ) {
        Return color;                       // Reached maximum trace depth.
    }
    // Calculate reflection direction and add in reflection color
    If ( ρ_rg ≠ 0 ) {           // if nonzero reflectivity
        Set r = u − 2(u · n)n;              // Eq. IX.2 with v = −u.
        Set color = color + ρ_rg*RayTrace(z, r, depth-1);
    }
    // Calculate transmission direction (if any) and add in transmitted color
    If ( ρ_tg ≠ 0 ) {           // if has transparency
        // Let η be the index of refraction.
        Set t = CalcTransmissionDirection(−u, n, η);
        If t is defined {                   // if not total internal reflection
            Set color = color + ρ_tg*RayTrace(z, t, depth-1);
        }
    }
    Return color;
}
```

The basic recursive ray tracing algorithms have now been completely defined with one notable exception; namely, we have not discussed how to find intersections of a ray with objects in the virtual scene. The basic idea is to model each object in the scene as a geometric object such as a sphere, cylinder, cone, or torus, or as a polygonal object with a surface comprising flat polygonal faces, or as being bounded by more general surfaces such as Bézier or B-spline patches. Then, we have to test the ray against each surface of each object for possible intersections. Further, it is important that the intersection testing algorithms be computationally efficient because we have to perform the test for every ray and every shadow feeler. Indeed, it is typically the case that the computation time required for intersection testing is the major portion of the execution time in ray tracing.

The discussion of how to perform the intersection tests for rays against common surfaces is left to Chapter X.

The basic ray tracing algorithm, with recursive calls and intersection testing, is much too slow for real-time rendering. Suppose, for instance, that the screen has about one million pixels and that each ray is traced to a depth of six bounces (i.e., starting with `maxDepth` set to 5). In the worst case, each intersection will spawn both a reflection ray and a transmission ray and so for each pixel we trace a total of $1 + 2 + 4 + \cdots + 2^5 = 63$ rays. In the best case, there is no transmission; consequently, each pixel requires us to trace six rays. In addition, for each light and each intersection point, we must intersect a shadow feeler against the scene. Thus, all in all, we may need to handle tens of millions, or even hundreds of millions, of rays, each ray needing to be tested for intersections with objects in the scene. It is common for this process to take several minutes on a modern-day personal computer. Given the amount of work being performed, one feels lucky that it takes only this long!

IX.2 Advanced Ray Tracing Techniques

IX.2.1 Distributed Ray Tracing

Distributed ray tracing, first introduced by (Cook, Porter, and Carpenter, 1984), is a collection of techniques used to extend the functionality of ray tracing by increasing the number of rays that are traced. Generally speaking, distributed ray tracing is significantly slower than basic recursive ray tracing; however, it can achieve a variety of additional effects. In this section, we describe some of the more common applications of distributed ray tracing.

Antialiasing with Multiple Eye-to-Pixel Rays
In the basic ray tracing model, only one ray is sent from the eye position to each pixel. This means that only a single ray determines the color of a given pixel. However, in actuality, a pixel covers a square region of the image, and sometimes one would obtain better visual effects if the pixel were colored as an average color of the region subtended by the pixel. This average color can be approximated by supersampling the pixel, namely, by tracing multiple rays through the pixel with the rays spread more or less evenly across the pixel and then assigning the pixel the average of the colors from the multiple rays.

Two prominent applications in which forming an average pixel color can help with antialiasing are (a) removing the "jaggies," or pixel-sized bumps, from lines, edges, or other object boundaries; and (b) viewing texture maps. We have already discussed two ad hoc solutions to these problems: (a) lines can be smoothed through blending and transparency, and (b) texture map aliasing can be minimized by using mipmapping. Distributed ray tracing gives a more general solution to these and other related problems.

Supersampling and stochastic supersampling were discussed earlier in Section V.1.4 in the context of texture maps. Supersampling consists of selecting multiple subpixel locations.

(a) No supersampling.

(b) Supersampling with jittered subpixel centers.

Figure IX.9. An example of antialiasing using jittered subpixel centers. (a) The scene rendered without supersampling; note the "jaggies" on the silhouettes of the balls, for instance. (b) The scene with pixels selectively supersampled up to a maximum of 40 times. See Color Plate 9.

Distributed ray tracing can trace separate rays from the eye to each subpixel location and then average the results. The strategies described in Section V.1.4 apply also to ray tracing; in particular, jittering is also a recommended method for selecting subpixel locations for distributed ray tracing (see Figure V.7 on page 134).

Figures IX.9 and IX.10 show an example of antialiasing with jittered pixel supersampling.

Depth of Field with Jittered Eye Positions
Depth of field is caused by a lens's focusing on objects at a given depth, thereby making objects that are either nearer or farther than the focus depth appear out of focus. This is particularly noticeable in movies when a camera switches from focusing up close to focusing far away or vice versa. Pinhole cameras and lenses with a very small aperture are not affected nearly so much by depth of field. Depth of field affects human eyes as well; however, your visual system compensates for this so that you do not notice it under normal circumstances. Computer graphics systems calculate images purely virtually and do not require physical focusing devices, and so of course they are not affected by depth-of-field focusing problems. Nonetheless, it is sometimes desirable to simulate depth of field in computer graphics.

Ray tracing allows depth-of-field effects by jittering the eye position while keeping the focal plane fixed. For this, you set up the virtual viewport in the plane of the image you wish to

(a) No supersampling.

(b) Supersampling with jittered subpixel centers.

Figure IX.10. Close-up views of the images in Figure IX.9. See Color Plate 10.

have in focus. Then, for each pixel, you trace multiple rays from jittered eye positions to the center of the pixel (the pixel's center being kept fixed in the focal plane). For instance, one possibility is to jitter the eye position to nine (or more) positions with the jittered positions obtained by moving the eye position up or down, and left or right. Then, from each jittered position, perform ray tracing as usual: the final color of the pixel is the average of the results of the multiple ray traces.

The effect of jittering the eye position is that objects that lie in the focal plane (and are visible to the eye) are always hit exactly, and each of the multiple ray traces hits the same point and yields essentially the same results. On the other hand, objects that are either nearer or farther than the focal plane are hit differently from different jittered eye positions, and the averaging tends to blur them. Figure IX.11 shows how the rays converge and diverge to focus objects in the focal plane and blur objects at other depths. Figure IX.12 shows an example of depth of field.

It is important that you choose the jittered positions for the eye separately for each pixel, that is, do not use the same jittered eye positions for all the pixels but instead use new jittered positions for each pixel. The problem with reusing the same jittered positions is that the result

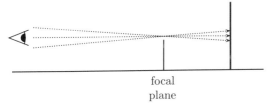

focal
plane

Figure IX.11. The rays from the jittered viewpoints converge at the focal plane but not at the back plane.

would be a composite of multiple copies of the scene from slightly different viewpoints rather than an actual blurring of the scene.

Motion Blur

Motion blur renders fast-moving objects as blurs or streaks to indicate their speed; an example is shown in Figure IX.13. Motion blur can be accomplished by jittering objects' positions backwards in time. This can be done as follows: each time the high-level ray tracing routine begins tracing a ray from the eye position to a pixel, the moving object(s) are moved back to their position at a small time, δt, in the past. The δt values should be chosen at random and independently. It probably would be best to adjust the probabilities so that small δt values are more likely than large ones. For instance, you could use the following algorithm to choose k jittered values for δt: First choose values a_i randomly and independently from the intervals $[\frac{i}{k}, \frac{i+1}{k}]$, for $0 \le i < k$. Then set b_i by

$$b_i = a_i^2.$$

Finally, set the ith jitter value δt equal to $b_i \Delta t$, where Δt is the time period over which the motion blur should extend. (That is, large Δt values make the motion blur trail longer.) Calculating the δt values using the b_i's instead of the a_i's has the effect of compressing them to be closer to zero: the intended visual effect is that the motion blur trail fades out smoothly.

Soft Shadows with Extended Lights and Jittered Shadow Rays

Up until now, we have discussed only point light sources. However, few light sources are modeled well by points. Most lights are either roundish or spherical (such as the sun or light

Figure IX.12. An example of depth of field. The front of the eight ball is the focal plane. Note also the blurring of the checkerboard plane. In this image, each pixel is selectively supersampled up to 40 times. The eye positions and the subpixel positions were independently jittered as described on page 249. See Color Plate 11.

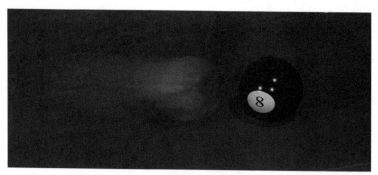

Figure IX.13. An example of motion blur. Pixels were selectively supersampled up to 40 times. Both motion supersampling and subpixel supersampling were used. See Color Plate 12.

bulbs) or are rectangularly shaped (such as fluorescent lights in the ceiling behind a plastic cover). The term "extended light" refers to any nonpoint source.

Extended lights differ from point lights in several important ways. Mainly, an extended light source may be *partially* occluded. As a consequence, an extended light will not cast perfectly sharp shadows and generally gives a softer, smoother lighting effect. Figure IX.14 illustrates how soft shadows work. It shows a spherical light source shining on a wall with an obstruction shadowing part of the wall. Where the obstruction blocks the entire light, the wall is completely in shadow. But there is a region, called the *penumbra*, where the obstruction blocks only part of the spherical light. In the penumbra, the shadowing transitions smoothly from completely shadowed to completely illuminated.

Ray tracing can be used to simulate penumbra effects by casting multiple shadow feelers instead of a single shadow feeler. The shadow feelers should be more or less evenly distributed across the extent of the light as seen from the point being illuminated. The fraction of shadow feelers not finding an obstruction between the point of illumination and the light can be used as an estimate of the fraction by which the light is occluded. The lighting from the that light is then reduced correspondingly by the same fraction.

As usual, one gets better effects by randomly choosing positions on the light's extent as seen by the point of illumination and then casting shadow feelers to those positions on the light. If you were to pick fixed points on the light as the targets for shadow feelers, then the penumbra would show banding: there would be noticeable changes in the shading where each fixed light point vanished from view. Jittering can be used to good effect to help distribute the shadow feeler targets evenly over the extent of the light.

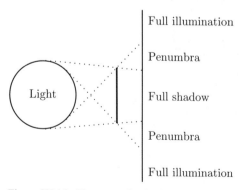

Full illumination

Penumbra

Full shadow

Penumbra

Full illumination

Figure IX.14. The penumbra is the area where the light is only partly blocked.

Using Multiple Techniques at Once

It is possible to combine multiple distributed ray tracing techniques to achieve more than one effect at once. For instance, you can render an image that has both antialiasing and depth of field. To do this, you would jitter subpixel locations for antialiasing and jitter the eye position for depth of field. At first glance, this might seem to require tracing many more rays. That is, if each pixel has nine jittered subpixel locations and nine jittered eye positions, then one might try casting $9^2 = 81$ rays from the eye to the pixel, one for each choice of eye position and pixel position. Fortunately, this large increase in the number of rays is not necessary. We can instead cast rays from each eye position and to each subpixel position but use only one ray for each eye position and choose one jittered subpixel position for each eye position. For best results, you need to make sure that the choices of jittered subpixel positions are independent of the jittered eye positions. In particular, suppose the jittered subpixel positions are chosen from square subpixels, as shown in Figure V.7 on page 134. Also suppose that the eye positions are chosen in a similar manner by jittering the centers of an array of squares around the central view position. Then you should choose a random assignment of subpixel positions to eye positions (i.e., a random one-to-one correspondence between subpixel positions and eye positions) and then recursively trace one ray from each eye position to its corresponding pixel position. The point of using the random assignment is to avoid having a correlation between the jittered eye positions and jittered pixel positions that could cause unwanted visual effects.

The high-level algorithm for this is as follows:

```
Variables:
    Array p[N]: An array for holding N subpixel positions.
    Array e[N]: An array for holding N eye locations.
    Array π[N]: An array that holds a permutation of [0,...,N − 1]
For each pixel: {
    Fill p[] with N jittered subpixel locations.
    Fill e[] with N jittered eye positions.
    Choose π a random permutation of [0,...,N − 1].
    For i = 0,...,N − 1 {
        Recursively ray trace with ray from e[i] to p[π[i]].
    }
}
```

To choose a random permutation of $[0, \ldots, N - 1]$, you can use the following code. We use the function RandInt(i) to compute a random integer in the range $0, \ldots, i$.

```
RandomPermutation(N) {
    For i = 0,...,N − 1 {
        Set π[i] = i;
    }
    For i = N − 1, N − 2,...,1 {
        Set j = RandInt(i);
        If j < i
            Swap values of π[j] and π[i];
    }
}
```

Similar methods can be used to combine other distributed ray tracing methods.

Multiple Colors

For greater realism, one can perform ray tracing for more colors than just the primary red, green, and blue colors. In addition, the speed of light in a medium typically depends on the wavelength of the light. For refraction, this means that the transmission direction varies with color: a good example of this is a prism splitting white light into a spectrum of wavelengths. In addition, in some local lighting models (such as Cook–Torrance, but not in the Phong model), the dominant reflection angle is also wavelength dependent. Thus, for more realistic results with multiple colors, one may wish to trace multiple reflection and transmission rays from a single ray–object intersection.

Path Tracing. Tracing Diffuse Reflection and Transmission

The basic ray tracing methods described so far are a hybrid of (a) a local lighting model that includes ambient and diffuse lighting terms, and (b) ray tracing perfect reflection and perfect transmission directions. This hybrid is far from physically correct and contains several undesirable features. For example, the local lighting model has a term for ambient light, which is needed because of our inability to trace all rays of light completely. Similarly, the basic ray tracing model does not allow the illumination of a diffuse surface to illuminate other surfaces in the scene. For instance, in the real world, a diffusely lit red wall will itself illuminate nearby objects with reddish light; ray tracing, however, will not simulate this because it only follows reflections in the direction of perfect, specular reflection.

It would be more physically realistic if we could completely subsume the ambient and diffuse lighting from the local lighting model into the global methods of ray tracing. In essence, this would mean trying to trace *all* the photons in the entire scene to track the entire flow of light throughout the scene. If this could be successfully done, then it would be possible to unify the local lighting models with the ray tracing model: for instance, one would use the same lighting models for both reflected and transmitted rays as for rays to light sources.

Several techniques are used to try to increase the realism of the ray tracing model by capturing more effects of diffuse and ambient reflection. The main idea behind these techniques is to try to follow reflection (and perhaps transmission) rays in all possible directions, not just in the direction of perfect reflection. Unfortunately, this requires spawning a huge number of reflection rays in hundreds, or thousands, of directions. This is often done via a technique called *path tracing*. In path tracing, one generates many rays starting at the eye position through a given pixel. At each intersection, the subsequent reflection direction is chosen by a random procedure. In this way, one attempts to sample a large number of representative paths by which light can reach the eye.

When tracing multiple reflection directions, one must also still trace shadow feelers to the lights and calculate direct illumination from the lights. Of course, this can be combined with extended lights and the use of multiple shadow feelers per light to create soft shadows.

The big drawback to tracing so many reflection directions is that it greatly increases the number of rays that must be traced by a factor of a thousandfold or more. These techniques are therefore very time consuming, and can require hours of computation time to trace a single image.

Path tracing can also be combined with so-called backwards ray tracing. Backwards ray tracing follows rays of light starting at the light source through one or more bounces and tracks the flow of light from the light source towards the eye. Backwards ray tracing is discussed briefly in the next section.

Another global lighting method, called *radiosity*, can also be used to simulate the flow of diffuse lighting through a scene. Radiosity is based on a method quite different from ray tracing and is covered in Chapter XI.

IX.2.2 Backwards Ray Tracing

Ray tracing as described so far has involved tracing paths of light starting at the eye position and ending at lights. It is also possible to trace light in the other direction by starting at light sources and tracing the paths taken by light from the light sources. This process is called *backwards ray tracing*. The name is somewhat misleading, since backwards ray tracing involves tracing the forward movement of light from the light source. The usual ray tracing, however, sometimes called *forward ray tracing*, traces backwards from the eye along the paths taken by light.

The difficulty with backwards ray tracing is that most of the light exiting light sources never reaches the eye position at all but instead either leaves the scene entirely or is attenuated by multiple bounces until it is insignificant. Thus, a pure backwards ray tracing algorithm would be much more computationally intensive than forward ray tracing. For this reason, backwards ray tracing is generally used in conjunction with forward ray tracing.

The most common methods use backwards ray tracing to track the overall distribution of light throughout the scene and then use forward ray tracing to view the lit scene. (Radiosity is another method with a similar idea.) The first such method was the method of *illumination maps* introduced by (Arvo, 1986). For illumination maps, all the surfaces of objects in the scene are parameterized and then gridded up into small patches. Then, numerous light rays are traced forward from the light sources through multiple bounces. Each time a light ray hits a surface, it is determined which surface patch is hit and the color and intensity of the illuminating light are applied to the patch. These color and intensity values are stored at the vertices of the patch, and the light color and intensity are distributed to each vertex roughly in proportion to the distance of the intersection point from the vertex (more precisely: by inverting linear or bilinear interpolation to get the weight coefficients). The corners of the surface patches are used as accumulators, and, at the end of the backwards ray tracing phase, they hold the sum of all the weighted illumination from all the light rays that hit neighboring patches. These vertices and their stored illumination values are together called an *illumination map*. After the illumination map has been created, forward ray tracing can be used to view the scene. For the forward ray tracing, the diffuse component of the lighting model is omitted; instead, the illumination map values are used for the diffuse lighting. More precisely, when a ray hits a patch, the intersection point is expressed as a weighted average of the corners of the patch, and the illumination levels at these vertices are combined using the corner weights to calculate the diffuse illumination at the intersection point.

A common visual effect that can be simulated well with illumination maps is the focusing of light through transparent objects. For example, light shining on a glass ball can create bright patterns on a surface under the glass ball, where the curvature of the ball has acted to focus many rays of light into a small area. Another visual effect that can be handled in this way is *caustics*. An example of caustics is seen in a pool of clear water in which small ripples on the surface of the water will bend light, creating rippling patterns of light on the bottom of the pool.

A more recent method of extending illumination maps is that of *photon maps* (Jensen, 2001; Jensen and Christensen, 1995). Unlike illumination maps, which store aggregate illumination levels at vertices on a surface, a photon map stores information about each individual light ray (i.e., photon) that hits the surface along with its color and intensity and possibly its direction.

Photon maps were originally invented to avoid needing to parameterize surfaces, but when they include direction information they can also be used to model specular light. An example of how direction information can help is when light is reflected off a mirror and then strikes a surface at point **x**. Then, a viewer looking at point **x** slightly off the direction of perfect specular reflection will still be able to see the specular highlight, for it can be calculated from the photon map.

Using a photon map allows one to drop both the diffuse and specular terms from the local lighting model. In fact, if the backwards ray tracing is carried out sufficiently far, through enough bounces, then sometimes even the ambient light term can be omitted from the local lighting formula. Photon maps are also used for illumination of volumes, for light scattering, and for translucency, see (Jensen, 2001).

Another form of backwards ray tracing is *bidirectional path tracing* (Lafortune and Willems, 1993; Veach and Guibas, 1994). In bidirectional path tracing, paths are traced both from light sources and from the eye and then are joined together.

Further Reading

Our treatment of the more advanced topics in ray tracing has been quite cursory. Some of the topics we have completely skipped are (a) Monte-Carlo methods for choosing ray trace directions, importance sampling, and more sophisticated probability distributions than jittered samples; (b) Russian roulette methods for deciding when to stop tracing rays (Arvo and Kirk, 1990); and (c) participating media, such as smoke, fog, or atmosphere, which scatter light.

There are several good sources for more information about these and other ray tracing topics. The book (Glassner, 1989) has a collection of introductory articles about the techniques of ray tracing as developed before 1990. The textbook (Watt and Watt, 1992) has several chapters devoted to advanced topics in ray tracing along with pointers to the literature. (Shirley, 2000) has a nice overview of ray tracing, including several advanced topics. (Glassner, 1995) covers many advanced topics relevant for ray tracing. The online newsletter *Ray Tracing News*, also maintained by Glassner, has a huge amount of material on developments in ray tracing. Finally, many of the recent developments in ray tracing can be found in conference proceedings and journals; the annual proceedings of the ACM Siggraph conference and the Eurographics conferences are good places to search for this literature.

Ray tracing was first developed by (Whitted, 1980): this seminal paper is remarkably readable and still relevant.

IX.3 Special Effects without Ray Tracing

Ray tracing is too complicated and too experimental to be included in a standard graphics API such as OpenGL. Indeed, if you want to write a ray tracing application in OpenGL, you must completely rewrite all the lighting models yourself, including standard routines like the calculation of Phong lighting. (However, a ray tracing package is included with this book and described in Appendix B.) On the other hand, many visual effects similar to those that can be achieved with ray tracing can also be obtained with much simpler and faster methods. We will discuss some of the more common of such methods in this section. Most of these can be done efficiently in OpenGL; the rest can generally be done efficiently by modern graphics hardware. Low-cost graphics boards for PCs are nowadays very sophisticated, have memory for computing and storing multiple textures, and even let the programmer download simple programs for remote real-time execution in the graphics pipeline. (Future releases of OpenGL are planned to allow the user to access these capabilities of graphics boards from OpenGL programs.)

Antialiasing Lines with Blending

OpenGL includes automatic use of blending to antialias lines, points, and polygons. These can be enabled by giving the commands

```
glEnable( { GL_POINT_SMOOTH
            GL_LINE_SMOOTH   } );
            GL_POLYGON_SMOOTH

glHint( { GL_POINT_SMOOTH_HINT
          GL_LINE_SMOOTH_HINT   }, GL_NICEST );
          GL_POLYGON_SMOOTH_HINT

glEnable(GL_BLEND);
glBlendFunc(GL_SRC_ALPHA, GL_ONE_MINUS_SRC_ALPHA);
```

These commands cause OpenGL to render pixels that lie at the border of, and are partially covered by, a point or edge as partly transparent. This is done by giving the partially covered pixels an alpha value between 0 and 1 equal to the fraction of the pixel that is covered. As these pixels are drawn, the blending operation averages the drawn color (the source color) with the color already stored for the pixel (the destination color).

Antialiasing in this way works reasonably well for line and points but does not work as well for filled polygons. You should see the OpenGL programming manual for a more sophisticated way to antialias polygon edges, but that method requires performing your own depth calculations instead of using the depth buffer for hidden surface removal.

Motion Blur and Depth of Field with the Accumulation Buffer

The OpenGL accumulation buffer is a memory region in which you can temporarily store and combine images. It is possible to render a scene multiple times, combine the results into the accumulation buffer, and finally display the composite image. OpenGL allows you to scale the accumulation buffer contents, and the accumulation buffer can be loaded from, and saved to, the current frame buffer.

By taking multiple snapshots and averaging them together into the frame buffer, you can obtain motion blur and depth of field similar to those that can be achieved with distributed ray tracing. For motion blur, you render the moving object several times at several intermediate positions in its motion. For depth of field, you render the complete scene from several different viewpoints. To get results comparable to distributed ray tracing you may need to use a larger number of repeated images to avoid having the results look like several superimposed snapshots, but this approach is still substantially faster than ray tracing.

Finally, because a scene may have only a few fast moving objects, you can often render the more static background once and then repeatedly render the moving objects in front of the static background to thus avoid the expense of repeatedly rendering the entire scene.

The OpenGL commands for manipulating the accumulation buffer are

```
glutInitDisplayMode( GLUT_ACCUM | other-options );
          { GL_ACCUM
            GL_LOAD
glAccum(  { GL_RETURN }, float factor );
            GL_MULT
            GL_ADD

glAccumClear( float red, float green, float blue, float alpha);
glClear(GL_ACCUM_BUFFER_BIT);
```

You must include the GLUT_ACCUM bit in the options to glutInitDisplayMode to request a rendering context with an accumulation buffer. The glAccumClear command sets the clear colors for the accumulator: the accumulator buffer is loaded with these values by the glClear command shown above. The call to glAccum with the GL_ACCUM operand adds into the accumulation buffer the contents of the current drawing buffer multiplied by the factor value. For superimposing multiple rendered images, you would use a loop of the following type:

```
glClear(GL_ACCUM_BUFFER_BIT);
For i = 1,...,n {
    glClear(GL_COLOR_BUFFER_BIT | GL_DEPTH_BUFFER_BIT);
    RenderScene( i );          // Render i-th version of scene
    glAccum(GL_ACCUM, 1.0/n);
}
glAccum(GL_RETURN, 1.0);
```

The subroutine RenderScene() must render the changing scene as usual but should not swap buffers to display it. The last line uses the GL_RETURN option to glAccum to place the contents of the accumulation buffer back into the rendering buffer. The factor, which is equal to 1 here, specifies another scaling value.

See the OpenGL programming manual for documentation on the rest of the operands to glAccum.

Depth of Field with z-Buffer–Based Blurring

The z-buffer contents contain the pseudo-distance from which one can determine the actual distance of the object from the eye. This distance information can be used to create depth of field effects. To do this, any pixel whose depth does not approximately match the focal depth can be blurred by replacing it with a weighted average of the surrounding pixels. The radius of the area from which the surrounding pixels are taken should depend on the distance of the pixel from the focal plane.

Reflections with Environment Mapping

Shiny, specular objects with reflections of the surrounding scene can be rendered using environment maps. The environment map is created by rendering the scene from the viewpoint of the shiny object and then using this to create an environment map. Typically, this is done by rendering the scene from the viewpoint of the shiny object up to six times and storing the environment map in the box projection format. Once an environment map is created from every shiny object, the final image can be rendered one further time from the eye position with the environment maps applied as textures to the objects. It is also possible to iterate this procedure to obtain multiple levels of reflection. Attenuated or blurry reflections can be handled by attenuating or blurring the environment map.

Environment maps were already discussed in more detail in Section V.3.

Using environment maps in this way cannot fully simulate reflections. First there is some error in the calculation of reflection because the environment map is formed from the viewpoint of only a single position (usually the center point) of the object. Further, this approach does not handle self-reflections; for instance, a shiny teapot would not show the reflection of the spout on its body, or vice versa, unless you treat the spout and the body as separate objects and calculate separate environment maps for them.

Mirror Reflections with Clones

Reflections from flat, mirrored surfaces can be created by rendering a mirror image of the world behind the mirror's plane. This involves first rendering the entire scene reflected across the plane of the mirror, then drawing the mirror as a transparent shape (using blending; see `glBlend` in the OpenGL programming manual), and then drawing the real scene. Attenuated reflections can be achieved by choosing blending value appropriately.

For small mirrors or for difficult geometric arrangements, you may need to use the OpenGL stencil buffer to restrict the mirror image to be rendered only behind the mirror, for otherwise the mirror image of the world would be visible around the mirror too. For this, you set up the stencil buffer by drawing the mirror shape, then render the mirror image of the scene with the stencil buffer enabled, and then disable the stencil buffer and render the mirror and then the rest of the scene again. The stencil buffer acts as a mask to prevent rendering outside of a defined area (for more details see the OpenGL programming manual).

Shadows

As we discussed already in Section II.3.4, shadows can be projected on a flat surface using projection transformations. For soft shadows, this process can be repeated with multiple light positions and blending.

Casting shadows on nonplanar surfaces is harder, but there are variety of methods that can render shadows in real time. Two of the most popular ways of rendering shadows in real time without ray tracing are the *shadow volume* method and the *shadow map* method. We give only brief descriptions of these methods, but you can consult the references mentioned below for more information.

The shadow volume method works by determining what regions in 3-space are in shadow. For each point light source ℓ_i, and each polygonal object, we determine the solid region that lies in the shadow cast by that object from light ℓ_i. This region is called a *shadow volume*. For positional lights, the shadow volume is a generalized truncated cone. For instance, if the object is a triangle, then its shadow volume is a three-sided, infinitely tall pyramid that is capped (truncated) by the triangle. For general polygonal objects instead of triangles, it suffices to find the "silhouette edges" and then the shadow volume is the infinite region bounded by the shadows cast by the silhouette edges and capped by the polygonal object. The side faces of the shadow volume are the boundaries of the shadow region as cast from the silhouette edges.

Standard implementations of shadow volumes proceed roughly as follows: First, the scene is rendered into the frame buffer as usual with all depth buffer information and either (a) with all lighting as usual, or (b) with ambient lighting only. Then, the shadow volumes' side faces are rendered, but instead of drawing them into the frame buffer, the (pseudo-)depths are compared with the depth buffer values in the frame buffer. By keeping track of the net number of front- and back-facing shadow volume faces that lie in front of a given pixel in the frame buffer, we can determine whether the pixel is in shadow. (The OpenGL stencil buffer can be used to keep track of the net number of front- and back-facing edges.) Third, once it is determined which pixels are in shadow, then either (a) all shadowed pixels are darkened to simulate shadows, or (b) Phong lighting is used to add diffuse and specular lighting to all nonshadowed pixels. These steps have to be repeated for each point light source.

The shadow volume method was first described by (Crow, 1977). It was generalized to more general shapes by (Bergeron, 1986) and adapted to handle soft shadows from extended lights by (Brotman and Badler, 1984). (Heidmann, 1991) describes efficient implementation of shadow volumes with the stencil buffer. (Everitt and Kilgard, 2002) also discuss implementations on modern graphics hardware along with optimizations that avoid problems with clipping planes.

The second method is that of shadow maps. A *shadow map* consists of the view of the scene as rendered from the perspective of a point light source (instead of from the viewpoint of the viewer). For each point light source, a shadow map is created with a depth buffer and with hidden surfaces removed. The shadow map can be used to determine the distance from the light source to the first object in the scene in any given direction (up the resolution of the shadow map). After the shadow maps are created, the scene is rendered as usual from the viewpoint of the viewer. Each pixel in the scene is rendered into screen space, with x- and y-coordinates and with a pseudodepth value z. These screen space coordinates can be inverted to obtain the position of the pixel's contents in the scene in 3-space.[3] Then the distance from the light in 3-space can be compared with the corresponding distance from the shadow map. If the object is farther away than the distance in the shadow map, it is shadowed; otherwise, it is not. (Usually, a bias value is added to the distance to avoid problems with self-shadowing caused by roundoff error.) Once it is known which pixels represent surfaces in shadow, then, as before, either shadowed pixels can be darkened or nonshadowed pixels can be illuminated with Phong lighting.

Shadow maps were introduced by (Williams, 1978). They can suffer from problems with aliasing and roundoff error; (Reeves, Salesin, and Cook, 1987) use a method called "percentage closer filtering" that can reduce aliasing and make softer shadows. (Agrawala et al., 2000) and (Chen and Williams, 1993) discuss ways to use shadow maps to render soft shadows with from jittered light sources.

(McCool, 2000) describes a hybrid method that combines shadow volumes and shadow maps by extracting shadow volume information from a shadow map.

Transparency, Blending, and Fog

OpenGL includes several features that allow some aspects of transparency to be rendered easily. The OpenGL functions `glBlendFunc` and `glFog` control these features.

Blending allows transparent objects to modify the colors of objects behind them. The alpha component of colors is used to control blending. To obtain good results with blending, it is usually necessary to first render all nontransparent objects and then render the transparent objects with the painter's algorithm, namely, to render the transparent objects sorted so that more distant objects are rendered first.

Fog allows more distant objects to "fade out," as from fog or other atmospheric interference. Fog has the advantage of providing "depth cueing," wherein the attenuation of images due to fog gives an indication of distance. In addition, fog can be used to obscure distant objects and thereby improve performance since obscured objects do not need to be rendered.

---

[3]   The OpenGL function `gluUnProject` can help with inverting the screen space coordinates.

Color Plate 1. (Figure I.1, page 2.) A pixel is formed from subregions or subpixels, each of which displays one of three colors.

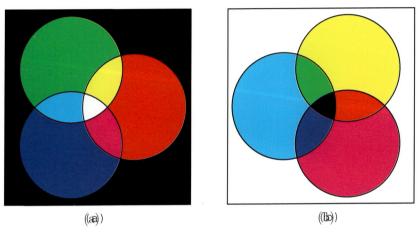

(a)   (b)

Color Plate 2. (Figure VI.1, page 149.) (a) The additive colors are red, green, and blue. (b) The subtractive colors are cyan, magenta, and yellow.

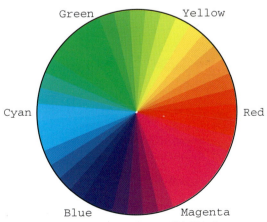

Color Plate 3. (Figure VI.2, page 152.) Hue is measured in degrees representing an angle around the color wheel. Pure red has hue equal to $0°$, pure green has hue equal to $120°$, and pure blue has hue equal to $240°$.

Color Plate 4. (Figure III.1, page 68.) Six teapots with various shading and lighting options. (a) Wireframe teapot. (b) Teapot drawn with solid color but no lighting or shading. (c) Teapot with flat shading with only ambient and diffuse lighting. (d) Teapot drawn with Gouraud interpolation with only ambient and diffuse reflection. (e) Teapot drawn with flat shading with ambient, diffuse, and specular lighting. (f) Teapot with Gouraud shading with ambient, diffuse, and specular lighting.

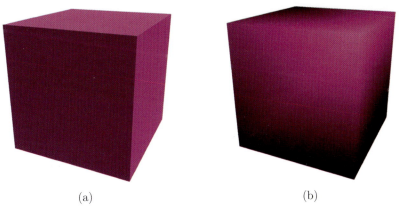

(a)   (b)

Color Plate 5. (Figure III.9, page 76.) Two cubes with (a) normals at vertices perpendicular to each face, and (b) normals outward from the center of the cube. Note that (a) is rendered with Gouraud shading, not flat shading.

Color Plate 6. (Figure V.8, page 135.) A bump-mapped torus. Note the lack of bumps on the silhouette. Four white lights are shining on the scene plus a low level of ambient illumination. This picture was generated with the ray tracing software described in Appendix B.

Color Plate 7. (Figure V.10, page 138.) An environment map mapped into a sphere projection. This is the kind of environment map supported by OpenGL. The scene is the same as is shown in Figure V.11. Note that the front wall has the most fidelity and the back wall the least. For this reason, spherical environment maps are best used when the view direction is close to the direction used to create the environment map.

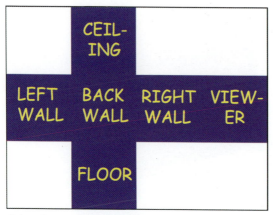

Color Plate 8. (Figure V.11, page 138.) An environment map mapped into a box projection consists of the six views from a point mapped to the faces of a cube and then unfolded to make a flat image. This scene shows the reflection map from the point at the center of a room. The room is solid blue except for yellow writing on the walls, ceiling, and floor. The rectangular white regions of the environment map are not used.

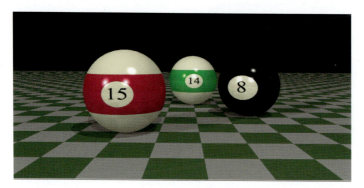

(a) No supersampling.

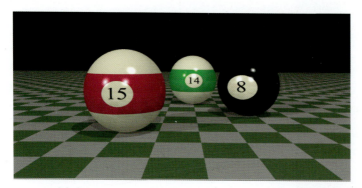

(b) Supersampling with jittered subpixel centers.

Color Plate 9. (Figure IX.9, page 245.) An example of antialiasing using jittered subpixel centers. (a) The scene rendered without supersampling; note the "jaggies" on the silhouettes of the balls, for instance. (b) The scene with pixels selectively supersampled up to a maximum of 40 times.

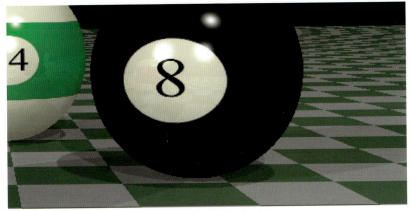

(a) No supersampling.

(b) Supersampling with jittered subpixel centers.

Color Plate 10. (Figure IX.10, page 246.) Closeup views of the images in figure IX.9.

Color Plate 11. (Figure IX.12, page 247.) An example of depth of field. The front of the eight ball is the focal plane. Note also the blurring of the checkerboard plane. In this image, each pixel is selectively supersampled up to 40 times. The eye positions and the subpixel positions were independently jittered as described on page 249.

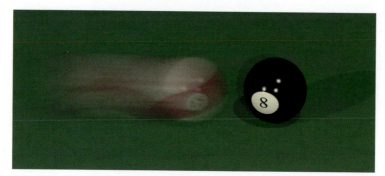

Color Plate 12. (Figure IX.13, page 248.) An example of motion blur. Pixels were selectively supersampled up to 40 times. Both motion supersampling and subpixel supersampling were used.

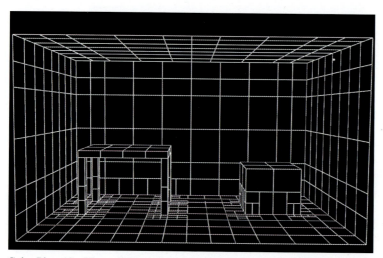

Color Plate 13. (Figure XI.1, page 273.) The patches used to render the radiosity scene of Figures XI.2 and XI.3.

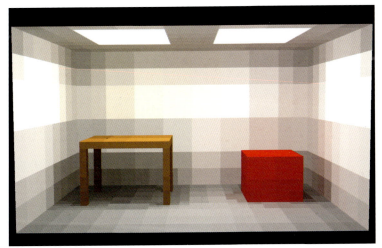

Color Plate 14. (Figure XI.2, page 274.) A radiosity-rendered figure with flat shading. It is evident that this image is based on the patches shown in Figure XI.1.

Color Plate 15. (Figure XI.3, page 274.) A radiosity-rendered figure with smooth shading of illumination. The red color of the box is reflected onto the nearby walls, giving them a slight reddish hue. This is based on the patches shown in Figure XI.1.

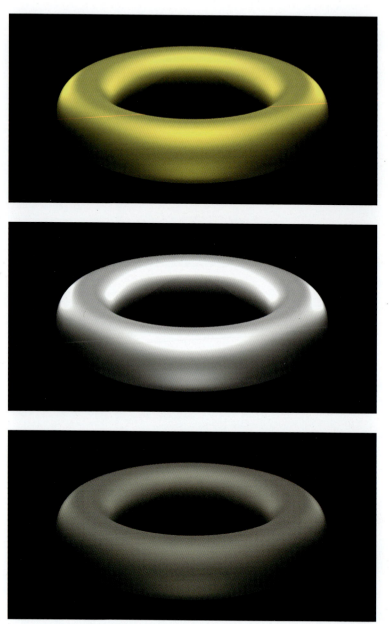

Color Plate 16. (Figure III.20, page 98.) Metallic tori with specular component computed using the Cook–Torrance model. The materials are, from top to bottom, gold, silver, and platinum. The roughness is $m = 0.4$ for all three materials. The tori are each illuminated by five positional white lights.

X

Intersection Testing

This chapter discusses issues in intersection testing and describes algorithms for intersecting rays with geometric objects. Intersection testing is one of the fundamental algorithms used in ray tracing, which usually requires intersecting a large number of rays against a large set of geometric objects. For this reason, it is often the case that the bulk of the computational time required for ray tracing is spent on intersection testing. Intersection testing has other applications besides ray tracing (for e.g., in motion planning and collision detection).

Intersection testing is a large and diverse field. In this chapter, we discuss only some of the first topics, namely, intersecting rays against simple geometric objects. We only briefly discuss methods such as bounding boxes and bounding spheres and global pruning methods such as octtrees and binary space partitioning. More information on intersection testing can be found in the book (Möller and Haines, 1999), which has two chapters devoted to this topic, including numerous references to the literature. The *Graphics Gems* volumes also contain many articles on intersection testing. For additional reading suggestions, see the end of this chapter.

Two important goals need be kept to in mind when designing software for intersection testing. The first design goal concerns *accuracy* and *robustness*. Clearly, it is important that the algorithms be accurate; even more so, the algorithms need to be free from occasional errors that may make visible artifacts, such as holes, or cause an occasional inconsistency in intersection status. For example, in ray tracing applications, it ought to be impossible for a path to be confused about being inside or outside a closed object such as a sphere. Similarly, for objects made up of multiple parts, say a cube made from six square faces, or a surface whose "faces" are Bézier patches, it should not be possible for roundoff error to allow a ray to pass through a "crack" between two faces without hitting the surface.

The second design goal for intersection testing is *speed*. It is often the case that intersection testing is the most computationally intensive part of a program. In particular, in ray tracing, most of the computation time is commonly spent on intersection testing. The reason for this is that there are typically numerous objects – hundreds, thousands, or perhaps many more – and one has to consider the possibility that each ray hits each object. Since the ray hits only one object, the time spent processing the actual hit is generally much less than the time spent determining which of the many objects is first hit. A subordinate principle is that what is really important is that one be able to determine very quickly when an intersection has *not* occurred. That is, it is often far more important to decide quickly when a ray does not hit an object than it is to decide quickly that a ray does hit an object.

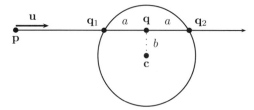

Figure X.1. The ray from **p** in direction **u** reaches its closest point to the center **c** of the sphere at **q**. The points $\mathbf{q}_1$ and $\mathbf{q}_2$ are the two places where the line intersects the sphere.

If a ray is being intersection tested against many objects, then it may be useful to preprocess the objects by arranging them hierarchically or by partitioning space with the use of octtrees or binary space partitioning trees. These techniques allow a quick rejection of many objects at once and thus intersection testing does not have to be performed against each individual object. We will discuss these techniques briefly at the end of the chapter; however, our main emphasis is on algorithms for testing whether a ray intersects an individual object.

X.1 Fast Intersections with Rays

In this section, we discuss algorithms for intersecting rays with several common surfaces in $\mathbb{R}^3$. We do not try to be encyclopedic in our coverage of intersection testing with rays but instead strive to show the issues and algorithms that arise in many common cases. We consider intersections of rays against spheres, planes, triangles, convex polytopes, cylinders, quadrics, and Bézier patches.

X.1.1 Ray versus Sphere Intersections

Assume that a ray and a sphere are fixed. The ray is specified by its starting position **p** and a unit vector **u** in the direction of the ray. That is, the ray is the set of points

$$\{\mathbf{p} + \alpha\mathbf{u} : \alpha \geq 0\}.$$

We will also talk about the *line* containing the ray, which we call the *ray-line*.

The sphere is specified by its center **c** and its radius $r > 0$ and is equal to the set of points at distance r from the center.

The ray–sphere intersection algorithm works by first finding the point **q** on the ray-line closest to the center of the sphere. (Refer to Figure X.1.) The point **q** will be equal to $\mathbf{p} + \alpha\mathbf{u}$, where α is a scalar measuring how far **q** is from **p** along the ray. A point **q** will be the closest point on the ray-line to the point **c** provided that the line from **q** to **c** is perpendicular to the ray; that is, the point **q** can be defined by

$$0 = (\mathbf{q} - \mathbf{c}) \cdot \mathbf{u} = (\mathbf{p} + \alpha\mathbf{u} - \mathbf{c}) \cdot \mathbf{u}.$$

Solving for α, using the fact that $\mathbf{u} \cdot \mathbf{u} = 1$, gives

$$\alpha = -(\mathbf{p} - \mathbf{c}) \cdot \mathbf{u}.$$

Therefore $\mathbf{q} = \mathbf{p} - ((\mathbf{p} - \mathbf{c}) \cdot \mathbf{u})\mathbf{u}$.

Once we have found **q**, we can check whether it lies inside the sphere by checking whether $||\mathbf{q} - \mathbf{c}|| \leq r$. Finding the norm of a vector involves calculating a square root, and so it is actually more efficient to check whether $||\mathbf{q} - \mathbf{c}||^2 \leq r^2$. The calculation of the square of the magnitude of a vector, say of $||\mathbf{w}||^2$, can be done with only three multiplications and two additions, and this is significantly more efficient than also using a square root. If **q** does not lie inside the sphere, then obviously the ray does not intersect the sphere.

When **q** does lie inside the sphere, let $b = ||\mathbf{q} - \mathbf{c}||$ and set $a = \sqrt{r^2 - b^2}$. Note that only the square of b is needed; however, a square root is needed to compute a. Then the ray-line intersects the sphere at the two points

$$\mathbf{q}_1 = \mathbf{p} + (\alpha - a)\mathbf{u} \qquad \text{and} \qquad \mathbf{q}_2 = \mathbf{p} + (\alpha + a)\mathbf{u}.$$

(See Figure X.1.) Now, if $\alpha - a \geq 0$, then the ray does actually hit the sphere at $\mathbf{q}_1$, and this is its first intersection with the sphere. However, if $\alpha < a$, then the point $\mathbf{q}_1$ lies in the wrong direction along the ray-line, that is, behind **p** on the line. In this latter case, we then check whether $\alpha + a > 0$; if so, then the point **p** lies inside the sphere and $\mathbf{q}_2$ is the point where the ray first hits the sphere.

Putting this together gives the following algorithm for ray–sphere intersection testing.

```
Ray-Sphere Intersection:
Input:  p and u describe a ray. u a unit vector.
        A sphere specified by center c and radius r.
Algorithm:
    Set α = -(p - c) · u;
    Set q = p + αu;
    Set bSq = ||q - c||²;
    If ( bSq > r² ) {
        Return "No intersection";
    }
    Set a = √(r² - bSq);
    If ( α ≥ a ) {
        Set q₁ = q - au;
        Return q₁;
    }
    If ( α + a > 0 ) {
        Set q₂ = q + au;
        Return q₂;
    }
    Return "No intersection";
```

As discussed in the introduction, the most important aspect of the computational speed of the algorithm is how fast it detects nonintersections. In the algorithm above, to get to the rejection test of $b^2 > r^2$ on line 4, one performs 9 multiplications, 11 additions, and 1 comparison on the assumption that the radius squared, r^2, has been precomputed.

If you know that the ray's beginning point **p** is never inside the sphere, it could be worthwhile to add a check for whether $\alpha > 0$ since $\alpha \leq 0$ means that the ray is not pointing towards the sphere at all. In ray tracing, this may be the case if the sphere is not transmissive. This extra test for nonintersection does not work so easily when it is possible for **p** to be inside the sphere. For that, you need to check both $\alpha > 0$ and $||\mathbf{p} - \mathbf{c}||^2 > r^2$, that is, check that **p** is outside the sphere and that the ray is pointing away from the sphere. This test then requires three extra multiplications, two extra additions, and two extra comparisons; thus, it is generally only marginally useful to perform this extra test.

Intersection tests for complicated geometric objects can be speeded up by giving the object a bounding sphere, which must completely enclose the object. To test whether a ray intersects

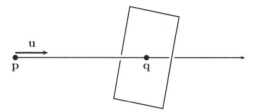

Figure X.2. The ray specified by its start position **p** and direction **u** intersects the plane at the point **q**.

the complicated object, you can first test whether the ray intersects the bounding sphere. If not, then it also does not intersect the geometric object. However, if the ray does intersect the bounding sphere, you must further test for intersection with the geometric object. The advantage of the bounding sphere is that it allows you to detect many cases of nonintersection *quickly*.

> **Exercise X.1** *Write an efficient pseudocode algorithm for bounding sphere testing. [Hint: Use the first part of the ray–sphere intersection algorithm, namely, the part through line 6 ending with the test for $b^2 > r^2$. Finish up by testing the condition "$\alpha > 0$ or $\alpha^2 \leq a^2$."]*

> **Exercise X.2**★ *An ellipsoid is specified by its center, three orthogonal axes, and three radii. The three orthognal axes and radii can be specified by three orthogonal vectors $\mathbf{v}_1$, $\mathbf{v}_2$, and $\mathbf{v}_3$, with each norm $||\mathbf{v}_i||$ equal to the inverse of the radius in the direction of $\mathbf{v}_i$: the ellipsoid is the set of points $\mathbf{x}$ such that $\sum_i ((\mathbf{x} - \mathbf{c}) \cdot \mathbf{v}_i)^2 = 1$. Formulate an efficient ray versus ellipsoid intersection algorithm.*

X.1.2 Ray versus Plane Intersections

A plane is specified by a normal vector **n** perpendicular to the plane and a scalar d. The plane is the set of points **x** satisfying $\mathbf{x} \cdot \mathbf{n} = d$.

If **p** and **u** specify a ray as usual, then, to intersect the ray with the plane, we first calculate the point **q** (if it exists) that is the intersection of the ray-line with the plane. This **q** will equal $\mathbf{p} + \alpha\mathbf{u}$ for α a scalar. To lie in the plane, it must satisfy

$$d \;=\; \mathbf{q} \cdot \mathbf{n} \;=\; \mathbf{p} \cdot \mathbf{n} + \alpha\mathbf{u} \cdot \mathbf{n}.$$

Solving for α yields

$$\alpha \;=\; \frac{d - \mathbf{p} \cdot \mathbf{n}}{\mathbf{u} \cdot \mathbf{n}}.$$

The quantities in this formula for α all have geometric meaning. If **n** is a unit vector, then the value $d - \mathbf{p} \cdot \mathbf{n}$ is the negative of the distance of **p** above the plane, where "above" means in the direction of **n**. For nonunit **n**, $(d - \mathbf{p} \cdot \mathbf{n})/||\mathbf{n}||$ is the negative of the distance of **p** above the plane. In particular, **p** is above (respectively, below) the plane if and only if $d - \mathbf{p} \cdot \mathbf{n}$ is negative (respectively, positive).

The dot product $\mathbf{u} \cdot \mathbf{n}$ is negative if the ray's direction is downward relative to the plane (with **n** defining the notions of "down" and "up"). If $\mathbf{u} \cdot \mathbf{n} = 0$, then the ray is parallel to the plane, and the usual convention is that in this case the ray does not intersect the plane at all. Even if the ray lies in the plane, it is usually desirable for applications to treat this as not intersecting the plane. The value of α is the signed distance of **q** from **p**. If $\alpha < 0$, then the ray does not intersect the plane.

These considerations give the following ray-versus-plane intersection algorithm:

```
Ray-Plane Intersection:
Input: p and unit vector u defining a ray.
       n and d defining a plane.
Algorithm:
  Set c = u · n;
  If ( c == 0 ) {
       Return "No intersection (parallel)";
  }
  Set α = (d − p · n)/c;
  If ( α < 0 ) {
       Return "No intersection";
  }
  Set q = p + αu;
  Return q;
```

Sometimes we want to intersect the ray-line against the plane instead, such as in the ray versus convex polytope intersection algorithm in Section X.1.4. This is even simpler than the previous algorithm, for we just omit the test for $\alpha \geq 0$:

```
Line-Plane Intersection:
Input: p and unit vector u defining a line.
       n and d defining a plane.
Algorithm:
  Set c = u · n;
  If ( c == 0 ) {
       Return "No intersection (parallel)";
  }
  Set α = (d − p · n)/c;
  Set q = p + αu;
  Return q;
```

Exercise X.3 *What would happen if we drop the requirement that the vector* **u** *be a unit vector? Show that the preceding algorithms would still compute the intersection point* **q** *correctly, but not the distance* α.

X.1.3 Ray versus Triangle Intersections

We next take up the intersection of a ray with a triangle. In principle, this can be taken as the fundamental intersection operation, because all surfaces can be approximated by planar patches – indeed by triangles.

A ray is, as usual, specified by its starting position **p** and direction **u**, with **u** a unit vector. A triangle can be represented by its three vertices v_0, v_1, and v_2, which are presumed to be noncollinear.

The first step in intersecting a ray with the triangle is to intersect it with the plane containing the triangle. Let **n** be a vector normal to the plane, and let d be the scalar so that the plane consists of those points **x** such that $\mathbf{n} \cdot \mathbf{x} = d$. By convention, the vector **n** is taken to be the "upward" direction, and we presume the triangle's vertices are ordered in the counterclockwise

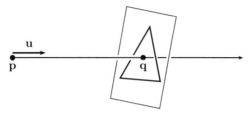

Figure X.3. Intersecting a ray with a triangle. The first step is to find the intersection $\mathbf{q}$ with the plane containing the triangle.

direction when the plane is viewed from above. Values for $\mathbf{n}$ and d can be computed by the following formulas:

$$\mathbf{n} = (\mathbf{v}_1 - \mathbf{v}_0) \times (\mathbf{v}_2 - \mathbf{v}_0)$$

$$d = \mathbf{n} \cdot \mathbf{v}_0.$$

The point $\mathbf{q}$ where the ray intersects the plane is found using the ray–plane intersection test of the previous section. This also gives the signed distance α from $\mathbf{p}$ to $\mathbf{q}$; if this test finds that $\alpha < 0$, then there is no intersection. By further examining the sign of either $\mathbf{u} \cdot \mathbf{n}$ or $d - \mathbf{p} \cdot \mathbf{n}$, one can determine whether the point $\mathbf{p}$ lies above or below the surface.

Once the point $\mathbf{q}$ has been found, we still need to determine whether $\mathbf{q}$ is inside or outside the triangle. One way to do this is by computing the barycentric coordinates of $\mathbf{q}$ relative to the triangle. They can be found using Equations IV.15 and IV.16 on page 107. To translate these equations to our present setting, we let $\mathbf{x} = \mathbf{v}_0$, $\mathbf{y} = \mathbf{v}_1$, $\mathbf{z} = \mathbf{v}_2$, and $\mathbf{u} = \mathbf{q}$. To find the barycentric coordinates of $\mathbf{q}$, we first calculate

$$\mathbf{e}_1 = \mathbf{v}_1 - \mathbf{v}_0$$

$$\mathbf{e}_2 = \mathbf{v}_2 - \mathbf{v}_0$$

$$a = \mathbf{e}_1^2$$

$$b = \mathbf{e}_1 \cdot \mathbf{e}_2$$

$$c = \mathbf{e}_2^2.$$

Here $\mathbf{e}_1$ and $\mathbf{e}_2$ are two of the edge vectors for the triangle. Then, calculate

$$D = ac - b^2$$

$$A = a/D$$

$$B = b/D$$

$$C = c/D.$$

Then let

$$\mathbf{u}_\beta = C\mathbf{e}_1 - B\mathbf{e}_2 \qquad \text{and} \qquad \mathbf{u}_\gamma = A\mathbf{e}_2 - B\mathbf{e}_1.$$

The barycentric coordinates α, β, γ, which represent $\mathbf{q}$ as $\mathbf{q} = \alpha\mathbf{v}_0 + \beta\mathbf{v}_1 + \gamma\mathbf{v}_2$ are found by

$$\beta = \mathbf{u}_\beta \cdot (\mathbf{q} - \mathbf{v}_0)$$

$$\gamma = \mathbf{u}_\gamma \cdot (\mathbf{q} - \mathbf{v}_0)$$

$$\alpha = 1 - \beta - \gamma.$$

The point $\mathbf{q}$ lies in or on the triangle provided that α, β, and γ are all nonnegative.

Putting this together gives the following algorithm. The algorithm is split into two phases. The precomputation calculates values that depend on the triangle only, and these values can be computed once and saved.

```
Ray-Triangle Intersection Algorithm
Input: p and unit vector u specifying a ray.
        v₀, v₁, v₂ specifying a triangle.
```
Precompute $\mathbf{n}$, d, $\mathbf{u}_\beta$, $\mathbf{u}_\gamma$:
```
    Set e₁ = v₁ − v₀;
    Set e₂ = v₂ − v₀;
    Set n = e₁ × e₂;
    Set d = n · v₀;
    Set a = e₁ · e₁;
    Set b = e₁ · e₂;
    Set c = e₂ · e₂;
    Set D = ac − b²;
    Set A = a/D;
    Set B = b/D;
    Set C = c/D;
    Set u_β = Ce₁ − Be₂;
    Set u_γ = Ae₂ − Be₁;
```
```
Main algorithm:
    Invoke Ray-Plane intersection algorithm to calculate q.
    If ( No ray-plane intersection exists ) {
        Return "No intersection";
    }
    Set r = q − v₀;
    Set β = u_β · r;
    If ( β < 0 ) {
        Return "No intersection";
    }
    Set γ = u_γ · r;
    If ( γ < 0 ) {
        Return "No intersection";
    }
    Set α = 1 − β − γ;
    If ( α < 0 ) {
        Return "No intersection";
    }
    Return q;
```

The algorithm above has been optimized for speed, not memory usage. Examination of the main algorithm shows that for each triangle we need to have the values $\mathbf{v}_0$, $\mathbf{n}$, d, $\mathbf{u}_\beta$, and $\mathbf{u}_\gamma$; this is four floating point numbers more than would be needed to store just the three vertices (but most applications would need to keep $\mathbf{v}_1$ and $\mathbf{v}_2$ too). There are several algorithms that use fewer precomputed numbers; see especially (Möller and Trumbore, 1997; Möller and Haines, 1999) for an algorithm that skips the stage of calculating $\mathbf{q}$. Those algorithms have the advantage of needing less memory, which can be important if there are many triangles; however, without storing the plane normal and scalar values, it is not possible to have such a quick intersection rejection test.

X.1.4 Ray versus Convex Polytope Intersections

A convex polytope in $\mathbb{R}^3$ is a region bounded by a finite number of planes.[1] In 3-space, convex polytopes are also called convex polyhedra, and examples include cubes, rectangular prisms (boxes), pyramids, and so on. In 2-space, the bounding planes are replaced by bounding lines, and so a convex polytope is the same as a convex polygon. The concept of polytope is easily extended to arbitrary dimension (in $\mathbb{R}^d$, the bounding planes are replaced by $(d-1)$-dimensional affine subspaces), and the algorithms we develop in this section apply equally well to all dimensions. However, to avoid confusion, we will just discuss the case of polytopes in $\mathbb{R}^3$.

Because we never consider nonconvex polytopes, we simplify terminology by omitting the adjective "convex" and using "polytope" to mean convex polytope.

After working out the rather complex algorithm for ray–triangle intersection in the previous section, one might fear that ray–polytope intersection algorithms would be even more complex. Surprisingly, and fortunately, this does not happen, and the algorithm for ray–polytope intersection is not particularly complicated.

Consider a fixed polytope. If there are k faces for the polytope, then the k planes bounding the polytope have normals $\mathbf{n}_i$ and scalars d_i for $1 \le i \le k$. By convention, the normals face outward from the polytope. Therefore, the polytope is the set of points $\mathbf{x}$ satisfying

$$\mathbf{x} \cdot \mathbf{n}_i \ \le \ d_i \qquad \text{for all } i = 0, 1, 2, \ldots, k.$$

That is to say, the polytope is the intersection of the k closed halfspaces bounded by the k planes.

To intersect a ray with a convex polytope, we first intersect the ray with each of the k bounding planes. For each plane i, we compute the intersection $\mathbf{q}_i$ of the ray-line with that plane along with the signed distance α_i from the originating point $\mathbf{p}$ to $\mathbf{q}_i$. In addition, we compute whether the ray-line hits the bounding plane from above or from below. By "from above," we mean that $\mathbf{u} \cdot \mathbf{n}_i < 0$ and that the ray direction vector $\mathbf{u}$ is pointing in the plane's downward direction. By "from below," we mean that $\mathbf{u} \cdot \mathbf{n}_i > 0$ and that the ray direction is pointing in the upward direction.

An intersection from above is also called a "front intersection," meaning that the ray-line has hit the plane from its front face and is entering the halfspace bounded by the plane. An intersection from below is also called a "back intersection," and the ray-line is hitting the back face and exiting the halfspace. The intersections are categorized as front or back intersections on the basis of the dot product $\mathbf{u} \cdot \mathbf{n}_i$ according to the following table:

Test	Meaning
$\mathbf{u} \cdot \mathbf{n}_i < 0$	Front intersection: ray-line entering halfspace
$\mathbf{u} \cdot \mathbf{n}_i > 0$	Back intersection: ray-line exiting halfspace
$\mathbf{u} \cdot \mathbf{n}_i = 0$ & $\mathbf{p} \cdot \mathbf{n}_i \le d_i$	Parallel ray below face: front intersection, $\alpha_i = -\infty$.
$\mathbf{u} \cdot \mathbf{n}_i = 0$ & $\mathbf{p} \cdot \mathbf{n}_i > d_i$	Parallel ray above face: back intersection, $\alpha_i = -\infty$.

The degenerate case of the ray's being parallel to the plane is treated by the convention that it hits the plane at $\alpha = -\infty$. However, in this case, it still needs treated as a front or a back intersection. This is consistent with the treatment of other front and back intersections in that it makes the following property hold:

---

[1] Generally, it is also required that the polytope be bounded, that is, not infinite in size; however, the algorithm we present does not require polytopes to be bounded.

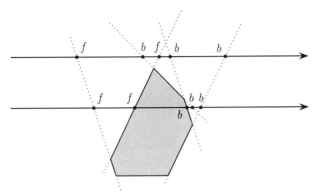

Figure X.4. The two rays are shown intersecting the bounding planes of the shaded polytope. Front intersections are labeled "*f* " and back intersections are labeled "*b*". The upper ray hits some back intersections before some front intersections and thus does not intersect the polytope. The lower ray hits all the front intersections before all the back intersections and thus does intersect the polytope.

Lemma X.1 *Let* $\mathbf{q}_i$ *and* α_i *be set for the* ith *plane as above. Let* $\mathbf{p}(\beta) = \mathbf{p} + \beta\mathbf{u}$. *Then,*

a. *If the intersection with the* ith *plane is a front intersection, then* $\mathbf{p}(\beta)$ *is in the halfspace bounded by the* ith *plane if and only if* $\beta \geq \alpha_i$.
b. *If the intersection with the* ith *plane is a back intersection, then* $\mathbf{p}(\beta)$ *is in the halfspace bounded by the* ith *plane if and only if* $\beta \leq \alpha_i$.

The proof of the lemma is immediate from the definitions.

The property of the lemma is the crucial idea behind the algorithm for intersecting a ray and a convex polytope. The algorithm calculates all the α_i and $\mathbf{q}_i$ values and categorizes them as either front or back intersections. It then lets

fMax $= \max\{\alpha_i : $ the ith intersection is a front intersection$\}$

bMin $= \min\{\alpha_i : $ the ith intersection is a back intersection$\}$.

The ray-line then intersects the polytope if and only if fMax $\leq$ bMin. If fMax ≥ 0, then the ray intersects the polytope boundary first at $\mathbf{p}($fMax$)$, and it is entering the polytope at this point. If fMax $< 0 \leq$ bMin, then $\mathbf{p}$ is inside the polytope, and the ray first hits the polytope boundary at $\mathbf{p}($bMin$)$; it is exiting the polytope at this point. If however, bMin < 0 or bMin $<$ fMax, then the ray does not intersect the polytope. Figure X.4 illustrates the idea for this intersection testing algorithm.

To verify all the assertions of the last paragraph, you simply note that, in order to be in the polytope it is necessary and sufficient to be inside all the half spaces simultaneously. The front intersections give the point where the line enters a half space, and the back intersections are where the line exits a half space.

We can now give the intersection algorithm based on the preceding constructions. We use $\pm\infty$ only as a shorthand notation for very large (in absolute value) positive and negative numbers.

```
Input:  A ray specified by p and a unit vector u
        k planes specified by normals nᵢ and scalars dᵢ.
Algorithm:
    Set fMax = −∞;
    Set bMin = +∞;
```

```
For i = 1, 2, ..., k {
    // Ray to plane intersection
    Set s = u · nᵢ;
    If (s == 0) {                        // If parallel to plane
        If ( p · nᵢ > dᵢ ) {
            Return "No intersection";
        }
        Else {
            Continue loop with next value of i;
        }
    }
    // If not parallel to plane
    Set α = (dᵢ − p · nᵢ)/s;
    If ( u · nᵢ < 0 ) {                   // If front intersection
        If ( α > fMax ) {
            If ( α > bMin ) {
                Return "No intersection";
            }
            Set fMax = α;
        }
    }
    Else {                               // Else, back intersection
        If ( α < bMin ) {
            If ( α < 0 or α < fMax ) {
                Return "No intersection";
            }
            Set bMin = α;
        }
    }
}                                        // End of for loop
If ( fMax > 0 ) {
    Set α = fMax;
}
else {
    Set α = bMin;
}
Return q = p + αu;
```

There are some notable special cases for which the preceding algorithm can be sped up. In particular, many common shapes like cubes, rectangular prisms, parallelepipeds, and k-DOP's (see Section X.2) have bounding planes that come in pairs with opposite faces parallel. For these, it is possible to speed up the algorithm by treating pairs of parallel faces simultaneously.

X.1.5 Ray versus Cylinder Intersections

The intersection of a ray with a cylinder can be done by combining the techniques for intersecting rays with spheres and polytopes. We consider only the case of right, circular, finite cylinders: such a cylinder is specified by a radius r, an axis $\mathbf{v}$, a center point $\mathbf{c}$, and a height $\mathbf{h}$. It is convenient to assume that $\mathbf{v}$ is a unit vector. The cylinder consists of the points that both lie within

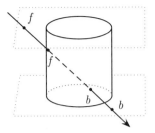

Figure X.5. A cylinder is the intersection of an infinite cylinder and the area between two parallel planes. The ray is shown hitting the top plane, then entering the (infinite) cylinder, then exiting the cylinder, and finally hitting the bottom plane. All the front intersections come before all the back intersections, and thus the ray does intersect the cylinder.

distance r of the line through $\mathbf{c}$ in the direction $\mathbf{v}$ and are between the two planes perpendicular to $\mathbf{v}$ that are distance $h/2$ away from the center $\mathbf{c}$. That is, the cylinder is the set of points

$$\{\mathbf{x} : ||\mathbf{x} - ((\mathbf{x} - \mathbf{c}) \cdot \mathbf{v})\mathbf{v} - \mathbf{c}||^2 \leq r^2\} \cap \{\mathbf{x} : ((\mathbf{x} - \mathbf{c}) \cdot \mathbf{v})^2 \leq (h/2)^2\}.$$

The cylinder is expressed as the intersection of two sets of points: the first set is the infinite height cylinder, and the second set is the region bounded between two parallel planes. Clearly, a cylinder is convex.

The algorithm to intersect a ray with this cylinder proceeds as follows. First, use essentially the method of Section X.1.1 to find where the ray-line intersects the infinite height cylinder: this gives zero, one, or two intersections. (Handle the case of the ray being parallel to the cylinder's axis as a special case.) If there is only one intersection, it is a glancing intersection and should be treated as being either zero or two intersections. If there are two intersections, categorize them as being front and back intersections much like what was done in the algorithm for ray-polytope intersection; the front intersection will always precede the back intersection. Otherwise, if the ray does not intersect the infinite cylinder, it also does not intersect the finite cylinder. Second, intersect the ray with the two parallel planes, getting its front and back intersections (the degenerate case of the ray parallel to the planes is best treated as a separate special case). Again, the front intersection will always precede the back intersection. Third, combine the (up to) four intersections in the same manner as was used for ray-polytope intersections. Figure X.5 illustrates the idea for this intersection testing algorithm.

> **Exercise X.4** *Fill in the details of the paragraph above and write an algorithm for ray–cylinder intersections.*

The `RayTrace` software package described in Appendix B includes more general cylinders, allowing them to have elliptical cross section and to have bounding planes that are not perpendicular to the central axis. We leave it to the reader as an exercise to work out efficient intersection algorithms for these.

X.1.6 Ray versus Quadric Intersections

A *quadric* is a surface in 3-space that consists of the points satisfying a polynomial of degree 2. That is, a quadric is a surface consisting of all points $\langle x, y, z \rangle$ satisfying an identity $f = 0$, where f is a function of the form

$$f(\langle x, y, z \rangle) = Ax^2 + By^2 + Cz^2 + Dxy + Exz + Fyz + Gx + Hy + Jz + K.$$

Examples of quadrics include spheres, ellipsoids, cylinders, paraboloids, and hyperboloids.

To intersect a ray with a quadric, let **p** and **u** specify the starting point and the direction of the ray as usual. Let $\mathbf{p}(\alpha)$ equal $\mathbf{p} + \alpha\mathbf{u}$. To find the points $\mathbf{p}(\alpha)$ that lie on the quadric, we need to find the values for $\alpha \geq 0$ such that $f(\mathbf{p}(\alpha)) = 0$. Since f is a polynomial of total degree two, the value of $f(\mathbf{p}(\alpha))$ is a polynomial of degree two,

$$f(\mathbf{p}(\alpha)) = a\alpha^2 + b\alpha + c.$$

Solving for values of α such that $f(\mathbf{p}(\alpha)) = 0$ can easily be done with the quadratic formula and yields 0, 1, or 2 solutions. The least nonnegative solution, if any, gives the first intersection of the ray with the quadric.

For ray tracing applications, you want to know not only the point of intersection but also the normal vector to the surface at that point. For a quadric, the normal vector can be found by using the method of Theorem III.2 on page 80 using the gradient of f. Except in degenerate cases, the gradient, ∇f, will be nonzero.

X.1.7 Ray versus Bézier Patch Intersections

Testing the intersection of a ray and Bézier patch can be a daunting task. In fact, there is no way to give a closed-form solution to the problem, and one must instead use iterative methods to find the intersection approximately.

There are several approaches to algorithms that perform ray-versus-Bézier-patch intersection testing. These basically fall into two categories: (a) Newton and quasi-Newton methods and (b) recursive subdivision methods.

Let a Bézier patch be given by a function $\mathbf{q}(u, v)$ that is, say, degree three in each of u and v, and let a ray be specified as usual by **p** and **u**. Finding an intersection is the same as finding values for u, v, and α so that $||\mathbf{q}(u, v) - \mathbf{p} + \alpha\mathbf{u}|| = 0$. Alternatively, one can define $d(\mathbf{q})$ to equal the distance from **q** to the ray-line. In this case, we are seeking values for u and v such that $d(\mathbf{q}(u, v)) = 0$. In both approaches, we are seeking the zeros of a function. Newton methods and quasi-Newton methods are methods that, at least in ideal situations, will iteratively compute points that converge rapidly to a solution. Papers that discuss (quasi-)Newton methods include (Toth, 1985) and (Joy and Bhetanabhotla, 1986).

Recursive subdivision algorithms are more straightforward but do not hold out the promise of fast quadratic convergence of the type that can be obtained from (quasi-)Newton methods. For this, a surface patch is given a bounding volume such as a bounding sphere or a bounding box. The ray is checked for intersections against the bounding volume. If an intersection occurs, then the Bézier patch is split into two subpatches using the de Casteljau subdivision algorithm, and the ray is recursively checked against both patches. The RayTrace software performs ray-versus-Bézier-patch intersections in this way using a bounding parallelepiped. The bounding parallelepiped is chosen so as to enclose the control points of the patch. This is sufficient, since the convex hull property guarantees that the entire Bézier patch lies in the convex hull of its control points.

A recursive subdivision algorithm for ray versus bicubic surface patch intersection was used already in the original publication on ray tracing (Whitted, 1980). A more sophisticated recursive subdivision algorithm is proposed by (Nishita, Sederberg, and Kakimoto, 1990), who subdivide Bézier patches into sizes smaller than half the size of the whole patch when this can be justified by convexity considerations. This allows for much faster convergence, particularly in cases in which the ray is hitting the patch at an angle significantly away from parallel to the surface.

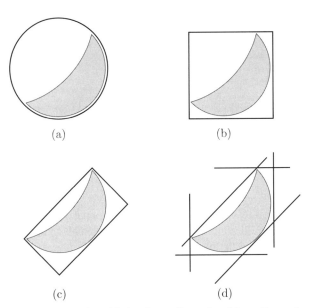

Figure X.6. Various kinds of two-dimensional bounding volumes enclosing a crescent shape. (a) A bounding sphere. (b) An axis-aligned bounded box (AABB). (c) An oriented bounding box (OBB). (d) A discrete oriented polygon (k-DOP) with $k = 3$.

X.2 Pruning Intersection Tests

We next discuss "pruning" methods that let us avoid having to perform so many intersection tests. For space reasons, we do not cover these in depth but instead give an overview of some of the more common techniques and provide some references at the end for further reading.

Several standard approaches are used to prune intersection tests. The first is to use bounding volumes to enclose objects. The bounding volumes are picked to be much simpler than the enclosed object and must completely enclose the object. If there is no intersection with the bounding volume, then there is also no intersection with the enclosed object. Common bounding volumes include bounding spheres, bounding boxes called AABBs and OBBs, and k-DOPs. Figure X.6 shows examples of these different types of bounding volumes. A bounding sphere is a sphere that completely encloses an object. An AABB is an *axis-aligned bounding box* and is a box whose edges are parallel to the standard x, y, z-axes. An OBB is an *oriented bounding box*: this is a box placed at an arbitrary orientation. Computing intersections against OBBs is more complex than against AABBs, but OBBs can sometimes more closely enclose an object and moreover have the flexibility to move with an object as it changes orientation. A k-DOP is a *discrete oriented polygon*: it is a convex polytope bounded by k planes, where the k-planes come in pairs so that opposite faces of the polytope are parallel (it is permitted for some planes to be extraneous and intersect the k-DOP in only a single point).

The second approach to pruning intersection tests involves partitioning space into regions. Each object lies in one or more regions. When a ray is tested for intersections with the set of all objects, the regions that the ray intersects are traversed one at a time: for each region that the ray enters, the ray intersection tests are performed for each object that intersects the region. There are a wide variety of ways to partition space. Representative methods include (a) room- or cell-based methods, (b) quadtrees or octtrees, (c) k-d trees, and (d) BSP trees.

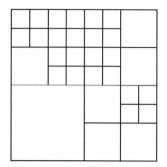

Figure X.7. A quadtree.

Room- or cell-based partitions apply well to situations in which space is partitioned into rooms or regions: typical applications that could use room-based partitions are 3-D models of houses or buildings and computer games where the player traverses rooms or other discrete regions. In a room-based partition, the extents of the rooms would usually be explicitly set by the designer of the 3-D model.

Quadtrees are used to partition 2-space hierarchically into square regions, as shown in Figure X.7. The root of a quadtree is an axis-aligned square containing the entire region of interest. It is split into the four subsquares obtained by dividing it into half horizontally and vertically. Each of these subsquares may themselves be split into four subsquares, and so on, recursively. The decision of whether to split a square into four sub-subsquares depends usually on how many objects intersect the region. The entire quadtree is stored as a tree structure, including pointers to allow traversal of the quadtree. Octtrees are the generalization of quadtrees to three dimensions: each node of an octtree is a cube and can be split into eight subcubes.

The k-d trees are generalizations of quadtrees and partition space (of any dimension) by using axis-aligned planes, as shown in Figure X.8. The root of a k-d tree is a rectangular box containing the region of interest. Each nonleaf node N in a k-d tree has two children (i.e., is split into two subregions). The two subregions are defined by choosing an axis and dividing the node N with a plane perpendicular to that axis. The most common way to choose the two subregions is by selecting a vertex v from an object in the region covered by N, choosing one axis, and splitting the region into two subregions based on v's coordinate for that axis. In 2-space this means choosing a vertical or horizontal line through v; in 3-space this means splitting the region with an axis-aligned plane through v. The advantage of k-d trees over quadtrees is that one can intelligently pick the vertex v and axis direction so as to try to divide

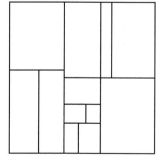

Figure X.8. A k-d tree in two dimensions. A region in a k-d tree can be subdivided by either a vertical or a horizontal line.

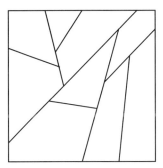

Figure X.9. A BSP tree in two dimensions.

into subregions that partition the objects into sets of approximately equal size. The hope is that the tree will have lower depth and be faster to traverse.

Binary space partitioning trees, known as BSP trees, generalize k-d trees by allowing the regions to be partitioned by an arbitrary plane rather than only axis-aligned planes (see Figure X.9.) Typically, the plane that divides a region is chosen so that it contains one of the faces of one of the objects in the region. The BSP trees were first introduced by (Fuchs, Abram, and Grant, 1983; Fuchs, Kedem, and Naylor, 1980), (see also the references in the Further Reading section below).

The third approach to pruning intersection tests is the use of hierarchical bounding volumes. This is actually a hybrid of the first two approaches. Typically, they work by first enclosing each individual object with a bounding volume, then enclosing pairs or small clusters of bounding volumes by another bounding volume, and recursively iterating this procedure until the entire scene in enclosed in a bounding volume. Oriented bounding boxes are a popular choice for these bounding volumes (see (Gottschalk, Lin, and Manocha, 1996)), but other types of bounding volumes can be used as well.

Further Reading: Some good textbooks that cover octtrees, BSPs, and related spatial data structures are (Samet, 1990a; 1990b) and (de Berg et al., 2000). (Möller and Haines, 1999) describe many algorithms for AABBs, OBBs, k-DOPs, and hierarchical methods.

This chapter has discussed only intersecting rays against three-dimensional objects. For many applications, one also wants to perform intersection tests on pairs of three-dimensional objects to determine if they have collided or interpenetrated: this is a much harder task in general. For an overview of intersecting three-dimensional objects, see (Möller and Haines, 1999), who discuss algorithms for intersecting simple objects such as spheres, boxes, and k-DOPs. Exact algorithms for intersection testing between general convex objects have been given by (Lin, 1993; Lin and Canny, 1991) and (Gilbert, Johnson, and Keerthi, 1988). As of this writing, at the University of North Carolina, the Geometry Group's Web site, http://www.cs.unc.edu/~geom, has numerous related papers and resources, including extensive downloadable software.

XI

Radiosity

Radiosity is a global lighting method that tracks the spread of diffuse light around a scene. As a *global* lighting method, it attempts to simulate the effect of multiple light reflection. Unlike basic ray tracing, which tracks only the specular transport of light, radiosity tracks only the diffuse transport of light.

The goal of a radiosity algorithm is to calculate the illumination levels and brightness of every surface in a scene. As an example, consider a scene of a classroom with fluorescent light fixtures, painted walls, a nonshiny tile floor, and desks and other furniture. We assume that there are no shiny surfaces, and thus no significant amount of specular light reflection. All the light in the room emanates originally from the ceiling lights; it then reflects diffusely from objects in the room, especially from the walls and floor, providing indirect illumination of the entire room. For instance, portions of the floor underneath the desk may have no direct illumination from any of the lights; however, these parts of the floor are only partly shadowed. Likewise, the ceiling of the room receives little direct illumination from the overhead lights but still is not dark. As a more extreme case, the bottom sides of the desk tops are partly shadowed but are certainly not completely dark: they are illuminated by light reflecting off the floor.

Another common example of a scene with diffuse lighting is a room lit by indirect light such as by a torchère. A torchère is a vertically standing, bright white light that shines up onto the ceiling of the room. The light reflects diffusely from the ceiling to illuminate the entire room even though essentially none of the room is directly visible to the light bulb. Radiosity can also model a room lit by indirect outdoor light.

Radiosity methods are, in many ways, complementary to ray tracing methods. Basic ray tracing tracks the global transport of specularly reflected light, whereas radiosity tracks the global transport of diffusely reflected light. Thus, radiosity is much better at softly lit scenes with subtle color shading, whereas ray tracing is better at rendering sharp shadows. Radiosity methods usually track the diffusely reflected light by starting at the light source and tracking the movement of illumination forward. Ray tracing generally starts at the view point position and tracks rays of light backwards (in the so-called forward ray tracing). For this reason, the results of ray tracing are view dependent, whereas the results of radiosity are view independent. Thus, radiosity can be used to preprocess a scene ahead of time, and once the radiosity algorithm is completed the scene can be traversed in real time without expensive computation. This means that radiosity is well suited to interactive walkthrough applications. By comparison, ray tracing cannot generally be viewed by a moving viewer in realtime, since the entire ray tracing procedure must be repeated for each change in the view position.

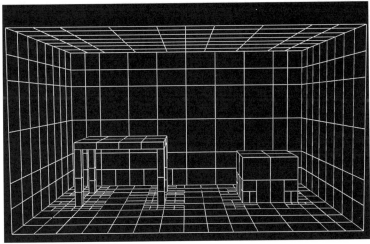

Figure XI.1. The patches used to render the radiosity scene of Figures XI.2 and XI.3. See Color Plate 13.

This chapter describes radiosity algorithms in some detail. However, before presenting the detailed mathematical algorithms, we give a high-level overview of radiosity algorithms.

Radiosity algorithms typically begin by breaking the scene into a set of flat polygons called "patches" (for an example, see Figure XI.1). The main goal of the radiosity algorithm is to compute an illumination level, or brightness, of each patch. For this, the radiosity algorithm assumes that each patch is uniformly lit. In addition, it is assumed that all light is reflected only diffusely; that is, it is only the total illumination of a given patch that is important, and the direction of the incoming illumination can be ignored. Some of the patches are light sources: these are called emissive patches. For the other polygons, we wish to determine illumination levels. This will be done by tracing the flow of all the light – from the light sources through multiple bounces – to determine the overall light levels for each patch.

After breaking the scene into patches, the radiosity algorithm computes "form factors." The form factors will be used to describe how much light reflects diffusely from one patch to another. For each pair of patches, their form factor measures the fraction of the light leaving the first patch that directly illuminates the second patch. For instance, if the first patch lies on the wall of the classroom and the second patch corresponds to one tile on the floor, the form factor would be equal to the percentage of the light leaving the wall's patch that goes directly to the tile.

Once the form factors have been determined, we set up equations that relate the patch illuminations and the form factors. These equations can be conveniently set up as a large system of linear equations. The remainder of the radiosity algorithm solves the system of equations to determine the level of illumination of each patch. Figure XI.2 shows an example of a scene with each patch illuminated according to the radiosity algorithm. In the figure, each patch is flat shaded, and so the scene does not look realistic. But, as the final step of the radiosity algorthm, an averaging procedure is applied to make each patch smoothly shaded. Figure XI.3 shows the result of smoothly shading the patches.

Although we will describe the radiosity algorithm as computing a single brightness value for each patch, in fact, we really mean for it to compute a different brightness level at each wavelength (typically, red, green, and blue). As a general rule, the same patches and the same form factors are used for all wavelengths.

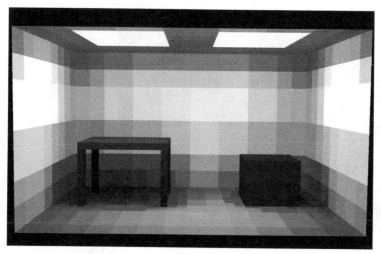

Figure XI.2. A radiosity-rendered figure with flat shading. It is evident that this image is based on the patches shown in Figure XI.1. See Color Plate 14.

XI.1 The Radiosity Equations

XI.1.1 Patches, Light Levels, and Form Factors

The first step in rendering a scene in the radiosity algorithm is to break the surfaces in the scene into a set of small flat patches. The main part of the radiosity algorithm will treat each patch as being uniformly illuminated, but in the end shading will be used to render the patches with smoothly varying illumination levels. It is important to choose patches sufficiently small that the assumption that each patch is uniformly illuminated will not cause too much error in the calculation. Thus, the illumination levels should not change very much between adjacent patches or within a single patch; otherwise, the radiosity algorithm may give poor results.

Figure XI.3. A radiosity-rendered figure with smooth shading of illumination. The red color of the box is reflected onto the nearby walls, giving them a slight reddish hue. This is based on the patches shown in Figure XI.1. See Color Plate 15.

An example of a scene broken into patches is shown in Figure XI.1, which shows a table and a box sitting in a room with the whole scene drawn as wireframe quadrilaterals. This is a particularly simple example of a scene to break into patches, for all the surfaces are already rectangular. However, complications arise even here because the changes in illumination levels are more pronounced near corners; thus, it helps to use smaller patches near corners.

Several important issues are involved in making a good choice for the patches. The smaller the patches, the more likely it is that the radiosity algorithm will succeed in calculating lighting levels well. On the other hand, the radiosity algorithm takes time at least $O(n^2)$, where n is the number of patches, and so the running time increases quadratically with the number of patches. Even worse, the memory usage is also $O(n^2)$. Thus, it is common to use some kind of adaptive meshing in which some patches are large and some patches are small. In Figures XI.1–XI.3, we used smaller patches near the sides of the room, near the box, and under the table: the idea is that patches should be smaller where the illumination levels are changing more rapidly.

We will not further discuss issues in how to choose patches (see (Cohen and Wallace, 1993; Sillion and Puech, 1994) for a discussion of good tactics for choosing patches). Instead, we henceforth assume that patches have already been chosen. We label the patches $P_1, P_2, \ldots, P_n$. We let A_i denote the area of patch P_i.

The central goal of the radiosity algorithm is to determine the average brightness of each patch P_i. For this, we define B_i to equal the light energy leaving patch P_i divided by the area of P_i. Thus, the brightness B_i measures the light energy per unit area averaged over patch P_i. Note that the B_i values are different from the intensity levels, denoted I, discussed in Chapter III. The intensities I were defined as light flux per unit area perpendicular to the direction of light propagation, whereas B_i equals light flux per unit of surface area. The reason for using brightness values instead of intensity levels is that we now are interested in the illumination levels for each individual patch rather than (at least for the moment) in the illumination that reaches a viewer. However, the assumption that the surfaces are Lambertian means the perceived brightness of a patch is proportional to its B_i value and independent of the viewing angle.

Often, the term "radiosity" is used for the values B_i, but we will use the more intuitive term "brightness."

We write B_i^{in} to denote the brightness of the total light shining onto patch P_i. The equation relating the incoming and outgoing brightnesses is

$$B_i = E_i + R_i \cdot B_i^{\text{in}}, \qquad\qquad \text{XI.1}$$

where E_i is the emissiveness of the patch and R_i is its reflectivity. Like the brightness values B_i and B_i^{in}, the emissiveness E_i is measured in terms of light energy per unit area. The factor E_i represents the amount of light being generated by the surface (as compared with being reflected by the surface). Positive values of E_i are used for patches that are light sources. For ordinary surfaces other than lights, E_i should equal zero. The reflectivity value R_i specifies the color of the patch. Since we are considering only a single wavelength, R_i is a scalar that equals the fraction of incoming light that is (diffusely) reflected by the patch. We require that $0 \le R_i < 1$. If $R_i = 0$, the patch is not reflective at all, and values of R_i close to 1 mean that the patch is highly reflective. Values of R_i close to 0 are appropriate for black surfaces, and values near 1 are appropriate for white surfaces.

Equation XI.1 gives a formula for the light leaving a patch in terms of the light incident on the patch. We also want to express the light incident to a patch in terms of the outgoing brightnesses of the rest of the patches. The light incident on a patch P_i should be equal to the total light leaving the other patches that directly illuminates patch P_i. To express this mathematically, let $F_{i,j}$ be the fraction of the light leaving patch P_i that shines directly onto patch P_j without reflecting off any intermediate patches. To handle the case of $i = j$, we let $F_{i,i} = 0$. The values $F_{i,j}$ are called *form factors*.

Since brightness is measured in terms of light energy per unit area, the total light leaving patch P_j is equal to $A_j B_j$. Likewise, the total light entering patch P_i is equal to $A_i B_i^{in}$. Therefore, the definition of form factors gives us

$$A_i B_i^{in} = \sum_{j=1}^{n} F_{j,i} A_j B_j. \qquad\qquad \text{XI.2}$$

We will see later that the form factors satisfy the following *reciprocity* equation:

$$A_i F_{i,j} = A_j F_{j,i}.$$

With this, equation XI.2 may be rewritten as

$$B_i^{in} = \sum_{j=1}^{n} F_{i,j} B_j. \qquad\qquad \text{XI.3}$$

Combining equations XI.1 and XI.3 gives the *radiosity equation*:

$$B_i = E_i + R_i \sum_{j=1}^{n} F_{i,j} B_j. \qquad\qquad \text{XI.4}$$

The radiosity equation can be rewritten in matrix form by letting

$$\mathbf{B} = \begin{pmatrix} B_1 \\ \vdots \\ B_n \end{pmatrix} \qquad \text{and} \qquad \mathbf{E} = \begin{pmatrix} E_1 \\ \vdots \\ E_n \end{pmatrix}$$

and letting M be the $n \times n$ matrix, $M = (R_i F_{i,j})_{i,j}$. Then, the matrix form of the radiosity equation is

$$\mathbf{B} = \mathbf{E} + M\mathbf{B}. \qquad\qquad \text{XI.5}$$

By letting I equal the $n \times n$ identity matrix, this can be rewritten as

$$(I - M)\mathbf{B} = \mathbf{E}.$$

The vector $\mathbf{E}$ of emissivities and the reflectivity values R_i are presumed to be known, and we will see how to compute the form factors $F_{i,j}$. It will then remain to compute the value of the brightness vector $\mathbf{B}$. One way to do this would be to invert the matrix $(I - M)$. However, matrix inversion is relatively time consuming and difficult, and so we discuss alternate, iterative methods of computing $\mathbf{B}$ in Section XI.3.

XI.1.2 High-Level Description of the Radiosity Algorithm

We can now describe the major steps in the basic radiosity algorithm. These are illustrated in Figure XI.4. The first step is to model the scene and break it into patches P_i. We presume that the emissivities E_i and the reflectivities R_i are given ahead of time.

The second step is to compute the form factors $F_{i,j}$. This typically is the computationally difficult part of the radiosity algorithm and consumes most of the time needed for the radiosity computation. We discuss a couple methods for computing form factors in Section XI.2. Once the form factors are computed, it is easy to compute the entries in the matrix M and set up the radiosity equation XI.5.

The third step is to solve the radiosity equation for the brightness levels $\mathbf{B}$. Several methods for solving this are presented in Section XI.3. These are iterative methods that mostly work

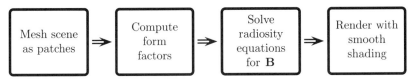

Figure XI.4. The four stages of the radiosity algorithm.

by chasing light around the scene from the light sources (i.e., patches with nonzero emissivity values) and calculating better and better estimates for the brightness levels of all the patches.

The fourth step is to render the scene. Each patch has been assigned a brightness (or color), but we do not merely want to render each patch as a flat color; instead, we want to use interpolation to render the surfaces with smooth shading. (Figures XI.2 and XI.3 illustrate the difference between flat and smooth shading.) To obtain smooth shading, we first use the brightness levels for each patch to set the brightness levels for each patch vertex. For instance, each patch vertex can be assigned a brightness equal to a weighted average of the brightness levels of the adjacent patches. Once the brightness level is set for each vertex, then the patches can be rendered by standard means using Gouraud interpolation. The use of interpolation and shading helps to smooth out the lighting and hide the fact that we computed a uniform average brightness level for each patch.

Several complications arise in the fourth step. First, the lighting levels will generally be only continuous – but not C^1-continuous – across patch boundaries, which can sometimes cause visible edges due to "Mach banding." The human eye is fairly sensitive to discontinuities in the first-order derivative of lighting levels, and this tends to make boundaries between patches more visible than expected. Second, if the patches are not uniform in size, one must be careful with adjacent patches that share an edge. This was already discussed at the end of Chapter II as well as on page 177 with Figure VII.15. If a larger patch shares part of an edge with another smaller patch, then the common edge should be split for rendering the larger patch too.

The first three stages of the radiosity algorithm in Figure XI.4 are *view independent*. The final, fourth state is view dependent of course, but this stage is computationally easy and efficient. For this reason, radiosity lends itself well to precomputation of lighting and allows interactive walkthroughs.

Figure XI.4 shows the most basic form of the radiosity algorithm. Frequently, one wishes to use adaptive methods to form patches: that is, on the basis of the quality of the solution obtained in the third stage, one may wish to refine the patches in areas where light levels are changing rapidly or where the solution otherwise needs more accuracy. Thus, sophisticated algorithms may alternate between solving the radiosity equations, and adding more patches and computing new form factors.

XI.2 Calculation of Form Factors

Recall that $F_{i,j}$ is equal to the fraction of the light leaving patch P_i that goes directly to patch P_j. Clearly, the values of $F_{i,j}$ are always in the interval [0, 1]. We assume that we have an enclosed environment so that all light leaving a patch hits some other patch; in other words,

$$\sum_{j=1}^{n} F_{i,j} = 1.$$

This holds without loss of generality, for, if necessary, we can add completely nonreflective black patches surrounding the environment.

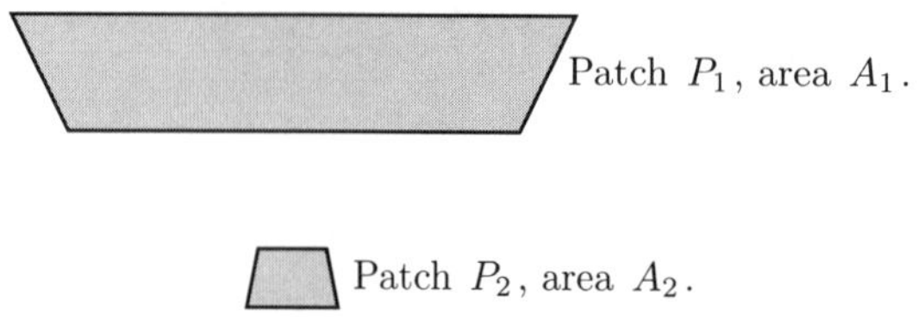

Patch P_1, area A_1.

Patch P_2, area A_2.

Figure XI.5. A large patch and small patch.

To aid our intuition about the values of $F_{i,j}$, consider the situation shown in Figure XI.5. Here, a small patch P_2 is facing upward, and centered above it is a large patch P_1 facing downward. We expect the value of $F_{1,2}$ to be small, since only a relatively small fraction of the light leaving the upper patch hits the small lower patch. Conversely, we expect the value of $F_{2,1}$ to be large because the larger patch P_1 fills much of the field of view of the smaller patch.

Now consider two small patches P_i and P_j obliquely facing each other, as shown in Figure XI.6. The distance between the centers of the patches is equal to d, and the normal vectors to the two patches make angles φ_i and φ_j with the line joining the centers of the two patches. Here we assume that φ_i and φ_j are both less than $90°$, for otherwise the two patches would not face each other and the form factors would be zero, $F_{i,j} = 0 = F_{j,i}$.

We make the further assumption that the patches are infinitesimally small so as to simplify estimation of the form factors. The patches have areas A_i and A_j. Consider the field of view of patch P_i. The other patch P_j has area A_j but is turned away at an angle of φ_j and is a distance d away. Consider what happens when patch P_j is projected towards P_i onto the unit sphere centered around P_i. The area that the projection of patch P_j occupies on that unit sphere is equal to $(\cos \varphi_j)A_j/d^2$. The area of the upper half of the unit sphere is equal to 2π; hence, the fraction of P_i's field of view that is occupied by patch P_j is

$$\frac{(\cos \varphi_j)A_j}{2\pi d^2}.$$

The surface of patch P_i is assumed to be Lambertian. A large Lambertian surface has the same apparent brightness from any viewing angle. But, as we remarked already on page 72, because of the foreshortening of areas when viewed obliquely the fraction of light that leaves the patch P_i in a direction at an angle φ_i from the normal is proportional to $\cos \varphi_i$. Therefore, the fraction $F_{i,j}$ of the light energy that leaves P_i in the direction of P_j is *proportional* to

$$\cos \varphi_i \frac{(\cos \varphi_j)A_j}{2\pi d^2}. \qquad\qquad \text{XI.6}$$

The constant of proportionality is set from the condition that the total light leaving patch P_i should of course be fraction 1 of the light. For this, we let S^{2+} denote the upper half of the

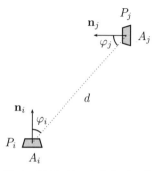

Figure XI.6. Two infinitesimally small patches P_i and P_j with areas A_i and A_j. The normals to the patches are $\mathbf{n}_i$ and $\mathbf{n}_j$.

unit sphere and, thinking of the patches A_j constituting the unit sphere around P_i, evaluate the integral

$$\int_{S^{2+}} \cos \varphi \, dA = \int_{\varphi=0}^{\pi/2} (\cos \varphi)(2\pi \sin \varphi) \, d\varphi = \pi.$$

Therefore, we need to drop the factor of 2 from Equation XI.6, and the form factor $F_{i,j}$ is equal to

$$F_{i,j} = \frac{(\cos \varphi_i)(\cos \varphi_j)A_j}{\pi d^2}. \qquad \qquad \text{XI.7}$$

One convenient property of the form factors is the reciprocity property that

$$F_{i,j}A_i = F_{j,i}A_j.$$

The reciprocity property is an immediate consequence of Equation XI.7. In some cases, the reciprocity property can effectively cut the work of computing form factors in half. Usually, the areas are known; thus, once the form factors $F_{i,j}$ with $i < j$ have been computed, the rest can be computed by using $F_{j,i} = F_{i,j}A_i/A_j$.

The preceding derivation of Formula XI.7 for the form factor is simple enough, but there are two potentially serious pitfalls. First, the formula was derived under the assumption that the two patches are infinitesimal but are separated by a noninfinitesimal distance d. Often this assumption does not hold, and, in this case, the actual form factor may be quite different from the value given by Formula XI.7. As a general rule, if the sizes of the patches are small compared with the distance d, then Equation XI.7 will be close enough to the correct value for practical purposes. Define the *diameter* of a patch to be the diameter of the smallest circle that contains the patch. Then if the distance d between the patches is at least five times the diameters of the patches, then Equation XI.7 is likely to be sufficiently accurate.

One might wish to have a better formula for the form factors that could be applied to (say) arbitrary rectangles. Such formulas can be derived for important special cases, but even in simple cases, such as two patches that share a common edge and meet at right angles, the formulas are quite complicated. Thus, if you want more accurate calculation for form factors, you must perform a double integral over the surfaces of the two patches. In practice, this means that the two patches are divided into multiple, sufficiently small subpatches, and the form factors between each subpatch of P_i and subpatch of P_j are computed using XI.7. These form factors are then combined to obtain the overall form factor $F_{i,j}$ for P_i and P_j.

The second pitfall in using Equation XI.7 concerns visibility. In other words, if there are other patches between P_i and P_j, then they can obstruct the light from P_i to P_j. Now, if the light from P_i to P_j is completely blocked, then $F_{i,j}$ is just equal to 0. On the other hand, if the light is only partially blocked, the form factor needs to be reduced by multiplying by the fraction of light from P_i that can reach P_j.

XI.2.1 The Ray Tracing Method

One method for computing the visibility between patches is to use ray tracing. We sketch a simple, and fairly robust, way to compute form factors with the aid of ray tracing.

The computation of the form factors will be based on Equation XI.7 but with an additional visibility term $V_{i,j}$, which is an estimate for the fraction of patch P_i that is visible from patch P_j. Note that we will have $V_{i,j} = V_{j,i}$. One way to compute $V_{i,j}$ is to cast rays from k positions on patch P_i towards k positions on patch P_j. Ray tracing is then used to determine if these rays intersect any intermediate objects. We then set $V_{i,j}$ equal to the fraction of rays that were not obstructed by intersections with intermediate objects.

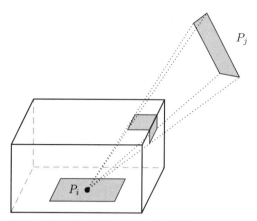

Figure XI.7. Projection onto a hemicube.

A good way to choose the k rays is to use the method of jittering discussed in Chapters V and IX. You can choose k jittered subpixel positions on each of P_i and P_j, then choose a random one-to-one correspondence between jittered positions in P_i and jittered positions in P_j, and cast rays between the corresponding points.

The rest of the form factor calculation is unchanged. We let $\mathbf{c}_i$ and $\mathbf{c}_j$ be the centers of P_i and P_j, let d be the distance from $\mathbf{c}_i$ to $\mathbf{c}_j$, and let φ_i and φ_j be the angles that the patches' normals make with the vector $\mathbf{c}_j - \mathbf{c}_i$. Then the form factor can be estimated by

$$F_{i,j} \;=\; V_{i,j} \frac{(\cos \varphi_i)(\cos \varphi_j) A_j}{\pi d^2}.$$

XI.2.2 The Hemicube Method

The hemicube method, introduced by (Cohen and Greenberg, 1985), is a method for computing form factors that takes advantage of hardware acceleration using the depth buffer algorithms present in most graphics chips. The hemicube algorithm computes the form factors for a particular patch P_i by rendering a view of the world from the viewpoint of patch P_i. For every other patch P_j, this rendered view can be used to determine what fraction of P_i's field of view is occupied by patch P_j. After compensating for distance and for the cosine factors, we obtain the form factor $F_{i,j}$.

The basic idea of the hemicube algorithm is illustrated in Figure XI.7. Here a virtual hemicube is placed over the center of an infinitesimal patch P_i. The hemicube is the top half of a cube with sides of length 2. The field of view occupied by patch P_j is projected towards P_i onto the hemicube. Clearly, the form factor $F_{i,j}$ is the same as the form factor from P_i to the projection of P_j.

This does not yet take visibility or occlusion into account. Now, for each of the five faces of the hemicube, the top and the four sides, we render a view of the scene from the center of P_i as seen through that face. This maps every other patch onto a (possibly empty) set of pixels of the viewscreen, and the depth buffer algorithm keeps track of which patches are visible in the direction of any given pixel. At the end of rendering the scene from the point of view of P_i, we do not display the rendered scene as usual but instead read the contents of the image buffer to determine which patch was visible at each pixel position.

We use a trick to determine which patch is visible in each pixel position. We do not render the patches in their correct color but instead assign to each patch P_j a distinct color C_j. Then,

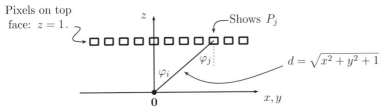

Pixels on top
face: $z = 1$.
Shows P_j
$d = \sqrt{x^2 + y^2 + 1}$

Figure XI.8. A row of pixels along the top of the hemicube. One pixel shows patch P_j. The origin is placed at the center of patch P_i. The top of the cube is the $z = 1$ plane.

P_j is visible at a given pixel position if and only if the pixel has been rendered with color C_j. Since there are typically $(256)^3$ many distinct colors, plenty of colors will be available to give each patch a distinct color.

The hemicube algorithm estimates the form factor $F_{i,j}$ as the sum of the form factors from P_i to the pixels showing P_j, namely, as

$$F_{i,j} = \sum_{\substack{\text{Pixels} \\ \text{showing } P_j}} (\text{fraction of } P_i\text{'s light that reaches pixel}). \qquad \text{XI.8}$$

Figure XI.8 shows the situation for a pixel in the top surface of the hemicube. Here a pixel containing the color of P_j is at coordinates $\langle x, y, 1 \rangle$ on the top surface of the hemicube, where the coordinates refer to the natural coordinatization of the hemicube relative to placing the origin at the center $\mathbf{c}_i$ of patch P_i. The distance from $\mathbf{c}_i$ to the pixel is $d = \sqrt{x^2 + y^2 + 1}$. The angles φ_i and φ_j are equal, and the cosine of this angle is equal to $1/d$. Thus, referring back to Equation XI.7, we find that the contribution to the summation XI.8 from pixels on the top of the hemicube is

$$\sum_{\substack{\text{Pixels on top} \\ \text{showing } P_j}} \frac{(1/d)(1/d)(Pixel\,Area)}{\pi d^2} = \sum_{\substack{\text{Pixels on top} \\ \text{showing } P_j}} \frac{(Pixel\,Area)}{\pi d^4},$$

where $d^4 = (x^2 + y^2 + 1)^2$. The "$Pixel\,Area$" value is equal to the area occupied by a single pixel on the top of the cube. Since the top of the cube is a 2×2 square, the pixel area will be $4/(w\,h)$, where h and w stand for "height" and "width," respectively, and are the dimensions of the image buffer measured in pixels.

Pixels from the view through the side faces of the hemicube contribute similarly to the form factor $F_{i,j}$. For instance, pixels on any of the four side faces of the hemicube, as shown in Figure XI.9, contribute the following amount to $F_{i,j}$:

$$\sum_{\substack{\text{Pixels on side} \\ \text{showing } P_j}} \frac{z(Pixel\,Area)}{\pi d^4},$$

where z is the z-component of the side face pixel.

There are some odd side effects that can arise when using the hemicube method. One phenomenon is that patches are treated asymmetrically when computing form factors. That is, when computing $F_{i,j}$ for i fixed and for all j's, we are essentially treating patch P_i as a single point, whereas we are treating the other patches as extended areas. Therefore, the reciprocity condition may no longer hold. On the other hand, it is still guaranteed that $\sum_j F_{i,j} = 1$; this is

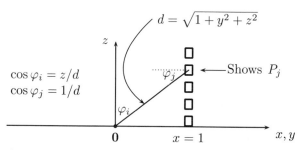

Figure XI.9. A row of pixels along the $x = 1$ side of the hemicube.

important because the convergence of the algorithms discussed in the next section for solving the radiosity equations depends on this fact. Finally, like any method based on discretization into pixels, the hemicube method is subject to errors involving aliasing.

XI.3 Solving the Radiosity Equations

We now assume that all patch geometry has been set and the form factors have all been computed; this means that the matrix M is completely known, and it remains to solve the radiosity equation XI.5 for the value of the brightness vector $\mathbf{B}$. The first section below will discuss theoretical issues, especially iterative methods that can obtain approximate values for $\mathbf{B}$. The basic iterative method, called Jacobi iteration, works by solving a fixed point equation by iterating a function. However, there are various ways to improve on this basic iteration. We give sketches of proofs that these various methods are guaranteed to converge. The remaining three sections describe the details of implementing successively better iterative methods for solving the radiosity equations.

XI.3.1 Iterative Methods

Recall that the matrix form of the radiosity equations is

$$(I - M)\mathbf{B} = \mathbf{E}.$$

The vectors $\mathbf{B}$ and $\mathbf{E}$ have n entries, M is an $n \times n$ matrix, I is the $n \times n$ identity matrix, and we assume that $\mathbf{E}$ and M are known. We wish to solve for the brightness vector $\mathbf{B}$.

Of course, one way to solve for $\mathbf{B}$ would be to invert the matrix $I - M$ and just set

$$\mathbf{B} = (I - M)^{-1}\mathbf{E}.$$

The problem with this is that inverting a large matrix can be computationally expensive and difficult to implement robustly. Because n is the number of patches in the scene, the matrix is indeed quite large, say on the order of $n = 10,000$ for moderately complex scenes. It is not hard to verify that the straightforward algorithms for matrix inversion require running time of $O(n^3)$, and so it would be prohibitively difficult to invert such a large matrix.

On the other hand, the matrix M enjoys several special properties, and there are iterative methods that can exploit these properties to get better and better approximations to the correct solution to the radiosity equation. These special properties of M are captured by the next lemma.

Definition The entry in the ith row and jth column of M is denoted $m_{i,j}$. We denote this by $M = (m_{i,j})_{i,j}$. Let $\max(M)$ be the maximum entry of M. Let $\text{RowSum}_i(M)$ be the sum of the entries in the ith row of M, that is,

$$\text{RowSum}_i(M) = \sum_{j=1}^{n} m_{i,j}.$$

Finally, let $\text{MaxRowSum}(M) = \max\{\,\text{RowSum}_i(M) : i = 1, \ldots, n\}$.

Lemma XI.1 *Let $M = (m_{i,j})_{i,j}$ be the matrix for the radiosity equation.*
(a) *For all i, j, $m_{i,j} \geq 0$.*
(b) *$0 \leq \text{MaxRowSum}(M) < 1$.*
(c) *Let $\alpha = \text{MaxRowSum}(M)$. For all $k \geq 0$,*

$$\text{MaxRowSum}(M^k) \leq \alpha^k.$$

In particular, $\max(M^k) \leq \alpha^k$.

Proof That (a) and (b) hold follows immediately from the definition of M. Each diagonal entry of M is zero, and each off-diagonal entry is equal to $m_{i,j} = R_i F_{i,j}$, which is certainly nonnegative. Thus, (a) holds. To prove (b), note that the sum of the entries in the ith row is equal to

$$\sum_{j=1}^{n} m_{i,j} = R_i \sum_{j=1}^{n} F_{i,j} = R_i.$$

As discussed in Section XI.1.1, the reflectances are strictly less than 1 for any realistic situation. Thus, each row sum is less than 1, and because there are finitely many rows the maximum row sum exists and is less than 1.

Now we prove (c). For k equal to 0 or 1, (c) is trivially true. The general case is proved by induction on k. First note that every entry in M^k is nonnegative. To prove the induction step, we need the following fact:

Claim *If $N = (n_{i,j})_{i,j}$ and $P = (p_{i,j})_{i,j}$ are arbitrary matrices containing only nonnegative entries, and if $\nu = \text{MaxRowSum}(N)$ and $\rho = \text{MaxRowSum}(P)$, then*

$$\text{MaxRowSum}(NP) \leq \nu\rho.$$

To prove the claim, note that the entry in row i and column k of the product NP is equal to

$$\sum_{j=1}^{n} n_{i,j} p_{j,k}.$$

Thus, $\text{RowSum}_i(NP)$ can be bounded by

$$\text{RowSum}_i(NP) = \sum_{k}\sum_{j} n_{i,j} p_{j,k} = \sum_{j} n_{i,j} \sum_{k} p_{j,k}$$

$$\leq \sum_{j} n_{i,j}\rho \leq \nu\rho.$$

That proves the claim, and now part (c) follows easily by using induction on k. $\qquad\square$

In particular, part (c) of the lemma implies that every entry in M^k is $\leq \alpha^k$. Thus, since $\alpha < 1$, the matrices M^k converge quickly to zero as k tends to infinity. With part (c) of the lemma proved, we are now able to establish that the matrix $I - M$ is invertible. One motivation for the next theorem comes from the Taylor series for the function $f(x) = 1/(1 - x)$. It is not hard to show, via the formula for Taylor series, that

$$\frac{1}{1-x} = 1 + x + x^2 + x^3 + x^4 + \cdots,$$

for all x such that $|x| < 1$. Thus, one might guess that a similar fact holds for the matrix $I - M$, namely,

$$(I - M)^{-1} = I + M + M^2 + M^3 + M^4 + \cdots,$$

where the role of the condition that $|x| < 1$ is now played by the property that MaxRowSum$(M) < 1$. This formula for matrix inverse does indeed hold, as the next theorem states.

Theorem XI.2 *Let M satisfy the properties of parts (a) and (b) of Lemma XI.1. Then $I - M$ is invertible, and its inverse is equal to the infinite sum*

$$I + M + M^2 + M^3 + M^4 + \cdots. \qquad \text{XI.9}$$

Proof We give a sketch of the proof. The first observation is that the summation XI.9 converges to a matrix N, where the limit N is a matrix in which all entries are finite. This is because each entry in M^k is in the range $[0, \alpha^k]$ and the geometric series $\sum_k \alpha^k$ has a finite limit.

Let N_k be the matrix equal to the first $k + 1$ terms in the series

$$N_k = I + M + M^2 + M^3 + \cdots + M^k.$$

As $k \to \infty$, $N_k \to N$, where N is the matrix given by XI.9. Now,

$$(I - M)N_k = (I - M)(I + M + \cdots + M^{k-1} + M^k)$$

$$= (I + M + \cdots + M^{k-1} + M^k) - (M + M^2 \cdots + M^k + M^{k+1})$$

$$= I - M^{k+1}.$$

Since $M^{k+1} \to 0$, we have $(I - M)N_k \to I$ as $k \to \infty$. By the continuity of matrix product, this means that $(I - M)N = I$. This proves the theorem. $\qquad \square$

An important consequence of Theorem XI.2 is that there is a unique solution **B** to the radiosity equation, namely, $\mathbf{B} = (I - M)^{-1}\mathbf{E}$. The theorem also suggests one method for approximating **B**: First, choose a value of k large enough so that M^k is expected to be sufficiently close to zero. Then, compute N_k, the first $k + 1$ terms of the power series. Then set $\mathbf{B} = N^k\mathbf{E}$, so that

$$\mathbf{B} = (I + M + M^2 + M^3 + \cdots + M^k)\mathbf{E}.$$

This would indeed work, but the runtime would still be much slower than we would like, for computing powers M^i of M requires iterated matrix multiplication and the usual algorithms for matrix multiplication have a fairly poor cubic runtime of $O(n^3)$ for $n \times n$ matrices. There are better algorithms for matrix multiplication, but even those are still not as good as we would like.

To find a faster algorithm, we cast the radiosity equation back into its original form $\mathbf{B} = \mathbf{E} + M\mathbf{B}$. We think of this as a *fixed point problem* by defining an operator Ω that acts on matrices by

$$\Omega(\mathbf{B}) = \mathbf{E} + M\mathbf{B}.$$

Then we are seeking a **B** (in fact, the unique **B**) such that

$$\Omega(\mathbf{B}) = \mathbf{B}.$$

We call such a **B** a *fixed point* of Ω. A standard way to solve fixed point problems is to choose an initial guess for the value of **B** and then repeatedly apply the operator Ω. If we are lucky (and we will be lucky in the present situation), repeatedly applying Ω yields a sequence of matrices that converge to a finite limit. In that case, the limit of the sequence will be a fixed point of Ω.

To make this more concrete, define a sequence of vectors $\mathbf{B}_0, \mathbf{B}_1, \mathbf{B}_2, \ldots$ by

$$\mathbf{B}_0 = \mathbf{0} \quad \text{(the zero vector)}$$

$$\mathbf{B}_{k+1} = \mathbf{E} + M\mathbf{B}_k,$$

for all $k \geq 0$. Thus, $\mathbf{B}_1 = \mathbf{E}$ and $\mathbf{B}_2 = \mathbf{E} + M\mathbf{E} = (I + M)\mathbf{E}$ and $\mathbf{B}_3 = \mathbf{E} + M\mathbf{E} + M^2\mathbf{E} = (I + M + M^2)\mathbf{E}$. For general k,

$$\mathbf{B}_{k+1} = (I + M + M^2 + \cdots + M^k)\mathbf{E}.$$

Therefore, by the earlier theorem and proofs, $\mathbf{B}_k$ converges to the solution of the radiosity equation as k increases.

The fixed point algorithm for approximating the solution **B** of the radiosity equation is mathematically equivalent to the power series algorithm. However, in the fixed point algorithm, each iteration uses only one matrix–vector product and one matrix addition. This takes time only $O(n^2 + n) = O(n^2)$ and is considerably faster than the power series algorithm, which required matrix multiplications.

There is a simple physical intuition for the meaning of the intermediate brightness vectors $\mathbf{B}_k$ obtained by the fixed point iteration method. The first nonzero one, $\mathbf{B}_1 = \mathbf{E}$, is just the directly emitted light. The second one, $\mathbf{B}_2 = \mathbf{E} + M\mathbf{E}$, is equal to the emitted light plus the illumination from a single bounce of the emitted light. The kth one, $\mathbf{B}_k$, is equal the lighting that results after $k - 1$ bounces of reflected light.

A useful property of the $\mathbf{B}_i$ vectors is that they are increasing. Let the notation $B_{k,i}$ represent the ith entry of $\mathbf{B}_k$. Then the increasing property states that, for all i, k, we have $B_{k,i} \leq B_{k+1,i}$. This is easy to prove by induction on k using the fact that every entry in the matrix M is nonnegative. Intuitively, this corresponds to the fact that the more reflection bounces that are taken into account, the brighter the scene gets.

The proofs of Theorem XI.2 and Lemma XI.1 give an estimate for the rate of convergence of the fixed point iterative algorithm. Namely, the errors of the entries N_k are bounded by $\sum_{i>k} \alpha^i = \alpha^{k+1}/(1 - \alpha)$, where α is the maximum reflectivity of the patches. Actually, the error tends to zero more like β^k, where β is the *average* of the reflectivities. Thus, not surprisingly, the lower the reflectivity values, the fewer the iterations that are needed to achieve a good accuracy. That is, the lower the reflectivities, the smaller the number of "bounces" that need to be followed.

The iterative fixed point method described above is the same as the Jacobi iteration given in more detail in the next section.

XI.3.2 Jacobi Iteration

The Jacobi method for solving the radiosity equation is just the iterative method described in the previous section. This algorithm successively computes $\mathbf{B}_1, \mathbf{B}_2, \mathbf{B}_3, \ldots$. Here is the algorithm expressed in terms of individual entries, rather than in terms of vectors.

```
JacobiIteration.
    // B[], E[] and Bnew[] are arrays. E[] is already set.
    // m[i,j] denotes m_{i,j}.
    // Initialization: set B = E.
```

```
For i = 1 to n {
  Set B[i] = E[i];
}
// Main loop.
While (not converged enough) {
  For i = 1 to n {
    Set Bnew[i] = E[i] + ∑ⁿⱼ₌₁m[i,j]*B[j];
  }
  For i = 1 to n {
    Set B[i] = Bnew[i];
  }
}
```

The algorithm uses the emissivity array **E** instead of the zero vector **0** for its initial brightness vector: this saves one iteration of the loop. The array Bnew[] is used to save a separate copy of B[] so that the previous values can be remembered long enough to compute the new values. Strictly speaking, there is no need to copy back the array values; instead, the two arrays could alternate roles on each iteration of the loop.

We have not shown any explicit test for whether the solution has converged sufficiently. Usually, this would just involve checking whether the change in value of B[*i*] is sufficiently small for all *i*. This can be tested by checking the values of Bnew[i]-B[i].

XI.3.3 Gauss–Seidel Iteration

The Gauss–Seidel method is an improvement of the Jacobi method that is easier to implement and converges to the solution faster. The new feature of the Gauss–Seidel method is that it does not save a copy of the old values of B[] but instead updates them immediately.

```
Gauss-Seidel Iteration.
  // B[] and E[] are arrays. E[] is already set.
  // m[i,j] denotes mᵢ,ⱼ.
  // Initialization: set B = E.
  For i = 1 to n {
    Set B[i] = E[i];
  }
  // Main loop.
  While (not converged enough) {
    For i = 1 to n {
      Set B[i] = E[i] + ∑ⁿⱼ₌₁m[i,j]*B[j];
    }
  }
```

The Gauss–Seidel method is sometimes called the *gathering method*. The reason for the name "gathering method" is that you can think of the computation's updating the brightness B_i of patch P_i (that is, B[i]) by setting[1]

$$B_i = E_i + \sum_j m_{i,j} B_j$$

as gathering together all the light from other patches to calculate the brightness of patch P_i. The difference with the Jacobi method is that we apply the update to B_i immediately instead

---

[1] This B_i should not be confused with the vector $\mathbf{B}_i$ (note the difference in font).

of waiting until the next loop iteration for the new value to take effect. Thus, the new value of B_i affects the updated values of B_j for $j > i$ in the same loop iteration.

It is not hard to show that the Gauss–Seidel algorithm converges to the correct solution of the radiosity equation. In fact, it is easy to prove, by induction on the number of gathering calculations, that the brightness values in the array B[] computed by the Gauss–Seidel method are less than or equal to the correct brightness values. In addition, if $\mathbf{B}_k$ denotes the brightness vector obtained after $k - 1$ iterations of the Jacobi algorithm loop, and $\mathbf{B}_k^{GS}$ the brightness vector obtained by $k - 1$ iterations of the Gauss–Seidel loop, then the entries in the vector $\mathbf{B}_k^{GS}$ are greater than or equal to the corresponding entries in $\mathbf{B}_k$. This fact is also easily proved by induction on k by again using the nonnegativity of the entries of M. Therefore, the Gauss–Seidel results are sandwiched between the results of the Jacobi iteration and the correct solution. Because the Jacobi algorithm converges to the correct solution, the Gauss–Seidel algorithm must also converge to the correct solution. In practice, the Gauss–Seidel method tends to converge noticeably faster than the Jacobi method.

XI.3.4 The Shooting Method

The shooting method, also known as the Southwell iteration method, is another iterative method for solving the radiosity equations. For both the Gauss–Seidel and Jacobi methods, a basic update step consists of choosing a single patch and updating its brightness level based on the brightnesses of all the other patches. The shooting method operates rather differently: the basic update step now chooses a single patch and sends (or "shoots") its brightness out to all the other patches. That is, instead of concentrating on a single receiving patch at a time, the shooting method concentrates on a single transmitting patch. To make this work, the shooting method must track, for each patch P_j, how much of its brightness level has not yet been taken into account by the brightness levels of the other patches P_i.

The shooting algorithm maintains two brightness values for each patch, B_i and ΔB_i. Both B_i and ΔB_i will always be nonnegative, and the overall brightness of the patch is equal to the sum $B_i + \Delta B_i$. The value ΔB_i represents the part of the brightness of patch P_i that has not yet been transmitted on to the other patches. The update loop consists of choosing a value for i and "shooting" the ΔB_i value to all the other patches, thereby updating the values of all the other patches to take into account the brightness due to ΔB_i.

The shooting algorithm is as follows.

```
Shooting_Method
     // B[] and ΔB[] and E[] are arrays.
     // Initialization.
     For i = 1 to n {
          Set B[i] = 0;
          Set ΔB[i] = E[i];
     }
     // Main loop
     While (not converged enough) {
          Choose j so that ΔB[j]*A_j is maximized;       // A_j = area of P_j
          Set B[j] = B[j] + ΔB[j];
          For i = 1 to n {
               Set ΔB[i] = ΔB[i] + m[i,j]*ΔB[j];
          }
          Set ΔB[j] = 0;
     }
```

```
// Finish up
For i = 1 to n {
    Set B[i] = B[i]+ΔB[i];
}
```

The choice of j was made so as to find the patch having the largest amount of outgoing light energy that has not been accounted for. Since the brightness values B[] are measured in terms of light energy per unit surface area, we multiply the unshot brightness value ΔB[i] times the patch area to measure the total outgoing light energy. Thus, this choice for j attempts to "shoot" the largest amount of light energy possible. Other choices for j could work well too, but it is important that every j value that still has unshot brightness get picked eventually.

The runtime of a single shooting operation is clearly just $O(n)$. For comparison, a single gather operation is also $O(n)$; the advantage of the shooting algorithm lies in the possibility that fewer shooting operations may be needed because the shooting algorithm concentrates its efforts on the patches with the most "unshot" light.

The test in the while loop for sufficient convergence would probably be based on a threshold value for the largest ΔB[i] * A_i value. The code written above assumes that the diagonal entries m[j,j] in the matrix are equal to zero.

> **Exercise XI.1** *Prove that, under the assumptions we have been making about the matrix M, the shooting method is guaranteed to converge to the correct answer. [Hint: Prove bounds on how fast the summation $\sum_i A_i \Delta B_i$ is decreasing. Use the reciprocity condition.]*

Further Reading: This chapter has covered only the most basic aspects of radiosity. Good sources for information on more advanced topics in radiosity are the books (Cohen and Wallace, 1993) and (Sillion and Puech, 1994). There is a hierarchical method of calculating form factors that can greatly reduce the computational work in very large scenes (Hanrahan, Salzman, and Aupperle, 1991) Advanced work in global lighting often combines techniques from radiosity and ray tracing.

(Ashdown, 1994) gives a theoretical description and complete code for a radiosity renderer.

XII

Animation and Kinematics

XII.1 Overview

The term *animation* refers to the process of specifying or controlling the movement of objects. Of particular concern to us in this chapter is the use of mathematical techniques to aid in the programming of animation.

Traditional animation techniques, used notably in movies, substantially predate computerized animation. Traditionally, animation requires drawing a series of pictures, each picture showing an instantaneous snapshot of objects in motion. These are then displayed in rapid succession, giving the visual effect of smooth motion. The same general idea applies to computer animation: a software program repeatedly renders a three-dimensional scene with each scene showing the objects at a particular point in time. These scenes are then displayed at a sufficiently fast frame rate to give the visual illusion of motion.

Nowadays, much of the work of animation is being taken over by computers. An artist will create objects, people, creatures, and so on as three-dimensional models in a CAD program. These models can include information about the formation and permissible motions of the objects. For instance, an object may have a skeleton of rigid links connected by joints, and the joints can be given characteristics that control their motion. The rest of the object can be controlled to move in synchronization with the skeleton. One such technique is called *skinning* and permits the "skin," or surface, of a creature to move in conjunction with the movement of the skeleton. Once a model has been properly created and the appropriate software is written, the task of an animator is simplified greatly: he or she needs to control only the motion of the skeleton to control the motion of the entire model. Furthermore, techniques such as *inverse kinematics* (IK) allow an even simpler interface for the animator; inverse kinematics permits the animator to set the positions or orientations of only a few selected portions of the skeleton, and the software can automatically control the rest of the skeleton.

The outline of this chapter is as follows. First, there is some general introductory discussion about topics including keyframing, motion capture, and applications of animation and of forward and inverse kinematics. Next, we discuss some problems in animation of position, including "ease-in" algorithms. Animation of orientation is covered next, including yaw, pitch, and roll, as well as an in-depth treatment of quaternions. The chapter concludes with forward and inverse kinematics for articulated rigid bodies (multibodies).

XII.1.1 Techniques Evolved from Traditional Animation

Many techniques from traditional animation are useful for computer animation. Space (and lack of knowledge) prevents us from covering very much traditional animation, but you can find extensive information on techniques traditionally used in animation in the books (Thomas and Johnston, 1981) and (White, 1986). (The former book has a thorough discussion of animation at Disney.) Traditional animation is certainly more of an art than a science, and considerable experience and talent were needed to devise styles of animation that produce visually pleasing results. Of course, using computers for animation is no less of an art than traditional animation.

Several mathematical aspects of computer animation are direct extensions of techniques used in traditional animation: two prominent examples are keyframing and motion capture.

Keyframing. *Keyframing* is the process of creating animated motion by specifying the positions of objects at *keyframes* and then filling in the motion in intermediate frames by interpolation. For traditional animation of movies, the keyframes, also called *keys*, are drawn by a senior animator. Other artists, *inbetweeners* and *inkers*, draw the intermediate frames and flesh out the complete detailed drawings. The keyframes typically show the extreme poses, or most critical poses. Initially, the keyframes can be in only rough form without complete details. The job of the inbetweener would be to draw the intermediate poses, being sure to make the motion look fluid and natural.

Keyframing is particularly important to the animation of full-length movies. A movie shows 24 frames per second, and thus there are too many frames for a single artist to draw all the frames in a movie. On the other hand, if multiple artists draw different parts of the movie, then consistency of style is lost. By employing a few senior animators to draw the keyframes and a larger number of inbetweeners and inkers, a movie can be drawn with a smaller number of senior animators. A single senior animator can handle the drawing of all keyframes for a particular character in the movie, providing more consistency of style.

The computerized analogue of keyframing and inbetweening is the use of splines for interpolating points. At keyframes, the positions, orientations, and shapes of objects in the scene are specified. Then, by using interpolating curves, one can obtain positions, orientations, and shapes of the objects as smooth functions of time. This often can be done fully automatically with Catmull–Rom or Overhauser splines, but manual editing can also be employed (e.g., using tension-continuity-bias splines).

Motion Capture. *Motion capture* is the measurement of the motion of (real-world) objects and the use of these measurements to guide animated motion. In early animated movies, motion capture consisted of filming live action. The filmed live action could be traced over to generate animated motion. For instance, to animate a fight scene, one might first film a movie of a two actors mock fighting. This could be translated into an animated fight by using the motion and timing of the filmed fight as the basis for the animated motion. Of course, the filmed motion capture does not need to be followed too slavishly. For instance, if one were animating a fight involving Daffy Duck, then one certainly would not want the movements of Daffy Duck to follow the motion of the actor exactly. Rather, the motions would be modified to reflect Daffy's physiology, and some aspects of the motion would be exaggerated for better artistic results. This kind of motion capture, when properly used, can greatly increase the fluidity and naturalness of the animated motion.

Modern versions of motion capture involve attaching sensors to actors that allow measurement of their three-dimensional motion. There are various types of motion capture sensors. Some motion capture systems work by using small devices (called diodes) that sense motion through electrical or magnetic fields; these magnetic sensors can provide both position and orientation data in real time. Optical motion capture systems work by attaching bright reflective spheres to the actors and tracking the spheres with multiple cameras: the multiple camera views can be combined to give three-dimensional positional information. Other systems work by attaching mechanical sensors to the actor's body that directly measure joint angles or bending, and so on. A small-scale example of this is the *data glove*, which can capture precise finger movements.

All approaches provide for measurement of the position of each sensor as a function of time. The motion capture data usually needs (often significant) processing to remove noise and distortion. After the motion capture data has been cleaned up, it can be translated into information about positions and joint angles. This detailed information about positions of parts of the bodies as a function of time can be used to control animated motion that is highly realistic. Typical applications include capturing the motion of actors performing movements such as walking, running, and fighting or of acrobats or athletes performing movements. These animated movements can be approximated by spline curves and played back to reproduce the captured motion as an animation.

XII.1.2 Computerized Animation

The kinds of systems that can be animated with the aid of computers include the following:

Particle Systems. Particle systems are collections of particles moving as a group. These can be used to simulate a wide range of phenomena, including smoke, fluids, and the flocking behavior of large crowds or large groups of creatures.

Rigid Bodies. A rigid body does not change shape as it moves but does change position and orientation. It may be controlled directly in terms of its position and orientation or indirectly in terms of velocity and angular velocity.

Articulated Rigid Bodies. Articulated rigid bodies, also called *multibodies*, are hierarchically connected assemblages of rigid bodies called *links*. The connections between the rigid bodies are generally joints. The joints may be rotational or translational; more complicated joints, such as screw joints, are also possible. Examples of objects that can be modeled as multibodies include skeletons of humans or other creatures; for this, the links are the bones of the skeletons. Other examples include robot arms and other mechanical linkages.

Flexible Objects. Flexible objects include cloth or rope as well as "squishy" or bendable objects.

Camera Viewpoint. An important element in many computer games is the use of a camera that follows the player around as he or she navigates an environment. The camera needs to follow the viewpoint of the player without having excessive jerkiness, oscillation, or other jitter.

Other Specialized Phenomena. Other applications of animation are diverse, including topics such as lightning, clouds, galaxy collisions, and many more.

The rest of the present chapter will be concerned with the animation of rigid bodies and of articulated rigid bodies.

The motion of rigid bodies can be completely described in terms of position and orientation. The specification of position is, at least from a mathematical viewpoint, quite straightforward. The position of an object is usually given by specifying the position of its center of mass, and the position consists of a single point in $\mathbb{R}^3$. Similarly, the velocity of an object (the velocity of the center of mass of the object, for instance) is just a single vector. Of course, both position and velocity will generally be functions of time. Section XII.2 will cover some simple topics involved in controlling the position of objects.

Specifying and controlling the orientation of a rigid body are more problematic. There are several possible ways to represent orientation, including rotation matrices, yaw-pitch-roll angles, and quaternions. Section XII.3 discusses these ways of representing rotation with particular attention to the theory of quaternions. It also discusses spherical linear interpolation (slerping) for interpolation between two quaternion specifications of orientation.

Articulated rigid bodies are taken up in Section XII.4. Techniques for animating articulated bodies can be divided roughly into two categories. The first category, *kinematics*, concerns the relationship between joint angles or, more generally, joint settings and the positions of the links. Typical concerns of kinematics include the relationships between, on the one hand, the joint angles and their rate of motion and, on the other hand, the positions and velocities of the links. The second category is *dynamics* and is concerned with physical properties such as forces, accelerations, energy, and so on. It is often convenient to subdivide techniques for animation of articulated objects further into four categories:

Forward Kinematics. The forward kinematics problem is as follows: Given settings for all the joint angles, determine the positions of all the links in the articulated structure.

Inverse Kinematics. The inverse kinematics, or IK, problem is as follows: Given a desired position for one or more links of an articulated object, determine settings for the joint angles that will achieve the desired position. For example, we set the position of one or more of the hands or feet of an animated person and then solve the IK problem to determine good settings for all the joints in the body that give the hands or feet the desired positions. Inverse kinematics allows an animator to set only the position of a small number of links; for instance, to simulate a person reaching for an object, the animator could specify the trajectory of the hand as a function of time and let the IK algorithm automatically determine the position of the joints and thereby the position of the rest of the body. Not surprisingly, the inverse kinematics problem is much more difficult than the forward kinematics problem.

Forward Dynamics. Forward dynamics is the same as physical simulation. If we are given the initial positions, orientations, velocities, and angular velocities (or essentially equivalently, if we are given the initial joint angles and rates of change of joint angles), and, if we are further given information about all external forces and torques, then we want to compute the movement of the articulated object as a function of time. This usually requires a physical simulation of the object's motion.

Inverse Dynamics. The inverse dynamics problem is usually considerably simpler than forward dynamics. Here, we are given the motions of all the links (or, equivalently, the motions of all the joint angles). The problem is to determine what forces must be applied, firstly at the joints and secondly from external sources, to obtain this motion.

Section XII.4 will treat the mathematical theory of forward and inverse kinematics. We will not discuss dynamics at all.

XII.2 Animation of Position

The position of an object at time u can be given by a single vector $\mathbf{q}(u)$. We have several tools for describing curves $\mathbf{q}(u)$, namely Bézier curves and B-splines. To animate position using keyframing, one picks times $u_0, u_1, \ldots, u_n$ and corresponding values for $\mathbf{q}(u_i)$ for each i. Then, Bézier or B-spline interpolation, as described in Sections VII.15 and VIII.13, can be used to describe the curve at arbitrary times u, for $u_0 \le u \le u_n$.

Often, one wants to animate nonpreprogrammed motion. By "nonpreprogrammed" we mean that the motion is not following a path determined in advance but is instead following a path in response to changing circumstances. A notable example of this is in interactive applications such as computer games. However, nonpreprogrammed motion can also be useful in noninteractive situations. A prime example of nonpreprogrammed motion is the motion of the camera, or viewpoint, in a computer game that must follow the movement of a player around a virtual world. The player could be a character moving on foot or could be a vehicle in a driving game, and so on. The camera then needs to follow behind the character, keeping the character and the environs in view. In addition, the camera needs to move smoothly without jerkiness.

One way to control a camera position is with techniques known as "ease-in." Ease-in refers to moving from a starting position to a desired position in a smooth, nonjerky fashion with no sudden changes in position or velocity and perhaps with an additional constraint of no sudden changes in acceleration. A real-world example of ease-in is the motion of a subway train or an airport tram as it stops at a station. The tram needs to stop smoothly with no sudden changes in acceleration that would jerk passengers, but it also needs to end up at a precise location so that the automatic doors line up correctly. The ease-in problem in computer graphics is much simpler to solve than the ease-in problem for trams because we do not have to deal with real-world considerations like brakes or with needing feedback to measure current velocity and position accurately.

XII.2.1 Ease In: Fixed Target

The *fixed-target ease-in* problem is as follows. At some time u_0, an object has position $\mathbf{p}_0$ and velocity $\mathbf{v}_0$. It is desired that at some future time u_1 the object have position $\mathbf{p}_1$ and stay there with velocity $\mathbf{0}$. The airport tram mentioned above is an example of the fixed-target ease-in problem.

A simple solution to this fixed-target ease-in problem can be given using degree three Hermite polynomials. (Hermite polynomials were defined in Section VII.5.) First, if $u_0 = 0$ and $u_1 = 1$, then we can let

$$\mathbf{q}(u) = \mathbf{p}_0 H_0(u) + \mathbf{v}_0 H_1(u) + \mathbf{p}_1 H_3(u)$$

and let $\mathbf{q}(u)$ specify the position at time u, $0 \le u \le 1$. It is easy to verify that this meets all the requirements of the ease-in problem. In addition, the position curve $\mathbf{q}(u)$ is a degree three polynomial and thus has a constant third derivative; consequently, the acceleration of the object is changing at a constant rate throughout the movement.[1]

For general $u_0 < u_1$, we need to make a change of variables by setting

$$J_i(u) = H_i\left(\frac{u - u_0}{u_1 - u_0}\right).$$

The functions J_i have properties similar to the Hermite functions but on the domain $[u_0, u_1]$ instead of on $[0, 1]$. Note, however, that the change of variables affects the first derivatives, and thus

$$J_1'(u_0) = \frac{1}{u_1 - u_0}.$$

---

[1] This solution would not be good enough for the above-mentioned tram example since the acceleration does not go smoothly to zero at $u = 1$.

The curve $\mathbf{q}(u)$ can then be defined for $u_0 \leq u \leq u_1$ by

$$\mathbf{q}(u) = \mathbf{p}_0 J_0(u) + (u_1 - u_0)\mathbf{v}_0 J_1(u) + \mathbf{p}_1 J_3(u).$$

Exercise XII.1 *The* fixed-target ease-out *problem is similar to the fixed-target ease-in problem but has initial position* $\mathbf{p}_0$ *and velocity* $\mathbf{0}$ *at time* u_0 *and needs to reach a target position* $\mathbf{p}_1$ *and velocity* $\mathbf{v}_1$ *at time* u_1. *Give a solution to the fixed-target ease-out problem based on Hermite polynomials.*

XII.2.2 Ease In: Moving Target

The moving target version of the ease-in problem is the problem of making an object both move smoothly and track a moving target. An example of this would be a camera position in a computer game; in a first-person exploration game, or in a driving game, the camera position needs to follow behind the player position smoothly. In this case, it is desirable for the camera to stay at a more-or-less fixed distance behind the player, but it is also important for the camera not to move too jerkily.

We will use the term "target position" to indicate the position we wish to track or approximate. The term "current position" means the current position of the object that is trying to track the target position. We assume that the animation is being updated in fixed time steps, each time step being of duration Δt. Let $\mathbf{t}_i$ denote the target position at time step i, that is, at time step $i \cdot \Delta t$. Let $\mathbf{c}_i$ be the current position of the tracking object at time step i. In each time step, we are given the target positions up through $\mathbf{t}_{i+1}$ and wish to compute $\mathbf{c}_{i+1}$.

We will discuss two versions of the moving-target ease-in problem. In the first case, suppose that neither the target nor the object has any inherent velocity. By "has inherent velocity," we mean that the object has enough mass or inertia that velocity should not change abruptly. In the case where neither the target nor the tracking device has inherent velocity, a very simple update is to set

$$\mathbf{c}_{i+1} = (1 - \alpha)\mathbf{c}_i + \alpha\mathbf{t}_{i+1}$$

for some fixed scalar α between 0 and 1. This defines the next position $\mathbf{c}_{i+1}$ as a weighted average of the current position $\mathbf{c}_i$ and the target position. The higher α is, the faster the object's position responds to changes in the target position but the greater the possibility of jumpy or jerky movement. The best value for α would depend on the time step Δt and on the particular application.

For the second case, suppose the target does not have a velocity, but the tracking object does. The current velocity of the tracking object can be approximated as

$$\mathbf{v}_i = \frac{\mathbf{c}_i - \mathbf{c}_{i-1}}{\Delta t}.$$

If the object were to keep moving at this velocity, then its next position would be

$$\mathbf{c}_i + \frac{\mathbf{c}_i - \mathbf{c}_{i-1}}{\Delta t}\Delta t = 2\mathbf{c}_i - \mathbf{c}_{i-1}.$$

However, we want also to incorporate the new target position so we can set

$$\mathbf{c}_{i+1} = (1 - \alpha) \cdot (2\mathbf{c}_i - \mathbf{c}_{i-1}) + \alpha \cdot \mathbf{t}_{i+1}.$$

This sets $\mathbf{c}_{i+1}$ to be an average of the target position and the position the object would reach if there were no change in velocity.

In both cases, the closer the value of α is to 1, the more tightly the object tracks the target; the closer α is to 0, the smoother, and less jerky, the motion of the object is.

XII.3 Representations of Orientations

We now turn to the problem of animating the orientation of objects. A rigid body's position in space can be completely specified in terms of the position of its center (its center of mass, say) and its orientation. The position of the center of the rigid body is specified by a single vector $\mathbf{q} \in \mathbb{R}^3$ and is readily amenable to keyframing and interpolation. Specifying the orientation of a rigid body is more problematic. There are several ways to represent orientations, and the best choice of representation depends on the application at hand.

Let us consider two examples of animation of orientation. As a first example, consider the orientation of a camera or viewpoint. The camera is given a position as usual, and then its orientation can specified by a view direction and an "up" direction, as was used by the gluLookAt command. Cameras usually have a preferred up direction, namely, pointing up along the y-axis as much as possible. As a second example, consider the orientation of a spacecraft traveling in deep space away from any planets or suns. There is no preferred "up" direction in space, and so the orientation of the spacecraft is essentially arbitrary when it is not moving. If the spacecraft is accelerating, or has nonzero velocity relative to its surroundings, the spacecraft has a preferred forward orientation direction; but even in this case, it would generally not have a preferred axial rotation (or roll amount).

This lack of a preferred up direction for spacecraft is somewhat counterintuitive to us, for we are so used to living on the surface of a planet. Indeed, in popular shows such as *Star Trek*, spacecraft always have an up direction and, furthermore, whenever two spacecraft meet in an episode of *Star Trek*, they always miraculously share the same up direction. That is, they never meet turned axially or facing each other upside down, and so on. Of course, this common up direction is unrealistic because there is no reason that there should be a shared "up" direction out in deep space. On the other hand, for spacecraft near a planet, there is of course a preferred up direction, namely away from (or towards) the planet. For instance, the U.S. space shuttle frequently orients itself so that its top side is facing the Earth.

When animating orientation, the decision of how to represent orientations is crucial. For applications that have a preferred up direction (such as cameras), it is probably useful to use the yaw, pitch, and roll representation. For applications that do not have a preferred up direction, and where it is necessary to blend or interpolate orientations, quaternions provide a good representation. We will discuss these representations, along with rotation matrices, in the next sections.

XII.3.1 Rotation Matrices

Specifying an orientation is essentially identical to specifying a rotation, namely, if we choose an initial orientation Ω_0, then any other orientation Ω can be specified in terms of the rotation that takes the body from Ω_0 to Ω. As was discussed in Chapter II, an orientation in 3-space can be described by an orthonormal 3×3 matrix that represents a rigid, orientation-preserving transformation.

A big drawback to using rotation matrices for animating orientation is that they cannot be interpolated or averaged in a straightforwardly. For instance, consider the following two rotation matrices:

$$\begin{pmatrix} 0 & 0 & 1 \\ 0 & 1 & 0 \\ -1 & 0 & 0 \end{pmatrix} \quad \text{and} \quad \begin{pmatrix} 0 & -1 & 0 \\ 1 & 0 & 0 \\ 0 & 0 & 1 \end{pmatrix}. \qquad \text{XII.1}$$

The first matrix represents a $90°$ rotation around the y-axis, and the second represents a $90°$ rotation around the z-axis. If you attempt to take the average of these two rotations by just adding the matrices and dividing by two, you obtain the matrix

$$\begin{pmatrix} 0 & -1/2 & 1/2 \\ 1/2 & 1/2 & 0 \\ -1/2 & 0 & 1/2 \end{pmatrix}.$$

The resulting matrix is not even orthonormal and certainly does not represent a rotation midway between the two initial rotations.

XII.3.2 Yaw, Pitch, and Roll

Yaw, pitch, and roll specify an orientation in terms of three successive rotations around the x-, y-, and z-axes. This is particularly useful for orientations in settings where there is a preferred up direction, such as for cameras or for airplane navigation.

Actually, yaw, pitch, and roll is only one example of a more general class of methods called *Euler angles*, which specify a rotation in terms of three rotations around three axes. There are many different forms of Euler angles depending (a) on the order in which the rotations are performed (i.e., on the order in which the axes x, y, and z are chosen for rotations), and (b) on whether the axes move with the object or remain fixed in global coordinates. Yaw, pitch, and roll performs rotation first around the y-axis (yaw), then around the x-axis (pitch), and finally around the z-axis (roll). The second and third rotations (pitch and roll) are around the local x- and z-axes that move with the object, not around the fixed x-, z-axes in world coordinates.[2] Figure XII.1 shows the effects of yaw, pitch, and roll on the orientation of an airplane.

So far, we have described the axes of rotations for yaw, pitch, and roll as being local axes that move with the object being rotated. An equivalent way to describe the rotations is as being made around the fixed x-, y-, and z-axes. By "fixed," we mean that the axes do not move with the object. However, as discussed in Section II.1.7, if fixed rotation axes are used, the rotations must be performed in the opposite order: first roll around the z-axis, then pitch around the x-axis, and finally yaw around the y-axis. This representation of yaw, pitch, and roll around fixed axes lets us give a formula for yaw, pitch, and roll. Let θ_y, θ_p, and θ_r be the yaw, pitch, and roll angles with directions of rotation determined by the right-hand rule. Then the effect of the yaw, pitch, and roll is the transformation

$$R_{\theta_y,\mathbf{j}} \circ R_{\theta_p,\mathbf{i}} \circ R_{\theta_r,\mathbf{k}}. \qquad\qquad\qquad\qquad \text{XII.2}$$

Exercise XII.2 *The methods of Chapter II let you express the rotations $R_{\theta_y,\mathbf{j}}$, $R_{\theta_p,\mathbf{i}}$, and $R_{\theta_r,\mathbf{k}}$ as 3×3 matrices. Use these to derive the formula for the rotation matrix of formula XII.2 in terms of the sines and cosines of the three angles. Your answer should have the form*

$$\begin{pmatrix} s_y s_p s_r + c_y c_r & s_y s_p c_r - c_y s_r & s_y c_p \\ c_p s_r & c_p c_r & -s_p \\ c_y s_p s_r - s_y c_r & c_y s_p c_r + s_y s_r & c_y c_p \end{pmatrix},$$

where $c_y = \cos\theta_y$, $s_y = \sin\theta_y$, etc.

---

[2] Our conventions for the names "yaw," "pitch," and "roll" and for the order in which the rotations occur are based on the assumption that the z-axis is the forward direction, the x-axis is the rightward direction, and the y-axis is the upward direction. The reader is warned that other conventions are often used.

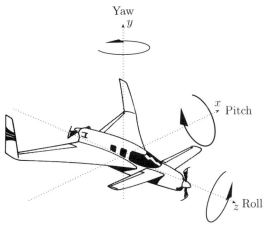

Figure XII.1. Yaw, pitch, and roll represent rotations around the y-axis, the x-axis, and the z-axis. If the axes move with the object, the rotations are performed in the order yaw, then pitch, and finally roll. If the axes are taken as fixed, then the rotations are performed in the opposite order: roll, then pitch, then yaw. Rotation directions are determined by the right-hand rule. The reader is warned that the rotation directions for pitch and yaw shown in the figure are opposite to customary usage in aviation. For us, a positive pitch means the nose dips down, and a positive yaw steers to the left. However, aviation conventions are that a positive pitch means the nose moves up, and a positive yaw means turning to the right. It is customary for positive roll to mean that the right wing dips, which agrees with our convention. In aviation conventions, the directions of the x and y axes are reversed with the x-axis pointing rightward and the y-axis pointing downward.

As we discuss in the next paragraph, yaw, pitch, and roll can sometimes lead to bad behavior of interpolation. On the other hand, yaw, pitch, and roll have the advantage of being intuitive. For instance, yaw, pitch, and roll are commonly used for airplane navigation since they correspond well to the controls available to a pilot. Yaw, pitch, and roll also work well for a camera. Actually, cameras usually do not use roll but instead keep roll equal to zero. The orientation for a camera can be given in terms of just yaw and pitch, and interpolating yaw and pitch values usually works well for interpolating camera orientation.

There are three ways in which the use of yaw, pitch, and roll can cause problems with interpolation. The first two are easy to circumvent, but the third one (gimbal lock) is more serious. First, when interpolating yaw, pitch, and roll, you need to keep in mind that if angles are changed by $360°$ the orientation is unchanged. For instance, when interpolating from a yaw angle of $170°$, to a yaw angle of $-170°$ (with pitch and roll both held fixed, say equal to zero), it is usually intended that the yaw vary by only $20°$ rather than rotating the other direction through $340°$. This is easily handled by adding $360°$ to the second angle and interpolating the yaw from 170 to $190°$. (The interpolated yaw values greater than $180°$ can of course have $360°$ subtracted back off if desired.)

The second potential pitfall with interpolating yaw, pitch, and roll is that every orientation has two distinct representations. Namely, the orientation represented by the angles θ_y, θ_p, and θ_r is identical to the orientation represented by the following yaw, pitch, and roll angles:

$$\theta_y' = \theta_y \pm 180°$$

$$\theta_p' = -\theta_p \pm 180° \qquad\qquad \text{XII.3}$$

$$\theta_r' = \theta_r \pm 180°,$$

where any combination of plus or minus signs may be used. Thus, care must be taken when interpolating yaw, pitch, and roll angles to decide properly whether to transform the angles according to Equations XII.3 before performing the interpolations.

The third, and most serious, problem with interpolation of yaw, pitch, and roll involves *gimbal lock*, which occurs when a degree of freedom is lost at particular angle settings (to be precise, at pitch equal to $\pm 90°$). As an example, consider interpolation between the following two orientations: Ω_1 is the "standard position" orientation given with yaw, pitch, and roll all equal to zero. Let Ω_2 be the orientation with yaw equal to $90°$, pitch equal to $-90°$, and roll equal to $-90°$. (You should visualize this! The airplane of Figure XII.1 in orientation Ω_2 would have its nose pointing up the y-axis and its bottom facing the positive z-axis.) The orientation Ω_2 suffers from gimbal lock since a degree of freedom has been lost: in particular, the yaw and roll axes have become effectively identical, and so changing either yaw or roll would have the same effect on the orientation Ω_2. Now suppose we try to use averaging to obtain an orientation midway between Ω_1 and Ω_2; straightforward averaging will give yaw equal to $45°$, pitch equal to $-45°$, and roll equal to $-45°$. This orientation is by no means intuitively midway between Ω_1 and Ω_2: indeed, the intuitive midway position would be obtained by rotating around the (global, fixed) x-axis. One could complain that this example is unfair, for it involves a pitch of $90°$ and results in gimbal lock; however, one could use instead a pitch very close to $90°$, say a pitch of $89°$, and then there would still be the same kinds of problems with interpolation.

> **Exercise XII.3** *Verify that yaw, pitch, and roll angles θ_y', θ_p' and θ_r' of Equations XII.3 represent the same orientation as θ_y, θ_p, and θ_r.*

XII.3.3 Quaternions

Quaternions provide a method of representing rotations by 4-tuples. Recall from Euler's theorem in Section II.2.4 that an arbitrary, rigid, orientation-preserving linear transformation can be expressed as a rotation around some fixed axis. Such a rotation is specified by a rotation angle θ and a rotation axis $\mathbf{u}$, where $\mathbf{u}$ is a unit vector: recall that this rotation was denoted $R_{\theta,\mathbf{u}}$. To represent $R_{\theta,\mathbf{u}}$ with a quaternion, let $c = \cos(\theta/2)$, $s = \sin(\theta/2)$, and $\mathbf{u} = \langle u_1, u_2, u_3 \rangle$. Then the 4-tuple q defined by

$$q = \langle c, su_1, su_2, su_3 \rangle$$

is called a *quaternion* and represents the rotation $R_{\theta,\mathbf{u}}$. We will see that quaternions provide a useful method of representing rotations in situations where there is no preferred up direction.

Most of the discussion to follow will give a theoretical development of quaternions. But before starting the theoretical treatment, we point out a few practical issues.

Note that the magnitude of the quaternion q as defined above is equal to one (strictly speaking this is not necessary, and we can also deal with nonunit quaternions; however, in practice, it is common to use only magnitude 1 quaternions). Conversely, suppose we are given an arbitrary 4-tuple of magnitude 1, say

$$r = \langle r_1, r_2, r_3, r_4 \rangle,$$

such that $r_1^2 + r_2^2 + r_3^2 + r_4^2 = 1$. Then, since $-1 \le r_1 \le 1$, we can set $\varphi = \cos^{-1}(r_1)$. Also, let $\mathbf{v} = \langle r_2, r_3, r_4 \rangle$ so that $||\mathbf{v}|| = \sqrt{1 - r_1^2}$. Since $\sin \varphi = \pm\sqrt{1 - r_1^2}$, the vector

$$\mathbf{u} = \frac{\mathbf{v}}{\sin \varphi}$$

is a unit vector. Finally, let $\theta = 2\varphi$. Then we have

$$r = \langle \cos(\theta/2), \sin(\theta/2)u_1, \sin(\theta/2)u_2, \sin(\theta/2)u_3 \rangle,$$

and so r is a quaternion representing the rotation $R_{\theta,\mathbf{u}}$. By this method, any unit 4-tuple represents a rotation. Nonunit 4-tuples can be normalized and thus also represent rotations.

Quaternions have the unexpected property that $-q$ represents the same rotation as q. This is because adding 360° to a rotation angle does not change the ending orientation. That is, $R_{\theta+360°,\mathbf{u}}$ is the same transformation as $R_{\theta,\mathbf{u}}$. Letting c, s, and q be defined from θ and $\mathbf{u}$ as above, we have $-c = \cos(\theta/2 + 180°)$ and $-s = \sin(\theta/2 + 180°)$. Thus, $-q$ is the quaternion that corresponds to the transformation $R_{\theta+360°,\mathbf{u}}$, and so $-q$ represents the same rotation as q.

We next take up the theoretical development of quaternions. The theoretical discussion culminates with practical considerations of how quaternions represent rotations and how to perform interpolation (slerping) with quaternions. For more discussion of how quaternions represent rotations, the reader can also consult (Hart, Francis, and Kauffman, 1994).

XII.3.4 Theoretical Development of Quaternions

Quaternions were developed by the mathematician W.R. Hamilton in 1843 to represent rotations in 3-space. The quaternions were invented (or discovered?) as a generalization of complex numbers. The complex numbers are of course obtained from the real numbers by including the number i, which is a square root of -1. Quaternions further extend the complex numbers by including a total of *three* square roots of -1, which are represented by i, j, and k. Thus, we have $i^2 = j^2 = k^2 = -1$. We wish to be able to multiply quaternions, and for this we need to define how the three new symbols i, j, k multiply with each other, namely,

$$
\begin{array}{lll}
i^2 = -1 & j^2 = -1 & k^2 = -1 \\
ij = k & jk = i & ki = j \\
ji = -k & kj = -i & ik = -j.
\end{array}
\qquad \text{XII.4}
$$

Note that this multiplication is not commutative; for example, $ij \neq ji$.

A quaternion q is defined to equal an expression of the form

$$d + ai + bj + ck,$$

where d, a, b, c are all scalars from $\mathbb{R}$. We also represent this quaternion by the 4-tuple $q = \langle d, a, b, c \rangle$.[3]

Two quaternions are defined to be *equal* if and only if they have exactly the same four components. (Two unequal quaternions may still represent the same rotation.) Addition of quaternions is defined component-wise, namely

$$
(d + ai + bj + ck) + (d' + a'i + b'j + c'k) = (d + d') + (a + a')i
$$
$$
+ (b + b')j + (c + c')k.
$$

The product of a scalar and quaternion is defined also as expected, namely,

$$\alpha(d + ai + bj + ck) = (\alpha d) + (\alpha a)i + (\alpha b)j + (\alpha c)k,$$

where $\alpha \in \mathbb{R}$. The product of two quaternions q_1 and q_2 is denoted $q_1 q_2$ (we reserve the dot product notation $q_1 \cdot q_2$ for the usual dot product). The definition of multiplication is more complicated than the definition of addition and is defined from the identities XII.4 using the

---

[3] There are various conventions on representing quaternions, and many authors put the scalar component last in the 4-tuple and might prefer the notation $\langle a, b, c, d \rangle$ for $d + ai + bj + ck$. Similarly, we later introduce the notation $\langle d; \mathbf{u} \rangle$, and these authors would typically prefer $\langle \mathbf{u}, d \rangle$ instead. We prefer to put the scalar component d first since it corresponds better to the way one treats complex numbers.

associative and distributive laws. This gives

$$(d + ai + bj + ck)(d' + a'i + b'j + c'k)$$

$$= dd' + da'i + db'j + dc'k + ad'i + aa'i^2 + ab'ij + ac'ik$$

$$+ bd'j + ba'ji + bb'j^2 + bc'jk + cd'k + ca'ki + cb'kj + cc'k^2$$

$$= (dd' - aa' - bb' - cc') + (da' + ad' + bc' - cb')i \qquad\qquad \text{XII.5}$$

$$+ (db' + bd' + ca' - ac')j + (dc' + cd' + ab' - ba')k.$$

This formula for multiplication is fairly messy but can be expressed more clearly with vector notation. Let $\mathbf{u}$ be the vector $\mathbf{u} = \langle a, b, c \rangle$. Then the notation $\langle d; \mathbf{u} \rangle$ is used as a shorthand notation for the quaternion $\langle d, a, b, c \rangle$. Letting also $\mathbf{u}' = \langle a', b', c' \rangle$, we can rewrite equation XII.5 as

$$(\langle d; \mathbf{u} \rangle)(\langle d'; \mathbf{u}' \rangle) \;=\; \langle dd' - \mathbf{u} \cdot \mathbf{u}'; d\mathbf{u}' + d'\mathbf{u} + \mathbf{u} \times \mathbf{u}' \rangle. \qquad\qquad \text{XII.6}$$

Thus, for $q = \langle d; \mathbf{u} \rangle$ and $q' = \langle d'; \mathbf{u}' \rangle$, the scalar component of the quaternion product qq' is equal to $dd' - \mathbf{u} \cdot \mathbf{u}'$, and the vector component is $d\mathbf{u}' + d'\mathbf{u} + \mathbf{u} \times \mathbf{u}'$.

Theorem XII.1 *Quaternion addition is commutative and associative. Quaternion multiplication is associative. The left and right distributive laws hold for quaternions, that is, for all quaternions q, r, s,*

$$q(r + s) = qr + qs \qquad and \qquad (r + s)q = rq + sq.$$

The theorem is proved by simple calculations, and we leave the proof to the reader.

On the other hand, we already mentioned that quaternion multiplication is not commutative; in Equation XII.6 the noncommutativity arises from the fact that $\mathbf{u} \times \mathbf{u}'$ is not generally equal to $\mathbf{u}' \times \mathbf{u}$. The noncommutativity may seem strange at first; however, you are already quite familiar with some other noncommutative systems. First, matrices (2×2 matrices, for instance) have addition and multiplication operations that satisfy properties similar to quaternions, and matrix multiplication is not commutative. As a second example, consider vectors over $\mathbb{R}^3$ with the usual vector addition and with cross product as the multiplication operation. Vector addition is of course associative and commutative. Furthermore, cross products are distributive over vector addition. However, the vector cross product is neither commutative nor associative.

The *norm*, or *magnitude*, of a quaternion $q = \langle d, a, b, c \rangle$ is defined to equal

$$||q|| \;=\; \sqrt{d^2 + a^2 + b^2 + c^2}.$$

We define the *conjugate*, q^*, of q to equal $q^* = \langle d, -a, -b, -c \rangle$. If $q = \langle d; \mathbf{u} \rangle$, then $||q|| = \sqrt{d^2 + \mathbf{u}^2}$, where $\mathbf{u}^2 = \mathbf{u} \cdot \mathbf{u}$. Also, $q^* = \langle d; -\mathbf{u} \rangle$. It is easily verified, from the definition of quaternion multiplication, that

$$qq^* \;=\; q^*q \;=\; \langle d^2 + \mathbf{u}^2; \mathbf{0} \rangle \;=\; ||q||^2. \qquad\qquad \text{XII.7}$$

A *unit quaternion* is a quaternion with norm equal to 1.

Exercise XII.4 *Let $q_1 = \langle \frac{\sqrt{2}}{2}, 0, \frac{\sqrt{2}}{2}, 0 \rangle$, $q_2 = \langle \frac{\sqrt{2}}{2}, 0, 0, \frac{\sqrt{2}}{2} \rangle$, and $q_3 = \langle 2, 0, 0, 0 \rangle$.*

a. Calculate $q_1 + q_2$, $q_1 - q_2$, and $q_1 + q_3$.
b. Calculate the products $q_1 q_2$, $q_2 q_1$, $q_1 q_3$, $q_3 q_1$, and $q_1(q_2 + q_3)$.
c. Calculate q_1^*, q_2^*, and q_3^*.
d. Calculate $||q_1||$, $||q_2||$, $||q_3||$, $||q_1 q_2||$, and $||q_1 q_3||$.

Exercise XII.5 *Give examples showing that the vector cross product is not commutative and not associative.*

A quaternion $\langle d; \mathbf{0} \rangle$ with zero vector component will be identified with the scalar $d \in \mathbb{R}$. This is compatible with the earlier definitions since the product dq is the same whether d is interpreted as a quaternion or as a scalar. Similarly, a vector $\mathbf{u} \in \mathbb{R}^3$ will be identified with the quaternion $\langle 0; \mathbf{u} \rangle$ with zero scalar component. Care should be taken when vectors are interpreted as quaternions because a vector cross product is *not* the same as a quaternion product. (Indeed, they could not be the same, for quaternion products are associative whereas vector cross products are not.) As an example, we have

$$(\mathbf{i} + \mathbf{j}) \times \mathbf{j} = \mathbf{k},$$

but,

$$(i + j)j = (\langle 0, 1, 1, 0 \rangle)(\langle 0, 0, 1, 0 \rangle) = \langle -1, 0, 0, 1 \rangle \neq \langle 0, 0, 0, 1 \rangle = k.$$

The next theorem discusses the scalar multiplication and multiplicative inverse properties for quaternions.

Theorem XII.2

a. *The scalar $1 = \langle 1; \mathbf{0} \rangle$ is the multiplicative identity, that is, $q = 1q = q1$ for all quaternions q.*

b. *Let $s = \langle s; \mathbf{0} \rangle$ be a scalar. Then $sq = qs$ for all quaternions q.*

c. *Let q be a nonzero quaternion. Then*

$$q^{-1} = \frac{1}{||q||^2} q^*$$

is the multiplicative inverse of q, that is, $qq^{-1} = q^{-1}q = 1$.

The proof of the theorem is by straightforward calculation; use Equation XII.7 to help prove part c. Note that if $q = \langle d; \mathbf{u} \rangle$ is a unit quaternion, then q^{-1} is very simply computable as $q^{-1} = \langle d; -\mathbf{u} \rangle$.

Exercise XII.6 *Let q_1, q_2, and q_3 be as in Exercise XII.4. Also, let $q_4 = \langle 1, 0, 1, 0 \rangle$. Calculate q_1^{-1}, q_2^{-1}, q_3^{-1}, and q_4^{-1}.*

Exercise XII.7 *Let q_1 and q_2 be arbitrary quaternions. Prove that $(q_1 q_2)^* = q_2^* q_1^*$ and that $(q_1 q_2)^{-1} = q_2^{-1} q_1^{-1}$.*

Exercise XII.8 *Let q_1 and q_2 be arbitrary quaternions. Prove that $||q_1 q_2|| = ||q_1|| \cdot ||q_2||$. [Hint: This can be proved with straightforward but messy algebraic manipulation; alternatively, a slick proof can be given using the previous exercise and Equation XII.7.]*

XII.3.5 Representing Rotations with Quaternions

We are now ready to (re)state the method by which quaternions represent rotations. Fix a unit vector $\mathbf{u}$ and a rotation angle θ. Recall that $R_{\theta, \mathbf{u}}$ is the rotation around axis $\mathbf{u}$ through angle θ with the rotation direction given by the right-hand rule. Let $c = \cos(\theta/2)$ and $s = \sin(\theta/2)$, and let q be the quaternion

$$q = \langle c, s\mathbf{u} \rangle = \langle c, su_1, su_2, su_3 \rangle.$$

The next theorem explains the basic method by which quaternions represent rotations: to rotate a vector $\mathbf{v}$ you multiply on the left by q and on the right by q^{-1}.

Theorem XII.3 *Let* **u**, θ, *and* q *be as above. Let* **v** *be any vector in* $\mathbb{R}^3$, *and set* $\mathbf{w} = R_{\theta,\mathbf{u}}\mathbf{v}$. *Then*,

$$q\mathbf{v}q^{-1} = \mathbf{w}. \qquad\qquad\qquad\qquad\qquad\qquad\qquad\qquad \text{XII.8}$$

Some comments are in order before we prove the theorem. First note that q, as defined above, is a unit quaternions, and so $q^{-1} = q^*$. So for unit quaternions we have $q\mathbf{v}q^* = \mathbf{w}$. Second, Equation XII.8 uses our convention on treating vectors as quaternions, and so another way of stating XII.8 is

$$q\langle 0;\mathbf{v}\rangle q^{-1} = \langle 0;\mathbf{w}\rangle.$$

Third, Equation XII.8 can also be used for nonunit quaternions. To see this, let α be a nonzero scalar and let $r = \alpha q$. Then $r^{-1} = (1/\alpha)q^{-1}$, and thus

$$r\mathbf{v}r^{-1} = (\alpha q)\mathbf{v}(\alpha^{-1}q^{-1}) = q\mathbf{v}q^{-1} = \mathbf{w}.$$

In other words, multiplying a quaternion by a nonzero scalar does not change the value of $q\mathbf{v}q^{-1}$. In this way, quaternions act very much like homogeneous coordinates since, if we are interested only in what rotation is represented by the formula $q\mathbf{v}q^{-1}$, multiplication by nonzero scalars has no effect. In most applications it is best to work with unit quaternions, which can be viewed as 4-tuples that lie on the unit sphere S^3 in $\mathbb{R}^4$. Conversely, each point on the unit sphere S^3 can be viewed as a quaternion.[4] Antipodal points on the sphere represent the same rotation, for q and $-q$ differ by a nonzero scalar factor.

In abstract algebra, a mapping of the form

$$\mathbf{v} \mapsto q\mathbf{v}q^{-1},$$

computed by multiplying on the left by a fixed element and on the right by its inverse is called an *inner automorphism*.

We now prove Theorem XII.3.

Proof (Theorem XII.3.) Let **u**, θ, and q be as in the statement of the theorem: in particular, **u** is a unit vector and q is a unit quaternion. Referring back to Figure II.14 on page 37, we write the vector **v** as a sum of two vectors $\mathbf{v} = \mathbf{v}_1 + \mathbf{v}_2$ such that $\mathbf{v}_1$ is parallel to **u** and $\mathbf{v}_2$ is perpendicular to **u**. By the distributive law, the map $\mathbf{v} \mapsto q\mathbf{v}q^{-1}$ is linear, that is,

$$q\mathbf{v}q^{-1} = q\mathbf{v}_1q^{-1} + q\mathbf{v}_2q^{-1} = \|\mathbf{v}_1\|(q\mathbf{u}q^{-1}) + q\mathbf{v}_2q^{-1}.$$

Therefore, it will suffice to prove

a. $q\mathbf{u}q^{-1} = \mathbf{u}$, and
b. $q\mathbf{v}_2q^{-1} = R_{\theta,\mathbf{u}}\mathbf{v}_2$ for $\mathbf{v}_2$ perpendicular to **u**.

First we prove a. by direct calculation:

$$\begin{aligned}
q\mathbf{u}q^{-1} &= [(\langle c; s\mathbf{u}\rangle)(\langle 0; \mathbf{u}\rangle)]q^{-1} \\
&= ((\langle 0 - s\mathbf{u}\cdot\mathbf{u}; c\mathbf{u} + s\mathbf{u}\times\mathbf{u}\rangle))q^{-1} \\
&= ((\langle -s; c\mathbf{u}\rangle))q^{-1} \\
&= ((\langle -s; c\mathbf{u}\rangle)(\langle c; -s\mathbf{u}\rangle))
\end{aligned}$$

---

[4]   The unit sphere S^3 is the set of points $\{\langle x, y, z, w\rangle : x^2 + y^2 + z^2 + w^2 = 1\}$. The superscript 3 means that the surface of the sphere is a three-dimensional manifold.

$$= \langle -cs + cs\mathbf{u} \cdot \mathbf{u}; s^2\mathbf{u} + c^2\mathbf{u} - cs\mathbf{u} \times \mathbf{u} \rangle$$

$$= \langle -cs + cs; (s^2 + c^2)\mathbf{u} \rangle$$

$$= \langle 0; \mathbf{u} \rangle = \mathbf{u}.$$

These calculations used the fact that $\mathbf{u}$ is a unit vector, and so $\mathbf{u} \cdot \mathbf{u} = 1$. In addition, $c^2 + s^2 = 1$ because $c = \cos(\theta/2)$ and $s = \sin(\theta/2)$.

We now prove b. We have $\mathbf{v}_3 = \mathbf{u} \times \mathbf{v}_2$ and $\mathbf{v}_3 \times \mathbf{u} = \mathbf{v}_2$, where $\mathbf{v}_3$ is defined as in Section II.2.3 (again, see Figure II.14 on page 37). We will explicitly compute $q\mathbf{v}_2 q^{-1}$. First,

$$q\mathbf{v}_2 = (\langle c; s\mathbf{u} \rangle)(\langle 0; \mathbf{v}_2 \rangle)$$

$$= \langle 0 - s\mathbf{u} \cdot \mathbf{v}_2; c\mathbf{v}_2 + s\mathbf{u} \times \mathbf{v}_2 \rangle$$

$$= \langle 0; c\mathbf{v}_2 + s\mathbf{v}_3 \rangle.$$

Then,

$$q\mathbf{v}_2 q^{-1} = (\langle 0; c\mathbf{v}_2 + s\mathbf{v}_3 \rangle)(\langle c; -s\mathbf{u} \rangle)$$

$$= \langle 0 + sc\mathbf{v}_2 \cdot \mathbf{u} + s^2\mathbf{v}_3 \cdot \mathbf{u}; 0 + c^2\mathbf{v}_2 + cs\mathbf{v}_3 - cs\mathbf{v}_2 \times \mathbf{u} - s^2\mathbf{v}_3 \times \mathbf{u} \rangle$$

$$= \langle 0; c^2\mathbf{v}_2 + cs\mathbf{v}_3 + cs\mathbf{v}_3 - s^2\mathbf{v}_2 \rangle$$

$$= \langle 0; (c^2 - s^2)\mathbf{v}_2 + (2cs)\mathbf{v}_3 \rangle.$$

$$= \langle 0; (\cos\theta)\mathbf{v}_2 + (\sin\theta)\mathbf{v}_3 \rangle$$

$$= R_{\theta,\mathbf{u}}\mathbf{v}_2.$$

The last equality follows from Equation II.8 on page 42. The next-to-last equality follows from the sine and cosine double angle formulas:

$$\cos(2\varphi) = \cos^2\varphi - \sin^2\varphi \quad \text{and} \quad \sin(2\varphi) = 2\cos\varphi\sin\varphi,$$

with $\varphi = \theta/2$. We have thus completed the proof of Theorem XII.3. $\qquad\square$

Using quaternions to represent rotations makes it easy to calculate the composition of two rotations. Indeed, if the quaternion q_1 represents the rotation $R_{\theta_1,\mathbf{u}_1}$ and if q_2 represents $R_{\theta_2,\mathbf{u}_2}$, then the product $q_1 q_2$ represents the composition $R_{\theta_1,\mathbf{u}_1} R_{\theta_2,\mathbf{u}_2}$. To prove this, note that

$$R_{\theta_1,\mathbf{u}_1} R_{\theta_2,\mathbf{u}_2}\mathbf{v} = q_1(q_2\mathbf{v}q_2^{-1})q_1^{-1} = (q_1 q_2)\mathbf{v}(q_2^{-1}q_1^{-1}) = (q_1 q_2)\mathbf{v}(q_1 q_2)^{-1}$$

holds by associativity of multiplication and by Exercise XII.7.

> **Exercise XII.9** *Let R_1 and R_2 be the two rotations with matrix representations given in the formulas XII.1 on page 295.*
>
> a. *What are the two unit quaternions that represent R_1? What are the two unit quaternions that represent R_2?*
> b. *Let $\mathbf{v} = \langle 1, 3, 2 \rangle$. Compute $R_1\mathbf{v}$ and $R_2\mathbf{v}$ using quaternion representations from part a. by the method of Theorem XII.3. Check your answers by multiplying by the matrices in XII.1.*

XII.3.6 Quaternion and Rotation Matrix Conversions

Because a quaternion represents a rotation, its action on $\mathbb{R}^3$ can be represented by a 3×3 matrix. We now show how to convert a quaternion q into a 3×3 matrix. Recall from the discussion on page 35 that a transformation $A(\mathbf{v})$ is represented by the matrix $(\mathbf{w}_1 \ \mathbf{w}_2 \ \mathbf{w}_3)$, where the columns $\mathbf{w}_i$ are equal to $A(\mathbf{i})$, $A(\mathbf{j})$, and $A(\mathbf{k})$. Thus, to represent a quaternion q by a matrix, we set

$$\mathbf{w}_1 = q\mathbf{i}q^{-1}, \qquad \mathbf{w}_2 = q\mathbf{j}q^{-1}, \qquad \text{and} \quad \mathbf{w}_3 = q\mathbf{k}q^{-1},$$

and then the matrix representation will be $(\mathbf{w}_1 \ \mathbf{w}_2 \ \mathbf{w}_3)$.

Let $q = \langle d, a, b, c \rangle$ be a unit quaternion. To compute $q\mathbf{i}q^{-1}$, first compute

$$(\langle d, a, b, c \rangle)(\langle 0, 1, 0, 0 \rangle) = \langle -a, d, c, -b \rangle.$$

Then, since $q^{-1} = \langle d, -a, -b, -c \rangle$, compute $q\mathbf{i}q^{-1}$ by

$$(\langle -a, d, c, -b \rangle)(\langle d, -a, -b, -c \rangle) = \langle 0, d^2 + a^2 - b^2 - c^2, 2ab + 2cd, 2ac - 2bd \rangle.$$

Similar computations give

$$q\mathbf{j}q^{-1} = \langle 0, 2ab - 2cd, d^2 - a^2 + b^2 - c^2, 2bc + 2ad \rangle$$

$$q\mathbf{k}q^{-1} = \langle 0, 2ac + 2bd, 2bc - 2ad, d^2 - a^2 - b^2 + c^2 \rangle.$$

Thus, the matrix representing the same rotation as the quaternion $\langle d, a, b, c \rangle$ is

$$\begin{pmatrix} d^2 + a^2 - b^2 - c^2 & 2ab - 2cd & 2ac + 2bd \\ 2ab + 2cd & d^2 - a^2 + b^2 - c^2 & 2bc - 2ad \\ 2ac - 2bd & 2bc + 2ad & d^2 - a^2 - b^2 + c^2 \end{pmatrix}. \qquad \text{XII.9}$$

A 3×3 matrix that represents a rotation can also be transformed into a quaternion. For this, we are given a matrix $M = (m_{i,j})$ and want to find a quaternion $q = \langle d, a, b, c \rangle$ such that M is equal to XII.9. Furthermore, the quaternion will be a unit quaternion with $d^2 + a^2 + b^2 + c^2 = 1$. Since q and $-q$ represent the same rotation, there are two possible answers.

There are several methods for converting M into a quaternion (see (Klumpp, 1976; Spurrier, 1978; Shepperd, 1978)). We follow the algorithm of (Shepperd, 1978). The algorithm is also similar to the one given in Section II.2.3 to convert a rotation matrix into a rotation axis and rotation angle.

The first step in the derivation of a quaternion from a matrix is to note the following identities:

$$\begin{aligned} m_{2,1} + m_{1,2} &= 4ab & m_{1,3} + m_{3,1} &= 4ac & m_{3,2} + m_{2,3} &= 4bc \\ m_{2,1} - m_{1,2} &= 4cd & m_{1,3} - m_{3,1} &= 4bd & m_{3,2} - m_{2,3} &= 4ad. \end{aligned} \qquad \text{XII.10}$$

If we know one of the values of d, a, b, c, and if this value is nonzero, then we can solve for the other three values by using the appropriate three of these six equations. For instance, if we have the value for d, then we can solve for a, b, c by using the bottom three equations; note that this requires dividing by d and thus works only if d is nonzero.

The *trace* of M is equal to the sum of its diagonal elements:

$$T = m_{1,1} + m_{2,2} + m_{3,3} = 3d^2 - a^2 - b^2 - c^2 = 4d^2 - 1,$$

where the last step used $d^2 + a^2 + b^2 + c^2 = 1$. It is convenient also to use the notation $m_{0,0}$ for the trace, that is, set $m_{0,0} = T$. Then, we have

$$2m_{0,0} - T = T = 3d^2 - a^2 - b^2 - c^2 = 4d^2 - 1$$

$$2m_{1,1} - T = -d^2 + 3a^2 - b^2 - c^2 = 4a^2 - 1$$

$$2m_{2,2} - T = -d^2 - a^2 + 3b^2 - c^2 = 4b^2 - 1$$

$$2m_{3,3} - T = -d^2 - a^2 - b^2 + 3c^2 = 4c^2 - 1.$$

We can use any of these four equations to solve for values of any of a, b, c, d; for instance,

$$a = \pm\frac{1}{2}\sqrt{2m_{1,1} - T + 1}.$$

However, there is the complication that we would not be able to determine the proper signs for a, b, c, and d in this way. In addition, this approach would require the computational expense of four square roots. Therefore, instead of using all four equations, we use just one of them to calculate one of a, b, c, or d : this value may arbitrarily be set to be either positive or negative since it will affect only the overall sign of the quaternion. Then we can use the appropriate equations from XII.10 to solve for the other three variables. To choose which of a, b, c, d to solve for first, recall that we want to avoid division by zero. Further, to avoid division by a value near zero, we can choose to solve for the one of a, b, c, d having the largest absolute value. It is evident from the four equations that this is done by choosing the largest $m_{i,i}$, for $0 \le i \le 3$ and using the corresponding equation.

We can write out the complete algorithm as follows:

```
Input: A rotation matrix M.
        M has entries m_{i,j}, for i = 1, 2, 3 and j = 1, 2, 3.
Output: A quaternion ⟨d, a, b, c⟩
Algorithm:
      Set m_{0,0} = m_{1,1} + m_{2,2} + m_{3,3};                 // Trace
      Set i so that m_{i,i} = max{m_{0,0}, m_{1,1}, m_{2,2}, m_{3,3}};
      Switch ( i ) {
      Case 0:                                                     // i == 0
            Set d = ½√(m_{0,0} + 1);
            Set a = (m_{3,2} − m_{2,3})/(4d);
            Set b = (m_{1,3} − m_{3,1})/(4d);
            Set c = (m_{2,1} − m_{1,2})/(4d);
            Return;
      Case 1:                                                     // i == 1
            Set a = ½√(2m_{1,1} − m_{0,0} + 1);
            Set d = (m_{3,2} − m_{2,3})/(4a);
            Set b = (m_{2,1} + m_{1,2})/(4a);
            Set c = (m_{1,3} + m_{3,1})/(4a);
            Return;
      Case 2:                                                     // i == 2
            Set b = ½√(2m_{2,2} − m_{0,0} + 1);
            Set d = (m_{1,3} − m_{3,1})/(4b);
            Set a = (m_{2,1} + m_{1,2})/(4b);
            Set c = (m_{3,2} + m_{2,3})/(4b);
            Return;
      Case 3:                                                     // i == 3
            Set c = ½√(2m_{3,3} − m_{0,0} + 1);
            Set d = (m_{2,1} − m_{1,2})/(4c);
            Set a = (m_{1,3} + m_{3,1})/(4c);
            Set b = (m_{3,2} + m_{2,3})/(4c);
            Return;
      }
```

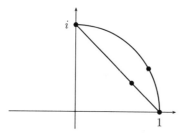

Figure XII.2. Lerping moves from 1 to i at a constant rate along the secant line. Slerping moves from 1 to i at a constant rate along the great circle. The points drawn on the secant line and on the great circle are obtained by lerping and slerping with $\alpha = \frac{1}{3}$. They do not correspond to the same rotation.

The algorithm returns a single quaternion $q = \langle d, a, b, c \rangle$; however, recall that $-q$ represents the same rotation. Depending on how you use the quaternion, you may need to determine which of q or $-q$ is more appropriate.

XII.3.7 Interpolation of Quaternions

Interpolation of quaternions is best done with the spherical linear interpolation introduced earlier in Section IV.6. Because every rotation is represented by a unit quaternion, we restrict our attention to unit quaternions. Recall that unit quaternions can be viewed as points on the unit sphere S^3 in $\mathbb{R}^4$. The only catch is that antipodal points on the sphere represent the same rotation; thus, each rotation has two possible representations as a unit quaternion. It is often important in applications to choose the more appropriate of the two possible representations.

Suppose we are given two unit quaternions q_1 and q_2 and a scalar $\alpha \in [0, 1]$, and wish to interpolate between q_1 and q_2. Because the quaternions lie on the unit sphere, it is better to use spherical linear interpolation instead of ordinary linear interpolation. Namely, one can interpolate with

$$q(\alpha) = \text{slerp}(q_1, q_2, \alpha).$$

The slerp function is computed by the method of Section IV.6.

What would go wrong if we used linear interpolation (lerping) instead of spherical linear interpolation (slerping)? First, of course, the results would not lie on the sphere and would need to be renormalized. Even more important, linear interpolation would not result in a constant rate of rotation. For example, in Figure XII.2, the two quaternions $1 = \langle 1, 0, 0, 0 \rangle$ and $i = \langle 0, 1, 0, 0 \rangle$ are shown. The latter quaternion corresponds to a $180°$ rotation around the x-axis. Both slerping and lerping can be used to move smoothly from the quaternion 1 to the quaternion i. However, using linear interpolation and computing $q(\alpha) = \text{lerp}(1, i)$ causes the quaternion $q(\alpha)$ to move along the straight line segment from 1 to i at a constant rate. On the other hand, setting $q(\alpha) = \text{slerp}(1, i, \alpha)$ causes $q(\alpha)$ to move along the great circle from 1 to i at a constant rate. So only slerping makes the orientation vary at a constant rate.

Recall from Equation IV.28 on pages 123–124 that the formula for spherical linear interpolation is

$$\text{slerp}(q_1, q_2, \alpha) = \frac{\sin((1 - \alpha)\varphi)}{\sin \varphi} q_1 + \frac{\sin(\alpha\varphi)}{\sin \varphi} q_2.$$

Here φ is the angle between q_1 and q_2. This angle can be computed by using the dot product $q_1 \cdot q_2$, which is equal to $\cos \varphi$. (You treat q_1 and q_2 as ordinary vectors in $\mathbb{R}^4$ to compute the dot product.) Alternately, you may also compute the sine of φ and then take the arctangent, as was done on page 124 in the second version of the `Precompute_for_Slerp`.

One typically is really interested in interpolating between rotations rather than between quaternions. That is say, one is typically given two orientations and is asked to interpolate between them. The orientations can be converted to quaternions by the method of the previous section, but then one has the choice of negating one of the quaternions to get a second quaternion representation of the same orientation. The question then is, Should one use

$$\text{slerp}(q_1, q_2, \alpha) \qquad \text{or} \qquad \text{slerp}(q_1, -q_2, \alpha)$$

for the interpolation? (Negating both quaternions just negates the results of the slerp function, and so these are really the only two choices.) The usual way to resolve this question is to consider the angle between q_1 and q_2. If this is less than or equal to $90°$, then slerp between q_1 and q_2. If it is greater than $90°$, then slerp between q_1 and $-q_2$. Physically, this corresponds to rotating in the shortest direction between the two orientations. To determine whether the angle is greater than $90°$, form the dot product $q_1 \cdot q_2$; the dot product is negative if and only if the angle is greater than $90°$.

Interpolation between quaternions can be used to create splinelike curves that take on quaternion values. The importance of this is that it allows orientation to be smoothly animated by a spline function in terms of control points. The main remaining technical difficulty is that slerping only interpolates between two quaternions at a time, but the usual definitions of Bézier and B-spline curves in terms of blending functions require taking a weighted average of multiple control points at a time. This problem can be circumvented by using de Casteljau and de Boor methods, which allow calculating the value of a Bézier curve or B-spline curve by a series of interpolations of two control points at a time. (Shoemake, 1985; 1987) employs this as the basis for some methods of using Catmull–Rom style curves that interpolate given quaternions, and several other authors have made similar suggestions. We have also proposed a method of forming the weighted average of multiple quaternions at a time in (Buss and Fillmore, 2001).

XII.4 Kinematics

The term "kinematics" refers to motion or movement without regard to physical properties such as mass or momentum. Instead, kinematics refers to the purely geometric properties of motion such as position, orientation, velocity, rotational velocity, and so forth.

We focus on the kinematics of hierarchies of simple, rigid, three-dimensional objects linked with perfect joints; such assemblages are also called *articulated objects* or *multibodies*. Applications include the animation of humans and other creatures by controlling their skeletal movement. These techniques can also be used for simulating chains or ropes by approximating them as a series of short rigid segments. Much of the theory of kinematics was developed for the analysis and control of mechanical linkages as well as for motion planning and control of robots.

The outline of the rest of this chapter is as follows. We first set up a framework for discussing rigid, articulated objects. This involves creating a tree structure of links, with each link connected to its parent by a single degree of freedom (1–DOF) joint. Next we examine *forward kinematics*: this involves methods for calculating positions and orientations of the rigid objects as functions of the joint positions. The final section will take up the harder topic of *inverse kinematics*, which provides methods to control the positions of the joints so as to achieve a desired motion.

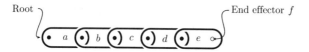

(a) A linear chain of links with 1-DOF rotational joints.

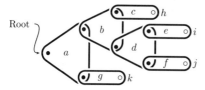

(b) A tree-like arrangement of links and 1-DOF joints. The
points h-k are end effector points.

Figure XII.3. Two examples of tree-like arrangements of links. The black dots represent 1-DOF rotational
joints. The small circles are end effector points.

XII.4.1 Rigid Links and Joints

We wish to model simple arrangements of rigid bodies, called links, connected by joints.
We make several simplifying assumptions. The first assumption is that the joints are purely
rotational and have a single degree of freedom (that is, they are 1–DOF joints). This assumption
is not so crucial in that it can be relaxed significantly without seriously affecting the difficulty
of either forward kinematics or inverse kinematics. The second assumption is that the links
are hooked up in a treelike fashion (i.e., there is no loop or closed chain of links). This second
assumption is crucial for our discussion of kinematics: Indeed any loop or closed chain would
imply dependencies among joint positions, and we would have no meaningful way to deal with
these dependencies kinematically (as compared with dealing with the dynamics or physics of
the bodies).

We assume therefore that we have a set L of links (rigid objects) connected by rotational
joints (see Figure XII.3). The links are organized as a tree; the nodes of the tree are the set
of links from L. One of the links is identified as the *root link*, and the leaves of the tree (i.e.,
links that do not have any children) are called *end links*. Each link is joined to its parent and
its children in the tree by 1–DOF rotational joints. A joint is attached to fixed positions on two
links and has a single axis of rotation; this is similar in effect to a door hinge, for example.
The axis of rotation of the 1–DOF joint is fixed relative to the two links that it joins. End links
are also called *end effectors*. For each end effector, we pick a fixed point on the link called an
end effector point. The end effector points are the points we are trying to control with inverse
kinematics. For example, for a robot arm, the end effector point could be the position of the
hand or other tool at the end of the robot arm, and we would like to control the position,
orientation, or both of the end effector.

XII.4.2 Forward Kinematics

To describe the positions of links mathematically, we need to set up a scheme for naming joints
and effectors their positions and orientations, and so on. Each link $x \in L$ has an *attachment
point*, which is the place where link x is attached to its parent. The root link also has an
attachment point, called the *base position*, where it is attached to a fixed point. We assume each
attachment point consists of a 1–DOF joint. A 1–DOF joint rotates around a single axis. This

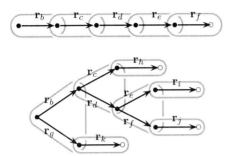

Figure XII.4. The relative position vectors $\mathbf{r}_x$ measure the relative rest positions of the links; $\mathbf{r}_a = \mathbf{0}$ and the other relative position vectors are as shown.

axis is fixed relative to the two adjacent links but of course may depend on other joint angles. We use the variable θ_x to denote the angle of the 1–DOF joint connecting link x to its parent.

The *relative positions* of the links (other than the root link) will be specified with variables $\mathbf{r}_x$. The relative position vectors $\mathbf{r}_x$ are *fixed* and are not functions of the joint angles. The relative positions $\mathbf{r}_x$ for a link x are defined as follows: if y is the parent link of link x, and if all the joint angles are set equal to zero, then $\mathbf{r}_x$ is equal the vector from the attachment point of y to the attachment point of x. This is illustrated in Figure XII.4. We also define $\mathbf{r}_x$ when x is an end effector point instead of a link. In this case, if x lies on link y, then $\mathbf{r}_x$ is defined to be the vector from the attachment point of y to the end effector point x. Examples of this in Figure XII.4 are $\mathbf{r}_f$ in the first figure and $\mathbf{r}_h$ through $\mathbf{r}_k$ in the second figure.

As discussed earlier in this section, the angle θ_x is measured in terms of the *relative orientation* of joint x to its parent. This means that if the parent link is rotated and θ_x is held fixed, then x moves and changes orientation with its parent (see Figure XII.5.) We will use vectors $\mathbf{v}_x$ to denote the rotation axis for the 1–DOF joint attaching x to its parent link (or, if x is the root link, attaching x to the base position). The vector $\mathbf{v}_x$ is equal to the unit vector along the axis of rotation of the joint when all the joint angles equal zero. Of course, as the joint angles θ_x vary, the joints' actual axes of rotation can change (we will denote these changing axes by $\mathbf{w}_x$ below in this section).

The vectors $\mathbf{r}_x$ and $\mathbf{v}_x$ give a description of the mechanical functionality of the links. These vectors are fixed and do not vary with the joint angles θ_x; in other words, they are static. We will shortly define values $\mathbf{s}_x$ and $\mathbf{w}_x$ that give the positions of the joints' attachment points and the joints' rotational axes as functions of the joint angles θ_x.

The basic problem of forward kinematics is to obtain a formula for end effector point positions as functions of the angles θ_x. We solve this problem by defining vectors $\mathbf{s}_x$ that equal

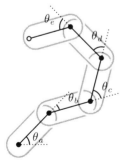

Figure XII.5. The angles of joints are measured relative to the two links that are joined.

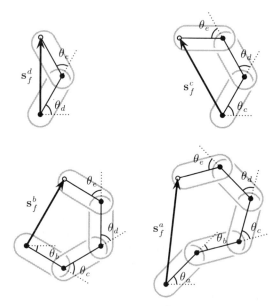

Figure XII.6. The definitions of $\mathbf{s}_f^y$ for the end effector f and the links $y = a, b, c, d$ of the linear chain shown in Figure XII.3.

the position of the attachment point of a link x or the position of an end effector x, where $\mathbf{s}_x$ is a function of the joint angles. A good way to define the vectors $\mathbf{s}_x$ is to traverse the tree of links starting from the end effectors up to the root. We will give formulas for intermediate vectors $\mathbf{s}_x^y$, where x is either a link or an end effector point and the link y is an ancestor of x in the tree. The meaning of $\mathbf{s}_x^y$ is as follows (also, refer to Figure XII.6). Let T_y be the set containing the link y and all the links z that are descendants of y in the tree, that is, T_y is the subtree rooted at y. Then $\mathbf{s}_x^y$ is a function of the angles θ_z such that $z \in T_y$. For a link x, $\mathbf{s}_x^y$ is the vector from the attachment point of y to the attachment point of x if it is assumed that the joint positions are set according to the values of the angles θ_z and that $\theta_{z'} = 0$ for all other links $z' \notin T_y$. For an end effector point x, $\mathbf{s}_x^y$ is the vector from the attachment point of y to the point x again on the assumption that the joint positions are set according to the values of the angles θ_z and that $\theta_{z'} = 0$ for all $z' \notin T_y$.

For a link x in the subtree T_y, we also define a vector $\mathbf{w}_x^y$ that describes the rotation axis for the joint attaching x. The vector $\mathbf{w}_x^y$ will be a function of the angles θ_z such that $z \in T_y$. The value of $\mathbf{w}_x^y$ is defined to be the unit vector along the axis of rotation for the 1–DOF joint connecting x to its parent (based on the angles θ_z, $z \in T_y$) under the same assumption that $\theta_{z'} = 0$ for $z' \notin T_y$.

It is fairly easy to give recursive formulas for $\mathbf{s}_x^y$ and $\mathbf{w}_x^y$. For $y = x$, we have

$$\mathbf{s}_x^x = \mathbf{0} \qquad \text{and} \qquad \mathbf{w}_x^x = \mathbf{v}_x.$$

And, for an end effector position x on the link y,

$$\mathbf{s}_x^y = \mathbf{r}_x.$$

Then, for y equal to the parent link of w and for x in T_w, we have

$$\mathbf{s}_x^y = R_{\theta_y, \mathbf{v}_y}(\mathbf{r}_w + \mathbf{s}_x^w),$$

$$\mathbf{w}_x^y = R_{\theta_y, \mathbf{v}_y}(\mathbf{w}_x^w).$$

As you should recall from Section II.2.3, $R_{\theta,\mathbf{u}}$ represents the linear transformation that performs a rotation of θ degrees around the axis $\mathbf{u}$.

These formulas for $\mathbf{s}_x^y$ and $\mathbf{w}_x^y$ suffice to solve the forward kinematics problem. For instance, the position of end effector f is given as a function of the joint angles by $\mathbf{s}_f^a$, where a is the root link.

To avoid excessive superscripts, we henceforth let $\mathbf{s}_x$ and $\mathbf{w}_x$ equal

$$\mathbf{s}_x \;=\; \mathbf{s}_x^a \qquad \text{and} \qquad \mathbf{w}_x \;=\; \mathbf{w}_x^a,$$

where a is the root link. Thus, $\mathbf{s}_x$ gives the position of the link or end effector point x as a function of the joint angles. Likewise, $\mathbf{w}_x$ gives the rotation axis for the joint at link x.

We now turn to the inverse kinematics problem, which is to find joint angles that will produce desired values for the end effector positions.

XII.4.3 Inverse Kinematics, Setting It Up

The inverse kinematics problem is the problem of, given desired positions for some of the links, finding appropriate joint angles that will place the links in these positions. Applications of inverse kinematics include motion planning in real-world applications, such as in robotics, and also include animation in graphical environments – especially of articulated figures such as humans or other creatures.

Our discussion of inverse kinematics is based loosely on (Girard and Maciejewski, 1985), who used inverse kinematics to animate the walking motion of legged creatures. See also the later paper (Zhao and Badler, 1994) for more advanced methods of inverse kinematics, applications to human figures, and references to related work.

In computer graphics, a typical application of inverse kinematics is animation of a creature. An animator may, for example, specify the desired positions of the hand and feet of a person, and then the inverse kinematics problem will be solved to find good positions for the joints of the entire body. If this works well, the job of the animator can be significantly simplified because this approach can eliminate the work of manually setting all the joint angles in a skeleton. Other applications include motion planning – either for robotics or in a virtual reality application. For instance, if it is desired to make an arm and hand reach out to grasp an object, then inverse kinematics can be used to find possible solutions for the movement. Of course, these possible solutions may need to take into account issues such as collision detection and avoidance, or joint forces and joint limits.

We discuss only the "pure" form of inverse kinematics: in particular, we do not consider issues like collision avoidance or limits on joint angles. Rather, we discuss solutions to the following problem: Given a set of joint angles, and thereby, from forward kinematics, given the positions and orientations of all the links, and given a set of desired new positions for *some* of the links, we want to find a way to change the joint angles so as to move the links' positions closer to the desired positions. This process can be iterated in such a way that each iteration moves the links' positions closer to their target positions until eventually new joint positions are reached that place the links close enough to their desired positions. The reason for using an iterative procedure is that it is usually too complicated to actually solve for joint angles, $\vec{\theta}$, in terms of the desired link positions. The iterative procedure will be easier to implement and, if it converges sufficiently well, can provide values for the joint angles that put the links arbitrarily close to their desired positions.

For a single step of the iterative procedure, we consider the function telling us how links' positions depend on joint angles (this function is obtainable from the forward kinematics of the last section). We then evaluate the partial derivatives of this function to find a linear

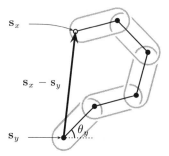

$\mathbf{s}_x$

$\mathbf{s}_x - \mathbf{s}_y$

$\mathbf{s}_y$

θ_y

Figure XII.7. The rate of change of the position $\mathbf{s}_x$ of point x with respect to the joint angle θ_y is calculated in terms of rotation around the axis $\mathbf{w}_y$ of the joint y as $\mathbf{w}_y \times (\mathbf{s}_x - \mathbf{s}_y)$. The axis $\mathbf{w}_y$ is pointing out of the page, and so $\mathbf{w}_y \times (\mathbf{s}_x - \mathbf{s}_y)$ has the right direction for the partial derivative. Since $\mathbf{w}_y$ is a unit vector, $\mathbf{w}_y \times (\mathbf{s}_x - \mathbf{s}_y)$ also has the right magnitude. This calculation works for any x and y, not for just end effectors and the root link.

approximation to the function. That is, we compute the rates of changes in links' positions with respect to the rates of changes in joint angles. These give a *Jacobian matrix* of partial derivatives. With some assumptions about the nonsingularity of the Jacobian matrix, we can then find a way to change the joints' angles so as to move the links' positions closer to the desired positions. Since the Jacobian gives only a linear approximation to the function, we have to iterate the process until it converges (we hope!) to a good solution.

Suppose that x is an end effector position or an attachment point of a link and that we are seeking to set the joint angles so as to set the position $\mathbf{s}_x$ of x equal to a target value $\mathbf{s}'_x$. More generally, we may have more than one x and be trying to make each x reach its target position $\mathbf{s}'_x$. We assume the links are already placed in some initial configuration with known joint angles $\vec{\theta}$, where $\vec{\theta}$ represents the vector of all the joint angles. The discussion in the previous section on forward kinematics gives us a formula for $\mathbf{s}_x$ in terms of the angles $\vec{\theta}$.

The first step in setting up the inverse kinematics problem is to define the Jacobian matrix, which will tell us how the position of x changes with respect to small changes in the angles $\vec{\theta}$; in other words, the matrix will contain the partial derivatives of $\mathbf{s}_x$ with respect to the variables $\vec{\theta}$.

To define the Jacobian matrix, we must define the partial derivatives of the functions $\mathbf{s}_x$ giving the link positions. We have $\mathbf{s}_x$ as a function of $\vec{\theta}$, that is, $\mathbf{s}_x = \mathbf{s}_x(\vec{\theta})$. For particular links x and y, we can define $\partial \mathbf{s}_x / \partial \theta_y$ as follows:

$$\frac{\partial \mathbf{s}_x}{\partial \theta_y} = \begin{cases} \mathbf{0} & \text{if } y = x \text{ or } x \notin T_y \\ \mathbf{w}_y \times (\mathbf{s}_x - \mathbf{s}_y) & \text{otherwise} \end{cases}$$

To see that this correctly defines the partial derivative, note the following: (a) If x is not a proper descendant of y, then the rotation of y's joint does not affect the position of x, and so $\partial \mathbf{s}_x / \partial \theta_y = \mathbf{0}$. (b) Otherwise, the vector from point y to point x is equal to $\mathbf{s}_x - \mathbf{s}_y$, and the rotation axis for angle θ_y is the axis $\mathbf{w}_y$. An infinitesimal rotation φ radians around the axis $\mathbf{w}_y$ centered at $\mathbf{s}_y$ will move the point x an infinitesimal distance given by the vector $\varphi \mathbf{w}_y \times (\mathbf{s}_x - \mathbf{s}_y)$. From this observation, the second part of the definition of $\partial \mathbf{s}_x / \partial \theta_y$ is obtained immediately. Figure XII.7 shows how to visualize the derivation of the formula for the partial derivative.[5]

---

[5] The formula for $\partial \mathbf{s}_x / \partial \theta_y$ is only correct if angles are measured in radians. If the angle θ is measured in units of α radians, then the equation for the partial derivative becomes $\alpha \mathbf{w}_y \times (\mathbf{s}_x - \mathbf{s}_y)$. For example, if angles are measured in degrees, then $\alpha = \pi/180$.

The vector version of the Jacobian matrix is then defined to equal the $m \times n$ matrix

$$\left(\frac{\partial \mathbf{s}_x}{\partial \theta_y}\right)_{x,y},$$

where the rows of the matrix are indexed by the m many links x whose position we are trying to set (often, x ranges over the set of end effectors, for instance) and the columns of the matrix are indexed by the set of all joints y.

The entries in the preceding matrix are 3-vectors; to convert the matrix into an ordinary matrix with real numbers as entries, we replace each vector-valued entry by its column form. This gives a matrix of dimension $(3m) \times n$. We call this $(3m) \times n$ matrix the *Jacobian matrix* and denote it J. Each row in J has length n and consists of partial derivatives of one of the x-, y-, or z-coordinates of one of the $\mathbf{s}_x$ values with respect to the n angles θ_y.

To finish setting up the inverse kinematics problem, we assume we are given current values for the angles $\vec{\theta}$. This gives values $\mathbf{s}_x$, and we denote the sequence of all these by $\vec{\mathbf{s}}$ (so $\vec{\mathbf{s}}$ is a sequence of m vectors and thus a sequence of $3m$ scalars). We also let $\mathbf{s}'_x$ be the desired values for these positions and let $\vec{\mathbf{s}}'$ denote the sequence of all these. Finally, let $\Delta\vec{\mathbf{s}}$ equal

$$\Delta\vec{\mathbf{s}} = \vec{\mathbf{s}}' - \vec{\mathbf{s}},$$

which equals the desired change in the links' positions.

To solve the inverse kinematics problem, we want to solve the following equation for $\Delta\vec{\theta}$:

$$\Delta\vec{\mathbf{s}} = J(\Delta\vec{\theta}). \qquad\qquad \text{XII.11}$$

This will give $\Delta\vec{\theta}$ as a first-order approximation to the change in values of $\vec{\theta}$ necessary to effect the desired change $\Delta\vec{\mathbf{s}}$ in positions.

The next section will describe an algorithm to find a solution $\Delta\vec{\theta}$ to Equation XII.11. Once we have this solution, we might be tempted to set $\vec{\theta}$ equal to $\vec{\theta} + \Delta\vec{\theta}$. This, however, will not work so easily and is likely to lead to unstable performance. The Jacobian matrix gives only a first-order approximation to the change in angles, and, unfortunately, the partial derivatives can change very rapidly with changes in the angles $\vec{\theta}$. A second problem is that when the links and joints are positioned badly, Equation XII.11 can be unstable; in particular, the matrix J may have rank less than n, or be close to having rank less than n, and this can cause instability and overshoot problems.

To keep these problems under control, it is recommended that you choose a small positive scalar $\epsilon < 1$ and update the joint angles $\vec{\theta}$ by adding $\epsilon\Delta\vec{\theta}$. Then proceed iteratively by recomputing the Jacobian based on the updated angles and positions, finding new values for $\Delta\vec{\theta}$ and again updating with a small fraction ϵ. This is repeated until the links x are sufficiently close to the desired positions. The question of how small ϵ needs to be depends on the geometry of the links; it would be a good idea to keep ϵ small enough so that the angles are updated by at most 5 or 10° at a time.

XII.4.4 Inverse Kinematics, Finding a Local Solution

The previous section reduced the inverse kinematics problem to the problem of solving Equation XII.11 for $\Delta\vec{\theta}$ in terms of $\Delta\vec{\mathbf{s}}$ and J. Of course, if we are very lucky, then J is a square matrix and is invertible. In that case, we can solve for $\Delta\vec{\theta}$ as

$$\Delta\vec{\theta} = J^{-1}(\Delta\vec{\mathbf{s}}).$$

However, we are not usually so lucky. First of all, J may well not be square. For example, if there is only one end effector, so $m = 1$, and there are $n > 3$ joints, then J is a $3 \times n$ matrix with more columns than rows. In this case, the rank of J is ≤ 3, and thus the columns cannot be linearly independent. A second way that things can go wrong is when the rows of J are not linearly independent, that is, the rank of J is $< 3m$. A simple example of this is seen in Figure XII.3(a) on page 308. Suppose the joints are all straight, as shown in the figure, and that the end effector is at the point f at the right end of the rightmost link. Let f_x measure the x-coordinate (horizontal position) of the end effector f. Then $\partial f_x / \partial \theta = 0$ for all the joint angles θ: in other words, the corresponding row of J is zero. Physically, this means that no infinitesimal change in joint angles can effect a change in the horizontal position of the end effector.

When J is not invertible, we will use the *pseudo-inverse* of J instead of the inverse of J. The pseudo-inverse is also sometimes called the *Moore–Penrose inverse*. Before defining the pseudo-inverse of J, we need to develop some background from linear algebra. (See Appendix A.3.3 for related background material.)

We define the *kernel* of J to be the set of vectors $\mathbf{v} \in \mathbb{R}^n$ such that $J\mathbf{v} = \mathbf{0}$. We define the *rowspan* of J to be the subspace of $\mathbb{R}^n$ spanned by the rows of J (i.e., the subspace of vectors that can be expressed as linear combinations of the rows of J). Then $\mathbb{R}^n$ is the direct sum of kernel(J) and rowspan(J); that is, every vector $\mathbf{v}$ in $\mathbb{R}^n$ can be written uniquely in the form

$$\mathbf{v} = \mathbf{k} + \mathbf{r} \qquad \text{with } \mathbf{k} \in \text{kernel}(J) \text{ and } \mathbf{r} \in \text{rowspan}(J). \qquad \text{XII.12}$$

Furthermore, the dot product $\mathbf{k} \cdot \mathbf{r}$ is equal to zero for all $\mathbf{k} \in \text{kernel}(J)$ and $\mathbf{r} \in \text{rowspan}(J)$. Since these conditions hold, kernel(J) and rowspan(J) are called *orthogonal complements*. It is an elementary fact from linear algebra that any subspace of $\mathbb{R}^n$ has a unique orthogonal complement.

Similarly, we let colspan(J) be the column span of J, and its orthogonal complement is kernel(J^{T}).[6] It is easy to check that colspan(J) is the same as the range of the linear map represented by J.

We henceforth let $k = 3m$ be the number of rows of J.

Definition Let J be a $k \times n$ matrix. Then the *pseudo-inverse* of J, denoted $J^\dagger$, is the $n \times k$ matrix such that

(a) For every $\mathbf{v} \in \text{kernel}(J^{\mathrm{T}})$, $J^\dagger \mathbf{v} = \mathbf{0}$.
(b) For every $\mathbf{v} \in \text{colspan}(J)$, $J^\dagger \mathbf{v} \in \text{rowspan}(J)$.
(c) For every $\mathbf{v} \in \text{colspan}(J)$, $J J^\dagger \mathbf{v} = \mathbf{v}$.

A crucial property of the pseudo-inverse is that $J^\dagger J$ is the projection mapping onto the subspace rowspan(J); namely, if Equation XII.12 holds, then $J^\dagger J \mathbf{v} = \mathbf{r}$. To prove this, note that applying condition (b) with $\mathbf{v}$ replaced by $J\mathbf{v}$, shows that $J^\dagger J \mathbf{v}$ is in rowspan(J). Further, by (c), $J J^\dagger J \mathbf{v} = J \mathbf{v} = J \mathbf{r}$. These two facts imply $J(J^\dagger J \mathbf{v} - \mathbf{r}) = \mathbf{0}$, and so $J^\dagger J \mathbf{v} - \mathbf{r} \in \text{kernel}(J)$. But also, $J^\dagger J \mathbf{v} - \mathbf{r} \in \text{rowspan}(J)$, and thus $J^\dagger J \mathbf{v} - \mathbf{r} = \mathbf{0}$, that is, $J^\dagger J \mathbf{v} = \mathbf{r}$.

By similar reasoning, it can also be shown that $J J^\dagger$ is the projection mapping onto colspan(J). By (a), $J J^\dagger$ maps kernel(J^{T}), the orthogonal complement of colspan(J), to zero. For $\mathbf{v} \in \text{colspan}(J)$, $J J^\dagger \mathbf{v} = \mathbf{v}$, by (c). Thus, $J J^\dagger$ is the projection mapping onto colspan(J).

To see that conditions (a)–(c) determine a unique matrix $J^\dagger$, note that for all $\mathbf{v} \in \text{colspan}(J)$, there is a unique $\mathbf{w} \in \text{rowspan}(J)$ such that $J\mathbf{w} = \mathbf{v}$. Thus, (a)–(c) uniquely determine $J^\dagger(\mathbf{v})$ for $\mathbf{v}$ in kernel(J^{T}) $\cup$ colspan(J). These are orthogonal complements, and so the linear map $J^\dagger$ is thereby uniquely specified for all vectors $\mathbf{v}$.

---

[6] J^{T} is the transpose of J.

An alternative, and equivalent, definition of the pseudo-inverse of J is as follows: for any vector $\mathbf{v} \in \mathbb{R}^k$, $J^\dagger \mathbf{v} = \mathbf{w}$, where $\mathbf{w} \in \mathbb{R}^n$ is the vector such that

(a') $||\mathbf{v} - J\mathbf{w}||$ is minimized, and
(b') $||\mathbf{w}||$ is the minimum among all $\mathbf{w}$ satisfying (a').

To see this equivalence, first note that because the range of J is colspan(J), the quantity $||\mathbf{v} - J\mathbf{w}||$ will be minimized if $J\mathbf{w}$ is the projection of $\mathbf{v}$ onto colspan(J). As just proved above, $JJ^\dagger$ is the projection mapping onto colspan(J), and thus condition (a') holds. Condition (b') now follows from (b).

Conditions (a') and (b') can be equivalently expressed in terms of minimizing the squares of the magnitudes, that is, minimizing $||\mathbf{v} - J\mathbf{w}||^2$ and $||\mathbf{w}||^2$. The square magnitude of a vector is, of course, the sum of the squares of the components of the vector. Therefore, (a') and (b') show that the pseudo-inverse $J^\dagger$ finds a solution that is as good as possible, where "good" is measured in terms of the sum of the squares. In other words, it solves the least-squares minimization problem.

> **Exercise XII.10*** *Suppose that $J^\dagger$ satisfies conditions (a') and (b'). Prove that it also satisfies conditions (a), (b), and (c).*

Now that we have defined the pseudo-inverse, we can give a solution for Equation XII.11, namely,

$$\Delta\vec{\theta} = J^\dagger(\Delta\vec{\mathbf{s}}). \qquad\qquad \text{XII.13}$$

By the characterization of pseudo-inverses through conditions (a') and (b'), we see that this is a reasonably good choice for $\Delta\vec{\theta}$.

It remains to explain how to compute $J^\dagger$. The next theorem gives a formula for finding $J^\dagger$ in the case where J has at least as many columns as rows and where the rows are linearly independent.

Theorem XII.4 *Suppose J is a $k \times n$ matrix and that J has rank k. Then JJ^T is nonsingular, and the pseudo-inverse $J^\dagger$ of J is*

$$J^\dagger = J^\mathsf{T}(JJ^\mathsf{T})^{-1}. \qquad\qquad \text{XII.14}$$

Proof We start by just assuming that JJ^T is nonsingular, and thus $(JJ^\mathsf{T})^{-1}$ exists. Let $J^\dagger$ be the matrix given by the right-hand side of equation XII.14.

Since J has rank k, the rows of J are linearly independent. Also, colspan(J) has dimension k. Thus, colspan(J) is equal to all of $\mathbb{R}^k$, and kernel(J^T) = $\{\mathbf{0}\}$. Therefore, condition (a) of the definition of the pseudo-inverse automatically holds for $J^\dagger$ without even using Equation XII.14. In addition, the range of J^T equals colspan(J^T), and therefore the range of $J^\mathsf{T}(JJ^\mathsf{T})^{-1}$ is certainly a subset of colspan(J^T). Since colspan(J^T) equals rowspan(J), condition (b) must hold for $J^\dagger$ defined by Equation XII.14. Finally, condition (c) holds since

$$JJ^\dagger = J(J^\mathsf{T}(JJ^\mathsf{T})^{-1}) = JJ^\mathsf{T}(JJ^\mathsf{T})^{-1} = \text{Identity}.$$

We have shown that if $J^\dagger$ is defined by Equation XII.14, then conditions (a)–(c) hold, and so it remains only to prove the assumption that $Z = JJ^\mathsf{T}$ is invertible. Note that Z is a $k \times k$ matrix and that the entries of Z are equal to

$$z_{i,j} = \mathbf{r}_i \cdot \mathbf{r}_j,$$

where $\mathbf{r}_i$ is the ith row of J and "$\cdot$" denotes a vector dot product. Suppose Z has rank $< k$ and thus that there is a linear dependence among the rows of Z. This means there are scalars α_i, not all zero, such that

$$0 = \sum_i \alpha_i z_{i,j} = \sum_i \alpha_i \mathbf{r}_i \cdot \mathbf{r}_j \qquad \text{for all } j = 1, 2, \ldots, k.$$

Then, for all j,

$$\left(\sum_i \alpha_i \mathbf{r}_i \right) \cdot \mathbf{r}_j = 0.$$

The vector in the parentheses is in the span of the rows of J and also has a dot product equal to zero with each of the rows $\mathbf{r}_j$. Therefore, the quantity in parentheses must be zero. This, however, contradicts the hypothesis that the rows of J are linearly independent. □

Very frequently, the Jacobian J does not have full row rank, that is, its rank is $< k$. In this case, Theorem XII.4 does not apply, and we must find another way to compute the pseudo-inverse $J^\dagger$. Let ℓ equal the rank of J. We wish to express J in the form

$$J = J_1 J_2 \qquad\qquad\qquad\qquad\qquad\qquad\qquad \text{XII.15}$$

where J_1 is a $k \times \ell$ matrix, J_2 is an $\ell \times n$ matrix, and both J_1 and J_2 have rank ℓ. When these conditions hold, the product $J = J_1 J_2$ is called the *full rank factorization* of J.

To find J_1 and J_2, first find ℓ rows of J that are linearly independent. Let $\mathbf{r}_{s_1}, \ldots, \mathbf{r}_{s_\ell}$ be these ℓ rows. Then, express all the rows of R as

$$\mathbf{r}_i = \sum_{j=1}^{\ell} \alpha_{i,j} \mathbf{r}_{s_j}.$$

The linearly independent rows $\mathbf{r}_{s_j}$ and the coefficients $\alpha_{i,j}$ can be found by a Gaussian elimination type procedure. Care should be taken here to have good criteria for deciding when a given row is the span of another set of rows, since to deal with roundoff errors and with matrices that are near-singular, one has to allow a row nearly equal to a linear combination of other rows to be treated as being a linear combination.

Once the values $\alpha_{i,j}$ have been found, let J_1 be the matrix with entries $\alpha_{i,j}$, and let J_2 be the matrix obtained from J by keeping the ℓ rows $\mathbf{r}_{s_1}$ through $\mathbf{r}_{s_\ell}$ and discarding the rest of the rows. Then, by inspection, $J = J_1 J_2$.

Theorem XII.5 *Let $J = J_1 J_2$ be such that J_1 is $k \times \ell$ and J_2 is $\ell \times n$ and suppose J (and thus J_1 and J_2) are rank ℓ. Then*

$$J^\dagger = J_2^{\mathrm{T}} (J_2 J_2^{\mathrm{T}})^{-1} (J_1^{\mathrm{T}} J_1)^{-1} J_1^{\mathrm{T}}. \qquad\qquad\qquad \text{XII.16}$$

Proof We already proved that $J_2 J_2^{\mathrm{T}}$ is invertible in the proof of Theorem XII.4. A similar argument shows that $J_1^{\mathrm{T}} J_1$ is invertible. Let $J^\dagger$ be the matrix defined by Equation XII.16: we must show that conditions (a)–(c) hold. Since $J^{\mathrm{T}} = J_2^{\mathrm{T}} J_1^{\mathrm{T}}$ and $\text{kernel}(J_2^{\mathrm{T}}) = \{\mathbf{0}\}$, we have $\text{kernel}(J^{\mathrm{T}}) = \text{kernel}(J_1^{\mathrm{T}})$. Therefore, condition (a) certainly holds. Similarly, because $\text{kernel}(J_1) = \{\mathbf{0}\}$, J and J_2 have the same kernel, and so $\text{rowspan}(J_2) = \text{rowspan}(J)$. Clearly, the range of $J^\dagger$ is a subset of $\text{colspan}(J_2^{\mathrm{T}}) = \text{rowspan}(J_2)$. Therefore, the range of $J^\dagger$ is a subset of $\text{rowspan}(J)$, and so condition (b) holds. Finally, suppose $\mathbf{v}$ is in $\text{colspan}(J)$, that is, $\mathbf{v}$ is in the range of J so that $\mathbf{v} = J(\mathbf{w})$ for some w. From this,

$$JJ^\dagger \mathbf{v} = JJ^\dagger J\mathbf{w}$$

$$= JJ_2^{\mathrm{T}} (J_2 J_2^{\mathrm{T}})^{-1} (J_1^{\mathrm{T}} J_1)^{-1} J_1^{\mathrm{T}} J\mathbf{w}$$

$$= (J_1 J_2) J_2^{\mathrm{T}} (J_2 J_2^{\mathrm{T}})^{-1} (J_1^{\mathrm{T}} J_1)^{-1} J_1^{\mathrm{T}} (J_1 J_2)\mathbf{w}$$

$$= J_1(J_2 J_2^T)(J_2 J_2^T)^{-1}(J_1^T J_1)^{-1}(J_1^T J_1)J_2\mathbf{w}$$

$$= J_1 J_2 \mathbf{w}$$

$$= J\mathbf{w}$$

$$= \mathbf{v},$$

and condition (c) is proved. □

Theorems XII.4 and XII.5 imply algorithms for finding the pseudo-inverse that are fairly efficient as long as k is small; that is, as long as the total number of links we are trying to force to a specified position is small. There are other iterative methods that find the pseudo-inverse by computing a singular value decomposition (c.f., (Press et al., 1986)). Quasi-Newton methods have also been used to solve the inverse kinematics problem (c.f., (Zhao and Badler, 1994)).

We have glossed over many important issues that are important for writing a functioning inverse kinematics system based on pseudo-inverse calculations. Perhaps the most significant of these issues are how to handle extra constraints such as joint limits and how to avoid unnecessarily reaching configurations of the links where the Jacobian has reduced row rank. One way to help avoid these problems was suggested by (Girard and Maciejewski, 1985). For each joint angle, we choose a "rest position," which is a desired value for the joint angle; preferably, this rest position would be in a partially flexed position away from any joint limits and away from configurations that lead to reduced row rank in the Jacobian. In a given configuration of the links, let $\Delta \vec{H}$ denote the change in the values of the joint angles $\vec{\theta}$ that would suffice to bring all the joints back to their rest positions. Then, after performing the pseudo-inverse calculation of $\Delta\vec{\theta}$, update the joint positions by

$$\epsilon[\Delta\vec{\theta} + (I - J^\dagger J)(\Delta\vec{H})]. \qquad \text{XII.17}$$

Recall that $J^\dagger J$ is the projection mapping onto the rowspan of J. Therefore, $(I - J^\dagger J)$ is the projection map onto the kernel of J, and we have

$$J(\Delta\vec{\theta} + (I - J^\dagger J)(\Delta\vec{H})) = J(\Delta\vec{\theta}).$$

Updating the joint positions by XII.17 thus tends to move the joint angles back to their rest positions as well as can be done without worsening the progress made towards the target positions of the links.

Weighting Joint Angles. Often, it is useful to weight joint angle changes to allow some joints to rotate more readily than others. For example, in a robot arm, it can be much easier to rotate a joint angle near an end link than a joint angle near the root. Analogously, for a human arm, it is generally much easier to rotate a finger joint through an angle of φ than to move a shoulder joint through the same angle φ. Indeed, it is generally preferable to change a finger joint by a relatively large angle rather than a shoulder joint through a relatively small angle.

The pseudo-inverse method described above does not incorporate any weighting of the costs of rotating different joints; however, it is fairly simple to modify it to do so. Let $\vec{\theta} = \langle \theta_1, \ldots, \theta_m \rangle^T$ be the joint angles (which are now indexed by integers instead of by links). We assign positive weights α_i, for $i = 1, \ldots, m$, to these joint angles, choosing the values α_i to be proportional to the cost of changing the angle θ_i. That is to say, the cost of changing angle θ_i by a small angle φ is equal to α_i / α_j times the cost of changing angle θ_j by the same amount φ. For instance, in the shoulder–finger example, the value of weight α would be much higher for the shoulder joint than for the finger joint. Another way to state the property satisfied by the weights α_i is that if $\alpha_i \Delta\theta_i = \alpha_j \Delta\theta_j$, then the costs of the changes to the two angles θ_i and θ_j are equal.

We introduce new variables $\psi_i = \alpha_i \theta_i$, and let $\vec{\psi}$ be the vector of values ψ_i. Note that $\theta_i = \psi_i / \alpha_i$, and $\Delta\theta_i = (\Delta\psi_i)/\alpha_i$, and so on. We now define a new Jacobian matrix $\widehat{J}$ using the variables $\vec{\psi}$, namely, $\widehat{J}$ is the Jacobian matrix whose entries are equal to

$$\frac{\partial \mathbf{s}_x}{\partial \psi_i}.$$

Since $(d\theta_i / d\psi_i) = 1/\alpha_i$, we have

$$\frac{\partial \mathbf{s}_x}{\partial \psi_i} = \frac{1}{\alpha_i} \frac{\partial \mathbf{s}_x}{\partial \theta_i}.$$

Therefore, the matrix $\widehat{J}$ can be obtained from the original Jacobian J by dividing the entries in each column i by α_i. Then we solve the least-squares problem but use the variables $\vec{\psi}$. To do this, form the pseudo-inverse $\widehat{J}^\dagger$ and set

$$\Delta\vec{\psi} = \widehat{J}^\dagger (\Delta\vec{\mathbf{s}}).$$

Finish by letting $\Delta\theta_i = (\Delta\psi_i)/\alpha_i$ and then proceed as before, choosing a small ϵ and incrementally updating the joint angles.

We have just shown that weighting joint angle costs corresponds to a very simple change of variables. Now, one should wonder why it is appropriate to use the multipliers α_i instead of some other value. This choice can be justified by the following simple example.

Suppose we want to solve

$$\theta_1 + \theta_2 = 1$$

subject to minimizing the quantity

$$(\alpha_1 \theta_1)^2 + (\alpha_2 \theta_2)^2.$$

That is, we are trying to minimize the sum of the squares of the costs of the angles with α_1 and α_2 specifying the relative costs. When we change to the variables ψ_1 and ψ_2, this is the same as solving for

$$\frac{\psi_1}{\alpha_1} + \frac{\psi_2}{\alpha_2} = 1$$

subject to minimizing the quantity

$$\psi_1^2 + \psi_2^2.$$

In other words, the problem becomes an ordinary least-squares problem with all weights equal to 1. Thus, the transformation from the variables θ_i to the variables ψ_i converts the weighted least-squares minimization problem into an unweighted least-squares minimization problem.

APPENDIX A

Mathematics Background

This appendix quickly reviews many of the mathematical prerequisites for this book. This material is mostly from a first-year calculus course with particular emphasis on vectors. The first section covers some preliminaries. Section A.2 covers vectors in $\mathbb{R}^2$ and then in $\mathbb{R}^3$, including dot products and cross products. The next section introduces 3×3 matrices and their connections to vector dot products and cross products. Matrix determinants and inverses and adjoints are covered after that. Then, fundamental properties of linear spaces and dimension are reviewed. The concluding sections discuss some of the basic concepts from multivariable calculus, including partial derivatives, gradients, vector-valued functions, and Jacobians.

Other prerequisites, not covered in this appendix, include basic topics from discrete math, most notably proofs by induction and simple facts about trees. There a few places where we presume knowledge of big-O notation, of the choice function $\binom{n}{k}$, and of geometric series. The reader is also expected to have prior knowledge of trigonometry and of the basics of single-variable calculus.

A.1 Preliminaries

The set $\mathbb{R}$ is the set of real numbers (also called *scalars*). For $k \geq 1$ an integer, $\mathbb{R}^k$ is the set of k-tuples of real numbers; these k-tuples are also called k-vectors when we want to emphasize that $\mathbb{R}^k$ is a vector space (vector spaces are discussed more below). A k-tuple is a sequence of length k and is represented by the notation

$$\langle a_1, a_2, \ldots, a_k \rangle,$$

using angle brackets.

For $a < b$, the set $[a, b]$ is the closed interval containing all points x such that $a \leq x \leq b$. The square brackets indicate the inclusion of the endpoints a and b. We use parentheses instead of square brackets when the endpoints are omitted; for example,

$$[a, b) = \{x \in \mathbb{R} : a \leq x < b\}$$

is a half-open interval. Exponent notation is used for tuples of elements from intervals too; for example,

$$[0, 1]^2 = [0, 1] \times [0, 1] = \{\langle a, b \rangle : a, b \in [0, 1]\}$$

is the unit square containing pairs of reals from $[0, 1]$.

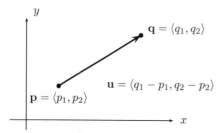

Figure A.1. Two points $\mathbf{p}$ and $\mathbf{q}$ and the vector $\mathbf{u} = \mathbf{q} - \mathbf{p}$.

The notation

$$f : A \to B$$

indicates that f is a function with domain A and with range contained in B. A function is also called a *mapping*. The *range* of f is the set of values $f(a)$ for a in the domain A; the set B is sometimes called the *codomain* of f. For example, the function $g : \mathbb{R} \to \mathbb{R}$ defined by $g(x) = \sin(x)$ has domain $\mathbb{R}$ and range $[-1, 1]$. The function $f : A \to B$ is *one-to-one* provided that for each $b \in B$ there is at most one $a \in A$ such that $f(a) = b$. The function is *onto* provided that the range of f is equal to all of B.

When the codomain B is $\mathbb{R}$, we define the *support* of f to be the set of elements a such that $f(a)$ is nonzero.

A.2 Vectors and Vector Products

A k-vector $\mathbf{u}$ is a sequence of k real numbers,

$$\mathbf{u} = \langle u_1, u_2, \ldots, u_k \rangle.$$

Our conventions are to use boldface letters, like $\mathbf{u}$ to denote vectors and italic symbols, like u or u_i, for scalar values.

In computer graphics, we are mostly concerned with vectors with 2, 3, or 4 components. For $k = 2$, a 2-vector represents a point in $\mathbb{R}^2$, the real plane. Going up a dimension, a 3-vector represents a point in $\mathbb{R}^3$, that is, in three-dimensional space. We use 4-vectors mostly to represent points in homogeneous coordinates (see Chapter II for information on homogeneous coordinates).

The space of all k-vectors is the k-dimensional vector space, sometimes called Euclidean space, and is denoted $\mathbb{R}^k$.

A.2.1 Vectors in $\mathbb{R}^2$

A vector in $\mathbb{R}^2$ is a pair of real numbers and is written $\mathbf{u} = \langle u_1, u_2 \rangle$. As an ordered pair, a vector can be viewed either as a point in the usual xy-plane or as a displacement between two points (see Figure A.1). It is sometimes useful to make a distinction between points and vectors since they are often used in different ways. However, they are both represented by a pair of scalars, and their similarities greatly outweigh their differences. Thus, we find it convenient to treat vectors and points as being the same kind of object, namely, as a pair of scalars.

The length of a vector, also called its *magnitude* or *norm*, can be defined in terms of the Euclidean distance function

$$\|\mathbf{u}\| = \sqrt{u_1^2 + u_2^2}.$$

A *unit vector* is a vector with magnitude equal to 1.

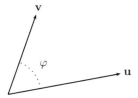

Figure A.2. The angle between **u** and **v** equals φ and is used for computing the dot product. Since $\cos\varphi = \cos(-\varphi) = \cos(360° - \varphi)$, it makes no difference which way the angle is measured for the purposes of computing the dot product.

The unit circle in $\mathbb{R}^2$, also called the 1-sphere, is the set of vectors with magnitude 1. Vector addition and vector subtraction are defined to act component-wise:

$$\mathbf{u} + \mathbf{v} = \langle u_1, u_2 \rangle + \langle v_1, v_2 \rangle = \langle u_1 + v_1, u_2 + v_2 \rangle,$$

$$\mathbf{u} - \mathbf{v} = \langle u_1, u_2 \rangle - \langle v_1, v_2 \rangle = \langle u_1 - v_1, u_2 - v_2 \rangle.$$

One could define a component-wise multiplication operation on vectors, but this turns out not to be a very useful operation. Instead, there are two much more useful ways to define multiplication on vectors, the dot product and the cross product:

$$\mathbf{u} \cdot \mathbf{v} = u_1 v_1 + u_2 v_2 \qquad \text{Dot product} \qquad\qquad \text{A.1}$$

$$\mathbf{u} \times \mathbf{v} = u_1 v_2 - u_2 v_1 \qquad \text{Cross product} \qquad\qquad \text{A.2}$$

Note that both the dot and cross products form the product of two vectors and produce a scalar as the result. If you have studied cross products before, you may remember their being defined only for vectors in $\mathbb{R}^3$ and giving another vector as the result. It is useful, however, to define cross products also for vectors in $\mathbb{R}^2$. In $\mathbb{R}^2$, the cross product of two 2-vectors is a scalar.

The dot product is sometimes called the *inner product*.

Dot Products in $\mathbb{R}^2$

The dot product was defined in (A.1) with the formula $u_1 v_1 + u_2 v_2$. An alternate definition can be given in terms of the magnitudes of **u** and **v** and the angle φ between the two vectors; that is, with reference to Figure A.2,

$$\mathbf{u} \cdot \mathbf{v} = ||\mathbf{u}|| \cdot ||\mathbf{v}|| \cos\varphi. \qquad\qquad \text{A.3}$$

It is fine to take equation A.3 on faith, but if you wish to see a proof you may work the next exercise.

Exercise A.1★ *Prove the correctness of equation A.3. [Hint: Let **u** make angle ψ with the x-axis. Therefore, **v** makes angle $\psi + \varphi$ with the x-axis. Express the vectors **u** and **v** component-wise with sines and cosines. Then compute the dot product according to the definition in equation A.1 and transform it using the sine or cosine angle sum formulas (or the angle difference formulas). Show that equation A.3 results.]*

Suppose **u** and **v** are nonzero. Then equation A.3 shows that $\mathbf{u} \cdot \mathbf{v}$ is equal to zero if and only if $\cos\theta$ equals zero. This happens if and only if the angle between **u** and **v** is a right angle. In this case, the two vectors are said to be *perpendicular*, or *orthogonal*.

When **u** is a unit vector, the dot product formula reduces to just $\mathbf{u} \cdot \mathbf{v} = ||\mathbf{v}|| \cos\varphi$. With reference to Figure A.3, this implies that, when **u** is a unit vector, $\mathbf{u} \cdot \mathbf{v}$ is the (signed) length

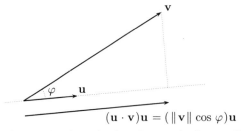

$$(\mathbf{u} \cdot \mathbf{v})\mathbf{u} = (\| \mathbf{v} \| \cos \varphi)\mathbf{u}$$

Figure A.3. The projection of $\mathbf{v}$ onto the line parallel to a unit vector $\mathbf{u}$, where φ is the angle between $\mathbf{u}$ and $\mathbf{v}$. How would the picture look if φ were between 90 and 180°?

of the *projection* of $\mathbf{v}$ onto the line in the direction of $\mathbf{u}$. The *projection of* $\mathbf{v}$ *onto* $\mathbf{u}$ is defined to equal

$$(\mathbf{u} \cdot \mathbf{v})\mathbf{u},$$

which is the component of $\mathbf{v}$ parallel to the vector $\mathbf{u}$. (This formula for projection is correct only if $\mathbf{u}$ is a unit vector.) Note that the projection is a vector parallel to $\mathbf{u}$.

We can also find a formula for the component of $\mathbf{v}$ perpendicular to $\mathbf{u}$. Namely, if we subtract the projection, the remaining part is perpendicular to $\mathbf{u}$. Thus, for a unit vector $\mathbf{u}$, the component of $\mathbf{v}$ perpendicular to $\mathbf{u}$ is equal to

$$\mathbf{v} - (\mathbf{u} \cdot \mathbf{v})\mathbf{u}.$$

It is easy to check that $\mathbf{u} \cdot \mathbf{u} = \|\mathbf{u}\|^2$. Thus, the magnitude of $\mathbf{u}$ is $\sqrt{\mathbf{u} \cdot \mathbf{u}}$. We use $\mathbf{u}^2$ as a shorthand notation for $\mathbf{u} \cdot \mathbf{u} = \|\mathbf{u}\|^2$.

Cross Products in $\mathbb{R}^2$

The cross product of vectors in $\mathbb{R}^2$ was defined as $\mathbf{u} \times \mathbf{v} = u_1 v_2 - u_2 v_1$. There are several alternate useful ways to think about cross products:

(a) If you are more familiar with cross products in three dimensions, we can restate the two-dimensional cross product in terms of the three-dimensional cross product. For this, we pad $\mathbf{u}$ and $\mathbf{v}$ with a third entry equal to zero and take the cross product in three dimensions. This yields

$$\langle u_1, u_2, 0 \rangle \times \langle v_1, v_2, 0 \rangle = \langle 0, 0, u_1 v_2 - u_2 v_1 \rangle.$$

Thus, the two-dimensional cross product is equal to the z-component of the cross product obtained by embedding $\mathbf{u}$ and $\mathbf{v}$ into three dimensions. The advantage of thinking about two-dimensional cross products in this way is that properties (c) and (d) below may already be quite familiar.

(b) In the two-dimensional setting, the vector cross product can be expressed as a dot product with a rotated vector. To explain, let, as usual, $\mathbf{u} = \langle u_1, u_2 \rangle$, and let $\mathbf{u}^{\text{rot}}$ be the vector $\mathbf{u}$ rotated counterclockwise 90°. Referring to Figure A.4, we see that $\mathbf{u}^{\text{rot}}$ is equal to

$$\mathbf{u}^{\text{rot}} = \langle -u_2, u_1 \rangle.$$

It is immediate from the definitions of cross and dot products that $\mathbf{u} \times \mathbf{v} = \mathbf{u}^{\text{rot}} \cdot \mathbf{v}$. That is, the cross product of $\mathbf{u}$ and $\mathbf{v}$ can be calculated by rotating $\mathbf{u}$ through a right angle and then forming the dot product with $\mathbf{v}$.

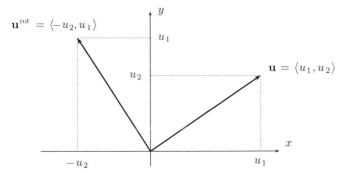

Figure A.4. The effect of rotating a vector $90°$ counterclockwise.

This tells us that $\mathbf{u} \times \mathbf{v}$ is equal to zero if and only if $\mathbf{u}$ and $\mathbf{v}$ are parallel (i.e., collinear). In other words, $\mathbf{u} \times \mathbf{v} = 0$ if and only if $\mathbf{u} = \alpha\mathbf{v}$ (or $\mathbf{v} = \alpha\mathbf{u}$) for some scalar α; or equivalently, if the angle between the vectors is equal to either 0 or $180°$.

(c) Let φ be the angle between $\mathbf{u}$ and $\mathbf{v}$: the angle φ must be measured in the counterclockwise direction from $\mathbf{u}$ to $\mathbf{v}$ as shown in Figure A.5. Then the cross product of the 2-vectors is equal to

$$\mathbf{u} \times \mathbf{v} = \|\mathbf{u}\| \cdot \|\mathbf{v}\| \sin\varphi.$$

(This can easily be proved from Equation A.3 and the fact that the cross product with $\mathbf{u}$ is equivalent to the dot product with $\mathbf{u}^{\mathrm{rot}}$.) Note that it is important that the angle φ be measured in the correct direction, for $\sin(-\varphi) = -\sin\varphi$. Indeed, the cross product is antisymmetric:

$$\mathbf{u} \times \mathbf{v} = -\mathbf{v} \times \mathbf{u}.$$

(d) There is an elegant interpretation of cross product in terms of area. Consider the parallelogram with sides equal to the vectors $\mathbf{u}$ and $\mathbf{v}$, as shown in Figure A.6. Then the (signed) area of the parallelogram is equal to

$$\text{Area} = \mathbf{u} \times \mathbf{v}.$$

To prove this, use the formula (base) · (height). If the base length is measured along $\mathbf{u}$, it is just equal to $\|\mathbf{u}\|$. Then, the height must be measured perpendicularly to $\mathbf{u}$ and is equal to $\|\mathbf{v}\| \sin\varphi$.

When the angle φ is greater than $180°$, then the cross product $\mathbf{u} \times \mathbf{v}$ is negative. In this case, the parallelogram can be thought of as having "negative height" and hence negative area.

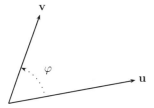

Figure A.5. The angle between $\mathbf{u}$ and $\mathbf{v}$ equals φ and is used for computing the cross product. The direction (sign) of the angle is important for the cross product.

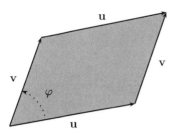

Figure A.6. In $\mathbb{R}^2$, the (signed) area of the parallelogram is equal to the cross product $\mathbf{u} \times \mathbf{v}$. In $\mathbb{R}^3$, the area of the parallelogram is equal to the magnitude of $\mathbf{u} \times \mathbf{v}$.

A.2.2 Vectors in $\mathbb{R}^3$

The three-dimensional Euclidean space is denoted by $\mathbb{R}^3$. A point or a vector $\mathbf{u}$ in $\mathbb{R}^3$ is specified by a triple of values, $\mathbf{u} = \langle u_1, u_2, u_3 \rangle$. In computer graphics, it is common to use x, y, z-axes that are oriented as shown in Figure I.4 on page 6: as shown there, the x-axis points rightward, the y-axis points upward, and the z-axis points toward the viewer. This is different from the usual conventions you probably learned in calculus class, but is still a right-handed coordinate system. (The main reason to work with a right-handed coordinate system rather than a left-handed coordinate system is that it makes the cross product obey the usual "right-hand rule.")

The length (usually called *magnitude* or *norm*) of a vector in $\mathbb{R}^3$ is given by the Euclidean distance formula

$$\|\mathbf{u}\| = \sqrt{u_1^2 + u_2^2 + u_3^2}.$$

A vector $\mathbf{u}$ is a *unit vector* provided $\|\mathbf{u}\| = 1$. The unit sphere in $\mathbb{R}^2$, also called the 2-sphere or S^2, is the set of vectors with magnitude 1.

A nonunit vector $\mathbf{u}$ is *normalized* by the process of replacing it with a unit vector pointing in the same direction. That is, $\mathbf{u}$ is normalized by calculating $\mathbf{u}/\|\mathbf{u}\|$. The terminology is a little confusing because the term "normal vector" is used to mean a nonzero vector that is perpendicular (that is, normal) to a surface. By definition, normal vectors are *not* required to be unit vectors. In other words, normal vectors do not always need to be normalized. Nonetheless, it is frequently helpful to use unit normal vectors – particularly in Chapter III for lighting applications.

Addition and subtraction of vectors in $\mathbb{R}^3$ are defined component-wise in much the same way as their definition in $\mathbb{R}^2$. Dot product and cross product are discussed next.

Dot Products in $\mathbb{R}^3$

The dot product of two vectors in $\mathbb{R}^3$ is defined by

$$\mathbf{u} \cdot \mathbf{v} = u_1 v_1 + u_2 v_2 + u_3 v_3.$$

This means that the dot product of two 3-vectors is a scalar.

If φ is the angle between the vectors $\mathbf{u}$ and $\mathbf{v}$, then

$$\mathbf{u} \cdot \mathbf{v} = \|\mathbf{u}\| \cdot \|\mathbf{v}\| \cos \varphi.$$

Suppose that $\mathbf{u}$ is a unit vector. Then the *projection* of the vector $\mathbf{v}$ onto the line containing the vector $\mathbf{u}$ has signed length equal to $\mathbf{u} \cdot \mathbf{v}$. (This can be proved in the way used for $\mathbb{R}^2$ using the characterization of the dot product in terms of $\cos \varphi$.) The *projection of* $\mathbf{v}$ *onto the unit vector* **u** is thus equal to the vector

$$(\mathbf{u} \cdot \mathbf{v})\mathbf{u}.$$

This is the component of **v** in the direction of **u**.

The component of **v** perpendicular to **u** is equal to

$$\mathbf{v} - (\mathbf{u} \cdot \mathbf{v})\mathbf{u}.$$

The magnitude or *norm* of a vector **u** is equal to $\sqrt{\mathbf{u}^2} = \sqrt{\mathbf{u} \cdot \mathbf{u}}$.

Cross Products in $\mathbb{R}^3$

The cross product of two vectors in $\mathbb{R}^3$ is the vector defined by

$$\mathbf{u} \times \mathbf{v} = \langle u_2v_3 - u_3v_2, \ u_3v_1 - u_1v_3, \ u_1v_2 - u_2v_1 \rangle.$$

To describe the definition of $\mathbf{u} \times \mathbf{v}$ in an alternate, geometric way, let φ be the angle from **u** to **v** measured in a direction such that $0 \le \varphi \le 180°$ (the direction to measure φ is unique for noncollinear **u** and **v**). Then, $\mathbf{u} \times \mathbf{v}$ has magnitude

$$||\mathbf{u}|| \cdot ||\mathbf{v}|| \sin \varphi,$$

and is perpendicular to both **u** and **v** with its direction given by the *right-hand rule*. The right-hand rule states that if you use the palm of your right hand to push **u** towards **v** with your thumb extended out at right angles, then your thumb will point in the direction of $\mathbf{u} \times \mathbf{v}$.

An equivalent way to state the geometric definition of the cross product is as follows. Let **u** and **v** both lie in a plane P. The plane P divides $\mathbb{R}^3$ into two half-spaces. Arbitrarily choose one of these half-spaces as being "above" the plane. Viewing the two vectors from above, let ψ be the angle from **u** to **v** measured in the counterclockwise direction. Then $\mathbf{u} \times \mathbf{v}$ is the vector with *signed* magnitude equal to

$$||\mathbf{u}|| \cdot ||\mathbf{v}|| \sin \psi, \qquad\qquad\qquad \text{A.4}$$

and $\mathbf{u} \times \mathbf{v}$ is pointing up perpendicularly to P. We called the value A.4 the signed magnitude because, if this value is negative, the cross product is pointing downwards from P.

Evidently, for nonzero **u** and **v**, the cross product is equal to zero if and only if **u** and **v** are collinear.

The parallelogram area property (d) of cross products in $\mathbb{R}^2$ still holds in $\mathbb{R}^3$. With reference to Figure A.6, the vectors **u** and **v** now lie in $\mathbb{R}^3$. The area of the parallelogram is equal to the length of $\mathbf{u} \times \mathbf{v}$.

A.3 Matrices

A matrix $M = (m_{i,j})_{i,j}$ is a rectangular array of scalars,

$$M = \begin{pmatrix} m_{1,1} & \cdots & m_{1,s} \\ \vdots & \ddots & \vdots \\ m_{r,1} & \cdots & m_{r,s} \end{pmatrix}.$$

Here M is $r \times s$ matrix, and $m_{i,j}$ is the entry in row i and column j.

If in addition N is an $s \times t$ matrix, then the matrix product of M times N is the $r \times t$ matrix P whose entries $p_{i,k}$ are obtained by taking the inner product of the ith row of M with the kth column of N, namely,

$$p_{i,k} = \sum_{j=1}^{s} m_{i,j} n_{j,k}.$$

The $r \times r$ identity matrix is the matrix I that has diagonal entries equal to 1, and off-diagonal entries equal to 0. There is a different identity matrix for each $r \geq 1$, but we use the same notation I for all of them because it should always be clear from the context what the dimension is.

The identity matrices have the property that

$$IM = M \qquad \text{and} \qquad MI = M.$$

The inverse of M is the matrix M^{-1} such that $MM^{-1} = M^{-1}M = I$. Only square matrices can have inverses, and not even all of them do. A matrix that is invertible is also said to be *nonsingular*.

The *transpose* of M is the matrix M^{T} obtained by swapping elements of M across the diagonal: for $M = (m_{i,j})_{i,j}$, an $r \times s$ matrix, its transpose $M^{\mathrm{T}} = (m_{j,i})_{i,j}$ is an $s \times r$ matrix. (Note the subscripts in reverse order!)

The following identities are easy to check:

$$M^{\mathrm{T}} N^{\mathrm{T}} = (NM)^{\mathrm{T}} \qquad \text{and} \qquad I^{\mathrm{T}} = I.$$

In addition, for invertible M, $(M^{\mathrm{T}})^{-1} = (M^{-1})^{\mathrm{T}}$.

The matrices used in the early chapters of this book are primarily small (of dimensions 2×2 through 4×4). Frequently, we are interested in how these matrices act on points or vectors. For this, points and vectors will be treated as being column vectors: namely, a 2-vector is a 2×1 matrix, and a 3-vector is a 3×1 matrix. For instance, our convention is that a 3-vector $\mathbf{u} = \langle u_1, u_2, u_3 \rangle$ is the same as the column vector

$$\begin{pmatrix} u_1 \\ u_2 \\ u_3 \end{pmatrix}.$$

In this way, we can take the product of a matrix and a vector and get a vector as a result. You should refer to Chapter II for more information on matrices and vectors in $\mathbb{R}^2$ and $\mathbb{R}^3$. As discussed in Chapter II, matrices are used extensively in computer graphics to transform vectors by multiplication.

A.3.1 Matrices and Vector Products in $\mathbb{R}^3$

It is possible to reexpress dot and cross products in terms of matrix products. As we just said, a vector $\mathbf{u} = \langle u_1, u_2, u_3 \rangle$ is, by convention, the same as a column vector (i.e., a 3×1 matrix). Therefore, the transpose of a vector is a 1×3 matrix or a row vector. That is,

$$\mathbf{u}^{\mathrm{T}} = (u_1 \ u_2 \ u_3).$$

It is easy to check that a dot product can be expressed as

$$\mathbf{u} \cdot \mathbf{v} = \mathbf{u}^{\mathrm{T}} \mathbf{v}.$$

Or, to write it out fully,

$$\langle u_1, u_2, u_3 \rangle \cdot \langle v_1, v_2, v_3 \rangle = (u_1 \ u_2 \ u_3) \begin{pmatrix} v_1 \\ v_2 \\ v_3 \end{pmatrix}.$$

To interpret this correctly, the left-hand side of each of the two equalities above is a dot product, and the right-hand side is a matrix product. (If one wanted to be overly precise, one could note that the right-hand side really denotes a 1×1 matrix, not a scalar, but it does no harm to treat a 1×1 matrix as being the same as a scalar.)

We just described how to reexpress a dot product as a matrix product using a 1×3 matrix. Similarly, a cross product operation can be expressed as a matrix product but now using a 3×3 matrix. Namely, let $M_{\mathbf{u} \times}$ be the matrix

$$M_{\mathbf{u} \times} = \begin{pmatrix} 0 & -u_3 & u_2 \\ u_3 & 0 & -u_1 \\ -u_2 & u_1 & 0 \end{pmatrix}.$$

Then it is easy to check that

$$(M_{\mathbf{u} \times})\mathbf{v} = \mathbf{u} \times \mathbf{v}$$

by using the first definition of cross product in $\mathbb{R}^3$.

The matrix version of a dot product allows us to express the projection operator as a matrix. Let $\mathbf{u}$ be a unit vector, and recall that the projection of $\mathbf{v}$ onto $\mathbf{u}$ is equal to $(\mathbf{u} \cdot \mathbf{v})\mathbf{u}$. This can be rewritten as

$$(\mathbf{u} \cdot \mathbf{v})\mathbf{u} = \mathbf{u}(\mathbf{u} \cdot \mathbf{v}) = \mathbf{u}(\mathbf{u}^{\mathsf{T}}\mathbf{v}) = (\mathbf{u}\mathbf{u}^{\mathsf{T}})\mathbf{v}.$$

(The last equality uses the associativity of matrix multiplication.) Thus, letting Proj_u be the matrix

$$\mathrm{Proj}_u = \mathbf{u}\mathbf{u}^{\mathsf{T}} = \begin{pmatrix} u_1 \\ u_2 \\ u_3 \end{pmatrix} \begin{pmatrix} u_1 & u_2 & u_3 \end{pmatrix} = \begin{pmatrix} u_1^2 & u_1 u_2 & u_1 u_3 \\ u_1 u_2 & u_2^2 & u_2 u_3 \\ u_1 u_3 & u_2 u_3 & u_3^2 \end{pmatrix},$$

we have that $(\mathrm{Proj}_u)\mathbf{v}$ is equal to the projection of $\mathbf{v}$ onto $\mathbf{u}$.

A.3.2 Determinants, Inverses, and Adjoints

Let M be a square $n \times n$ matrix. For $i, j \in \{1, \ldots, n\}$, the matrix $M_{i,j}$ is defined to be the $(n-1) \times (n-1)$ matrix obtained by deleting the ith row and the jth column from M.

We now define the *determinant* $\det(M)$ of M. The definition of the determinant proceeds by induction on the dimension of M. When $n = 1$, M is just a 1×1 matrix, and $\det(M)$ is equal to its sole entry $m_{1,1}$. For $n > 1$, the determinant of M is equal to

$$\det(M) = m_{1,1}\det(M_{1,1}) - m_{1,2}\det(M_{1,2}) + m_{1,3}\det(M_{1,3})$$

$$-m_{1,4}\det(M_{1,4}) + \cdots \pm m_{1,n}\det(M_{1,n})$$

$$= \sum_{j=1}^{n}(-1)^{1+j}m_{1,j}\det(M_{1,j}). \qquad \text{A.5}$$

The definition A.5 defines the determinant in terms of its expansion along the first row of the matrix. More generally, the determinant can also be defined with an expansion along any row i as

$$\det(M) = \sum_{j=1}^{n}(-1)^{i+j}m_{i,j}\det(M_{i,j}),$$

as well as in terms of an expansion along any column j:

$$\det(M) = \sum_{i=1}^{n}(-1)^{i+j}m_{i,j}\det(M_{i,j}).$$

The value $(-1)^{i+j} \det(M_{i,j})$ is called the *cofactor of M at* (i, j). Thus, the determinant is expressed in terms of an inner product of the entries in a given row (or column) of the matrix and its cofactors along the same row (or column).

The *adjoint* of M is the matrix N that is the transpose of the cofactors of M. Namely, N is the matrix with entries

$$n_{i,j} = (-1)^{i+j} \det(M_{j,i}).$$

It is always the case that

$$MN = NM = \det(M)I,$$

for N the adjoint of M. Therefore, if $\det(M) \neq 0$, then M is invertible and

$$M^{-1} = \frac{1}{\det(M)} N.$$

This gives a formula for inverting any invertible matrix, for a matrix M is invertible if and only if its determinant is nonzero.

A.3.3 Linear Subspaces⋆

(Knowledge of linear subspaces is needed only for the discussion of inverse kinematics in Chapter XII and, to a lesser extent, for the material on projective geometry in Chapter II.)

Let $k \geq 1$ and consider $\mathbb{R}^k$. A subset $A \subseteq \mathbb{R}^k$ is called a *linear subspace* provided that A is closed under addition and under scalar multiplication.[1] That is, A is a linear subspace if and only if, for all $\mathbf{x}$ and $\mathbf{y}$ in A and for all scalars α, $\mathbf{x} + \mathbf{y}$ and $\alpha\mathbf{x}$ are also in A.

The vectors $\mathbf{x}_1, \mathbf{x}_2, \ldots, \mathbf{x}_n$ are said to be *linearly independent* provided there is no sequence of scalars $\alpha_1, \ldots, \alpha_n$, not all zero, such that

$$\alpha_1\mathbf{x}_1 + \alpha_2\mathbf{x}_2 + \cdots + \alpha_n\mathbf{x}_n = \mathbf{0}.$$

(Here, $\mathbf{0}$ is the zero vector.) The *dimension* of a linear subspace A is the largest value n for which A contains n linearly independent vectors. When $A \subseteq \mathbb{R}^k$, the dimension of A can be at most k.

Let $\mathbf{x}_1, \ldots, \mathbf{x}_n$ be vectors in $\mathbb{R}$. The *span* of these vectors is the linear subspace that contains all linear combinations of the vectors $\mathbf{x}_i$. In other words, the span of $\mathbf{x}_1, \ldots, \mathbf{x}_n$ is the following subspace:

$$\text{span}(\vec{\mathbf{x}}) = \{\alpha_1\mathbf{x}_1 + \cdots + \alpha_n\mathbf{x}_n : \alpha_1, \ldots, \alpha_n \in \mathbb{R}\}.$$

It is easy to check that this is closed under addition and scalar multiplication and thus is indeed a linear subspace. If $\mathbf{x}_1, \ldots, \mathbf{x}_n$ are linearly independent, then every vector in their span can be expressed as a linear combination of $\mathbf{x}_1, \ldots, \mathbf{x}_n$ in a unique way.

Theorem A.1 *Let* $A \subseteq \mathbb{R}^k$ *be a linear subspace of dimension n. Suppose* $\mathbf{x}_1, \ldots, \mathbf{x}_n$ *are in A and are linearly independent. Then* $\text{span}(\vec{\mathbf{x}})$ *is equal to A.*

Let A and B be linear subspaces of $\mathbb{R}^k$. We say that A and B are *orthogonal* if and only if, for all $\mathbf{x} \in A$ and all $\mathbf{y} \in B$, $\mathbf{x} \cdot \mathbf{y} = 0$. We say that A and B are *orthogonal complements* if they are orthogonal and if for every $\mathbf{u} \in \mathbb{R}^k$ there are $\mathbf{x} \in A$ and $\mathbf{y} \in B$ such that $\mathbf{u} = \mathbf{x} + \mathbf{y}$. In this case, $\mathbf{x}$ and $\mathbf{y}$ are uniquely determined by $\mathbf{u}$; in fact, $\mathbf{x}$ and $\mathbf{y}$ are the orthogonal projections of $\mathbf{u}$ onto the subspaces A and B.

---

[1] Vector spaces are usually defined very generally. However, we only use vector spaces that are subspaces of $\mathbb{R}^k$ for some k and therefore make the corresponding simplifications in the discussion of linear subspaces.

Theorem A.2 *Let A be a linear subspace of $\mathbb{R}^k$. Then there is a unique subspace B such that A and B are orthogonal complements. In fact,*

$$B = \{\mathbf{y} : \text{for all } \mathbf{x} \in A, \, \mathbf{x} \cdot \mathbf{y} = 0\}.$$

We use $A^\perp$ to denote the orthogonal complement of A.

Now, we return to matrices. Let M be an $r \times s$ matrix. If $\mathbf{x}$ is an s-vector, then $M\mathbf{x}$ is an r-vector. Therefore, the mapping

$$f_M : \mathbf{x} \mapsto M\mathbf{x}$$

is a function with domain $\mathbb{R}^s$ and codomain R^r. We often conflate the matrix M with the mapping f_M and use M to refer to both the matrix and the mapping. It is easily seen that the range of M is exactly equal to the span of the columns of M. That is, let M have as columns the r-vectors $\mathbf{u}_1, \ldots, \mathbf{u}_s$; then the range of M is equal to span($\vec{\mathbf{u}}$).

The *kernel* of M (or of f_M, to be more proper), is the set of vectors $\mathbf{x} \in \mathbb{R}^s$ such that $M\mathbf{x} = \mathbf{0}$. Let the rows of M be the s-vectors $\mathbf{v}_1, \ldots, \mathbf{v}_r$. Clearly, the kernel of M is the set of vectors $\mathbf{x}$ such that $\mathbf{x} \cdot \mathbf{v}_i = 0$ for all $i = 1, \ldots, r$. From the previous theorem, it follows easily that the kernel of M is the linear subspace that is the orthogonal complement of the span of the rows of M; namely, the kernel of M is equal to $(\text{span}(\vec{\mathbf{v}}))^\perp$.

We call span($\vec{\mathbf{u}}$) the *column span* of M and span($\vec{\mathbf{v}}$) the *row span* of M. These are also denoted colspan(M) and rowspan(M).

The *rank* of the matrix M is defined to be the dimension of rowspan(M) and of colspan(M). (It is a theorem that these both have the same dimension.) The rank can also be defined as being equal to the maximum number of linearly independent rows (or, columns) of M.

A.4 Multivariable Calculus

A.4.1 Multivariable Functions

A *multivariable* function is a function with multiple inputs. For now, we consider only real-valued multivariable functions, that is, functions with domain $\mathbb{R}^k$ and codomain $\mathbb{R}$. Simple examples of such functions include

$$f(x, y) = x^2 + y^2,$$

which can be visualized as a paraboloid surface, as well as functions of three variables such as $f(x, y, z) = x^2 + y^2 + z^2$. The latter function is hard to visualize because it would require four dimensions to graph it properly.

In addition, functions that take vectors as inputs can be viewed as multivariable functions. For example, the vector magnitude function $\mathbf{u} \mapsto ||\mathbf{u}||$ can be viewed as a function of the three scalar values u_1, u_2, u_3. Likewise, the distance function $f(\mathbf{u}, \mathbf{v}) = ||\mathbf{u} - \mathbf{v}||$ can be viewed as a function with domain $\mathbb{R}^6$, taking six scalar inputs.

Fix some function $f = f(x_1, \ldots, x_k)$ with k inputs. We sometimes slightly abuse notation and also write f as $f(\mathbf{x})$, where $\mathbf{x} = \langle x_1, \ldots, x_k \rangle$. The *partial derivative* of f with respect to x_i is the multivariable function

$$\frac{\partial f}{\partial x_i}(x_1, \ldots, x_k)$$

that equals the rate of change in values of f with respect to changes in the value of x_i while keeping the rest of the input values fixed. To express this formally with limits, the partial derivative is the function satisfying

$$\frac{\partial f}{\partial x_i}(x_1, \ldots, x_k) = \lim_{h \to 0} \frac{f(x_1, \ldots, x_{i-1}, x_i + h, x_{i+1}, \ldots x_k) - f(x_1, \ldots, x_i, \ldots x_k)}{h}.$$

The partial derivative is undefined where this limit does not exist.

The *total derivative* of f is given by the expression

$$df = \frac{\partial f}{\partial x_1} dx_1 + \frac{\partial f}{\partial x_2} dx_2 + \cdots + \frac{\partial f}{\partial x_k} dx_k.$$

A good way to visualize what the total derivative means is to think of it as providing a way to approximate f in the neighborhood of a point $\langle x_1, \ldots, x_k \rangle$:

$$f(x_1 + \Delta x_1, \ldots, x_k + \Delta x_k) - f(x_1, \ldots, x_k) \approx \frac{\partial f}{\partial x_1} \Delta x_1 + \cdots + \frac{\partial f}{\partial x_k} \Delta x_k. \qquad \text{A.6}$$

We can write this more suggestively as

$$\Delta f \approx \frac{\partial f}{\partial x_1} \Delta x_1 + \cdots + \frac{\partial f}{\partial x_k} \Delta x_k.$$

For well-behaved functions, this approximation is first-order accurate, which is to say that the error in the approximation is only $O(\Delta x_1^2 + \cdots + \Delta x_k^2)$. Therefore, the approximation is very accurate for sufficiently small values of Δx_i.

The *gradient* of $f(x_1, \ldots, x_k)$ is the vector-valued function

$$(\nabla f)(\mathbf{x}) = \left\langle \frac{\partial f}{\partial x_1}(\mathbf{x}), \frac{\partial f}{\partial x_2}(\mathbf{x}), \ldots, \frac{\partial f}{\partial x_k}(\mathbf{x}) \right\rangle.$$

The gradient function has k scalar inputs, and its value is a k-vector.

The motivation for the definition of the gradient is that it plays the role of the first derivative of $f(\mathbf{x})$. Indeed, using the gradient function, we can rewrite the first-order approximation of Equation A.6 in vector notation as

$$f(\mathbf{x} + \Delta \mathbf{x}) - f(\mathbf{x}) \approx (\nabla f) \cdot (\Delta \mathbf{x}).$$

The right-hand side of this approximation is a vector dot product.

A *level set* of a function f is a set of the points $\langle x_1, \ldots x_k \rangle$ satisfying $f(x_1, \ldots, x_k) = c$ for some fixed constant c. In this book, we only work with level sets of functions of three variables (i.e., $k = 3$). Such sets are also called *implicitly defined surfaces*. For example, the equation $x^2 + y^2 + z^2 - 1 = 0$ is an implicit definition of the unit sphere in $\mathbb{R}^3$.

In "nice" situations, an implicitly defined surface is a two-dimensional surface lying inside $\mathbb{R}^3$ (think of the unit sphere, for instance). Of course, there are pathological cases of surfaces that have cusps, discontinuities, or self-intersections; however, in most cases that are of interest to us, an implicitly defined surface is (at least locally) a smooth, well-behaved surface.

Let S be an implicitly defined surface in $\mathbb{R}^3$ and $\mathbf{x}$ be a point on S. A vector $\mathbf{n}$ is said to be normal to the surface S at the point $\mathbf{x}$ provided that $\mathbf{n}$ is perpendicular to the surface at that point. If the gradient vector $\nabla f(\mathbf{x})$ is nonzero, then it is normal to the surface at $\vec{x}$. In this case,

$$\mathbf{n} = \frac{(\nabla f)(\mathbf{x})}{||(\nabla f)(\mathbf{x})||}$$

is a unit normal for the surface. It is harder to compute a normal vector when the gradient vector is zero; in fact, the surface may have a cusp or other strange behavior and may not have any normal vector at all.

As an example of computing **n**, consider the implicit definition of a flattened ellipsoid by $4x^2 + y^2 + 4z^2 = 4$. Here, $\nabla f(x, y, z) = \langle 8x, 2y, 8z \rangle$ is nonzero for any point $\langle x, y, z \rangle$ on the ellipsoid and hence is normal to the ellipsoid at that point.

A.4.2 Vector-Valued Functions

A vector-valued function is a function whose values are vectors. We often use the convention of writing vector-valued functions in boldface – for instance $\mathbf{f}(x)$, to distinguish them from scalar-valued functions. (Less commonly, we also use uppercase, such as $P(x)$, for the same purpose.) An example of a vector-valued function is a function $\mathbf{p}(t)$ that gives the position of a point at time t. For a point moving in the xy-plane, $\mathbf{p}(t)$ would be in $\mathbb{R}^2$; for a point moving in $\mathbb{R}^3$, $\mathbf{p}(t)$ would be in $\mathbb{R}^3$.

The components of a vector-valued function $\mathbf{f}$ are scalar-valued functions, $f_1(x), \ldots, f_n(x)$. Thus,

$$\mathbf{f}(x) = \langle f_1(x), f_2(x), \ldots, f_n(x) \rangle.$$

The first derivative of $\mathbf{f}$ is calculated component-wise. Namely, the first derivative is equal to

$$\mathbf{f}'(x) = \langle f_1'(x), f_2'(x), \ldots, f_n'(x) \rangle.$$

For example, the derivative of a position function $\mathbf{p}(t)$ is the velocity function $\mathbf{v}(t) = \mathbf{p}'(t)$. The second derivative of $\mathbf{p}(t)$ is the acceleration function.

A *parametric curve* is defined by a vector-valued function $\mathbf{f}(x)$. The curve is the set of points $\{\mathbf{f}(x) : x \in \mathbb{R}\}$. If the values of the function $\mathbf{f}$ are k-vectors, then the parametric curve lies in $\mathbb{R}^k$. The first derivative $\mathbf{f}'(x)$ will be tangent to the curve at the point $\mathbf{f}(x)$ provided it is nonzero.

A.4.3 Multivariable Vector-Valued Functions

A vector-valued multivariable function is a function that has as input a sequence of reals and produces a vector as its value.

Let $\mathbf{f} : \mathbb{R}^k \to \mathbb{R}^n$. Then we can write $\mathbf{f}$ in terms of its n components as

$$\mathbf{f}(\mathbf{x}) = \langle f_1(\mathbf{x}), f_2(\mathbf{x}), \ldots, f_n(\mathbf{x}) \rangle,$$

where $\mathbf{x} = \langle x_1, \ldots, x_k \rangle$. Note that each f_i is a scalar-valued, multivariable function.

The first derivative of $\mathbf{f}$ is called the *Jacobian* of $\mathbf{f}$. Intuitively, the first derivative of $\mathbf{f}$ should be the vector of first derivatives of its n components. However, from Section A.4.1, the first derivative of a component f_i is actually the gradient function ∇f_i, which is a k-vector valued function. Thus, the first derivative of $\mathbf{f}(\mathbf{x})$ becomes an $n \times k$ matrix called the Jacobian matrix.

The Jacobian matrix is defined to be the matrix whose ith row is equal to the gradient of $f_i(\mathbf{x})$. This can be written explicitly as

$$J(\mathbf{x}) = \left(\frac{\partial f_i}{\partial x_j} \right)_{i,j} = \begin{pmatrix} \dfrac{\partial f_1}{\partial x_1} & \cdots & \dfrac{\partial f_1}{\partial x_k} \\ \vdots & \ddots & \vdots \\ \dfrac{\partial f_n}{\partial x_1} & \cdots & \dfrac{\partial f_n}{\partial x_k} \end{pmatrix}.$$

The first-order approximation formula for values of $\mathbf{f}$ in a neighborhood of $\mathbf{x}$ is then

$$\mathbf{f}(\mathbf{x} + \Delta \mathbf{x}) - \mathbf{f}(\mathbf{x}) \approx J \, \Delta \mathbf{x}.$$

APPENDIX B

RayTrace Software Package

B.1 Introduction to the Ray Tracing Package

I have written a ray tracing package that implements basic recursive ray tracing. This software and its source code are freely available and can be downloaded from this book's Web site.

The ray tracing software uses an object-oriented approach to rendering and ray tracing. The object-oriented design includes base classes for materials, for geometric shapes, for lights, and for textures. This provides considerable flexibility in adding features since it allows the addition of new geometric shapes without affecting the functionality of older code; similarly, new kinds of lighting models, new kinds of textures, and so on, can be added without needing to change the structure of the software.

The material and lighting classes supported by the software include the usual material properties such as ambient, diffuse, and specular color and specular exponents. In addition, the material classes include reflection and transmission color coefficients for use in recursive ray tracing. The complete Phong model for local lighting is supported, including all the OpenGL-type features such as spotlights and attenuation. A version of the Cook–Torrance model is also supported.

The ray tracing software supports a range of geometric shapes, including spheres, triangles, parallelograms, cones, cylinders, tori, ellipsoids, parallelepipeds, and Bézier patches. Collectively, these geometric shapes are called *viewable objects*. The viewable object classes are responsible for detecting intersections of rays against a particular geometric shape. The viewable object classes also calculate normals and keep track of the material of an object. In addition, they calculate u and v coordinates for texture mapping purposes.

The texture mapping classes are in essence implemented as "callback" routines. This means that it is easy to add algorithmic texture maps in addition to the more traditional bitmap (table lookup) texture maps. Three kinds of texture maps are currently supported: texture maps formed from RGB images read from bitmap (.bmp) files, procedurally generated checkboard patterns, and bump maps.

To make the ray tracing software more modular, as well as easier to use, the software is split into three levels (in separate C++ projects). These levels are as follows:

Top Level: Ray Tracing. The top level routines implement the recursive ray tracing algorithm and the high-level scene description. In the sample implementation, this is split into two parts. First, the program RayTraceData makes function calls to set up the lights and the geometric shapes and their materials and textures. Second, the program RayTrace implements the high-level recursive ray tracing algorithm. A similar set of

332

high-level routines, `RayTrace2` and `RayTraceData2`, are also provided; these are similar but use a more complex scene with more kinds of geometric shapes.

These high-level routines are intended to be easy to modify without the programmer's having to understand the internal structure of the intermediate and low levels. In fact, the high-level routines have been left in a fairly preliminary state: the software was developed for teaching purposes, and students are asked to improve on the high-level routines, for instance, by implementing distributed ray tracing. The intermediate- and low-level routines are more polished and are not really intended to be modified.

Intermediate Level: Geometry and Rendering. The intermediate level routines handle lights, geometric shapes, materials, and texture maps. In addition, they include code for local lighting calculation (Phong and Cook–Torrance lighting are both supported). The lights include all the usual OpenGL style features such as ambient, diffuse, and specular light components, attenuation, and spotlight effects. The materials encompass the usual OpenGL material properties, including ambient, diffuse, and specular colors and shininess, plus additional properties such as reflection and transmission coefficients. The geometric shapes are implemented with a C++ base class called `ViewableBase`; derived classes include many shapes. These geometric classes incorporate efficient routines for calculating intersections with rays. They also calculate normals and u, v coordinates for texture mapping. Texture maps are also C++ classes and are implemented somewhat like callback routines: a texture map is attached to a viewable object, and when an object is intersected by a ray the texture map routines are called. This provides a flexible framework for texture mapping.

Low-Level Routines: Linear Algebra. These routines are in the project `VrMath` and include linear algebra routines for 2-vectors, 3-vectors, and 4-vectors. The intermediate- and high-level routines have been written to isolate the low-level routines, allowing modifications to the high-level routines to require little knowledge of the low-level routines.

B.2 The High-Level Ray Tracing Routines

The high-level ray tracing routines are illustrated by the example code in `RayTrace.cpp` and `RayTraceData.cpp`, or in `RayTrace2.cpp` and `RayTraceData2.cpp`. We will first discuss the `RayTrace` routines, which control the recursive ray tracing procedures.

RayTraceView: This is the highest level routine that initiates the ray tracing procedure. It functions in much the same way as the routine `RayTraceMain` on page 242. `RayTraceView` loops over all the pixels in the view window. For each pixel, it calculates the view ray from the view position towards the center of the pixel and then calls the recursive routine `RayTrace` to calculate the color value to render the pixel. The `RayTrace` routine returns the value `curPixelColor`, which is stored into the pixel array. After calculating all the pixel colors, the pixel array's `Draw` routine is called to store the pixel colors into the rear OpenGL rendering buffer; then the buffers are swapped to show the ray traced scene.

RayTrace: This is the routine that recursively traces rays and combines color values. It is the heart of the recursive ray tracing algorithm. Its parameters consist of (a) a trace depth, (b) a starting position for the ray, (c) a unit vector giving the direction of the ray, (d) a 4-vector `VectorR4` in which a color value is returned, and (e) an avoidance number that specifies what object the ray originates from.

RayTrace begins by calling `FindIntersection`, which calculates whether the ray intersects some viewable object. If not, then the ray is presumed to have passed completely out of the scene and the default background color is returned. Otherwise, an intersection point is returned by `FindIntersection` as an object of type `Visible-Point`. The `VisiblePoint` class includes information about the position, the normal, and the material properties of the intersected point. `RayTrace` calls the routine `CalcAllDirectIllum` to calculate the illumination of the intersected point with the local lighting model, which incorporates the effect of global ambient lighting and of direct illumination from lights (the latter is usually computed according to the Phong lighting model). Then, if the trace depth has not been exhausted, `RayTrace` spawns reflection and transmission rays. Reflection rays have their direction computed by Equation IX.2 on page 238. `RayTrace` is called recursively with the reflection ray. Whatever color is returned is then filtered by the reflective color (the ρ_{rg} values) of the material at the intersection point and added to the color as already calculated according to the direct illumination. Finally, a transmission ray may be spawned. The direction of the transmission ray is calculated by a routine `CalcRefractDir` that implements the algorithm given on page 241; transmission rays are otherwise handled in the same manner as reflection rays.

When examining the routine `RayTrace`, you will note that it uses some C++ classes `VectorR3` and `VectorR4`. These are vectors of real numbers, and their members are accessed via `A.x`, `A.y`, `A.z`, and `A.w`. The main reason for their use in the high-level ray trace routines is that positions and directions in 3-space are conveniently stored in a single `VectorR3`, which greatly simplifies the interfaces for the ray trace routines. The alternative would be to pass arrays of floating point numbers, which would be somewhat less elegant and certainly more prone to errors owing to the lack of compile time type-checking. If you are modifying only the high-level ray tracing routines, you can probably avoid using much of the `VectorR3` or `VectorR4` classes.

SeekIntersection: This routine loops through the array of viewable objects, checking each one for an intersection with a ray. The ray is specified in terms of its starting position and a unit vector giving its direction. The first thing done is to move the starting position a very small distance in the direction of the ray: this is to avoid having a repeated intersection with the same point owing to roundoff error. (This is not guaranteed to work always but has worked in all cases tried so far.) `SeekIntersection` checks every viewable object for intersections with the ray and returns the closest intersection found.

CalcAllDirectIllum: This routine takes as input a view position and a visible point. It is presumed that the visible point is in fact visible from the view position. (The view position may be the position of the actual viewer or may be a position from whence a traced ray has been reflected or refracted.) The direct illumination of the point includes the following components: any emissive color of the visible point, color due to global ambient lights, and, for each light, the color due to direct illumination. Before any illumination from a light is calculated, a shadow feeler is traced from the visible point to the light position. If the shadow feeler is not intersected by any viewable object (as determined by the routine `ShadowFeeler`), the light is presumed to be shining on the visible point; otherwise, the light is deemed to have its direct light completely blocked. In either case, the value of `percentLit` is set, as appropriate, to either 0 or 1, indicating the fraction of the light illuminating the visible point. The illumination from each light is calculated with `DirectIlluminateViewPos` whether or not it is shadowed, since even shadowed lights contribute ambient lighting.

ShadowFeeler: This routine works in much the same way as `SeekIntersection`. However, it does not need to return a visible point. Since it returns only `true` or `false` depending on whether an intersection is found, this routine can stop as soon as any intersection is found without needing to continue searching for a closer intersection.

The program `RayTraceData` contains routines for describing the virtual scene to be rendered. First, there is the routine `SetUpMainView`, which describes information about the main view position (i.e., the position of the camera). This first creates a new `CameraView` and sets its position and direction of view. The direction of view is specified by any nonzero vector (in this case as stored in an array of `double`'s). The camera view is conceptualized by envisioning the camera as pointing at the center of a viewscreen of pixels. The viewscreen is thought of as being positioned in a rectangular array in 3-space. The distance to the viewscreen is set by a call to `SetScreenDistance`, and its width and height by a call to `SetScreenDimensions`. However, the routine `ResizeWindow` in `RayTrace` will resize the array of pixels as necessary to keep the entire viewscreen in view. If the aspect ratio of the OpenGL rendering window is different from the aspect ratio of the viewscreen, then the pixels are positioned so that the entire viewscreen area is rendered.

Neither a near-clipping plane or a far-clipping plane is used. However, the variable `MAX_DIST` should be set to be at least as large as the diameter of the scene because rays are traced only to that distance.

Second, there is a call to `SetUpMaterials`. This creates an array of pointers to materials. Each material is created with the C++ operator `new` and then has its material properties set. These material properties include ambient color, diffuse color, specular color, reflection color, and transmissive color, as well as shininess and index of refraction. If the reflection color is set to zero (but by default it is not zero), then the object does not generate reflection rays. If the transmission color is zero (and zero is its default value), then the object does not generate transmission rays. The index of refraction is used only for transmission rays, of course. Good values for the index of refraction would be numbers like 1.33, which is approximately the index of refraction of water, or 1.5, which is approximately the index of refraction for glass.

The color values for materials are specified by giving three or four floating point numbers for the red, green, blue, and possibly alpha values of the color. (The alpha values are just ignored for ray tracing purposes but were included in case future versions of the software will to exploit them.) The color values can be specified either by giving an array of floating point numbers, similar to the convention used by OpenGL, or, alternatively, by passing in a `VectorR3` or `VectorR4` object. This means that a wide variety of interfaces are supported to set color values, and you may use whatever one seems most convenient.

For example, here are the eight possible ways to set the ambient color of a material `M` (the alpha value defaults to 1.0):

```
M.SetColorAmbient(0.2,0.3,0.4);

M.SetColorAmbient(0.2,0.3,0.4,1.0);

double c[3]={0.2,0.3,0.4};
M.SetColor3Ambient(&c[0]);

double c[4]={0.2,0.3,0.4,1.0};
M.SetColor4Ambient(&c[0]);

float c[3]={0.2,0.3,0.4};
M.SetColor3Ambient(&c[0]);

float c[4]={0.2,0.3,0.4,1.0};
M.SetColor4Ambient(&c[0]);

M.SetColorAmbient( VectorR4(0.2,0.3,0.4,1.0) );
```

The next routine that is called is `SetUpLights`. It defines one or more lights and sets their properties, which include the usual ones such as position and ambient, diffuse, and specular color. It is also possible to set attenuation constants and spotlight effects of exactly the same kind as are supported by OpenGL. In addition, the lights can be made directional instead of positional.

The next routine that is called is `SetUpViewableObjects`. The viewable objects are geometric shapes defined by `ViewableBase` objects. The `SetUpViewableObjects` routine defines the various objects and their positions and orientations; it also assigns material to the objects' surfaces. See Section B.3.5 for information on how to set up viewable objects.

Every viewable object supports texture maps, which are applied by using objects of type `TextureMap`. You may have separate texture maps for the front and back surfaces of objects. Each type of object has its own system of assigning texture coordinates, and in a few cases, such as spheres and ellipses, there is more than one way for texture coordinates to be calculated.

B.3 The `RayTrace` API

B.3.1 Specifying Lights

The ray tracing package supports lights that are very similar to OpenGL's lights. This includes the use of separate ambient, diffuse, and specular light as well as distance attenuation and spotlights.

Lights are C++ objects of type `Light`. A new light is allocated by declarations of one of the following two forms:

```
Light* lightPtr = new Light();

Light myLight;
```

The first form allocates a light in the C++ heap with `lightPtr` a pointer to the light; the second allocates a light on the stack.

By default, lights are positional and are placed at the origin; to place the light elsewhere, you use one of the following routines:

```
SetPosition( double x, double y, double z );
SetPosition( double *position );
SetPosition( float *position );
SetPosition( VectorR3& position );
```

These routines are all functionally equivalent: they make the light positional and place it at the location specified. In each case, three numeric values are given for x, y, z-components of the position. These numeric values are given explicitly in the first form of `SetPosition` and are given by a pointer to a list of three `double`'s or `float`'s in the next two forms of `SetPosition` or by a single `VectorR3` in the final form of `SetPosition`. These different ways of setting values are provided in the ray tracing package since different ways of setting values may be more convenient in different settings.

To make a light directional, call one of the following routines to set a light to shine in a particular direction:

```
SetDirectional( double x, double y, double z );
SetDirectional( double *direction );
SetDirectional( float *direction );
SetDirectional( VectorR3& direction );
```

The next important property to set for a light is its color. Just as in the Phong lighting model used by OpenGL, each light has ambient, diffuse, and specular colors. To set the ambient color, use one of the following routines:

```
SetColorAmbient( double red, double green, double blue);
SetColor3Ambient( double *color );
SetColor3Ambient( float *color );
SetColor4Ambient( double *color );
SetColor4Ambient( float *color );
SetColor4Ambient( VectorR4& color );
```

The color contains red, green, and blue components as usual plus an optional α component. The α component is currently ignored by the ray tracing software and defaults to 1. The difference between the `SetColor3*` and `SetColor4*` routines is that the former expects an array of length three and the latter expects an array of length 4.

To set the diffuse and specular colors, use similar routines but with "`Ambient`" replaced by "`Diffuse`" and "`Specular`". You can also use `SetColorAmbientDiffuse` to set the ambient and diffuse colors simultaneously or use "`SetColor`" to set all three colors at once.

Lights support the same kind of distance attenuation as used in OpenGL. The attenuation coefficients are set by calling

```
SetAttenuation(double aConst, double aLinear, double aQuadratic);
```

Spotlights are also supported with exactly the same kinds of features as are supported by OpenGL. The spotlight characteristics are set by the following routines:

```
SetSpotCutoff( double cutoffCosine ):
SetSpotExponent( double spotExponent );
SetSpotDirection( double x, double y, double z );
SetSpotDirection( double* direction );
SetSpotDirection( float* direction );
SetSpotDirection( VectorR3& direction );
```

Calling any of these routines turns the light into a spotlight. To deactivate the spotlight effects, use `ResetSpotlight()`.

B.3.2 Defining the Viewport and Camera Positions

We now describe how to set the camera position, the virtual viewport position, and the array of pixel positions. The ray trace software works only in global coordinates, and does not incorporate any use of model view or projection transformations. Thus, the software expects you to give camera position and direction, light positions and directions, and viewable object positions and orientations in global coordinates.

To set up a camera position and direction plus a screen position and size, use a sequence of commands such as

```
double Cpos[3] = {0.0,0.0,25.0}; // Position of camera
double Cdir[3] = {0.0,0.0,-1.0}; // Direction of camera
double Cdist = 25.0; // Distance to "screen"
double width = 5.0, height=4.0; // Width and height of the screen
int pixelWidth=640, pixelHeight=480; // Screen dimensions
CameraView* cv = new CameraView();
cv->SetPosition( Cpos );
```

```
cv->SetDirection( Cdir );
cv->SetScreenDistance( Cdist );
cv->SetScreenDimensions( width, height );
cv->SetScreenPixelSize( pixelWidth, pixelHeight );
```

These calls specify the position of the camera, its view direction, and the distance from the camera to the virtual viewport. The "up" direction of the view is always as much "upward" along the y-axis as possible. This is the natural upward direction for a camera; if $\mathbf{v}$ is the view direction, then the up direction is given by the vector $\mathbf{v} \times (\mathbf{j} \times \mathbf{v})$.

For convenience, these commands have several different formats that give the same functionality:

```
SetPosition( double x, double y, double z );
SetPosition( double* pos );
SetPosition( float* pos );
SetPosition( VectorR3& pos );

SetDirection( double x, double y, double z );
SetDirection( double* dir );
SetDirection( float* dir );
SetDirection( VectorR3& dir );

SetScreenPixelSize( int i, int j );
SetScreenPixelSize( PixelArray& pixelarray );
```

You can also make the viewer either directional or positional using the commands

```
SetLocalViewer();
SetNonLocalViewer();
```

The default is a local (i.e., positional) viewer. Nonlocal viewers are used for directional (orthographic) camera views; nonlocal viewers must be given a finite position since the position helps determine the location of the viewport.

For ray tracing, it is convenient to know the position in space where a pixel position lies in order to be able to shoot a ray from the eye position through a pixel position. The `CalcPixel Direction` routine takes as input the coordinates of a pixel and returns the unit vector pointing in the direction from the eye to the given pixel. This command (a member function of `CameraView`) has the syntax:

```
CalcPixelDirection( double i, double j, double* dir);
CalcPixelDirection( double i, double j, float* dir);
CalcPixelDirection( double i, double j, VectorR3* dir );
```

The `dir` value is the returned unit vector. The pixel coordinates `i` and `j` are floating point numbers, which makes it easy to use subpixel locations for distributed ray tracing applications.

For directional (or, orthographic) cameras, rays traced from the eye position have a fixed direction but start at different locations. These are calculated for you by the `CalcView Position` routine, which has the calling syntax

```
CalcViewPosition( double i, double j, double* pos);
CalcViewPosition( double i, double j, float* pos);
CalcViewPosition( double i, double j, VectorR3* pos );
```

The `pos` value is the returned position.

The following routines can obtain the position of a pixel in the viewport:

```
CalcPixelPosition( double i, double j, double* pos);
CalcPixelPosition( double i, double j, float* pos);
CalcPixelPosition( double i, double j, VectorR3* pos );
```

If you modify the high-level routines to use distributed ray tracing with jittered eye positions, you should *not* move the position of the eye with SetPosition, for this would move the positions of the viewport pixels too. Instead, you should calculate the jittered eye position and then call CalcPixelPosition to get a pixel position. The ray direction can then be computed by taking the difference of these two positions and normalizing.

B.3.3 Working with the Pixel Array

A PixelArray object holds an array of pixel values. You can allocate a new pixel array of a given size by using the command

```
PixelArray px = new PixelArray( width, height);
```

The size can be changed by the SetSize or ResetSize method. The former command explicitly sets the dimensions of the pixel array; the latter uses the size of the current GLUT rendering window to determine the size of the pixel array. The PixelArray class takes care of reallocating memory for the pixel array when the size of the array increases.

Each pixel in the pixel array holds red, green, and blue values as floating point numbers. These can be set by any of the following commands, which are member functions of Pixel Array:

```
SetPixel( int i, int j, float* color );
SetPixel( int i, int j, double* color );
SetPixel( int i, int j, VectorR4& color );
SetPixel( int i, int j, VectorR3& color );
```

In each case, values for red, green, and blue are stored. There is no alpha value in the pixel array. A member function GetPixel will return the color values of a single pixel.

Finally, there is the important Draw() function, which copies the contents of the pixel array into the current rendering window. This is invoked by

```
px->Draw();
```

B.3.4 Defining Materials

A Material object encapsulates the reflective, transmissive, and emissive properties of a surface. A Material consists of the attributes listed below. Except for the last two, these values are set separately for red, green, and blue. The first four coefficients are used for the Phong lighting calculations and apply to both reflected and transmitted direct illumination.

- ρ_a Ambient illumination coefficients.
- ρ_d Diffuse illumination coefficients.
- ρ_s Specular illumination coefficients.
- ρ_e Emissive color.
- ρ_{rg} Global reflection coefficients.
- ρ_{tg} Global transmission coefficients.
- η Index of refraction – same for all colors.
- f Specular shininess exponent.

For convenience, several different ways exist to set these values. For example, the ambient illumination coefficient may be set with any of the following member functions:

```
SetColorAmbient( double r, double g, double b );
SetColorAmbient( double r, double g, double b, double alpha );
SetColor3Ambient( double* color );
SetColor4Ambient( double* color );
SetColor3Ambient( float* color );
SetColor4Ambient( float* color );
SetColorAmbient( VectorR4& color );
```

The alpha component of color is ignored by the current software implementation but is reserved for future use. It defaults to the value 1. The same kinds of commands work for the other material coefficients, and the function names are formed by replacing "`Ambient`" with "`Diffuse`," "`AmbientDiffuse`," "`Specular`," "`Emissive`," "`Reflective`," or "`Transmissive`." The only exception to this naming scheme is that the reflective and transmissive values do not have alpha components, and so the routines that set four components do not apply to them.

The index of refraction and the shininess exponent are set by the member functions

```
SetIndexOfRefraction( double eta );
SetShininess( double exponent );
```

The default values for of all these are identical to the default OpenGL value. The default value for the global reflectivity coefficients is 0.5, and for the global transmission coefficients is 0. That is, by default surfaces are 50 percent reflective and are not transparent at all.

B.3.5 Defining Viewable Objects

The "viewable objects" are the various geometric shapes that can be used in a scene. A viewable object generally contains the following information:

1. *Geometric information, such as size, position, orientation, and shape.* Each type of viewable object has its own unique specifications; for example, a sphere is specified by giving its center position and its radius, a triangle is specified by its three vertices, and so on.
2. *Materials for the surfaces of the object.* Most objects have two or more surfaces. Flat objects such as triangles and parallelograms have front and back surfaces. Solid objects such as spheres and tori have inner and outer surfaces. Each viewable object type allows a different material to be assigned to each surface, and thus each viewable object type has at least two materials that need to be specified. The most common way of specifying material is with member functions

```
SetMaterial( Material *material );
SetMaterialOuter( Material *outermat );
SetMaterialInner( Material *innermat );
```

For solid objects, including spheres, ellipses, tori, and parallelepipeds, these functions set the materials for the inner and outer surfaces. The first function, `SetMaterial`, sets both the inner and outer materials.

Flat objects, such as triangles, parallelograms, and Bézier patches, also have two materials, but they are called the "front" and "back" materials rather than the "outer" and "inner" materials.

The more complicated shapes, such as cones and cylinders, have the ability to specify separate materials for the sides, bottom, and, in the case of a cylinder, the top.

3. *Texture maps* can be applied to all the surfaces of viewable objects. These are set with the following member functions:

```
TextureMap( TextureMapBase* texture );
TextureMapFront( TextureMapBase* texture );
TextureMapBack( TextureMapBase* texture );
```

The first command sets both the front and back texture maps. For objects with insides, such as spheres, "front" and "back" are synonyms for "outer" and "inner," respectively.

When texture maps are assigned to a surface, texture coordinates are also needed. Fortunately, the ray tracing software will automatically calculate texture coordinates for all viewable objects. Each viewable object class provides customized methods for controlling how texture coordinates are assigned. Viewable objects always return texture map coordinates in the unit square $[0, 1]^2$. Geometries with more than one face, such as parallelepipeds, cylinders, and so on, also return a *face number*.

B.3.6 Viewable Spheres

A sphere has type `ViewableSphere`; its geometry is set simply by giving its center and radius. These are set with the following member functions:

```
SetRadius( double radius );

SetCenter( double x, double y, double z );
SetCenter( double *center );
SetCenter( float *center );
SetCenter( VectorR3& center );
```

The various forms of `SetCenter` all have the same functionality.

The geometry of the sphere becomes a little more complicated if texture coordinates need to be used. First, an orientation for the sphere needs to be defined. The standard orientation for a sphere has the positive y-axis as the up direction and the positive z-axis as the forward direction. Then u and v coordinates are set so that $v = 1$ means the point at the top of the sphere (in the up direction, i.e., at the "North Pole") and $v = 0$ means the point in the down direction, at the "South Pole." The value $u = \frac{1}{2}$ is used for direction of the positive z-axis. That is, a sphere centered at the origin in standard position has texture coordinates $\langle u, v \rangle = \langle \frac{1}{2}, \frac{1}{2} \rangle$ at the point in the front of the sphere, namely, the point where the positive z-axis intersects the sphere.

General orientations are specified by giving two axes. The first axis, called `AxisA` specifies the front direction, that is, the direction towards a viewer who is looking at the front of the sphere; its default value is **k** (the z-axis). The second axis, called `AxisC` is the up direction, and it defaults to **j**. These axes are set with any of the commands

```
SetuvAxes( double* axisA, double* axisC);
SetuvAxes( float* axisA, float* axisC);
SetuvAxes( VectorR3& axisA, VectorR3& axisC);
```

In each case, the axis is specified by three floating point numbers; it is not necessary that the axis directions be unit vectors. They should be nonzero, however, or a divide-by-zero will occur. In addition, they should be orthogonal.

Recall from Section V.1.2 that there are two natural ways to calculate texture coordinates for spheres, as given by Equations V.2 and V.3 on page 131. Either of these methods can be used; they are enabled by the member functions

```
SetuvSpherical();
SetuvCylindrical();
```

The default is the `SetuvSpherical` mode, as in Equation V.2.

B.3.7 Viewable Triangles and Parallelograms

Triangles and parallelograms are perfectly flat with zero thickness. By default, they can be seen from both the front and the back. The classes for triangles and parallelograms are `View-ableTriangle` and `ViewableParallelogram`. Each is specified with three vertices; for the parallelogram, the fourth vertex is calculated from the other three. The member functions that can be used to set the three vertices are

```
Init( double* vertexpositions);
Init( float* vertexpositions);
Init( VectorR3& vA, VectorR3& vB, VectorR3& vC );
```

The first two forms take an array of nine floating point numbers that specify the three vertices. The three vertices are given in counterclockwise order, as viewed from the front. For the parallelogram, the fourth vertex will be opposite the second specified vertex.

The materials for the front and back faces are set by the commands

```
SetMaterial( Material* material );
SetMaterialFront( Material* frontmaterial );
SetMaterialBack( Material* backmaterial );
```

The first form of the command sets both materials. If the back material pointer is equal to 0, then the back face is invisible and is never intersected (i.e., is culled).

The points on the triangle and parallelogram are assigned texture coordinates using linear interpolation. The three vertices A–C of the triangle are given texture coordinates $\langle 0, 0 \rangle$, $\langle 1, 0 \rangle$, and $\langle 0, 1 \rangle$ in that order. The vertices A–D of the parallelogram are assigned texture coordinates $\langle 0, 0 \rangle$, $\langle 1, 0 \rangle$, $\langle 1, 1 \rangle$, and $\langle 0, 1 \rangle$. You cannot change the texture coordinates assigned to the vertices, but you can achieve the same effect by using `TextureAffineXform` and `TextureBilinearXform` objects, which allow texture coordinates to be modified by a linear or bilinear mapping.

B.3.8 Viewable Ellipsoids

An axis-aligned ellipsoid with center at the origin is specified by three radius values, α, β, γ and is the set of points

$$\left\{ \langle x, y, z \rangle : \frac{x^2}{\alpha^2} + \frac{y^2}{\beta^2} + \frac{z^2}{\gamma^2} = 1 \right\}.$$

This ellipsoid is a sphere stretched to have dimensions $\alpha \times \beta \times \gamma$. More generally, ellipsoids can be translated away from the origin and can be oriented so as to not be axis aligned.

An object of type `ViewableEllipsoid` is a general ellipsoid. Its center position is specified by any of the member functions

```
SetCenter( double x, double y, double z );
SetCenter( double *center );
SetCenter( float *center );
SetCenter( VectorR3& center );
```

A circular ellipsoid is one that has circular cross sections, that is, two of its three radii are equal. A circular ellipsoid is set by using the functions

```
SetCentralAxis( VectorR3& axisC );
SetRadii( double radiusC, double radiusAB );
```

The first function sets the central axis (the default is the y-axis). The second command sets the height of the ellipsoid along its central axis and the radius of the central circular cross section.

You may also specify noncircular ellipsoids. These have three axes with three separate radii. The functions to set these values are

```
SetAxes( VectorR3& axisC, VectorR3& axisA );
SetRadii( double radiusC, double radiusA, double radiusB );
```

The inner and outer materials for the ellipsoid are set in the usual way. Texture coordinates are calculated in much the same way as the texture coordinates on the sphere. In particular, the height along the center axis, AxisC, controls the v texture coordinate. The axis AxisA intersects the ellipsoid at the front, at the $u = \frac{1}{2}$ position.

Just as for spheres, SetuvSpherical and SetuvCylindrical specify the method for computing texture coordinates for ellipsoids.

B.3.9 Viewable Cylinders

The ViewableCylinder class supports a broad range of cylindrical shapes. The simplest cylinders are the circular right cylinders. "Circular" means that the cross sections parallel to the central axis are circular. A "right" cylinder is one in which the top and bottom faces are perpendicular to the central axis. The next simplest kind of cylinder is a noncircular, right cylinder. Finally, you may also define cylinders that are neither right nor circular. Noncircular cylinders have elliptical cross sections; nonright cylinders may have arbitrary planes bounding the top and bottom faces.

Every cylinder needs its center and its central axis specified: these are given with the functions

```
SetCenterAxis( double x, double y, double z );
SetCenterAxis( double* axisC );
SetCenterAxis( float* axisC );
SetCenterAxis( VectorR3& axisC );

SetCenter( double x, double y, double z );
SetCenter( double* center );
SetCenter( float* center );
SetCenter( VectorR3& center );
```

A right cylinder is further specified by giving its height and radius with the member functions

```
SetHeight( double height );
SetRadius( double radius );
```

A noncircular right cylinder has two radii, and you must specify another axis direction, AxisA. The third axis direction, AxisB, is computed for you as the cross product of the central axis and AxisA. To initialize a noncircular right cylinder, you first call SetCenterAxis and SetCenter and then call the following three functions:

```
SetHeight( double height );
SetRadialAxis( VectorR3& axisA );
SetRadii(double radiusA, double radiusB);
```

For general nonright cylinders, you use the preceding commands to set the radius or the radial axes and their radii. But instead of using the SetHeight method, the following two functions are called to define the plane equations for the top and bottom faces of the cylinder:

```
SetBottomFace( VectorR3& planenormal, double planecoef );
SetTopFace( VectorR3& planenormal, double planeCoef );
```

The plane normals are vectors that are perpendicular to the plane containing the top or bottom face. If **n** is the normal for the top (respectively, the bottom) face, and if **c** is the center axis axisC, then it is required that $\mathbf{n} \cdot \mathbf{c} > 0$ (respectively, that $\mathbf{n} \cdot \mathbf{c} < 0$). The plane coefficient is a scalar d. The plane is the set of points **x** satisfying $\mathbf{x} \cdot \mathbf{n} = d$.

For a cylinder, you specify six materials: one for each of the inner and outer surfaces of the cylinder's side, top face, and bottom face. These six materials can be set individually with the member functions

```
SetMaterialSideInner(Material *material);
SetMaterialSideOuter(Material *material);
SetMaterialTopInner(Material *material);
SetMaterialTopOuter(Material *material);
SetMaterialBottomInner(Material *material);
SetMaterialBottomOuter(Material *material);
```

Several functions let you set multiple materials at once. These are:

```
SetMaterial(Material *material);
SetMaterialInner(Material *material);
SetMaterialOuter(Material *material);
```

`SetMaterial` sets all six materials at once, `SetMaterialOuter` sets all three outer materials, and so forth.

Texture coordinates are assigned separately for the side and for the top and bottom faces. For the side of the cylinder, the axis AxisA, points in the direction of the $u = 1/2$ line, and the v coordinate measures distance up and down the cylinder. Texture coordinates for the side are returned with u, v values in $[0, 1]^2$. Texture coordinates for the top and bottom faces are returned with u, v values lying in the circle with radius $1/2$ centered at $\langle \frac{1}{2}, \frac{1}{2} \rangle$. For both the top and the bottom, the texture coordinates are from the viewpoint of a viewer outside the cylinder looking along the center axis with the u-axis pointing along the positive AxisB axis.

The top face, the bottom face, and the side of a cylinder are assigned different face numbers: the side is face number 0, the bottom is face 1, and the top is face 2. The face numbers can be used by texture maps to apply different textures to different faces (by using a `TextureMultiFaces` object).

B.3.10 Viewable Cones

Cones are objects of type `ViewableCone`. The interface for cones is mostly similar to the interface for cylinders. Cones can be right cones, with the bottom face perpendicular to the central axis, or can be nonright, with any plane for the bottom face. (Truncated cones are not supported, however.) Further, cones may have either circular or elliptical cross section.

Every cone has an apex position and a central axis. These are specified by the functions

```
SetCenterAxis( double x, double y, double z );
SetCenterAxis( double* axisC );
SetCenterAxis( float* axisC );
SetCenterAxis( VectorR3& axisC );
```

```
SetApex( double x, double y, double z );
SetApex( double* apexPos );
SetApex( float* apexPos );
SetApex( VectorR3& apexPos );
```

The apex is the position of the point at the top of the cone. The `AxisC` central axis points up out of the top of the apex. It does not need to be a normal vector and will be automatically normalized.

In addition, every cone has the steepness of its sides set in terms of their slope. For right circular cones, you use the function

```
SetSlope( double slope );
```

The `slope` value is the slope of the sides measured by the change in distance from the center axis divided by the distance along the center axis from the apex. The slope should be positive.

Noncircular cones have elliptical cross sections. For these, you specify a second, radial axis, called `AxisA`. The third axis, `AxisB`, is calculated as the cross product of the center axis and `AxisA`. The radial axis is set by the function

```
SetRadialAxis( VectorR3& axisA );
```

The central axis must be set before the radial axis. An elliptical cone has two slopes, one along `AxisA` and the other along `AxisB`. These are set with the functions

```
SetSlopes(double slopeA, double slopeB);
```

A *right cone* is one whose base is perpendicular to its central axis. The height of a right cone is set by using the member function

```
SetHeight(double height);
```

For nonright cones, you may make any plane be the base by calling

```
SetBaseFace( VectorR3& planenormal, double planecoef );
```

The `SetBaseFace` function works in much the same way as the commands that specify the top and base face of a cylinder. The `planenormal` should be pointing out of the base (so its dot product with `axisC` should be negative), and the apex of the cone should therefore be below the plane.

A cone has four distinct materials; one for each of the inner and outer faces of the cone's side and base. These are set individually by the functions

```
SetMaterialSideInner(Material *material);
SetMaterialSideOuter(Material *material);
SetMaterialBaseInner(Material *material);
SetMaterialBaseOuter(Material *material);
```

or, as with cylinders, multiple materials can be set at once with the functions

```
SetMaterial(Material *material);
SetMaterialInner(Material *material);
SetMaterialOuter(Material *material);
```

Texture coordinates for cones are similar to texture coordinates of cylinders. The side of the cone has texture coordinates in $[0, 1]^2$. The base has texture coordinates that lie in the circle of radius $1/2$ centered at $\langle \frac{1}{2}, \frac{1}{2} \rangle$. The side is face number 0, and the base is face number 1.

B.3.11 Viewable Parallelepipeds

A parallelepiped is a solid object bounded by six planar faces with opposite faces parallel. This includes as special cases cubes and rectangular prisms (that is, boxes), but, more generally, any kind of linear transformation of a cube or rectangular prism is a parallelepiped.

The geometry for an object of type `ViewableParallelepiped` is specified by giving four of its vertices (corners). The first corner `VertexA` is surrounded by the three vertices `VertexB`, `VertexC`, and `VertexD`. For help with visualizing the vertices' positions, and for later assignment of face numbers, the following table lists, for each vertex, the identity of the corresponding corner of the parallelepiped:

Vertex	Position on Parallelepiped
VertexA	bottom left front vertex
VertexB	bottom right front vertex
VertexC	top left front vertex
VertexD	bottom left back vertex

The four vertices are specified with one of the functions

```
SetVertices( double *verts );
SetVertices( float *verts );
SetVertices( VectorR3& vertA, VectorR3& vertB, VectorR3& vertC,
                                VectorR3& vertD );
```

The argument to the first two forms of the function is a pointer to an array of 12 floating point numbers.

Materials are set as usual with the `SetMaterial`, `SetMaterialOuter`, and `SetMaterialInner` commands. There is currently no provision for giving separate materials to the six faces. Texture coordinates are set by mapping each face to the unit square [0, 1]. The face numbers for the six faces are given in the following table:

Face	Face Number
Front face	0
Back face	1
Top face	2
Bottom face	3
Right face	4
Left face	5

The top and bottom faces have texture coordinates set with the u-axis pointing "rightward," and the four sides have texture coordinates set with the v-axis pointing "upward."

B.3.12 Viewable Tori

The geometry of a torus, an object of type `ViewableTorus`, is given by specifying (a) the position of its center, (b) the axis of symmetry of the torus, and (c) the major and minor radius of the torus. The center can be set by any of the following member functions:

```
SetCenter( double x, double y, double z );
SetCenter( double *centerpos );
SetCenter( float *centerpos );
SetCenter( VectorR3& centerpos );
```

The central axis direction, also known as `AxisC`, is set by one of the member functions

```
SetAxis( double* centralaxis );
SetAxis( float* centralaxis );
SetAxis( VectorR3& centralaxis );
```

It is not necessary that the central axis direction be a unit vector. To set the two radii, use the member function

```
SetRadii( double majorradius, double minorradius );
```

The major radius is the radius of the circle that forms the center of the torus's tube. The minor radius is the radius of the tube.

The inner and outer materials are set in the usual fashion with `SetMaterial`, `SetMaterialInner`, and `SetMaterialOuter`.

To set texture coordinates, you also need to choose a radial axis: this is done by setting `AxisA`, which is the axis pointing out the front of the torus. This axis intersects the front of the torus where the texture coordinate u is equal to $1/2$. This axis is set with the member function

```
SetRadialAxis( VectorR3& axisA );
```

The v-axis for texture coordinates runs vertically around the torus. The texture coordinates are calculated by the method asked for in Exercise V.2 on page 131.

B.3.13 Viewable Bézier Patches

Bézier patches are geometrically a good deal more complicated than the rest of the viewable objects. In fact, Bézier patches are more general than the other geometric shapes, since spheres, cones, tori, and so on can all be realized as Bézier patches. Corresponding to this fact, Bézier patches are algorithmically much more difficult to process, and computation speeds for Bézier patches are worse than for simpler geometric objects by about an order of magnitude.

The ray tracing software supports both rational and nonrational Bézier patches and patches of orders three and four. In addition, patches can have order three with respect to one variable and order four with respect to the other variable.

Objects of type `ViewableBezierSet` hold a set (i.e., a collection) of Bézier patches. It is intended that a single `ViewableBezierSet` hold Bézier patches that are clustered together: for example, a teapot composed of Bézier patches would probably use a single `ViewableBezierSet` to holds its patches. If one were modeling multiple teapots, then each teapot would probably have its own `ViewableBezierSet`.

The only purpose of `ViewableBezierSet` is to hold a group of Bézier patches and surround them with a single bounding sphere. The bounding sphere is used to prune intersection testing to speed up the processing of rays that do not come near the patches. Thus, the decision of what `ViewableBezierSet`'s to use and which patches to include in which set depends mostly on the question of which patches could profitably be surrounded by a single bounding sphere. A secondary consideration is that every patch in a `ViewableBezierSet` is given the same texture map object (however, the different patches are assigned different face numbers and so can be distinguished by a texture map).

To create a new `ViewableBezierSet`, you use a constructor of one of the forms

```
ViewableBezierSet myBezierSet;

ViewableBezierSet* myBezierSetPtr = new ViewableBezierSet();
```

The set is created without any patches. You must add patches one at a time to the set using the commands `AddPatch`, `AddRationalPatch`, or both. These commands have the following forms:

```
AddPatch( int uOrder, int vOrder, float* controlPts );
AddRationalPatch( int uOrder, int vOrder, float* controlPts );
AddPatch( int uOrder, int vOrder, double* controlPts );
AddRationalPatch( int uOrder, int vOrder, double* controlPts );
```

The parameters `uOrder` and `vOrder` must equal either 3 or 4 (it is permitted for them to be different), and they give the orders of the cross-sectional slices of the Bézier patch in the u and v directions. Recall that the order of a Bézier curve is one greater than the degree of the curve.

The pointer `controlPts` points to an array of floating point numbers. For `Rational` patches, the floating point numbers come in groups of four values, giving the $x, y, z,$ w-components of the control points in homogeneous representation. For nonrational patches, the floating point numbers come in groups of three, specifying x, y, z-coordinates of the control points.

The control points are denoted $\mathbf{p}_{i,j}$, where $0 \leq i <$ `uOrder` and $0 \leq j <$ `vOrder`. The default assumption is that the control points come in the order $\mathbf{p}_{0,0}, \mathbf{p}_{1,0}, \mathbf{p}_{2,0}, \ldots$ with the i subscript changing faster than the j subscript (see below for how to change this order).

It is also possible to use `VectorR3` and `VectorR4` formats for control points. The relevant forms of the `AddPatch` commands are

```
AddPatch( int uOrder, int vOrder, VectorR3* controlPts );
AddPatch( int uOrder, int vOrder, VectorR4* controlPts );
```

The first of these uses nonrational control points, and the second uses rational control points.

You may also specify the order of the control points by giving different forms of the `AddPatch` commands:

```
AddPatch( int uOrder, int vOrder, float* controlPts,
                        int uStride, int vStride );
AddRationalPatch( int uOrder, int vOrder, float* controlPts,
                        int uStride, int vStride );
AddPatch( int uOrder, int vOrder, double* controlPts,
                        int uStride, int vStride );
AddRationalPatch( int uOrder, int vOrder, double* controlPts,
                        int uStride, int vStride );
AddPatch( int uOrder, int vOrder, VectorR3* controlPts,
                        int uStride, int vStride );
AddPatch( int uOrder, int vOrder, VectorR4* controlPts,
                        int uStride, int vStride );
```

The `uStride` and `vStride` parameters give the number of steps (the stride) between successive control points in the u and v directions. In other words, if `controlPts+m` points to the beginning of the control point $\mathbf{p}_{i,j}$, where m is an integer, then `controlPts+m+uStride` and `controlPts+m+vStride` point to the control points $\mathbf{p}_{i+1,j}$ and $\mathbf{p}_{i,j+1}$, respectively. For example, the default values of `uStride` and `vStride` for the first of the six `AddPatch` commands are `uStride=3` and `vStride=3*uOrder`. The factor 3 signifies that each nonrational point uses three floating point numbers: it would be replaced by 4 for rational control points.

For the final two forms of the AddPatch commands, the default values are uStride=1 and vStride = uOrder.

Face numbers are assigned to patches in numerical order; in addition, the AddPatch functions return face numbers.

You can set the material of Bézier patches by using the commands (member functions of ViewableBezierSet),

```
SetMaterial( Material *material );
SetMaterialFront( Material *frontMaterial );
SetMaterialBack( Material *backMmaterial );
```

As usual, the first command sets both the front and back materials. The material specifications will affect all subsequent patches added to the set and remain in effect until the next material specification. Thus, different patches in the same ViewableBezierSet may have different materials.

Texture coordinates can be set by the command

```
SetUvRange (double uMin, double vMin, double uMax, double vMax);
```

For the purpose of reporting texture coordinates, this command makes *u* vary from uMin to uMax, and *v* vary from vMin to vMax. The default values for the minimum and maximum values are 0 and 1. Like the SetMaterial commands, SetUvRange affects subsequent patches added to the ViewableBezierSet. When using textures, you would usually need to call SetUvRange for each patch.

The texture map itself is specified as usual with the TextureMap, TextureMapFront, and TextureMapBack commands. Every patch in the ViewableBezierSet shares the same texture map.

In some circumstances, you may wish to use SetBoundingSphereCenter command to explicitly specify the center position for the bounding sphere used to hold the set of Bézier patches. If this command is not given, then the bounding sphere center and radius are automatically calculated the first time an attempt is made to trace a ray and intersect it with the set of patches.

B.3.14 Texture Maps

The ray tracing software supports several basic texture mapping features. At present, it supports a checkerboard pattern, texture maps that apply bitmap images, and bump mapping. It also incorporates several methods for transforming texture map coordinates, for sequentially applying multiple texture maps to a surface, and for applying different texture maps based on face numbers.

The checkerboard pattern consists of infinitely repeating rectangles of two different materials. A checkered texture map is an object of type TextureCheckered and is specified by giving two materials and the width and height of the rectangles in the check pattern. The two materials are specified by the following member functions of TextureCheckered:

```
SetMaterials( Material* mat1, Material* mat2 );
SetMaterial1( Material* mat1 );
SetMaterial2( Material* mat2 );
```

The first function subsumes the other two calls. The width and height of the rectangles are set by the member function

```
SetWidths(double uwidth, double vwidth);
```

Here `uwidth` and `vwidth` mean the width and height, which are measured in the direction of the u and v coordinates, respectively.

A `TextureRgbImage` texture map contains a texture map loaded from a bitmap. You can create a new `TextureRgbImage` by the command

```
TextureRgbImage* tRgb = new TextureRgbImage( "filename.bmp" );
```

where `filename.bmp` is the name of the bitmap format file containing the texture map image. Many common drawing programs support the bitmap file format, and thus this file format is relatively easy to create. When the texture map `tRgb` is applied to a surface, it overwrites the ambient and diffuse reflectivity coefficients with the color from the texture map. The specular reflectivity coefficient of the surface is left unchanged. The texture map is applied before the lighting calculation; consequently, the effect of the texture map is to make the ambient and diffuse colors of the surface equal the values from the texture map. The colors of specular highlights are unchanged by the texture map, however.

You may specify whether the texture map is repeating by the commands

$$\texttt{SetWrapMode(} \left\{ \begin{array}{l} \texttt{TextureRgbImage::WrapUV} \\ \texttt{TextureRgbImage::ClampUV} \end{array} \right\} \texttt{);}$$

These allow you set whether the texture map repeats or whether it clamps to the color of the border. In addition to these two wrap modes, you can also set a background color to be used instead of the border colors when not wrapping. This background color is set by

```
SetWrapMode( VectorR3& color );
```

A `BumpMapFunction` texture map can be used to create a bump map. This allows you to specify a function that computes the bump map height function d, as discussed in Section V.2. The most common way to create a `BumpMapFunction` is to invoke it with the constructor

```
BumpMapFunction( f );
```

where f is a function of type `double f(double u, double v)`. The function f will be called as needed by the bump map, and it must compute the height function d. Optionally, you may call the member function `SetBorderType()` to set the way the height function wraps around at the borders of the unit square [0, 1]. The default setting is that the height function $f(u, v)$ is defined for all values of u and v. In the current implementation, a `BumpMapFunction` will not work correctly if it is applied subsequently to a texture map that transforms texture coordinates, such as the `TextureAffineXform` and `TextureBilinearXform` functions described below, because the calculation of the partial derivatives for bump mapping does not (at present) take into account the effects of these transformations.

A `TextureSequence` combines several texture maps into a single texture map that applies the constituent texture maps sequentially. It can be created by one of the constructors

```
TextureSequence( int numMaps, TextureMapBase* texMaps[] );

TextureSequence( TextureMapBase* texMap1, ...,
                        TextureMapBase* texMapn );
```

Here `texMaps` should be an array of pointers to texture maps, and the `texMap`i's should be pointers to texture maps (n can be 2, 3, or 4). The specified texture maps will be applied sequentially by the `TextureSequence` object. The component texture maps can be changed by using the `SetTexture` member function. The total number of texture maps cannot be changed, but null pointers can be used for disabling texture maps.

A `TextureMultiFaces` texture map allows you to apply different texture maps to different faces; for example, different faces of a cylinder can receive different textures. The texture map can be created with one of the constructors:

```
TextureMultiFaces( int numMaps, TextureMapBase* texMaps[] );

TextureMultiFaces( TextureMapBase* texMap1, ...,
                        TextureMapBase* texMapn );
```

Here, n may be 2, 3, 4, or 6. The ith texture map is applied to face number i. For face numbers greater than or equal to `numMaps`, the last texture map is applied.

Note that `TextureSequence` and `TextureMultiFaces` are themselves texture map objects (i.e., are subclasses of the `TextureMapBase` class).

Several of the viewable objects in the previous section have special methods for specifying axes that determine the way texture coordinates are assigned. The sphere, for instance, has methods for setting two "u–v"-axes, whereas the cylinder, cone, and torus use a "center axis" and an "AxisA" and "AxisB." Finally, the ellipsoid uses axes A, B, and C. To keep in mind how these work, think of the default as being that axis A is the z-axis, axis B is the x-axis, and axis C is the y-axis. Axis C is often the axis of symmetry and in this case is called the center axis. The texture coordinates are set so that if the axes have their default values, and if the viewer is looking straight down the z-axis towards the center of the object, then he or she will see the v-component of the texture coordinates varying from bottom to top on the surface in front and the u-coordinates varying from left to right with $u = 1/2$ in the center of the view.

Sometimes the default assignments of texture coordinates are not what you want, and one may then use several special texture maps that let you remap texture coordinates by linear or bilinear transformations. These texture maps do not actually apply any texture but instead can be combined with other texture maps using a `TextureSequence` object.

A `TextureAffineXform` allows you to apply an arbitrary affine transformation to texture coordinates. There are four options for defining a `TextureAffineXform`:

```
SetScaling( uFactor, vFactor );

SetLinearMatrix( a11, a21, a12, a22 );

SetAffineMatrix( a11, a21, a12, a22, a13, a23 );

SetTriangleCoords( Ax, Ay, Bx, By, Cx, Cy);
```

The `SetScaling` function makes the affine map a simple scaling linear transformation that applies different scaling values to u and v coordinates. The `SetLinearMatrix` function allows you to set an arbitrary linear map by setting the four entries of a 2×2 matrix – the operands are given in *column* order. The `SetAffineMatrix` function allows you to set an arbitrary affine map by giving the six entries of a 2×3 matrix (in column order) that define an affine map: these six entries are the top two rows of a 3×3 matrix that has bottom row (0 0 1) as is usual for matrices acting on homogeneous coordinates.

The function `SetTriangleCoords` is a convenience function that defines the affine map that maps the canonical texture coordinates for the vertices of a triangle (namely the points $\langle 0, 0 \rangle$, $\langle 1, 0 \rangle$, and $\langle 0, 1 \rangle$) to the texture coordinates $\langle Ax, Ay \rangle$, $\langle Bx, By \rangle$, and $\langle Cx, Cy \rangle$. This is convenient for defining a texture map on a triangle or parallelogram by linear interpolation (and linear extrapolation).

A `TextureBilinearXform` object lets you define texture coordinates by bilinear interpolation from four vertices of a rectangle. A bilinear transformation is defined by setting four texture coordinate values $\langle u_i, v_i \rangle$, with $i = 0, 1, 2, 3$. The transformation maps the four corners of the unit square, $\langle 0, 0 \rangle$, $\langle 1, 0 \rangle$, $\langle 1, 1 \rangle$, and $\langle 0, 1 \rangle$ to the four specified values (in that order) and computes texture coordinates at other points by bilinear interpolation. To set the four texture coordinate values you may use one of the functions

```
SetTextureCoordinates( double &txcoords[0] );

SetTextureCoordinates( float &txcoords[0] );
```

where `txcoords[]` is an array of eight floating point values. Alternatively, you may give the following four commands:

```
SetTextureCoordA( double u₀, double v₀ );
SetTextureCoordB( double u₁, double v₁ );
SetTextureCoordC( double u₂, double v₂ );
SetTextureCoordD( double u₃, double v₃ );
```

Bibliography

M. Agrawala, R. Ramamoorthi, A. Heirich, and L. Moll, *Efficient image-based methods for rendering soft shadows*, in Computer Graphics Proceedings, ACM, 2000, pp. 375–384. SIGGRAPH'2000.

E. Angel, *OpenGL: A Primer*, Addison–Wesley, Boston, 2002.

J. Arvo, *Backwards ray tracing*, in Developments in Ray Tracing, 1986. SIGGRAPH'86 Course Notes, Volume 12.

J. Arvo and D. Kirk, *Particle transport and image synthesis*, Computer Graphics, 24 (1990). SIGGRAPH'90.

I. Ashdown, *Radiosity: A Programmer's Perspective*, John Wiley, New York, 1994.

R. H. Bartels, J. C. Beatty, and B. A. Barsky, *An Introduction to Splines for Use in Computer Graphics and Geometric Modeling*, Morgan Kaufmann, Los Altos, CA, 1987. Forewords by P. Bézier and A.R. Forrest.

P. Beckmann and A. Spizzichino, *The Scattering of Electromagnetic Waves from Rough Surfaces*, Macmillan, New York and Pergamon Press, Oxford, UK, 1963.

P. Bergeron, *A general version of Crow's shadow volumes*, IEEE Computer Graphics and Applications, 6 (1986), pp. 17–28.

R. S. Berns, F. W. Billmeyer, and M. Saltzman, *Billmeyer and Saltzman's Principles of Color Technology*, John Wiley, New York, 3rd ed., 2000.

P. E. Bézier, *Mathematical and practical possibilities of UNISURF*, in Computer Aided Geometric Design, Proceedings of Conference held at the University of Utah, Salt Lake City, March 1974, R. E. Barnhill and R. F. Riesenfeld, eds., Academic Press, New York, 1974, pp. 127–152.

——, *How Renault uses numerical control for car body design and tooling*, in Society of Automotive Engineers' Congress, 1968. SAE paper 680010.

E. A. Bier and K. R. Sloan Jr., *Two-part texture mappings*, IEEE Computer Graphics and Applications, 6 (1986), pp. 40–53.

J. Blinn, *Models of light reflection for computer synthesized pictures*, Computer Graphics, 11 (1973), pp. 192–193. SIGGRAPH'77.

——, *Simulation of wrinkled surfaces*, Computer Graphics, 12 (1978). SIGGRAPH'78. Reprinted in (Wolfe, 1998).

——, *What, teapots again?*, IEEE Computer Graphics and Applications, 7 (1987), pp. 61–63. Reprinted in (Blinn, 1998), pp. 17–20.

——, *Hyperbolic interpolation*, IEEE Computer Graphics and Applications, 12 (1992), pp. 89–94. Reprinted in (Blinn, 1996).

——, *Jim Blinn's Corner: A Trip Down the Graphics Pipeline*, Morgan Kaufmann, San Francisco, 1996.

——, *Jim Blinn's Corner: Dirty Pixels*, Morgan Kaufmann, San Francisco, 1998.

W. Böhm, *Inserting new knots into B-spline curves*, Computer-Aided Design, 12 (1980), pp. 199–201.

W. Böhm and H. Prautsch, *The insertion algorithm*, Computer-Aided Design, 17 (1985), pp. 58–59.

P. J. Bouma, *Physical Aspects of Colour: An Introduction to the Scientific Study of Colour Stimuli and Colour Sensations*, Philips Technical Library, Macmillan, London, 2nd ed., 1971. Edited by W. de Groot, A.A. Kruithof, and J.L. Guweltjes.

L. S. Brotman and N. I. Badler, *Generating soft shadows with a depth buffer algorithm*, IEEE Computer Graphics and Applications, 4 (1984), pp. 5–12.

S. R. Buss and J. Fillmore, *Spherical averages and applications to spherical splines and interpolation*, ACM Transactions on Graphics, 20 (2001), pp. 95–126.

S. E. Chen and L. Williams, *View interpolation for image synthesis*, Computer Graphics, 27 (1993), pp. 279–288. SIGGRAPH'92.

E. Cohen, T. Lyche, and R. F. Riesenfeld, *Discrete B-splines and subdivision techniques in computer-aided geometric design and computer graphics*, Computer Graphics and Image Processing, 14 (1980), pp. 87–111.

M. F. Cohen and D. P. Greenberg, *The hemi-cube: A radiosity solution for complex environments*, Computer Graphics, 19 (1985), pp. 31–40.

M. F. Cohen and J. R. Wallace, *Radiosity and Realistic Image Synthesis*, Academic Press, Boston, 1993. Includes a chapter by P. Hanrahan.

R. L. Cook, T. Porter, and L. Carpenter, *Distributed ray tracing*, Computer Graphics, 18 (1984), pp. 137–145. SIGGRAPH'84.

R. L. Cook and K. E. Torrance, *A reflectance model for computer graphics*, ACM Transactions on Graphics, 1 (1982), pp. 7–24.

M. G. Cox, *The numerical evaluation of B-splines*, Journal of the Institute of Mathematics and Its Applications, (1972), pp. 134–149.

H. S. M. Coxeter, *Projective Geometry*, Springer-Verlag, New York, second ed., 1974.

F. C. Crow, *Shadow algorithms for computer graphics*, Computer Graphics, 11 (1977), pp. 242–248. SIGGRAPH'77.

H. B. Curry and I. J. Shoenberg, *On spline distributions and their limits: The Pólya distribution function*, Abstract 308t, Bulletin of the American Mathematical Society, 53 (1947), p. 1114.

M. Daniel and J. C. Daubisse, *The numerical problem of using Bézier curves and surfaces in the power basis*, Computer Aided Geometric Design, 6 (1989), pp. 121–128.

M. de Berg, M. H. Overmars, M. V. Krevald, and O. Schwartzkopf, *Computational Geometry: Algorithms and Applications*, Springer-Verlag, Berlin, 2nd ed., 2000.

C. de Boor, *On calculating with B-splines*, Journal of Approximation Theory, 6 (1972), pp. 50–62.

P. de Casteljau, *Outillages méthodes calcul*. Technical report, 1959.

——, *Courbes et surfaces à poles*. Technical report, 1963.

C. Everitt and M. J. Kilgard, *Practical and robust stenciled shadow volumes for hardware-accelerated rendering*. Manuscript at http://developer.nvidia.com, 2002.

M. D. Fairchild, *Color Appearence Models*, Addison–Wesley, Reading, MA, 1998.

H. S. Fairman, M. H. Brill, and H. Hemmendinger, *How the CIE 1931 color-matching functions were derived from Wright–Guild data*, Color Research and Application, 22 (1997), pp. 11–23.

G. Farin, *Curves and Surfaces for Computer Aided-Geometric Design: A Practical Guide*, Academic Press, San Diego, 4th ed., 1997. Contains chapters by P. Bézier and W. Böhm.

R. T. Farouki, *On the stability of transformations between power and Bernstein polynomial forms*, Computer Aided Geometric Design, 8 (1991), pp. 29–36.

R. T. Farouki and V. T. Rajan, *On the numerical condition of polynomials in Bernstein form*, Computer Aided Geometric Design, 4 (1987), pp. 191–216.

——, *Algorithms for polynomials in Bernstein form*, Computer Aided Geometric Design, 5 (1988), pp. 1–26.

R. T. Farouki and T. Sakkalis, *Real rational curves are not "unit speed,"* Computer Aided Geometric Design, 8 (1991), pp. 151–157.

J. Ferguson, *Multivariable curve interpolation*, Journal of the Association for Computing Machinery, 11 (1964), pp. 221–228.

R. P. Feynman, *Lectures on Physics, Volume I*, Addison–Wesley, Redwood City, CA, 1989. Chapters 35 and 36.

J. FOLEY, A. VAN DAM, S. K. FEINER, AND J. F. HUGHES, *Computer Graphics: Principles and Practice*, Addison–Wesley, Reading, MA., 2nd ed., 1990.

H. FUCHS, G. D. ABRAM, AND E. D. GRANT, *Near real-time shaded display of rigid objects*, Computer Graphics, 17 (1983). SIGGRAPH'83.

H. FUCHS, Z. KEDEM, AND B. F. NAYLOR, *On visible surface generation by a priori tree structures*, Computer Graphics, 14 (1980), pp. 124–133. SIGGRAPH'80.

E. G. GILBERT, D. W. JOHNSON, AND S. S. KEERTHI, *A fast procedure for computing the distance between objects in three-dimensional space*, IEEE J. Robotics and Automation, RA-4 (1988), pp. 193–203.

M. GIRARD AND A. A. MACIEJEWSKI, *Computational modeling for the computer animation of legged figures*, Computer Graphics, 19 (1985), pp. 263–270. SIGGRAPH'85.

A. GLASSNER, ed., *An Introduction to Ray Tracing*, Academic Press, London, 1989.

——, *Andrew Glassner's Notebook : Recreational Computer Graphics*, Morgan Kaufmann, San Francisco, 1999.

——, *Principles of Digital Image Synthesis*, Morgan Kaufmann, San Francisco, 1995. Two volumes.

S. GOTTSCHALK, M. C. LIN, AND D. MANOCHA, *OBBTree: A hierarchical structure for rapid interference detection*, Computer Graphics, 30 (1996), pp. 171–180. SIGGRAPH '96.

H. GOURAUD, *Continuous shading of curved surfaces*, IEEE Transactions on Computers, 20 (1971), pp. 623–629.

B. GRÜNBAUM, *Convex Polytopes*, Interscience, London, 1967.

R. HALL, *Illumination and Color in Computer Generated Imagery*, Springer-Verlag, New York, 1989.

P. HANRAHAN, D. SALZMAN, AND L. AUPPERLE, *A rapid hierachical radiosity algorithm*, Computer Graphics, 25 (1991), pp. 197–206. SIGGRAPH'91.

J. C. HART, G. K. FRANCIS, AND L. H. KAUFFMAN, *Visualizing quaternion rotation*, ACM Transactions on Graphics, 13 (1994), pp. 256–276.

X. D. HE, K. E. TORRANCE, F. X. SILLION, AND D. P. GREENBERG, *A comprehensive physical model for light reflection*, Computer Graphics, 25 (1991), pp. 175–186. SIGGRAPH'91.

P. S. HECKBERT AND H. P. MORETON, *Interpolation for polygon texture mapping and shading*, in State of the Art in Computer Graphics: Visualization and Modeling, D. F. Rogers and R. A. Earnshaw, eds., Springer-Verlag, New York, 1991, pp. 101–111.

T. HEIDMANN, *Real shadows real time*, Iris Universe, 18 (1991), pp. 28–31. Silicon Graphics, Inc.

N. J. HIGMAN, *Accuracy and Stability of Numerical Algorithms*, Society for Industrial and Applied Mathematics, Philadelphia, 1996.

F. S. HILL, *Computer Graphics Using OpenGL*, Prentice–Hall, Upper Saddle River, NJ, 2001.

J. HOSCHEK AND D. LASSER, *Fundamentals of Computer Aided Geometric Design*, AK Peters, Wellesley, MA., 1993. Translated from German by L. Schumaker.

R. JACKSON, L. MACDONALD, AND K. FREEMAN, *Computer Generated Colour: A Practical Guide to Presentation and Display*, John Wiley, Chichester, UK, 1994.

H. W. JENSEN, *Realistic Image Synthesis Using Photon Mapping*, A.K. Peters, Natick, MA, 2001.

H. W. JENSEN AND N. J. CHRISTENSEN, *Photon maps in bidirectional Monte Carlo ray tracing of complex objects*, Computers and Graphics, 19 (1995), pp. 215–224.

K. I. JOY AND M. N. BHETANABHOTLA, *Ray tracing parametric surface patches utilizing numerical techniques and ray coherence*, Computer Graphics, 20 (1986), pp. 279–285. SIGGRAPH'86.

J. T. KAJIYA, *Anisotropic reflection models*, Computer Graphics, 19 (1985), pp. 15–21. SIGGRAPH'85.

A. R. KLUMPP, *Singularity-free extraction of a quaternion from a direction-cosine matrix*, Journal of Spacecraft and Rockets, 13 (1976), pp. 754–755.

D. H. U. KOCHANEK AND R. H. BARTELS, *Interpolating splines with local tension, continuity and bias control*, Computer Graphics, 18 (1984), pp. 33–41. SIGGRAPH'84.

E. P. LAFORTUNE AND Y. D. WILLEMS, *Bi-directional path tracing*, in Proc. 3rd International Confernence on Computational Graphics and Visualization Techniques (Compugraphics '93), ACM, 1993, pp. 145–153.

E. LEE, *Rational Bézier representation for conics*, in Geometric Modeling: Algorithms and New Trends, G. E. Farin, ed., Philadelphia, 1987, SIAM, pp. 3–19.

M. Lin, *Collision Detection for Animation and Robotics*, Ph.D. thesis, U.C. Berkeley, 1993.

M. C. Lin and J. F. Canny, *Efficient algorithms for incremental distance computation*, in IEEE Conference on Robotics and Automation, 1991, pp. 1008–1014.

M. D. McCool, *Shadow volume reconstruction from depth maps*, ACM Transactions on Graphics, 19 (2000), pp. 1–26.

T. Möller and E. Haines, *Real-Time Rendering*, AK Peters, Natick, MA, 1999.

T. Möller and B. Trumbore, *Fast, minimum storage ray–triangle intersection*, Journal of Graphics Tools, 2 (1997), pp. 21–28.

W. M. Newman and R. F. Sproull, *Principles of Interactive Computer Graphics*, McGraw–Hill, New York, second ed., 1979.

T. Nishita, T. W. Sederberg, and M. Kakimoto, *Ray tracing trimmed rational surface patches*, Computer Graphics, 24 (1990), pp. 337–345. SIGGRAPH'90.

M. Oren and S. K. Nayar, *Generalization of Lambert's reflectance model*, Computer Graphics, 28 (1994), pp. 239–246. SIGGRAPH'94.

——, *Generalization of the Lambertian model and implications for machine vision*, International Journal of Computer Vision, 14 (1995), pp. 227–251.

A. Overhauser, *Analytic definition of curves and surfaces by parabolic blending*, tech. rep., Ford Motor Company, 1968.

B. T. Phong, *Illumination for computer generated pictures*, Communications of the ACM, 18 (1975), pp. 311–317.

L. Piegl and W. Tiller, *A menagerie of rational B-spline circles*, IEEE Computer Graphics and Applications, 9 (1989), pp. 48–56.

L. Piegl and W. Tiller, *The NURBS Book*, Springer-Verlag, Berlin, 2nd ed., 1997.

H. Prautsch, *A short proof of the Oslo algorithm*, Computer Aided Geometric Design, 1 (1984), pp. 95–96.

W. H. Press, B. P. Flannery, S. A. Teukolsky, and W. T. Vetterling, *Numerical Recipes: The Art of Scientific Computing*, Cambridge University Press, Cambridge, 1986.

W. T. Reeves, D. H. Salesin, and R. L. Cook, *Rendering antialiased shadows with depth maps*, Computer Graphics, 21 (1987), pp. 283–291. SIGGRAPH'87.

D. F. Rogers, *An Introduction to NURBS: With Historical Perspective*, Morgan Kaufmann, San Francisco, 2001.

H. Samet, *Applications of Spatial Data Structures: Computer Graphics, Image Processing and GIS*, Addison–Wesley, Reading, MA, 1990.

——, *The Design and Analysis of Spatial Data Structures*, Addison–Wesley, Reading, MA, 1990.

C. Schlick, *An inexpensive BRDF model for physically-based rendering*, Computer Graphics Forum, 13 (1994), pp. 233–246. Proceedings, Eurographics'94.

D. Schreiner, ed., *OpenGL Reference Manual: The Official Reference Document to OpenGL, Version 1.2*, OpenGL Architecture Review Board, Addison–Wesley Developers Press, Reading, MA, third ed., 1999.

P. Schröder, and D. Zorin, et al., *Subdivision for Modeling and Animation*, SIGGRAPH'98 Course Notes #36, ACM, 1998.

L. L. Schumaker, *Spline Functions: Basic Theory*, Wiley, New York, 1981.

H.-P. Seidel, *Knot insertion from a blossoming point of view*, Computer Aided Geometric Design, 5 (1988), pp. 81–86.

——, *A new multiaffine approach to B-splines*, Computer Aided Geometric Design, 6 (1989), pp. 23–32.

S. W. Shepperd, *Quaternion from rotation matrix*, Journal of Guidance and Control, 1 (1978), pp. 223–224.

P. Shirley, *Realistic Ray Tracing*, AK Peters, Natick, MA, 2000.

K. Shoemake, *Animating rotation with quaternion curves*, Computer Graphics, 19 (1985), pp. 245–254. SIGGRAPH'85.

——, *Quaternion calculus and fast animation*, in SIGGRAPH'87 Course Notes on State of the Art Image Synthesis, ACM, 1987, pp. 101–121.

I. J. Shoenberg, *Contributions to the problem of approximation of equidistant data by analytic functions, Part A – On the problem of smoothing or gradation, a first class of analytic approximation formulae,* Quarterly of Applied Mathematics, 4 (1946), pp. 45–99.

——, *On spline functions,* in Inequalities, Proceedings of a Symposium held at Wright–Paterson Air Force Base, August 19–27, 1965, O. Shisha, ed., New York, 1967, Academic Press.

F. X. Sillion and C. Puech, *Radiosity and Global Illumination,* Morgan Kaufmann, San Francisco, 1994.

R. A. Spurrier, *Comment on "Singularity-free extraction of a quaternion from a direction-cosine matrix,"* Journal of Spacecraft and Rockets, 15 (1978), pp. 255–256.

F. Thomas and O. Johnston, *Disney Animation: The Illusion of Life,* Abbeville Press, New York, 1981.

D. L. Toth, *On ray tracing parametric surfaces,* Computer Graphics, 19 (1985), pp. 171–179. SIGGRAPH'85.

Y. S. Touloukian and D. P. Witt, *Thermal Radiative Properties: Metallic Elements and Alloys,* Thermophysical Properties of Matter, Vol. 7, IFI/Plenum, New York, 1970.

——, *Thermal Radiative Properties: Nonmetallic Solids,* Thermophysical Properties of Matter, Vol. 8, IFI/Plenum, New York, 1972.

Y. S. Touloukian, D. P. Witt, and R. S. Hernicz, *Thermal Radiative Properties: Coatings,* Thermophysical Properties of Matter, Vol. 9, IFI/Plenum, New York, 1972.

T. S. Trowbridge and K. P. Reitz, *Average irregularity representation of a rough surface for ray reflection,* Journal of the Optical Society of America, 65 (1975), pp. 531–536.

E. Veach and L. Guibas, *Bidirectional estimators for light transport,* in Proceedings, Fifth Eurographics Workshop on Rendering, New York, 1994, Springer-Verlag, pp. 147–162.

J. Warren and H. Weimer, *Subdivision Methods for Geometric Design: A Constructive Approach,* Morgan Kaufmann, San Francisco, 2002.

A. Watt, *3D Computer Graphics,* Addison–Wesley, Reading, MA, 2nd ed., 1993.

A. Watt and M. Watt, *Advanced Animation and Rendering Techniques: Theory and Practice,* Addison–Wesley, Reading, MA, 1992.

T. White, *The Animator's Workbook,* Phaidon Press, Oxford, UK, 1986.

T. Whitted, *An improved illumination model for shaded display,* Communications of the ACM, 23 (1980).

L. Williams, *Casting curved shadows on curved surfaces,* Computer Graphics, 12 (1978), pp. 270–274. SIGGRAPH'78.

——, *Pyramidal parametrics,* Computer Graphics, 17 (1983), pp. 1–11. SIGGRAPH'83.

R. Wolfe, ed., *significant Seminal Papers of Computer Graphics: Pioneering Efforts that Shaped the Field,* Association for Computing Machinery, New York, 1998.

L. B. Wolff and D. J. Kurlander, *Ray tracing with polarization parameters,* IEEE Computer Graphics and Applications, 10 (1990), pp. 44–55.

M. Woo, J. Nieder, T. Davis, and D. Schreiner, *OpenGL Programming Guide: The Official Guide to Learning OpenGL, Version 1.2,* OpenGL Architecture Review Board, Addison–Wesley Developers Press, Reading, MA, third ed., 1999.

R. S. Wright Jr., *OpenGL SuperBible,* Waite Group, Indianapolis, 2nd ed., 1999.

G. Wyszecki and W. S. Stiles, *Color Science: Concepts and Methods, Quantitative Data and Formulae,* John Wiley & Sons, New York, 2nd ed., 1982.

J. Zhao and N. I. Badler, *Inverse kinematics positioning using nonlinear programming for highly articulated figures,* ACM Transactions on Graphics, 13 (1994), pp. 313–336.

G. M. Ziegler, *Lectures on Polytopes,* Springer-Verlag, New York, 1995.

Index